AMSCO®

ADVANCED PLACEMENT® EDITION

English Language and Composition

Abdon
Freitas
Peterson

PERFECTION LEARNING®

Authors

Brandon Abdon, Senior Author, Doctor of Arts, English

Brandon Abdon worked for five years as Director of Curriculum, Instruction, and Assessment for the AP® English courses at The College Board, during which time he collaborated with experts from around the country to develop the Course and Exam Descriptions (CEDs) now in use. This work was a culmination of more than 15 years' experience in high schools and universities, teaching both the AP® English Language and Composition and the AP® English Literature and Composition courses as well as college composition and literature and teacher education courses. He has also taught or trained thousands of teachers around the country. He has served as an AP® Reader, led many professional developments, and offered dozens of conference presentations. Currently, he serves as professional development consultant for the Advanced Placement® program and works as an Education Specialist and Curriculum Coach in Cincinnati, Ohio.

Timothy Freitas, Master of Arts in Teaching, Secondary English Education

Timothy Freitas, a College Board-endorsed AP® English Language and Composition consultant, has been teaching AP® English Language and Composition for more than a decade and AP® English Literature and Composition for almost as long. He has also been an AP® Reader and in 2017 was invited to work on the College Board's Instructional Design Team for the new AP® English Language and Composition framework. Timothy works as a consultant and professional development facilitator for Massachusetts Math and Science Initiative (now Mass Insight Education) and is typically assigned to work in New York City when consulting for the National Math and Science Initiative. Timothy teaches in Massachusetts, currently at Whitinsville Christian School and formerly at Blackstone Valley Tech.

Lauren Peterson, Master of Arts, Education

Lauren Peterson has been teaching AP® English Language and Composition in a number of states for more than ten years, most recently at Highlands High School in Fort Thomas, Kentucky, where she is also the schoolwide literacy leader. Before this position, Lauren served as a curriculum and instructional coach in Duval County, Florida. Lauren worked for College Board on a pilot curriculum designed to both remediate common AP® English Language challenges and also prepare students for Microsoft Office Specialist Certification. As an independent consultant for the National Math and Science Initiative, Lauren has written diverse curricula used by students across the country as well as training materials for beginning and experienced AP® English Language teachers. Lauren served as an AP® English Language Reader and continues to work as an AP® English Language trainer for new and experienced teachers.

Senior Consultants

Tricia Ebarvia, M.S. Ed.

Tricia Ebarvia is an AP® English teacher, author, a National Writing Project Fellow, Heinemann Fellow, and #DisruptTexts Co-Founder. A fierce advocate for literacy instruction rooted in equity and liberation, Ebarvia is also a professional development provider, consulting on topics such as reading/writing workshop, digital literacies, anti-bias pedagogy, and curriculum design.

Senior Consultants (continued)

Jennifer Fletcher, Ph.D.

Jennifer Fletcher is a Professor of English at California State University, Monterey Bay, where she coordinates the undergraduate program for future English teachers. Her twenty-five years of experience in education include a decade as a high school teacher. Jennifer is the author of the books *Teaching Arguments* (2015), *Teaching Literature Rhetorically* (2018), and the forthcoming *Writing Rhetorically* (2021).

Darrin Pollock, M.A. Ed.

Darrin Pollock served at the College Board as Director, Instructional Design for AP® English Language and Composition for two years. He has more than 15 years of public high school teaching experience in diverse districts in Kentucky, where he has taught both AP® English Literature and Composition and AP® English Language and Composition as well as other courses for grades 9–12.

Reviewers

Erica Griffin, Ed.S.
AP® English Content Director
AP® English Reader
A+ College Ready
Birmingham, Alabama

Ryan Hale, NBCT, M.A.
AP® Literature, Language, Seminar, Research
College Board/ETS AP® Literature
AP® English Reader/Table Leader
Western Hills High School
Frankfort, Kentucky

Angela Houston, M.A. Ed.
English Language Arts Instructional Coach
Cincinnati Public Schools
Cincinnati, Ohio

Jim Jordan, M.A. Ed.
AP® English Language and Composition Workshop Consultant
AP® Reader/Table Leader
Sacred Heart Cathedral Preparatory
San Francisco, California

Chris Judson, M.S.
English Content Director
AP® Teacher Investment Program
University of Notre Dame
Goshen, Indiana

Tom Reynolds, M.A.
AP® English Language and Literature Teacher
Hononegah High School
Rockton, Illinois

Melissa Alter Smith, NBCT
AP® English Teacher
AP® English Reader
Lake Norman Charter High School
Huntersville, North Carolina

Kristy Strickland Seidel, B.S.
AP® English Language and Composition Question Leader
Suncoast Community High School
Riviera Beach, Florida

Jacqueline N. Stallworth, M.A.
College Board Consultant
AP® Literature
Founder of Stallworth Educational Consulting Team
Alexandria, Virginia

For Angie and John

Please visit our website at:
www.perfectionlearning.com

When ordering the student book, please specify:
ISBN: 978-1-6903-8554-7 or **T3241**
eBook ISBN: 978-1-6903-8559-2 or **T3241D**

5 6 7 8 DR 26 25 24 23 22

Printed in the United States of America

Contents

Essential Questions: *As a reader, how can you identify a writer's position and the way that position is supported? As a writer, how can you develop and support your own positions?*

Essential Question: *How does a text create unity and coherence and use transitions to guide readers through a line of reasoning?*

UNIT 7—Style as Substance

Essential Question: *How can sentences express relationships among ideas?*

UNIT 8—Using Style Strategically

PREFACE

AMSCO® English Language and Composition: Advanced Placement® Edition develops skills and concepts necessary for both introductory college writing and performance on the Advanced Placement® English Language and Composition exam. While the College Board's 2019 release of the Course and Exam Description (CED) was not a redesign of the course, it did—for the first time in the forty-plus year history of the course—identify the specific skills and knowledge that students need for demonstrating their understanding of key reading and writing concepts. The CED also—again for the first time—suggests an order for teaching those skills and knowledge to provide foundations on which students and teachers can build. This book is organized to align with the CED, providing students the opportunity to work with a diverse array of writers and speakers, a variety of text types and levels, and a colorful mix of topics. Students will closely read, analyze, and write about professional texts they encounter in this book. They will also study drafts of student texts and choose revisions to improve them. They will then apply the skills they are learning about reading and revising to their own writing. In this way, skills of reading and writing are combined, just as they are in a college writing course and on the national exam.

This book fills the gap between test prep handbooks and costly English textbooks and anthologies. Most important, while it uses the CED as a framework and provides exam practice, its focus is to make students better readers and writers. It is thorough enough to be a student's main book and flexible enough to be used along with other print and online resources.

First thanks go to my parents and grandparents as readers and my gran as a (and my!) teacher. Next, I would like to thank my co-writers and colleagues Lauren and Timm for their candor and patience; English professors Sarah Cooper, Jennifer Fletcher, Mary Trachsel, Liz Wright, Duku Anokye, Asao Inoue, Octavio Pimental Sheila Carter-Tod, Michael Neal, Cheryl Glenn, and David Kirkland for their inspiration; and colleagues Becky McFarland and Darrin Pollock for picking up their phones. Special thanks to the Senior Consultants for this book—Darrin Pollock, Jennifer Fletcher, and Tricia Ebarvia—whose perspectives provided meaningful guidance. Thanks to all the reviewers listed on page iii for their insightful contributions. Also, Lily, Paul, Patrick, Carl, Kevin, Jen, Jodi, Alfonso, Carlos, Angela—you're all in here. Special thanks go to John Williamson and Brian Robinson as colleagues and mentors.

Enough cannot be said for the kind professionalism of our chief editor Carol Francis and the crew of Andrea Stark, Jamie Charlton, and Sue Thies (yes, we know you're there, Sue) who all shared a vision but are thoughtful enough to let it grow and evolve throughout the process—"getting it right, not just getting it done."

But more than anything, thanks to Colin and Jennifer—as well as Angie, Hilton, and Dorian—for the sacrifices that allowed this book to become a reality.

Brandon Abdon, Senior Author
May 2020

INTRODUCTION

Writing is thinking on paper. The goal of writing is to communicate your thoughts, and the goal of reading is to understand others'. By accepting the challenge of the Advanced Placement® English Language and Composition course, you have become a scholar of the tools of rhetoric—what makes writing work. All college students begin their college career with a course much like this one, in which they sharpen their reading and writing skills to allow them to become literate members of the community of thinkers. This book will encourage you to express and improve your ideas as you write, and it will help you to better navigate the ideas of others as you read.

Writing is a process. In writing this book, for example, my co-authors and I drafted parts, shared them with others, took feedback, made revisions, improved what we were doing, and then repeated the process again—and again. This is what writers do. The writing you do for this exam does not allow for rounds of revisions; instead, the exam captures writing you do under a time limit and expects that you produce the best first draft that you possibly can. The best first draft should always be the goal when you write—but in the real world you would be able to revisit that draft and improve it. To help you prepare for writing in the real world, this course provides opportunities to practice the full writing process—from developing your first ideas to polishing a final draft after rounds of revision. This book will regularly challenge you to apply what you learn to your own writing process.

Writing is always part of a communication situation, which includes an audience of readers and a purpose. The types of writing you may be familiar with in school have been called "mutt genres" because they don't have a real audience or real purpose—they are school assignments you write for your teacher or your classmates. In this course you will think a lot about what you want to accomplish with your writing, who reads your writing, and why your purpose and audience matter in how you express yourself. Even though on the exam you will write for a defined set of purposes and for an audience of teachers and professors, the exam readers want to see that you have tried to consider the impact of audience on expressing your thoughts. They know that you are writing on an exam and will give you the benefit of the doubt. This book will repeatedly ask you to think about the bigger situation of your writing and how choices you make in your writing affect and are affected by it.

By enrolling in this class, you are accepting the challenge to become a scholar in one of the subjects that you can carry with you into study of anything else or even into efforts to improve society as a whole. *AMSCO® English Language and Composition: Advanced Placement® Edition*, in alignment with the latest course and exam description from the College Board, will help you build mastery of the fundamental concepts and skills of reading and writing.

This introduction explains the course design and test format. In the nine skills-building units that follow, you will find extensive discussions built on the enduring understandings fundamental to reading and writing, diverse readings and tasks that both teach and challenge you to apply skills and knowledge, a number of practice questions and prompts to help you get used to what and how you will be asked to respond on the exam, as well as multiple opportunities to address your own growth as a reader and writer and not just as a test taker.

The College Board's Advanced Placement Program started in 1955. The AP® English Language and Composition course began in 1979 as an offshoot of the AP® English Literature and Composition course. As of 2019, the exam for this course had been taken by more students than any other AP® exam—more than half a million worldwide. More than 3,000 colleges accepted these scores and awarded either credit in place of course work or advanced placement into a higher-level college course meant to make students even stronger writers and scholars.

However, this course may not be only for those who are going to college straight out of high school. The skills that make for better readers and writers—and better critical thinkers in general—are essential to anyone in any profession. They are also essential to all members of society as people are daily exposed to a variety of media that seek to get their attention and sway their opinion. Skills related to effectively sharing your ideas and interacting with others' ideas—and weeding out slanted or untrustworthy information—make everyone better members of our complex society.

The exam is given in early May, but you must register near the beginning of the year. Check your school's guidance department or the College Board's website for details, fees, deadlines, and necessary supplies.

Design of the English Language and Composition Course

The College Board published the new Course and Exam Description (CED) in 2019. Though the course has not been redesigned, it has been articulated and focused so that there is little question about the skills and knowledge necessary to learn for the course. These skills, knowledge, and understandings are all directly drawn from previous exams and course descriptions and verified by college professors and writing experts from around the country. The CED focuses on depth rather than breadth and offers detailed enduring understandings meant to clarify the conceptual learning expected in the course. In fact, these enduring understandings and the big ideas they define are important for all writers, not just students in this course. They include: (1) Rhetorical Situation, (2) Claims and Evidence, (3) Reasoning and Organization, and (4) Style.

However, effective writing and reading do not reside in any one of these alone. Effective writing incorporates skills and knowledge from all of the big ideas. For this reason, the CED introduces material at appropriate points, encourages practice, and then builds on that material in later units by repeating the same skills but with new knowledge and higher expectations.

"Choices" are the overwhelming focus of the CED: understanding why a writer may have made certain choices in a text and also making very thoughtful and strategic choices about your own writing. This focus directly relates to the newest type of multiple-choice question—the composition question—which asks test takers to make the best choice for revising a given text to achieve a certain effect. You are expected to read like a writer and write like a reader.

To hone your writing skills, write a lot, read a lot, and write and read different texts. These activities mark the difference between taking the course just for the sake of passing a test and taking the course to develop the necessary skills for reading and writing so that when you do take the exam—and pursue reading and writing in college and beyond—you will do well. Some practice with test examples and the process of thinking through an exam are necessary—that is why they appear in this book—but this course will help you use those skills beyond the exam.

English Language and Composition Content

This course is like a college-level introductory course in writing or composition. The key word here is "introductory." Many colleges have only about 45 hours of classwork for a course, so they are able to focus on development of the most essential skills and understandings in the course. With an average of 140 hours of instruction in a school year, high schools have the opportunity to teach these same skills in much more depth, with much more practice and much more teacher feedback. Overarching questions that inform the instruction include the following: Why do writers make certain choices in their writing? How are writers influenced by the situation to make those choices? How do certain choices affect readers? How do others' perspectives affect the choices a writer makes?

Enduring Understandings The course content is developed from enduring understandings—statements that synthesize the important concepts in a discipline area and have lasting value even beyond that discipline area. For example, the College Board has articulated this enduring understanding (EU) derived from the big idea of *Reasoning and Style*:

> "Writers guide understanding of a text's lines of reasoning and claims through the text's organization and integration of evidence."

Why is that an enduring understanding? It highlights the fundamental responsibility of a writer to guide the readers' understanding of their ideas by making certain choices in organizing their writing and using evidence including information from others. Every student taking any writing class should clearly have that understanding at the end of the course. Without this understanding, writers might not make choices necessary for their writing to clearly reach a reader. Each unit in this book begins with a listing of the enduring understandings relevant to that unit.

Skills To help students fully develop those enduring understandings, the College Board has also articulated skills, the tools students are expected to use to show they understand the concepts in the big ideas and enduring understandings. To make the purpose of the skills in the course clearer, most of them have also been divided into Reading and Writing. For example, these are skills related to the enduring understanding above:

> "Reading—Describe the line of reasoning and explain whether it supports an argument's overarching thesis."
>
> "Writing—Develop a line of reasoning and commentary that explains it throughout an argument."

These skills tie to the enduring understanding by providing specific tasks students must be able to do as the reader and writer of any text. Each unit begins with a list of the skills tied to the unit's enduring understandings.

Essential Knowledge Mastering these skills or learning objectives requires content knowledge. The College Board has homed in on what it and its advisors of teachers and professors consider essential knowledge (EK). Here is an example of essential knowledge tied to the above skills:

> "The body paragraphs of a written argument make claims, support them with evidence, and provide commentary that explains how the paragraph contributes to the reasoning of the argument."

This essential knowledge statement outlines what you need to know to fulfill the learning objective, so you can focus your study on the most relevant information. If a writer doesn't have this knowledge about paragraphs and what they do in an argument, then that writer may think of a paragraph only the way an elementary school student once described it: "3–5 sentences and the first one is indented."

Rhetoric This term is thousands of years old. For eons it referred to the way language is used to communicate and even persuade. Today, however, you hear it in the media often used negatively to refer to the way language is used to manipulate or even hide the truth. This course considers rhetoric in the first way—the thoughtful study and use of language and communications. It considers rhetoric in the setting of a series of conversations to find the truth, conversations in which you agree with some and disagree with others as you and others gradually refine and express your understanding of a truth.

The study of rhetoric and composition differs from the study of English Literature (fiction: novels, stories, plays, poetry) on which many English classes focus. While study and analysis of English Literature usually ends in interpretation of meaning for the reader, the purpose of analysis and study of rhetoric is to better understand how language affects us and how we can use language to affect others. Nobel Prize-winning Irish poet William Butler Yeats may have summed up the differences between rhetoric and literature better than anyone else in his statement that

> "Out of the quarrel with others we make rhetoric; out of the quarrel with ourselves we make poetry."

Communication with other people and communication within ourselves is at the root of the difference.

Texts in This Course and in This Book What you read in this book may differ from texts you have read in your English classes. The course focuses on nonfiction, specifically how nonfiction presents an argument of some kind in speeches, articles, essays, and other texts. The texts presented here are part of the proof of professor Andrea Lunsford's claim that "everything is an argument."

This book has a variety of texts, from excerpts of famous speeches to chapters of books and even short articles from local newspapers. It also includes an array of topics, some chosen to be interesting and some chosen because they represent the type of reading that people must do every day, even if they are not especially interesting. Finally, the texts in this book represent a wide assortment of experiences and perspectives: different cultural backgrounds, nationalities, faiths, and politics. The authors have taken this diversity of perspectives very seriously since it is a way to promote understanding and cooperation.

Writing in This Course While you will write throughout this course, what and how you write will differ as you progress. You will write in response to a variety of tasks and prompts, applying the skills you are learning as you go. Near the end of each unit, you will encounter writing activities that build across the entire course as your skills accumulate.

As you write in the course, reflect back on the lessons you have learned with previous writing tasks and activities and consider how you can use those skills with the next text you write. Helping you know how to transfer those skills to new situations and use them to make better decisions as you write is one of the goals of this course. We hope that you will take the skills you learned and sharpened in the imagined situations of the classroom and the exam and transfer them to writing in real-world situations.

The Design of This Book

This book explains college level writing and reading in straightforward terms and with many memorable analogies and examples for understanding. It is the result of the authors' experiences in teaching both the AP® course and college writing course, working directly with the College Board, serving as a Reader for the AP® Exams, and engaging with real-world scholarship in literacy. All of these provide perspective for much of the explanations that follow.

The unit sequence in this book corresponds to the order in the CED. However, the units' main points and concepts can be understood in isolation. As with any skills-based book, there is overlap among the units, and we have included cross-references where appropriate.

Nine Units

This book contains nine units.

Unit One: The Unending Conversation introduces the rhetorical situation and the essentials of argument. As the first unit, it provides the foundation upon which all other units will build as it also offers prompts and activities that encourage practice of fundamentals before expecting a more advanced performance in later units.

Unit Two: Selecting Evidence to Motivate an Audience begins to focus on strategic choices related to the audience of a text. Still an early unit, it continues to offer some foundational skills but begins to emphasize the writer's responsibility for choices and awareness of audience.

Unit Three: Connecting an Argument focuses on the relationships of ideas within arguments and how they develop a claim throughout a text. The line of reasoning features prominently here as different pieces of evidence and methods of developing an argument become the focus of a writer's choices.

Unit Four: Structuring and Organizing Arguments begins the shift to revising and refining arguments and understanding how and why writers make choices to improve their writing. Most skills for the course have been introduced by this point; the rest of the course will focus on improving them.

Unit Five: Structuring and Supporting Coherent Arguments continues foundations laid in earlier units regarding the line of reasoning but also begins to closely examine specific language. Cohesion and coherence become the focus of learning, including careful and strategic choices of words.

Unit Six: Synthesizing Perspectives and Refining Arguments looks more closely at the role of other people's perspectives in shaping and refining an argument. The importance of this unit to the development of thoughtful, critical, yet empathetic readers and writers cannot be overstated.

Unit Seven: Style as Substance takes aspects of writing often disregarded as flourishes and simple polish and examines them as essential choices to refining an argument. Clarity, coherence, and reasoning all feature prominently as the effects of choices about advanced revisions and edits come into the spotlight.

Unit Eight: Using Style Strategically builds from unit seven as seemingly stylistic choices become more strategic based on the audience and different possible perspectives. While unit seven focused on sentences and conventions, this unit looks even more granularly at parts of sentences and their effect on the argument.

Unit Nine: Contributing to the Conversation ends the book where it began: exploring how to contribute to ongoing conversations on topics of interest and importance using all of the new skills and understandings. Consideration of others and how they affect the argument, including how the argument can change over time and perspectives can change, is the main focus of this final unit.

Thematic Approach

While themes are not the main method of organizing this book, each unit does use anchor texts that revolve around certain themes relevant to a contemporary study of language and rhetoric. You will notice an intentional combination of abstract and concrete subjects.

Unit One:	Climate Change
Unit Two:	Education
Unit Three:	Fast Food
Unit Four:	Homelessness
Unit Five:	Freedom
Unit Six:	Lies
Unit Seven:	Technology
Unit Eight:	Morality
Unit Nine:	Tradition

In addition to the anchor texts, each unit also contains a number of shorter texts or excerpts, some to demonstrate certain rhetorical concepts and others to serve as readings for the practice synthesis and rhetorical analysis activities in the unit review. These can be grouped across units in a variety of themes.

In Each Unit

Each unit relies on organizing factors that help make information in this user-friendly book easy to find.

The Unit Overview does exactly what its name suggests: it provides a high-level explanation of concepts that are covered in the unit. More important, it offers a real-life scenario or example that helps to illustrate the importance of the material in that unit, from colorful reviews of the movie *Titanic* and the Superbowl halftime show put on by Shakira and J. Lo and many other high-interest, relevant narratives.

Anchor Texts are the primary texts the unit will refer to as new skills and knowledge are introduced. These include an excerpt from a professional text for reading practice and a thematically related student draft for practice with revision questions.

"What Do You Know?" is an essential tenet of this book. It asks you to challenge yourself to answer questions on concepts within anchor texts that the book hasn't yet covered. Asking yourself and answering questions on a subject before formally learning it will enhance learning. These questions are not meant to be scored. Instead, this practice will prepare you to learn and get you thinking about the anchor texts in possibly new ways. Don't worry if these are difficult—view this as productive frustration. You usually don't know what you don't know until you know you don't know it. (And you may surprise yourself by knowing more than you think.) This strategy is well supported by learning science as an effective way to learn.

The **Parts** of the unit are where the learning and practice happen. These include **Essential Questions** tied to the skills covered for each section that will help you focus your learning. They also include a chart of **Key Terms** you will encounter. Since the course is designed to lay a foundation and then build layers of increasing skill and complexity on that foundation, many of the key terms from unit to unit are the same, but with each advancing unit you will have a deeper understanding.

Inside the parts of each unit are smaller sections that provide instruction in specific essential knowledge to help apply the relevant skills and see their relationship with the enduring understandings. Also within each part are **Checkpoints** with practice tasks specific to the content in that part as well as AP® Exam-style questions on **close reading** and **evaluating writing** tied to the specific content in that part.

Composing on Your Own provides an opportunity for you to move beyond the world of the classroom and apply the content from different parts of the unit to your own writing. These activities encourage habitual revisiting, revising, and refining your own writing as you work through the book. These skills are essential to being an effective writer in school and in life.

Apply What You Have Learned tasks occur at the end of each part and ask you to take the skills, knowledge, and understandings that you have been practicing and apply them to a different text—sometimes outside of this book—to provide you with more practice. This task also helps the transfer of skills from both this book and this course into the real world.

The Unit Review has three main parts to further develop your skills and also help prepare you for the AP® exam and the challenges of college reading and writing.

- **Section I** offers a brief professional text and a student draft and a set of **multiple-choice questions** for each to give you another opportunity to apply what you have learned. These are in the format of the questions on the AP® exam.
- Inserted between Section I and Section II is a feature called **Join the Conversation** whose purpose is to provide guided and layered instruction on responding to the free response questions of the type that appear on the exam: Synthesis, Rhetorical Analysis, and Argument. The instruction builds unit by unit, each time adding complexity to the tasks until they reach the level of complexity of the free-response prompts on the exam.
- **Section II** returns to the AP® exam format and provides those **free-response prompts**.

The **Practice Examination** is the final portion of the text. This exam gives you an opportunity to answer the same number and types of questions as you will encounter on the actual exam, under the same time limits if you choose to impose them.

The Exam

You can earn college credit or placement into a different college course (depending on the institution you attend) for your work in the course upon your successful performance on the national AP® English Language and Composition exam given in early May. This three-hour test consists of 45 five-option multiple-choice questions and 3 free-response questions. You will have 60 minutes (1 hour) to complete the multiple-choice questions and then 135 minutes (2 hours, 15 minutes) for the free-response questions. The free-response questions are worth 55% of the course, with the multiple-choice worth the remaining 45%. A talented team of college faculty and experienced AP® teachers draft the questions and create the exam each year. The exam questions are also field-tested with actual college students and then revised accordingly to ensure they are testing what is necessary for the college-level course. A parallel practice exam is included at the end of this book. On the test, you can earn a score of 1 through 5. The College Board considers a score of 3 as "qualified," but some colleges require a 4 or even a 5 for consideration. To learn more about how colleges regard the exam, check out this website: https://apstudent.collegeboard.org/creditandplacement/search-credit-policies.

Multiple-Choice Questions

The 45 multiple-choice questions on both the practice exam and the actual exam appear in two unique forms and always have five options, A through E. There will be only one correct answer. The two forms are designed to test both your reading analysis skills and your writing revision skills, with 23–25 reading questions and 20–22 writing questions. These questions spread across two professional reading passages and three "student-drafted" writing passages. Since this book is organized by skills, most of the questions in the Unit Review relate to the skills and knowledge of that particular unit, although questions related to other units are also included, as they are in the Practice Examination beginning on page 601.

Reading the passages completely is essential to answering the multiple-choice questions. Be especially careful to finish it completely before thinking you understand it. Pay close attention to shifts in the passage (more on this later in the book), as they often indicate what the actual purpose of the passage may be. If you read the passage and have trouble understanding it, then you might use the questions to help guide your understanding. Sometimes, even reading the questions first can be a helpful strategy. As with most multiple-choice tests, determine what exactly the question is asking and then select the best answer. If an early option in (A) or (B) looks extremely obvious, continue to read and consider the remaining options to confirm or reconsider your first impressions. For questions you cannot immediately answer, use the process of elimination. Rule out and actually mark through the unlikely options to narrow your choices. Finally, as the directions on the actual exam will remind you, "pay particular attention to the requirements of questions that contain the words NOT, LEAST, or EXCEPT."

When you see a challenging or time-consuming question, remember time is limited. You have a little more than a minute and a half per question—this includes time for reading the passage and the question and then sorting answers. Some will take you less time; some will take you more. Because the reading questions come first and will likely take you less time than the writing questions, you should complete the reading questions in about 20-25 minutes. Skip the occasional tough question (be sure to leave that spot blank on the answer form) and continue through the test. Return and answer those challenging questions after you have gone through all 55. Since there is no added penalty for guessing, if you do not know the answer, make your best guess. Never leave any responses blank.

If you're just beginning your preparation, the example questions that follow may be challenging. Don't worry if you do not know the correct answer; the following nine units will teach you. These examples are to show you the formats of the questions. You could elect to revisit these questions as part of your review as exam day approaches.

All questions on the exam are keyed to the CED. That is, they test only those items that are included in the Course and Exam description. They are designed to test your understanding of all levels of the CED: Enduring Understandings, Skills, and Essential Knowledge. The following example questions include a key to show what aspects of the CED are tested in each question. You can look up the codes on a copy of the Course and Exam Description available on the College Board website.

Reading Analysis Questions are designed to test how you think and interact with others' writing. You will be given two different nonfiction passages between 600–750 words long. Unlike some tests, the questions are not meant to see how well you read the passage or what information you comprehend from it. Instead, you are asked to closely consider the choices that the writer of the passage has made and then answer questions about why those choices *may* have been made or how those choices affect the writing. These questions require that you go back and reread certain sections to be able to choose the right answer.

Example of a Reading Analysis Question

(Please note that this passage is not as long as an actual exam passage, and the paragraphs may not be numbered on the exam.)

Questions 1-4 refer to the passage below. Read the following passage carefully before you choose your answers.

(Following is an excerpt from congressional testimony given in 2007 by Army Private First Class Jessica Lynch, who was captured and later rescued during the Iraq war.)

(1) When I remember those difficult days, I remember the fear. I remember the strength. I remember that hand of that fellow American soldier reassuring me that I was going to be okay. At the same time, tales of great heroism were being told. [My] parents' home in Wirt County, West Virginia, was under siege by media all repeating the story of the little girl Rambo[1] from the hills of West Virginia who went down fighting.

(2) It was not true.

(3) I have repeatedly said, when asked, that if the stories about me helped inspire our troops and rally a nation, then perhaps there was some good. However, I'm still confused as to why they chose to lie and tried to make me a legend when the real heroics of my fellow soldiers that day were legendary: people like Lori Piestewa and First Sergeant Dowdy who picked up fellow soldiers in harm's way; or people like Patrick Miller or Sergeant Donald Walters who actually did fight until the very end.

(4) The bottom line is the American people are capable of determining their own ideals for heroes and they don't need to be told elaborate lies. My hero is my brother, Greg, who continues to serve his country today. My hero is my friend, Lori Piestewa, who died in Iraq but set an example for a generation of Hopi and Native American women and little girls everywhere about the contributions that just one soldier can make. My hero is every American who says, "my country needs me" and answers that call to fight.

1. Which of the following best describes the effect of the speaker's repetition of the phrase "I remember" in the first paragraph?

(A) It demonstrates the reliability of her memory in recalling the events of her capture.

(B) It allows her to establish a contrast between what she remembers and the untrue stories spread about her experience.

(C) It becomes essential to her definition of a hero.

(D) It prevents others from doubting her story because it comes from her memories and no one else's.

(E) It provides a foundation for her memory not being reliable.

(This question keys to Unit 5, Enduring Understanding (EU) REO-1, Skill 5.B, Essential Knowledge (EK) REO-1.)

1 **Rambo**: an exceptionally tough or aggressive person named for a fictional Vietnam war veteran

2. Which of the following best explains the speaker's use of the qualifier "repeatedly" in the first sentence of the third paragraph?
   (A) The audience expects her to say something different, yet she refuses.
   (B) Like her memories, she wants people to know that she does remember having said these things before.
   (C) She fears that her heroism will be forgotten.
   (D) She wants to emphasize that she has constantly denied the stories as fiction but accepted that some good may come.
   (E) Other soldiers mentioned in the passage cannot speak for themselves, so she feels a responsibility to speak for them.

(This question keys to Unit 7, EU CLE-1, Skill 3.C, EK CLE-1.X.)

3. Which of the following choices accurately describes what is most likely a strategic stylistic decision that the speaker makes in the third paragraph?
   (A) Using subordinate clauses in each sentence to provide even more emphasis on the independent clauses in each sentence
   (B) Contradicting each of her sentences with the sentences that follow so she can demonstrate the general confusion created by constantly contradictory stories and statements
   (C) Using complex sentences in order to illustrate the complexity of the situation in which she finds herself
   (D) Adding that she had to be asked about these things so she can make it clear just how shy and humble she is
   (E) Stating that she saw the stories about her as possibly good, but then explaining her confusion about their spread so she can emphasize the failure to recognize the true heroics of other soldiers

(This question keys to Unit 7, EU STL-1, Skill 7.B, EK STL-1.H.)

4. It becomes apparent throughout the excerpt that she assumes the audience is familiar with
   (A) "the story of the little girl Rambo from the hills of West Virginia who went down fighting" (paragraph 1, sentence 5)
   (B) "the real heroics of [her] fellow soldiers" (paragraph 3, sentence 2)
   (C) "people like Patrick Miller or Sergeant Donald Walters" (paragraph 3, sentence 2)
   (D) "Lori Piestewa, who died in Iraq but set an example for a generation of Hopi and Native American women" (paragraph 3, sentence 1)
   (E) "their own ideals for heroes" (paragraph 4, sentence 1)

   (This question keys to Unit 2, EU RHS-1, Skill 1.B, EK RHS-1.F.)

5. The excerpt as a whole claims
   (A) that the media always lie to people just to sell a story
   (B) the American people do not need to be told what to value in a hero
   (C) soldiers deserve more attention for their sacrifices than anyone else
   (D) fear and strength are the most overwhelming memories people can experience
   (E) lies can perhaps do some good

   (This question keys to Unit 1, EU CLE-1, Skill 3.A, EK CLE-1.A.)

Following is an answer key with an explanation of why each correct answer is correct.

#	Answer	Rationale
1	B	By stating everything that she does remember, Lynch is able to establish a direct contrast with parts of the stories told about her that are not true. That is, she remembers things and feelings but the stories people spread are not things that she remembers because they did not happen. This contrast then allows her to emphasize what was not true and eventually make her point about heroism and the ideals of the American people. The EU/Skill/EK combination refers to the relationship between the reasoning of the argument and the organization of the text, specifically how a text's organization creates unity and coherence. In this case, repetition (a concept from the EK) develops the relationship between remembered parts of her story and their lies. This distinction is significant to the reasoning of her argument as she eventually comes to what should really be remembered and honored—true heroism based on what people really value, not what they are told to value (e.g., the lies told about her experience).

(continued)

#	Answer	Rationale
2	D	The qualifier "repeatedly" describes how she has over and over again, constantly, stated that she hoped the stories would result in some good. This illustrates her insistence that she has never accepted her hero status but resolved herself to accept that some good may come of it. The EU/Skill/EK combination relates to the way a writer modifies a claim to better position it in the line of reasoning. The skill focuses on how a writer chooses certain qualifiers while the EK emphasizes the intention and strategy of the choice of certain qualifiers. That she has chosen to use the word "repeatedly" very likely indicates that she has been determined to communicate the same message and must—again—communicate the same here.
3	E	The organization of the sentences in this paragraph creates the strategic effect of admitting that she could see where these stories might be useful but at the same time she calls them "lies" and turns her focus on the "real heroics" of others. The EU/Skill/EK relationship begins with choices a writer makes based on the rhetorical situation. In this case, her choices are how to organize those sentences. For example, she could have left the first sentence of that paragraph out and started with "I'm still confused..." and it would have still made sense. Instead, the inclusion of that sentence and placement of it with the others highlights her interest in the truth and confusion about the lies.
4	A	She offers this almost humorous label of the stories without further explanation in this excerpt, so the audience likely was familiar with these stories beforehand. The EU/Skill/EK relationship relies on how an audience's prior knowledge in a rhetorical situation affects the writer's choices. In this case, her audience is aware of her circumstances, so she can make certain choices about what to include and what not to include. This awareness allows her to more quickly come to her comments about the true heroes and true heroism.
5	B	Though the excerpt addresses different topics, the phrase "the bottom line is..." indicates her claim. She follows it with examples that illustrate it so the audience can see her claim in action. This EU/Skill/EK foundation provides the source of all claims and the related evidence or examples. In this case, she comes to this claim after having almost already defended it and then provides more examples after the fact. These all align with the expectations of the Skill and EK that a claim requires a defense and can be explained with its evidence as support.

Writing Revision Questions ask you to consider a possible revision that a student writer would like to make and why he or she would like to make it. You will be given three different short drafts of student writing (two of them 250–350 words and one of them a bit shorter at 150–250 words). These questions are not asking you to make corrections on grammar or use of language. Instead, you are asked to closely consider the choices that the student writer is considering and why they are being considered and then you must choose the option that best accomplishes what the writer wants to accomplish in the draft. These questions also require that you reread portions of the draft to understand in context the choice the writer is trying to make. ***Note:*** *In this book, a rhetorical situation is provided for the student writer so that you can assess choices in relation to audience and purpose. You will not see this rhetorical situation on the exam.*

Example of a Writing Revision Question

Questions 6–10 refer to the passage below. Read the following passage carefully before you choose your answers.

(The passage below is a draft)

(1) While most people attest to having a hero, few really understand the most important qualities of heroism. (2) One quality with which few disagree is that heroes put others before themselves. (3) This quality may not be obvious to some people as they consider people that many people call heroes.

(4) One person often said to symbolize the heroism of everyday people is the late Rosa Parks, a Black citizen of Montgomery, Alabama. (5) After she was arrested in 1955 for refusing to surrender her bus seat to a White man, her resistance led to the Montgomery Bus Boycott—one of the most significant moments of the civil rights era. (6) Though many call her heroic for resisting what she saw as morally wrong, at first it may be difficult to see her actions as selfless. (7) However, Mrs. Parks had a history of working for civil rights and reported that she knew what she was doing by staying in her seat. (8) She accepted an arrest and a fine to bring attention to the larger injustices of racial segregation. (9) She surrendered her individual freedom for the sake of others.

(10) Often, heroes like Rosa Parks claim that they are just doing what they are supposed to do to help others. (11) But those same heroes often do things far beyond what people in their positions are asked to do. (12) Take for example Corporal Desmond Doss, a soldier in the U.S. Army during World War II. (13) While Doss wanted to serve in the military, he had a personal belief against killing and refused to pick-up a weapon of any sort, even during training. (14) He ended up serving with a combat medical team tasked with treating and saving soldiers during battle. (15) What Doss did, though, went far beyond that. (16) In one battle, he saved the lives of nearly one hundred men—including enemy soldiers—by lowering their injured bodies to safety over a nearly four-hundred-foot cliff.

(17) Naming a heroic act that does not involve the hero sacrificing something for others is difficult.

6. The writer wants to revise sentence 1 (reproduced below) to be less abrasive toward the audience.

While most people attest to having a hero, few really understand the most important qualities of heroism.

Which version of the underlined clause best accomplishes this goal?

(A) (as it is now)

(B) true heroes can never exist because no one will ever agree on what makes someone a hero

(C) the qualities that people value in a hero vary

(D) everyone's heroes are too different to compare

(E) only fools can expect to have a common definition about what makes someone a hero

(This question keys to Unit 2, EU RHS-1, Skill 2.B, EK RHS-1.G.)

7. The writer wants to revise sentence 3 (reproduced below) to avoid confusion at this point in the passage.

This quality may not be obvious to some people as they consider people that many people call heroes.

Which of the following revision best accomplishes this goal?

(A) (as it is now)

(B) This quality may not be obvious to some people as they think about those whom many others call heroes.

(C) This quality may not be obvious to people who think about people who others see as heroes.

(D) Some people simply have not considered the people that other people call heroes and the value of this quality.

(E) Some people do not consider this quality as they consider people regarded as heroes by others.

(This question keys to Unit 5, EU STL-1, Skill 8.A, EK STL-1.C.)

8. The writer is considering the following revision to sentence 8 (reproduced below) to qualify the punishment Parks received.

She accepted a few hours in jail and a $14 fine to bring attention to the larger injustices of racial segregation.

Should the writer make this revision?

(A) Yes, it clarifies the mistreatment she received.

(B) Yes, it prevents the reader from taking her treatment too seriously.

(C) Yes, it provides a way to consider her treatment from a 21st century perspective

(D) No, it makes it seem as though she wanted to be arrested and fined.

(E) No, it lessens the effect of her being arrested and fined.

(This question keys to Unit 9, EU CLE-1, Skill 4.C, EK CLE-1.Z.)

9. The writer is consider adding the following sentence to the end of the third paragraph (sentences 10–16).

There is no doubt that Doss put others before himself as he was injured four times while rescuing those soldiers, including by a gunshot that fractured his left arm and an explosion which left seventeen pieces of metal lodged in his body.

Should the writer add this sentence?

(A) Yes, because it explains the recklessness with which Doss acted during battle.

(B) Yes, because it prevents anyone from doubting that heroes must be selfless.

(C) Yes, because it provides an example of the consequences faced by heroes who put others first.

(D) No, because it simply rephrases information already provided earlier in the paragraph.

(E) No, because it would confuse the reason for including Doss' story in the passage.

(This question keys to Unit 3, EU REO-1, Skill 6.A, EK REO-1.C.)

10. The writer wants to add a clause to sentence 17 (reproduced below) to both clarify the purpose of the passage and bring the ending back around to the beginning.

Naming a heroic act that does not involve the hero sacrificing something for others is difficult.

Which choice (adjusting for punctuation as needed) best accomplishes this goal?

(A) (as it is now)
(B) as people rarely have the opportunity to meet their heroes
(C) even though people around the world claim to have heroes
(D) because heroism begins with the quality of selflessness
(E) but doing so would prove this entire argument invalid

(This question keys to Unit 7, EU RHS-1, Skill 2.A, EK RHS-1.J.)

Following is an answer key with an explanation of why each correct answer is correct.

#	Answer	Rationale
6	C	This option allows for an audience that may not agree with the writer and admits that others may call people heroes for a number of reasons. In making this choice, the writer allows for a conversation about the qualities of heroism before getting into the claim of the writing. The EU/Skill/EK combination emphasizes strategic choices that are attuned to the audience and that appeal to the audience's emotions and values. An audience that feels judged—as though being called ignorant, as the original clause suggests—will be less likely to remain cooperative or receptive.
7	B	The original sentence repeated the same pronoun three times but in reference to a different set of people each time. This option at least provides different pronouns in reference to the different groups who are involved in the sentence. The EU/Skill/EK relationship is about how the rhetorical situation of a text affects the choices a writer makes, including the specific words chosen and how they can create confusion if not chosen carefully. In this case, the correct answer still has pronouns, yet they have been revised to more clearly refer to different groups.

(continued)

#	Answer	Rationale
8	E	If the writer added this information, the reader may actually question Parks's treatment—claiming it not as severe as it has been made out to be. This interpretation would miss the point that she was arrested and fined for something most people today would see as not problematic. The EU/Skill/EK relies on justifying the claim using evidence that supports the reasoning of the argument, including qualifying certain parts of the argument. In this case, the evidence and details about her arrest and fine would neither support nor complement the thesis and, instead, would weaken it by suggesting that her punishment wasn't all that bad, especially if read by someone who already disagrees.
9	C	Because the consequences of Rosa Parks's resistance were discussed in the previous paragraph and because the audience needs to see that heroes do suffer for their selflessness, the audience also needs to see Doss as one who suffered as a result of his actions. The EU/Skill/EK relationship focuses on the value of explaining how the examples and evidence provided in the passage relate directly to the claims about heroes and heroism. In this case, Doss's injuries are mentioned in order to demonstrate his vulnerability as a person, which serves to only increase his legend. This addition also directly relates Doss's story to that of Rosa Parks.
10	D	This question is about the role of a conclusion in an argument. Here, the suggested line draws a direct connection to the introduction of the passage. The EU/Skill/EK combination focuses on the strategic choices necessary for a conclusion. Moreover, it emphasizes the appropriateness of the conclusion material to the rest of the text as well as the entire rhetorical situation.

Free-Response Questions

The free-response question (FRQ) section of the exam consists of three prompts you must respond to in 135 minutes. Though it comes down to about 45 minutes per response, during that time you need to read a number of texts and source materials, so develop a plan to use this time in ways that best suit you.

There are three types of free-response prompts on the exam: Synthesis, Rhetorical Analysis, and Argument. These responses are often called essays, but they differ from what you may be writing as essays in the actual course or in other classes. The goal of these prompts is to demonstrate your response in a set amount of time, showing that you have all the necessary skills, knowledge, and understanding to produce effective writing. You do not need to worry too much about the style of your writing on these responses. It does matter, but not nearly as much as your claim, your reasoning, your organization, and your use of evidence and examples. Even introductions and conclusions are not strictly required. While they may help, they also may take away time you will need to develop a successful argument.

In short, write a very good first draft of an essay you would expand later if you had the time.

Scoring the FRQ involves a scoring rubric that analyzes certain parts of your response to see if you have earned points across three different "rows."

Row A: Thesis (0–1 point)

Row B: Evidence and Commentary (0–4 points)

Row C: Sophistication (0–1 point)

Total possible points: 6

Though there are a total of 6 points possible, getting a 4 or 5 out of 6 is still a good score. The points get more difficult to get as you move down the rubric, meaning that the thesis point should be the easiest to get while the sophistication point is the most difficult. In fact, the sophistication point relies on so many different parts of the response working together that it is not only difficult, but *very* difficult to get. This means that a score of 1 in Row A, 4 in Row B, and 0 in Row C would get a total score of 5/6—which is a pretty good score.

Synthesis This type of free-response question will provide you with a topic along with a brief introduction to the rhetorical situation of that topic. You are then also provided 6 or 7 sources from the real world. These will always include 2 visuals, one of which must be quantitative (graph or chart, for example) while the other could be quantitative or qualitative. All of the reading sources will be either easily or moderately accessible.

Example of a Synthesis Prompt

Below is how the directions for the Synthesis prompt will appear on the exam:

In your response you should do the following:

- Respond to the prompt with a thesis that presents a defensible position.
- Select and use evidence from at least three of the provided sources to support your line of reasoning. Indicate clearly the sources used through direct quotation, paraphrase, or summary. Sources may be cited as Source A, Source B, etc., or by using the description in parentheses.
- Explain how the evidence supports your line of reasoning.
- Use appropriate grammar and punctuation in communicating your argument.

Specifics on Scoring the Synthesis FRQ

Row-by-Row

A. THESIS: Must have a thesis focused on the prompt. It must provide a claim, be clearly defensible, and not simply restate the prompt or summarize the situation. (0–1 point)

B. EVIDENCE AND COMMENTARY: To get 2 or more points, you must have 3 or more sources. If you only summarize the evidence but do not connect it to the argument, then you cannot score above a 2. Scores of 3 and 4 in this row are for responses that use very specific evidence, and a 4 is for responses that consistently explain how that evidence supports the reasoning of the argument. (0–4 points)

C. SOPHISTICATION: While there are several factors to consider across all of the FRQ types, for Synthesis in particular, the sophistication point may depend on: "Crafting a nuanced argument by consistently identifying and exploring complexities or tensions across the sources." (0–1 point)

Rhetorical Analysis A second type of free-response question resembles the reading multiple-choice questions, except in this case you are given a prompt to respond to creating an analysis of the entire passage. As with the Synthesis FRQ, you will be provided with a brief introduction to the topic and the rhetorical situation of the passage. You will then be asked to read and analyze the choices that the speaker or writer makes to accomplish a specific goal.

Example of a Rhetorical Analysis Prompt

Below is how the Rhetorical Analysis prompt will appear on the exam:

In your response you should do the following:

- Respond to the prompt with a thesis that analyzes the writer's rhetorical choices.
- Select and use evidence to support your line of reasoning.
- Explain how the evidence supports your line of reasoning.
- Demonstrate an understanding of the rhetorical situation.
- Use appropriate grammar and punctuation in communicating your argument.

Specifics on Scoring the Rhetorical Analysis FRQ

Row-by-Row

A. THESIS: Must have a thesis that provides at least the general choices made in the reading that will be analyzed. (0–1 point)

B. EVIDENCE AND COMMENTARY: To get 2 or more points, explain at least some of the evidence you provide and not just summarize it. If you only summarize the evidence but do not connect it to the argument, then you cannot score above a 2. Scores of 3 and 4 in this row will be for responses that provide very specific evidence and explain how one or more choices contribute to the argument/purpose/message of the passage, and a 4 will be for responses that consistently explain how that evidence supports the reasoning of the argument. (0–4 points)

C. SOPHISTICATION: While there are several factors to consider across all of the FRQ types, for Rhetorical Analysis in particular, the sophistication point may depend on: "Explaining the significance or relevance of the writer's rhetorical choices (given the rhetorical situation)" and "explaining a purpose or function of the passage's complexities or tensions." (0–1 point)

Argument The final type of free-response question provides you with a topic and very brief introduction to the rhetorical situation. You then are asked to write a response that argues your position on some aspect of the topic provided. This task is very similar to what you are asked to do on the Synthesis FRQ, but in this case you are not given sources. Instead, you must draw upon evidence and examples from your experiences with the world around you (via media, personal experience, and history, for example).

Example of an Argument Prompt

Below is how the Argument prompt will appear on the exam:

In your response you should do the following:

- Respond to the prompt with a thesis that presents a defensible position.
- Provide evidence to support your line of reasoning.
- Explain how the evidence supports your line of reasoning.
- Use appropriate grammar and punctuation in communicating your argument.

Specifics on Scoring the Argument FRQ

Row-by-Row

A. THESIS: Must have a thesis focused on the prompt. It must provide a claim, be clearly defensible, and not simply restate the prompt or summarize the situation. (0–1 point)

B. EVIDENCE AND COMMENTARY: To get 2 or more points, explain at least some of the evidence you provide and not just summarize it. If you only summarize the evidence but do not connect it to the argument, then you cannot score above a 2. Scores of 3 and 4 in this row will be for responses that use very specific evidence, and a 4 will be for responses that consistently explain how that evidence supports the reasoning of the argument. (0–4 points)

C. SOPHISTICATION: While there are several things to consider across all of the FRQ types, for Rhetorical Analysis in particular, the sophistication point may depend on: "Crafting a nuanced argument by consistently identifying and exploring complexities or tensions" and "articulating the implications or limitations of an argument by situating it within a broader context." (0–1 point)

Overall Scoring and Credit

The exams are scored in early June and reported back to you and your high school in mid-summer. You can earn between 0 and 5 points.

Many colleges award credit for a score of 3 or better; some require a 5; and occasionally prestigious universities do not recognize AP exam performance. The College Board equates a score of 5 to an A in a college-level class, a 4 to an A-, B+, or B, and a 3 to roughly a B-, C+, or C.

Be realistic about expectations: In 2019, just over 10 percent of those taking the exam earned a score of 5. Of the nearly 600,000 students who took the exam, only two students earned all of the possible points. That means they got all of the multiple choice correct and then got the highest possible scores of their essays, too. These students represent about .000003% of students taking the exam. A score of 3 is realistic to qualify for credit, but for some people a score of 2 will be honorable.

A Final Note

Language matters. Every day, people are bombarded with posts, tweets, reports, or other texts in which someone says something the wrong way. Every day, someone reads something in a way the author didn't mean. In both cases conflict is the unfortunate result. Sometimes people simply neglect to be as thoughtful with their words as they should be. Even worse, sometimes people use language as a weapon to hurt or mislead people.

Regardless of your score on the exam, this class—and all English classes—are about being responsible users of language. Now more than ever, responsible rhetoric that makes a sincere effort to understand others with an open mind and takes care to express ideas as precisely and respectfully as possible may lift civil discourse and point the way to better understanding of issues that matter.

Review Schedule

Set up a review schedule as you prepare for the exam in the weeks before the test. Start a study group with some of your classmates to intensify your review by talking about the concepts and quizzing one another.

Below is a sample of an eight-week review schedule, including information on the units in this book that cover the content to review. Because AP® tests are given during the first two full weeks of May, this review schedule assumes you begin your review in mid-March.

PROPOSED REVIEW SCHEDULE		
Week	Content	Units
1	The Unending Conversation (Rhetorical Situation) Selecting Evidence to Motivate an Audience	1 2
2	Connecting an Argument	3
3	Structuring and Organizing Arguments	4
4	Structuring and Supporting Coherent Arguments	5
5	Synthesizing Perspectives and Refining Arguments	6
6	Style as Substance	7
7	Using Style Strategically	8
8	Contributing to the Conversation (Engaging Counterarguments)	9

Other Review Suggestions

Use every possible way to make the material your own—read it, take notes on it, talk about it, create visualizations of it, and relate the ideas in this book to your prior experience and learning. In other words, think about how it connects to ideas in your other courses and to your personal life experiences. The following approaches will help you accomplish this goal:

- Start preparing for the AP® English Language and Composition exam the first day of class.
- Form a weekly study group. Use the Essential Question from each unit part as the starting point for your discussion, focusing on how the material you learned during the week helps to answer that question. Ask questions about anything you do not understand. The weekly meetings ensure that you will prepare on a regular basis, and they also give you a chance to speak about and listen to the concepts you are learning in addition to reading and writing about them.
- Work collaboratively in other ways, such as doing the open response activities in the Checkpoints
- Use the techniques of the cognitive scientists (cognitive psychologists) at http://www.learningscientists.org/. They offer free and more detailed information on the six strategies outlined on the next page, which have been proven in research to help people learn.

RESEARCH-BASED LEARNING STRATEGIES	
Distributed Practice	Spread out your studying over the entire course in manageable amounts.
Retrieval	After every class, or on another regular schedule, close your book and try to recall the important points, using a practice called retrieval. You can use the Reflect on the Essential Question feature at the end of each part as a framework. Write whatever you can't retrieve from memory alone by going back into the book for the missing pieces. Whether you use sample multiple-choice questions, flash cards, or an online program such as Quizlet, take the time to test yourself with a friend or on your own.
Elaboration	When studying, ask yourself questions about what you are reading. How does this material connect to other material in the unit? As you learn material, elaborate on it by connecting it to what you are experiencing in your daily life.
Interleaving	Few exams go in the order of how topics are presented in the text. The AP® English Language and Composition exam certainly does not. When you study, interleave the material. Switch up the order of your review. For example, when reviewing Units 1–3, change the order of your study. Switch it up to 2, 1, and 3. Then during your next review session, follow a different order—3, 2, and 1, for example. Use this technique only occasionally.
Concrete Examples	Write down all concrete examples your teacher uses in class. Note the examples given in this book. Use these examples to understand the application of the abstract concepts and ideas you are studying.
Dual Coding	Use dual coding, different ways of representing the information. Take notes or write reflections on a segment of text. Then create a visual representation of the same knowledge using graphic organizers, concept maps, drawings with labels, or other graphics.

UNIT 1

The Unending Conversation

Part 1: The Rhetorical Situation
Part 2: Claims and Evidence

ENDURING UNDERSTANDINGS AND SKILLS: Unit One

Part 1

Understand

Individuals write within a particular situation and make strategic writing choices based on that situation. (RHS-1)

Demonstrate

Identify and describe components of the rhetorical situation: the exigence, audience, writer, purpose, context, and message. (Reading 1.A)

Part 2

Understand

Writers make claims about subjects, rely on evidence that supports the reasoning that justifies the claim, and often acknowledge or respond to other, possibly opposing, arguments. (CLE-1)

Demonstrate

Identify and explain claims and evidence within an argument. (Reading 3.A)

Develop a paragraph that includes a claim and evidence supporting the claim. (Writing 4.A)

Source: *AP® English Language and Composition Course and Exam Description*

Unit 1 Overview

In 2013, a White female executive for a large company boarded a plane in London for an 11-hour flight to South Africa. Before her plane took off, she tweeted what to her was a joke about AIDS that implied she wouldn't get the disease because she was White. While she was on the flight, she had no Internet access, so she could not immediately see that social media exploded in response to her tweet, nor could she see her bosses' tweet that "we are taking appropriate action," implying that she had been fired. Her bosses saw an immediate need to step in and defend the company's public image even before talking to her.

The executive, ironically employed as an expert in corporate communications, may have thought that her audience was her 170 followers on

Twitter at the time, who very well might have found her comment amusing. But because of the viral spread of her tweet, thousands of people outside her circle saw it and condemned it. With the widening of her audience, the executive had stumbled into ongoing conversations about AIDS and race and money and fairness for which she was not prepared. She found herself engaged with others who were already in those conversations and who knew much more—and took the subject much more seriously—than she did. At that point, she entered the broader conversation intentionally, issuing an apology "for being insensitive to this crisis—which does not discriminate by race, gender, or sexual orientation, but which terrifies us all uniformly—and to the millions of people living with the virus, I am ashamed."

Entering Conversations Ongoing conversations are everywhere—in every country, every family, every school, every business, and every community that faces any kind of challenge. Each of these conversations arises out of a unique situation—how to spend tax money, whether to get a dog, whether to shut down school in the face of a contagious virus, whether to change an intersection to a roundabout. The words and ideas within these conversations have power to advance understanding, but as the example of the privileged executive illustrates, they can also set it back when used to diminish others.

Philosopher and literary critic Kenneth Burke created a metaphor that describes arguments as an unending or enduring conversation.

> Imagine that you enter a parlor. You come late. When you arrive, others have long preceded you, and they are engaged in a heated discussion, a discussion too heated for them to pause and tell you exactly what it is about. In fact, the discussion had already begun long before any of them got there, so that no one present is qualified to retrace for you all the steps that had gone before. You listen for a while, until you decide that you have caught the tenor of the argument; then you put in your oar. Someone answers; you answer him; another comes to your defense; another aligns himself against you, to either the embarrassment or gratification of your opponent, depending upon the quality of your ally's assistance. However, the discussion is interminable. The hour grows late, you must depart. And you do depart, with the discussion still vigorously in progress.
> —*The Philosophy of Literary Form*, 1941

Developing Positions As you develop your writing and argumentation skills, everything you create becomes part of an ongoing conversation. Almost all writing is in response to something—from a simple thank-you note for a birthday gift to an inspiring graduation speech. In academic writing, almost all writing is in response to something you have read and likely discussed with your peers. As you consider where your ideas fit into the conversation, you begin to develop your own position, and as you learn more about a topic, you develop an understanding that allows you to reason through the evidence.

Writers throughout history have grappled with many of the same issues that concern contemporary writers and have added their voices to the unending conversation. This course will help prepare you to add yours.

Describe the figures at this table. What perspectives might these people have had on the issues of their times? Why is it important to have a variety of perspectives "in the parlor"?

This unit will provide an explanation of the situation out of which writing emerges—the *rhetorical situation*. It will also explore how writers establish their own position on a subject by developing a claim, supporting that claim with evidence, and clearly showing the thinking and reasoning that relates to that position. These are the fundamental tools for reading and writing effective arguments: recognizing and asserting claims, analyzing and using experiences and evidence from reliable sources to support the claims, and understanding where each argument fits into the "unending conversation."

To help you develop these tools, this book will give you practice in

- **close reading**, a careful analysis of the details and patterns within a text that shape its purpose and effect
- **evaluating writing**, a critical look at drafts of writing to evaluate the strategies and choices of writers and how they might be improved
- **composing,** the creation of your own written work as you apply what you have learned through close reading and evaluating writing

To provide this practice, each unit includes

- an "anchor text," a high-quality written (or spoken) piece for you to analyze carefully, respond to in writing, and show comprehension by answering AP®-style multiple-choice questions. An anchor icon like the one on the following page accompanies each of these texts.
- an "anchor student draft," a work-in-progress for you to examine critically and evaluate the writing choices of others. You will also answer multiple-choice questions on this text that are similar to those found on the AP® test.
- writing activities as well as a writing prompt like those you will see on the AP® exam to provide practice in creating your own compositions

The three goals and elements of each unit are interconnected. Close reading will help you become a better writer; evaluating the writing of others will help you become a better reader and writer; and writing your own compositions will help you improve not only your writing but also your close-reading skills.

Close Reading: Professional Text
Greta Thunberg's Speech to the United Nations

Following is a speech Greta Thunberg, a climate activist from Sweden, gave when she was 16 years old. After starting protests outside of her own country's parliament calling for "school-strikes" until governments act against climate change, she was invited to speak to a gathering of representatives at the United Nations. She sailed across the ocean to avoid pollution caused by airplanes and then she delivered this speech on September 23, 2019. You will return to this anchor text throughout the unit. For now, read it to understand the main or central ideas Thunberg expresses as she contributes to the conversation about climate change.

1 "This is all wrong. I shouldn't be up here. I should be back in school on the other side of the ocean. Yet you all come to us young people for hope. How dare you!

2 "You have stolen my dreams and my childhood with your empty words. And yet I'm one of the lucky ones. People are suffering. People are dying. Entire ecosystems are collapsing. We are in the beginning of a mass extinction, and all you can talk about is money and fairy tales of eternal economic growth. How dare you!

3 "For more than 30 years, the science has been crystal clear. How dare you continue to look away and come here saying that you're doing enough, when the politics and solutions needed are still nowhere in sight.

4 "You say you hear us and that you understand the urgency. But no matter how sad and angry I am, I do not want to believe that. Because if you really understood the situation and still kept on failing to act, then you would be evil. And that I refuse to believe.

5 "The popular idea of cutting our emissions in half in 10 years only gives us a 50% chance of staying below 1.5 degrees [Celsius], and the risk of setting off irreversible chain reactions beyond human control.

6 "Fifty percent may be acceptable to you. But those numbers do not include tipping points, most feedback loops, additional warming hidden by toxic air pollution or the aspects of equity and climate justice. They also rely on my generation sucking hundreds of billions of tons of your CO_2 out of the air with technologies that barely exist.

7 "So a 50% risk is simply not acceptable to us—we who have to live with the consequences.

8 "To have a 67% chance of staying below a 1.5 degree global temperature rise—the best odds given by the [Intergovernmental Panel on Climate Change]—the world had 420 gigatons of CO_2 left to emit back on Jan. 1st, 2018. Today that figure is already down to less than 350 gigatons.

9 "How dare you pretend that this can be solved with just 'business as usual' and some technical solutions? With today's emissions levels, that remaining CO_2 budget will be entirely gone within less than 8 ½ years.

10 "There will not be any solutions or plans presented in line with these figures here today, because these numbers are too uncomfortable. And you are still not mature enough to tell it like it is.

11 "You are failing us. But the young people are starting to understand your betrayal. The eyes of all future generations are upon you. And if you choose to fail us, I say: We will never forgive you.

12 "We will not let you get away with this. Right here, right now is where we draw the line. The world is waking up. And change is coming, whether you like it or not.

13 "Thank you."

Composing on Your Own

Respond to the ideas in Thunberg's speech by writing your own thoughts on climate change. Write freely. Ask yourself questions to generate ideas and thoughts. You will develop these ideas throughout this unit, so save your work for future use.

Evaluating Writing: Student Draft
Climate Change

Following is the anchor student draft you will use in this unit to practice evaluating and editing writing. A student wrote it for an Earth Day project in which seniors were invited to submit short writings for an environmental website called "Dear Parents." This draft still needs work. As you read it, think about what it contributes to the conversation on climate change and compare it to the ideas you wrote down. Later you will have an opportunity to suggest ways the writing might be improved.

> (1) Though few experts disagree that climate change is happening, there are some who argue the actual causes of it. (2) For many, evidence that it is caused by people is clear, while some see it as a natural cycle of warming and cooling. (3) Regardless of the cause, climate change is happening. (4) "The entirety of many island nations and large portions of other countries with low-lying coastal lands, including the United States, will be underwater." (5) Millions will relocate inland, increasing housing costs and adding pressure to inland cities to support these new residents. (6) Agreement that the climate is changing is only the beginning of preparing for the changes it will cause. (7) While many people argue over the cause and who to blame, people must recognize that the world is going to change. (8) Only then can we begin trying to fix what is clearly broken.

What Do You Know?

This unit will explore the rhetorical situation and the claims and evidence that make arguments effective in particular contexts. Before digging in, assess what you already know about the rhetorical situation, claims, and evidence by answering questions about the anchor text by Greta Thunberg and the student draft on climate change. Answering questions on subjects before formally studying them is a good way to learn, according to learning scientists.

CLOSE READING: PROFESSIONAL TEXT

1. What was Thunberg's exigence, or motivation, for this speech?
2. What does she hope to accomplish with this speech? How do you know?
3. What claims does she make, and what evidence supports those?

EVALUATING WRITING: STUDENT DRAFT

1. What is the exigence for this writer's work?
2. In what ways are the audience for this writing and Thunberg's speech similar?
3. In what ways are the audience for this writing and Thunberg's speech different?

Greta Thunberg addresses climate strikers at Civic Center Park in Denver, Colorado, on October 11, 2019.

Most of the attendees standing behind Thunberg in this photo are Native Americans. What might their presence suggest about Thunberg's message?

Part 1

The Rhetorical Situation

Enduring Understanding and Skill

Part 1

Understand

Individuals write within a particular situation and make strategic writing choices based on that situation. (RHS-1)

Demonstrate

Identify and describe components of the rhetorical situation: the exigence, audience, writer, purpose, context, and message. (Reading 1.A)

Source: *AP® English Language and Composition Course and Exam Description*

Essential Question: What are the components of the rhetorical situation?

Understanding the rhetorical situation is important to you as both a reader and a writer. As a reader, you identify the parts of the rhetorical situation to fully understand the author's message and to evaluate how effective the writing is. If you don't know the purpose of the writing and for whom it was written, how can you determine if it is successful?

As a writer, you identify the rhetorical situation to position your ideas in relation to others' within the "unending conversation" on the subject you are writing about. To whom are you responding? What has sparked you to write? What do you hope to achieve? Why are you the person to write this? Without knowing the rhetorical situation, how would you know what to say or how to say it?

KEY TERMS

audience	purpose
context	rhetorical situation
exigence	speaker
message	writer

1.1 Elements of the Rhetorical Situation | RHS-1.A

Whether a tweet, text, email, or essay, all written communication takes place within a rhetorical situation. The **rhetorical situation** of a text collectively refers to the exigence, purpose, audience, writer, context, and message. Writers make key decisions about what to say and how to say it based on their specific situation.

The Communication Situation

As Kenneth Burke vividly described in the parlor metaphor (see Unit Overview), every essay and every speech become part of an ongoing conversation. Yet each operates within a unique rhetorical situation, which includes the

- **exigence** (the problem the essay or speech addresses; the impetus)
- **purpose** (the goals the writer or speaker wants to achieve)
- **audience** (receivers of the message who often have a variety of values and beliefs)
- **writer or speaker** (a unique voice with values and beliefs)
- **context** (the time, place, and occasion)
- **message** (the substance of the writer's or speaker's main points)

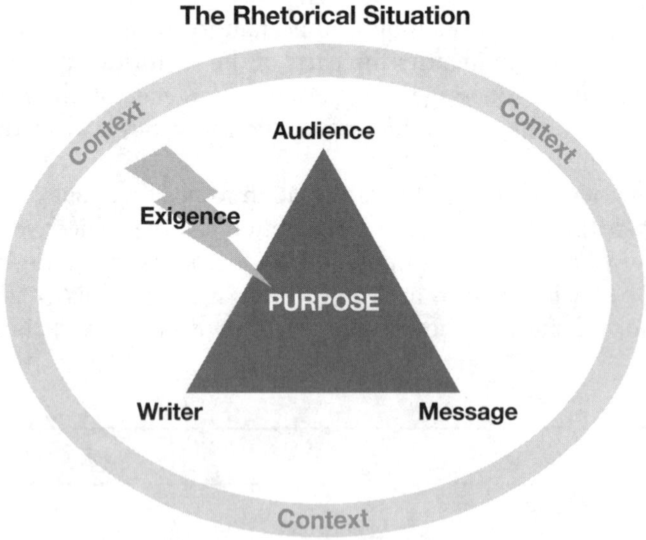

Figure 1-1

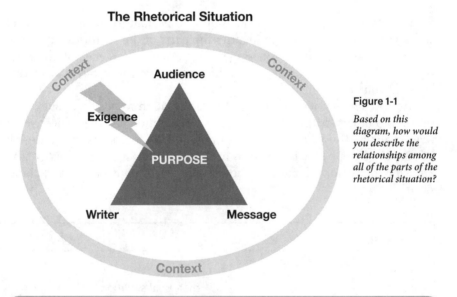

Based on this diagram, how would you describe the relationships among all of the parts of the rhetorical situation?

Remember: The rhetorical situation of a text collectively refers to the exigence, purpose, audience, writer, context, and message. (RHS-1.A)

1.1 Checkpoint

Close Reading: Professional Text

Though you will learn much more about each one of the elements of the rhetorical situation in the pages that follow, try to complete the following task and answer the multiple-choice question.

1. On separate paper, make an illustration similar to Figure 1.1 on the previous page, but for each element ,write the specific details related to Greta Thunberg's speech. For example, under "Writer" you would write "Greta Thunberg."

The multiple-choice questions in the Checkpoint sections are modeled on those on the AP® English Language and Composition exam.

2. Which of the following best describes Thunberg's purpose within her rhetorical situation?
   (A) to speak to representatives of the United Nations
   (B) to promote her status as a young environmental activist
   (C) to persuade world leaders to address climate change
   (D) to employ language that scolds world leaders
   (E) to rally young people to her cause

1.2 Exigence | RHS-1.B

In general use, the word *exigence* means "a case or situation that demands prompt action or remedy." It carries the idea of an urgent task or an emergency. In the rhetorical situation, the exigence may not be quite so urgent, but it does refer to the impetus or problem that evokes a response. The exigence prompts a **writer** or **speaker** to address the situation.

The Impetus

As Figure 1-1 on the previous page shows, the spark that ignites the need for the writer to write (or the speaker to speak) is the **exigence**, the problem or situation that propels the act of creating a text. Anything can be an exigence if it makes a person feel the need to respond to it in writing or formal speech:

- An invitation to a graduation party may prompt a relative to write a congratulatory note.
- A low test score may cause a student to write an email to the teacher.
- The behavior of a student in an elementary school may compel a teacher to call the parents.
- Decisions by a local school board to change grading policies may motivate a student (or group of students) to write to the board or even speak at a meeting.

Think of exigence and writing as a cause and effect relationship.

The Exigence of Rhetoric

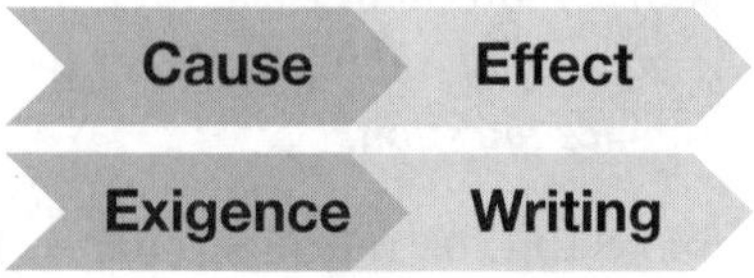

Figure 1-2

> **Remember:** The exigence is the part of a rhetorical situation that inspires, stimulates, provokes, or prompts writers to create a text. (RHS-1.B)

1.2 Checkpoint

Close Reading: Professional Text
Reread Greta Thunberg's speech and consider what you know about her. Then answer the following open response and multiple-choice questions.

1. How would you describe Thunberg's exigence? That is, what prompted her to speak?

2. Can you identify more than one exigence? If so, how might they relate?

3. Which of the following best describes the author's exigence in the speech?
   (A) her desire to persuade young people to become environmentally conscious
   (B) her concern that world leaders are ignoring the devastating consequences of climate change
   (C) her dissatisfaction with the economic consequences of climate change
   (D) her hope to devise an effective economic response to climate change for future generations
   (E) her belief that world leaders are well-intentioned people

Evaluating Writing: Student Draft
Reread the student draft on climate change on page 5. Find and explain two examples of how the differences in exigence affect Thunberg's language choices and the student writer's choices.

1.3 Purpose | RHS-1.C

A key part of evaluating a text is understanding the writer's **purpose**, or goal, for writing.

Writer's Goal

If the exigence is the writer's motivation, the purpose is what the writer wants to happen as a result of the writing. The writer may issue a "call to action," urging readers to take an action to bring about change. Or the writer may simply argue for readers to reconsider an issue and affirm that the writer's position is valid.

The method a writer chooses depends in part on that writer's purpose. For example, if the purpose is to entertain, a writer might tell an engaging story. If the purpose is to inform readers, a writer might compare something—the difference between the terms "climate change" and "climate crisis," for example—or explain or describe a subject in another way.

Whether a call to action or a desire to influence, inform, or entertain, purpose is intentional. Sometimes readers can find purpose explicitly in the text—they can point to where the writer makes it clear—while sometimes the writer only implies a purpose that is suggested at various points in the text. In either case, the writer wants something to happen in response to the exigence and decides to enter the conversation on a subject in order to make that happen.

Remember: The purpose of a text is what the writer hopes to accomplish with it. Writers may have more than one purpose in a text. (RHS-1.C)

1.3 Checkpoint

Close Reading: Professional Text

Reread Greta Thunberg's speech, and then answer the following open response and multiple-choice questions.

1. What does Thunberg want to make happen as a result of her speech? In other words, what is her purpose?

2. Is Thunberg's purpose explicitly stated or implied? Explain your answer with details from the speech.

3. Which of the following best characterizes Thunberg's purpose in the passage?
   (A) to reject the authority of the United Nations
   (B) to show the correlation between economic and environmental issues
   (C) to persuade listeners that some world leaders may be evil
   (D) to urge leaders to significantly cut emissions instead of following their current policies
   (E) to convince listeners that CO_2 emissions are the single greatest threat to the environment

1.4 Audience | RHS-1.D

A writer's purpose may be thought of as the *why* of the text. A writer must also think about *who* the audience is. A writer's **audience** is the people who will be reading or hearing the message. The audience could be young or old, rich or poor, powerful or vulnerable, male or female or nonbinary. The audience could also be a mix of these. The audience will likely have both shared and unique values, needs, and backgrounds.

Targeting Your Message

The exigence and purpose for writing an argument are intertwined with the intended audience. To get a message across, you need to understand and assess the target of your message. The easiest way to assess an audience is to look closely at their values. People usually make decisions about what they do and say based on the principles they value most. Consider their beliefs, their history or background, and their needs and desires.

Taking these things into account, a writer will be able to make decisions about what to say and how to say it—decisions that will make the argument reach its intended audience. This skill is at the heart of "rhetoric," as the famous Greek philosopher Aristotle explained it: ". . .the faculty of observing, in any given case, the available means of persuasion." The more a writer takes the audience into account, the more tools that writer has available to make a persuasive argument.

Consider how audience influences a writer's choices by looking on the next page at the two different text message conversations a student might have on a Friday night. Notice that the facts are the same in each exchange—the student doesn't lie to her mom. The reactions and content of the different exchanges are "adjusted," though, based on the two different audiences. In this example, the mom values the daughter's safety above all and the daughter knows it, so she is certain to give a detailed response to her mom's first question. In the second conversation, Izzy values her friendship and having fun and the student knows it, so she reacts accordingly with excitement and anticipation.

Figure 1-3

If the student above gave all of the facts to her mom, including Julio's interest in her, then the exchange may have turned into an argument. Instead, without lying, the daughter made strategic communication choices knowing what would concern her mother. While writers generate their ideas and positions from their own values and concerns, they also take the values and concerns of their audience seriously, a key strategy for persuasion.

Remember: An audience of a text has shared as well as individual beliefs, values, needs, and backgrounds. (RHS-1.D)

The person in this picture appears deep in thought as she reads something on her phone. What are some things to consider about your audiences when writing text messages or social media posts?

Source: Getty Images

1.4 Checkpoint

Close Reading: Professional Text

Review Thunberg's speech. Then answer the following open response and multiple-choice questions.

1. What does Thunberg assume her audience values? How do you know?

2. Based on those values, what are some of the strategic choices that Thunberg makes in her speech?

3. In paragraph 9, Thunberg asks, "How dare you pretend that this can be solved with just 'business as usual' and some technical solutions?" This question shows that Thunberg assumes her audience

(A) is making serious investments in technological solutions to the climate crisis

(B) believes that the problem is not as extreme as she paints it and that substantial action is not needed

(C) recognizes the existential challenge of climate change and is committed to addressing it

(D) takes her and the younger generation seriously as agents for change

(E) values the future and is willing to make "business as usual" sacrifices for long-term good

4. The use of the pronoun "you" throughout the speech refers to

(A) citizens from Sweden and Swedish political leaders

(B) children of the speaker's generation and the generation following hers

(C) officially appointed members of the United Nations the author considers "evil"

(D) global leaders and United Nations representatives

(E) international school children, especially the children of political leaders

5. In addressing her audience, the author speaks to them as if they were

(A) irresponsible children

(B) intentional hypocrites

(C) cruel and evil

(D) responsible adults

(E) compassionate politicians

6. Much of Thunberg's speech assumes that her environmental concerns have largely been treated by her central audience with a sense of

    (A) cautiousness
    (B) fear
    (C) urgency
    (D) sincerity
    (E) indifference

1.5 Context and Message | RHS-1.E

Writers know that the idea they want to convey—their **message**—is strongly influenced by the **context** of the writing, which includes the time, place, and occasion.

When, Where, and What

Writing doesn't happen in a vacuum. That is, any writing happens within a context, or situation, that helps shape the writing. The immediate *when, where*, and *what* of a context are the time, place, and occasion for the writing. A broader context also includes the ongoing conversations—what other people have written and talked about—on the subject of the writer's message.

For example, the executive who sent the insulting tweet did not consider the context of "the Twittersphere" or the broad topics of AIDS and racial injustice, so her message not only failed in its original purpose but also came back to hurt her. To achieve their purposes, writers consider both the immediate context as well as the broader context as they make choices about what they will say and how they will say it.

Immediate and Broader Context		
Message: Insulting tweet about AIDS and race		
	Immediate Context	**Broader Context**
Time	Right before an 11-hour flight	A time when hundreds a day were being infected with AIDS in Africa alone
Place	London and South Africa and the Twittersphere	A developed and wealthy country vs. some developing and poorer countries in Africa, and a social media platform known for viral messages
Occasion	Leaving on a family trip	Arriving in a country with a history of racial oppression under apartheid

Table 1-1

Context also extends to broad categories of thought. To determine the broader categories a subject may fit into, imagine in what section of the library different books on that subject might be shelved.

Categories for Context	
History Popular Culture Art/Literature Science	Sports Current Events Philosophy or Religion Government and Politics

Table 1-2

Consider this example: Suppose a school board will soon be voting on whether to require school uniforms. A student developing an argument about school uniforms must take into account the immediate context—in this case, the possibility of addressing the school board before they vote on requiring school uniforms—as well as broader contexts that may relate to school uniforms. Ideas from these broader contexts might influence the argument.

Broader Contexts for School Uniforms

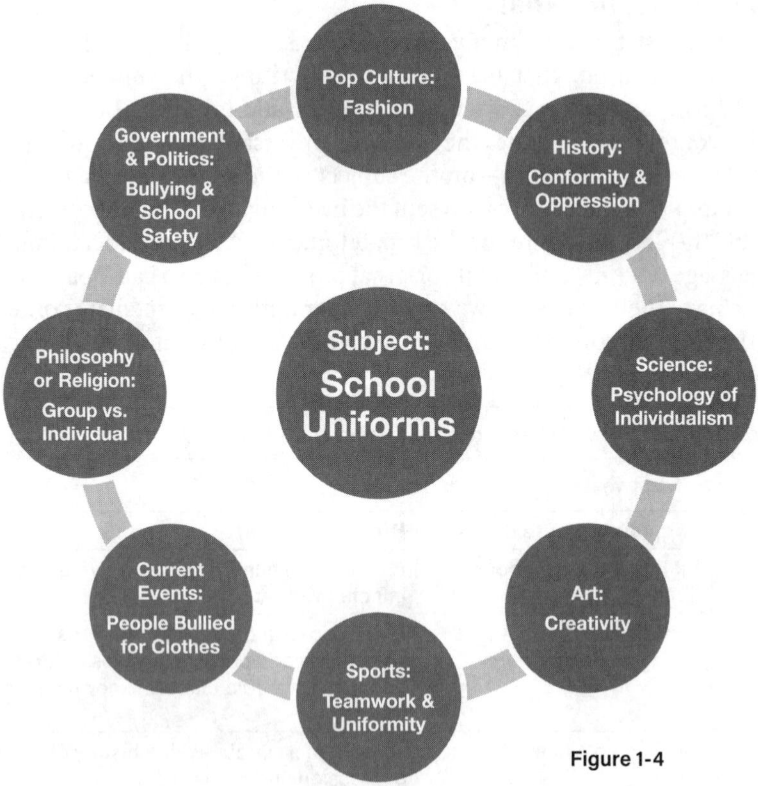

Figure 1-4

These broader contexts are sometimes called the "worlds" of the argument. Connecting to one or more of these worlds adds a universal dimension to your argument.

The way items are arranged in a graphic often reflects their relationship. What does the arrangement of the satellite circles say about their relationship to the center circle?

Information and ideas from these (and many other) categories contribute to the larger context of the discussion about school uniforms. Many people already having that conversation have considered these factors and taken them into account in their arguments. When new people join the conversation, they must take time to consider these—to learn about the context that surrounds the conversation—and then begin making choices that will allow them to join the ongoing conversation in a meaningful way.

The student considered what she could learn from the broader contexts, and, based on what she learned, she decided to support school uniforms. Here's how she might have thought through the ways in which context would affect her message and the choices she should make in presenting her argument.

Effects of Context on Message		
Message: The school board should vote to require school uniforms.		
	Context	**Effect on Message**
Immediate context	School board meeting on Thursday night at 7:30 p.m. in the auditorium with a vote scheduled for 9:00 p.m.	The audience will be adults, and the situation is formal, so the message should be respectful and formal, unlike the Thunberg speech.
Broader contexts	**Sports:** Uniforms have a unifying effect. **Current events:** Students are bullied for clothes they wear. **Government:** School safety is at stake.	By referring to these contexts, the student can provide reasons beyond simple opinions to back up her position by pointing to their effect on the school community. Her message might therefore include some examples of schools where uniforms made a positive difference.

Table 1-3

Remember: Writers create texts within a particular context that includes the time, place, and occasion. (RHS-1.E)

1.5 Checkpoint

Close Reading: Professional Text

Reread Greta Thunberg's speech and the paragraph that introduces it on page 4. Then answer the following open response and multiple-choice questions.

1. What is the immediate context of Thunberg's speech?

2. How might the immediate context have influenced Thunberg's choices?

3. Review the categories of broader context in the figure on page 16. What categories of context are relevant to Thunberg's speech? What research could you do to better understand the different contexts of her speech? Explain your answer.

4. What other details about the context of the speech may have affected Thunberg's choices? What details about the context affect the way you read it?

5. Which rhetorical choice in Thunberg's speech has the **LEAST** relevance to her awareness of the context in which her arguments will be heard?
   (A) her decision to not introduce herself formally
   (B) the tone of reprimand she directs at her audience
   (C) her emphasis on generational consequences
   (D) references to specific dates and time frames
   (E) citing statistics from recognized authorities

6. Which of the following broader contexts does Thunberg address in her speech?
   (A) morality and the arts
   (B) popular culture and science
   (C) arts and history
   (D) science and current events
   (E) sports and popular culture

Evaluating Writing: Student Draft
Reread the student draft on climate change on page 5. Explain how the context of the student's writing might have influenced the student writer's choices.

Composing on Your Own
Review the writing you started on climate change. Also think about some of the other subjects mentioned in Part 1: AIDS, racial injustice, communication with friends and family, and school uniforms. Choose one of these subjects or a different one not listed. In writing, develop and explain your position on the subject you chose. Save your work for future use.

Part 1 Apply What You Have Learned

Read the speech "A Whisper of AIDS" by Mary Fisher at americanrhetoric.com or another site. Bookmark the site so you can return to it. Make a two-column chart with the elements of the rhetorical situation in the left-hand column. In the right-hand column, identify each element in Mary Fisher's speech.

Reflect on the Essential Question Write a brief response that answers this essential question: *What are the components of the rhetorical situation?* In your answer, explain the key terms listed on page 7.

Part 2

Claims and Evidence

Enduring Understanding and Skills

Part 2

Understand

Writers make claims about subjects, rely on evidence that supports the reasoning that justifies the claim, and often acknowledge or respond to other, possibly opposing, arguments. (CLE-1)

Demonstrate

Identify and explain claims and evidence within an argument. (Reading 3.A)

Develop a paragraph that includes a claim and evidence supporting the claim. (Writing 4.A)

Source: *AP® English Language and Composition Course and Exam Description*

Essential Questions: As a reader, how can you identify a writer's position and the way that position is supported? As a writer, how can you develop and support your own position?

Two parents and two teenage girls are sitting at a kitchen table. The teenagers look mad at each other. One parent is explaining to the other, "Erin claims that she and Maddy were late for school because Maddy wanted to take time to shoot basketball in the park on the way to school. Maddy claims they were late for school because Erin thought she lost her phone and retraced her steps to try to find it, even though it turned out to be at the bottom of her backpack."

Both teens have different positions and are not willing to abandon their points of view. Their claims reflect their positions, and each of them must prove her claim by providing evidence or by explaining how her ideas are reasonable. In other words, each must explain how her own argument makes sense and how her sister's argument does not.

The word *claim* carries a sense of uncertainty. It is not a statement of fact. A claim needs proof to be believed and accepted. Claims are proven or supported through convincing evidence and logical thinking (reasoning). This section will help you identify and explain how writers make their positions clear through claims and support those claims with evidence and reasoning. It will also provide instruction in writing a paragraph that includes a clearly stated claim and effective supporting evidence.

KEY TERMS

analogies	expert opinions	quote
anecdotes	facts	reasoning
claims	illustrations	statistics
evidence	paraphrase	summarize
examples	personal observations	testimonies
experiments	position	

2.1 Claims | CLE-1.A

Writers convey their positions through one or more claims. Because these claims are not necessarily factual but instead are asserted to be true, they need to be backed up with evidence.

Stating Positions

Often, as you begin digging into a subject, you will find information that causes you to think about the subject in a certain way. You begin to ask questions about the subject. As you answer these questions, you develop a position and, ultimately, a specific claim about the subject.

When writers formulate a **position**, they gather and arrange their ideas about an issue and determine how their views relate to others' positions on the same issue in the "unending conversation." For others in the conversation to understand them, writers need to clearly convey their positions. They express their positions through **claims**—statements asserted to be true that are not obviously facts. Because a claim is not true by itself, it must be defended.

Suppose, for example, you are on a school improvement team trying to decide if continuing to require physical education is a good policy. Before you attend the meeting, you give some thought to the topic and do some research. You might begin with some general ideas and then gradually develop a more specific position. You might arrive at the claim that requiring physical education (PE) may be more harmful than helpful.

Narrowing a Subject to a Defensible Claim
Broad Subject: Physical Education
Narrowed Subject (in the form of a question): Should physical education be required in high schools?
Specific Position: It's not a good idea to require PE in high schools.
Defensible Claim: Requiring PE in high schools harms many students more than it helps them.

Table 1-4

The way the claim is worded implies that the idea is true. However, without any evidence or logical reasoning to back it up, the members of the school improvement team will likely see this claim as merely a suggested idea. Convincing them to accept this claim will require you to defend it.

The best claims are usually those that are interesting and somewhat provocative—those that make a reader really take notice. (See 2.4 for more on effective claims.)

Remember: Writers convey their positions through one or more claims that require a defense. (CLE-1.A)

2.1 Checkpoint

Close Reading: Professional Text

Reread Greta Thunberg's speech to the UN. Then answer the following open response and multiple-choice questions.

1. Thunberg's broad subject is climate change, but what might be her more narrow subject in the context of her speech?

2. What is her position?

3. Identify one of Thunberg's claims. Is it clearly stated (explicit) or is it implied?

4. Which of the following statements from the text best represents Thunberg's central position in the speech as a whole?

   (A) "You have stolen my dreams and my childhood with your empty words." (paragraph 2, sentence 1)

   (B) "For more than 30 years, the science has been crystal clear. How dare you continue to look away and come here saying that you're doing enough, when the politics and solutions needed are still nowhere in sight." (paragraph 3)

   (C) "The popular idea of cutting our emissions in half in 10 years only gives us a 50% chance of staying below 1.5 degrees [Celsius], and the risk of setting off irreversible chain reactions beyond human control." (paragraph 5)

   (D) "But those numbers do not include tipping points, most feedback loops, additional warming hidden by toxic air pollution . . . ." (paragraph 6, sentence 2)

   (E) "With today's emissions levels, that remaining CO_2 budget will be entirely gone within less than 8 ½ years." (paragraph 9, sentence 2)

Evaluating Writing: Student Draft

Reread the student draft on page 5. Then answer the following open response and multiple-choice questions.

1. The broad subject is climate change, but what might be the more narrow subject in the context of the writing assignment?

2. What is the writer's position?

3. Identify one of the writer's claims. Revise the claim to make it clearer.

4. The writer is considering adding the following sentence to the passage on page 5 to clarify a position.

   It will undoubtedly affect millions of lives around the world.

   Where would the sentence best be placed?

   (A) After sentence 1

   (B) After sentence 2

   (C) After sentence 3

   (D) After sentence 4

   (E) After sentence 6

Composing on Your Own

As you have read, the elements of the rhetorical situation greatly influence a writer's choices. Take time now to choose or create a rhetorical situation for the writing you have been developing in this unit. Choose or adapt any of the following contexts, audiences, and purposes or create your own. (You are always free to use the rhetorical situation you are *actually* in: context—assignment; audience—teacher and/or peers; purpose—to demonstrate your skill). With your rhetorical situation in mind, try to express your key idea in a claim that might serve as the basis of an argument. To arrive at your claim, go through the process of narrowing a subject shown in Table 1-4 on page 20. Save your work for future use.

Contexts/Formats
▪ Essay for a high school website ▪ Article to a local publication ▪ Speech at a school board meeting
Audiences
▪ Well-educated adults ▪ Friends and neighbors ▪ Students and faculty
Purposes
▪ Present a strong expression of yourself and issues you care about ▪ Engage readers with an informative text ▪ Present a reasoned argument

2.2 Evidence and Reasoning | CLE-1.B

Writers defend their claims with evidence and/or reasoning. Without those, their claims would just be opinions with no grounding in facts or logic.

Developing and Explaining Proof

As you read in 2.1, you usually don't form a claim first and then look for **evidence**—information to prove an idea is valid. Instead, you spend time thinking about a topic and the information related to it, and then you use what you learn to develop a position and claim. Once you have developed a claim, the information that originally introduced you to the subject becomes evidence for supporting the claim. To strengthen support for your claim, you find more evidence. (You will read about types of evidence in Part 2.3.)

Information or evidence on its own, however, is not sufficient to defend a claim. Defending a claim requires **reasoning**—showing your audience how you think through your argument and how the evidence supports the claim.

Reasoning both leads to and extends from the claim. The entire process of gathering information, formulating a claim, providing evidence to support the claim, and using reasoning to explain how the evidence relates to the claim is a cycle. The process is similar to what takes place in the unending conversation in the parlor metaphor (see Unit Overview), but in this case, much of the conversation is with yourself as you learn more about your subject.

The graphic below illustrates the cyclical nature of the argumentation process. Follow it all the way around the circle from 1 to 8 until you understand it well enough to be able to explain it to someone else.

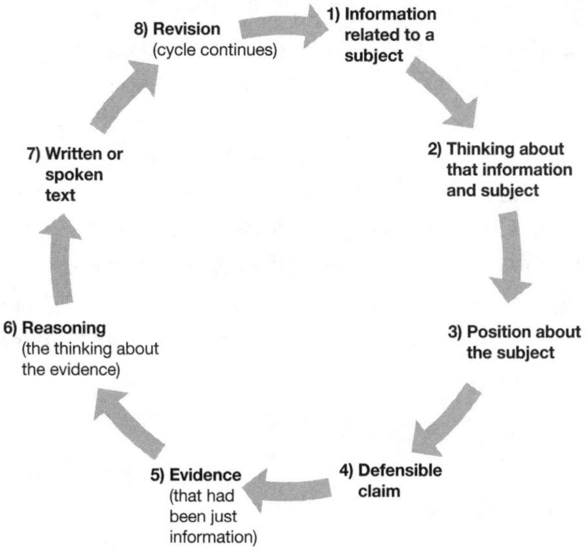

Figure 1-5

This graphic is sometimes called a "feedback loop" because steps in the process are "fed back" into the process. Why might a feedback loop be important to this process of thinking and reasoning? What are some other feedback loops that might occur in the process of writing?

Remember: Writers defend their claims with evidence and/or reasoning. (CLE 1.B)

2.2 Checkpoint

Close Reading: Professional Text

Reread Greta Thunberg's speech to the UN on pages 4–5. Then answer the following open response and multiple-choice questions.

1. What in Thunberg's position or claims requires defense?
2. What evidence does she use?
3. How does Thunberg use reasoning to connect her claims and evidence (or to explain what she's thinking)?
4. Which of the following statements from the passage functions more as interpretation than as evidence for the claims or arguments Thunberg makes about climate change in her speech?
   (A) "People are suffering. People are dying. Entire ecosystems are collapsing. We are in the beginning of a mass extinction. . . ." (paragraph 2, sentences 3–6)
   (B) "Because if you really understood the situation and still kept on failing to act, then you would be evil. And that I refuse to believe." (paragraph 4, sentences 3 and 4)
   (C) ". . . cutting our emissions in half in 10 years only gives us a 50% chance of staying below 1.5 degrees . . . ." (paragraph 5, sentence 1)
   (D) "To have a 67% chance of staying below a 1.5 degrees global temperature rise—the best odds given by the [Intergovernmental Panel on Climate Change]—the world had 420 gigatons of CO_2 left to emit back on Jan. 1st, 2018." (paragraph 8, sentence 1)
   (E) "With today's emissions levels, that remaining CO_2 budget will be entirely gone within less than 8 ½ years." (paragraph 9, sentence 2)

Evaluating Writing: Student Draft

Reread the student draft on page 5. Then answer the following open response and multiple-choice questions.

1. Which details in the current draft could be used as evidence?
2. What other evidence would be helpful?

3. Where could the writing include more reasoning to tie the evidence to the claim(s)?

4. The writer is considering revising sentence 5 (reproduced below) from the passage on page 5 to clarify the reasoning related to the information in sentences 4 and 5.

   Millions will relocate inland, increasing housing costs and adding pressure to inland cities to support these new residents.

   Which of the following versions of the underlined text best achieves this purpose?

   (A) (as it is now)

   (B) The loss of this land will force millions to relocate inland

   (C) This land was useful

   (D) Millions will relocate have to move

   (E) The United States will suffer greatly

2.3 Types of Evidence | CLE-1.C

Writers support their arguments with many different types of evidence (see the chart on page 26). These different types of evidence serve different purposes and have varying degrees of reliability and usefulness.

Evaluating Evidence

A variety of types of evidence can be used to support an argument. For example, suppose your friend complains that AP® Psychology won't fit into his schedule because he has to take a PE class. His personal experience may cause you to begin thinking about whether requiring all students to take PE is a good idea. You think about other friends who feel out of place in gym class as well—and you come to the conclusion that requiring PE is not a good idea.

At this point your specific claim emerges: "Requiring PE in high schools harms many students more than it helps them." You can support your claim with your friends' personal experiences, but those are only two examples, not enough evidence to create a solid argument. To create a well-rounded argument likely to be accepted by a diverse audience, you would do well to include additional types of evidence—facts and expert opinions, for example. Table 1-5 on the following page outlines the various types of evidence you can use and their strengths and weaknesses.

Types of Evidence and Definition	Pros	Cons
Facts: objective information	Facts are hard to disagree with.	Readers may not agree with what constitutes a proven fact.
Anecdotes: short, real-life stories used to illustrate a point	Anecdotes show how a claim might matter in the real world.	Readers may not agree on what the anecdote proves.
Analogies: comparisons between two things used to explain or clarify a point	Analogies make something unfamiliar or complex more understandable.	Readers may not understand the things being compared, causing them to reject the argument.
Statistics: numerical facts or data	Statistics are easy to accept because they show trends to support claims.	Readers may not trust the source or may believe that the statistics have been unfairly manipulated.
Examples: specific instances that demonstrate something relevant to the claim	Examples make abstract concepts understandable and relatable.	Readers may believe the examples are not relevant.
Details: relevant facts, descriptions, items, or features	Details provide visual images, making the claim real and substantial.	Readers may not relate to writer's chosen details.
Illustrations: examples meant to clarify or prove something	Illustrations make the claim feel more realistic, similar to the effects of using examples and details.	Readers may not accept them or the claim if the illustrations are unfamiliar.
Expert Opinions: statements made by people with special knowledge of the topic	Expert opinions build trust in the writer and in the claim.	Readers may not trust the experts or may reject the ideas as just opinions.
Personal Observations and Personal Experiences: writer's conclusions based on their experiences	Personal observations make the writer appear more relatable and trustworthy.	Readers may believe they are biased and unreliable.
Testimonies: formal written or spoken statements provided as evidence	Testimonies humanize the claim, making it real and relevant, similar to the effect of personal observation, personal experiences, and anecdotes.	Readers may believe they are biased and unreliable.
Experiments: scientific procedures that test hypotheses and rely on observable, measurable, and reproducible results	Experiments indicate that an objective process for gathering evidence and making claims was used.	Depending on the circumstances and the experiments being done, readers may reject the results.

Table 1-5

As with all other aspects of an argument, the evidence a writer chooses to use will depend on the specific elements of the rhetorical situation. Take the example of a person arguing against requiring PE in high school. What kinds of evidence would work best?

Element of Rhetorical Situation	Type of Evidence
Exigence	A writer should choose evidence that shows or closely relates to the motivation for writing. **Example:** Personal anecdotes might bring the issue closer to home.
Purpose	The evidence chosen should demonstrate what the writer hopes to accomplish. If the writer is arguing against a claim, then evidence related to the other argument should likely be addressed. **Example:** Expert opinions against requiring PE might counterbalance the argument in favor of requiring PE.
Writer	A writer should include evidence that he or she understands and can explain thoroughly. **Example:** Personal experience and observation about PE is something the writer knows firsthand.
Context	A writer should choose evidence that is appropriate for the time, place, and occasion. The writer needs to understand the audience's view of the context, which may be different from the writer's view. **Example:** Statistics may be appropriate for the formal and academic setting of a school board meeting whose members are used to evaluating data.
Message	A writer should include evidence that supports the reasoning that justifies the claim, but recognizing different views can strengthen the message and engage those in the audience who may not agree. **Example:** Anecdotes and analogies might help bridge the gap between the beliefs of some audience members and the position of the writer.

Table 1-6

Remember: Types of evidence may include facts, anecdotes, analogies, statistics, examples, details, illustrations, expert opinions, observations, personal experiences, testimonies, or experiments. (CLE-1.C)

2.3 Checkpoint

Close Reading: Professional Text

Reread Greta Thunberg's speech to the UN on pages 4–5. Then answer the following open response and multiple-choice questions.

1. What types of evidence does Thunberg use? Give examples of three types.

2. Why do you think she relied on those types of evidence?

3. What other type of evidence could she have used?

4. Where and why could she have used a different type of evidence?

5. Thunberg's most frequent and persuasive evidence is from
   - (A) analogies
   - (B) statistics
   - (C) personal observations
   - (D) details
   - (E) testimonies

Evaluating Writing: Student Draft

Reread the student draft on page 5. Then answer the following open response and multiple-choice questions.

1. What types of evidence did the student use in this passage?

2. Where could the student include a different type of evidence?

3. Why might the student want to use a different type of evidence?

4. The writer wants to add more information to the passage on page 5 to serve as evidence of future dangers of climate change. Which of the following statistics best helps accomplish this purpose?
   - (A) It is estimated that worldwide 150 million people are living in areas that will be underwater by 2050.
   - (B) At the end of the last century, three million people had already been displaced by climate change.
   - (C) Three out of five people believe that humans are causing climate change.
   - (D) Loss of land already includes millions of acres of farmland needed to sustain our population.
   - (E) Ice in the arctic is already melting a full two weeks earlier than it was just 30 years ago.

Composing on Your Own

Review the claim you developed as the basis of an argument (see page 22) and the information in Table 1-2 and Figure 1-4 that shows different categories of thought and how they might be sources of evidence. Also review the choices you made about your rhetorical situation. Keep those in mind as you complete this activity.

Make a chart like the one below to gather evidence you can use to support your claim. Use sources from a variety of materials, not just your own experience. You may end up not using all of your evidence. Refer to Table 1-5 on page 26 and use as many rows as you need. A few rows have been started for you. Save your work for future use.

Types of Evidence	Examples that Support Your Claim	Reasoning Explaining how the Evidence Supports your Claim
Facts		
Anecdotes		
Examples		
Statistics		

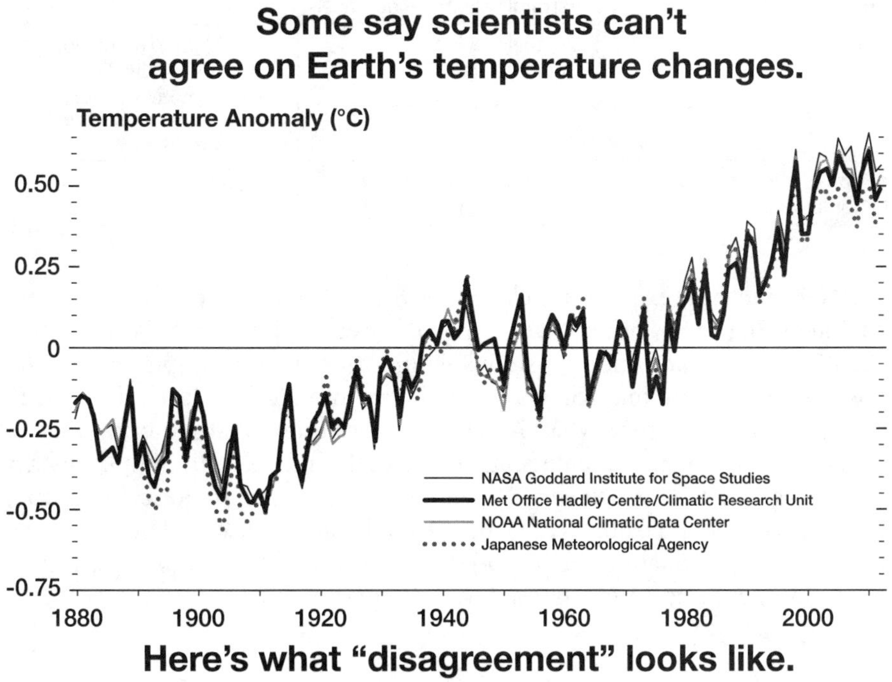

Source: NASA

Graphics like the one above can make forceful points. Explain what this graphic conveys and how someone might use it in an argument about climate change.

2.4 Defensible and Interesting Claims | CLE-1.D

Effective claims stir interest and call for a defense rather than simply present an obvious, known fact that would cause little or no disagreement.

Sharpening the Edge

As you read in 2.1, a claim must be defensible. If a claim isn't defensible, it is either completely untrue (cannot be defended or is just nonsensical) or it is a fact or generally accepted as a fact. As you gather evidence to support a claim, you should also be reviewing and, if necessary, revising your claim to be sure it has the edge or sharpness of a genuine claim. Consider the following examples:

Statement	Claim? Why or Why Not?	How Can the Statement be Revised into a Claim?
All children should receive an education.	No, this is generally accepted as true.	▪ Could specify what kind of education ▪ Could claim that some children should not be educated
Requiring PE in high schools harms some students more than it helps them.	Yes, claiming that something many educators think is beneficial is actually harmful requires a defense.	
People can vote when they turn 18.	No, this is a fact in the United States.	▪ Could state a position on the voting age ▪ Could state a position about who should be allowed to vote
People who don't vote should be penalized.	Yes, people could argue against such a penalty.	

Table 1-7

Notice that the examples of claims above are also refined enough to express an interesting view rather than a trite or oversimplified one. Issues worth debating always have more positions within them than a simple pro or con. For example, a claim that schools should not require PE is, as it stands, general, overly familiar, and somewhat dull. However, claiming that requiring PE can actually be harmful to some students adds a level of interest and complexity that will engage readers or listeners. When considering your rhetorical situation, anticipate the possible points of view, objections, and values held by the people reading your argument to help you refine your claim. Sometimes an effective claim produces discomfort in those who disagree with it.

Remember: Effective claims provoke interest and require a defense, rather than simply stating an obvious, known fact that requires no defense or justification. (CLE-1.D)

2.4 Checkpoint

Close Reading: Professional Text

Reread Greta Thunberg's speech to the UN on pages 4–5. Then answer the following open response and multiple-choice questions.

1. What claims does Thunberg make that provoke the interest of the listeners or readers?
2. Explain what makes Thunberg's claims complex rather than trite or oversimplified.
3. Which of the following statements best shows Thunberg's approach to sharpening the edge of her claim?
    (A) If world leaders fail to listen to young activists, environmental damage may be irreparable.
    (B) World leaders who are aware of the facts and urgency of climate change but who fail to act are behaving immorally.
    (C) People who live in small island nations will bear the burden of the climate crisis if current leaders fail to act now.
    (D) Overly concerned with their public images, world leaders ignore the devastating impact of climate change.
    (E) Many ecosystems worldwide are under threat because political leaders do not trust science.

Evaluating Writing: Student Draft

Reread the student draft on page 5. Then answer the following open response and multiple-choice questions.

1. Is there a claim that is defensible and that provokes interest? Copy it on your paper, or explain why you think there is not a claim that is defensible and interesting.
2. How might the passage be revised so the claim is more effective—defensible and interesting or complex? Write your revision on your paper.

3. The writer wants to revise sentence 7 (reproduced below) from the draft on page 5 to better articulate a claim that both requires defense and provokes interest.

While many people argue over the cause and who to blame, people must recognize that the world is going to change.

Which of the following versions of the underlined text best achieves this purpose?

(A) (as it is now)

(B) people must prepare now for the inevitable consequences of climate change.

(C) the effects go uncontrolled.

(D) people pay too little attention to the effects of climate change on animals and plants.

(E) people must consider these changes as the world population continues to grow.

Composing on Your Own

Review the claim you developed as the basis of an argument. Revise it as needed to make sure it is defensible, complex, provocative, and appropriate for your rhetorical situation. Depending on how you revise your claim, review the evidence to make sure it is still relevant. Save your work.

2.5 Source Materials | CLE-1.E

In academic contexts, most types of evidence come from source material—information found in books, articles, conversations, blogs, and many other documents, videos, or recordings. Evidence from firsthand observation or experience is also used in academic settings. Writers relate source material to their own argument by syntactically embedding, or weaving in, particular quoted, paraphrased, or summarized information from one or more sources into their own ideas. When you **quote** a source, you use an author's exact words. When you **paraphrase**, you rewrite the author's ideas in your own words. When you **summarize**, you condense key information from a source in your own words, leaving out some details.

Weaving in Others' Ideas

At the beginning of the argumentation process, a writer's thinking may be shaped by information from informal sources, such as conversations with classmates and posts on social media. However, once a writer has established a position and a claim, more concrete evidence is needed to make the argument convincing to a varied audience. (See 2.3.) When the writer's own observation or experience does not provide sufficient or appropriate evidence, the writer looks for other reliable sources for information to justify the claim.

Combining Writer and Source Ideas Good information from outside sources needs to be woven into a writer's argument. Deftly synthesizing source information with your own ideas strengthens your argument by demonstrating that experts agree with your position. The information you get from outside sources may shape the wording of the claim. It also may become evidence, or it may become part of the reasoning that explains how the evidence supports the claim. However you use it, new information should blend seamlessly with your own word choice and writing style. Study the following diagram.

WRITER'S OWN IDEA

I have seen a lot of students get bullied in PE class.

SOURCE INFORMATION

" . . . bullying situations have a negative impact on students' enjoyment of PE, leading to detrimental consequences for their physical and psychological health."

"Physical education and school bullying: a systematic review," *Physical Education and Sport Pedagogy Journal*, Volume 25, 2020

COMBINED WRITER AND SOURCE STATEMENT

Many students experience bullying in PE classes, which leads to "detrimental consequences for their physical and psychological health" (*Physical Education and Sport Pedagogy Journal*).

Figure 1-6

Source: Getty Images

Photographers, like writers, make choices. What does this image convey? What details "tell the story"? What choices did the photographer make to convey that message?

Drawing Inferences from Source Information Inferences are conclusions based on evidence and reasoning. Educator and author Jim Burke used the following formula to explain how an inference is made:

Known Information + New Information = Inference, or New Idea

When developing an argument, writers synthesize, or mix together, information from outside sources with their own ideas in order to arrive at a new idea, or an inference. Study the example below.

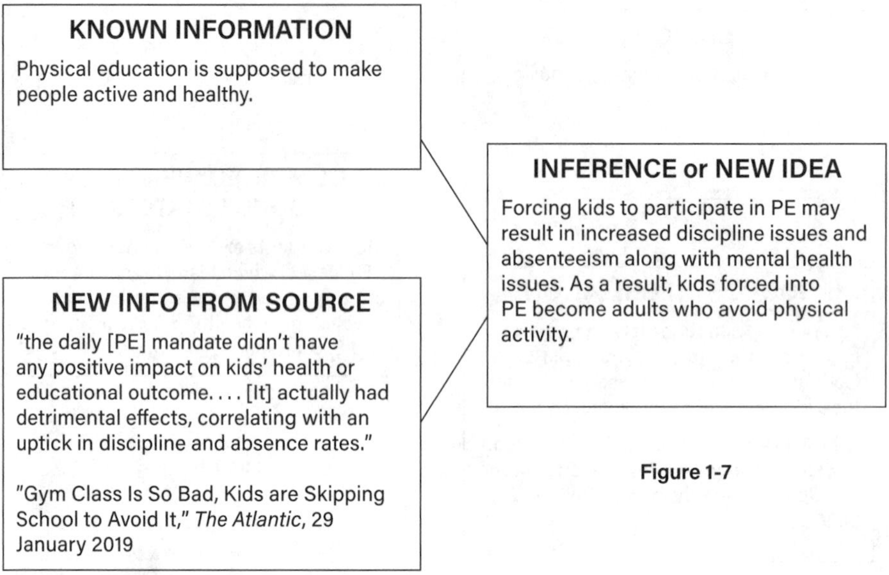
KNOWN INFORMATION
Physical education is supposed to make people active and healthy.
NEW INFO FROM SOURCE
"the daily [PE] mandate didn't have any positive impact on kids' health or educational outcome. . . . [It] actually had detrimental effects, correlating with an uptick in discipline and absence rates."
"Gym Class Is So Bad, Kids are Skipping School to Avoid It," *The Atlantic*, 29 January 2019
INFERENCE or NEW IDEA
Forcing kids to participate in PE may result in increased discipline issues and absenteeism along with mental health issues. As a result, kids forced into PE become adults who avoid physical activity.

Figure 1-7

Inferences such as the one above connect evidence to the writer's claim—in other words, they provide the reasoning that supports the argument. This connection is crucial for making a convincing argument.

Quoting, Paraphrasing, and Summarizing

In Figure 1-6 on page 33, the writer chose to quote a source directly. The writer could have paraphrased the information but probably thought that using a direct quotation would be more convincing.

You can synthesize sources into your own writing three different ways: by quoting, by paraphrasing, and by summarizing. Which method you choose will depend on the amount of information needed and the specific details of that information. Table 1-8 on the next page shows how and when an original text can be quoted, paraphrased, and summarized.

Original Text
"School-based physical education (PE) is recommended by The Community Guide as an effective strategy to promote physical activity among youth. Unfortunately, many have speculated that PE exposure has declined precipitously among U.S. students in the past decade. Limited resources and budgets, prioritization of core academic subjects, and several other barriers have been cited as potential drivers of these claims." (health.gov)

Quoting	Use when . . .
Even though PE classes have been losing out to "core academic subjects," they are still recommended by The Community Guide, a government task force, as "an effective strategy to promote physical activity among youth" (health.gov).	▪ the exact language of the original text is an especially good expression of the idea ▪ you want to disagree with an author's argument ▪ you want to highlight and clarify specific points of data ▪ you want to include information that is shocking or unlikely to be believed by the audience
Paraphrasing	**Use when . . .**
Though PE classes are losing ground to subjects deemed more important, they are still key to promoting physical activity among students.	▪ you want to communicate the main ideas in a clear, logical order ▪ the language or syntax of the source isn't appropriate for the audience
Summarizing	**Use when . . .**
PE is recommended to encourage physical activity among youth. However, many think that PE enrollment has likely declined significantly in the U.S. in the last ten years. Concerns about school funding and academic priorities are the major reasons PE may be in decline.	▪ only the main points of the source need to be explained ▪ you want to explain an idea found in multiple sources

Table 1-8

Remember: Writers relate source material to their own argument by syntactically embedding particular quoted, paraphrased, or summarized information from one or more sources into their own ideas. (CLE-1.E)

2.5 Checkpoint

Close Reading: Professional Text

Reread Greta Thunberg's speech to the UN on pages 4–5. Then answer the following open response and multiple-choice questions.

1. Where does Thunberg embed evidence into her reasoning?

2. How does she explain how the evidence relates to and helps support one of her claims?

3. Which of the following examples shows Thunberg's use of embedding source information to support her own ideas?

(A) "For more than 30 years, the science has been crystal clear." (paragraph 3, sentence 1)

(B) "Because if you really understood the situation and still kept on failing to act, then you would be evil." (paragraph 4, sentence 3)

(C) "They also rely on my generation sucking hundreds of billions of tons of your CO_2 out of the air with technologies that barely exist." (paragraph 6, sentence 3)

(D) "To have a 67% chance of staying below a 1.5 degrees global temperature rise—the best odds given by the [Intergovernmental Panel on Climate Change]—the world had 420 gigatons of CO_2 left to emit back on Jan. 1st, 2018." (paragraph 8, sentence 1)

(E) "There will not be any solutions or plans presented in line with these figures here today, because these numbers are too uncomfortable." (paragraph 10, sentence 1)

4. Many of the statistics Thunberg provides for her audience are chosen to

(A) prove beyond a doubt that the tipping point has been reached

(B) dismiss economics as a possible part of the solution

(C) balance her impassioned speech with the weight of science

(D) offer hope to younger generations

(E) highlight the details of the mass extinction

Evaluating Writing: Student Draft

Reread the student draft on page 5. Then answer the following open response and multiple-choice questions.

1. Where did the writer use outside evidence in this draft?

2. How could the use of this evidence be revised to better embed it with the writer's own ideas?

3. The writer wants to add to the beginning of sentence 4 (reproduced below) in the draft on page 5 (adjusting the capitalization and punctuation as needed) to better embed the quoted material within the writer's ideas in the passage.

"The entirety of many island nations and large portions of other countries with low-lying coastal lands, including the United States, will be underwater."

Which of the following would best accomplish this goal?

(A) Severe changes will arrive sooner than expected as

(B) Climate change simply cannot be stopped because

(C) Experts agree that

(D) While many argue that

(E) The effects of climate change on ecosystems around the world cannot be stopped because

Source: Getty Images

Coastal erosion caused these houses to slide into the sea.

Visuals such as photographs can provide persuasive evidence. Like any evidence, though, photographs usually need some commentary from the writer to explain how they fit with the claim. How might this photo be used to support what Thunberg or the student writer (page 5) is claiming? What aspects of the photograph would need to be explained?

Composing on Your Own

Write a paragraph-long draft of the argument you have been building through these exercises. Include three pieces of evidence. You may wish to use a table like the one below for guidance. Embed source materials by quoting, paraphrasing, or summarizing. Keep your rhetorical situation in mind as you write. Save your work.

Argument Paragraph Drafting Organizer
Claim:
Evidence 1
Explain how the evidence supports the reasoning that justifies that claim
Evidence 2
Explain how the evidence supports the reasoning that justifies that claim
Evidence 3
Explain how the evidence supports the reasoning that justifies that claim
Draft of Paragraph

Table 1-9

Part 2 Apply What You Have Learned

Reread or listen to the speech "A Whisper of AIDS" by Mary Fisher at americanrhetoric.com or another site you bookmarked, and review the chart you made for Part 1. Write a paragraph identifying the claim Fisher makes and the evidence she uses to back it up.

Reflect on the Essential Questions Write a brief response that answers these essential questions: *As a reader, how can you identify a writer's position and the way that position is supported? As a writer, how can you develop and support your own position?* In your answer, correctly use at least eight of the key terms listed on page 20.

Unit 1 Review

Section I: Multiple Choice

Section II: Free Response

Section I: Reading

Questions 1–13. Read the following passage carefully before you choose your answers.

(This passage is excerpted from an article titled "Why Chinatown Still Matters" that appeared on *The New York Times* website in 2016.)

1 There is one thing we do not see in a compelling 1982 self-portrait by Dean Wong: his face. Taken in Seattle's Chinatown, the photograph zeroes in on the back of a metal helmet, polished to a mirrorlike finish. In it is reflected a crowd of neighborhood residents—a metaphor for the people and hometown community that have shaped and fascinated Mr. Wong.

2 The image appears in Mr. Wong's new book, *Seeing the Light: Four Decades in Chinatown* (Chin Music Press), which centers on Seattle but includes images from other cities, including San Francisco, New York and Vancouver, British Columbia. Juxtaposing photographs with short, anecdotal essays, the book serves as a powerful corrective to decades of one-dimensional and blinkered reporting on neighborhoods generally represented in the cultural mainstream as exotic, insular or irrelevant, as places to order a quick meal or marvel at the colorful rituals of the Chinese New Year. . . .

3 Mr. Wong started photographing Seattle's Chinese-American community in the early 1970s, while working for the International District Emergency Center, a grassroots neighborhood services organization. Later, as a photojournalist for the *International Examiner*, a Seattle-based Asian-American newspaper, he continued to focus on Chinatown. "I photographed meetings, did portraits, went to community celebrations, and roamed the streets of Chinatown looking for anything that caught my eye," he later recalled.

4 Among the many contributions of *Seeing the Light* is its eloquent documentation of complex and evolving communities, neighborhoods that exist not for tourists, but as cultural, political, and historic sanctuaries for the Asian-American community.

5 "For me, Chinatown has been a kind of compass by which to find where I belong in this country," the writer Bonnie Tsui observed in her groundbreaking book, *American Chinatown: A People's History of Five Neighborhoods*. "I haven't always felt at ease in my identity as a Chinese-American, and as a young adult it was comforting to know that there was a place I could go in my city where everyone else looked like me."

6 If *Seeing the Light* affirms the role of Chinese-American communities in empowering a people, their history has been fraught, complicated by racism, xenophobia[1] and, more recently, the threats of urban renewal and gentrification.[2] In the mid-19th century, Chinese migration to the United States began when natural catastrophes across China inspired some of its more intrepid citizens to go to Gum Shan, "Gold Mountain," the Chinese nickname for California, and the western regions of North America, stoked by news of gold-rich land and economic opportunity.

7 But as the economy weakened in the United States, the Chinese labor force came to be viewed by white Californians as a threat. Racism and repressive legislation drove Chinese-Americans to self-segregate and form a sanctuary neighborhood in San Francisco: a so-called Chinatown, where close-knit families and benevolent associations sustained a spurned minority. As new businesses thrived within this community, however, the city's white residents continued to view Chinese-Americans as a danger to the region's fragile economy.

8 It was not until the mid-20th century that Chinese-Americans began to enter the nation's mainstream, with Chinatowns in cities as diverse as New York, Seattle, Washington, Los Angeles and Boston flourishing. But in recent years, gentrification has encroached on some communities, outpricing many Asian-Americans from neighborhoods that had served as cultural havens for

---

1 **xenophobia:** dislike of or prejudice against people from other countries

2 **gentrification:** process of changing the character of a neighborhood through the influx of more affluent residents and businesses

decades. At its peak, for example, Chinatown in the District of Columbia was once home to about 3,000 Chinese-Americans. That number has dwindled to 300.

9 In light of this history, Mr. Wong's vignettes[3] and photographs—including images of community activism, local businesses and organizations, political leaders, children playing, celebratory rituals and, on a more personal level, reminiscences about his family and student life—speak to the cultural nuances, complexity and necessity of Chinatown, well beyond the touristic fascination with swirling paper dragons, countless restaurants and trinket shops.

---

1. Which of the following best describes the writer's exigence in the passage?

(A) the declining population of Chinatowns

(B) the gentrification of ethnic neighborhoods

(C) the publication of Dean Wong's book, *Seeing the Light*

(D) the publication of Bonnie Tsui's book, *American Chinatown*

(E) growing racism and xenophobia

2. Paragraph 7 contributes to the ongoing conversation about Chinatowns by

(A) demonstrating how the formation of Chinatowns relates to the American history of racism and repression

(B) exploring the relationship between Chinatown's history and economic hardships in New York City

(C) demonstrating the racism of Chinese-Americans

(D) admitting the fear that large groups of like-minded people could create in a society

(E) exploring concerns that early Chinese immigrants shared about their acceptance and treatment

3 **vignettes:** brief evocative descriptions, accounts, or episodes

Questions 3–6 are covered in Units 2 and 5.

3. Which line(s) most nearly resemble(s) a thesis for this passage?

(A) "I haven't always felt at ease in my identity as a Chinese-American, and as a young adult it was comforting to know that there was a place I could go in my city where everyone else looked like me." (paragraph 5, sentence 2)

(B) ". . . natural catastrophes across China inspired some of its more intrepid citizens to go to Gum Shan, 'Gold Mountain,' the Chinese nickname for California . . . ." (paragraph 6, sentence 2)

(C) ". . . the city's white residents continued to view Chinese-Americans as a danger to the region's fragile economy." (paragraph 7, sentence 3)

(D) "But in recent years, gentrification has encroached on some communities, outpricing many Asian-Americans from neighborhoods that had served as cultural havens for decades." (paragraph 8, sentence 2)

(E) " . . . Mr. Wong's vignettes and photographs . . . speak to the cultural nuances, complexity and necessity of Chinatown . . . ." (paragraph 9, sentence 1)

4. Much of the passage suggests that the author assumes his audience

(A) desires to learn more about Dean Wong's biography

(B) shares the narrow views many Chinatown tourists have

(C) has little understanding of the goals shared by photographic artists

(D) knows little about the history of Chinese-American communities

(E) wants him to speak on behalf of the Chinese-American community

5. The author views the "gentrification" of Chinatowns as

(A) inevitable

(B) regrettable

(C) culturally insignificant

(D) necessary

(E) a form of racism

6. The tourists' views on the significance of Chinatowns are best represented by which of the following?
   (A) "places to . . . marvel at the colorful rituals" (paragraph 2, sentence 2)
   (B) "historic sanctuaries" (paragraph 4)
   (C) "a kind of compass" (paragraph 5, sentence 1)
   (D) "communities . . . empowering a people" (paragraph 6, sentence 1)
   (E) "cultural havens" (paragraph 8, sentence 2)

Questions 7–9 are covered in Unit 4.

7. In the opening paragraphs, the author expresses admiration for the work of Dean Wong because it
   (A) exposes the long-overlooked racism directed at Chinese-Americans
   (B) expands the public's awareness about Chinese-Americans
   (C) emboldens Chinese-Americans and their political fight for civil rights
   (D) provides the American reading public with a new source of entertainment
   (E) reveals the truth about the oppression of Chinese-American citizens in North America

8. The author's first sentence in the passage captures the audience's attention by
   (A) showing how a unique image reflects Dean Wong's identity
   (B) alluding to a world-famous photograph
   (C) mentioning Dean Wong by name
   (D) making an unconventional use of a colon
   (E) using the second person to address the audience directly

9. The author's concluding claim that Dean Wong's photographs "speak to the cultural nuances, complexity and necessity of Chinatown, well beyond the touristic fascination with swirling paper dragons" is best supported by the final sentence of
   (A) paragraph 1
   (B) paragraph 2
   (C) paragraph 3
   (D) paragraph 6
   (E) paragraph 7

Questions 10–12 are covered in Unit 5.

10. The phrase "blinkered reporting" in paragraph 2 implies that the media have historically portrayed Chinese-Americans

(A) through narrow stereotypes

(B) in an openly racist manner

(C) objectively and fairly

(D) in ways that oppress their communities

(E) cruelly and harmfully

11. Which of the following word or phrase from the passage is most consistent with the writer's attitude toward the work of Mr. Wong?

(A) "compelling" (paragraph 1, sentence 1)

(B) "new" (paragraph 2, sentence 1)

(C) "one-dimensional" (paragraph 2, sentence 2)

(D) "cultural mainstream" (paragraph 2, sentence 2)

(E) "irrelevant" (paragraph 2, sentence 2)

12. Quoting writer Bonnie Tsui in paragraph 5 serves to

(A) illustrate the cultural importance of Chinatowns to Chinese-Americans

(B) demonstrate why many Chinese-Americans have rejected Chinatowns

(C) present alternative arguments on the importance of Chinatowns

(D) deny any claim that Chinatowns are not real

(E) explain why many Chinese immigrants originally settled in these places

Question 13 is covered in Unit 5.

13. In relation to the passage as a whole, the transitional phrase at the beginning of the last paragraph refers to which of the following ideas?

(A) Immigrant stories

(B) Chinese-American values

(C) Spread of Chinatowns across America

(D) Tourists' interest in Chinatowns

(E) Chinatowns' troubling history

Section I: Writing

Questions 14–18. Read the following passage carefully before you choose your answers.

(The passage below on the subject of synthetic turf is a draft.)

(1) According to the Synthetic Turf Council, there are more than 12,000 fake athletic fields across the United States. (2) With no need to water, fertilize, or mow, synthetic surfaces mean that many sports can go year-round while also allowing sports fields where there could be no grass fields before. (3) In fact, New York City itself contains more than 160 synthetic turf fields throughout its parks.

(4) You are likely familiar with this green plastic grass turf with tiny specs of black "crumb rubber" meant to stand in as soil and provide a firm yet bounceable surface. (5) These types of surfaces are an innovative leap from previous synthetic fields that were little more than concrete with padding and a green-as-grass surface on top. (6) Often referred to as AstroTurf because of its famous use in the Houston Astrodome indoor stadium, this type of surface was patented in 1965. (7) AstroTurf eventually met with serious criticisms that it was changing the games played on it and leading to more injuries. (8) It needed to evolve. (9) Since the late 1990s, several companies, including the original AstroTurf company, have innovated to create "more natural," grasslike, crumb rubber fields with which many are now familiar.

(10) Today there are many questions about the safety of these new synthetic surfaces. (11) The most harrowing questions revolve around the use of crumb rubber. (12) Made from recycled tires, it is known to contain chemicals that can be harmful to humans. (13) Some even claim it causes cancer, citing an increase in the number of soccer goalies (who spend a lot of time on the ground getting crumb rubber all over their bodies) who have recently been diagnosed with cancer. (14) All of these concerns point to larger issues with synthetic turf. (15) Considering the criticism of the original AstroTurf surfaces and the unanswered questions emerging about these newer synthetic surfaces, it is obvious that these "advances" should be more closely scrutinized before they are used on such a large scale.

14. The writer wants to add more information to the third paragraph (sentences 10–15) to support the main argument of the paragraph. Which of the following information would best serve that purpose?

(A) Cancer develops when some outside influence such as chemicals or radiation changes a person's genes and causes cells to begin reproducing rapidly.

(B) The number of soccer goalies developing cancer has increased significantly since the introduction of synthetic turf with crumb rubber.

(C) Players on teams that regularly practice and play on synthetic surfaces are more likely to become injured than others.

(D) Some athletes are choosing to give up team sports altogether in order to avoid playing on synthetic surfaces.

(E) For every piece of black crumb rubber you can see, there are hundreds of microscopic pieces of the same material that you don't see—that you breathe in and even swallow.

Question 15 is covered in Unit 3.

15. The writer is considering moving the second paragraph (sentences 4–9) to become the first paragraph. Should the writer make this revision?

(A) Yes, that will help contextualize synthetic turf for readers, allowing them to better understand where these surfaces come from.

(B) Yes, the criticism should be introduced first so that the reader can begin to understand the reasoning of the argument being made.

(C) Yes, in order to create a cause and effect relationship that supports the argument being made, the paragraph should be moved.

(D) No, the first paragraph relies on the second to develop the reasoning introduced in the first paragraph.

(E) No, the second paragraph relies on the first paragraph to introduce how widespread synthetic turf is.

Question 16 is covered in Unit 5.

16. Which of the following, if placed at the beginning of sentence 10 (and adjusting for punctuation and capitalization), would create the most coherent transition between paragraph 2 (sentences 4–9) and paragraph 3 (sentences 10–15)?

(A) Evolution and innovation go hand in hand, and

(B) Crumb rubber may be softer, but

(C) The original AstroTurf company could not have foreseen the problems they would create since

(D) Innovation rarely comes without a cost, however, and

(E) However, innovation always produces positive results and

Question 17 is covered in Unit 7.

17. The author is considering adding information about the low maintenance costs of synthetic turf to sentence 2. Should the writer make this revision?

(A) Yes, all subjects have something to do with money.

(B) Yes, economic perspectives always generate reader interest.

(C) Yes, a brief mention of cost will help explain why synthetic surfaces are widely used.

(D) No, the additional information would not help the readers understand the popularity of synthetic turf.

(E) No, the lower costs are already implied in the opening portion of sentence 2.

Question 18 is covered in Unit 8.

18. In an attempt to avoid any bias and maintain the style of the passage, the writer wants to revise the underlined word in sentence 1 (reproduced below).

According to the Synthetic Turf Council, there are more than 12,000 fake athletic fields across the United States.

Which of the following would be the best choice to replace the underlined word?

(A) plastic

(B) artificial

(C) harmful

(D) scientific

(E) sham

JOIN THE CONVERSATION: THE ARGUMENT ESSAY (PART 1)

Before you move on to answering the free-response prompts in Section II of the Unit Review, take the time to understand the tasks they require by completing the activities in this "Join the Conversation" guide, which will appear in this spot in Units 1–8. Since Unit 1 focused on claims and evidence, the first type of prompt explained here is the argument essay (the final prompt on the AP® exam), which assesses your ability to use evidence and reasoning to support a claim. In this guide, the argument prompt for Units 1–5 is on the same topic but will require your using increasingly more complex writing skills. Study the sample prompt below.

> For decades, movies and music have included messages or labels to signal that they contain content that some people may find troubling. Advocates for such labeling argue this is important to prevent people from being exposed to things they do not want to encounter. However, Erika Christakis, a lecturer at the Yale Child Study Center, says that "free speech and the ability to tolerate offense are the hallmarks of a free and open society."
>
> Write a paragraph that argues your position on the use of warning labels or warning messages to signal potentially troubling content.
>
> In your response you should do the following:
>
> - Respond to the prompt with a claim that presents a defensible position.
> - Provide evidence to support your line of reasoning.
> - Explain how the evidence supports your line of reasoning.
> - Use appropriate grammar and punctuation in communicating your argument.

The first part of the prompt provides background, the second states your task, and the third provides a checklist for fulfilling the requirements. Everything the prompt asks you to do has been covered in Unit 1.

To develop a defensible claim required by the **first bullet**, think about experiences related to warning labels and warning messages. You might recall a time you were upset by something unexpected in a movie. Or you might think about a child having nightmares about a scary movie character. Maybe you will think about the warning labels on medications and other products, such as cigarettes. These ideas will lead you to your claim (see 2.1 and 2.4). State the claim clearly. For example, your claim might be: *Warning labels are necessary to prevent both emotional and physical harm.*

To address the **second bullet**, list evidence to support your claim. In this case, your evidence is the examples you thought of to reach your claim, such as "children have nightmares" and "some products are harmful." Try to tie your personal examples to the broader contexts, or "worlds," of an argument (Unit 1, Part 1.5, page 16). These connections will help you widen your appeal by linking your argument to abstract ideas, such as popular culture (movies) and science (health warnings).

The **third bullet** requires you to explain how your ideas support your reasoning behind the claim. For example, if you use the child with nightmares as evidence, show clearly how this example supports your claim. You might say, for example, "A child with nightmares suffers very real and possibly lasting fears that could have been prevented by a movie rating that would have stopped parents from allowing their child to see the movie." Filling in an organizer like the one below will help you keep track of your claim, evidence, and reasoning. Use it while responding to this prompt.

When you finish your draft, check it over to make sure you meet the requirements of each bullet point in the prompt. The **final bullet** reminds you to use appropriate grammar and punctuation, so double-check for possible grammatical and punctuation errors.

Argument Paragraph Drafting Organizer
Claim: Warning labels are necessary to prevent both emotional and physical harm.
Evidence 1 A child who has nightmares because of watching a movie with scary images
Explain how the evidence supports the reasoning that justifies that claim A child with nightmares suffers very real and possibly lasting fears that could have been prevented by a movie rating that would have stopped parents from allowing their child to see the movie.
Evidence 2 Warning labels on cigarettes
Explain how the evidence supports the reasoning that justifies that claim Warnings on cigarette packages explain that smoking causes cancer and other diseases, and as a result many people choose not to smoke.
Additional Evidence
Explain how the evidence supports the reasoning that justifies that claim
Draft of Paragraph

Apply

Follow the same process to respond to the argument prompt on the next page. For current free-response prompt samples, visit the College Board website.

Section II: Free Response

The first free-response question on the AP® exam is a synthesis task. For guided practice in writing a synthesis essay, see Join the Conversation on pages 364–373, 448–455 and 540–544. You will be provided synthesis prompts in Units 6–9.

Rhetorical Analysis: "Why Chinatown Still Matters"

The second free-response question on the exam is a rhetorical analysis. For guided practice in writing rhetorical analysis, see Join the Conversation on pages 104–106, 178–180, 232–235, and 290–295.

In May of 2016, research professor Maurice Berger wrote a review of the artist Dean Wong's new book of photographs. The review appeared on *The New York Times* website.

Read the passage carefully. Write an essay or short response that analyzes the rhetorical choices Berger makes to convey his message about the contribution Wong's book makes to understanding Chinatowns. Consider how the writer embeds evidence within his own ideas about "Why Chinatown Still Matters."

In your response you should do the following:

- Respond to the prompt with a thesis that analyzes the writer's rhetorical choices.
- Select and use evidence to support your line of reasoning.
- Explain how the evidence supports your line of reasoning.
- Demonstrate an understanding of the rhetorical situation.
- Use appropriate grammar and punctuation in communicating your argument.

Argument: Speeding Tickets Based on Income

Some European countries have laws that vary the amount of money fined for breaking some laws, such as speeding, based on the income of the person getting the ticket. This means that a wealthy person getting a speeding ticket will pay more for that ticket than a person doing the same speed who makes less money.

Write a paragraph that argues your position on attaching legal fines to the amount of money someone makes.

In your response you should do the following:

- Respond to the prompt with a claim that presents a defensible position.
- Provide evidence to support your line of reasoning.
- Explain how the evidence supports your line of reasoning.
- Use appropriate grammar and punctuation in communicating your argument.

UNIT 2

Selecting Evidence to Motivate an Audience

Part 1: Relating to an Audience
Part 2: Strategic and Sufficient Evidence
Part 3: Identifying a Thesis

ENDURING UNDERSTANDINGS AND SKILLS: Unit Two

Part 1

Understand

Individuals write within a particular situation and make strategic writing choices based on that situation. (RHS-1)

Demonstrate

Explain how an argument demonstrates understanding of an audience's beliefs, values, or needs. (Reading 1.B)

Demonstrate an understanding of an audience's beliefs, values, or needs. (Writing 2.B)

Part 2

Understand

Writers make claims about subjects, rely on evidence that supports the reasoning that justifies the claim, and often acknowledge or respond to other, possibly opposing, arguments. (CLE-1)

Demonstrate

Identify and explain claims and evidence within an argument. (Reading 3.A)

Develop a paragraph that includes a claim and evidence supporting the claim. (Writing 4.A)

Part 3

Understand

Writers make claims about subjects, rely on evidence that supports the reasoning that justifies the claim, and often acknowledge or respond to other, possibly opposing, arguments. (CLE-1)

Demonstrate

Identify and describe the overarching thesis of an argument, and any indication it provides of the argument's structure. (Reading 3.B)

Write a thesis statement that requires proof or defense and that may preview the structure of the argument. (Writing 4.B)

Source: *AP® English Language and Composition Course and Exam Description*

Unit 2 Overview

In August 2000, punk band Squad Five-O released *Bombs over Broadway*, their debut album for Tooth and Nail Records. The cover shows airplanes flying low over the streets of New York City. Smoke obscures two prominent buildings in the background—the twin towers of the World Trade Center. Seemingly, the cover eerily predicts a great tragedy in American history: the terrorist attacks on 9/11/2001 just over a year later.

Not only was this image prophetic, but the lyrics to the title track also include references to "New York City. Broadway, going up in flames" and "Ground zero . . . we never saw it coming." After the tragedy, the band decided to temporarily change their album art to a picture of band members and suspend live performances of their title track. Squad Five-O did, however, begin playing the song again once the tensions died down.

Relating to an Audience The record label spent enormous resources to rebrand the album, and the band chose not to play its premier piece. What would cause the record company and the band to make these dramatic choices? Both choices were made because the label and band had one thing in mind: audience. They knew many people would find the cover and song disrespectful to the families of the thousands of victims. Because they wanted to reach the greatest number of people, the band adjusted the message of their album art and their performances to match the values and needs of their audience.

Choosing Strategic Evidence In a similar way, effective writers assess the situation in which they write and then make strategic choices based on that situation. When writers understand the values and beliefs of their audience, they strategically select evidence most likely to "speak to" the audience. Writers use evidence to support their thinking by amplifying a point, providing examples, clarifying ideas, or setting a mood. High-quality evidence in good measure can also increase a writer's credibility and power to persuade.

Defending a Thesis The primary purpose of evidence, however, is to support the writer's central claim. While a central claim may extend over multiple sentences, a **thesis statement** often captures it clearly and concisely. A thesis statement may have more parts than the claim alone, but it always includes the overarching claim of the argument.

Close Reading: Professional Text
Malala Yousafzai's Speech to the UN Youth Assembly

The following speech was delivered on "Malala Day"—July 12, 2013—by Malala Yousafzai to the first "Youth Take Over the UN" assembly, an initiative that brings together young leaders from all over the world to promote education. This was the first speech Yousafzai gave since she had been shot by the Taliban in her home country of Pakistan. As you read the speech (or watch it on YouTube), focus on understanding the main ideas Yousafzai contributes to the conversations about education and women's rights and the way she relates to her audience.

1 In the name of God, the most beneficent, the most merciful.

2 Honorable UN Secretary General Mr. Ban Ki-moon, respected president of the General Assembly Vuk Jeremic, honorable UN envoy for global education Mr. Gordon Brown, respected elders and my dear brothers and sisters: Assalamu alaikum. [Peace be with you.]

3 Today it is an honor for me to be speaking again after a long time. Being here with such honorable people is a great moment in my life and it is an honor for me that today I am wearing a shawl of the late Benazir Bhutto.[1] I don't know where to begin my speech. I don't know what people would be expecting me to say, but first of all thank you to God for whom we all are equal and thank you to every person who has prayed for my fast recovery and new life.

4 I cannot believe how much love people have shown me. I have received thousands of good wish cards and gifts from all over the world. Thank you to all of them. Thank you to the children whose innocent words encouraged me. Thank you to my elders whose prayers strengthened me. I would like to thank my nurses, doctors and the staff of the hospitals in Pakistan and the UK [United Kingdom] and the UAE [United Arab Emirates] government who have helped me to get better and recover my strength.

5 I fully support UN Secretary General Ban Ki-moon in his Global Education First Initiative and the work of UN Special Envoy for Global Education Gordon Brown and the respectful president of the UN General Assembly Vuk Jeremic. I thank them for the leadership they continue to give. They continue to inspire all of us to action. Dear brothers and sisters, do remember one thing: Malala Day is not my day. Today is the day of every woman, every boy and every girl who have raised their voice for their rights.

6 There are hundreds of human rights activists and social workers who are not only speaking for their rights, but who are struggling to achieve their goal of peace, education and equality. Thousands of people have been killed by the terrorists and millions have been injured. I am just one of them. So here I stand. So here I stand, one girl, among many. I speak not for myself, but so those without a voice can be heard. Those who have fought for their rights. Their right to live in peace. Their right to be treated with dignity. Their right to equality of opportunity. Their right to be educated.

7 Dear friends, on 9 October 2012, the Taliban[2] shot me on the left side of my forehead. They shot my friends, too. They thought that the bullets would silence us, but they failed. And out of that silence came thousands of voices. The terrorists thought they would change my aims and stop my

---

1 Benazir Bhutto was Prime Minister of Pakistan from 1988 to 1990 and 1993 to 1996. She was the first woman to lead a democratic government in a Muslim majority nation. She was assassinated in 2007.

2 The Taliban is a fundamentalist Sunni Islamic military group in Afghanistan seeking to take power and establish Sharia, or traditional Muslim law.

ambitions. But nothing changed in my life except this: weakness, fear and hopelessness died. Strength, power and courage were born.

8 I am the same Malala. My ambitions are the same. My hopes are the same. And my dreams are the same. Dear sisters and brothers, I am not against anyone. Neither am I here to speak in terms of personal revenge against the Taliban or any other terrorist group. I am here to speak for the right of education for every child. I want education for the sons and daughters of the Taliban and all the terrorists and extremists. I do not even hate the Talib who shot me. Even if there was a gun in my hand and he was standing in front of me, I would not shoot him. This is the compassion I have learned from Mohammed, the prophet of mercy, Jesus Christ and Lord Buddha. This [is] the legacy of change I have inherited from Martin Luther King, Nelson Mandela[3] and Mohammed Ali Jinnah.[4]

9 This is the philosophy of nonviolence that I have learned from Gandhi,[5] Bacha Khan[6] and Mother Teresa.[7] And this is the forgiveness that I have learned from my father and from my mother. This is what my soul is telling me: be peaceful and love everyone.

10 Dear sisters and brothers, we realize the importance of light when we see darkness. We realize the importance of our voice when we are silenced. In the same way, when we were in Swat, the north of Pakistan, we realized the importance of pens and books when we saw the guns. The wise saying, "The pen is mightier than the sword." It is true. The extremists are afraid of books and pens. The power of education frightens them. They are afraid of women. The power of the voice of women frightens them. This is why they killed 14 innocent students in the recent attack in Quetta [a city in central Pakistan]. And that is why they kill female teachers. That is why they are blasting schools every day because they were and they are afraid of change and equality that we will bring to our society. And I remember that there was a boy in our school who was asked by a journalist, "Why are the Taliban against education?" He answered very simply by pointing to his book. He said, "a Talib doesn't know what is written inside this book."

11 They think that God is a tiny, little conservative being who would point guns at people's heads just for going to school. These terrorists are misusing the name of Islam for their own personal benefit. Pakistan is a peace loving, democratic country. Pashtuns[8] want education for their daughters and sons. Islam is a religion of peace, humanity and brotherhood. It is the duty and responsibility to get education for each child, that is what it says. Peace is a necessity for education. In many parts of the world, especially

---

3 Nelson Mandela (1918–2013) led the resistance to apartheid in South Africa and was president of the post-apartheid nation from 1994–1999.

4 Mohammed Ali Jinnah (1876–1948) was the first Governor-General of independent Pakistan.

5 Mahatma Gandhi (1869–1948) was the leader of the nonviolent resistance movement in India.

6 Abdul Ghaffar Khan (1890–1988) was a Pakistani activist who fought against British colonial rule in India.

7 Mother Teresa (1910–1997) was an Albanian-Indian Roman Catholic nun known for her charitable and humanitarian work.

8 Pashtuns are Eastern-Iranian people in Afghanistan and Pakistan whose first language is Pashto.

Pakistan and Afghanistan, terrorism, war and conflicts stop children from going to schools. We are really tired of these wars. Women and children are suffering in many ways in many parts of the world.

12 In India, innocent and poor children are victims of child labor. Many schools have been destroyed in Nigeria. People in Afghanistan have been affected by extremism. Young girls have to do domestic child labor and are forced to get married at an early age. Poverty, ignorance, injustice, racism and the deprivation of basic rights are the main problems, faced by both men and women.

13 Today I am focusing on women's rights and girls' education because they are suffering the most. There was a time when women activists asked men to stand up for their rights. But this time we will do it by ourselves. I am not telling men to step away from speaking for women's rights, but I am focusing on women to be independent and fight for themselves. So dear sisters and brothers, now it's time to speak up. So today, we call upon the world leaders to change their strategic policies in favor of peace and prosperity. We call upon the world leaders that all of these deals must protect women and children's rights. A deal that goes against the rights of women is unacceptable.

14 We call upon all governments to ensure free, compulsory education all over the world for every child. We call upon all the governments to fight against terrorism and violence. To protect children from brutality and harm. We call upon the developed nations to support the expansion of education opportunities for girls in the developing world. We call upon all communities to be tolerant, to reject prejudice based on caste, creed, sect, color, religion or agenda to ensure freedom and equality for women so they can flourish. We cannot all succeed when half of us are held back. We call upon our sisters around the world to be brave, to embrace the strength within themselves and realize their full potential.

15 Dear brothers and sisters, we want schools and education for every child's bright future. We will continue our journey to our destination of peace and education. No one can stop us. We will speak up for our rights and we will bring change to our voice. We believe in the power and the strength of our words. Our words can change the whole world because we are all together, united for the cause of education. And if we want to achieve our goal, then let us empower ourselves with the weapon of knowledge and let us shield ourselves with unity and togetherness.

16 Dear brothers and sisters, we must not forget that millions of people are suffering from poverty and injustice and ignorance. We must not forget that millions of children are out of their schools. We must not forget that our sisters and brothers are waiting for a bright, peaceful future.

17 So let us wage, so let us wage a glorious struggle against illiteracy, poverty and terrorism; let us pick up our books and our pens; they are the most powerful weapons. One child, one teacher, one book and one pen can change the world. Education is the only solution. Education first. Thank you.

Composing on Your Own

Write freely a personal response to Yousafzai's ideas about education and women's rights. Describe your own experiences with or observations about education and women's rights. What have you read on these topics? What ideas made a strong impression? What would you like to know more about? You will be developing these ideas throughout the unit, so save your work.

Source: Wikimedia Commons

In 2014, Malala Yousafzai (third from left) and Kaliash Satyarthi (second from left) were jointly awarded the Nobel Peace Prize for their fight for the right of every child to receive an education.

Viewers can draw conclusions from details in a picture. In what way can you see that Malala is different from the others on the stage? What might this difference say about Malala and her accomplishments?

Evaluating Writing: Student Draft
Global Education

Read the following draft of a student's essay, which will be published on the school website on National Education and Sharing Day, a day of observance founded by President Jimmy Carter in 1978. This is another anchor text, one you will be referring to and answering questions about to practice skills of evaluating writing. This draft still needs work. As you read it, think about what it contributes to the conversation about education, and compare it to the ideas you wrote down in response to Yousafzai's speech. Later you will have an opportunity to suggest ways the writing might be improved.

(1) In every state in the United States, school attendance is compulsory. (2) Different states are given the freedom to mandate different entrance ages; however, in most states, a child is to be enrolled in an approved educational program by the age of six. (3) Many U.S. students—along with their other

first-world counterparts—take for granted the educational opportunities that are presented to them as rights. (4) In fact, they often either view going to school as a boring burden, or they just neglect to consider how less fortunate areas and countries do not have similar requirements for their own populations. (5) In all of the world, Africa has the "10 lowest-ranked countries" in relation to a child's ability to access educational services. (6) The number of underserved children is further influenced by the amount of turmoil that pervades areas like Niger, Chad, and Djibouti. (7) Over the past two decades, increased international efforts have been working to open new doors for the children in these destitute areas. (8) These efforts will equip them with voices so that they too may be granted what is rightfully theirs: an opportunity to learn, which is an opportunity for hope.

What Do You Know?

This unit will explore the importance of audience as writers make strategic choices about evidence to back up their theses. Before proceeding, assess what you already know about choices writers make to reach their audience by answering questions about the anchor text by Malala Yousafzai and the student draft on education for children. According to learning scientists, quizzing yourself on subjects before formally studying them can help you focus your learning.

CLOSE-READING: PROFESSIONAL TEXT

1. What does Yousafzai's audience value? How do you know?
2. Identify three or four sentences from her speech that help the reader infer Yousafzai's thesis.
3. What evidence does Yousafzai provide to support her thesis? Which evidence seems the most convincing and of the highest quality?

EVALUATING WRITING: STUDENT DRAFT

1. What sentence(s) help the reader infer the writer's thesis about global education?
2. Identify the claims made in the student draft.
3. Which claim(s) have sufficient evidence?
4. Which claim(s) are less convincing? Are they less convincing because they do not have sufficient evidence, because they have low-quality evidence, or because of some other reason? Explain.

Part 1

Relating to an Audience

Enduring Understanding and Skills

Part 1

Understand

Individuals write within a particular situation and make strategic writing choices based on that situation. (RHS-1)

Demonstrate

Explain how an argument demonstrates understanding of an audience's beliefs, values, or needs. (Reading 1.B)

Demonstrate an understanding of an audience's beliefs, values, or needs. (Writing 2.B)

Source: *AP® English Language and Composition Course and Exam Description*

Essential Question: How does an audience influence the writer's choices?

As you read in Unit 1, the success of an argument depends on a writer's ability to produce evidence and reasoning that readers will find appealing and engaging. Just listing evidence is not enough. An effective writer connects the dots between claims and evidence by providing commentary: convincing explanations of how evidence supports a claim.

Writers rely on proven methods to motivate an audience. These methods, or modes of persuasion, appeal to the audience's emotions, reason, and trust in the writer. For example, consider how presidential candidates might change their appeals depending on whether they are speaking about educational funding to a group of parents or to a group of school administrators. They might focus on emotions as they share stories of student successes with a group of parents; they might focus on logic and reason as they present school administrators with statistics about rising test scores and graduation rates. This section will explain how readers and writers can use these modes of persuasion effectively.

KEY TERMS

arguments	ethical appeal	rhetorical choices
background	logical appeal	purpose
beliefs	modes of persuasion	values
emotional appeal	needs	

1.1 Relating to an Intended Audience | RHS-1.F RHS-1.G

An audience is made up of people who have distinct values, beliefs, backgrounds, and needs. Writers adapt their message to an intended audience's emotions and values in order to achieve their purpose for writing or speaking.

Adapting to An Audience

The interplay between a writer and reader is complex. Each comes to the rhetorical situation with a set of **values**, **beliefs**, and **needs**. These qualities vary from person to person, although people with similar **backgrounds** may share some commonalities in their values, beliefs, and needs. The chart below shows what a writer or speaker needs to consider when trying to reach an audience.

Audience Characteristics			
Term	**Definition**	**Example**	**Questions to Ask**
values	priorities, principles held in high regard	education, freedom, inclusivity, personal rights	What ideals does the audience hold dear? What is their highest priority?
beliefs	morals, standards, codes of conduct, religious beliefs	ideas in religious texts such as the Koran, Torah, and Bible; ideas in the Constitution; personal codes of belief	What convictions do they live by? What beliefs motivate their thinking about right and wrong?
needs	requirements for life and well-being	food, shelter, clothing, safety, human connection	What does the audience need for safety and fulfillment?
background	total of one's experiences, knowledge, education, and family life	economic status, first language, highest level of education completed, home culture, gender, race, ethnicity	How similar are the backgrounds and experiences of the audience? What advantages or disadvantages do they face?

Table 2-1

A writer steps into the rhetorical situation with a **purpose**. The writer wants to convince the audience to change their minds about a subject or even to take action. To achieve this purpose, the writer makes rhetorical choices to appeal to the concerns of the audience. **Rhetorical choices** made in the service of the audience affect all elements of an argument, including the content, tone, and word choice. The tone of a written work reveals an author's attitude or feelings about the subject matter and can reveal the author's perspective.

Sometimes a writer will affirm an audience. Other times, a writer wants to change an audience and motivate them to take a certain action. Effective writers, however, know they will likely achieve that purpose if they first create a feeling of solidarity with the audience before trying to change their minds.

Think back to the text message from Unit 1, page 13. When the student responds to her mother, she knows from prior experience (background) that her mom values her safety and does not want her to stay out late. The daughter makes the rhetorical choice to omit information—that Izzy's mom is partying with her friends—to reduce her mom's fear that she may not be well supervised. These choices show the student understands her mother's values and needs.

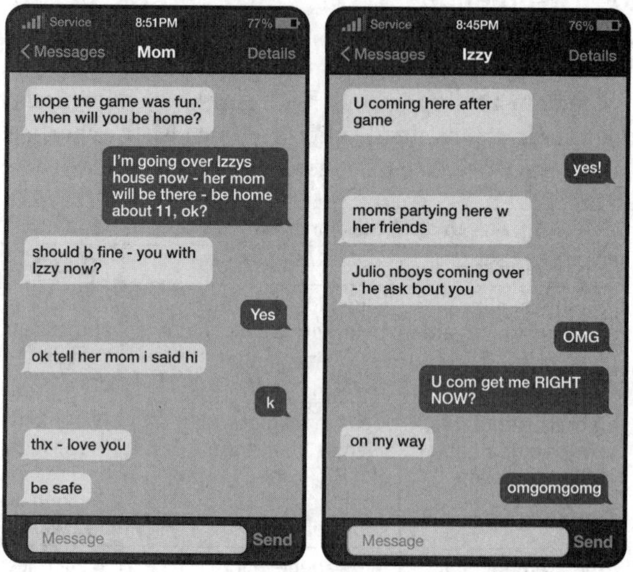

Figure 2-1

The chart below provides an analysis of the student's rhetorical choices.

Evidence from Text Message	Rhetorical Choices	What the Writer Believes about the Mom's Background, Values, Beliefs, Needs
I'm going over to Izzys house now—<u>her mom will be there</u>. . . Student does not mention <u>Izzy's "moms partying here w her friends"</u>	The student confirms the presence of an authority figure and omits questionable information.	Her mother values her daughter's safety, so the daughter chooses to state that Izzy's mom will be there. Mentioning the possibly lax supervision might mean the daughter would not be allowed to go to Izzy's.
. . .-be home <u>about 11. . .ok</u>?	The student offers a reasonable time frame or suggests a curfew and seeks her mom's approval.	Her mother values her daughter's safety and obedience.
[in response to "tell her mom i said hi"] - <u>k</u>	The student agrees to her mother's request.	Her mother values her daughter's responsibility and trust.

Table 2-2

Recognizing the rhetorical choices the student makes and how each relates to her mother's values and needs is the same skill needed to analyze the texts you encounter in college and on the AP® Language test. As you read a text, ask:

- How do the rhetorical choices in this text or text portion relate to the audience's values, beliefs, needs, and/or backgrounds?

When you are clear on the answers to that question, express your analysis in writing, since that is what you will be required to do as you advance in English Language and Composition. A written analysis of the texter's rhetorical choices, for example, might be worded this way: *The student confirms the presence of an authority figure at Izzy's house in order to anticipate and satisfy her mother's need for her daughter's safety.* This sentence effectively identifies the writer's choice and ties it to meaning. It also employs a strong verb, "confirms," instead of a weak verb such as "uses."

Remember: Writers' perceptions of an audience's values, beliefs, needs, and background guide the choices they make. To achieve a purpose, writers make choices in an attempt to relate to an intended audience's emotions and values. (RHS-1.F,G)

1.1 Checkpoint

Close Reading: Professional Text

Use what you have learned about how writers make choices in relation to their audience's backgrounds, values, beliefs, and needs to complete the following open response activity and answer the multiple-choice questions.

1. On separate paper, create a three-column chart like the one below. Then use Malala Yousafzai's speech on pages 53–55 to complete the chart with at least four more rows. In the first column, identify textual evidence showing how Yousafzai relates to the values, beliefs, needs, and/or background of her audience. In the second column, identify the rhetorical choice Yousafzai makes, and in the third column, clarify how this choice relates to the background, values, beliefs, or needs of Yousafzai's audience. One row is done for you.

Examples (Textual Evidence)	Rhetorical Choice What is the writer doing?	What Yousafzai Believes about the Audience's Background, Values, Beliefs, or Needs
"Today it is an honor for me to be speaking again after a long time."	Acknowledges privilege of her current position	Audience values humility in a speaker

2. Which of the following best illustrates Yousafzai's respect for leaders from diverse backgrounds?
   (A) "So here I stand, one girl, among many." (paragraph 6, line 4)
   (B) "This the legacy of change I have inherited from Martin Luther King, Nelson Mandela and Mohammed Ali Jinnah." (paragraph 8, line 12)
   (C) "Dear sisters and brothers, we realize the importance of light when we see darkness." (paragraph 10, line 1)
   (D) "We call upon all governments to ensure free, compulsory education all over the world for every child." (paragraph 14, line 1)
   (E) "Our words can change the whole world because we are all together, united for the cause of education." (paragraph 14, line 6)

3. Yousafzai most likely repeats the phrase "brothers and sisters" throughout the passage to
   (A) separate herself and the audience from those who deny others the right of education and abuse human rights
   (B) highlight the moral superiority of fighting for global education
   (C) unite her audience in a manner that encourages all parties to work together
   (D) stress the equality of males and females
   (E) appeal to ubiquitous nature of human rights

4. Yousafzai's awareness of her international audience is most evident in her
   (A) focus on politics and economic issues
   (B) references to multiple faiths and countries
   (C) direct address and appeals to women leaders
   (D) allusions to the Taliban and the Talib
   (E) personal story of being shot by an extremist

5. Sentence 3 in paragraph 9 ("This. . . love everyone") gives the audience the impression that Yousafzai views her desire to forgive as
   (A) a law prescribed by her religion
   (B) a strictly irrational and emotional response
   (C) a form of spiritual inspiration
   (D) an embodiment of womanhood
   (E) a sign that terrorists are incapable of love

6. The first two sentences of the speech establish Yousafzai's desire to
   (A) create a tone of goodwill and respect for her listeners
   (B) prove her technical authority for the remarks she will make
   (C) set a somber and serious mood for sorrowful remarks that follow
   (D) direct her comments primarily to those with conventional religious beliefs
   (E) evoke a sense of guilt or regret in representatives from the United Nations

Evaluating Writing: Student Draft

Use the student draft about global education on pages 56–57 to complete the following exercises.

1. Identify at least two instances showing the writer's attempt to address the backgrounds, needs, beliefs, or values of the audience. Explain your answers.

2. Identify a place to insert a new sentence or add a phrase to a current sentence to strengthen the writer's connection to the audience's backgrounds, needs, beliefs, or values. Write your addition and explain how your sentence or phrase improves the writing.

3. The writer wants to add to the end of sentence 3 (reproduced below), adjusting the punctuation as needed, to clarify why students take their educational opportunities for granted.

   Many U.S. students—along with their other first-world counterparts—take for granted the educational opportunities that are presented to them as rights.

   Which of the following choices best accomplishes this goal?
   (A) because they live in areas where compulsory and free education is the norm.
   (B) because they fail to appreciate their rights.
   (C) many students around the world misunderstand the lives of others.
   (D) this assumption highlights how different most students are.
   (E) yet, since free education is guaranteed by the government, many don't desire the privilege.

Composing on Your Own

Review the writing you started in Composing on Your Own on page 56. Choose a topic such as women's rights, education, or another topic related to Yousafzai's speech. Also think about the other subjects mentioned in Part 1.1, such as parent-child relations and the safety of teens. Choose one of these subjects or another that interests you. In writing, develop and explain your position on your chosen subject. Also determine to which audience you would most like to present your ideas. For example, will you be writing for other people your age? A teacher? Your Congressperson? A newspaper editor? Write a brief description of your chosen audience's values, beliefs, needs, and background. Answer the questions about your audience from the fourth column of Table 2-1 on page 59.

Use the following chart to help you decide on other aspects of your rhetorical situation. Write down the choices you make and save your work for future use.

Contexts/Formats
▪ Letter to the editor ▪ Submission to campus publication ▪ Citizen input before city hall ▪ Personal blog
Purposes
▪ Convince someone to support a cause ▪ Engage readers with informative article ▪ Urge people to vote for or against a new law ▪ Convince readers to take action

1.2 Modes of Persuasion | RHS-1.H

Writers present arguments to persuade and motivate their audiences. To strengthen their arguments, they appeal to the audience's emotions and their audience's sense of reason and logic. They also try to present themselves as reliable and trustworthy sources, appealing to the audience's sense of character. These appeals are called the **modes of persuasion**. As you build your skills of rhetorical analysis, which you will need to demonstrate on the AP® exam, you will identify and accurately express how writers use these modes to strengthen their arguments.

Three Modes

The different modes of persuasion address different ways readers or listeners respond to a message. The three main appeals, articulated in the 4th Century B.C.E. by Greek philosopher Aristotle in his book Rhetoric, are ethical (ethos, appealing to the character of the speaker), emotional or pathetic (pathos, appealing to emotions), and logical (logos, appealing to logic and reason). These three modes of persuasion often work together, each playing a role in persuading listeners or readers.

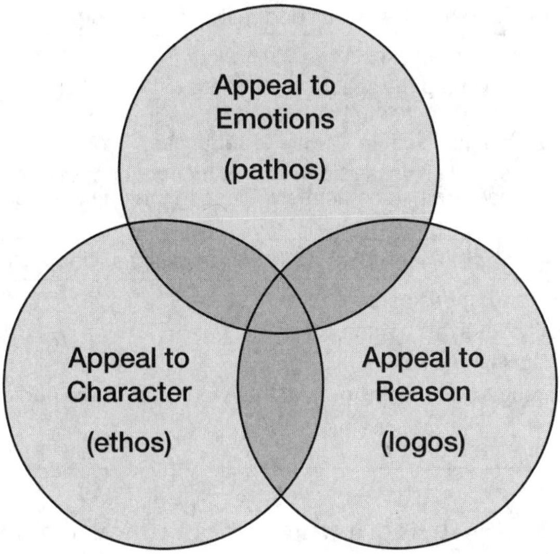

Figure 2-2

Many writers and speakers use a combination of appeals to persuade their audiences.

In this visual, identify the places representing a combination of 1) ethos and pathos, 2) ethos and logos, 3) logos and pathos, and 4) all three appeals.

Ethical Appeals (Ethos)

Ethical appeals are attempts by writers or speakers to convey the credibility of their character to the reader. Aristotle called this appeal *ethos*; the English word is *ethical*. Writers use ethical appeals to establish their credentials and win the trust of their audience. They may be experts in the area they are discussing, or they may have and use information from well-established experts to support their ideas. Writers may also establish trust because they are in a position of authority that implies trust, such as a teacher, parent or guardian, or community leader. Sometimes the writer's position or status is so lofty and prestigious that the audience accepts the message simply because of who the writer is. For example, when a Supreme Court justice writes an opinion, her role as a judge in the highest court in the country provides instant ethos. Finally, writers may earn readers' trust through ethical appeals by demonstrating that their motives for arguing their position are high-minded rather than self-serving and recognizing that their position may not be the only valid one.

Source: Library of Congress

Thurgood Marshall was the first African American Supreme Court justice, appointed in 1967 by President Lyndon B. Johnson. Marshall's stature as a Supreme Court justice conferred immediate credibility on his writing.

The chart below shows what textual details to look for and what questions to ask when analyzing a text for ethos.

Writers establish ethos and build trust by using . . .
▪ references or quotations from experts on the topic ▪ inclusive language indicating the speaker can relate to the audience and has shared values: *we, us, together, in common* ▪ description of personal qualifications or life experiences ▪ acknowledgment of any weaknesses in their argument or concession that an opposing viewpoint has some good points, indicating that the writer is forthright and honest
A reader can evaluate a writer's ethos by asking . . .
▪ Why should readers trust this person? ▪ With what authority does this person speak? ▪ What are this person's motives? ▪ What are the character traits of this person that would cause the audience to trust him or her? ▪ What is this person's reputation?

Table 2-3

When writing an analysis of a writer's use of ethical appeals, identify your observations and write about them with precision. Avoid saying, *the writer appeals to his own character, the writer establishes her credibility,* or *the writer uses ethos.* Instead, use specific language to identify the character traits the writing is demonstrating, including negative ones. For example, if you were writing a rhetorical analysis of Izzy's text messages to her mother, you might write the following:

> The student *agrees to her mother's request* and in doing so *showcases her willingness to obey,* even if it's an easy, seemingly insignificant gesture to her mom's authority. However, the student also *chooses to omit questionable information* and in doing so—to the onlooker who knows—she *highlights her dishonest nature.*

These two examples highlight the student's character: one choice has a positive effect; the other is negative.

Appeals to Emotion (Pathos)

Emotional appeals are writers' efforts to motivate or persuade the audience by evoking their emotions and passions. The Greek term is *pathos*; related English terms are *sympathy* and *empathy*. *Pathos* relates to appealing to emotions and evoking empathy—moving the audience to feel what the writer feels. Emotions are powerful and extremely motivating, and they can be evoked through references to cherished (or feared) abstract ideas, such as country, patriotism, health and well-being, freedom, or threats to any of those. Good writers seek to relate to the audience's emotions; however, writers walk a fine line between engaging an audience's emotions and using emotions to manipulate.

For example, during the debate about expanding health insurance through the Patient Protection and Affordable Care Act (2010), often called

Obamacare because it was President Barack Obama's signature legislation, political proponents and opponents both made emotional appeals to win support by publicizing compelling stories of real people, stories that engaged people's feelings of empathy and concern. Proponents highlighted stories of families forced into "medical debt" because their healthcare costs were so high. Opponents held up stories of people who would have to pay a consequential penalty if they chose not to purchase health insurance.

Sometimes, though, appeals to emotion cross the line into propaganda. In 1950, Senator Joseph McCarthy appealed to people's fears when he claimed in a speech that the U.S. State Department was "infested" with Communists. The word "infested" was an intentional rhetorical choice that helped set off the "Red Scare," disrupting American life and ruining the careers of the falsely accused.

The chart below shows what textual details to look for and what questions to ask when analyzing a text for pathos.

Writers establish pathos and empathy by using . . .
• personal stories or anecdotes • allusions to people, places, and events that evoke strong feelings • symbols that represent certain abstract ideals, such as freedom and hope • words with strong connotations • sensory details, figurative language, and comparisons
A reader can evaluate a writer's emotional appeals by asking . . .
• Who is the audience? • What are the collective values, needs, and beliefs of the audience? • Why should the audience care about the arguments? • What emotions does the writer want the reader to experience? • What details make the audience feel these emotions? • What is the audience supposed to do because of these emotions?

Table 2-4

When writing an analysis of emotional appeals, use specific language. Avoid saying, *a writer uses pathos to make the audience emotional,* and avoid clichés such as, *the writer pulls on the heartstrings.* Instead, identify the author's choices and the emotional response the writer desires from the audience, as in the following analysis of part of Thunberg's speech to the United Nations (UN).

Rhetorical Analysis of Thunberg's Speech (Unit 1)

> Thunberg repeatedly accuses the adult UN representatives of inaction to try to evoke a sense of shame. Thunberg's accusations also stress the idea that world leaders, who should act as public servants, are failing in their duty—an abstract idea—and will be judged accordingly: "The eyes of all future generations are upon you, and if you choose to fail us, I say: We will never forgive you." Finally, Thunberg's use of blunt language to address her audience—such as saying "You are failing us"—emphasizes the gravity of ignoring climate change.

Consider another speech to the UN given by Eleanor Roosevelt in 1948 when the UN was establishing an International Bill of Rights. Former First Lady

Eleanor Roosevelt was a tireless champion for human rights. Note the specific words she uses and abstract ideas she evokes to connect with the emotions of her audience in the following excerpt:

> We must not be confused about what freedom is. Basic human rights are simple and easily understood: freedom of speech and a free press; freedom of religion and worship; freedom of assembly and the right of petition; the right of men to be secure in their homes and free from unreasonable search and seizure and from arbitrary arrest and punishment.
>
> We must not be deluded by the efforts of the forces of reaction to prostitute the great words of our free tradition and thereby to confuse the struggle. Democracy, freedom, human rights have come to have a definite meaning to the people of the world which we must not allow any nation to so change that they are made synonymous with suppression and dictatorship.

An effective rhetorical analysis of Roosevelt's emotional appeals would refer to specific examples of pathos and the effects they have on the audience. Note that the final sentence acknowledges another type of appeal as well.

Rhetorical Analysis of Roosevelt's Speech

In her speech, Roosevelt uses a forthright, declarative approach, repeating the phrase "we must not," thereby encouraging her audience to never give up the struggle for freedom while also emphasizing the need for clarity on fundamental issues of human rights. She associates attempts to confuse the meaning of freedom with prostitution, evoking negative feelings with that word choice. Her use of "forces of reaction," "suppression," and "dictatorship" reminds her listeners of the terrible war the world had just endured. Knowing that her audience is anxious about the post-war future and newly nuclear world, Roosevelt's emotional appeal highlights the immediate need to secure democracy and equal rights throughout the world. Her stature as a former First Lady and internationally known champion for equal rights strengthens her message with an appeal to ethos—she has earned the right to be trusted.

Appeals to Logic (Logos)

The third appeal is to **logic**. The English term *logic* is derived from the Greek word *logos*. Generally, appeals to logic focus on a line of reasoning that asserts a claim and backs up the claim with evidence, including facts, statistics, data, examples, and expert testimony.

Effective writers carefully select evidence and correlate it with their claims. If they explain the evidence clearly enough, the audience should be able to follow a logical line of reasoning and then, ultimately, arrive at the same conclusion as the writer. For example, in her full speech at the UN (which you can read online at americanrhetoric.com), Roosevelt states her thesis in her first sentence: "I have come this evening to talk with you on one of the greatest issues of our time—that is the preservation of human freedom." Yet her statement would not carry weight unless she logically tied her argument to examples that reveal the power of a free society. She clearly lays out fundamental principles of a free society—"freedom of speech and a free press; freedom of religion and worship"—and later in the speech, she contrasts those freedoms with the severe limitations imposed by authoritarian regimes: "The totalitarian state typically places the will of the people second to decrees promulgated by a few men at the top." Logically, Roosevelt portrays the fundamentals of freedom and then reveals what happens when those freedoms are denied.

The chart below shows what textual details to look for and what questions to ask when evaluating the logic of an argument.

Writers establish logic by using . . .
▪ claims that state an opinion or point of view ▪ reasoning to draw inferences and conclusions ▪ evidence, including statistics and data ▪ expert opinions
A reader can evaluate a writer's logical appeals by asking . . .
▪ Is the argument reasonable? ▪ What evidence is provided? ▪ How is the evidence organized? ▪ Where does the writer explain the relationship between the evidence and the argument? ▪ Does the evidence adequately support the claim? ▪ Are the writer's explanations plausible? ▪ How does the argument progress and transition between central ideas?

Table 2-5

Answering the above questions will help you evaluate a writer's line of reasoning as you develop a written analysis of a text. A line of reasoning includes carefully chosen and organized evidence that deftly defends claims within an argument. Good written analysis of logic delineates a writer's specific choices and references, examples of evidence, organization, and/or commentary from the text. Consider this piece of evidence from Greta Thunberg's speech to the UN from Unit 1:

> To have a 67% chance of staying below a 1.5 degree global temperature rise—the best odds given by the [Intergovernmental Panel on Climate Change]—the world had 420 gigatons of CO_2 left to emit back on Jan. 1st, 2018. Today that figure is already down to less than 350 gigatons."
>
> "How dare you pretend that this can be solved with just 'business as usual' and some technical solutions? With today's emissions levels, that remaining CO_2 budget will be entirely gone within less than 8 ½ years.

Following is an example of a sentence that effectively analyzes the logical appeal.

> Thunberg supports her claim that the UN is not doing all it can to stop climate change by citing evidence from the Intergovernmental Panel on Climate Change that indicates how quickly the world is depleting the regulated amount of CO_2.

Writers rarely use only one mode of persuasion. Good writers will use all the tools available to influence their audience. Effective rhetoric relies on a careful blending of logos, pathos, and ethos, according to the needs of the audience. In the excerpt above, Thunberg appeals to all three: she appeals to pathos when she says, "How dare you pretend that this can be solved with just 'business as usual' and some technical solutions?" She appeals to logos by including pertinent statistics, "With today's emissions levels, that remaining CO_2 budget will be entirely gone within less than 8 ½ years." That is such a shocking statistic that it also would likely appeal to emotions. And her ready knowledge of that statistic strengthens her credibility, an appeal to ethos.

Modes of persuasion bring together the key players in the rhetorical situation: the writer, the audience, and the message. The diagram below shows the fundamental question each mode of appeal raises and how the three modes of appeals work together in a complex way within the rhetorical situation to answer those questions.

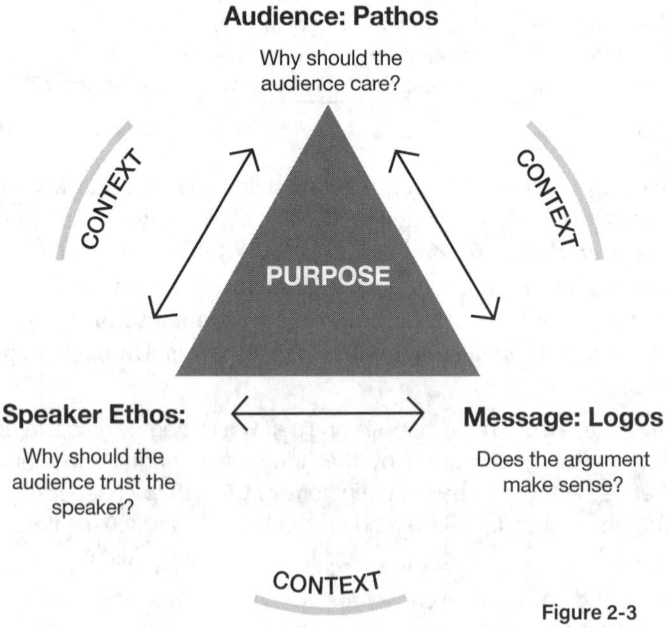

Figure 2-3

Remember: Arguments seek to persuade or motivate action through appeals—the modes of persuasion. (RHS-1.H)

1.2 Checkpoint

Close Reading: Professional Text

Review the speech by Malala Yousafzai on pages 53–55. Then complete the open response activities and answer the multiple-choice questions.

1. On separate paper, create a chart like the one below. Then fill in the chart by identifying the choices Yousafzai makes in her speech that help establish her character and/or credibility as a speaker as she appeals to ethos.

Textual Evidence	Rhetorical Choice: What is the writer doing?	Influence on Character/Credibility: How does this demonstrate her character or credibility?

2. Next create a modified chart to analyze Yousafzai's appeals to pathos. Fill in the chart by identifying the choices Yousafzai makes in her speech that appeal to different emotions in her audience.

Textual Evidence	Rhetorical Choice: What is the writer doing?	Emotion(s) of Audience: What emotion does this inspire in her audience?

3. Which of the following best characterizes Yousafzai's primary mode of persuasion throughout the passage?

(A) She confronts opponents and blatantly disparages their viewpoints.

(B) She repeats the need for international relief in countries devastated by natural disasters.

(C) She exposes the logical missteps of others.

(D) She highlights her credibility by consistently referring to only her experience.

(E) She empathizes with the audience by referencing common beliefs and experiences.

4. Which of the following lines in Yousafzai's speech appeal to the audience's emotions through figurative language and comparisons?
   (A) "I fully support UN Secretary General Ban Ki-moon in his Global Education First Initiative and the work of UN Special Envoy for Global Education Gordon Brown and the respectful president of the UN General Assembly Vuk Jeremic. I thank them for the leadership they continue to give." (paragraph 3, sentences 1 and 2)
   (B) "So today, we call upon the world leaders to change their strategic policies in favor of peace and prosperity. We call upon the world leaders that all of these deals must protect women and children's rights." (paragraph 3, sentences 4 and 5)
   (C) "Thank you to my elders whose prayers strengthened me. I would like to thank my nurses, doctors and the staff of the hospitals in Pakistan and the UK [United Kingdom] and the UAE [United Arab Emirates] government who have helped me to get better and recover my strength." (paragraph 4, sentences 7 and 8)
   (D) ". . . we realize the importance of light when we see darkness. We realize the importance of our voice when we are silenced. In the same way, when we were in Swat, the north of Pakistan, we realized the importance of pens and books when we saw the guns." (paragraph 10, sentences 1 and 2)
   (E) "We call upon all governments to ensure free, compulsory education all over the world for every child. We call upon all the governments to fight against terrorism and violence." (paragraph 14, sentences 1 and 2)

5. Yousafzai's remarks in paragraphs 3 and 4 portray her primarily as a speaker who
   (A) understands the importance of history
   (B) may not have prepared herself for the occasion of her speech
   (C) lacks the deep understanding of her faith possessed by her audience
   (D) recognizes the importance of gratitude and kindness
   (E) seeks to provoke a sense of self-pity that connects her to her audience

Evaluating Writing: Student Draft

Reread the student draft on pages 56–57. Then answer the following open response and multiple-choice questions.

1. What is the writer's primary mode of persuasion?
2. What textual evidence shows that mode of persuasion?
3. Which of the following sentences, if added after sentence 5, would motivate the audience to recognize the severity of educational injustice and logically transition to sentence 6?
    (A) Though there are some educational mandates in these countries, they can't be enacted.
    (B) Because many children can't access their educational needs, the laws offer no penalties for not delivering.
    (C) In these less fortunate areas, if the legal educational requirements exist, they are often neglected and consequently leave many children behind.
    (D) Most students in these areas are children of those with the most money or who have wealthy families, so only the rich are being educated.
    (E) Although many have tried to provide education for their youth, few laws make this even possible.

Composing on Your Own

Return to the writing you started (page 64) and review the description you wrote of your audience and other elements of your rhetorical situation. Then, on separate paper, complete a chart like the one below showing how you could use each mode of persuasion to reach your audience. In each column, write a few specific examples related to your subject and audience.

Your position on your subject:		
Your chosen audience:		
Appeals to Character	**Appeals to Logic**	**Appeals to Emotion**

Part 1 Apply What You Have Learned

Read or listen to former First Lady Hillary Rodham Clinton's remarks to the Fourth United Nations Conference on Women in Beijing, China, in 1995. (You can easily find it online. Bookmark the site so you can return to it for later activities.) On separate paper, use a chart like the one below to identify specific examples of rhetorical appeals. Use your findings to write a rhetorical analysis of the speech that accurately and precisely presents Clinton's modes of persuasions that motivate her audience to trust her and engage with her message about women.

Textual Evidence	Rhetorical Choice What is the writer doing?	Is this related to character/ credibility, emotion, or logic?

Reflect on the Essential Question: Write a brief response that answers this essential question: *How does an audience influence the writer's choices?* In your answer, correctly use the key terms listed on page 58.

Source: National Archives and Records Administration

In her speech on September 5, 1995, Hillary Clinton delivered these now famous words: "If there is one message that echoes forth from this conference, let it be that human rights are women's rights and women's rights are human rights, once and for all."

Look closely at the photo. What details relate directly to the statement Mrs. Clinton makes about human rights?

Part 2

Strategic and Sufficient Evidence

Enduring Understanding and Skills

Part 2

Understand

Writers make claims about subjects, rely on evidence that supports the reasoning that justifies the claim, and often acknowledge or respond to other, possibly opposing, arguments. (CLE-1)

Demonstrate

Identify and explain claims and evidence within an argument. (Reading 3.A)

Develop a paragraph that includes a claim and evidence supporting the claim. (Writing 4.A)

Source: *AP® English Language and Composition Course and Exam Description*

Essential Question: How does strategically selected and sufficient evidence strengthen an argument?

Imagine you want to borrow a car on a Friday night to head out to a friend's house. However, when you mention that you're taking the car, your parents say "No." You quickly retort, "You never let me take the car!" Your parents remind you that you take the car to school every day and that they have loaned it to you for three of the last five weekends so that you could go out with your friends.

Besides the fact that your original claim is a terribly broad generalization, where did you go wrong? The downfall in your argument is a lack of evidence.

The next section will help you select and use evidence effectively to create a convincing argument.

KEY TERMS

amplify	illustrate
associate	mood
clarify	quality
credibility	quantity
exemplify	validity

2.1 Strategic Evidence | CLE-1.F CLE-1.G

Writers strategically select evidence to strengthen the validity and reasoning of an argument. Evidence can be used to amplify and clarify main points, illustrate arguments, and highlight the writer's character and credibility. Effective evidence also appeals to the emotions and values of the audience.

Purpose of Evidence

As you read in Unit 1, writers have many types of evidence to use in arguments, including facts, anecdotes, analogies, statistics, examples, details, illustrations, and personal observations and experiences. With so many possibilities, how does a writer decide which evidence to use? Effective writers first consider their purpose—what they want to accomplish with their argument as a whole. Then they choose evidence that will help them achieve that purpose. Writers use valid evidence to strengthen or bolster claims, to set a mood and relate to the emotions of their audience, and to establish their credibility.

Bolstering Claims

When analyzing the evidence in a text, ask these questions: Why did the writer include this? What is he or she trying to accomplish with the argument? You will find that writers use evidence strategically and purposefully to illustrate, clarify, exemplify, associate (align it with other arguments or topics), or amplify a point in order to bolster or strengthen their claims.

Consider the Declaration of Independence, for example. It opens with logical reasons to explain why the colonies are severing their ties with Great Britain. Then, at the end of the second paragraph, the writers include a list of "Facts" that outline King George's "repeated injuries and usurpations" against the colonies. This list of detailed injuries includes keeping standing armies in the country without the legislature's consent, dissolving the representative houses, and taking away individual colony charters. If you ask yourself why the writers include a list of more than 20 examples of the British king's offenses, you can see that the list provides specific examples to support the claim that the king has established an "absolute Tyranny over these States." These details **illustrate**, or provide explanation through examples, to solidify the case against King George.

This extensive list of the King's offenses also serves to **amplify**, or intensify, the writers' point that there have been so many wrongs that taking action is required. When writers use amplifying evidence, they are trying to make the case for their claim more convincing by increasing the amount and intensity of the evidence. When writers use evidence to amplify, they rely on the volume, or amount, of evidence to further support their argument. Adding more evidence makes the claim more valid and harder to disagree with.

Later in the Declaration, the writers use evidence to **associate** their behavior with that of their British brethren. "We have appealed to their native justice and magnanimity, and we have conjured them by the ties of our common kindred to disavow these usurpations . . . . They too have been deaf to the voice of justice . . . ." In other words, the writers show how they have tried to live up to common standards while their British overlords have not.

The table below explains these and other purposes of evidence. It also details what to look for in a text when analyzing how an author is using evidence.

Purpose of Evidence	What does this look like in a text?	Transitional Language to Introduce Evidence	How does this motivate the reader to accept the argument?
Illustrate or Exemplify	Specific details that explain a larger idea or concept Hypothetical or real stories or testimonies	*To illustrate this point,* *For example,* *For instance,*	Offers concrete proof for general or abstract aspects of a claim and specific instances that validate a claim
Clarify	Definitions of unfamiliar terms or concepts or rephrasing in simpler terms	*To clarify,* *More specifically,* *In other words,*	Anticipates possible misunderstandings of the audience and makes rhetorical choices to help
Amplify	Examples that build in emotional intensity, emphasize the severity of a problem, and show a greater need for action Evidence that broadens the scope of problem	*Furthermore,* *To further highlight (insert argument),* *In addition,* *To make matters worse,*	Adds to preexisting evidence to make the argument more universal and strengthen its impact
Associate (or disassociate)	Comparisons and contrasts	*In a similar sense,* *In the same way,* *Unlike [ ],* *In contrast,*	Helps the reader make connections in the writer's argument through comparisons and contrasts

Table 2-6

Setting Mood

Writers also use evidence to create a mood. **Mood** is the emotional atmosphere created by the writer and experienced by the audience. Mood ties directly to the pathetic appeal (pathos), and writers can use mood effectively to move an audience toward accepting a claim. Certain types of evidence appeal to emotions more than other types. For example, personal experiences and testimonies have more emotional impact than statistics. Writers use different types of evidence to shift the mood throughout a text, often causing emotion to build to a climax and motivating the reader to take action or at least affirm the writer's position.

Consider how the writer of the Declaration of Independence sets the mood in its opening section:

Source: United States Capitol

John Trumbull's painting, *Declaration of Independence*, depicts the five-man drafting committee of the Declaration of Independence presenting their work to the Congress. The drafters of the declaration knew they had to persuade the colonists themselves to break from Britain, so the colonists were as much the audience as the British king and the rest of the world.

> When in the Course of human events, it becomes necessary for one people to dissolve the political bands which have connected them with another, and to assume among the powers of the earth, the separate and equal station to which the Laws of Nature and of Nature's God entitle them, a decent respect to the opinions of mankind requires that they should declare the causes which impel them to the separation.

The writer's language is academic and formal. He appeals to the "Laws of Nature and of Nature's God," grounding his argument in philosophy and core beliefs about humanity and setting a somber mood. This language matches the seriousness of the document. After all, the writer is trying to convince people to rebel against their established ruler, the king of England, and persuade people around the world that their cause is just. In addition, the phrases "the separate and equal station" and "entitles them" evoke positive emotions related to personal freedom and individual rights. The mood is serious and scholarly, as is appropriate for the rhetorical situation.

Consider a more recent example that uses less formal language to discuss the serious issue of racial injustice. During the historical March on Washington for Jobs and Freedom in 1963, Josephine Baker, a well-known entertainer, addressed the crowd just before Dr. Martin Luther King Jr. gave his famous "I Have a Dream" speech. The American-born Baker established her reputation as a singer, dancer, and actor while living in France. When she returned to the United States, she was shocked that she and her husband were turned away at hotels because of their skin color, and she publicly called out famous people for allowing that injustice. She began to use her fame to publicize the widespread segregation in the United States and to work for change through the civil rights movement. On that August day in 1963, Baker likely knew King would give a soaring oratory, so she opted for a different mood in her speech:

> Friends and family . . . you know I have lived a long time and I have come a long way. And you must know now that what I did, I did originally for myself. Then later, as these things began happening to me, I wondered if they were happening to you, and then I knew they must be. And I knew that you had no way to defend yourselves, as I had. And as I continued to do the things I did, and to say the things I said, they began to beat me. Not beat me, mind you, with a club—but you know, I have seen that done too—but they beat me with their pens, with their writings. And friends, that is much worse. . . . When I was a child and they burned me out of my home, I was frightened and I ran away. Eventually I ran far away.

Baker begins her speech with the phrase "Friends and family," which creates an inviting mood and encourages a close bond between Baker and her audience. Baker uses the second-person "you" to address the crowd, suggesting that she is talking directly to each person who is listening. In addition, she chooses evidence from her own experience, illustrating and exemplifying the prejudice she faced and then generalizing from it to the experience of racial injustice shared by her audience: "And I knew that you had no way to defend yourself, as I had." Although Baker discusses severe examples of racial repression—such as beatings and burnings—her speech maintains an approachable mood that quickly connects with the historical and emotional background of her audience.

As you write arguments, use evidence with your purpose in mind: to convince the audience to accept your claim. Ask yourself:

- Am I trying to illustrate, clarify, exemplify, associate, or amplify my point?
- Which of the above will be most convincing? Which will make my line of reasoning more convincing?
- How can I use evidence to create a mood? Based on my audience's background, emotions, and values, what mood should I create in order to persuade the audience?
- How can I arrange the evidence in an order that will enhance the mood and lead the audience to accept and act on my claim?

Using Valid Evidence

Not all evidence is created equal. Writers who have a wealth of evidence at their disposal should strategically select only the best and most useful evidence. The best evidence will strengthen the validity and reasoning of the argument, relate to their unique audience's emotions and values, and increase the writer's credibility. Although personal experience and anecdotal examples may connect with a reader's emotions, effective writers substantiate emotional appeals with evidence from reliable sources, such as subject-area experts and scientific studies, if that is what their audience requires. Certain audiences will find some evidence more convincing than other evidence.

When choosing valid evidence, then, a writer considers if the audience will accept the evidence as true and factual. Some common assumptions are universally believed; almost all people everywhere will accept some statements as true. One example of an assumption considered valid because of its broad acceptance is this statement from the Declaration of Independence: "We hold these truths to be self-evident, that all men are created equal." During the Enlightenment, when philosophers sought to apply scientific methods to social organization, many people believed, as they do today, that kings had no more worth than other people, that "all men are created equal." If this evidence is valid, then the reasoning that builds on it strengthens the claim that the colonies have the right to be independent from Great Britain.

Baker also includes a broadly accepted claim later in her speech as she addresses the thousands of young people among the crowd gathered at the Washington Monument:

> You must get an education. You must go to school, and you must learn to protect yourself. And you must learn to protect yourself with the pen, and not the gun.

Education is universally recognized as a positive means of empowerment. In fact, Baker's claim is nearly identical to Yousafzai's use of the adage: "The pen is mightier than the sword." In both cases, the speakers know that their statements will be widely accepted; that acceptance helps bolster the reasoning behind their appeals for equality and justice for all people.

Relating to the Audience's Emotions

Effective evidence also relates to the audience's emotions and values. For example, imagine a school administrator who must address a group of angry parents about cuts to the school budget. The parents value their children's education. The administrator's goal is to assure the audience that their children's education will not suffer under a more limited budget. To assuage the parents' fear that school budget cuts may mean that their children will not receive a high-quality education, the administrator chooses to present data, such as high test scores, and examples of student activism as evidence that the school is already providing a quality education. Through this evidence, the administrator wants the parents to understand that the school, like the parents, values high-quality instruction for all of the students. The administrator can then focus on evidence that reflects other audience values, including how the impact of the cuts will be reduced by decreasing spending in areas that don't directly affect students or teachers.

Establishing Credibility

Finally, effective evidence increases the writer's **credibility**, the quality of being believable and trustworthy. Evidence that the audience perceives as biased or from a source the audience considers prejudiced or unreliable will weaken the argument. If a writer relies on questionable evidence, the audience may challenge the integrity of the writer and the validity of the argument itself.

By the same reasoning, evidence that reflects a writer's knowledge or authority on the subject or issue can enhance credibility. Writers can maintain credibility by using evidence from sources that are reliable. They avoid using sources with unreasoned bias or that do not carefully vet or fact-check their articles.

Another method for maintaining credibility is to include counterarguments that acknowledge a different point of view. When writers admit that opposing viewpoints have some valid points and evidence, they appear more honest and trustworthy to their audience.

Remember: Writers use evidence strategically and purposefully to illustrate, clarify, set a mood, exemplify, associate, or amplify a point. Strategically selected evidence strengthens the validity and reasoning of the argument, relates to an audience's emotions and values, and increases a writer's credibility. (CLE-1.F, G)

2.1 Checkpoint

Close Reading: Professional Text

Review Yousafzai's speech. Then complete the open response activity and answer the multiple-choice questions.

1. On separate paper, make a chart like the one below. Use the chart to analyze Yousafzai's argument. Start by identifying her claim. Then in the first column record evidence she uses to prove her claim. You will fill in the second column in the next activity.

Yousafzai's Claim:	
Evidence	**Function of the Evidence (illustrate, clarify, set a mood, exemplify, associate, or amplify a point)**

2. Review the evidence from Yousafzai's speech that you documented in the chart you made. Then, in the second column, write a sentence that offers an analysis of Yousafzai's evidence. A model of how to word the analysis is provided below:

    (Writer)'s presentation of (insert summary of evidence) serves to (choose one: illustrate, clarify, exemplify, associate, amplify, set a mood) (insert explanation of the evidence's function).

    Example: Thunberg's presentation of the sharp decline of available gigatons of CO_2 that can still be pumped into the atmosphere before a terrible climate event happens serves to set a mood of immense urgency.

    While you may use the model as a template, you may also use your own words to express your ideas. For instance, in a single sentence, you might explore how the *mood* in Thunberg's speech helps *amplify* her main idea: *Thunberg's repetition of the phrase "how dare you?" creates a confrontational mood and amplifies the importance of recognizing the seriousness of global warming.*

    Whether you use the model or your own words, remember to logically support your analysis to show how Yousafzai builds her argument with evidence that helps illustrate, clarify, set a specific mood, exemplify, associate, or amplify a point.

3. Identify evidence from Yousafzai's speech that does the following:
    - strengthens the validity of the argument
    - relates to the audience's emotions and values
    - increases her credibility

4. In paragraph 7, Yousafzai mentions her attempted assassination to
    (A) create an ominous and foreboding atmosphere
    (B) present her experience to exemplify claims throughout her speech about standing up for rights
    (C) provide evidence related to the good wishes she mentioned at the beginning of her speech
    (D) amplify the idea that violence is widespread in the world
    (E) suggest that her suffering is the result of a uniquely cruel act of terrorism

5. In paragraph 12, Yousafzai's evidence most likely indicates her awareness of
   (A) the international makeup of her audience
   (B) the privileges of more developed nations
   (C) the responsibilities all nations share in protecting the rights of women and children
   (D) the audience's tendency to be ignorant of injustices in developing nations
   (E) the dismissive attitudes of male leaders in impoverished countries

Evaluating Writing: Student Text

Reread the student draft on pages 56–57. Then answer the following open response and multiple-choice questions.

1. Review the claims and the evidence that you identified in the student draft in the Evaluating Writing exercise on page 57. State whether or not each claim is supported with evidence. Then list some possible sources in which the writer could find additional credible evidence. Explain why each source would help the writer seem more credible and make the argument more reasonable to the writer's audience. Also explain how the evidence would relate to other elements of the rhetorical situation.

2. The writer is considering adding the following to the end of sentence 5, adjusting the punctuation as needed.

   as exemplified "in the United Nations' Human Development Report Education Index."

   Should the writer add this segment, and why or why not?
   (A) Yes, because more evidence always strengthens a writer's argument
   (B) Yes, because quoted material refers to a valid source which amplifies the credibility of the writer and argument
   (C) Yes, because the addition emphasizes an emotional appeal
   (D) No, because this evidence serves to contradict the evidence that comes before, thus limiting the validity of the argument
   (E) No, because it doesn't serve to maintain the mood created throughout the piece

Composing on Your Own

Return to the writing you started and review the description you wrote of your audience. Then, on separate paper, complete a chart like the one below listing evidence you could use for varying purposes. In the third column, describe the likely effect of that evidence. Also consider the appropriateness of your evidence in light of the context and your purpose. Save your work for later use.

Your position on your subject:		
Your chosen audience:		
Purposes of Evidence	**Evidence You Could Use**	**Effect (on the audience's emotions, the validity of your argument, or your credibility)**
To illustrate		
To clarify		
To set a mood		
To exemplify		
To associate		
To amplify a point		

2.2 Sufficient Evidence | CLE-1.H

Effective arguments contain sufficient evidence to support their ideas and justify their claims. In strong arguments, a sufficient quantity of high-quality evidence leaves little room for readers or listeners to disagree.

Providing Abundant Support

When the COVID-19 pandemic first spread throughout the world, scientists worked at unprecedented speeds to try to find a treatment to help people recover or a vaccine to prevent infection. The news media offered frequent descriptions of one promising approach after another. Yet in most cases the story of the early efforts ended in one of two ways (or in both ways). One way the story ended was with the idea that an insufficient number of patients had been involved in the experimental study to draw meaningful conclusions. A second way the story ended was with the idea that the experiment was not designed in the most rigorous way—it didn't contain a control group who received only a placebo (sugar pill) to compare with the experimental group who received the treatment. In other words, the quality of the study was not to the highest scientific standards. In most of the reports of early efforts, the stories ended in both ways: the sample size was too small, and the methodology was not of high quality.

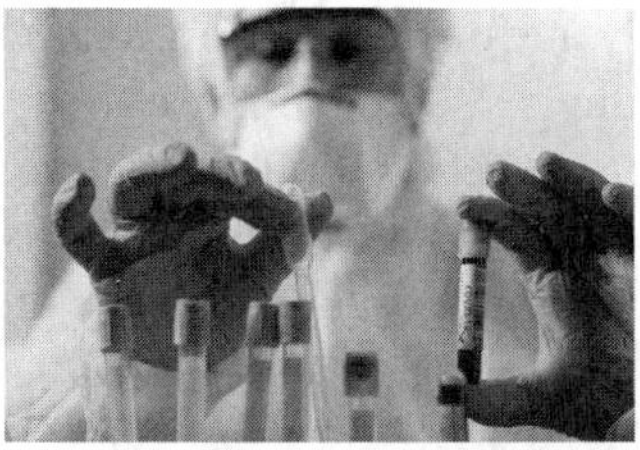

Source: Getty Images

Scientists raced to find a cure or vaccine for COVID-19 in the early months, but experiments repeatedly fell short in two ways—they did not provide sufficient evidence, and they did not provide quality evidence.

What do details captured by this photographer suggest about the person featured in the photo?

Even though in most cases the arguments you write will not have lives hanging in the balance, arguments on any subject require what these early studies lacked: high quality evidence and lots of it.

Quality of Evidence

The better the evidence, the more likely a writer will be to convince an audience. Evidence has high **quality** if it is appropriate for the context and exigence and if the audience is likely to find it valid and relevant. For these reasons, writers always evaluate their rhetorical situation when selecting evidence to support their argument. Think about the quality of evidence in Greta Thunberg's speech. Imagine if, instead of citing quantitative data from the Intergovernmental Panel on Climate Change, she had used anecdotal evidence from a high school friend who reported that the temperature was 30 degrees Celsius in the middle of the winter. The audience would no doubt have had an easy time dismissing this young girl who relied on such scanty evidence. Clearly, the objective and scientific context of Thunberg's speech mandated that she use quality evidence from internationally recognized and peer-reviewed scientific sources.

Quality evidence is also timely. Writers take into account when the evidence was generated. In arguments that may rely on scientific or academic evidence, newer research is a necessity for establishing the quality of an argument. However, when engaging in philosophical debates, sources from classic authors whose ideas have stood the test of time and are still being discussed and debated today in academic settings would be more appropriate than some modern thinkers.

Finally, quality evidence is from authoritative sources. Here are some questions to ask when evaluating sources for authority:

- What is the author's education, training, and experience as it relates to the information in the source? Is the author well known and respected in his or her field?
- What organization is behind this source? Is it a respected and widely accepted educational (.edu), governmental (.gov) or nonprofit source, or does it have a known bias?
- Is the information from a scholarly journal, and has it undergone a rigorous peer review process?

If the answers are yes, the source is probably authoritative. However, some people may not accept quality, authoritative evidence if it is strongly opposed to their values, needs, or beliefs, especially if it is presented without consideration of the audience's feelings. If people feel attacked, they will go on the defensive, making your argument that much more difficult. Carefully introduce strong evidence in a way that is sensitive to the audience.

Quantity of Evidence

Quantity of evidence is the amount of evidence a writer uses. How much evidence a writer needs depends on the purpose and the persuasive power of available evidence. For example, the Intergovernmental Panel on Climate Change (IPCC) publishes many reports to guide policymaking in governments all over the world. One report published in 2014 is 167 pages—the summary alone, filled with facts, data, and graphs, is 31 pages. Such a publication for such a purpose required a large quantity of evidence. However, if the goal is to make a memorable point about climate change in a short speech, as Greta Thunberg did before the United Nations (see pages 4–5), a smaller quantity of evidence may be sufficient. Thunberg refers to information published by the IPCC but needs no more than a few pieces of information to fulfill her purpose. In both cases, the quantity of evidence is appropriate for the rhetorical situation.

How much evidence a writer needs also depends on the audience. A skeptical audience will require more evidence to be convinced of a claim. If the audience is already sympathetic to the argument, the writer may not need as much evidence. The consideration of how much evidence to provide is another way in which writers need to understand the background and values of the audience.

The chart below contains common questions to evaluate the quantity and quality of evidence.

Questions to Ask about Evidence
Is the source credible, from an organization that can be trusted to be unbiased?
Is it current—published in the last five years for most topics? For science and technology topics, was it published in the previous one or two years?
Is it from a primary source—that is, does it contain first-hand accounts and information? If yes, might the source contain any bias?
Does it directly relate to other evidence?
Does it specifically and directly address the claim?
Is the quantity of evidence sufficient to build a convincing argument?

Table 2-7

Remember: An effective argument contains sufficient evidence; evidence is sufficient when its quantity and quality provide apt support for the argument. (CLE-1.H)

2.2 Checkpoint

Close Reading: Professional Text

Review Yousafzai's speech to the UN on pages 53–55. Then answer the following open response and multiple-choice questions.

1. Identify two claims Yousafzai makes and explain why her evidence is sufficient (or insufficient) in its quality and quantity to support them.

2. In paragraph 12, Yousafzai's evidence serves to
   (A) persuade her audience to focus on a specific region that is in need of change
   (B) amplify her desire to maintain the status quo through education
   (C) generate a mood of hope by discussing individual children
   (D) include contemporary examples to clarify a misconception her audience held
   (E) present illustrations of young people needlessly suffering

3. In paragraph 10, Yousafzai's evidence implicitly argues that violent extremists are
   (A) greedy
   (B) irreligious
   (C) uneducated
   (D) immoral
   (E) sadistic

4. The comments in paragraph 11 suggest Yousafzai believes actions that incite violence and deny a child an education are
   (A) issues unique to Pakistan
   (B) violations of Islamic faith
   (C) more common in developing nations than in those more developed
   (D) targeted specifically at Pashtuns
   (E) more pronounced in Islamic nations

Evaluating Writing: Student Draft

Reread the student draft about global education on pages 56–57. Then answer the open response and multiple-choice questions that follow.

1. Evaluate the quantity and quality of the evidence offered to support the argument's claims. Then recommend changes the writer should make to strengthen the argument.

2. The writer wants to replace the underlined section of sentence 7 (reproduced below) to provide evidence that proves there is increased hope for greater global educational equality.

Over the past two decades, increased international efforts have been working to open new doors for the children in these destitute areas.

Which of the following revisions to the underlined text best achieves this purpose?

(A) efforts by the United Nations (UNESCO and UNICEF), Education International, Save the Children, and other international organizations

(B) initiatives to study the problem in nations around the world

(C) diplomatic missions by state departments to the hardest hit areas

(D) efforts governed by NATO and other international collaborative treaties

(E) efforts by organizations such as the Asian Security Alliance and UN Department for Peace Keeping

Composing on Your Own

Return to the writing you started and review your evidence chart from page 84 in which you listed evidence you could use for varying purposes. Evaluate your evidence. Is it appropriate to the rhetorical situation? Do you have sufficient evidence, and is it of high quality? Refine your collection of evidence until you are satisfied you have a solid source of support for your position. Continue to consider your chosen context and purpose. Save your work for later use.

Part 2 Apply What You Have Learned

Reread or listen again to former First Lady Hillary Rodham Clinton's remarks to the Fourth United Nations Conference on Women. Write a response that identifies two or three examples of Clinton's choice of evidence and how they illustrate, clarify, set the mood, exemplify, associate, or amplify her point.

Reflect on the Essential Question: Write a brief response that answers this essential question: *How does strategically selected and sufficient evidence strengthen an argument?* In your answer, correctly use the key terms *mood, validity, credibility, quantity, quality.*

Part 3

Identifying a Thesis

Enduring Understanding and Skills

Part 3

Understand

Writers make claims about subjects, rely on evidence that supports the reasoning that justifies the claim, and often acknowledge or respond to other, possibly opposing, arguments. (CLE-1)

Demonstrate

Identify and describe the overarching thesis of an argument, and any indication it provides of the argument's structure. (Reading 3.B)

Write a thesis statement that requires proof or defense and that may preview the structure of the argument. (Writing 4.B)

Source: *AP® English Language and Composition Course and Exam Description*

Essential Question: How can you describe an argument's overarching thesis and what it suggests about the argument's structure?

A house has strong walls that hold up a roof and a foundation that supports those walls. The roof covers all the walls, but it can't stand without those strong, well-built walls, and those walls can't stand without that solid foundation. An argument is like a house. The foundation is the evidence that supports the reasoning represented by the walls; the roof is the overarching claim, or thesis, held up by the evidence and reasoning.

Part 3 explores the relationships among claims, thesis statements, reasoning, and the structure of an argument. Some thesis statements provide clues to how the writer will structure the argument. Others are not explicitly stated but instead emerge from the overall presentation of claims and evidence.

Not all arguments follow the same structure, just as not all houses have the same design. If developed thoughtfully, many variations in structure and presentation can result in a solidly built argument.

KEY TERMS

argument structure	thesis
claim	thesis statement

3.1 Thesis Statements | CLE-1.I CLE-1.J

A writer's overarching claim is called a **thesis**. A clearly expressed thesis is called a **thesis statement**. A writer defends his or her thesis by using reasoning supported by evidence.

Stating a Thesis

Gathering different kinds of evidence for different purposes (see pages 76–81) is an essential step in constructing an argument. Which evidence to use and how to use it depends in part on how you present your thesis.

In 1946, in the aftermath of World War II, George Orwell wrote an essay called "Politics and the English Language." He begins his essay this way, building up to his thesis statement at the end of the second paragraph:

> Most people who bother with the matter at all would admit that the English language is in a bad way, but it is generally assumed that we cannot by conscious action do anything about it. Our civilization is decadent,[1] and our language—so the argument runs—must inevitably share in the general collapse. It follows that any struggle against the abuse of language is a sentimental archaism,[2] like preferring candles to electric light or hansom cabs[3] to [air]planes. Underneath this lies the half-conscious belief that language is a natural growth and not an instrument which we shape for our own purposes.
>
> Now, it is clear that the decline of a language must ultimately have political and economic causes: it is not due simply to the bad influence of this or that individual writer. But an effect can become a cause, reinforcing the original cause and producing the same effect in an intensified form, and so on indefinitely. A man may take to drink because he feels himself to be a failure, and then fail all the more completely because he drinks. It is rather the same thing that is happening to the English language. It becomes ugly and inaccurate because our thoughts are foolish, but the slovenliness of our language makes it easier for us to have foolish thoughts. The point is that the process is reversible. Modern English, especially written English, is full of bad habits which spread by imitation and which can be avoided if one is willing to take the necessary trouble. If one gets rid of these habits one can think more clearly, and to think clearly is a necessary first step towards political regeneration: so that the fight against bad English is not frivolous and is not the exclusive concern of professional writers.

In these two paragraphs, Orwell asserts a number of claims:

- The English language is in a bad way.
- Most people think there's nothing that can be done to change that.

---

1 **decadent:** in moral decline
2 **archaism:** old-fashioned idea
3 **hansom cabs:** horse-drawn carriages

- The decline of language has political and economic causes.
- There is a cycle of decline: with sloppy language, thoughts become sloppy; with sloppy thoughts, language gets even sloppier.
- It is possible to reverse this process by breaking bad writing habits.
- Getting rid of bad writing habits will help lead to clearer thinking.
- Thinking clearly is the "necessary first step towards political regeneration."
- The fight against bad English is not frivolous.

Each of these statements is arguable and defensible, the necessary qualities of a claim. However, not all of them carry the same weight. The overarching claim, or **thesis**, is that clear writing and thinking are possible and that they are necessary for political regeneration, or renewal. All the other claims work to support that thesis.

In many written arguments, the writer clearly states a central claim in a single, explicit statement, as Orwell does in the final sentence of this excerpt. This is often called a **thesis statement**. It might also include the claim and other elements important to the argument. Other times the reader must infer the writer's thesis based on the evidence and reasoning presented. A reader may have to read the entire text in order to discover the thesis.

Orwell wrote the novel *1984* about a dystopian world where "doublespeak" and other travesties of language are used to maintain tyranny.

Text and graphics together amplify messages. How does the text affect the way you see the image?

Often, profiles of historical people and events will include an implied thesis. A writer may feel that stating an immediate thesis confines the narrative into a limited structure, while implying a thesis allows the writer more room to explore his or her subject matter. For example, John Hersey's book *Hiroshima* tells the stories of six people who survived the atomic bombing of the city of Hiroshima. The book details the six people's harrowing experiences of survival and follows them as they attempt to rebuild their lives.

The author clearly believes that the bombing was an unimaginable injustice ignored by much of the world; yet instead of stating this idea as a thesis, he allows the events and characters to speak for themselves. Through the course of the book, the reader learns that the six people profiled were able to rebuild meaningful lives. How the writer chooses to report on the six lives within his book—the details he leaves in or leaves out—gradually builds his thesis through the reader's recognition of the challenges the people face and overcome.

For the arguments in this course, however, present your overarching claim explicitly in a thesis statement. The statement will serve as a guide for both you and your audience. Traditionally, but not always, this sentence appears early in the essay. A clearly articulated thesis is required in the essays on the AP® exam.

Previewing the Structure of an Argument

In addition to laying out the main idea, a thesis statement may also provide clues about the **argument structure**, the organizational pattern you use to defend your thesis. Reread the last few lines of Orwell's second paragraph. What does it lead you to expect from the rest of the essay? If you are like most readers, you might expect Orwell to explain what those bad habits are, how you can break them, and in doing so how you can help regenerate politics. If you came to that conclusion, you did so probably on the basis of all the reading experience you have had, since Orwell does not explicitly say he will do this. Instead, he suggests a structure that experienced readers will likely notice.

Experienced writers rarely if ever announce their purpose and structure as directly as the following: "In this essay, I will show how language and thinking are linked, and then I will suggest bad habits that are clouding our thinking, and then I will make suggestions about how to break them." Writers may well *think* statements like that so they keep their purpose and organization clear in their minds, but when they start writing, they typically take the "I" out of the statement and just assert their claim, often suggesting an organization: "Because language and thought are so closely linked, sloppiness in language can turn into sloppiness in thought. But breaking bad language habits can be done, and it can lead to clearer thinking and more honest politics."

For another example, read the following introduction to an essay by Robert Benchley called "Advice to Writers" collected in his 1922 book *Love Conquers All.* Identify his thesis statement. What does it suggest to you about the structure of his essay?

> Two books have emerged from the hundreds that are being published on the art of writing. One of them is "The Lure of the Pen," by Flora Klickmann, and the other is "Learning to Write," a collection of [well-known writer Robert Louis] Stevenson's meditations on the subject, issued by Scribners. At first glance one might say that the betting would be at least eight to one on Stevenson. But for real, solid, sensible advice in the matter of writing and selling stories in the modern market, Miss Klickmann romps in an easy winner.

Although Benchley does not directly say, "In this essay I will compare Klickmann's book and Stevenson's book and show you why Klickmann's is better," he makes the point clearly enough through his thesis statement, the final sentence in the paragraph.

Remember: A thesis is the main, overarching claim a writer is seeking to defend or prove by using reasoning supported by evidence. A writer's thesis is not necessarily a single sentence or an explicit statement and may require a thorough reading of the text to identify, but when a thesis is directly expressed, it is called a thesis statement. (CLE-1.I,J)

3.1 Checkpoint

Close Reading: Professional Text

Carefully review Yousafzai's speech on pages 53–55. Then complete the following open response tasks and answer the multiple-choice questions.

1. Write a thesis statement that you could insert near the beginning of the speech. When constructing the thesis, include Yousafzai's overarching claim and project her argument's structure.

2. Yousafzai recounts her experiences and the suffering of others to support the thesis that
    - (A) the world is a harsh place that works to oppress the rights of minorities
    - (B) the world's youth is consistently looked down upon and belittled
    - (C) even those who have been unfairly injured deserve an education
    - (D) education is the solution to many of the world's problems and misunderstandings
    - (E) the UN needs to do something in order to prevent tragedies from happening

Why might the photographer have chosen such a starkly black background in this photo of Yousafzai? What might it convey about the photographer's attitude toward her?

Source: Wikimedia Commons

3. Which of the following lines best articulates the thesis for Yousafzai's whole speech?

    (A) "Today is the day of every woman, every boy and every girl who have raised their voice for their rights." (paragraph 5, sentence 5)
    (B) "Dear brothers and sisters, we must not forget that millions of people are suffering from poverty and injustice and ignorance." (paragraph 12, sentence 2)
    (C) "Today I am focusing on women's rights and girls' education because they are suffering the most." (paragraph 13, sentence 1)
    (D) "We call upon all the governments to fight against terrorism and violence." (paragraph 14, sentence 2)
    (E) "Education is the only solution." (paragraph 17, sentence 3)

Evaluating Writing: Student Draft
Reread the student draft about global education on pages 56–57. Then complete the free response activity and answer the multiple-choice question.

1. Write two possible alternate thesis statements for the evidence in this draft. One of them should indicate a possible structure for the draft.

2. The writer is considering adding the following sentence to the passage in order to emphasize the thesis.

    However, all is not lost.

    Where would the sentence best be placed?

    (A) After sentence 2
    (B) After sentence 3
    (C) After sentence 5
    (D) After sentence 6
    (E) After sentence 7

Composing on Your Own
Review your refined collection of evidence and the position you have taken. Considering your audience, context, and purpose, choose the three most compelling pieces of evidence. (Be prepared to explain your choices.) Then develop a thesis statement that clearly articulates your position and suggests the structure you will use to defend it. Draft your paragraph, using an organizer like the one on the next page.

Argument Paragraph Drafting Organizer		
Thesis statement, including structure for defending it:		
Evidence	**Evidence**	**Evidence**
Explain how that evidence supports the reasoning that justifies the thesis	Explain how that evidence supports the reasoning that justifies the thesis	Explain how that evidence supports the reasoning that justifies the thesis
Draft of paragraph		

Use the checklist below to revise your draft.

Checklist for Composing and Revising
✓ Did you make strategic rhetorical choices with the values, beliefs, needs, and background of your audience in mind? (1.1)
✓ Did you use the mode(s) of persuasion best suited to your audience and purpose? (1.2)
✓ Did you use evidence strategically and purposefully to illustrate, clarify, set a mood, exemplify, associate, or amplify a point? Does your evidence strengthen the validity and reasoning of your argument, relate to your audience's emotions and values, and increase your credibility? (2.1)
✓ Did you use abundant, high quality evidence sufficient to support your argument? (2.2)
✓ Do you have a clear thesis statement that expresses the overarching claim your argument seeks to defend or prove? Does your thesis statement preview the structure of your argument? (3.1)
✓ Did you check your writing for mistakes in spelling and mechanics and make an effort to correct them?

Table 2-8

Part 3 Apply What You Have Learned

Reread or listen again to former First Lady Hillary Rodham Clinton's remarks to the Fourth United Nations Conference on Women. Write a response that defines Clinton's thesis and explains how she defends it. Be sure to cite the evidence Clinton uses in her speech.

Reflect on the Essential Question: Write a brief response that answers this essential question: *How can you describe an argument's thesis statement and what it suggests about the argument's structure?* In your answer, correctly use the key terms *claim, thesis, thesis statement,* and *argument structure.*

Unit 2 Review

Section I: Reading

Questions 1–9. Read the following passage carefully before you choose your answers.

(The following is excerpted from an article appearing in the *Boston Globe.*)

1 Technology is an easy target for our ire. If you've ever cursed at a television or a laptop, you know this. The same is true in sports with instant replay. It's easy to villainize video replay in a pique[1] of anthropomorphic angst,[2] lamenting how it has altered sports, and not for the better. . . .

2 Here's the thing. Video replay isn't getting it wrong. It's not ruining sports. We are. Don't blame the technology. It doesn't make any decisions. Blame the people applying it. Like most technology, video replay is only as helpful or harmful as the human beings employing it. It's easy to rail against replay, but the real problem is human error. . . .

3 There is no play in sports that causes my blood to boil like a Major League Baseball review of a safe/out call at second base. You know the play. The baserunner has beaten the tag, but the laws of physics cause his momentum to lift him off the bag for a millisecond while a too-late tag is still being applied, an imperceptible and technical out. But here comes the manager's challenge. Suddenly, that player is out. It's absurd, a pure perversion of why replay was instituted in baseball in the first place.

4 The baserunner made no attempt to advance. He merely succumbed to motion and momentum. Baseball could fix this detestable play tomorrow. But it ignores it.

---

1 **pique:** feeling of irritation
2 **anthropomorphic angst:** dread so strong that it takes on human-like characteristics

So, now we have players who purposefully hold the tag on baserunners longer than the final *Lord of the Rings* movies in hopes of stealing an out. If I could banish this play from the planet for eternity, I would.

5 This is the problem. Like people misusing e-mail in phishing scams to hack an account or Facebook being repurposed to spread false political propaganda, technology has unintended consequences and unforeseen negative effects in the hands of human beings. So, we're stuck with replay being used to highlight venial[3] transgressions and picayune[4] violations. We're left with it being the "gotcha" of sports.

6 Replay was designed to correct injustices in sports, not create them.

7 Twice in these NHL playoffs, the fragility of the rectitude[5] of replay when funneled through the prism of human application has been exposed. The aforementioned Avalanche no-goal on May 8 stands out. In the second period of Game 7 of the Western Conference semifinals, Colorado's Colin Wilson netted the apparent game-tying goal. However, the San Jose Sharks challenged the play for being offsides.

8 In fuzzy pixels on the opposite side of the blue line from where San Jose turned over the puck and Colorado flicked it into the zone, it appeared that Avalanche captain Gabriel Landeskog had one skate inside the zone as he stepped off the ice for a line change. Instead of a 2-2 game, the goal was overturned for offsides. Colorado lost, 3-2. The actual score of the game was: Technicality 1, Common Sense 0.

9 Is this replay's fault? Nope. . . .

10 It's only going to get worse as replay technology improves and as its uses in sports expand to more equivocal matters. Replay is the Rubin's vase[6] of sports viewing. What you see is colored by perception.

11 The NFL's decision to extend the use of instant replay in the coming season to include offensive and defensive pass interference penalties, including retroactively putting a flag on the field when one wasn't thrown, is an abomination waiting to happen. Like a foul in the NBA, you could find technical pass interference on almost every pass play in an NFL game.

---

3 **venial:** slight
4 **picayune:** petty
5 **rectitude:** righteousness
6 **Rubin's vase:** A black and white optical illusion that appears to some as two white profiles facing each other and to others as a vase.

12 The NFL already has the most capricious, time-consuming, and confusing application of video replay review, thanks in part to senior vice president of officiating Alberto "Reverse' em All" Riveron and his gut-feeling rulings. . . . His overturning of a Buffalo Bills touchdown against the Patriots in 2017 remains a replay travesty. His replay applications of the catch rule were so technical that season that the NFL had him tone it down for that season's Super Bowl.

13 The worst part of the NFL's new pass interference replay review rule is that it's entirely in response to a controversial non-call that hurt the New Orleans Saints in the NFC Championship game. Replay was instituted to improve the accuracy of officiating and make sports contests fairer, not to settle old scores and address grievances.

14 Replay is supposed to remove human error from the equation, a technological Band-Aid for bad judgment. But as long as human beings are the ones overseeing replay, it will always be subject to misuse, poor judgment, and human error.

---

1. The writer uses the pronouns *you* and *our* in the first paragraph in order to

(A) establish technology's lack of social and practical value

(B) offer multiple examples of firmly established beliefs

(C) engage multiple perspectives about the topic at hand

(D) contextualize the paradoxical need for technology in sports

(E) connect with his audience around commonly held viewpoints

2. The writer references multiple sports-related examples throughout the piece primarily to

(A) suggest that the misuse of instant replay plagues all sports

(B) amplify his credentials as a sportswriter

(C) establish a critical mood

(D) appeal to the general preferences of the audience

(E) associate instant replay with other administrative technicalities and protocols

3. Throughout the piece, the writer's main purpose is to

(A) suggest the NFL's use of replay review technology is slowly improving

(B) propose multiple solutions to the problem of replay review

(C) justify his complaints and concerns about human misuse of replay review technology

(D) expose the depths of human folly and arrogance

(E) imply that professional sports organizations are governed by hypocrites

4. Which of the following sentences from the passage best represents the writer's central or overarching argument or thesis?

(A) "Technology is an easy target for our ire." (paragraph 1, sentence 1)

(B) "It's easy to villainize video replay in a pique of anthropomorphic angst, lamenting how it has altered sports, and not for the better." (paragraph 1, sentence 4)

(C) "It's absurd, a pure perversion of why replay was instituted in baseball in the first place." (paragraph 3, sentence 6)

(D) "The NFL's decision to extend the use of instant replay in the coming season to include offensive and defensive pass interference penalties, including retroactively putting a flag on the field when one wasn't thrown, is an abomination waiting to happen." (paragraph 11, sentence 1)

(E) "But as long as human beings are the ones overseeing replay, it will always be subject to misuse, poor judgment, and human error." (paragraph 14, sentence 2).

Question 5 is covered in Units 1 and 2.

5. The writer's evidence throughout the passage depends primarily on

(A) appeals to various authorities

(B) hearsay and rumor

(C) anecdotal descriptions

(D) ethical appeals

(E) personal biases and prejudices

Question 6 is covered in Unit 4.

6. Which of the following statements best describes the function of the passage's final paragraph?

(A) It seeks to summarize the reasons why human judgment makes video replay problematic.

(B) It mocks humanity's efforts to perfect sports.

(C) It persuades sports fans to embrace officiating errors.

(D) It asks readers to reject the use of instant replay reviews.

(E) It highlights the need for instant replay but with improvements.

Questions 7 and 8 are covered in Unit 5.

7. The writer's perspective most likely differs from that of the majority of the audience in that
   (A) fans demand new rules to address past errors, whereas he believes past errors should not lead to rule changes
   (B) the author and most fans embrace replay review technology, but the author appreciates human officiating more
   (C) most fans accept instant replay's use in sports, whereas the author finds no value in it
   (D) though most agree technology is detrimental to sporting events, the author finds it necessary for fairness
   (E) many people attack replay review technology, whereas the author criticizes how people misuse it

8. The writer primarily objects to replay review judgments because they
   (A) lack entertainment value
   (B) involve too many commercial breaks
   (C) take too long to conclude
   (D) are filtered through subjective human perception
   (E) rely too much on little-known technical rules

Question 9 is covered in Unit 8.

9. Which of the following statements best captures the central irony the writer exposes about the use of replay review technology?
   (A) Improving the quality of sports officiating will always involve a human element.
   (B) The desire for technological improvements in sports officiating undermines professional sports.
   (C) Efforts to improve sports officiating are always doomed to failure.
   (D) The fans' demands for justice and fairness in sports officiating makes sports less entertaining.
   (E) Replay review technology sometimes leads to rule changes based on past officiating mistakes.

Section I: Writing

Questions 10–13. Read the following passage carefully before you choose your answers.

The passage below on the subject of space waste is a draft.

(1) Space exploration, with its overt cost and discouraging projections, merely encourages the celebration of misguided idealism, something humanity is unable to afford at this point in history.

(2) The ridiculous financial burden of space travel implies that it's okay to take valuable, limited funds and spend them superfluously on hypothetical causes. (3) A recent breakdown of governmental spending suggests that space funding is not necessarily as high as one would think because space research is slated to receive "0.4% of the $4.7 trillion dollar federal budget"; however, what this amounts to is a ballpark number of about "$22.6 billion for fiscal year 2020." (4) In a world dealing with a global recession, and in a world that is laden with its own issues, it doesn't seem right to spend an astronomically large amount of money on something that won't be able to quickly solve more tangible and immediate issues like helping the "736 million people liv[ing] below the poverty line," which, by the way, is calculated by a UN-established ridiculously low wage of "$1.90 a day."[1] (5) By federally funding something as arbitrary as space exploration, national leaders are setting an example that it's okay to blatantly and irresponsibly ignore the complex issues that pervade the globe for the erroneous hope of finding something: who knows what? (6) The value of life is of utmost importance, so funding and exploring what is known to have a track record of success is a moral obligation.

(7) Space exploration accomplishes the opposite of its goal. (8) Such funding, no matter how small, should be put into solving deeper concerns that plague the national and global community. (9) It should even be argued that rather than looking for ways to increase the national budget, the government should attempt to save on some of its expenditures so it can address an even bigger problem: the irresponsible national debt of about "$23 trillion."[2]

---

1 https://www.un.org/en/sections/issues-depth/poverty/index.html
2 https://www.treasurydirect.gov/NP/debt/current

10. In sentence 1 (reproduced below), the writer wants to introduce the structure of the argument to come.

Space exploration, with its overt cost and discouraging projections, merely encourages the celebration of misguided idealism, something humanity is unable to afford at this point in history.

Which version of the underlined element would best serve this purpose?

(A) (as it is now)

(B) Space exploration, hardly meeting its return on investment, merely encourages the celebration of misguided idealism, something humanity is unable to afford at this point in history.

(C) Space exploration, though offering a semblance of hope, merely encourages the celebration of misguided idealism, something humanity is unable to afford at this point in history.

(D) Space exploration, with its negligent and oppressive policies and practices, merely encourages the celebration of misguided idealism, something humanity is unable to afford at this point in history.

(E) Space exploration, though consistently assisting medical research and other valuable studies, merely encourages the celebration of misguided idealism, something humanity is unable to afford at this point in history.

11. The writer would like the quotations in sentence 3 (reproduced below) to help establish greater credibility for the argument.

A recent breakdown of governmental spending suggests that space funding is not necessarily as high as one would think because space research is slated to receive "0.4% of the $4.7 trillion dollar federal budget"; however, what this amounts to is a ballpark number of about "$22.6 billion for fiscal year 2020."

Which of the following additions to the end of the sentence, adjusting punctuation as needed, would best accomplish this goal?

(A) as revealed by a government official who agreed to speak anonymously about the issue.

(B) this is much more than what many private space organizations like Space X receive from governmental subsidies.

(C) as quoted in multiple recent tabloids.

(D) which is a considerable amount of money for any organization to receive.

(E) according to the most recent official publications.

12. The writer is looking to revise sentence 7 (reproduced below) by adding the following underlined text.

Space exploration accomplishes the opposite of its goal: <u>rather than promoting exploration, it impedes human development.</u>

Should the writer add this text?

(A) Yes, because it serves to amplify the writer's main claim and clarifies a prior ambiguity.

(B) Yes, because the writer needs to highlight the greater needs for medical and economic funding.

(C) Yes, because the language repeats and reinforces the writer's claim and provides a strong example.

(D) No, because the language makes the argument too vague.

(E) No, because the language doesn't signify a shift to a new paragraph and the content it explores.

13. The writer wants to add the following sentence to highlight the contrasting value of humanitarian agencies when compared to space agencies.

In doing so, they are tearing funds from other more beneficial agencies like the Administration for Community Living, the Health Resources and Services Administration, or even the National Cancer Institute.

Where would the sentence best be placed?

(A) Before sentence 2

(B) Before sentence 3

(C) After sentence 5

(D) After sentence 6

(E) After sentence 8

Source: Wikimedia Commons

The launch of the SpaceX Falcon Heavy at the Kennedy Space Center in Florida, on February 6, 2018

JOIN THE CONVERSATION: RHETORICAL ANALYSIS (PART 1)

Before you move on to answering the free-response questions in Section II of the Unit 2 Review, take the time to understand the tasks they require by completing the activities in this "Join the Conversation" guide.

One type of free-response prompt on the AP® exam (the second question) is a **rhetorical analysis** task. The exam gives you a passage and asks you to read it closely, identify rhetorical choices the writer or speaker makes to convey his or her argument, message, or purpose, and then explain how those choices convey that message. In Units 2-5 in this "Join the Conversation" guide, the same prompt for rhetorical analysis will be repeated to allow you to practice and apply the new, increasingly complex skills you learned in the unit. As you do, you will see how your analysis and essay improve. Following is the prompt you will work on.

The speech on pages 53–55 was delivered on "Malala Day"—July 12, 2013—by Malala Yousafzai, a girls' and children's education rights activist who survived an assassination attempt in 2012 when she was 15. She delivered this speech to the "Youth Take Over the UN" assembly, a campaign that stressed the importance of global education rights. This was the first speech she delivered since the assassination attempt.

Read the passage carefully. Write a paragraph that identifies some of the rhetorical choices Yousafzai makes and briefly explain how those choices convey her message that all children around the world deserve an equal education.

In your response you should do the following:

- Respond to the prompt with a claim that analyzes the writer's rhetorical choices.
- Select and use evidence to support your line of reasoning.
- Briefly explain how the evidence supports your line of reasoning.
- Use appropriate grammar and punctuation in communicating your argument.

Like the argument prompt introduced in Unit 1 (and continued on page 107), the rhetorical analysis prompt has three parts: the first paragraph provides background, the second paragraph states your task, and the third provides a checklist to make sure your response fulfills the requirements. Everything this prompt asks you to do has been covered in Units 1 and 2.

Unlike the task in the argument essay, however, your task in the rhetorical analysis, identified in the second paragraph of the prompt, is to develop a defensible claim not about *what* the writer conveys but rather about *how* the writer conveys her message and the strategic rhetorical choices she makes. In this unit you learned about rhetorical choices related to appealing to the beliefs and values of an audience, methods of persuasion, types and purposes of different evidence, and expressing a thesis statement.

Here's how your thought process might go: When you first read Yousafzai's speech, maybe you were struck with all the renowned people she acknowledges at the beginning of her speech and the inclusive language she uses (brothers and sisters). You might now recognize these as part of an ethical appeal, a rhetorical choice about how to relate to her audience. Maybe you also were taken with her use of a dramatic personal story to convey her message. You might now recognize that as a type of evidence, another rhetorical choice. From these ideas you might develop a claim such as the following: "Demonstrating awareness of her audience through ethical appeals and a powerful personal story, Yousafzai skillfully got across her message about the importance of global education." When you get to this point in your thinking, you have completed the requirements of the **first two bullets** in the third part of the prompt—presenting a defensible claim and selecting and using evidence to support it—though you likely began with the evidence and worked backward, a reasonable way to proceed.

The **third bullet** instructs you to explain the connection between your evidence and reasoning. Discuss each choice and explain *how* it helps to convey Yousafzai's message. For example, you might say that her personal story of being attacked but recovering and not being silenced helps her to convey her message by showing her commitment to her cause. This evidence appeals to the audience by raising sympathy for her and building trust in her as a speaker, since she continues to literally risk her life for this cause. Yousafzai brings the audience to pity her only for a moment before they see the strength she continues to have despite the attempted assassination. This explanation goes beyond saying that her story made the audience trust her; instead, it explains *how* her story persuades the audience to trust her (ethical appeal) and how this evidence might emotionally affect the audience as they take in her entire speech.

When you finish your draft, check it over to make sure you meet the requirements of each bullet point in the prompt. The **final bullet** reminds you to use appropriate grammar and punctuation, so double check for possible grammatical and punctuation errors.

Using an organizer like the one on the following page may help you gather your thoughts and remind you to address each required aspect of the prompt as you draft your response. Save your completed draft for further development in Unit 3.

Unit 2: Rhetorical Analysis (Part 1) Drafting Organizer
Claim: Demonstrating awareness of her audience through ethical appeals and a powerful personal story, Malala Yousafzai skillfully got across her message about the importance of global education.
<u>Choices the writer makes to convey the message</u> her use of references to highly respected people known the world over for their honor and commitment to social justice and her use of inclusive language
<u>Explain how that evidence supports the reasoning that justifies that claim</u> Yousafzai's use of references to such highly respected people as Benazir Bhutto (she is even wearing her shawl), Nelson Mandela, and Mother Teresa places her in the company of people who would be well known at the UN for their global impact in standing up to oppression and violence. By so doing she establishes herself as someone whose message has value. But she does not set herself apart. She repeatedly uses inclusive language ("brothers and sisters," "we"), creating a bond with the audience. Through these ethical appeals, she shows her sensitivity to her audience as she attempts to motivate them to act.
<u>Choices the writer makes to convey the message</u> her personal story of being attacked but recovering
<u>Explain how that evidence supports the reasoning that justifies that claim</u> Yousafzai's personal story of being attacked but recovering and not being silenced helps her to convey her message by showing her commitment to her cause. This effective use of a compelling story as evidence strengthens her connection to her audience in a way that creates a trust in her as a speaker—she continues to literally risk her life for this cause.
<u>Draft of Paragraph</u> Malala Yousafzai uses references to highly respected and well-known people and her terrifying personal story to convey her message that all children around the world deserve an equal education. Putting herself in the company of people well-known in the international community for their bravery and principled resistance to inequality, she gives the audience reason to believe her. She is even literally wearing the shawl of the first female leader of a Muslim nation. Yet she does not set herself apart. She repeatedly uses inclusive language (brothers and sisters, we), creating a bond with the audience. Through these ethical appeals, she shows her sensitivity to her audience as she attempts to motivate them to act. Also, her personal story of being attacked but recovering and not being silenced helps her to convey her message by showing her commitment to her cause This effective use of a compelling story as evidence strengthens her connection to her audience in a way that creates trust in her as a speaker, since she continues to literally risk her life for this cause.

Apply

Follow the same process as above to respond to the rhetorical analysis prompt on page 110. For current free-response prompt samples, check the College Board's website.

JOIN THE CONVERSATION: THE ARGUMENT ESSAY (PART 2)

The final free-response task on the exam is an argument essay, which you first began working on in Unit 1, page 48. The practice prompt for Unit 2 is much like the prompt in Unit 1. In the example of the warning label topic from Unit 1, only one part of the task is different (explained below).

The first part of the prompt provides background, just as it did before. The second states your task, just as it did before.

> For decades, movies and music have included messages or labels to signal that they have material in them that some people may find troubling. Advocates for such warnings argue they are important to prevent people from being exposed to things they do not want to encounter. However, Erika Christakis, a lecturer at the Yale Child Study Center, says that "free speech and the ability to tolerate offense are the hallmarks of a free and open society."
>
> Write an essay that argues your position on the use of warning labels or warning messages to signal potentially troubling content.
>
> In your response you should do the following:
>
> - Respond to the prompt with a <u>thesis</u> that presents a defensible position.
> - Provide evidence to support your line of reasoning.
> - Explain how the evidence supports your line of reasoning.
> - Use appropriate grammar and punctuation in communicating your argument.

The third part once again provides a checklist to make sure your response fulfills the requirements. The items are the same as they were in Unit 1 except for the first bullet point, with the key word change underlined above. In Unit 1, the word was *claim*.

However, even though the remaining bullet points are the same, you have developed more sophisticated abilities through the activities in this unit, especially in regard to strategic and thoughtful use of evidence and commentary, and you are expected to demonstrate the development of these abilities. This time you will write a two-paragraph draft. Everything the prompt asks you to do has been covered in Units 1 and 2.

In Unit 1, the **first bullet** of paragraph three of the prompt reminded you to develop a defensible claim. Now, as you just read, you are required to express your claim as a *thesis*. One way to do so is to develop an appeal to emotions by attaching the claim to an abstract or universal idea, as

Thunberg does when she evokes the ideal of duty or as Yousafzai does when she places her argument in the context of "a glorious struggle against illiteracy, poverty and terrorism." Another is to place it within one of the broader contexts related to it (see page 16, Figure 1-4) and approach it through the perspective of one of those contexts. Both approaches highlight a key element of an effective thesis: it has enough universal appeal to make it worthy of a reader's consideration.

For example, if your claim was that warning labels are necessary, try to contextualize that within a concept or context with universal appeal. Perhaps you attach it to the idea of protection—how the government should protect consumers, how companies should protect customers, how adults should protect children. Or perhaps you contextualize it within the idea of personal liberty—the warning labels do not prevent people from purchasing the product, a liberty many want to protect, but they do make sure those decisions are at least informed decisions. Try to express your connection to an abstract idea in a statement to keep in mind as you draft.

The **second bullet** is worded the same way it was in Unit 1, but by now you have more experience with the types and purposes of evidence, so you would be expected to strategically choose evidence that enhances your credibility and shows your understanding of rhetorical choices. For example, keeping your audience in mind, you might decide that today's readers would be more interested in vaping than in cigarette smoking and shift the focus of your evidence to that subject. Use sufficient evidence to flesh out your argument and avoid repetition.

As you select evidence and develop commentary that explains how that evidence supports your line of reasoning according to the directions of the **third bullet**, consider how you will appeal to your audience to change their minds or motivate them to take action. For example, by adding an anecdote about how your grandfather's smoking led to his death, you would likely grab the reader emotionally. Talking about your own experience with smoking or vaping may help build trust with the audience. Some statistics or statements from experts about the danger of cigarettes or vaping may help the audience to see the logic of your example. The organizer on the next page will help you keep track of your thoughts and put them in good order.

When you finish your draft, check it over to make sure you meet the requirements of each bullet point in the prompt. The **final bullet** reminds you to use appropriate grammar and punctuation, so double check for possible grammatical and punctuation errors.

In the organizer on the next page, the claim, abstract idea statement, thesis, and first paragraph are fleshed out. How might you complete the second paragraph? Create a draft and save it for future use.

Unit 2: Argument Essay (Part 2) Drafting Organizer
Claim: Warning labels are absolutely necessary. **Abstract Idea**: Protection **Abstract Idea Statement**: Government and society should protect the most vulnerable people.
Thesis: Warning labels prove absolutely necessary to protect people from being exposed to things that might harm them without their knowing—from scary movies for children to dangerous and addicting products for adults. These potential harms demonstrate the need for government and society to protect the most vulnerable.
Evidence 1 Movie ratings
Explain how that evidence supports the reasoning that justifies that claim *and appeals to the audience.* Children who are exposed to certain images and events in movies may have nightmares. Movie ratings act as a kind of warning label for parents about what they should be careful allowing their children to watch. Because movies are advertised as appealing and interesting to a wide range of people, children may easily become ensnared in the excitement about a movie they really should not see. Though they are interested, the movie may have an inappropriate level of violence, sexuality, and/or language. When I was about nine years old, I slept over at my friend's house. We sneaked into his older brother's room to find a DVD to watch and ended up choosing the movie *Saw*. We felt like we were grown-ups watching the R-rated movie in my friend's basement, hidden from his parents. That night I didn't sleep at all. When I went home, I started having a lot of bad dreams about things that happened in it. Eventually, I admitted to my mom one night, in tears, that I had seen it, and we talked about what I had seen. Film ratings allow parents and others to make informed decisions about what they allow their children to see. It may not mean stopping the children from seeing a questionable movie altogether, but it may mean that the parents can have conversations with their children about those scenes. Without those rating labels, parents would have to rely on their observations about the movie. With so much media in the world, parents would have the nearly impossible task of keeping up with all of the available movies. The government and society in general use these ratings as just one more way to protect the most vulnerable.
Evidence 2 Cigarette/Vaping Warning Labels
Explain how that evidence supports the reasoning that justifies that claim *and appeals to the audience*.
2-Paragraph Draft

Apply

Follow the same process as above to respond to the argument prompt on page 110. For current free-response question samples, check the College Board's website.

Section II: Free Response

The first free-response question on the AP® exam is a synthesis task. For synthesis practice, see pages 364–373, 448–455 and 540–544. You will be provided synthesis prompts in Units 6–9.

Rhetorical Analysis: "Replay in Sports Isn't the Problem—Judgment Is"

Christopher L. Gaspar is a graduate of Boston University and was sportswriter for *The Boston Globe* before moving to television reporting in 2020. In 2019 he wrote an article for *The Boston Globe* about the use of instant replays in sports. In the article he explores where to lay the blame when instant replays do not serve their intended purpose.

Read the passage on pages 96–98 carefully. Write a paragraph that analyzes the rhetorical choices Gaspar makes to engage his audience and convey his message about the misuses of instant replays.

In your response you should do the following:

- Respond to the prompt with a claim that analyzes the writer's rhetorical choices.
- Select and use evidence to support your line of reasoning.
- Briefly explain how the evidence supports your line of reasoning.
- Use appropriate grammar and punctuation in communicating your argument.

Argument: Time on Learning

After observing flat or sinking educational trends, some educators have tried to increase "time on learning" by extending school days or the school year. Some argue, though, that trends would improve if students had more active and less structured time, not more "time on learning."

Consider these viewpoints. Write an essay that argues your position on the need for more time on learning.

In your response you should do the following:

- Respond to the prompt with a thesis that presents a defensible position.
- Provide evidence to support your line of reasoning.
- Explain how the evidence supports your line of reasoning.
- Use appropriate grammar and punctuation in communicating your argument.

UNIT 3

Connecting an Argument

Part 1: Connecting and Explaining Claims and Evidence
Part 2: Line of Reasoning
Part 3: Introduction to Methods of Development

ENDURING UNDERSTANDINGS AND SKILLS: Unit Three

Part 1

Understand

Writers make claims about subjects, rely on evidence that supports the reasoning that justifies the claim, and often acknowledge or respond to other, possibly opposing arguments. (CLE-1)

Demonstrate

Identify and explain claims and evidence within an argument. (Reading 3.A)

Develop a paragraph that includes a claim and evidence supporting the claim. (Writing 4.A)

Part 2

Understand

Writers guide understanding of a text's lines of reasoning and claims through that text's organization and integration of evidence. (REO-1)

Demonstrate

Describe the line of reasoning and explain whether it supports an argument's overarching thesis. (Reading 5.A)

Develop a line of reasoning and commentary that explains it throughout an argument. (Writing 6.A)

Part 3

Understand

Writers guide understanding of a text's lines of reasoning and claims through that text's organization and integration of evidence. (REO-1)

Demonstrate

Recognize and explain the use of methods of development to accomplish a purpose. (Reading 5.C)

Use appropriate methods of development to advance an argument. (Writing 6.C)

Source: *AP® English Language and Composition Course and Exam Description*

Unit 3 Overview

Arguments in the context of an "unending conversation," which stretches back to the earliest human thinkers, may seem distant and academic. But arguments are all around you, all the time. They do not appear only in essays or books on the great questions of humanity, but also in everyday life on more mundane but still interesting topics. Movie reviews are one example of these everyday arguments. Their purpose is to develop an argument on the value of a movie by stating a claim and backing it up with evidence. Roger Ebert (1942–2013) was a movie reviewer for the *Chicago Sun-Times* and one of the most famous movie critics in the United States. Read the opening to his review of the 1997 movie *Titanic.*

> Like a great iron Sphinx on the ocean floor, the Titanic faces still toward the West, interrupted forever on its only voyage. We see it in the opening shots of "Titanic," encrusted with the silt of 85 years; a remote-controlled TV camera snakes its way inside, down corridors and through doorways, showing us staterooms built for millionaires and inherited by crustaceans.
>
> These shots strike precisely the right note; the ship calls from its grave for its story to be told, and if the story is made of showbiz and hype, smoke and mirrors—well, so was the Titanic. She was "the largest moving work of man in all history," a character boasts, neatly dismissing the Pyramids and the Great Wall. There is a shot of her, early in the film, sweeping majestically beneath the camera from bow to stern, nearly 900 feet long and "unsinkable," it was claimed, until an iceberg made an irrefutable reply.
>
> <u>James Cameron's 194-minute, $200 million film of the tragic voyage is in the tradition of the great Hollywood epics. It is flawlessly crafted, intelligently constructed, strongly acted and spellbinding.</u> If its story stays well within the traditional formulas for such pictures, well, you don't choose the most expensive film ever made as your opportunity to reinvent the wheel.

Ebert gave the movie *Titanic* a four-star rating—his highest—so readers knew he had a strongly favorable view of the movie. If they were interested only in whether the movie was worth seeing, the rating would probably be enough. But moviegoers and those who love culture and the arts are interested in how a movie critic arrives at a rating—they are interested in the reasoning behind the argument. Ebert provides that reasoning in his review. He uses evidence from the movie to formulate a specific position that he expresses in his thesis (underlined in the excerpt above). In the rest of his review, Ebert explains each claim within his thesis (it is in the tradition of Hollywood epics; it is flawlessly crafted; it is intelligently structured; it is strongly acted; and it is spellbinding). He previews his line of reasoning in his thesis and spends the rest of the essay developing his argument by providing evidence to support it and commentary to explain how the evidence supports his reasoning and justifies his claims.

Some of the commentary comes from evidence Ebert had been collecting for decades before writing the *Titanic* review. Over many years, Ebert had researched and studied and analyzed many movies from many time periods. In those years of thinking and research and writing, Ebert was forming viewpoints about what makes a movie good. Each new review he wrote contributed to his depth of understanding of movies and also helped shape his response to new movies. Writers often use the evidence in their commentary they have collected from their experience to demonstrate connections between their thesis and claims.

In this unit you will continue to identify overarching patterns in evidence that will help you craft a good thesis statement. You will also see how to use commentary to explain and logically connect the evidence to your claim. Finally, you will recognize, explain, and use traditional methods of developing an argument to help readers trace your reasoning.

Close Reading: Professional Text
"What We Eat" from the Introduction to Fast Food Nation: The Dark Side of the All-American Meal *by Eric Schlosser*

The following excerpt is from the introduction to Eric Schlosser's book, *Fast Food Nation: The Dark Side of the All-American Meal* (2001). Schlosser, an investigative journalist, examines the local and global influence of the fast food industry in the United States. The anchor icon next to the heading reminds you that this is the reading you will return to throughout this unit. For now, read it to understand the main or central ideas Schlosser expresses as he contributes to the conversation about what people eat.

What We Eat

1 Over the last three decades, fast food has infiltrated every nook and cranny of American society. An industry that began with a handful of modest hot dog and hamburger stands in southern California has spread to every corner of the nation, selling a broad range of foods wherever paying customers may be found. Fast food is now served at restaurants and drive-throughs, at stadiums, airports, zoos, high schools, elementary schools, and universities, on cruise ships, trains, and airplanes, at K-Marts, Wal-Marts, gas stations, and even at hospital cafeterias. In 1970, Americans spent about $6 billion on fast food; in 2001, they spent more than $110 billion. Americans now spend more money on fast food than on higher education, personal computers, computer software, or new cars. They spend more on fast food than on movies, books, magazines, newspapers, videos, and recorded music—combined.

2 Pull open the glass door, feel the rush of cool air, walk in, get in line, study the backlit color photographs above the counter, place your order, hand over a few dollars, watch teenagers in uniforms pushing various buttons, and moments later take hold of a plastic tray full of food wrapped in colored paper and cardboard. The whole experience of buying fast food has become so routine, so thoroughly unexceptional and mundane, that

it is now taken for granted, like brushing your teeth or stopping for a red light. It has become a social custom as American as a small, rectangular, hand-held, frozen, and reheated apple pie.

3 This is a book about fast food, the values it embodies, and the world it has made. Fast food has proven to be a revolutionary force in American life; I am interested in it both as a commodity and as a metaphor. What people eat (or don't eat) has always been determined by a complex interplay of social, economic, and technological forces. The early Roman Republic was fed by its citizen-farmers; the Roman Empire, by its slaves. A nation's diet can be more revealing than its art or literature. On any given day in the United States about one-quarter of the adult population visits a fast food restaurant. During a relatively brief period of time, the fast food industry has helped to transform not only the American diet, but also our landscape, economy, workforce, and popular culture. Fast food and its consequences have become inescapable, regardless of whether you eat it twice a day, try to avoid it, or have never taken a single bite.

4 The extraordinary growth of the fast food industry has been driven by fundamental changes in American society. Adjusted for inflation, the hourly wage of the average U.S. worker peaked in 1973 and then steadily declined for the next twenty-five years. During that period, women entered the workforce in record numbers, often motivated less by a feminist perspective than by a need to pay the bills. In 1975, about one-third of American mothers with young children worked outside the home; today almost two-thirds of such mothers are employed. As the sociologists Cameron Lynne Macdonald and Carmen Sirianni have noted, the entry of so many women into the workforce has greatly increased demand for the types of services that housewives traditionally perform: cooking, cleaning, and child care. A generation ago, three-quarters of the money used to buy food in the United States was spent to prepare meals at home. Today about half of the money used to buy food is spent at restaurants—mainly at fast food restaurants.

5 The McDonald's Corporation has become a powerful symbol of America's service economy, which is now responsible for 90 percent of the country's new jobs. In 1968, McDonald's operated about one thousand restaurants. Today it has about thirty thousand restaurants worldwide and opens almost two thousand new ones each year. An estimated one out of every eight workers in the United States has at some point been employed by McDonald's. The company annually hires about one million people, more than any other American organization, public or private. McDonald's is the nation's largest purchaser of beef, pork, and potatoes—and the second largest purchaser of chicken. The McDonald's Corporation is the largest owner of retail property in the world. Indeed, the company earns the majority of its profits not from selling food but from collecting rent. McDonald's spends more money on advertising and marketing than any other brand. As a result it has replaced Coca-Cola as the world's most famous brand. McDonald's operates more playgrounds than any other private entity in the United States. It is one of the nation's largest

distributors of toys. A survey of American schoolchildren found that 96 percent could identify Ronald McDonald. The only fictional character with a higher degree of recognition was Santa Claus. The impact of McDonald's on the way we live today is hard to overstate. The Golden Arches are now more widely recognized than the Christian cross.

6 In the early 1970s, the farm activist Jim Hightower warned of "the McDonaldization of America." He viewed the emerging fast food industry as a threat to independent businesses, as a step toward a food economy dominated by giant corporations, and as a homogenizing influence on American life. In *Eat Your Heart Out* (1975), he argued that "bigger is *not* better." Much of what Hightower feared has come to pass. The centralized purchasing decisions of the large restaurant chains and their demand for standardized products have given a handful of corporations an unprecedented degree of power over the nation's food supply. Moreover, the tremendous success of the fast food industry has encouraged other industries to adopt similar business methods. The basic thinking behind fast food has become the operating system of today's retail economy, wiping out small businesses, obliterating regional differences, and spreading identical stores throughout the country like a self-replicating code.

7 America's main streets and malls now boast the same Pizza Huts and Taco Bells, Gaps and Banana Republics, Starbucks and Jiffy-Lubes, Foot Lockers, Snip N' Clips, Sunglass Huts, and Hobbytown USAs. Almost every facet of American life has now been franchised or chained. From the maternity ward at a Columbia/HCA hospital to an embalming room owned by Service Corporation International—"the world's largest provider of death care services," based in Houston, Texas, which since 1968 has grown to include 3,823 funeral homes, 523 cemeteries, and 198 crematoriums, and which today handles the final remains of one out of every nine Americans—a person can now go from the cradle to the grave without spending a nickel at an independently owned business.

8 The key to a successful franchise, according to many texts on the subject, can be expressed in one word: "uniformity." Franchises and chain stores strive to offer exactly the same product or service at numerous locations. Customers are drawn to familiar brands by an instinct to avoid the unknown. A brand offers a feeling of reassurance when its products are always and everywhere the same. "We have found out . . . that we cannot trust some people who are nonconformists," declared Ray Kroc, one of the founders of McDonald's, angered by some of his franchisees. "We will make conformists out of them in a hurry. . . . The organization cannot trust the individual; the individual must trust the organization."

9 One of the ironies of America's fast food industry is that a business so dedicated to conformity was founded by iconoclasts[1] and self-made men, by entrepreneurs willing to defy conventional opinion. Few of the people who built fast food empires ever attended college, let alone business

1 **iconoclasts:** people who attack established institutions

school. They worked hard, took risks, and followed their own paths. In many respects, the fast food industry embodies the best and the worst of American capitalism at the start of the twenty-first century—its constant stream of new products and innovations, its widening gulf between rich and poor. The industrialization of the restaurant kitchen has enabled the fast food chains to rely upon a low-paid and unskilled workforce. While a handful of workers manage to rise up the corporate ladder, the vast majority lack full-time employment, receive no benefits, learn few skills, exercise little control over their workplace, quit after a few months, and float from job to job. The restaurant industry is now America's largest private employer, and it pays some of the lowest wages. During the economic boom of the 1990s, when many American workers enjoyed their first pay raises in a generation, the real value of wages in the restaurant industry continued to fall. The roughly 3.5 million fast food workers are by far the largest group of minimum wage earners in the United States. The only Americans who consistently earn a lower hourly wage are migrant farm workers.

Source: Wikimedia Commons

The oldest McDonald's restaurant in existence, in Downey, California, opened in 1953. ***What do details in this photo suggest about how fast food has changed?***

10 A hamburger and french fries became the quintessential American meal in the 1950s, thanks to the promotional efforts of the fast food chains. The typical American now consumes approximately three hamburgers and four orders of french fries every week. But the steady barrage of fast food ads, full of thick juicy burgers and long golden fries, rarely mentions where these foods come from nowadays or what ingredients they contain. The birth of the fast food industry coincided with Eisenhower-era glorifications

of technology, with optimistic slogans like "Better Living through Chemistry" and "Our Friend the Atom." The sort of technological wizardry that Walt Disney promoted on television and at Disneyland eventually reached its fulfillment in the kitchens of fast food restaurants. Indeed, the corporate culture of McDonald's seems inextricably linked to that of the Disney empire, sharing a reverence for sleek machinery, electronics, and automation. The leading fast food chains still embrace a boundless faith in science—and as a result have changed not just what Americans eat, but also how their food is made.

11 The current methods for preparing fast food are less likely to be found in cookbooks than in trade journals such as *Food Technologist* and *Food Engineering*. Aside from the salad greens and tomatoes, most fast food is delivered to the restaurant already frozen, canned, dehydrated, or freeze-dried. A fast food kitchen is merely the final stage in a vast and highly complex system of mass production. Foods that may look familiar have in fact been completely reformulated. What we eat has changed more in the last forty years than in the previous forty thousand. . . . [T]oday's fast food conceals remarkable technological advances behind an ordinary-looking façade. Much of the taste and aroma of American fast food, for example, is now manufactured at a series of large chemical plants off the New Jersey Turnpike.

12 In the fast food restaurants of Colorado Springs, behind the counters, amid the plastic seats, in the changing landscape outside the window, you can see all the virtues and destructiveness of our fast food nation. I chose Colorado Springs as a focal point for this book because the changes that have recently swept through the city are emblematic of those that fast food—and the fast food mentality—have encouraged throughout the United States. Countless other suburban communities, in every part of the country, could have been used to illustrate the same points. The extraordinary growth of Colorado Springs neatly parallels that of the fast food industry: during the last few decades, the city's population has more than doubled. Subdivisions, shopping malls, and chain restaurants are appearing in the foothills of Cheyenne Mountain and the plains rolling to the east. The Rocky Mountain region as a whole has the fastest-growing economy in the United States, mixing high-tech and service industries in a way that may define America's workforce for years to come. And new restaurants are opening there at a faster pace than anywhere else in the nation.

13 Fast food is now so commonplace that it has acquired an air of inevitability, as though it were somehow unavoidable, a fact of modern life. And yet the dominance of the fast food giants was no more preordained than the march of colonial split-levels, golf courses, and man-made lakes across the deserts of the American West. The political philosophy that now prevails in so much of the West—with its demand for lower taxes, smaller government, an unbridled free market—stands in total contradiction to the region's true economic underpinnings. No other region of the United States has been so dependent on government subsidies for so long, from

the nineteenth-century construction of its railroads to the twentieth-century financing of its military bases and dams. One historian has described the federal government's 1950s highway-building binge as a case study in "interstate socialism"—a phrase that aptly describes how the West was really won. The fast food industry took root alongside that interstate highway system, as a new form of restaurant sprang up beside the new off-ramps. Moreover, the extraordinary growth of this industry over the past quarter-century did not occur in a political vacuum. It took place during a period when the inflation-adjusted value of the minimum wage declined by about 40 percent, when sophisticated mass marketing techniques were for the first time directed at small children, and when federal agencies created to protect workers and consumers too often behaved like branch offices of the companies that were supposed to be regulated. Ever since the administration of President Richard Nixon, the fast food industry has worked closely with its allies in Congress and the White House to oppose new worker safety, food safety, and minimum wage laws. While publicly espousing support for the free market, the fast food chains have quietly pursued and greatly benefited from a wide variety of government subsidies. Far from being inevitable, America's fast food industry in its present form is the logical outcome of certain political and economic choices.

14 In the potato fields and processing plants of Idaho, in the ranch-lands east of Colorado Springs, in the feedlots and slaughterhouses of the High Plains, you can see the effects of fast food on the nation's rural life, its environment, its workers, and its health. The fast food chains now stand atop a huge food-industrial complex that has gained control of American agriculture. During the 1980s, large multinationals—such as Cargill, ConAgra, and IBP—were allowed to dominate one commodity market after another. Farmers and cattle ranchers are losing their independence, essentially becoming hired hands for the agribusiness giants or being forced off the land. Family farms are now being replaced by gigantic corporate farms with absentee owners. Rural communities are losing their middle class and becoming socially stratified, divided between a small, wealthy elite and large numbers of the working poor. Small towns that seemingly belong in a Norman Rockwell painting are being turned into rural ghettos. The hardy, independent farmers whom Thomas Jefferson considered the bedrock of American democracy are a truly vanishing breed. The United States now has more prison inmates than full-time farmers.

15 The fast food chains' vast purchasing power and their demand for a uniform product have encouraged fundamental changes in how cattle are raised, slaughtered, and processed into ground beef. These changes have made meatpacking—once a highly skilled, highly paid occupation—into the most dangerous job in the United States, performed by armies of poor, transient immigrants whose injuries often go unrecorded and uncompensated. And the same meat industry practices that endanger these workers have facilitated the introduction of deadly pathogens, such as *E. coli* 0157:H7, into America's hamburger meat, a food aggressively

marketed to children. Again and again, efforts to prevent the sale of tainted ground beef have been thwarted by meat industry lobbyists and their allies in Congress. The federal government has the legal authority to recall a defective toaster oven or stuffed animal—but still lacks the power to recall tons of contaminated, potentially lethal meat.

16 I do not mean to suggest that fast food is solely responsible for every social problem now haunting the United States. In some cases (such as the malling and sprawling of the West) the fast food industry has been a catalyst and a symptom of larger economic trends. In other cases (such as the rise of franchising and the spread of obesity) fast food has played a more central role. By tracing the diverse influences of fast food I hope to shed light not only on the workings of an important industry, but also on a distinctively American way of viewing the world.

17 Elitists have always looked down at fast food, criticizing how it tastes and regarding it as another tacky manifestation of American popular culture. The aesthetics of fast food are of much less concern to me than its impact upon the lives of ordinary Americans, both as workers and consumers. Most of all, I am concerned about its impact on the nation's children. Fast food is heavily marketed to children and prepared by people who are barely older than children. This is an industry that both feeds and feeds off the young. During the two years spent researching this book, I ate an enormous amount of fast food. Most of it tasted pretty good. That is one of the main reasons people buy fast food; it has been carefully designed to taste good. It's also inexpensive and convenient. But the value meals, two-for-one deals, and free refills of soda give a distorted sense of how much fast food actually costs. The real price never appears on the menu.

18 The sociologist George Ritzer has attacked the fast food industry for celebrating a narrow measure of efficiency over every other human value, calling the triumph of McDonald's "the irrationality of rationality." Others consider the fast food industry proof of the nation's great economic vitality, a beloved American institution that appeals overseas to millions who admire our way of life. Indeed, the values, the culture, and the industrial arrangements of our fast food nation are now being exported to the rest of the world. Fast food has joined Hollywood movies, blue jeans, and pop music as one of America's most prominent cultural exports. Unlike other commodities, however, fast food isn't viewed, read, played, or worn. It enters the body and becomes part of the consumer. No other industry offers, both literally and figuratively, so much insight into the nature of mass consumption.

19 Hundreds of millions of people buy fast food every day without giving it much thought, unaware of the subtle and not so subtle ramifications of their purchases. They rarely consider where this food came from, how it was made, what it is doing to the community around them. They just grab their tray off the counter, find a table, take a seat, unwrap the paper, and dig in. The whole experience is transitory and soon forgotten. I've written this book out of a belief that people should know what lies behind the

shiny, happy surface of every fast food transaction. They should know what really lurks between those sesame-seed buns. As the old saying goes: You are what you eat.

Composing on Your Own

Respond to Schlosser's ideas by writing your own thoughts on fast food in American life, or choose a related topic of special interest to you. Write freely, asking yourself questions to generate ideas and thoughts. You will develop these initial ideas throughout this unit, so save your work.

Evaluating Writing: Student Draft
Fast Food

Following is the anchor text you will use in this unit to practice evaluating writing. It was written as an entry on a blog for new drivers called "On the Road." This draft still needs work. As you read it, think about what it contributes to the conversation on fast food, and compare it to the writing you did after you read the excerpt from Schlosser's introduction to *Fast Food Nation*. Later you will have an opportunity to suggest ways the writing might be improved.

(1) My friends have all started to get their driver's licenses and we often find ourselves asking, "What should we do?" or "Where should we go?" (2) Driving down the main road of our town, the flashing lights of the different fast food chains taunt us and, most often, we end up sitting in the back corner of a McDonald's or Panera. (3) While it is understood that the consumption of fast food is a leading cause of our nation's deteriorating health, many exonerate fast food companies' fault and claim that it is the choice of the consumer to eat unhealthy fast foods. (4) In fact, Americans are making this choice more frequently. (5) The increased spending on fast food proves that our addiction to fast food is a cultural choice: one that has been dictated by a desire for efficiency. (6) Healthier options have shown up in the industry to help consumers make healthier choices. (7) McDonald's menu has not changed minus the addition of a few salads, but why? (8) McDonald's has tried to add healthier options, such as McLean Deluxe that claimed to be 91% fat-free. (9) Once consumers discovered that the chain had added carrageenan, or seaweed extract, to the patty to replace the lost fat, all sales stopped and the item was removed from the menu. (10) Although a new chain, Panera's marketing focuses on fresh and healthy options, promising to use healthy ingredients and no hormones. (11) It is evident that we have healthier fast-food options to still fuel our busy lifestyles, but it is up to each of us to assume responsibility for healthy (or unhealthy) choices.

What Do You Know?

This unit will explore how evidence supports the reasoning in an argument and how that reasoning then justifies the claim. It will also explore methods of developing an argument. Before digging in, assess what you already know about these concepts by answering questions about the text by Eric Schlosser and the student draft on fast food. Learning scientists have shown that answering questions on subjects before formally studying them is a good way to learn.

CLOSE READING: PROFESSIONAL TEXT

1. Identify at least one possible thesis statement in Schlosser's introduction. (Hint: Writers often, though not always, place their thesis statement early in their essay.)

2. In paragraph 4, what method or organization does Schlosser use to develop the topic sentence of that paragraph (the first sentence)?

3. Where did Schlosser include words and ideas from another source? What effect did that reference to a source have on your understanding of the argument?

EVALUATING WRITING: STUDENT DRAFT

1. What evidence or explanations does the writer use to back up his or her claim? Where would you revise to add more evidence or explanations?

2. Where are the lapses in the writer's line of reasoning? In other words, where do you have to think on your own to see how the evidence connects to the claim?

Top 10 Fast Food Locations by Number of Locations, 2019

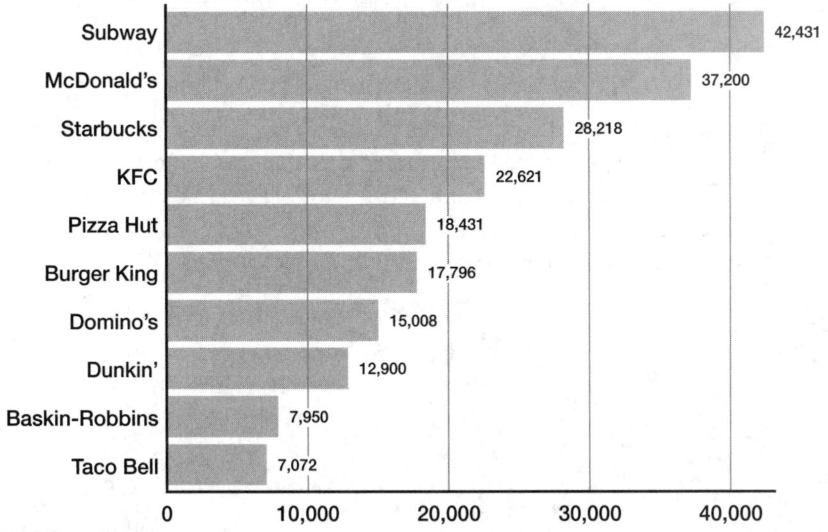

Source: Deseret News

To understand bar graphs such as the one above, you must consider the information on both the x-axis (horizontal or side-to-side) and y-axis (vertical or up-and-down).

Based on this chart, what claim might you be able to make about American tastes for fast food? How would you use information from this chart to support that claim?

Part 1

Connecting and Explaining Claims and Evidence

Enduring Understanding and Skills

Part 1

Understand

Writers make claims about subjects, rely on evidence that supports the reasoning that justifies the claim, and often acknowledge or respond to other, possibly opposing, arguments. (CLE-1)

Demonstrate

Identify and explain claims and evidence within an argument. (Reading 3.A)

Develop a paragraph that includes a claim and evidence supporting the claim. (Writing 4.A)

Source: *AP® English Language and Composition Course and Exam Description*

Essential Questions: As a reader, how do you understand the thinking behind writers' arguments—the relationships between their evidence and their claim? As a writer, how can you integrate source material to strengthen your argument?

An argument has several key elements, including a claim and evidence. Neither element, when presented to readers as an independent and unconnected statement, effectively communicates a writer's message. Like the pieces of a quilt, the pieces of an argument need to be stitched together in a skillful way that creates meaning, reinforces connections, and closes gaps.

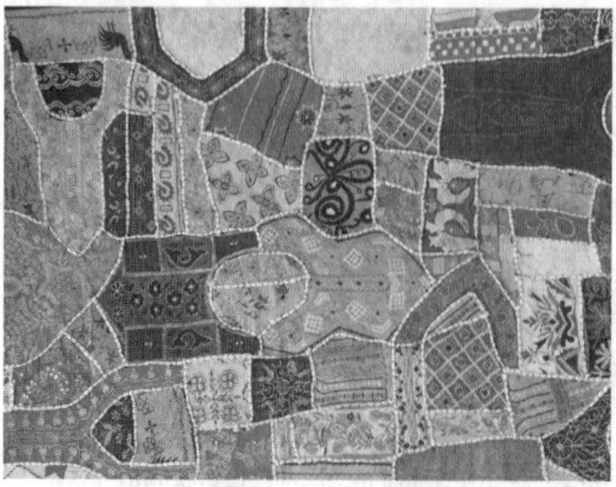

Source: Getty Images

The pieces of an argument are held together through a writer's skillful connections of ideas. The pieces of this quilt from Rajasthan, India, like many interesting arguments, do not necessarily follow a predictable pattern, but they all hold together well to form a satisfying whole.

Commentary is the thread that connects the elements of an argument. A writer's commentary explains how the evidence "proves" the claim so that readers see and understand the logic of the writer's reasoning. Writers also use commentary to stitch source material—the work of other writers—into their arguments, giving their own arguments more weight and validity. In Part I, you will continue to practice identifying claims and evidence. You will also learn how a writer uses commentary to explain relationships and integrate and acknowledge source material.

KEY TERMS

attribution	commentary	source material
citation	reference	synthesis

1.1 Using Commentary Effectively | CLE-1.K

Effective arguments often rely on evidence. However, the relationship between the evidence and the claims of the argument is often not clear by itself. Simply making a claim and then listing some evidence to support it is not enough. The way a writer thinks about the evidence supporting the claim—the reasoning—must be evident, too. Commentary provides the reasoning and logically connects evidence to the claim it justifies, creating a convincing argument. It shows what was in the writer's mind when developing the argument.

Connecting the Pieces

Readers come to argumentative writing as interested bystanders at best and as skeptic nay-sayers at worst. Additionally, readers may not have spent hours of research and study on the topic at hand. Connections that may seem obvious to a writer, who may have lived and breathed a subject for weeks, may not seem obvious or valid to a reader. The writer's job, then, is to help the reader see how the argument makes sense by connecting the evidence to the claim in a convincing way. **Commentary**—explanations that guide the reader to link claims, evidence, and reasoning and that acknowledge and integrate sources—establishes these connections. (You will read more about reasoning in Part 2.)

Notice how Schlosser uses commentary to explain his thinking and connect evidence to a claim about fast food and the West in the paragraph from *Fast Food Nation* on the next page.

Text	Commentary
Fast food is now so commonplace that it has acquired an air of inevitability, as though it were somehow unavoidable, a fact of modern life. And yet the dominance of the fast food giants was no more preordained than the march of colonial split-levels, golf courses, and man-made lakes across the deserts of the American West. The political philosophy that now prevails in so much of the West—with its demand for lower taxes, smaller government, an unbridled free market—stands in total contradiction to the region's true economic underpinnings. **(1)** No other region of the United States has been so dependent on government subsidies for so long, from the nineteenth-century construction of its railroads to the twentieth-century financing of its military bases and dams. One historian has described the federal government's 1950s highway-building binge as a case study in "interstate socialism"—a phrase that aptly describes how the West was really won. The fast food industry took root alongside that interstate highway system, as a new form of restaurant sprang up beside the new off-ramps. **(2)** Moreover, the extraordinary growth of this industry over the past quarter-century did not occur in a political vacuum. It took place during a period when the inflation-adjusted value of the minimum wage declined by about 40 percent, when sophisticated mass marketing techniques were for the first time directed at small children, and when federal agencies created to protect workers and consumers too often behaved like branch offices of the companies that were supposed to be regulated. **(3)** Ever since the administration of President Richard Nixon, the fast food industry has worked closely with its allies in Congress and the White House to oppose new worker safety, food safety, and minimum wage laws. While publicly espousing support for the free market, the fast food chains have quietly pursued and greatly benefited from a wide variety of government subsidies. **(4)** Far from being inevitable, America's fast food industry in its present form is the logical outcome of certain political and economic choices—and as a result have changed not just what Americans eat, but also how their food is made	**Evidence** **(1)** The region has depended on government subsidies (examples: railroad construction, military bases and dams, and highway building). **Commentary** **(2)** Explanation of the context in which these developments took place **Evidence** **(3)** Since Nixon, the fast food industry has worked closely with political allies (examples: to oppose worker safety, food safety, and minimum wage laws). **Claim** **(4)** The fast food industry is the logical outcome of certain choices.

Table 3-1

Schlosser's evidence alone—that the West accepted subsidies and other government support and that the food industry had strong political connections to influence policy—may not have been sufficient to explain the dominance of fast food giants if those were the only forces, if they had unfolded "in a political vacuum." To link his evidence to his claim, he provides commentary describing the social and economic context in which these forces operated. He cites the decline in real minimum wage, mass marketing to small children, and federal agencies representing the companies rather than the consumers.

His commentary shows his reasoning and the logical relationship between his evidence and his claim.

When analyzing arguments, ask yourself these questions:

- What is the claim?
- What is the writer's reasoning? That is, what line of thinking does the writer follow to justify the claim?
- What evidence supports that reasoning?
- How does commentary explain the evidence and justify the claim?

The answers to those questions about the Schlosser passage on the previous page are:

- The *claim* is that America's fast food industry is the logical outcome of certain political and economic choices.
- Schlosser suggests his *reasoning* in his wording of the claim. By referring to a "logical outcome," he shows that his reasoning will be based on cause and effect. If the fast food industry is indeed the logical outcome of political and economic choices, then tracing backward will show the causes.
- Schlosser provides *evidence* of government subsidies and political connections that would affect the "logical outcome."
- Further, he provides *commentary* about the social and economic context and its effect on the cause-and-effect pattern.

Remember: Effective use of evidence uses commentary to establish a logical relationship between the evidence and the claim it supports. (CLE-1.K)

1.1 Checkpoint

Close Reading: Professional Text

Reread the excerpt below from *Fast Food Nation* and pay special attention to the writer's use of commentary. Then complete the open response activity and answer the multiple-choice questions.

> The current methods for preparing fast food are less likely to be found in cookbooks than in trade journals such as *Food Technologist* and *Food Engineering*. <u>Aside from the salad greens and tomatoes, most fast food is delivered to the restaurant already frozen, canned, dehydrated, or freeze-dried</u>. A fast food kitchen is merely the final stage in a vast and highly complex system of mass production. Foods that may look familiar have in fact been completely reformulated. <u>What we eat has changed more in the</u>

last forty years than in the previous forty thousand. . . . **[T]oday fast food conceals remarkable technological advances behind an ordinary-looking façade.** Much of the taste and aroma of American fast food, for example, is now manufactured at a series of large chemical plants off the New Jersey Turnpike.

1. The claim in this paragraph is in bold type. The evidence is underlined. Explain how the other sentences in the paragraph, the writer's commentary, show the relationship between the claim and evidence.

2. In context, which of the following evidence from the text best supports the claim that the "fast food industry has helped to transform not only the American diet, but also our . . .economy . . ."?
   (A) "The whole experience of buying fast food has become so routine . . . that it is now taken for granted, like brushing your teeth or stopping for a red light." (paragraph 2, sentence 2)
   (B) "The basic thinking behind fast food has become the operating system of today's retail economy, wiping out small business, obliterating regional differences, and spreading identical stores throughout the country like a self-replicating code." (paragraph 6, sentence 7)
   (C) "America's main streets and malls now boast the same Pizza Huts and Taco Bells, Gaps and Banana Republics, Starbucks and Jiffy-Lubes, Foot Lockers, Snip N' Clips, Sunglass Huts, and Hobbytown USAs." (paragraph 7, sentence 1)
   (D) "The key to a successful franchise . . . can be expressed in one word: 'uniformity.' " (paragraph 8, sentence 1)
   (E) "In the fast food restaurants of Colorado Springs, behind the counters, amid the plastic seats, in the changing landscape outside the window, you can see all the virtues and destructiveness of our fast food nation." (paragraph 12, sentence 1)

3. In paragraph 13, much of Schlosser's evidence is used to
   (A) accuse the fast food industry of immoral business practices
   (B) refute the belief that the fast food industry's growth was unavoidable
   (C) illustrate declining political and economic influence of the American West
   (D) defend the position that government interference in business is always harmful
   (E) create a tone of despair regarding the decline of the food service industry

4. What evidence does Schlosser provide for his claim that McDonald's has come to symbolize America's service economy?
   (A) He tells us that, after 1973, the hourly wage of the average U.S. worker steadily declined for 25 years.
   (B) He tells us that half the money used to buy food is spent at restaurants.
   (C) He tells us that an estimated one out of eight U.S. workers has at some point been employed by McDonald's.
   (D) He tells us that McDonald's is the largest owner of retail property in the world.
   (E) He tells us that only Santa Claus is more recognizable by American schoolchildren than Ronald McDonald.

Evaluating Writing: Student Draft

Reread the student draft on page 120. Complete the open response activity and answer the multiple-choice question.

1. On separate paper, complete the third column of the chart by writing commentary that connects the claim to any of the pieces of evidence.

Claim	Evidence	Commentary
Although some of the blame in the rise in popularity of fast food lies with the companies, it is the choice of the consumer that is ultimately driving the success of the industry.	Healthier options have shown up in the industry to help consumers make healthier choices. McDonald's menu has not changed minus the addition of a few salads. McDonald's has tried to add healthier options.	

2. The writer wants to add specific evidence to support the claim that fast food consumers have choices. Which detail would best support this claim if included after sentence 6?
   (A) Subway and Panera have changed their marketing and their menus to include healthier fast food options.
   (B) My friends and I usually end up at the McDonald's because that is where everyone is used to going.
   (C) Usually, the healthier options are more expensive, which makes it harder to make the right choice.
   (D) Panera's advertisements focus on the ripest and best produce for their customers.
   (E) Burger King, for example, has introduced "Satisfries," a healthier version of French fries.

Composing on Your Own

The anchor text focuses on just one issue in the broader conversation of ethical eating practices. In addition to Schlosser's concern over how fast food has changed society, other concerns relating to food ethics include environmental impact, exploitive labor practices, inhumane treatment of food animals, government subsidies and food policy, food deserts, fair trade, and many more. Choose one of these topics or another that interests you and begin to research it. Keep notes about where you find your information—the titles of books or articles, websites, or other sources—as well as the authors and their credentials. Develop and explain an arguable position or claim about the subject you choose.

As you have read, the elements of the rhetorical situation greatly influence the choices a writer makes. Take time now to choose or create a rhetorical situation. Choose or adapt any of the following contexts, audiences, and purposes or create your own. Write down the choices you make and save your work for future use.

Contexts/Formats
• Class debate about healthy or humane food choices • Opinion piece for a school newspaper • Efforts to improve lunch options in the school cafeteria
Audiences
• Fellow students • Students and teachers • School administrators
Purposes
• Persuade others that your position concerning food choices is valid • Encourage mindfulness of eating habits and sources of food • Change the types of food the school buys for student hot lunches

1.2 Integrating and Acknowledging Source Material

CLE-1.L CLE-1.M CLE-1.N

In addition to tying claims to evidence, writers also use commentary to introduce source material into their arguments. **Source material** includes words, music, ideas, images, texts, or any other intellectual property that is used in research. Commentary properly integrates ideas from other people and sources into a writer's line of reasoning, a process called **synthesis**. Writers must acknowledge the sources of ideas, images, text, and other intellectual property they use and give proper credit.

Voices of Support

In an argument, the writer's position and voice should be prominent and clear. Writers should maintain their own voice throughout an argument and not become lost in a fog of facts, quotes, and name-dropping. But writers also must draw on other sources and voices to strengthen and validate their claims. You have practiced this skill since childhood when you used the phrase "Mom says" in order to give importance to your ideas and make your brother or sister pause and listen to what you had to say.

Using Commentary to Integrate Sources

When writers turn to an expert or authority and introduce source material into an argument, they should do so with consideration and care. Writers use commentary to introduce source material into their argument in a way that smoothly continues their line of reasoning and enhances their position. Integrating others' arguments into your own is called *synthesizing*. Synthesis requires

- consideration—giving careful thought to how someone else's words or ideas can support your ideas
- explanation—making clear to the reader how another's views correspond to yours
- integration—smoothly weaving the other sources into your text

In the example below, Schlosser synthesizes the material he uses from Jim Hightower with his own writing.

Text	Explanation
(1) In the early 1970s, the **(2)** farm activist Jim Hightower warned of **(3)** "the McDonaldization of America." **(4)** He viewed the emerging fast food industry as a threat to independent businesses, as a step toward a food economy dominated by giant corporations, and as a homogenizing influence on American life. **(5)** In *Eat Your Heart Out* (1975), he argued that "bigger is not better." Much of what Hightower feared has come to pass. The centralized purchasing decisions of the large restaurant chains and their demand for standardized products have given a handful of corporations an unprecedented degree of power over the nation's food supply.	Schlosser introduces the source material by providing some context **(1)**. He then gives Hightower's credentials **(2)** before integrating the key quote **(3)**. Schlosser then paraphrases Hightower's opinion **(4)** and raises Hightower's stature by referring to his book **(5)**.

Table 3-2

Schlosser weaves Hightower's source material into his own argument thoughtfully, enhancing his opinion and keeping the focus on his claim.

Acknowledgment

In the example above, Schlosser gives Jim Hightower credit for the phrase "McDonaldization of America" along with another quote and ideas. Giving credit where credit is due is essential and ethical when integrating others' arguments into your own. Failing to do so and passing off someone else's words and ideas as your own is *plagiarism*, a serious offense that carries significant consequences.

Writers use a number of conventions to show their debt to other writers' ideas, including attribution, citation, and reference.

Attribution is the act of acknowledging the source of an idea, statistic, fact, observation, image, or other intellectual property by ascribing, or attributing, it to its creator. Writers use attribution by including the contributor's name and any other pertinent information in their commentary. Schlosser's introductory commentary about Jim Hightower's words and ideas (above) is an attribution of credit to Hightower's intellectual property.

When you attribute an idea to an author, convey what makes that source credible. For example, Schlosser says:

> As the sociologists Cameron Lynne Macdonald and Carmen Sirianni have noted, the entry of so many women into the workforce has greatly increased demand for the types of services that housewives traditionally perform: cooking, cleaning, and child care.

The identification of Macdonald and Sirianni as sociologists provides a credential for them and elevates their credibility. Without that brief description, readers might wonder, "Who are they, and why should I trust or believe them?" When writers integrate others' ideas into their own to strengthen their arguments, they want supportive voices readers will respect.

Attributions are usually included within the body of a text to identify the source of such material. A **citation** is a more formal documentation of another's work, research, and words and often appears as a footnote or endnote. The following formal citation appears at the back of Schlosser's book. It includes enough information for the reader to be able to find the source and check it independently.

> [5] "*the McDonaldization of America*": Jim Hightower, *Eat your Heart Out: Food Profiteering in America* (New York: Crown, 1975), p. 237.

A **reference** is like a citation, but it does not refer to a specific page or chapter number in a source. Instead it provides the basic publishing information about a source. References to all the works an author has consulted often appear at the end of a book in a list called a *bibliography*.

Acknowledging others' intellectual property through attribution, citation, and/or reference is an essential step for validating your evidence, including diverse perspectives, and adding credibility to your own position. For specific ways to use commentary to synthesize others' ideas into your own writing, refer to Table 1-8 in Unit 1 on page 35 on quoting, paraphrasing, and summarizing.

Remember: Writers introduce source material by using commentary to properly integrate it into their line of reasoning. Synthesis requires consideration, explanation, and integration of others' arguments into one's own argument. Writers must acknowledge words, ideas, images, texts, and other intellectual property of others through attribution, citation, or reference. (CLE-1.L–N)

1.2 Checkpoint

Close Reading: Professional Text

Reread the excerpt from the introduction to *Fast Food Nation.* Then complete the open response activity and answer the multiple-choice questions.

1. Suppose you are writing your own text about the fast food industry and you want to use Schlosser as a source. Your claim is "*Fast food corporations are responsible for replacing independent food growers and farmers.*" Below are quotes you identified from Schlosser's text that support your reasoning and justify your claim. Practice synthesizing these details into a paragraph-long argument. Be sure to give credit to Schlosser, including his name and what makes him credible.

   Quotes from Schlosser that support your claim:

   - "Farmers and cattle ranchers are losing their independence, essentially becoming hired hands for the agribusiness giants or being forced off the land."
   - "Family farms are now being replaced by gigantic corporate farms with absentee owners."
   - "Rural communities are losing their middle class and becoming socially stratified, divided between a small, wealthy elite and large numbers of the working poor."
   - "The United States now has more prison inmates than full-time farmers."

2. In the fourth paragraph, Schlosser introduces sociologists Cameron Lynne Macdonald and Carmen Sirianni primarily to
   (A) strengthen his argument that the fast food industry has caused significant changes in American society
   (B) spotlight the significance of his counter-argument about fast food in a larger context to give credit to his claim
   (C) offer an alternative perspective about the influence of fast food chains on American culture
   (D) question the motives of those who ignore the financial struggles of workers in the fast food industry
   (E) offer additional research to support people in their attempt to make healthier meals at home

3. Schlosser cites the sociologist George Ritzer (paragraph 18, sentence 1) to suggest that
   (A) McDonald's is most responsible for the ethical flaws in the fast food industry
   (B) the fast food industry's focus on business efficiency blinds it to the greater good
   (C) the fast food industry would be better served if its business practices were regulated
   (D) without critics to attack and monitor the fast food industry, its abuses would grow worse
   (E) McDonald's success occurred at the expense of human rights

4. Which of the following does Schlosser do to establish a sense of ethical credibility with his readers?
   (A) He attacks elitists for looking down on the fast food industry and acting snobbishly.
   (B) He points out the irony in the fact that the fast food industry, which is dedicated to conformity, was founded by nonconformists.
   (C) He describes the hypocrisy of the American West, with its demands for smaller government and lower taxes as it profits from government subsidies.
   (D) He acknowledges some beneficial consequences resulting from the fast food industry's success.
   (E) He tells us that the hamburger and french fries became the quintessential American meal in the 1950s.

Evaluating Writing: Student Draft

Reread the student draft on page 120 and answer the following open response and multiple-choice questions.

1. Where does the writer introduce factual information that likely came from source materials?

2. How could the writer make better use of commentary in this draft?

3. The writer is considering adding the following sentence to the draft passage to better support the claim.

   According to Eric Schlosser, Americans spent more than $110 billion on fast food in 2001 compared to the $6 billion in 1970.

   Where would the sentence best be placed?

   (A) After sentence 2

   (B) After sentence 3

   (C) After sentence 4

   (D) After sentence 5

   (E) After sentence 7

Composing on Your Own

Return to the research and writing you did on food ethics or another topic of your choice. Write a paragraph on your topic that includes an arguable claim and provide evidence to support the claim. As you integrate the information from your research, be sure to introduce the information from your sources with commentary that makes clear how it fits into your line of reasoning. Also review the choices you made about your rhetorical situation and keep them in mind as you complete this activity.

Part 1 Apply What You Have Learned

In March 1989, Cesar Chavez gave a speech on the perils of pesticides at Pacific Lutheran University in Tacoma, Washington. Read the excerpt reprinted here. Then answer the questions that follow.

1 What is the worth of a man or a woman? What is the worth of a farm worker? How do you measure the value of a life?

2 Ask the parents of Johnnie Rodriguez.

3 Johnnie Rodriguez was not even a man; Johnnie was a five-year-old boy when he died after a painful two-year battle against cancer.

4 His parents, Juan and Elia, are farm workers. Like all grape workers, they are exposed to pesticides and other agricultural chemicals. Elia worked in the table grapes around Delano, California, until she was eight months pregnant with Johnnie.

4 Juan and Elia cannot say for certain if pesticides caused their son's cancer. But neuroblastoma is one of the cancers found in McFarland, a small farm town only a few miles from Delano, where the Rodriguezes live.

5 "Pesticides are always in the fields and around the towns," Johnnie's father told us. "The children get the chemicals when they play outside, drink the water or when they hug you after you come home from working in fields that are sprayed.

6 "Once your son has cancer, it's pretty hard to take," Juan Rodriguez says. "You hope it's a mistake, you pray. He was a real nice boy. He took it strong and lived as long as he could."

7 I keep a picture of Johnnie Rodriguez. He is sitting on his bed, hugging his Teddy bears. His sad eyes and cherubic face stare out at you. The photo was taken four days before he died.

8 Johnnie Rodriguez was one of 13 McFarland children diagnosed with cancer in recent years; and one of six who have died from the disease. With only 6,000 residents, the rate of cancer in McFarland is 400 percent above normal.

9 In McFarland and in Fowler childhood cancer cases are being reported in excess of expected rates. In Delano and other farming towns, questions are also being raised.

10 The chief source of carcinogens in these communities are pesticides from the vineyards and fields that encircle them. Health experts believe the high rate of cancer in McFarland is from pesticides and nitrate-containing fertilizers leaching into the water system from surrounding fields.

Source: Wikimedia Commons, Creative Commons License **Credit:** Tomas Castelazo

These grape pickers migrate from field to field in northern Mexico and California.

What details in this photograph provide information about the working conditions of these migrant grape pickers?

11 Last year California's Republican Governor, George Deukmejian, killed a modest study to find out why so many children are dying of cancer in McFarland. "Fiscal integrity" was the reason he gave for his veto of the $125,000 program, which could have helped 84 other rural communities with drinking water problems.

12 Last year, as support for our cause grew, Governor Deukmejian used a statewide radio broadcast to attack the grape boycott.[1]

13 There is no evidence to prove that pesticides on grapes and other produce endanger farm workers or consumers, Deukmejian claimed.

14 Ask the family of Felipe Franco.

15 Felipe is a bright seven-year-old who is learning to read and write. Like other children, Felipe will someday need to be independent. But Felipe is not like other children: he was born without arms and legs.

16 Felipe's mother, Ramona, worked in the grapes near Delano until she was in her eighth month of pregnancy. She was exposed to Captan, known to cause birth defects and one of the pesticides our grape boycott seeks to ban.

17 "Every morning when I began working I could smell and see pesticides on the grape leaves," Ramona said.

18 Like many farm workers, she was assured by growers and their foremen how the pesticides that surrounded her were safe, that they were harmless "medicine" for the plants.

19 Only after Ramona took her son to specialists in Los Angeles was she told that the pesticides she was exposed to in the vineyards caused Felipe's deformity. The deep sadness she feels has subsided, but not the anger.

1. Identify places where Chavez uses commentary to establish a relationship between evidence and a claim.
2. Analyze how Chavez introduces and synthesizes source material into his argument. How does the inclusion of source material affect the argument?

Reflect on the Essential Questions: Write a brief response that answers the essential questions: *As a reader, how do you understand the thinking behind writers' arguments—the relationships between their evidence and their claim? As a writer, how should you use source material to strengthen your argument?* Use the key terms on page 123 in your answer.

1 **grape boycott:** In 1984, the United Farm Workers launched their third and longest boycott of grapes, urging people to refuse to buy table grapes picked by workers unprotected from dangerous chemicals. The boycott ended in 2000.

Part 2

Line of Reasoning

Enduring Understanding and Skills

Part 2

Understand

Writers guide understanding of a text's lines of reasoning and claims through that text's organization and integration of evidence. (REO-1)

Demonstrate

Describe the line of reasoning and explain whether it supports an argument's overarching thesis. (Reading 5.A)

Develop a line of reasoning and commentary that explains it throughout an argument. (Writing 6.A)

Source: *AP® English Language and Composition Course and Exam Description*

Essential Questions: As a reader, how can you determine if an argument's line of reasoning supports the thesis and is logical? As a writer, how can you organize a text to help communicate your line of reasoning?

Sometimes when people in a conversation are interrupted, they might say, "Oh, now I've lost my train of thought." By that they mean that the sequence of their thoughts was uncoupled somewhere along the line and they lost the path to their main point. Fortunately, in writing you are not likely to be interrupted, and you can map out your train of thought carefully, explaining the reasoning that led you to your main point and adjusting each twist and turn to guide readers to the destination you desire: understanding and accepting your thesis as valid and meaningful, even if they disagree.

KEY TERMS

commentary	sequence
line of reasoning	significance
relevance	thesis

2.1 A Line of Reasoning | REO-1.A REO-1.B REO-1.C REO-1.D REO-1.E

As its name suggests, a **line of reasoning** is the logical sequence of the writer's claim, evidence, and commentary that leads a reader to or from the writer's conclusion. The most effective lines of reasoning are clear and logical. If the line of reasoning is flawed or incomplete, the argument loses credibility.

The Line of Logic

Reasoning is the writer's thinking put on paper—the writer's inferences, conclusions, predictions, and logic, among other aspects of thinking. The writer's claim, evidence, and commentary communicate the line of reasoning to the reader. Each writer decides which line of reasoning suits his or her topic, audience, and message best, but much writing tends to follow a few common patterns of reasoning. Whichever pattern the writer uses, transitional words and phrases serve as guideposts or turn signals to keep readers on track.

Following are examples of different patterns of reasoning as well as the words that flag them, alerting the reader to slow down and pay attention. These words are part of the writer's commentary as an argument unfolds.

Common Reasoning Patterns

There are many patterns of reasoning. The ones listed below are the ones you are most likely to come across.

- **Deductive Reasoning:** Reasoning from a general concept or assumption to show how a specific example relates to that concept
  Example: Fast foods contain high degrees of fat. Foods high in fats pose health problems, such as obesity, high blood pressure, and heart disease. For this reason, we can conclude that fast foods pose health problems.
  Signal Words: *if, then, since, for this reason, conclude, therefore*

- **Inductive Reasoning:** Reasoning from specific examples or observations to a general conclusion based on them
  Example: In February 2020, the toys in kids' meals at Wendy's were "Wild, Wild Animals." In addition, in the same month, Burger King's kids' toys were "Feisty Pets," while McDonald's offered "Spirit" toys based on the movie about a horse. From these examples we can conclude that animals are popular toys in kids' fast food meals.
  Signal Words: *in addition, also, for example, therefore*

- **Causal Reasoning:** Reasoning that something causes something else
  Example: Several developments have caused fast food chains to offer healthier options. One was the rise of fast food drive-throughs that offered only healthy food, such as Salad and Go in Arizona, at the same prices as regular fast food chains. A second was the requirement by the U.S. Food and Drug Administration that all large chains must list nutrition information, including calorie content of foods, on their

menus. Making that information available publicly puts pressure on chains to offer foods with lower calories.
Signal Words: *because, consequently, for this reason, explains, supports, caused, therefore, as a result*

- **Analogic or Comparative Reasoning**: Reasoning that something is like or unlike something else
Example: Efforts to market fast food to children continue with few regulations, cementing the presence of fast foods in American culture. In 2018, the fast food industry spent $29 million lobbying lawmakers to make sure those regulations stay away. And as children get older, they face a similar level of marketing from the makers of e-cigarettes, now largely owned by the big tobacco companies, who spend an average of $23 million each year lobbying lawmakers. As dollars spent on unregulated marketing to youth have increased, so has the use of e-cigarettes among teens and young adults, and so has apparent harm to health.
Signal Words: *in the same way, like, in contrast, for the same reasons, similar*

In high-quality writing, patterns of reasoning are usually more complex than the examples above, but they still follow the same overall patterns.

Reasoning to a Claim or Thesis

Sometimes writers of high-quality texts begin by laying out a line of reasoning that will lead readers to the **thesis,** the overarching claim, following the inductive reasoning process. Consider the example on the next page from the Afterword to the 2012 edition of Schlosser's book. In it Schlosser talks about some of the problems that remained as well as some changes that had occurred since his book first came out in 2001. He explains that a food movement has developed—an effort to grow, buy, and eat healthier and less processed foods. As you read the excerpt, follow Schlosser's line of reasoning to his thesis, which is printed in bold type.

Source: Getty Images

Farmers' markets throughout the country focus on locally grown, often organic, food that bypasses agribusinesses and provides healthy whole foods at a reasonable price.

In what ways does the photo suggest a path different from "the McDonaldization" of the food industry?

Text	Key Points in Line of Reasoning
(1) At the moment, the main problem with the food movement is how few Americans can enjoy its benefits. **(2)** Although the amount of money spent on organic food has increased more than 20-fold since the early 1990s, it currently accounts for only 4 percent of the nation's total spending on food. The annual revenue of McDonald's Corp. is roughly equal to those of America's entire organic-food industry. **(3)** Organic food is more expensive. **(4)** Families in which both parents work outside the home often don't have the time to prepare meals from scratch. **(5)** And more than 23 million low-income Americans now live in "food deserts" that lack supermarkets. As upper-middle-class and well-educated people increasingly reject fast food, the industry has responded much like the tobacco industry once did when that demographic group decided to quit smoking. **(6)** The fast-food chains, like the tobacco companies, are now aggressively targeting African-Americans, Latinos, and the poor. America's low-income communities now boast the highest proportion of fast-food restaurants—as well as the highest obesity rates and the highest rates of diabetes. **Two vastly different food cultures now coexist in the United States.** While some Americans eat free-range chicken and organic produce, exercise regularly, and improve their health, most are consuming inexpensive processed foods, drinking large amounts of soda, and reducing their life expectancy. The contrast between the thin, fit, and well-to-do and the illness-ridden, poor, and obese has no historical precedent. The wealthy used to be corpulent, while the poor starved.	**(1)** The food movement leaves out a lot of people. **(2)** Sales figures provide evidence that spending on organic food is very low, though it has increased. **(3)** One reason more people are not part of the food movement is because organic food is more expensive. **(4)** Another is that families with two working parents don't have time to cook from scratch. **(5)** Another is that millions of low-income Americans live in neighborhoods without supermarkets. **(6)** These are the people the fast food industry is targeting now. Commentary compares tactics of the fast food industry to those of the tobacco industry. **Thesis:** Privileged people can afford to eat healthy food; poor people can only afford less healthy options, resulting in two different food cultures. Commentary notes that the traditional divisions between wealthy and poor and thin and fat have reversed.

Table 3-3

In this passage, Schlosser leads the reader through evidence and **commentary**, or explanations, to his conclusion. Follow his reasoning process in the chart below.

Reasoning to the Claim
If **idea 1** is true (Healthy food is expensive) and **idea 2** is true (Healthy food takes more time to prepare than families with two working parents have) and **idea 3** is true (Millions of Americans live in neighborhoods without supermarkets but with plenty of fast food restaurants)
Then a **logically drawn conclusion** from them is also true. (Two vastly different food cultures coexist)

Table 3-4

Reasoning from a Claim or Thesis

Schlosser also uses deductive reasoning, another common pattern. Many of Schlosser's paragraphs begin with a claim and then continue with a line of reasoning that justifies the claim. In his commentary, Schlosser takes care to explain how his evidence is both *significant* and *relevant*. (See page 141.) Consider the example below.

Text	Key Points in Line of Reasoning
The McDonald's Corporation has become a powerful symbol of America's service economy, which is now responsible for 90 percent of the country's new jobs. In 1968, McDonald's operated about one thousand restaurants. Today it has about thirty thousand restaurants worldwide and opens almost two thousand new ones each year. An estimated one out of every eight workers in the United States has at some point been employed by McDonald's. The company annually hires about one million people, more than any other American organization, public or private. McDonald's is the nation's largest purchaser of beef, pork, and potatoes—and the second largest purchaser of chicken. The McDonald's Corporation is the largest owner of retail property in the world. Indeed, the company earns the majority of its profits not from selling food but from collecting rent. McDonald's spends more money on advertising and marketing than any other brand. As a result it has replaced Coca-Cola as the world's most famous brand. McDonald's operates more playgrounds than any other private entity in the United States. It is one of the nation's largest distributors of toys. A survey of American schoolchildren found that 96 percent could identify Ronald McDonald. The only fictional character with a higher degree of recognition was Santa Claus. The impact of McDonald's on the way we live today is hard to overstate. The Golden Arches are now more widely recognized than the Christian cross.	Schlosser begins the paragraph with a claim (bold type). Through the rest of the paragraph he provides his reasoning, which is that the overwhelming dominance of McDonald's in the fast food industry explains why it is the most powerful symbol of the nation's service economy (number of restaurants; number of past, present, and future employees; scope of purchasing of beef, pork, potatoes, and chicken; extent of retail property; reach of advertising; number of playgrounds; distributor of toys). Schlosser uses commentary to explain the connections between the evidence and the claim. When he points out that McDonald's hires more people than any other organization, public or private, he is showing how the evidence ("the company annually hires about one million people") is *significant* to the claim that the "McDonald's Corporation has become a powerful symbol of America's service economy." Schlosser also uses commentary to point out that because McDonald's uses advertising to extensively target children, they recognize Ronald McDonald nearly as frequently as they recognize Santa Claus. This shows how the evidence about the vast numbers of playgrounds and toys is *relevant* to his claim.

Table 3-5

In this passage, Schlosser starts with the claim and then leads the reader through evidence and **commentary**, or explanations, to his conclusion. His line of reasoning is to build up statistics that show McDonald's unique position of power, economically and culturally.

Starting with the Claim
This **general, overarching claim** is true (McDonald's has become a powerful symbol). It's true because
Evidence 1 is true (Has 30,000 restaurants and 2,000 more each year) and **Evidence 2** is true (Hires more than one million workers a year) [commentary that shows significance: that's more than any other public or private enterprise] **Evidence 3** is true (Is largest purchaser of meat) **Evidence 4** is true (Owns more retail property) **Evidence 5** is true (Outreach to children through advertising, playgrounds, and toys) [commentary that shows relevance: Ronald McDonald is almost as recognizable to children as Santa]

Table 3-6

Commentary and Line of Reasoning

Just as commentary can smoothly interweave ideas from other sources into an argument (see pages 32–35), it can also smoothly explain how evidence relates to claims and help guide the flow of reasoning in an argument. Commentary is especially useful to help readers understand the importance, or **significance**, of evidence. It can also clearly show the **relevance** of evidence, the precise way evidence works to support the reasoning behind the claim.

The following excerpt is from a health policy journal article titled "Obesity prevention: the role of policies, laws and regulations" by Boyd A. Swinburn.

Source: Getty Images

In his report, Swinburn notes a cause and effect relationship between healthy food choices in the school cafeteria and healthy food choices elsewhere.

Swinburn's Text	Commentary
Many parallels have been drawn between other epidemics and the obesity epidemic. Tobacco control is the usual analogy and this is rebutted by the food industry with the statement that food and tobacco are completely different. It is true that the products are completely different but the observed patterns of corporate responses to the public health pressure for regulations and the required spectrum of solutions for the epidemics, including regulatory and fiscal interventions, are remarkably similar.	Swinburn's commentary communicates his thinking that the obesity epidemic and tobacco use are similar. He uses comparative reasoning to show how they are similar. This commentary also shows the significance of the evidence to Swinburn's line of reasoning, since the dangers of smoking and the regulations put in place to reduce it are well understood as successful health initiatives.
Even though legislation for obesity prevention could not be directly aimed at eating and physical activity behaviors, any "rule-based" approach (even at the level of school or home rules) is likely to be a powerful way of changing social norms and attitudes. For example, a policy banning high fat or sugar food and beverages from school [cafeterias] . . . can be expected to accelerate the transition in norms from [cafeterias] full of foods high in fat, sugar and salt to [cafeterias] with foods that match those promoted in a school's nutrition curriculum. While only a few percent of children's total yearly energy intake comes from the school [cafeteria], having visible icons of healthy food are likely to be very important in influencing eating patterns outside school. Such policy interventions could be considered "lighthouse" interventions because they cast their light far and wide and show children and parents the way forward for healthy eating.	Swinburn's commentary again shows his use of causal reasoning. If students have healthy examples of eating in the school cafeteria, then they are likely to make healthy choices outside of school. He also shows the relevance of having healthy food visible at school to his reasoning about how to achieve the larger goal of healthy eating in general.

Table 3-6

Sequencing Paragraphs

The entire organization and structure of an argument, even the order of the sentences and paragraphs, are tools to communicate line of reasoning. In the two-paragraph excerpt above, each topic sentence is a claim which the other sentences in the paragraph support, and their arrangement helps convey the line of reasoning. In the same way as sentences work together within a paragraph, paragraphs work together within an essay. The topic sentence of a paragraph in a longer argument often introduces a *supporting claim*, a statement that backs up the overarching thesis. Each paragraph plays a role in supporting or leading to the thesis.

Examine the **sequence,** or order, of the paragraph topics in the anchor text as outlined below. The structure and sequence of the entire text reveal Schlosser's line of reasoning.

Paragraph	Paragraph Claim	Line of Reasoning
Paragraphs 1–2	Fast food has infiltrated every nook and cranny of American society. It has become almost a custom.	The writer introduces the topic of fast food and reminds the readers how ubiquitous it is.
Paragraph 3	Fast food has become a revolutionary force in American life. (thesis)	The writer states his overarching claim, or thesis.
Paragraph 4	The growth rate of fast food is due to fundamental changes in American society.	Historical context: how did we get here?
Paragraph 5	The McDonald's Corporation is a powerful symbol of America's service economy.	The writer uses the next ten paragraphs to provide evidence and commentary to support his overarching claim. Each paragraph discusses an important aspect of American society (e.g., service economy, business competition, conformity v. nonconformity, capitalism, technology). Read each paragraph's claim. Note how each paragraph supports the thesis, revealing a logical line of reasoning that continues through the entire text.
Paragraphs 6–7	Fast food threatens small businesses as chains take over independent stores.	
Paragraph 8	Successful fast food chains thrive on conformity.	
Paragraph 9	Fast food chains embody the best and worst of capitalism: innovation, and a widening gulf between rich and poor.	
Paragraphs 10–11	Technological advances have contributed to mass production and a disconnect between food sources and food service.	
Paragraph 12	Back to Cheyenne Mountains: the growth of the Colorado population mirrors the growth of the fast food industry.	
Paragraph 13	The fast food industry's success is due, in part, to certain political and economic choices like government subsidies.	
Paragraph 14	The fast food industry now controls many of the choices surrounding American agriculture, which has negatively affected rural areas and small towns.	
Paragraph 15	Fast food chains' rise to power has changed how cattle are raised and processed, making the meatpacking industry dangerous.	
Paragraph 16	The fast food industry and some of the peripheral issues, such as "malling and sprawling" and obesity, exhibit a distinctly American viewpoint.	
Paragraph 17	Fast food has impacted ordinary American lives, even children's lives.	
Paragraph 18	The fast food industry is gaining popularity outside America and provides insight into mass consumption.	Now what? The author explains how the fast food phenomenon in America is spreading across the globe. Perhaps this is the exigence for engaging in this important conversation.
Paragraph 19	The purpose of the book is to raise awareness for the complex and concerning issues involved in the fast food industry.	

Table 3-7

Remember: Writers may lead readers through a line of reasoning and then arrive at a thesis. Writers may express a claim and then develop a line of reasoning to justify the claim. Writers explain their reasoning through commentary that connects chosen evidence to the claim. Commentary explains the significance and relevance of evidence in relation to the line of reasoning. The sequence of paragraphs in a text reveals the argument's line of reasoning. (REO-1.D–F)

2.1 Checkpoint

Close Reading: Professional Text

Reread the following excerpt from Schlosser's Introduction to *Fast Food Nation.* Then answer the open response and multiple-choice questions that follow.

> Fast food is now so commonplace that it has acquired an air of inevitability, as though it were somehow unavoidable, a fact of modern life. And yet the dominance of the fast food giants was no more preordained than the march of colonial split-levels, golf courses, and man-made lakes across the deserts of the American West. The political philosophy that now prevails in so much of the West—with its demand for lower taxes, smaller government, an unbridled free market—stands in total contradiction to the region's true economic underpinnings. No other region of the United States has been so dependent on government subsidies for so long, from the nineteenth-century construction of its railroads to the twentieth-century financing of its military bases and dams. One historian has described the federal government's 1950s highway-building binge as a case study in "interstate socialism"—a phrase that aptly describes how the West was really won. The fast food industry took root alongside that interstate highway system, as a new form of restaurant sprang up beside the new off-ramps. Moreover, the extraordinary growth of this industry over the past quarter-century did not occur in a political vacuum. It took place during a period when the inflation-adjusted value of the minimum wage declined by about 40 percent, when sophisticated mass marketing techniques were for the first time directed at small children, and when federal agencies created to protect workers and consumers too often behaved like branch offices of the companies that were supposed to be regulated. Ever since the administration of President Richard Nixon, the fast food industry has worked closely with its allies in Congress and the White House to oppose new worker safety, food safety, and minimum wage laws. While publicly espousing support for the free market, the fast food chains have quietly pursued and greatly benefited from a wide variety of government subsidies. Far from being inevitable, America's fast food industry in its present form is the logical outcome of certain political and economic choices.

1. How does this paragraph contribute to the overall line of reasoning that supports the author's claim that "Fast food and its consequences have become inescapable"?

2. Analyze the structure of this paragraph. How does the line of reasoning support the claim?

3. Which sentence from the excerpt on the previous page best explains the significance or relevance of evidence?

4. In the excerpt from *Fast Food Nation*, which of the following is an example of the writer's use of causal reasoning?
   (A) The author shows how the western expansion of freeways led to more fast food restaurants.
   (B) The author shows that the reduction in minimum wage led to reduced choices in food.
   (C) The author shows how the development of more human-made structures led to the development of fast food chains.
   (D) The author shows how development of new government agencies led to the government overregulating people's lives.
   (E) The author shows how the West's dependence on subsidies led to the public's dependence on fast food.

5. Which of the following excerpts best expresses the author's commentary regarding the government's relation to the fast food industry?
   (A) "Fast food is now so commonplace that it has acquired an air of inevitability, as though it were somehow unavoidable, a fact of modern life." (sentence 1)
   (B) "No other region of the United States has been so dependent on government subsidies for so long, from the nineteenth-century construction of its railroads to the twentieth-century financing of its military bases and dams." (sentence 4)
   (C) "One historian has described the federal government's 1950s highway-building binge as a case study in 'interstate socialism'—a phrase that aptly describes how the West was really won." (sentence 5)
   (D) "Moreover, the extraordinary growth of this industry over the past quarter-century did not occur in a political vacuum." (sentence 7)
   (E) "Ever since the administration of President Richard Nixon, the fast food industry has worked closely with its allies in Congress and the White House to oppose new worker safety, food safety, and minimum wage laws." (sentence 9)

Evaluating Writing: Student Draft
Reread the student draft on page 120. Then answer the open response and multiple-choice questions that follow.

1. Trace the writer's line of reasoning by condensing it down to four sentences in the following way. First summarize sentences 1 and 2 in one sentence. Do the same for sentences 3–5, 6–9, and 10–11. Based on your summary, what can you conclude about the line of reasoning in this draft?

2. Make a suggestion about the best line of reasoning this writer should follow—deductive, inductive, causal, or comparative—based on how the essay begins. Then list some appropriate topics for the next two or three paragraphs of this student's writing on fast food that would develop that line of reasoning.

3. Which transitional word or phrase would best underscore the relationship between sentences 5 and 6 in order to maintain the line of reasoning?
   (A) Consequently,
   (B) However,
   (C) Also,
   (D) In addition,
   (E) Furthermore,

4. The writer wants to add specific evidence to support the claim asserted in sentence 6. Which detail would best support this claim and maintain the line of reasoning?
   (A) because individuals are realizing the life-altering health problems—such as obesity and heart issues—tied to their choices.
   (B) because the industry knows that obesity is harming people.
   (C) and change the culture of American values by encouraging people live healthier and lead a less busy lifestyle.
   (D) because we have more means to do so now than we did when fast food first appeared in the market 30 years ago.
   (E) For example, the McLean Deluxe no longer uses carcinogens to pretend to be a healthier option.

Composing on Your Own
Return to the paragraph you wrote about food ethics or another topic of interest to you. Examine your line of reasoning. Create a two-column chart like the one on page 142 with your text in the first column and your train

of thought in the second. Evaluate your line of reasoning and ask if it keeps the elements of your rhetorical situation in mind. Is it logical, complete, sequential, and clear? If you notice any gaps, introduce commentary to fill them in. When you are satisfied that the essential elements are in place, add more commentary to explain the significance and relevance of your evidence. Also consider how to best position your claim. Will you begin your paragraph with the claim and use a line of reasoning to justify it? Or will you present a line of reasoning that will lead to a thesis? Experiment with each type of structure as you write your paragraph. Save your work for later use.

2.2 Flaws in Reasoning | REO-1.F

A logical line of reasoning is the backbone of a strong and valid argument. But what happens when the reasoning wears thin, or even breaks? Flaws in a line of reasoning can cause significant harm to an argument's validity or a writer's credibility.

Broken Lines

In a classic episode of Fox Broadcasting Company's *The Simpsons,* the character Ned Flanders spots a bear on the street. This sighting launches a citywide crusade against bears and prompts the creation of the Bear Patrol. In the following conversation, Homer Simpson commends the success of the Bear Patrol in keeping bears away. Read the exchange between Homer and his daughter, Lisa.

> *Homer*: Not a bear in sight. The Bear Patrol must be working like a charm.
> *Lisa*: That's specious reasoning, Dad.
> *Homer*: Thank you, dear.
> *Lisa*: By your logic I could claim that this rock keeps tigers away.
> *Homer*: Oh, how does it work?
> *Lisa*: It doesn't work.
> *Homer*: Uh-huh.
> *Lisa*: It's just a stupid rock.
> *Homer*: Uh-huh.
> *Lisa*: But I don't see any tigers around, do you?
> [Homer thinks about this and then pulls out some money.]
> *Homer*: Lisa, I want to buy your rock.
> [Lisa refuses at first, then takes the money.]

This example of faulty reasoning, although illogical and nonsensical, illustrates how so-called "experts," backwards thinking, and unsubstantiated claims can fool people into accepting false ideas and jumping to conclusions. Careful readers are always on guard for signs of faulty reasoning as they follow an argument's line of reasoning. And writers must make sure that their arguments are grounded in facts and a logical train of thought. Schlosser's argument doesn't have flaws in the line of reasoning to render it illogical or **specious**—seemingly accurate at first but on closer inspection clearly wrong. But for the sake of your writing and critical reading, learn to recognize such flaws and the false claims to which they lead. The following sections show some ways each common line of reasoning can go wrong.

Deductive Flaws

Maybe you have come across the popular way of explaining deductive reasoning: the syllogism. The syllogism draws a conclusion from two statements (premises) assumed to be true.

Major premise: All men are mortal.
Minor premise: Aristotle was a man.
Conclusion: Aristotle was mortal.

This syllogism is sound and valid—in other words, logical—because both premises are true and the conclusion follows logically from them. But what about the following?

Major premise: All men are mortal.
Minor premise: Aristotle was a man.
Conclusion: All men are Aristotle.

That is an example of flawed reasoning, because even though the premises are true, the conclusion does not follow logically.

Or consider this flawed reasoning.

Major premise: All men are dogs.
Minor premise: Aristotle was a man.
Conclusion: Aristotle was a dog.

In this case, the conclusion follows logically from the premises—that is, if the major premise and the minor premise are true, then the conclusion is also true—but one of the premises is false, creating an invalid argument.

Read this example of flawed reasoning related to fast food. Where is the flaw, in the premises or in the conclusion?

> Fast food is inexpensive. Inexpensive foods are unhealthy. For this reason, we can conclude that fast foods are unhealthy.

In this case, the flaw is in the second sentence, or premise. While it is true that some healthy food is more expensive than fast food, there are many examples of healthy food that are also inexpensive. Nothing inherent in inexpensive foods makes them unhealthy.

Inductive Flaws

As you read, inductive reasoning moves from specific examples or observations to a general conclusion based on them. An earlier example of logical inductive reasoning (page 137) focused on toys in kids' meals. What about the following paragraph makes the reasoning flawed?

> In February 2020, the toys in kids' meals at Wendy's were "Wild, Wild Animals." In addition, in the same month, Burger King's kids' toys were "Feisty Pets," while McDonald's offered "Spirit" toys based on the movie about a horse. From these examples we can conclude that fast food chains always give animals as toys in kids' fast food meals.

In this case, the flaw is that the conclusion is overly general given the limited examples provided. One month's worth of toys from three fast food chains is nowhere near enough evidence to make such a broad conclusion. Words suggesting absolute, far-reaching conclusions, such as *always, never, most, least, best*, and *worst*, are red flags that the logic is likely faulty.

Causal Flaws

The most common flaw in causal reasoning is assuming that if something happens before something else, the first happening caused the second.

> In 1992, the United States Department of Agriculture issued the first "food pyramid," a guide to balancing food groups for optimal healthy eating. That development led to the requirement passed in 2018 that fast food chains needed to publish nutritional information.

While these two events may be related in a general way, both having to do with government involvement in food and health, the first did not cause the second even though it came before it. The 2018 requirement was issued by the Food and Drug Administration, a different bureaucratic entity, and many events and developments in between may have influenced the outcome.

Comparative Flaws

A common flaw in comparative reasoning is drawing a conclusion about one thing based on a conclusion about a similar thing when the two things are not alike enough to justify the common conclusion.

> One purpose of government regulation is to protect the vulnerable, who are often children unable to make decisions for themselves. For this reason, fast food marketing to children should be carefully regulated, because eating too much fast food often leads to obesity and other lifelong health problems. However, fast food is not the only threat to children. Many books children are assigned to read in school have themes that are not appropriate for children, challenging their faith and possibly leaving lifelong damage. Government regulations are needed here as much as in fast food marketing; local governments should have the right to ban any book they feel would be harmful to a child.

Assessing the ill effects of eating fast food, which can be quantified in health statistics, is very different from trying to gauge the effect of a provocative book on a young person. The latter is likely much more subjective. The situations are similar in that they both relate to government protection of children, but the conclusion drawn for one does not apply to the other because of fundamental differences between them.

Other Common Flaws

Schlosser's logic is solid. But if the underlined statements had somehow slipped into his writing, they would be logically faulty. Read the altered text and the explanation of the flaws in reasoning.

Text	Logical Flaws
A hamburger and french fries became the quintessential American meal in the 1950s, thanks to the promotional efforts of the fast food chains. The typical American now consumes approximately three hamburgers and four orders of french fries every week. But the steady barrage of fast food ads, full of thick juicy burgers and long golden fries, **(1)** never mention where these foods come from nowadays or what ingredients they contain. **(2)** "We have the meats" declares Arby's, which is a disgusting and barbaric slogan in the first place. **(3)** But where do the meats come from and did the animals die humanely, or were they tortured? **(4)** If you enjoy fast food you are either ignorant about animal rights or you don't care. The birth of the fast food industry coincided with Eisenhower-era glorifications of technology, with optimistic slogans like "Better Living through Chemistry" and "Our Friend the Atom." The sort of technological wizardry that Walt Disney promoted on television and at Disneyland eventually reached its fulfillment in the kitchens of fast food restaurants. **(5)** Television is directly responsible for the obesity epidemic and should be banned or at least highly regulated. Indeed, the corporate culture of McDonald's seems inextricably linked to that of the Disney empire, sharing a reverence for sleek machinery, electronics, and automation. The leading fast food chains still embrace a boundless faith in science—and as a result have changed not just what Americans eat, but also how their food is made	**(1) Overgeneralization:** using absolutes such as, *always, never, all, most*, and *every* to falsely enhance an argument **(2) *Ad hominin*:** Latin for "against the man"; attacking a specific person (or in this case, restaurant franchise) instead of addressing the argument **(3) Red herring:** skipping to a new and irrelevant topic which confuses or manipulates perspective on an issue **(4) Either-or fallacy:** also called false dilemma; presenting two extreme options as the only choices **(5) Nonsequitur:** Latin for "it does not follow"; lacking a logical connection between the claim and the evidence. This could also be an example of oversimplification. Clearly the obesity epidemic has varied and complex causes.

Table 3-8

You don't need to memorize the names and definitions of these fallacies to improve your close reading or writing skills. But understanding the fallacies themselves will help you evaluate others' and your own lines of reasoning for clarity, completeness, logic, and order. When you write an argument, avoid these flaws when providing explanation of your reasoning to your audience. Your argument will be strong and valid when you provide evidence and use commentary to communicate your logical line of reasoning that justifies your claim.

Remember: Flaws in a line of reasoning may render an argument specious or illogical. (REO-1.F)

2.2 Checkpoint

Close Reading: Constructed Text

Read the following passage, which was written to demonstrate logical flaws, and answer the open response questions below it.

1 Despite its bad reputation, fast food is actually good for you. Think about a healthy home-cooked meal. It might consist of mashed potatoes, beef, rolls and butter, and salad. Now think about a typical fast food meal. It too might consist of potatoes, beef, a bun, and "the works" on the patty—lettuce, tomato, onions. These are the same ingredients as in the home-cooked meal. If it's healthy at home, it's healthy at the restaurant.

2 Furthermore, the people who have written books and made documentaries about the negative side of the fast food industry have made fortunes from their efforts. It's clear they have a profit motive for their criticisms of the fast food industry, so readers and viewers should be skeptical of everything they say.

3 However, one documentary maker took a different approach. Like the maker of *Super Size Me,* a film critical of the fast food industry, the maker of *Fat Head* also ate nothing but McDonald's for 30 days. He actually lost weight, and his cholesterol went down. That proves that fast food itself is not the problem.

4 The fast food industry is also criticized for its marketing to children but is never given credit for the benefits it provides. Many McDonald's restaurants have a "play place" that children love and that gives them a chance to burn off calories. McDonald's also has food children love, and their meals tend to be inexpensive. Furthermore, McDonald's gives many young people their first jobs, and while the pay might not be great, whose first job does pay well?

5 During the COVID-19 pandemic, McDonald's also went out of its way to start a "microsite" where employees could connect globally to share stories of inspiration. The site is called Our McFamily in the Community and it's full of great ideas. For example, in Australia, drive-through customers

can also pick up such basic foods as milk and bread. In Israel, some drive-throughs have been turned into testing sites.

6 All of these examples show that fast food has been misunderstood and can even be good for you. It's time to rethink our attitudes toward the companies that keep America fed.

1. Where is the breakdown of logic in the first paragraph?
2. What is the logical flaw in the second paragraph?
3. Explain the flawed thinking in paragraph 3.
4. Identify two more logical flaws in paragraphs 4–6.

Evaluating Writing: Student Draft

Reread the student draft on page 120. Then answer the following open response and multiple-choice questions.

1. Identify any examples of flaws in the writer's line of reasoning. How would you revise the writing to make the argument stronger?
2. Which of the following statements would best connect the ideas in sentences 9 and 10 to maintain the writer's line of reasoning as it relates to their thesis?
   (A) Instead, consumers went back to buying the traditional hamburger and fries sold at every fast food chain.
   (B) Because the branded healthy items did not sell, the fast food industries realized that consumers wanted real healthy options, not just additives disguised as healthy options.
   (C) More and more fast food chains have tried to offer healthier menu items and they are starting to sell and more and more, like the new salads offered at Wendy's.
   (D) In addition to America's growing concerns about health, there has also been a question about the working conditions in fast food chains.
   (E) There are only a few fast food chains that are trying to offer healthy options, and some restaurants are trying to rebrand themselves as healthy, such as Taco Bell offering Fresco-style tacos that leave off the cheese.

Composing on Your Own

Return to the paragraph you are developing on food ethics or another topic. Analyze your paragraph to be sure it is appropriate for your rhetorical situation and note any flaws in your line of reasoning. Check your writing carefully to be sure you have not used absolute language and have not used limited evidence to jump to unsubstantiated conclusions. Save your work for later use.

Part 2 Apply What You Have Learned

Reread the excerpt from Chavez's speech "The Perils of Pesticides" on pages 133–135.

Write a paragraph that explains the line of reasoning Chavez uses in his speech. How does the structure of his argument work to reveal the line of reasoning?

Reflect on the Essential Question: Write a brief response that answers these essential questions: *As a reader, how can you determine if an argument's line of reasoning supports the thesis and is logical? As a writer, how can you use a text's organization to communicate your line of reasoning?* In your answer, explain the key terms listed on page 136.

Part 3

Introduction to Methods of Development

Enduring Understanding and Skills

Part 3

Understand

Writers guide understanding of a text's lines of reasoning and claims through that text's organization and integration of evidence. (REO-1)

Demonstrate

Recognize and explain the use of methods of development to accomplish a purpose. (Reading 5.C)

Use appropriate methods of development to advance an argument. (Writing 6.C)

Source: *AP® English Language and Composition Course and Exam Description*

Essential Questions: How are methods of development used to accomplish a writer's purpose? How can I use methods of development to advance my argumentative writing?

When a dad opens a book with his preschool daughter on his lap and reads "Once upon a time," both father and daughter have a good idea what to expect next. They expect that they will hear a story that shows characters working through some kind of conflict but in the end living "happily ever after." Or when you look for a recipe for *pan de muerto* (bread of the dead) as the holiday *Dia de los Muertos* approaches, you would expect to see the recipe presented in a certain way—needed ingredients followed by step-by-step instructions for combining them. When you look up an unfamiliar animal in a nature encyclopedia—a pangolin, for example—you would expect to see certain categories of thought explained: what species the animal belongs to (mammal—the only one completely covered in scales); the animal's habitat (hollow trees or burrows); how the animals raise their young (pups ride on their mother's tail for about three months). All of these are conventional ways to structure and develop stories, instructions, and information.

In the same way, writers use and readers recognize conventional patterns of organizing an argument. Those patterns help to advance an argument and accomplish the writer's purpose.

KEY TERMS

- cause-effect
- comparison-contrast
- definition
- description
- methods of development
- narration

3.1 Methods of Development | REO-1.G REO-1.H

Writers develop and organize their arguments in a variety of ways so that an audience can trace their reasoning. These patterns of organization are collectively called **methods of development**. Some common methods of developing an argument include narration, cause-effect, comparison-contrast, definition, and description.

Patterns of Arrangement

Throughout the introduction of *Fast Food Nation* Schlosser uses narrative anecdotes to illustrate the broadening scope of the impact of the fast food industry to include the West, the whole of the United States, and finally the globe. Narration, like other methods of development, provides the audience with a means to trace the development of his ideas. Writers use narration, compare and contrast, cause and effect, and other methods of development to arrange their arguments to accomplish their purpose. These methods are recognizable to an audience and help them make sense of the information.

Writers make decisions about the structure of their argument based on the elements of the rhetorical situation. Recognizing the various methods of development will help you trace the reasoning of arguments that you read and help you leave a clear line for your audience to follow when you write. You may find holes in your reasoning that can be explained by a definition, or you may discover an important piece of evidence that might seem even more powerful when compared or contrasted with something else. Often, you will combine a variety of argumentative structures to support your claim. Most writers use a number of different methods of development in one text.

Table 3-9 on the next page shows some common methods of development and their purpose in a text.

Method of Development	Purpose
Narration	To explain information about your topic as a series of events in story format
Cause-Effect	To explain what caused (cause) something to happen (effect) related to your topic
Comparison-Contrast	To show how two or more areas of your topic are similar (comparison) or different (contrast) or both
Definition	To define a word or concept about your topic using synonyms, essential definition, or extended definitions
Description	To create a picture in words (vivid, specific details) to help the reader visualize something a writer has seen, heard, or done

Table 3-9

Remember: Methods of development are common approaches writers frequently use to develop and organize the reasoning of their arguments. A method of development provides an audience with the means to trace a writer's reasoning in an argument. Some typical methods of development are narration, cause-effect, comparison-contrast, definition, and description. REO-1.G, H

3.1 Checkpoint

Close Reading: Professional Text

Review Schlosser's introduction to *Fast Food Nation.* On separate paper, make a chart like the one below, leaving several lines between each method of development, and fill in the second column. Then answer the multiple-choice questions.

1. Find an example where Schlosser uses each method of development in his introduction to *Fast Food Nation.*

Method of Development	Example from the Text
Narration	
Cause-Effect	
Comparison-Contrast	
Definition	
Description	

2. In paragraph 8, Schlosser includes the word "uniformity" primarily to
   (A) define and clarify the meaning of the word in relation to the fast food industry
   (B) describe how the fast food industry has spread throughout the world
   (C) reveal that the fast food industry is similar to other industries
   (D) show how the word defines a guiding principle behind the fast food industry
   (E) compare how the fast food industry views food to how customers usually view food

3. According to Schlosser, what is the main reason for the growth of the fast food industry?
   (A) the growth of suburban communities
   (B) main streets and malls filled with franchises and chain stores
   (C) multinational corporations such as Cargill, ConAgra, and IBP
   (D) increased social stratification between a wealthy elite and the working poor
   (E) fundamental changes in American society

4. Which of the following best describes Schlosser's primary method for developing his arguments in the passage as a whole?
   (A) He describes the reasons for the fast food industry's growth and its consequences for society.
   (B) He relays personal anecdotes regarding his experiences with the fast food industry.
   (C) He attacks the negative impact of the fast food industry and proposes solutions to the problems it has caused.
   (D) He describes the causes of the fast food industry's growth followed by warnings about how the industry will one day collapse.
   (E) He moves back and forth between describing the benefits of the fast food industry's growth and giving examples of its negative impact on human health.

Evaluating Writing: Student Draft

Reread the student draft on page 120. Then answer the following open response and multiple-choice questions.

1. Identify where the writer uses narration as a method for developing his or her argument.

2. Edit the narration so that it offers insights and reflections on the writer's experience in order to advance the argument. Feel free to include your own experience and details.

3. The writer is looking to describe life as a teenager. Which of the following would best define the commonalities of teenagers and serve as the first sentence of the paragraph?
   (A) Teenagers who want a job can usually only work in the fast food industry because of their age, hours, and experience.
   (B) The life of a teenager is busy and often demands that we eat fast food so we can get to practices and special events.
   (C) Teenagers are often not aware of fast food's influence on their health.
   (D) Teenagers are eager to exercise their new adult freedoms, but they do not always know how to make the best use of them.
   (E) Teenagers are often ill-equipped to make healthy decisions, which is why the fast food industry caters to them the most.

Composing on Your Own
Review your draft on food ethics or another topic. Analyze your writing to determine what method(s) of development you recognize in your draft. Always keep your rhetorical situation in mind—are your choices appropriate for your audience and purpose? Save your analysis and draft for later use.

3.2 Methods of Development: Narration | REO-1.I

When writers develop their ideas through narration, they draw on details from real-life experiences. They not only tell the stories of those experiences, but they also offer interpretations of the importance or meaning of those experiences.

Stories of Significance

The purpose of **narration** is to tell a story or relate an event. Narration can be especially useful when attaching a personal anecdote to an argument or when assembling a logical order to an argument.

Narration gives a face, an experience, a humanity to an argument. Through those personal details, writers use an appeal to pathos (see pages 66–68) and the audience feels emotionally connected. For example, in "The Perils of Pesticides," Cesar Chavez skillfully uses narration to introduce his topic with compelling real-life experiences that quickly connect with the emotions and ethics of his audience.

Writers also use narration to offer reflection or insight on the significance of a real-life experience. Read the following excerpt from an essay that appeared in *The Atlantic*. In the essay, the author Ta-Nehisi Coates suggests that Black artists may lose aspects of their identities when they try to assimilate into White culture. While the majority of his essay focuses on Kanye West, Coates uses his introduction to narrate his own youthful experience of first viewing Michael Jackson on TV:

> I could only have seen it there, on the waxed hardwood floor of my elementary-school auditorium, because I was young then, barely 7 years old, and cable had not yet come to the city, and if it had, my father would not have believed in it. Yes, it had to have happened like this, like folk wisdom, because when I think of that era, I do not think of MTV, but of the futile attempt to stay awake and navigate the yawning whiteness of *Friday Night Videos,* and I remember that there were no VCRs among us then, and so it would have had to have been there that I saw it, in the auditorium that adjoined the cafeteria, where after the daily serving of tater tots and chocolate milk, a curtain divider was pulled back and all the kids stormed the stage. And I would have been there among them, awkwardly uprocking, or worming in place, or stiffly snaking, or back-spinning like a broken rotor, and I would have looked up and seen a kid, slightly older, facing me, smiling to himself, then moving across the floor by popping up alternating heels, gliding in reverse, walking on the moon.

Coates focuses on the corrosive effects of Black artists like Kayne West and Michael Jackson choosing to adopt the identity of the dominant White culture. Coates uses a story from his childhood to introduce his subject matter, effectively building a bridge between his claim and his own background. When Coates describes trying to "navigate the yawning whiteness of *Friday Night Videos*," the reader learns of the identity struggles Coates faced in his own life. Coates poignantly contrasts himself in school—his boyhood awkwardness and gawkiness—with the effortless movements of Michael Jackson "gliding in reverse, walking on the moon." While not all readers may share Coates's cultural experiences, many can relate to the insecurities and frustrations of adolescence. As a result, Coates's story situates readers in the familiar territory of shared experience, and they recognize how those experiences work to build adult identities. Although Coates later accuses Michael Jackson of "dying to be white," his narrative shows the appeal of Jackson when seen through the eyes of a young African American boy who was trying to find his own place in the world.

Read the following example from *The New Yorker* in which Casey Cep uses narration to argue for the importance of the postal service:

> I am probably one of the least consequential things my mother has ever delivered. She has two other daughters, for starters—one's a public servant and the other is a special-education teacher. But she's also spent her working life delivering love letters, college acceptances, medications, mortgage papers, divorce filings, gold bars, headstones, ashes, and care packages. In her thirty-eight years as a rural letter carrier with the United States Postal Service, she's delivered just about everything you can legally send through the mail.

> For twenty-seven of those years, she's driven the same fifty miles five or six days every week, starting out at the post office and tracing Rural Route 5, bringing letters and packages to her five hundred and forty-five customers. Her best advice from all that driving is to carry duct tape, which can fix anything, and can even be made into a leash if you happen to find a lost dog. Her best day, she says, was a few years ago, when a retirement community got added to her route—a hundred and fifty-seven new customers, with stories and the time to tell them. The retirement home comes early in her fifty miles, but some days she stops again on her way home for longer visits, or heads back there on weekends for birthdays and anniversaries or to welcome someone home from the hospital.

Cep could simply state her claim: *we should maintain a working postal service because it is one of the oldest and most important public goods in American history.* But readers might find this approach bland and uninteresting. Instead, the author chooses to connect with her audience by introducing a narrative from her own personal experience. In the narration, readers meet the author's mother, a postal worker, and as they learn about the wide variety of essential goods she delivers, they realize the Postal Service is a key lifeline to her rural community. In addition, rather than simply stating facts and figures about the Postal Service delivering mail, the author's narrative reveals that her mother's personal interactions with customers—particularly at a "retirement community"—are a key part of her job. This unique insight reveals that the postal workers deliver essential goods and, just as importantly, form an integral human part of the "stories" that bind communities together. As a result, the narration appeals to both the readers' emotions and their sense of the writer's character.

When writing your own argument, consider how narration might improve it. Look for areas where a narrative could add both interest and content to your essay. A narrative might help develop support for a position or provide an illustration of a challenging concept. With its ability to pull in readers or listeners who relate to personal experiences, narration is a method of development that can powerfully advance an argument. However, when assessing the quality of an argument, be aware that narratives are often based on only one person's anecdotal experiences. These experiences are subject to personal memories and emotions. As a result, while narratives may be powerful, they may not reflect the findings of scientific studies and the opinions of experts. For this reason, effective writers support narration with evidence from reliable sources.

Remember: When developing ideas through narration, writers offer details about real-life experiences and offer reflections and insights on the significance of those experiences. (REO-1.I)

3.2 Checkpoint

Close Reading: Professional Text

Reread the excerpt from Schlosser's introduction to *Fast Food Nation*. Then answer the following open response and multiple-choice questions.

1. Reread the following example of narration from Schlosser's introduction to *Fast Food Nation*. Identify where in this paragraph Schlosser uses narration. What purpose does it serve?

> Elitists have always looked down at fast food, criticizing how it tastes and regarding it as another tacky manifestation of American popular culture. The aesthetics of fast food are of much less concern to me than its impact upon the lives of ordinary Americans, both as workers and consumers. Most of all, I am concerned about its impact on the nation's children. Fast food is heavily marketed to children and prepared by people who are barely older than children. This is an industry that both feeds and feeds off the young. During the two years spent researching this book, I ate an enormous amount of fast food. Most of it tasted pretty good. That is one of the main reasons people buy fast food; it has been carefully designed to taste good. It's also inexpensive and convenient. But the value meals, two-for-one deals, and free refills of soda give a distorted sense of how much fast food actually costs. The real price never appears on the menu.

2. In paragraph 2, Schlosser includes a narrative about buying fast food primarily to
   (A) show that fast food negatively affects people's health
   (B) reveal that buying fast food is a routine part of people's lives
   (C) explain how fast food restaurants have become part of the American landscape
   (D) describe how the fast food industry dehumanizes workers
   (E) suggest that healthy eating options are not available at fast food restaurants

Evaluating Writing: Student Draft

Reread the student draft on page 120. Complete the following open response activity and answer the multiple-choice questions.

1. Edit the narration in sentences 1–3 so it offers more reflection and insight about the significance of the personal experience. Add details from your own experiences that help heighten the emotional or ethical appeal.

2. The writer wants to add more narrative detail to the paragraph to increase the sophistication of the development.

I can picture, even now, the McDonald's Arches and the life-sized clown of Ronald McDonald staring at me while I tried to tell my best friend what happened at school that day while drinking my McFlurry.

Where would the sentence best be placed?

(A) After sentence 1
(B) After sentence 2
(C) After sentence 4
(D) After sentence 5
(E) After sentence 10

Composing on Your Own

Review the draft you have been working on. If you haven't used narration, introduce it as a method of developing your argument. For example, try beginning your paragraph with an anecdote or personal experience, or offer an insight or reflection that advances your position. As you experiment with these techniques, keep your rhetorical situation in mind—are they effective for your audience, purpose, and message? Save your work for later use.

3.3 Methods of Development: Cause-Effect | REO-1.J

Another method of developing an argument is the cause-effect arrangement. When developing ideas through cause-effect, writers present a cause, show the effects or results of that cause, or present a series of causes and the effect(s) that follow.

Reasons and Consequences

The driver got into an accident because he was texting. If I drink coffee I can focus better. She came home late and as a result got grounded. The dog tore up the slippers since someone left them on the floor. Complete your homework so that you can perform better on your test. These statements all express cause-effect relationships. The purpose of the cause-effect method is to explain the reason (cause) why a consequence (effect) happened in a specific situation. Key words that signal the cause-effect method of development include *so, so that, thus, because, consequently, therefore, since, as a result, if,* and *reason.*

The cause-effect argument can be developed in a variety of ways. Entire texts are sometimes organized using this method, with the cause presented at the beginning of the argument and the effects following. Use the cause-effect method of development in your arguments when there are obvious and important relationships to establish. Use the key words above to signal these revealing correlations to your audience.

Pay attention to the use of cause-effect development as you read this excerpt from Malala Yousafzai's Speech to the UN Youth Assembly.

> Dear friends, on 9 October 2012, the Taliban shot me on the left side of my forehead. They shot my friends, too. They thought that the bullets would silence us, but they failed. And out of that silence came thousands of voices. The terrorists thought they would change my aims and stop my ambitions. But nothing changed in my life except this: weakness, fear and hopelessness died. Strength, power and courage were born.
>
> I am the same Malala. My ambitions are the same. My hopes are the same. And my dreams are the same. Dear sisters and brothers, I am not against anyone. Neither am I here to speak in terms of personal revenge against the Taliban or any other terrorist group. I am here to speak for the right of education for every child. I want education for the sons and daughters of the Taliban and all the terrorists and extremists. I do not even hate the Talib who shot me. Even if there was a gun in my hand and he was standing in front of me, I would not shoot him. This is the compassion I have learned from Mohammed, the prophet of mercy, Jesus Christ and Lord Buddha. This [is] the legacy of change I have inherited from Martin Luther King, Nelson Mandela and Mohammed Ali Jinnah.

Malala presents a cause: She was shot by the Taliban on October 9, 2012. She then explains the effects and consequences of the cause: She is no longer weak and fearful; she is using her voice and position to stand for equal rights in education; she remains peaceful and compassionate. In this case Malala is using the cause-effect method of development to highlight some unexpected and extraordinary effects. Readers or listeners might expect that the effect of violence would be fear, isolation, or defeat. But here Malala uses the common approach of cause-effect to show an uncommon result. In this case, one cause resulted in many effects.

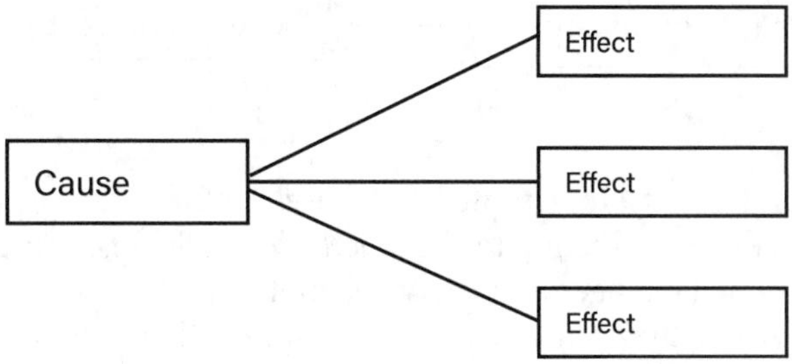

Figure 3-1

The cause-effect method of development can be used in many ways. For example, a series of causes can be followed by a series of effects. The following example explains three causes and three effects of those causes.

In the COVID-19 pandemic, a number of factors contributed to the quick spread and danger of the disease. First, people with the disease might show no symptoms, yet they are still able to infect others. Exposure to people with hidden infection greatly aided the fast spread of the virus. Second, even after stay-at-home orders were in place, many people ignored them, including young people who celebrated spring break on crowded beaches of Florida. The result of this behavior was that many of those people returned home infected and caused infections in people exposed to them. Finally, low supplies of personal protective equipment—masks, gloves, and gowns—for frontline healthcare workers and of ventilators and medications for the seriously ill resulted in overwhelmed medical facilities where doctors and nurses became sick, reducing the size of the healthcare workforce, and some patients needing ventilators did not get them and died.

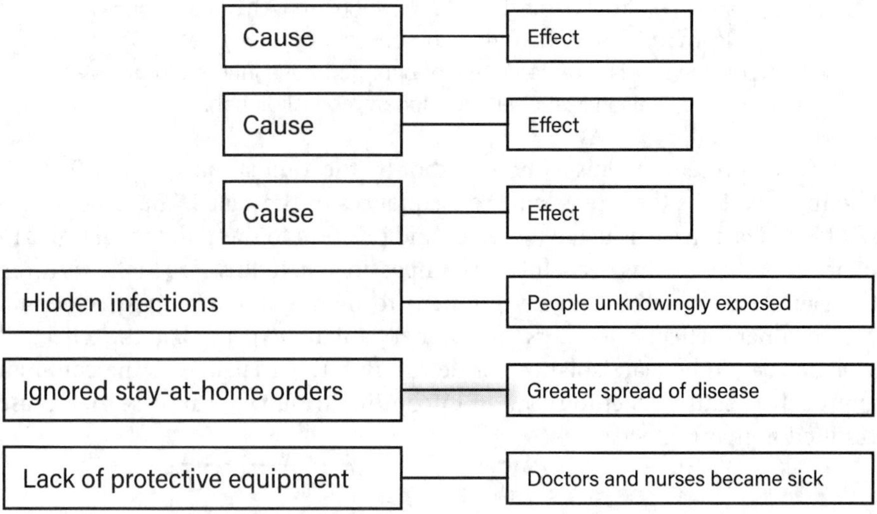

Figure 3-2

Schlosser and many other writers also use another form of cause-effect development. In the introduction to *Fast Food Nation,* Schlosser presents many causes—fundamental changes in society, technological advances, government subsidies to farmers, the trend toward uniformity—that produce one effect: fast food and its consequences have become inescapable.

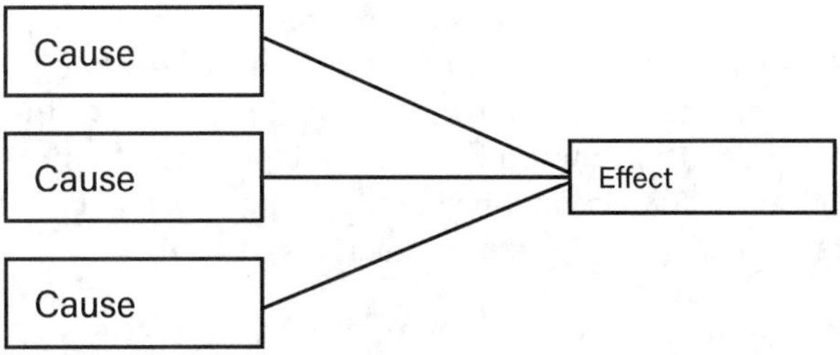

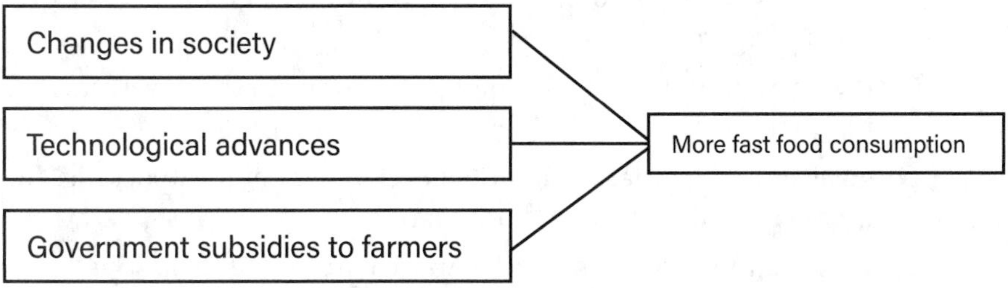

Figure 3-3

Remember: When developing ideas through cause-effect, writers present a cause, assert effects or consequences of that cause, or present a series of causes and subject effect(s). (REO-1.J)

3.3 Checkpoint

Close Reading: Professional Text

Reread the excerpt from Schlosser's introduction to *Fast Food Nation*. Then answer the following open response and multiple-choice questions.

1. Reread the following example of cause-effect development from Schlosser's introduction to *Fast Food Nation.* Explain how this method of development is situated within Schlosser's line of reasoning. How does this use of cause-effect advance Schlosser's claim?

> The extraordinary growth of the fast food industry has been driven by fundamental changes in American society. Adjusted for inflation, the hourly wage of the average U.S. worker peaked in 1973 and then steadily declined for the next twenty-five years. During that period, women entered the workforce in record numbers, often motivated less by a feminist perspective than by a need to pay the bills. In 1975, about one-third of American mothers with young children worked outside the home; today almost two-thirds of such mothers are employed. As the sociologists Cameron Lynne Macdonald and Carmen Sirianni have

noted, the entry of so many women into the workforce has greatly increased demand for the types of services that housewives traditionally perform: cooking, cleaning, and child care. A generation ago, three-quarters of the money used to buy food in the United States was spent to prepare meals at home. Today about half of the money used to buy food is spent at restaurants—mainly at fast food restaurants.

2. Schlosser uses cause-effect development to show a relationship between
   (A) promotional advertising and patterns of American food choices
   (B) the entry of more women into the workforce and the decline of hourly wages
   (C) the growth of the fast food industry and increased government regulations
   (D) government regulation and the development of meatpacking into a highly skilled, highly paid occupation
   (E) food technology and healthier, more natural menu options

3. According to Schlosser, which of the following is a major effect of the growth of the fast food industry in America?
   (A) More women entering the American workforce
   (B) The expansion of the interstate highway system
   (C) Safer working conditions in meatpacking plants
   (D) Uniformity, standardization, and conformity in business practices
   (E) Improved federal regulation of the meat industry to prevent the sale of contaminated meat

4. Which of the following events or trends from the 1950s does Schlosser cite as an essential cause of the fast food industry's growth and success?
   (A) the demand for lower taxes and smaller government
   (B) the construction of the interstate highway system
   (C) the rise of the Baby Boomer generation
   (D) the invention and spread of television and entertainment
   (E) the increasing student enrollment in American universities

Evaluating Writing: Student Draft

Reread the student draft on page 120. Then complete the following open response activities and answer the multiple-choice questions.

1. Identify sentences where the writer uses a cause-effect method of development to explain an idea.

2. Which of the cause-effect ideas could be more fully developed to advance the argument? Explain.

3. Which of the following would be the best addition to the paragraph in order for the writer to establish a cause-effect method of development that supports the claim and maintains the line of reasoning?
   (A) Thirty years ago, when women began entering the workforce at a rapid pace, American culture shifted to a fast-paced lifestyle that fueled the desire for fast food.
   (B) If there were more healthy options for teenagers' lifestyles, perhaps they wouldn't find themselves hanging out inside fast food restaurants.
   (C) Because traditional fast food restaurants are allowing new chains like Panera and Subway to cater to health-conscious consumers, the service industry is able to offer more choices to support a wide variety of customers.
   (D) The leading cause for Americans' fast food consumption is their busy lifestyle and lack of education when it comes to the choices that surround their food options.
   (E) The increased focus on health education in high schools has had little impact on teens' food choices outside of school.

Composing on Your Own

Return to your draft in progress on food ethics or another topic. Keeping your rhetorical situation in mind, consider how the cause-effect method of development could advance your argument. Draw on and experiment with the different cause-effect models presented on the previous pages, using specific details to fill in the "cause" and "effect" boxes based on your topic. Observe how the changes in structure affect your argument. Then make a final draft of your paragraph using the following checklist as a guide.

Checklist for Composing
✓ Did you develop an arguable position and do research to support it, noting your sources' credentials? (1.1)
✓ As you drafted your paragraph, did you use your sources to support your line of reasoning and credit them appropriately? (1.2)
✓ Did you visualize your line of reasoning and experiment with different approaches to choose the best one? (2.1)
✓ Did you check your work for flaws in reasoning, especially using absolute terms and jumping to conclusions with insufficient evidence? (2.2)
✓ Did you analyze your draft to determine the method of development you used? (3.1)
✓ Did you introduce narration to enhance your argument? (3.2)
✓ Did you experiment with cause-effect arrangements to determine if they are appropriate for your paragraph? (3.3)
✓ Did you check your writing for mistakes in spelling and mechanics and make an effort to correct them?

Table 3-10

Part 3 Apply What You Have Learned

Reread Cesar Chavez's speech on the perils of pesticide on pages 133–135. Then answer the following questions.

1. What methods of development can you identify in Chavez's speech?
2. What methods of development in Chavez's speech are the most powerful and why?

Reflect on the Essential Questions: Write a brief response that answers the following essential questions: *How are methods of development used to accomplish a writer's purpose? How can I use methods of development to advance my argumentative writing?* Include the key words on page 155 in your response.

Unit 3 Review

Section I: Multiple Choice

Section II: Free Response

Section I: Reading

Questions 1–7. Read the following passage carefully before you choose your answers.

(M. R. O'Connor is a journalist who writes about science, technology, and ethics and is the author of *Wayfinding: The Science and Mystery of How Humans Navigate the World*.)

1 It has become the most natural thing to do: get in the car, type a destination into a smartphone, and let an algorithm using GPS data show the way. Personal GPS-equipped devices entered the mass market in only the past 15 or so years, but hundreds of millions of people now rarely travel without them. These gadgets are extremely powerful, allowing people to know their location at all times, to explore unknown places and to avoid getting lost.

2 But they also affect perception and judgment. When people are told which way to turn, it relieves them of the need to create their own routes and remember them. They pay less attention to their surroundings. And neuroscientists can now see that brain behavior changes when people rely on turn-by-turn directions.

3 In a study published in *Nature Communications* in 2017, researchers asked subjects to navigate a virtual simulation of London's Soho neighborhood and monitored their brain activity, specifically the hippocampus, which is integral to spatial navigation. Those who were guided by directions showed less activity in this part of the brain than participants who navigated without the device. "The hippocampus makes an internal map of the environment and this map becomes active only when you are engaged in navigating and not using GPS," Amir-Homayoun Javadi, one of the study's authors, told me.

4 The hippocampus is crucial to many aspects of daily life. It allows us to orient in space and know where we are by creating cognitive maps. It also allows us to recall events from the past, what is known as episodic memory. And, remarkably, it is the part of the brain that neuroscientists believe gives us the ability to imagine ourselves in the future.

5 Studies have long shown the hippocampus is highly susceptible to experience. (London's taxi drivers famously have greater gray-matter volume in the hippocampus as a consequence of memorizing the city's labyrinthine streets.) Meanwhile, atrophy in that part of the brain is linked to devastating conditions, including post-traumatic stress disorder and Alzheimer's disease. Stress and depression have been shown to dampen neurogenesis—the growth of new neurons—in the hippocampal circuit.

6 What isn't known is the effect of GPS use on hippocampal function when employed daily over long periods of time. Javadi said the conclusion he draws from recent studies is that "when people use tools such as GPS, they tend to engage less with navigation. Therefore, brain area responsible for navigation is less used, and consequently their brain areas involved in navigation tend to shrink."

7 How people navigate naturally changes with age. Navigation aptitude appears to peak around age 19, and after that, most people slowly stop using spatial memory strategies to find their way, relying on habit instead. But neuroscientist Véronique Bohbot has found that using spatial-memory strategies for navigation correlates with increased gray matter in the hippocampus at any age. She thinks that interventions focused on improving spatial memory by exercising the hippocampus—paying attention to the spatial relationships of places in our environment—might help offset age-related cognitive impairments or even neurodegenerative diseases.

8 "If we are paying attention to our environment, we are stimulating our hippocampus, and a bigger hippocampus seems to be protective against Alzheimer's disease," Bohbot told me in an email. "When we get lost, it activates the hippocampus, it gets us completely out of the habit mode. Getting lost is good!" Done safely, getting lost could be a good thing.

9 Saturated with devices, children today might grow up to see navigation from memory or a paper map as anachronistic as rote memorization or typewriting. But for them especially, independent navigation and the freedom to explore are vital to acquiring spatial knowledge that may improve hippocampal function. Turning off the GPS and teaching them navigational skills could have enormous cognitive benefits later in life.

10 There are other compelling reasons outside of neuroscience to consider forgoing the GPS.

11 Over the past four years, I've spoken with master navigators from different cultures who showed me that practicing navigation is a powerful form of engagement with the environment that can inspire a greater sense of stewardship. Finding our way on our own—using perception, empirical observation and problem-solving skills—forces us to attune ourselves to the world. And by turning our attention to the physical landscape that sustains and connects us, we can nourish "topophilia," a sense of attachment and love for place. You'll never get that from waiting for a satellite to tell you how to find a shortcut.

---

1. In the opening paragraph, the writer begins with a hypothetical scenario in order to

(A) explain the importance of the research that will follow

(B) suggest that we all use technology in the same way

(C) emphasize the common, shared experience of using a GPS

(D) underscore the power of technology in all aspects of life

(E) highlight the challenges with modern-day technology

2. Which of the following best characterizes the writer's position on the use of GPS-equipped devices?

(A) Because the GPS is so powerful, it has made exploration and navigation easier.

(B) Because the GPS is so powerful, people continue to use the data because they are able to know their location, not get lost, and know where others are at all times.

(C) Because the GPS has the power to dictate directions, the brain's behavior changes and is likely to have lasting consequences on cognitive function.

(D) Although the brain's hippocampus is "highly susceptible to experience," the brain is still able to recognize common routes even when using a GPS device.

(E) Because the GPS invites people to rely on turn-by-turn directions, the brain area responsible for navigation is not used and becomes dormant.

3. The writer's inclusion of a study published in *Nature Communications* in 2017 (paragraph 3) serves primarily to

(A) question the motives of others' research on the topic of technology's effect on brain function

(B) introduce the effects of technology on the hippocampus by using a real-world example

(C) affirm the validity of the writer's thesis

(D) support the writer's claim by situating his position in a larger context

(E) spotlight the growing interest in the long-term effects of technology on the brain

4. Toward the end of the passage, Bohbot uses "if . . . then" construction (paragraph 8) in order to

(A) provide two possible explanations for the deterioration of the hippocampus

(B) offer two alternative methods for avoiding GPS use

(C) assert that brain health is promoted when the hippocampus is stimulated

(D) imply that Alzheimer's disease is a result of daily use of a GPS navigation system

(E) suggest that getting lost will help restore gray matter in the hippocampus

Question 5 is covered in Unit 1.

5. Which of the following best describes the writer's exigence in the passage?

(A) Consumers are not interested in investing in tech tools.

(B) The trend of using technology to make life easier is growing.

(C) Limited resources are available for the elderly who wish to live independently.

(D) Increasing evidence shows that people may experience long-term effects resulting from their reliance on technology.

(E) The disparity between the younger and older generations' use of technology is widening.

Question 6 is covered in Unit 5.

6. In the context of the passage, which of the following words or phrases refers to the same idea as the word *hippocampus*?

(A) "gray matter"

(B) "labyrinthine"

(C) "internal map"

(D) "neurogenesis"

(E) "topophilia"

Question 7 is covered in Unit 6.

7. According to the writer and the sources she cites, the two possible benefits of getting lost and navigating one's way without using digital satellite technology are most likely to be

(A) a personal connection with one's environment and cognitive function

(B) learning to think independently while developing a sense of autonomy

(C) reducing gray matter in the brain and providing physical exercise

(D) fostering a sense of imagination and improving creative problem-solving skills

(E) slowing down the aging process and memory loss while developing the intellect

Section I: Writing

Questions 8–14. Read the following passage carefully before you choose your answers. (The passage below on the role of technology is a draft.)

(1) Technology is everywhere we look, everywhere we go, and connected to everything that we do. (2) I use computers on a daily basis at school. (3) I get the news about what is happening in my community or in the world from notifications that come across my phone. (4) I am able to stay in contact with friends and family from other places because of technology.

(5) Technology's influence on our culture is becoming too strong. (6) Technology has allowed me to stay in touch with family and friends from all over; it has also weakened some of these relationships. (7) Often, text messages and posts online can be misinterpreted, which leads to additional conflict. (8) I see parents who resort to technology to communicate with their child or who don't know how to help their child manage technology, which can be dangerous for the child. (9) While technology has made research easier, it has resulted in more distracted students and students who have a harder time studying. (10) Also, their spelling and grammar has suffered since technology, Microsoft Word, fixes a lot of these mistakes for them. (11) Additionally, while technology has made transportation easier, it has also increased the amount of pollution and that hurts our environment.

(12) For each advantage that technology has offered us, there is an equally important disadvantage. (13) Technology should not be the panacea, but a tool to help facilitate growth and progress.

---

8. The writer wants to add more detail to offer additional commentary about the evidence introduced at the beginning of the paragraph:

For example, I think that I know what is going on in their lives because of what they post on social media.

Where would this sentence best be placed?

(A) After sentence 4

(B) After sentence 5

(C) Before sentence 7

(D) After sentence 7

(E) After sentence 8

9. Which of the following underlined revisions would best maintain the line of reasoning between sentences 8 and 9?

(A) (8) I see parents who resort to technology to communicate with their child or who don't know how to help their child manage technology, which can be dangerous for the child. (9) Furthermore, while technology in schools has made research easier, it has resulted in more distracted students and students who have a harder time studying.

(B) (8) I see parents who resort to technology to communicate with their child or who don't know how to help their child manage technology, which can be dangerous for the child. (9) For example, while technology has made research easier, it has resulted in more distracted students and students who have a harder time studying.

(C) (8) I see parents who resort to technology to communicate with their child or who don't know how to help their child manage technology which can be dangerous for the child. (9) This technology has resulted in more distracted students and students who have a harder time studying.

(D) (8) I see parents who resort to technology to communicate with their child or who don't know how to help their child manage technology, which can be dangerous for the child. (9) Even though technology has made research easier, it has resulted in more distracted students and students who have a harder time studying.

(E) (8) I see parents who resort to technology to communicate with their child or who don't know how to help their child manage technology, which can be dangerous for the child. (9) This has resulted in more distracted students and students who have a harder time studying.

10. The writer wants to include others' arguments to support his thesis. The author is considering adding the following research:

"Kids who are being put in front of screens are showing delayed development," said lead researcher Sheri Madigan, the research chair of child development with the University of Calgary's department of psychology.

Where would this sentence best be integrated into this paragraph to connect the evidence and the writer's claim?

(A) After sentence 5

(B) After sentence 7

(C) After sentence 8

(D) After sentence 10

(E) After sentence 12

11. Which of the following revisions best incorporates the words of the lead researcher, Sheri Madigan, from question 10?

(A) Sheri Madigan, the research chair of child development at the University of Calgary's department of psychology, argues that "kids who are being put in front of screens are showing delayed development."

(B) Sheri Madigan said, "Kids who are being put in front of screens are showing delayed development."

(C) A famous lead researcher who is the research chair of child development with the University of Calgary's department of psychology, in Canada, said that "kids who are being put in front of screens are showing delayed development."

(D) Sheri Madigan agrees that kids who are put in front of screens at young ages are delayed in their development.

(E) "Kids who are being put in front of screens are showing delayed development," said lead researcher Sheri Madigan, who published an article on WebMD in 2019.

12. Which of the following underlined revisions to the end of sentence 12 best confirms the writer's claim in this paragraph?

(A) (as it is now)

(B) For each advantage technology offered, there <u>are disadvantages and we as a society need to recognize these disadvantages and make adjustments accordingly</u>.

(C) For each advantage that technology has offered us, there is an equally important disadvantage <u>like technology being used too much in schools</u>.

(D) For each advantage that technology offers, there is a greater disadvantage <u>because technology is not a panacea, but only a tool that sometimes leads to progress</u>.

(E) For each advantage that technology has offered us, there is an equally important disadvantage <u>and the disadvantages are becoming greater and greater</u>.

Questions 13 and 14 are covered in Unit 5.

13. The writer wants an effective transition from the introductory part of the paragraph to the claim:

While technology has these great benefits, with such advantages come disadvantages.

Where would this sentence best be placed in order to achieve this purpose?

(A) Before sentence 1

(B) After sentence 4

(C) After sentence 5

(D) After sentence 11

(E) After sentence 13

14. Which of the following phrases best establishes a contrast at the beginning of sentence 6?

(A) Even though

(B) For example,

(C) In fact,

(D) Furthermore,

(E) Similarly,

JOIN THE CONVERSATION: RHETORICAL ANALYSIS (PART 2)

Before moving on to the rhetorical analysis prompt in the free-response portion of the unit review, spend more time on the practice prompt you started in Unit 2. The rhetorical analysis prompt for Unit 3 is much like the prompt in Unit 2. In the example based on Malala Yousafzai's speech in Unit 2 (see pages 53–55), the first part of the prompt (background) and the second part (description of task) are the same. The third part once again provides a checklist to make sure your response fulfills the requirements. The items are similar to those in Unit 2, but now you are expected to respond to the prompt with a *thesis*, not just a claim, and to show your awareness of the *rhetorical situation*. Everything the prompt asks you to do has been covered in Units 1–3.

The speech on pages 53–55 was delivered on "Malala Day"—July 12, 2013—by Malala Yousafzai, a girls' and children's education rights activist who survived an assassination attempt in 2012, when she was 15. She delivered this speech to the "Youth Take Over the UN" assembly, a campaign that stressed the importance of global education rights. This was the first speech she delivered since the assassination attempt.

Read the passage carefully. Write a paragraph that identifies some of the rhetorical choices Yousafzai makes and briefly explain how those choices convey her message that all children around the world deserve an equal education.

In your response you should do the following:

- Respond to the prompt with a thesis that analyzes the writer's rhetorical choices.
- Select and use evidence to develop and support your line of reasoning.
- Briefly explain how the evidence supports your line of reasoning.
- Demonstrate an understanding of the rhetorical situation.
- Use appropriate grammar and punctuation in communicating your argument.

The first time you tried the rhetorical analysis prompt, you were asked to write a claim. Now, for the **first bullet**, you are expected to develop a thesis. As with other kinds of arguments, you can develop a thesis by considering the broader contexts or universal ideas and significance of her speech:

> Malala Yousafzai uses appeals to ethos and her terrifying personal story to convey her message that all children around the world deserve an equal education and to illustrate the value of education to develop independent and self-sufficient people.

Even though the **second and third bullets** are the same as they were in Unit 2, you have developed more sophisticated abilities through the activities in this unit. Use what you learned about line of reasoning and methods of development to improve the draft you started in Unit 2.

The **fourth bullet** instructs you to demonstrate an understanding of the rhetorical situation. To do so, take into account the exigence, audience, context, message, and the speaker herself. These naturally connect to rhetorical choices, the focus of your analysis.

Return to the draft you started in Unit 2 and use the chart on the next page to help organize your evidence, reasoning, and commentary and "upgrade" your draft to demonstrate your new learning.

When you finish your draft, check it over to make sure you meet the requirements of each bullet point in the prompt. The **final bullet** reminds you to use appropriate grammar and punctuation, so double-check for possible grammatical and punctuation errors.

Save your completed draft for continued development in Unit 4.

Unit 3: Rhetorical Analysis (Part 2) Drafting Organizer
Thesis: Malala Yousafzai uses appeals to ethos and her terrifying personal story to convey her message that all children around the world deserve an equal education, and to illustrate the value of education to develop independent and self-sufficient people.
Choices the writer makes to convey the message Yousafzai's references to highly respected people uplift the message she is conveying, while at the same time she establishes solidarity with the audience with her inclusive language, such as "Dear brothers and sisters."
Explain how that evidence supports the reasoning that justifies that claim Yousafzai's appeals to ethos and inclusive language help emphasize certain points in her speech, especially because while she associates her own efforts with those of some of the most respected heroes of social reform, she simultaneously associates herself with her audience through inclusive language and in the process lifts up everyone. By inspiring solidarity she makes her audience receptive to her arguments.
Choices the writer makes to convey the message Her personal story of being attacked but recovering
Explain how that evidence supports the reasoning that justifies that claim Her personal story of being attacked but recovering and not allowing herself to be silenced helps her to convey her message by showing her commitment to her cause. This story appeals to the audience in a way that creates a trust in her as a speaker—she continues to literally risk her life for this cause. In doing so, Yousafzai brings the audience to empathize with her for a moment before they see the strength she continues to have despite the attempted assassination.
Draft of Paragraph

Apply

Follow the same process as above to respond to the rhetorical analysis prompt on page 184. For current free-response question samples, visit the College Board website.

JOIN THE CONVERSATION: THE ARGUMENT ESSAY (PART 3)

The argument prompt for Unit 3 is very similar to the prompt in Unit 2. In fact, the first two parts are identical. However, one seemingly small change in the third part (third bullet) actually requires a big change in how developed your essay must be. In Unit 2, the third bullet began with the word "Briefly." That word is gone now. You will be expected to *fully* explain how your evidence supports your line of reasoning. This list will now remain the same until the end of the course. You will also see it on the exam.

For decades, movies and music have included messages or labels to signal that they have material in them that some people may find troubling. Advocates for such things argue this is important to prevent people from being exposed to things they do not want to encounter. However, Erika Christakis, a lecturer at the Yale Child Study Center, says that "free speech and the ability to tolerate offense are the hallmarks of a free and open society."

Write an essay that argues your position on the use of warning labels or warning messages to signal potentially troubling content.

In your response you should do the following:

- Respond to the prompt with a thesis that presents a defensible position.
- Provide evidence to support your line of reasoning.
- Explain how the evidence supports your line of reasoning.
- Use appropriate grammar and punctuation in communicating your argument.

The prompt for Unit 3 focuses on the way you use evidence within your essay and how you develop the all-important line of reasoning. You have developed more sophisticated abilities through the activities in this unit, and you should demonstrate those in your response. For this reason, your response to the prompt should be a *multi-paragraph essay*, not just a single paragraph. Everything the prompt asks you to do has been covered in Units 1–3.

To fulfill the requirements of the **first bullet**, you will use what you have learned about how to develop a strong, defensible thesis. The **second and third bullets** require you to provide evidence to support your line of reasoning and to develop commentary that explains how the evidence you have thoughtfully and strategically selected supports the claim in your thesis. For example, using the movie ratings prompt from pages 48 and

197, you would need to go beyond simply saying that those ratings protect the vulnerable. Now you need to explain *how* they protect the vulnerable.

When you use evidence or examples, you are expected to genuinely integrate them into your argument, not simply drop them into the essay. Integrating evidence in a genuine way not only creates an appealing and easier-to-read style; it also helps to better connect the ideas from the evidence—and possibly others' ideas or even opposing viewpoints—to your own ideas.

As you develop multiple paragraphs with more examples and evidence, be sure to connect them to reflect a coherent line of reasoning, with no paragraph out of place. If you can move one paragraph to come before or after another without changing the meaning much, then those paragraphs are not thoughtfully enough connected within the line of reasoning in the essay. For example, simply mentioning movie ratings, cigarette labels, and potential trigger warnings on college courses may not immediately reveal how they all relate. However, when you see those in the context of the abstract idea in your drafted thesis ("Government and society should protect the most vulnerable"), then you can find the words and concepts to connect them. Each paragraph should connect back to that abstract idea and build on it so that the essay follows the reasoning of both the argument and the examples used to make it.

Return to the draft you worked on in Unit 2 and use the chart on the next page to help organize your evidence, reasoning, and commentary into a multi-paragraph essay.

When you finish your draft, check it over to make sure you meet the requirements of each bullet point in the prompt. The **final bullet** reminds you to use appropriate grammar and punctuation, so double-check for possible grammatical and punctuation errors.

Save your completed draft for continued development in Unit 4.

<table>
<tr><th colspan="4">Unit 3: Argument (Part 3) Multi-Paragraph Drafting Organizer</th></tr>
<tr><td></td><td colspan="2">Thesis:</td><td rowspan="13">Abstract Idea that runs throughout (What is it really about?)</td></tr>
<tr><td rowspan="4">Paragraph 1</td><td>Supporting Claim 1</td><td>Connection to abstract idea in thesis</td></tr>
<tr><td>Lead-in to evidence/example</td><td>Describe evidence/example</td></tr>
<tr><td colspan="2">Explain how that evidence/example supports the reasoning that justifies that claim and appeals to the audience.</td></tr>
<tr><td>How does it build and connect to the next paragraph?</td><td>Reconnect to abstract idea in thesis</td></tr>
<tr><td rowspan="4">Paragraph 2</td><td>Supporting Claim 2</td><td>Connection to abstract idea in thesis</td></tr>
<tr><td>Lead-in to evidence/example</td><td>Describe evidence/example</td></tr>
<tr><td colspan="2">Explain how that evidence/example supports the reasoning that justifies that claim and appeals to the audience.</td></tr>
<tr><td>How does it build upon or connect to previous paragraph?</td><td>Reconnect to abstract idea in thesis</td></tr>
<tr><td rowspan="4">Paragraph 3</td><td>Supporting Claim 3</td><td>Connection to abstract idea in thesis</td></tr>
<tr><td>Lead-in to evidence/example</td><td>Describe evidence/example</td></tr>
<tr><td colspan="2">Explain how that evidence/example supports the reasoning that justifies that claim and appeals to the audience.</td></tr>
<tr><td>How does it build upon or connect to previous paragraph?</td><td>Reconnect to abstract idea in thesis</td></tr>
<tr><td></td><td colspan="3">Multi-paragraph Draft</td></tr>
</table>

Apply

Follow the same process as above to respond to the argument prompt on page 184. For current free-response question samples, visit the College Board website.

Section II: Free Response

The first free-response question on the AP® exam is a synthesis task. For guided practice in writing a synthesis essay, see pages 364–373, 448–455, and 540–544. You will be provided synthesis prompts in the Units 6–9.

Rhetorical Analysis: "Ditch the GPS. It's Ruining Your Brain"

The second free-response question on the exam is a rhetorical analysis. For guided practice in writing rhetorical analysis, see pages 104–106, 178–180, 232–235, and 290–295.

In June of 2019, journalist M. R. O'Connor wrote an op-ed for the Washington Post. O'Connor usually writes about science, technology, and ethics. In this article, "Ditch the GPS. It's Ruining Your Brain," she reflects on the immediate and lasting effects of relying on a GPS device for navigating.

Read the passage on pages 169–171 carefully. Write an essay that analyzes the rhetorical choices O'Connor makes to convey her message about the negative effects of GPS.

In your response you should do the following:

- Respond to the prompt with a thesis that analyzes the writer's rhetorical choices.
- Select and use evidence to support your line of reasoning.
- Briefly explain how the evidence supports your line of reasoning.
- Demonstrate an understanding of the rhetorical situation.
- Use appropriate grammar and punctuation in communicating your argument.

Argument: The Role of Technology

The influx of technology has influenced much of our culture, from medical advancements to transportation to how we monitor finances to how we vote and find ourselves as members of a global community. How we choose and how we use technology is, perhaps, a reflection of our values.

Consider which tech tools play the biggest role in your life. Write an essay that argues your position on the extent to which the tech tools we use show our individual and cultural values.

In your response you should do the following:

- Respond to the prompt with a thesis that presents a defensible position.
- Provide evidence to support your line of reasoning.
- Explain how the evidence supports your line of reasoning.
- Use appropriate grammar and punctuation in communicating your argument.

UNIT 4

Structuring and Organizing Arguments

Part 1: Introductions and Conclusions
Part 2: Thesis and Structure
Part 3: Comparison, Contrast, Definition, and Description

ENDURING UNDERSTANDINGS AND SKILLS: Unit Four

Part 1 Introductions and Conclusions

Understand

Individuals write within a particular situation and make strategic writing choices based on that situation. (RHS-1)

Demonstrate

Identify and describe components of the rhetorical situation: the exigence, audience, writer, purpose, context, and message. (Reading 1.A)

Write introductions and conclusions appropriate to the purpose and context of the rhetorical situation. (Writing 2.A)

Part 2 Thesis and Structure

Understand

Writers make claims about subjects, rely on evidence that supports the reasoning that justifies the claim, and often acknowledge or respond to other, possibly opposing, arguments. (CLE-1)

Demonstrate

Identify and describe the overarching thesis of an argument, and any indication it provides of the argument's structure. (Reading 3.B)

Write a thesis statement that requires proof or defense and that may preview the structure of the argument. (Writing 4.B)

Part 3 Comparison, Contrast, Description, and Definition

Understand

Writers guide understanding of a text's lines of reasoning and claims through that text's organization and integration of evidence. (REO-1)

Demonstrate

Recognize and explain the use of methods of development to accomplish a purpose. (Reading 5.C)

Use appropriate methods of development to advance an argument. (Writing 6.C)

Source: *AP® English Language and Composition Course and Exam Description*

Unit 4 Overview

Jigsaw puzzles delight many people, from children who proudly complete their first six-piece puzzle to older teens and adults anticipating the final picture the puzzle reveals. The idea is simple: there is a picture on the puzzle box, and you have a number of pieces that need to be put together (or "pieced together") to create that picture. Almost always, puzzlers know what the picture is supposed to look like. They know where certain parts of the image go and try to follow that guide to complete the puzzle.

Source: Getty Images

Sometimes pictures represent metaphors or can be viewed metaphorically. The relationship of this picture to this unit overview may be clear, but what else could this picture represent?

Jigsaw puzzlers often begin by finding edge or corner pieces. With their easily identifiable straight edges, these pieces stand out of the jumble, helping the puzzler to create the "frame" of the puzzle that they then gradually fill in with the remaining pieces. In this way, the picture is framed and the other parts of the image slowly develop as they are discovered and fit together—piece by piece.

When you write an argument, you follow a similar process. You have developed a thesis and selected information that you are confident will support both your thinking and that thesis. In effect, you have framed your argument for the reader. Now you just have to fit the remaining pieces of your argument together to complete the picture for your reader.

The Importance of Structure In contrast to puzzlers, though, readers do not have a picture to see ahead of time to know what your argument will look like. Your reader expects you to put the pieces together in a way that makes the picture clear. The structure of an argument plays an important role in bringing the whole picture into focus. How well you introduce and preview the picture for your reader, organize the pieces, and help the reader finish the picture determines in part how effective your argument will be.

In this unit, you will examine choices writers make to engage an audience and address other aspects of the rhetorical situation early in an argument, to effectively organize the points they are making in the body of an argument, and to wrap up an argument so that it leaves a lasting effect.

Professional Text | Government Report GAO-10-702: *"Homelessness: A Common Vocabulary Could Help Agencies Collaborate and Collect More Consistent Data"*

Following is an excerpt from a report published in 2010 by the United States Government Accountability Office (GAO), a government agency that provides auditing, evaluation, and investigative services for the United States Congress. The anchor icon next to the heading tells you that this is a reading you will return to throughout this unit. In this passage, the writer explains the problems with multiple government agencies attempting to work on the problem of "homelessness" and offers suggestions for addressing some of those problems. For now, read it to understand the main or central ideas the report expresses as it contributes to the conversation about homelessness.

1 For many years, the federal government has attempted to determine the extent and nature of homelessness. As part of this effort, [the departments of] Education, Health and Human Services (HHS), and Housing and Urban Development (HUD) have systems in place that require service providers involved in the homelessness programs they administer to collect data on those experiencing homelessness and report these data in various ways to the agencies. However, while the data currently being collected and reported can provide some useful information on those experiencing homelessness, because of difficulties in counting this transient population and changes in methodologies over time, they are not adequate for fully understanding the extent and nature of homelessness. In addition, the data do not track family composition well or contribute to an understanding of how family formation and dissolution relate to homelessness. Further, because of serious shortcomings and methodologies that change over time, the biennial[1] point-in-time counts have not adequately tracked changes in homelessness over time. While these data systems have improved, it still is difficult for agencies to use them to understand the full extent and nature of homelessness, and addressing their shortcomings could be costly. For example, one shortcoming of HUD's point-in-time count is that it relies on volunteer enumerators[2] who may lack experience with the population, but training and utilizing professionals would be very costly.

2 In part because of data limitations, researchers have collected data on narrowly defined samples that may not be useful for understanding homelessness more generally or do not often consider structural factors, such as area poverty rates, which may be important in explaining the prevalence and causes of homelessness. In addition, because complete and accurate data that track individuals and families over time do not exist, researchers generally have not been able to explain why certain people experience homelessness and others do not, and why some are homeless for a single, short period and others have multiple episodes of homelessness or remain homeless for a long time.

---

1 **biennial:** taking place every other year
2 **enumerators:** workers employed to count people, as in a census

3 However, those who have experienced or might experience homelessness frequently come in contact with mainstream programs that are collecting data about the recipients of their services. While homelessness is not the primary focus of these programs, if they routinely collected more detailed and accurate data on housing status, agencies and service providers could better assess the needs of program recipients and could use these data to help improve the government's understanding of the extent and nature of homelessness. This would allow for comparison of the experiences of those being served by those programs based upon their status as homeless or not. Researchers also could potentially use these data to better define the factors associated with becoming homeless or to better understand the path of homelessness over time. Collecting these data in existing or new systems might not be easy, and agencies would incur costs in developing questions and providing incentives for accurate data to be collected. Collecting such data may be easier for those programs that already collect some housing data on individuals, families, and youths who use the programs and report those data on an individual or aggregate basis to a federal agency, such as HHS's Substance Abuse Treatment and Prevention Block Grant program or Head Start. For those mainstream programs that do not currently report such data, collecting it may be a state or local responsibility, and the willingness of states to collect the data may vary across locations. For example, HHS has reported that about half of the states that do collect homelessness data do not consider it burdensome to do so through their TANF[3] and Medicaid[4] applications, and would be willing to provide data extracts to HHS for research purposes. States or localities and researchers could find these data useful even if they are not collected on a federal or national level. However, concerns exist about resource constraints and data reliability. Therefore, the benefits of collecting data on housing status for various programs would need to be weighed against the costs.

4 Federal efforts to determine the extent and nature of homelessness and develop effective programs to address homelessness have been hindered by the lack of a common vocabulary. For programs to collect additional data on housing status or homelessness or make the best use of that data to better understand the nature of homelessness, agencies would need to agree on a common vocabulary and terminology for these data. Not only would this common vocabulary allow agencies to collect consistent data that agencies or researchers could compile to better understand the nature of homelessness, it also would allow agencies to communicate and collaborate more effectively. As identified in 2011 budget proposals, [the departments of] Education, HHS, and HUD are the key agencies that would need to collaborate to address homelessness, but other agencies that also belong to the Interagency Council—a venue for federal collaborative efforts—such as Department

3 **TANF:** Temporary Assistance for Needy Families, a government program that assists families with children when the parents or other responsible relatives cannot provide for the family's basic needs

4 **Medicaid:** the U. S. public health insurance program that provides health care coverage to low-income families or individuals

of Labor and Department of Justice might need to be involved as well. However, agency staff may find it difficult to communicate at a federal or local level when they have been using the same terms to mean different things. For example, agencies might want to avoid using the term *homelessness* itself because of its multiple meanings or the stigma attached to it. Instead, they might want to list a set of housing situations explicitly. The agencies could begin to consider this as part of the proceedings Congress has mandated that the Interagency Council convene after this report is issued. Once agencies have developed a common vocabulary, they might be able to develop a common understanding of how to target services to those who are most in need and for whom services will be most effective. In addition, with a common vocabulary, local communities could more easily develop cohesive plans to address the housing needs of their communities.

Composing on Your Own

After you read, respond to those ideas by writing your own thoughts on homelessness. What experiences have you had with people who are homeless or people who work to provide assistance to the homeless? Use freewriting and brainstorming to record your thoughts. You will be developing these ideas throughout the unit, so save your work for future use.

Evaluating Writing: Student Draft | *Homelessness*

Following is the student anchor text you will use in this unit to practice evaluating and editing writing. A student wrote it for the Opinion section of a local newspaper that invited graduating seniors to write short essays on the theme of "Freedom of Choice." This draft still needs work. As you read it, think about what it contributes to the conversation on homelessness and compare it to the ideas you wrote down. Later you will have an opportunity to suggest ways the writing might be improved.

(1) Though the number of homeless Americans has declined slightly over the last decade, the National Alliance to End Homelessness still reports that more than half a million Americans remain homeless. (2) People must be careful not to jump to such hasty conclusions. (3) When asked what the most common misconception is about people experiencing homelessness, Mental Health Center of Denver, Colorado supportive housing provider Takisha Keesee knew her answer right away: "That they want to be homeless."

(4) Sadly, most people disregard homelessness as a choice made by the homeless person. (5) As with most assumptions, looking more closely at details related to homelessness reveals that there are more complicated and complex causes to these problems than most people expect and that many homeless are not, in fact, choosing to be homeless.

(6) According to the National Center on Family Homelessness, among industrialized nations, there are more homeless women and children in

the United States than any other country in the world. (7) Rarely is it the case that these women are choosing to be homeless while caring for their children. (8) In fact, many of these women report that leaving their homes was actually a way of caring for their children. (9) These mothers have been forced from their homes as a way to protect themselves and their children from abusive partners. (10) In these ways, leaving the home was not really a "choice," as the mothers really had no other option.

(11) In some cities, even those with jobs are forced into situations of homelessness. (12) A 2019 study conducted by the National Low-Income Housing Coalition showed that an individual making minimum wage in an average city like Cincinnati, Ohio would need to work 78 hours per week to afford a two-bedroom rental home. (13) That's eleven hours a day, every day, which probably means two jobs. (14) Just a quick look at these numbers makes clear the effect that high housing prices can have and the significant stress placed on low-wage workers to keep a roof over their head—homelessness is literally one paycheck away.

(15) Until more is done to educate the public on the causes and possible solutions for homelessness, people will continue to denigrate homeless people as irresponsible and poor decision makers who are choosing to live how they live.

What Do You Know?

This unit will explore the structural and organizational choices writers make to present the best case for their arguments. Before moving on, take stock of what you already know about these concepts by answering questions about the anchor text and student draft on homelessness. Assessing what you already know about a topic you are about to study helps provide a framework for new learning.

CLOSE READING: PROFESSIONAL TEXT

1. What is the purpose of the first two paragraphs of the government report on homelessness?

2. What two concrete recommendations does the report make?

EVALUATING WRITING: STUDENT DRAFT

1. What is one strategy the student writer uses to engage the audience early in the essay?

2. In paragraphs three and four, what strategy does the writer use to support the argument?

3. In the last paragraph, what revisions might help call the audience to act, suggest a change in behavior or attitude, or propose a solution?

Part 1

Introductions and Conclusions

Enduring Understanding and Skills

Part 1

Understand

Individuals write within a particular situation and make strategic writing choices based on that situation. (RHS-1)

Demonstrate

Identify and describe components of the rhetorical situation: the exigence, audience, writer, purpose, context, and message. (Reading 1.A)

Write introductions and conclusions appropriate to the purpose and context of the rhetorical situation. (Writing 2.A)

Source: *AP® English Language and Composition Course and Exam Description*

Essential Question: How does a writer address the purpose and context of the rhetorical situation in an introduction and conclusion of an essay?

Recall the metaphorical parlor (Unit 1) where conversations on a variety of topics have been ongoing for centuries. You yourself have participated in some of those conversations and have developed positions of your own. Suppose that before sharing your ideas and positions with people outside the parlor, you extend an invitation to others to enter the parlor and meet some of the voices and ideas who have shaped the conversation and your views on a topic. By the time your guests leave the parlor, they have a grounding in your topic and their minds are open to hearing your views.

Introductions in essays and other texts serve the same purpose as these invitations. They metaphorically walk readers around the parlor and lay out the scope of the topic. They also point the way to what you will focus on in your essay. Some introductions explicitly lay out a main claim, or thesis, that the rest of the essay will support and defend. However, as you may remember from Unit 2, some introductions include aspects of the main claim, but the essay as a whole gradually builds the argument throughout the writing. Instead of laying out an immediate claim, these introductions may begin with a question or a narrative—commonly called a "hook"—that helps interest the reader in the subject.

Either way, your introduction gets the audience in the parlor. Then you can begin to logically develop and support your ideas by using all the rhetorical strategies at your disposal, including references to ongoing conversations on the subject.

At the end of your essay, after making your case persuasively, you look for a way to distinguish your voice from all the others participating in the conversations as you take leave of your audience. A strong conclusion provides the opportunity to leave an impression, highlight key points, and even call for action from the audience.

In argumentative essays, introductions and conclusions frequently rely on one another and make the essay come full circle. Often a conclusion links back to the introduction and an introduction suggests the conclusion. These connections convey completeness and finality to the argument and often help the audience understand and appreciate the argument in full. However, no essay can ever be complete in itself since each is always part of larger, ongoing conversation.

KEY TERMS

- audience
- context
- conclusion
- introduction
- purpose

1.1 Introductions | RHS-1.I

Like every part of an essay, the **introduction** of an argument plays a distinct role. It's the readers' first impression of the writer and an introduction to the subject, and it often includes the thesis. Frequently, the introduction invites the audience to join the writer in a conversation. Depending on the audience and **context**, the writer may loop readers in by presenting quotations, intriguing statements, anecdotes, questions, statistics, data, contextualized information, or a scenario. For example, if a speaker is at City Hall arguing for a specific proposal, he or she might immediately introduce a clear thesis that includes statistics and expert opinions. But if a speaker is giving an informal speech to a group that has shared interests, he or she may use an interesting and amusing anecdote as an introduction. Introductions are well-crafted ways of saying "this is what I am going to talk about and this is why you should be interested in it," though never in those words. Throughout an essay, writers can add perspectives and support that may expand on the introduction, but the introduction still serves as an entry point that situates the reader and presents the subject matter.

Addressing the Rhetorical Situation

An effective introduction usually takes into account key aspects of the rhetorical situation. The following chart shows questions to ask yourself about how to address each element.

Element of Rhetorical Situation	A Writer Asks: How Can an Introduction Address That Element?
Audience	Who is my audience (consider age, gender, needs, values)? How can I engage the audience by making the subject interesting? What does my audience understand or not understand about the subject? What position (if any) does my audience already have on the subject?
Writer	How can I reveal something about myself as a writer to develop trust and give the reader a reason to accept what is coming?
Message	How can I preview my specific position and defensible claim?
Purpose	How can I reveal or preview the purpose of the essay? What do I want my audience to do or think about the subject? Which emotions do I want my audience to feel when considering this subject?
Exigence	How can I explain or suggest what motivated me to write?
Context	How can I provide background the audience may need to know to understand the world of the argument?

Table 4-1

Consider, for example, the first few paragraphs of this unit on page 186. They address the elements of the rhetorical situation in the following ways:

- **Audience**—The jigsaw example gets readers thinking about the purpose of an introduction and provides an image for the reader to consider.
- **Writer**—The tone is straightforward and communicates an eagerness to help readers understand.
- **Message**—This introduction narrows the focus from writing in general to the structure of writing and its importance.
- **Purpose**—The purpose of examining structure is explicitly stated.
- **Exigence**—The writer wants the audience to avoid the problems caused by the lack of a cohesive structure or strong introduction and conclusion.
- **Context**—The writer relates structure and introductions and conclusions to the other parts of arguments (thesis and evidence) that have been covered in earlier units.

Orienting, Focusing, and Engaging an Audience

How well an introduction engages the intended **audience** can determine the readers' response to your argument. Look at the chart below, which offers suggestions that may help you orient, focus, and engage an audience. Which of the suggested strategies and openings would make you most interested in reading on? What do they suggest about the direction the essay might take? Based on your own discussions and reading, you may also be familiar with other ways of effectively engaging an audience.

Suggested Ways to Orient, Focus, and Engage an Audience	
What You Can Convey	**Examples**
Interesting example	To some people, the word *homeless* brings certain images to mind—beggars on street corners, people sleeping under cardboard shelters, alcohol and drug abuse. But for people in the Skid Row neighborhood of Los Angeles, another image comes to mind: the Skid Row Running Club. Founded by a judge (and runner) who mediated cases between the Los Angeles Police Department and the homeless community in Skid Row, the club uses the discipline, camaraderie, and exhilaration of participating in running events to help people regain control over their lives, especially those battling addiction.
Quotation	"Today's society is wanting in such a way that Honor, Integrity, Trust, Compassion, Empathy are left for the homeless and their pets." With these words, Solange Nicole, a Latina influencer and founder of a line of beauty products committed to humane treatment of animals, raises important questions about the values of mainstream culture.
Intriguing statement	Many observers think of people who live on the street as "the other," people who are very different from themselves. In fact, many homeless people may have had similar thoughts—maybe even as recently as a few weeks ago—before they were suddenly laid off, or evicted because medical debt made them unable to pay rent, or kicked out of a family home because of an addiction to pain pills originally prescribed for a broken ankle.
Anecdote	Keith had been living on the streets for three months. Although I didn't know his name then, I would pass him on my way to the red line station at Wilson Avenue in Chicago almost every day. He sat against a weather-stained brick wall, baseball cap upside down in front of him, hoping people would fill it with money so he could eat that day. I always gave him a dollar. For a few days, I didn't see him and started to worry. But he was soon back at a corner near where he used to sit. Now, though, he was standing. He was selling *Streetwise*, a weekly publication that helps put homeless people to work as writers, artists, and vendors. That's when I began talking to Keith, learning his name and his story. As a vendor of *Streetwise* he was now employed—he bought the issues he sold for $.90 and sold them for $2.00, keeping the profit.
Questions	What do you do when you come across apparently homeless persons begging for money? Do you give them money even if you think they might use it to buy alcohol or drugs? Do you give them the name and location of an agency that could help them find housing or shelter them temporarily? Do you walk by as if you didn't see them?

(continued)

Suggested Ways to Orient, Focus, and Engage an Audience	
What You Can Convey	**Examples**
Statistics or data	According to the National Center on Family Homelessness, "a staggering 2.5 million children are now homeless each year in America. This historic high represents one in every 30 children in the United States."
Contextualized information	Advocates for homeless people take as good news the decline in homelessness in 29 states from its high in 2010. Yet for the third straight year, in 2019 the homeless rate rose again. The steady decreases over the years since 2010 were offset by a 22.5% increase in homelessness in California, where housing prices are astronomically high.
Scenario	Picture a printer that stands 11 feet high and 28 feet wide. Picture 4–6 workers, tablets in hand, controlling the actions of the printer with a touch on the screen. Now fast forward, but not very far, to 27 hours ahead. In that time, the printer will have produced the foundation and walls for a "tiny house," leaving the remaining items like roofing and siding for carpenters. The end result is a promising solution to homelessness—a complete house for about $10,000 start to finish that can be made available through a variety of funding options to people who would otherwise be homeless.

Table 4-2

Remember: The introduction of an argument introduces the subject and/or writer of the argument to the audience. An introduction may present the argument's thesis. An introduction may orient, engage, and/or focus the audience by presenting quotations, intriguing statements, anecdotes, questions, statistics, data, contextualized information, or a scenario. (RHS-1.I)

1.1 Checkpoint

Close Reading: Professional Text

Review the anchor text on pages 187–189. Then complete the open response activity and answer the multiple-choice questions.

1. Reread the first paragraph of the anchor text (page 187). On separate paper, recreate the frame of Table 4-1 to show how the introduction addresses elements of the rhetorical situation. Show how the text answers the questions in column 2 of the table by using quotes from the anchor text. Some elements in the table may not be included in the anchor text.

2. Which of the following statements from the introduction (paragraph 1) best serves to introduce the reader to the argument of the passage?
   (A) "…the federal government has attempted to determine the extent and nature of homelessness." (sentence 1)
   (B) "…Education, Health and Human Services (HHS), and Housing and Urban Development (HUD) have systems in place that require service providers involved in the homelessness programs they administer to collect data…." (sentence 2)
   (C) "…while the data currently being collected and reported can provide some useful information on those experiencing homelessness, because of difficulties in counting this transient population and changes in methodologies over time, they are not adequate for fully understanding the extent and nature of homelessness." (sentence 3)
   (D) "Further, because of serious shortcomings and methodologies that change over time, the biennial point-in-time counts have not adequately tracked changes…." (sentence 5)
   (E) "…one shortcoming of HUD's point-in-time count is that it relies on volunteer enumerators…." (sentence 7)

3. Which of the following statements describes the function of the third sentence in the passage's introductory paragraph?
   (A) It appeals to the reader's sense of sympathy for the plight of homeless people.
   (B) It creates a cause-effect line of reasoning for the author's argument.
   (C) It establishes a sense of the author's credibility to speak on the sensitive issue of homelessness.
   (D) It introduces readers to the author's central concern in the passage as a whole.
   (E) It discusses further challenges regarding the difficulties of collecting accurate data on homeless people.

Evaluating Writing: Student Draft

Reread the student draft on pages 189–190. Then answer the following open response and multiple-choice questions.

1. What revisions might you make to the first paragraph to better address the audience, purpose, and context?

2. The writer wants to add a sentence before sentence 2 to provide a transition and suggest the purpose of the passage. Which of the following sentences accomplishes that goal?
   (A) With this many homeless, some people easily make simplistic assumptions about the causes of homelessness: drug/alcohol abuse, mental illness, ignorance, laziness, or even choice.
   (B) Usually, people just assume that the homeless simply don't want jobs or that they are unmotivated to try to find work.
   (C) Clearly, homelessness continues to be an issue that government agencies are largely ignoring.
   (D) Although many people assume homelessness is getting better, the numbers tell a different story.
   (E) Without a doubt, extensive job training and educational opportunities would help alleviate the issue of homelessness and give hope to the many homeless people who want to improve their circumstances.

Composing on Your Own

As you have read, the elements of the rhetorical situation greatly influence the choices a writer makes. Take time now to choose or create a rhetorical situation. Choose or adapt any of the following contexts, audiences, and purposes or create your own. (You can always choose the rhetorical situation you are actually in: context—class assignment; audience—teacher; purpose—to learn about and demonstrate your understanding of introductions.) Write down the choices you make. Then review the writing you did after you read the GAO report. Identify a main idea to develop and try out a few different ways you might introduce it. Choose three different introduction strategies from Table 4-2 on pages 194–195 and draft an introductory sentence or two for each one of those ways. Save your work for future use.

Contexts/Formats
▪ Debate ▪ Opinion piece on YouTube ▪ Meeting of task force on community issues
Audiences
▪ Students and teachers ▪ General public ▪ People you disagree with
Purposes
▪ Convince audience of your position on homelessness ▪ Encourage people to become more active in responding to serious social issues ▪ Propose solutions to problems facing homeless families

1.2 Conclusions | RHS-1.J

The **conclusion** of an argument often ties together the writer's main claims, providing a sense of closure or completeness. Frequently, it reiterates key ideas from the argument's thesis while also engaging the audience in a variety of ways. These include explaining the significance of the argument within a broader context, making connections, calling the audience to act, suggesting a change in behavior or attitude, or proposing a solution. The conclusion may also leave the audience with a compelling image, explain implications, summarize the argument, or connect to the introduction. The conclusion may end the essay by unifying the writer's ideas, but it does not necessarily end the argument, because it may provide additional ideas or questions for the audience to consider. In some respects, a good conclusion could form the thesis for an additional essay, because it invites the audience to continue participating in an ongoing conversation.

The Goals of Conclusions

Effective conclusions fulfill key goals. They bring the argument full circle by connecting to the introduction. Often, a conclusion brings an argument to an end by advancing the writer's purposes, addressing the audience's needs, and logically unifying the argument. In addition, a conclusion may offer a compelling idea that leaves the reader with something to think about.

Consider the following introduction and conclusion from an essay titled "Living Like Weasels" by Pulitzer Prize-winning writer Annie Dillard, who became widely known when she published a collection of nonfiction essays, *Pilgrim at Tinker Creek*, which detailed her experiences living in a cabin in the woods. In her essays focusing on the natural world, Dillard often explores how the restorative and destructive aspects of nature are intertwined. When reading her essay, you will notice some words in italic type and some phrases underlined. These serve as connectors between the introduction and the conclusion.

> **[Introduction]**
>
> A weasel is wild. Who knows what he thinks? He sleeps in his underground den, his tail draped over his nose. Sometimes he lives in his den for two days without leaving. Outside, he stalks rabbits, mice, muskrats, and birds, killing more bodies than he can eat warm, and often dragging the carcasses home. ***Obedient*** to instinct, he bites his prey at the neck, either splitting the jugular vein at the throat or crunching the brain at the base of the skull, and <u>he does not let go</u>. One naturalist refused to kill a weasel who was socketed into his hand deeply as a rattlesnake. The man could in no way pry the tiny weasel off and he had to walk half a mile to water, the weasel ***dangling*** from his palm, and soak him off like a stubborn label.

> And once, says Ernest Thompson Seton—once, a man shot an eagle out of the sky. He examined the ***eagle*** and found the dry skull of a weasel fixed by the jaws to his throat. The supposition is that the ***eagle*** had pounced on the weasel and the weasel swiveled and bit as instinct taught him, tooth to neck, and nearly won. I would like to have seen that eagle from the air a few weeks or months before he was shot: was the whole weasel still attached to his feathered throat, a fur pendant? Or did the ***eagle*** eat what he could reach, gutting the living weasel with his talons before his breast, bending his beak, cleaning the beautiful airborne bones?

In the essay that follows this introduction, Dillard creates an extended comparison between weasels that live wild and by instinct and humans who live by choices. Ultimately, she says she "would like to live as [she] should, as the weasel lives as he should," wild and by instinct, without constraints of society. She moves easily from this comparison into a conclusion about grasping life and living it wildly.

> **[Conclusion]**
> I think it would be well, and proper, and ***obedient,*** and pure, to grasp your one necessity and not let it go, to ***dangle*** from it limp wherever it takes you. Then even death, where you're going no matter how you live, cannot you part. Seize it and let it seize you up aloft even, till your eyes burn out and drop; let your musky flesh fall off in shreds, and let your very bones unhinge and scatter, loosened over fields, over fields and woods, lightly, thoughtless, from any height at all, from as high as ***eagles***.

Take another look at the italicized words and underlined phrases that directly connect the conclusion to the introduction. Repeating or echoing words, phrases, and ideas is a good way to unify an essay.

Also notice that the word "weasel" does not appear in the conclusion. Instead, Dillard expands to more universal ideas, talking directly to the reader with the pronoun "you," illustrating that the reader should be more like the weasel—never giving up. An essay that begins with discussion of the viscous stubbornness of weasels becomes a call for the reader to live life with that same stubbornness. In this way, Dillard fulfills key goals of a conclusion: she brings the argument full circle by connecting to the introduction and makes the argument matter by connecting to something beyond the essay itself. Dillard doesn't simply repeat her introduction about the tenacity of weasels but instead leaves the reader something to think about, encouraging the reader to consider how human behavior is a balance between raw instinct and personal choice.

Like introductions, conclusions may address the rhetorical situation by

- leaving a lasting impression on the *audience*
- solidifying the credibility of the *writer*
- driving home the *message*
- showing the fulfillment of the writer's *purpose*

- clarifying the *exigence*
- broadening the *context* to beyond the essay

The chart below shows some useful strategies for writing a conclusion and gives examples of how Dillard uses some of them and not others.

Effective conclusions . . .	Dillard's conclusion . . .
Explain the significance of the argument within a broader context	Although she does not state the significance explicitly, Dillard implies that there are life lessons for humans in the stubbornness of the weasel.
Make connections to something beyond the essay	Dillard reaches to the something beyond the essay when she takes on the thought of death—the reality that colors so many human choices.
Call the audience to act	Dillard calls on the audience to "grasp [their] one necessity and not let it go" so they will really live the life that they want without giving up too easily.
Suggest a change in behavior or attitude	In a way similar to her call of action, Dillard makes the suggestion that people should see life as something they can take hold of and not let go.
Propose a solution	Dillard's writing is poetic rather than practical. She is addressing a way of approaching life, not trying to solve a problem like homelessness.
Leave the audience with a compelling image	The image of the weasel's grasping the eagle (from the introduction) and not letting go, even after the "flesh falls off in shreds" leaves a powerful picture in the reader's mind on the value of tenacity even in the face of mortal danger.
Explain implications	Dillard lets her vivid language speak for her, avoiding over-explanation, while essayists on other topics may choose not to. They might want direct commentary on the effects or implications of their arguments.
Summarize the argument	Though it should not ever be the only purpose of a conclusion, a summary can help readers remember and process a complex line of reasoning. Dillard's essay would in fact be weakened by a summary since she is tapping as much into the emotional as the rational side of thinking.
Connect to the introduction	Through shared images and words, Dillard echoes and connects directly back to the introduction. More than that, however, she has moved the ideas from the introduction forward—they now mean more than they did at the beginning of the essay as a result of her developing ideas and extending them beyond the essay.

Table 4-3

Remember: The conclusion of an argument brings the argument to a unified end. A conclusion may present the argument's thesis. It may engage and/or focus the audience by explaining the significance of the argument within a broader context, making connections, calling the audience to act, suggesting a change in behavior or attitude, proposing a solution, leaving the audience with a compelling image, explaining implications, summarizing the argument, or connecting to the introduction. (RHS-1.J)

1.2 Checkpoint

Close Reading: Professional Text

Reread the last paragraph of the anchor text (page 189). Then answer the open response and multiple-choice questions.

1. Recreate Table 4-3 on the previous page, completing the second column with details from the anchor text. If a concluding technique is not included, add a brief explanation of why the author may have chosen not to use it. When you are finished, write a summary of the conclusion using your own words, and explain whether you found the conclusion convincing.

2. Which of the following statements best describes the purpose of the next to last sentence in the passage ("Once agencies . . . be most effective," paragraph 4, sentence 9)?

   (A) It represents the author's core suggestion in addressing the problem of homelessness.

   (B) It expresses the author's frustration about a lack of coordination among agencies collecting data on homelessness.

   (C) It acts as the author's final appeal to the reader's sense of sympathy for the homeless.

   (D) It criticizes governmental agencies that lack the will to track data about homelessness.

   (E) It illustrates how difficult it will be to find new ways to collect data on homelessness.

Evaluating Writing: Student Draft

Reread the student draft on pages 189–190. Then answer the following open response and multiple-choice questions.

1. What revisions might you make to the last paragraph to improve the conclusion? In particular, consider whether the author addresses the needs of the audience by proposing workable solutions.

2. Which of the following sentences, if added to the end of the last paragraph, would best connect the conclusion to the introduction?
    (A) In fact, both homeless people and the public in general need better education on how to overcome the problems of homelessness.
    (B) Most people are shocked to hear of the number of homeless people who are school-aged children.
    (C) It's only a problem with lack of job training, and politicians with plans to get more people to work will be the final cure for homelessness in America.
    (D) These people need to realize that it is, in fact, uncontrollable mental-health issues that cause most people to be homeless in the first place.
    (E) It is not a voluntary choice to be homeless, though being homeless may be the result of difficult choices in difficult situations.

Composing on Your Own

Return to the writing you did on the subject of homelessness based on the GAO report. After reviewing the introductions you wrote, use three strategies from Table 4–3 on page 200 to draft three brief conclusions. In one of your conclusions, you may use a strategy that you devised on your own. When writing your conclusions, be sure to logically connect with your introduction and keep the rhetorical situation in mind, including your audience, context, and purpose. Save your work for later use.

Part 1 Apply What You Have Learned

The year 2019 marked the 50th anniversary of the Apollo moon landing, and a number of books were published evaluating the impact of that iconic event. Jill Lepore, Harvard professor, staff writer at *The New Yorker*, and author of many books, reviewed a number of the books released in that anniversary year in an essay in the *New York Times* (June 14, 2019) titled "Fifty Years Ago We Landed on the Moon. Why Should We Care Now?"

Following are both the introduction and conclusion of that essay. Read the passages carefully. Then write an essay that analyzes the rhetorical choices Lepore uses to achieve the purposes of engaging her audience and unifying the introduction and conclusion.

[Introduction]

The footprints are still there, the striped tread of Neil Armstrong's boots, caked into dust. There's no atmosphere on the moon, no wind and no water. Footprints don't blow away and they don't wash away and there's no one up there to trample them. Superfast micrometeorites, miniature particles traveling at 33,000 miles per hour, are bombarding the surface of the moon all the time, but they're so infinitesimal that they erode things only at the more or less unobservable rate of 0.04 inches every million years. So unless those footprints are hit by a meteor and blasted into a crater, they'll last for tens of millions of years.

This summer marks half a century since Armstrong first walked on the moon, though cosmologically, that was a mere snap of the fingers ago. "Man on the moon!" cried Walter Cronkite on CBS television news, gasping, while the world watched, rapt. Kids away at summer camp were marched from their tents deep in the woods to mess halls to plop down in front of a little screen, while camp counselors tinkered with rabbit-ear antennas. "That's one small step for man," Armstrong said, immortally, as he stepped off the ladder of the Lunar Module on July 20, 1969, "one giant leap for mankind." And then Armstrong pressed his gray-and-white boot into the dust, and left that first trace.

But what really lasts from that moment? What was the mission for? And what did it leave behind, here on Earth? Fifty years later, floods made more frequent by the changing of the climate have begun to wash away the Kennedy Space Center in Florida, from which Apollo 11 was launched (NASA has been shipping in sand to try to shore up devastated dunes), and hurricanes worsened by the rising of the seas threaten the site of Apollo 11's mission control, the Johnson Space Center in Texas. Houston, we have a problem.

[Conclusion]

One small step for man, one giant leap for mankind. The lasting legacy of the voyage to the moon lies in the wonder of discovery, the joy of knowledge, not the gee-whizzery of machinery but the wisdom of beauty and the power of humility. A single photograph, the photograph of Earth taken from space by William Anders, on Apollo 8, in 1968, served as an icon for the entire environmental movement. People who've seen the Earth from space, not in a photograph but in real life, pretty much all report the same thing. "You spend even a little time contemplating the Earth from orbit and the most deeply ingrained nationalisms begin to erode," Carl Sagan once described the phenomenon. "They seem the squabbles of mites on a plum." This experience, this feeling of transcendence, is so universal, among the tiny handful of people who have ever felt it, that scientists have a term for it. It's called the Overview Effect. You get a sense of the whole. Rivers look like blood. "The Earth is like a vibrant living thing," the Chinese astronaut Yang Liu thought, when he saw it. It took Alan Shepard by surprise. "If somebody'd said before the flight, 'Are you going to get carried away looking at the Earth from the moon?' I would have said, 'No, no way.' But yet when I first looked back at the Earth, standing on the moon, I cried." The Russian astronaut Yuri Artyushkin put it this way: "It isn't important in which sea or lake you observe a slick of pollution or in the forests of which country a fire breaks out, or on which continent a hurricane arises. You are standing guard over the whole of our Earth."

That's beautiful. But here's the hitch. It's been 50 years. The waters are rising. The Earth needs guarding, and not only by people who've seen it from space. Saving the planet requires not racing to the moon again, or to Mars, but to the White House and up the steps of the Capitol, putting one foot in front of the other.

Source: NASA

Astronaut Edwin "Buzz" Aldrin took this photograph of Commander Neal Armstrong's footprint on the moon to study the nature of lunar dust. It has become a symbol for Apollo 11, the mission that landed the first humans on the moon on July 21, 1969.

Reflect on the Essential Question: Write a brief response that answers this essential question: *How does a writer address the elements of the rhetorical situation in the introduction and conclusion of an essay?* In your answer, correctly use the key terms listed on page 192.

Part 2

Thesis and Structure

Enduring Understanding and Skills

Part 2

Understand

Writers make claims about subjects, rely on evidence that supports the reasoning that justifies the claim, and often acknowledge or respond to other, possibly opposing, arguments. (CLE-1)

Demonstrate

Identify and describe the overarching thesis of an argument, and any indication it provides of the argument's structure. (Reading 3.B)

Write a thesis statement that requires proof or defense and that may preview the structure of the argument. (Writing 4.B)

(See also Unit 2)

Source: *AP® English Language and Composition Course and Exam Description*

Essential Question: How might a thesis statement preview a line of reasoning?

The lights dim and the audience settles down, but the feature film does not yet begin. Instead, in two-and-a-half-minute "mini-movies," previews for upcoming movies fill the screen and try to entice you to come back and see the movies when they are released. The first part of the preview lays out the premise of the movie, the second hints at the problems that develop as the plot unfolds, and the third usually sets up an emotional "grab" using music and striking images from the movie. In those few minutes, the preview has given you a good idea of what to expect from the movie and, if successful, has raised your interest.

Movie previews are the product of sophisticated marketing techniques designed to manipulate consumers, and they exist in a commercial world very different from the world of academic writing. Yet certain strategies are effective in communicating wherever they are used. Thesis statements, like movie previews, present the premise of the argument, suggest the line of reasoning and structure the argument may follow, and attempt to grab readers with a provocative edge to their position. Part 2 will explore the way the thesis statement in an essay may preview an argument's line of reasoning.

KEY TERMS

structure	thesis
line of reasoning	thesis statement

2.1 Thesis Statement and Line of Reasoning | CLE-1.O

While not every argument may have a direct statement of the **thesis**—or **thesis statement**—those that do sometimes suggest a **structure** the essay will follow. However, thesis statements come in many varieties. Not all of them the list points of an argument, ideas to be analyzed, and specific evidence.

Developing an Overarching Thesis Statement

As you read in Units 2 and 3, a thesis statement is an overarching claim a writer attempts to defend through evidence and commentary. All the points within the essay serve to support that overarching claim. You might visualize a simplified thesis statement in the following figure.

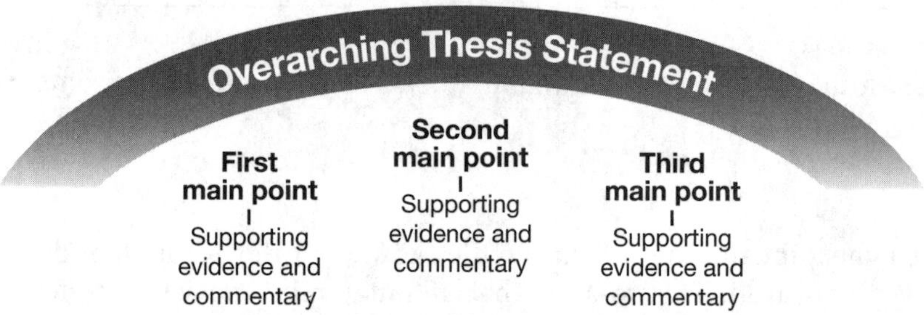

Figure 4-1

You have also read, though, that the process of developing a thesis statement and the evidence and commentary to accompany it may not be as straightforward as it appears in the figure above. The figure suggests that the writer already knows what the first, second, and third main points are going to be and what evidence to use to support them. If the writer does indeed know the substance of the essay, writing a thesis statement is a fairly straightforward task.

However, few writers think briefly about a subject, quickly write a thesis statement that takes into account all they want to say about a subject, and then just fill in the details. Instead, writers typically take time to get to know a subject. They collect evidence, examine it, look for patterns within it, align it with other knowledge they have, and keep mulling ideas until they develop a position they are interested in defending or until an exigence compels them to produce an essay or other written or spoken piece and a rhetorical situation—in particular, audience, context, and purpose—emerges.

Eric Schlosser, for example, whose introduction to the book *Fast Food Nation* you read in Unit 3, explains that he didn't set out to "write a muckraking exposé of the dark side" of America's fast food industry. His writing began as an assignment from *Rolling Stone* magazine to find out how fast food giants operate. He had no preconceived ideas about the industry—he was just doing what he knows how to do: collecting information about a subject. However, he describes the turn his research took when someone gave him confidential files about McDonald's advertising campaigns, which struck him as "cynical and manipulative." Then later when he visited meatpacking facilities in Greeley, Colorado, the "story became much darker" for him.

Schlosser's research took place over years, and during those years he was continually learning and refining his ideas and judgments about the impact of the fast food industry. Your evidence collection and thinking for this course and many of your college courses will take place over a much shorter period of time, but the process still needs to happen. You start with a general idea about something, collect evidence, and gradually a position requiring support or defense will come into focus for you.

You can take the following steps toward discovering a thesis as you collect your evidence.

Steps for Developing a Thesis Statement that Requires Proof or Defense
1. Ask yourself questions. These might include ▪ What perspective do I, with my unique experiences, bring to the subject? ▪ What are some conventional ways of looking at my subject? Where might there be flaws in those approaches? ▪ What have I read about my subject or learned about through some other medium (movies, online discussion groups)?
2. Brainstorm, free write, or make mind maps or cluster diagrams to explore the ideas you have and the connections between them. Keep track of your writing so you can watch your ideas unfold.
3. Review your writing and identify themes or ideas that keep appearing or that hold special interest for you.
4. Try to pull those ideas into a draft thesis statement to get you started in developing the main points you will make to defend your position and the evidence and commentary you will need to do so. Your thesis is likely to continue to evolve. (See Unit 9 for more on revising your thesis in the light of new evidence or compelling counterarguments.)

Table 4-4

Previewing the Line of Reasoning

As Table 4-4 shows, you usually develop a thesis that outlines a **line of reasoning** *after* you finish prewriting and carefully considering all the available evidence. Only after you have followed the steps above will you have enough raw material to use to develop an overarching thesis statement that will reign over all your ideas.

The example that follows demonstrates the way an overarching thesis statement previews the line of reasoning. It is a speech President George W. Bush made after meeting at the Islamic Center of Washington, D.C., with Islamic religious leaders from across the country and around the world less than a week after the September 11, 2001, attacks on the United States. With those leaders at his side, he gave a short speech that became known as the "Islam is Peace" speech.

As you read the speech, note where you sense a preview of the rest of the speech.

1 Thank you all very much for your hospitality. We've just had a wide-ranging discussion on the matter at hand. Like the good folks standing with me, the American people were appalled and outraged at last Tuesday's attacks. And so were Muslims all across the world. Both Americans and Muslim friends and citizens, tax-paying citizens, and Muslims in nations were just appalled and could not believe what we saw on our TV screens.

2 These acts of violence against innocents violate the fundamental tenets of the Islamic faith, and it's important for my fellow Americans to understand that.

3 The English translation is not as eloquent as the original Arabic, but let me quote from the Koran,[1] itself: "In the long run, evil in the extreme will be the end of those who do evil. For that they rejected the signs of Allah and held them up to ridicule."

4 The face of terror is not the true faith of Islam. That's not what Islam is all about. Islam is peace. These terrorists don't represent peace. They represent evil and war.

5 When we think of Islam we think of a faith that brings comfort to a billion people around the world. Billions of people find comfort and solace and peace. And that's made brothers and sisters out of every race—out of every race.

6 America counts millions of Muslims amongst our citizens, and Muslims make an incredibly valuable contribution to our country. Muslims are doctors, lawyers, law professors, members of the military, entrepreneurs, shopkeepers, moms, and dads. And they need to be treated with respect. In our anger and emotion, our fellow Americans must treat each other with respect.

7 Women who cover their heads in this country must feel comfortable going outside their homes. Moms who wear covers must not be intimidated in America. That's not the America I know. That's not the America I value.

8 I've been told that some fear to leave [their homes]; some don't want to go shopping for their families; some don't want to go about their ordinary daily routines because, by wearing covers, they're afraid they'll be intimidated. That should not and that will not stand in America.

---

1 **Koran:** the holy book of Islam

9 Those who feel like they can intimidate our fellow citizens to take out their anger don't represent the best of America; they represent the worst of humankind, and they should be ashamed of that kind of behavior.

10 Now, this is a great country. It's a great country because we share the same values of respect and dignity and human worth. And it is my honor to be meeting with leaders who feel just the same way I do. They're outraged. They're sad. They love America just as much as I do.

11 I want to thank you all for giving me a chance to come by. And may God bless us all.

President George W. Bush speaks at The Islamic Center of Washington, D.C. on September 17, 2001.

What might the details in this photo imply about the situation it captures? How could it add to an understanding of the speech?

After the brief welcome and introduction in the first paragraph, President Bush provides his thesis statement in paragraph 2: "These acts of violence against innocents violate the fundamental tenets of the Islamic faith, and it's important for my fellow Americans to understand that."

This thesis states Bush's supporting claim, and it also previews the line of reasoning that he will follow throughout the speech. The paragraphs after the thesis generally trace two connected claims that make up the line of reasoning: 1) The terrorists' actions violate fundamental beliefs about peace that characterize Islam and Muslims, and 2) Americans must understand and respect that. Reread the speech and look closely at how the paragraphs are organized to follow President Bush's line of reasoning. Then study the visual representation of the speech on the next page, noting the line of reasoning proceeding from the first claim and the line of reasoning proceeding from the second claim.

Notice that the President does not make a long list of specifics when he previews the reasoning in his thesis statement; in fact, he makes only a brief statement to preview, allowing the two main points in the body of the speech to engage the audience. The president subtly links them by showing that America's respect for Islam as a religion of peace constitutes a key part of American identity. In other words, if a key part of American identity is the respect for fellow citizens' religious freedoms, then Americans must respect Islam.

Remember: A thesis statement may preview the line of reasoning of an argument. This is not to say that a thesis statement must list the points of an argument, aspects to be analyzed, or specific evidence to be used in an argument. (CLE-1.O)

Thesis:
These acts of violence against innocents violate the fundamental tenets of the Islamic faith and it's important for my fellow Americans to understand that.

Supporting claim within line of reasoning:
violate the fundamental tenets of the Islamic faith

Paragraph 3: *The English translation is not as eloquent as the original Arabic, but let me quote from the Koran, itself: "In the long run, evil in the extreme will be the end of those who do evil. For that they rejected the signs of Allah and held them up to ridicule."*

Paragraph 4: *The face of terror is not the true faith of Islam. That's not what Islam is all about. Islam is peace. These terrorists don't represent peace. They represent evil and war.*

Paragraph 5: *When we think of Islam we think of a faith that brings comfort to a billion people around the world. Billions of people find comfort and solace and peace. And that's made brothers and sisters out of every race—out of every race.*

Supporting claim within line of reasoning:
it's important for my fellow Americans to understand that

Paragraph 6: *America counts millions of Muslims amongst our citizens, and Muslims make an incredibly valuable contribution to our country. Muslims are doctors, lawyers, law professors, members of the military, entrepreneurs, shopkeepers, moms, and dads. And they need to be treated with respect. In our anger and emotion, our fellow Americans must treat each other with respect*

Paragraph 7: *Women who cover their heads in this country must feel comfortable going outside their homes. Moms who wear cover must not be intimidated in America. That's not the America I know. That's not the America I value.*

Paragraph 8: *I've been told that some fear to leave [their homes]; some don't want to go shopping for their families; some don't want to go about their ordinary daily routines because, by wearing cover, they're afraid they'll be intimidated. That should not and that will not stand in America.*

Paragraph 9: *Those who feel like they can intimidate our fellow citizens to take out their anger don't represent the best of America, they represent the worst of humankind, and they should be ashamed of that kind of behavior.*

Figure 4-2

2.1 Checkpoint

Close Reading: Professional Text

Reread the anchor text on homelessness on pages 187–189. Then complete the open response activity and answer the multiple-choice questions.

1. Recreate Figure 4-2 on the previous page using a statement from the introduction paragraph to identify and track the line of reasoning in the passage.

2. Which of the following statements best summarizes the line of reasoning of the passage?
   (A) Government agencies simply do not adequately support the homeless of this country, which is evident in the unwillingness of those agencies to collect or share data on homelessness.
   (B) The lack of common vocabulary in the discussion of homelessness is one major factor that many government agencies could actually help to fix, despite the general inability for those agencies to communicate with one another because of failures in both funding and leadership.
   (C) Government agencies fail to collect data on homelessness, even though reliable data is necessary when considering how the government can improve its data-collection processes to help the homeless community.
   (D) Though the current data on homelessness is often inaccurate and insufficient, the various government programs that serve the homeless could develop systems for collecting more reliable data and, as a result, improve the services the government can provide.
   (E) The departments of Education, HHS, HUD, and other agencies could be doing much more to collect data on the homeless with whom they come into contact.

3. In the second paragraph, the author suggests that the current data collected to measure homeless is too
   (A) excessive
   (B) limited
   (C) subjective
   (D) impersonal
   (E) broad

Evaluating Writing: Student Draft
Reread the student draft on pages 189–190. Then answer the following open response and multiple-choice questions.

1. What is the line of reasoning according to the organization of the paragraphs?

2. The writer would like to relocate sentence 2 (reproduced below) to better preview the line of reasoning for the passage.

   People must be careful not to jump to such hasty conclusions.

   Where would be the best place to move the sentence?

   (A) Before sentence 1

   (B) After sentence 2

   (C) After sentence 3

   (D) After sentence 4

   (E) After sentence 1

Composing on Your Own
Review the writing you did on the subject of homelessness after reading the GAO report, including your sample introductions and conclusions. Then use free writing, brainstorming, or other techniques that work for you to explore your subject. Keep the elements of your rhetorical situation in mind during this process. Do research as necessary and fold what you learn from your research into your thinking and writing. Continue working until you can develop a thesis statement that 1) requires defense and 2) suggests a line of reasoning. Remember that a thesis may be a single statement and may be introduced as a line of reasoning that will be further developed in the article as a whole. Save your work for later use.

Part 2 Apply What You Have Learned

Reread the following sample introductions from pages 194–195. Determine if they include a potential thesis statement, and, if so, identify it. Describe in a few sentences what you might expect the line of reasoning to be in an essay that thesis statement introduces.

1. The word *homeless* no doubt brings certain images to mind—beggars on street corners, people sleeping under cardboard shelters, alcohol and drug abuse. But for people in the Skid Row neighborhood of Los Angeles, another image comes to mind: the Skid Row Running Club. Founded by a judge (and runner) who mediated cases between the Los Angeles Police Department and the homeless community in Skid

Row, the club uses the discipline, camaraderie, and exhilaration of participating in running events to help people regain control over their lives, especially those battling addiction.

2. What do you do when you come across apparently homeless persons begging for money? Do you give them money even if you think they might use it to buy alcohol or drugs? Do you give them the name and location of an agency that could help them find housing or shelter them temporarily? Do you walk by as if you didn't see them?

3. Picture a printer that stands 11 feet high and 28 feet wide. Picture 4–6 workers, tablets in hand, controlling the actions of the printer with a touch on the screen. Now fast forward, but not very far, to 27 hours ahead. In that time, the printer will have produced the foundation and walls for a "tiny house," leaving the remaining items like roofing and siding for carpenters. The end result is a promising solution to homelessness—a complete house for about $10,000 start to finish that can be made available through a variety of funding options to people who would otherwise be homeless.

Reflect on the Essential Question: Write a brief response that answers this essential question: *How might a thesis statement preview a line of reasoning?* In your answer, explain the key terms listed on page 206.

Part 3

Comparison-Contrast, Description, and Definition

Enduring Understanding and Skills

Part 3

Understand

Writers guide understanding of a text's lines of reasoning and claims through that text's organization and integration of evidence. (REO-1)

Demonstrate

Recognize and explain the use of methods of development to accomplish a purpose. (Reading 5.C)

Use appropriate methods of development to advance an argument. (Writing 6.C)

(See also Unit 3)

Source: *AP® English Language and Composition Course and Exam Description*

Essential Question: As a reader, how do I recognize and explain the methods of development a writer uses to achieve a purpose? As a writer, how can I advance my argument with appropriate methods of development?

No single arrangement is right for every written argument, so you will likely use multiple arrangements—or methods—to develop your essay. In Unit 3 you read about two common methods: narration and cause-effect. This unit will explore several other methods.

How to organize your paragraphs and evidence depends on several factors. These include

- your topic
- your argument
- your evidence
- your audience
- your purpose

An audience may find your argument more convincing if they can easily trace the reasoning that led you to your thesis.

KEY TERMS

comparison-contrast	description
definition	methods of development

3.1 Methods of Development: Comparison-Contrast | REO-1.G REO-1.K

Methods of development are approaches writers frequently use to develop and organize the reasoning of their arguments. A **method of development** provides an audience with a way to trace a writer's reasoning in an argument.

Analyzing Similarities and Differences

When developing ideas through **comparison-contrast**, writers tell how something—an idea, concept, policy, proposal—is similar to (comparison) or different from (contrast) other related things. This reasoning process is often used to show how something unfamiliar is like or unlike something familiar, so the unfamiliar becomes easier for the audience to understand.

When analyzing similarities and/or differences, be sure you are making comparisons or contrasts in similar categories. For example, if you are comparing homelessness among adults to homelessness among children, you would need to be sure that your basis of comparison is the same. That is, you can't compare the *number* of homeless adults in the United States with the *percentage* of homeless children in the United States. Those are two different categories of statistics. To see their relationship, you would have to look at total numbers for both groups or percentages for both groups.

Writers have a number of ways to structure comparison-contrast. Suppose, for example, you were comparing homeless adults and homeless youth. You could present your comparisons and contrasts in these ways:

- **Whole-by-whole**: First, present all your points and information about homeless adults. Then present all your information about homeless children, noting differences/similarities with homeless adults as you go.

- **Similarities vs. differences:** Present all the ways in which homeless children and homeless adults are alike and then show how homeless adults and homeless children are different.

- **Point-by-point**: Present comparisons and contrasts one point at a time. For example, focus on the causes of homelessness for adults and children, both similarities and differences, and then move on to the next point (medical care, for example) following the same pattern.

Whatever method you use, make your comparisons clear by using words and phrases that signal comparison (such as *like, also, just as, similarly)* and contrast (such as *in contrast, unlike, conversely, instead, rather than, differ*).

Study how Schlosser uses comparison-contrast in his introduction (see page 114, paragraph 5). Then, practice explaining *why* this was an effective choice based on the context of the introduction as a whole.

First, Schlosser explores the influence of fast food over the past 30 years, using a whole-by-whole method—first discussing the past and then discussing the present.

Past: In 1968, McDonald's operated about one thousand restaurants.
Present: Today it has about thirty thousand restaurants worldwide and opens almost two thousand new ones each year. An estimated one out of every eight workers in the United States has at some point been employed by McDonald's.

Explanation of Rhetorical Choices

Schlosser presents a quantitative (numbers-based) comparison of franchises McDonald's owned in 1968 with franchises owned 30+ years later. To substantiate how many 30,000 restaurants actually is, Schlosser adds additional quantitative evidence that supports the incredible growth of the franchise, but in a different way—now focusing on people who have had a job at McDonald's at some point in their lifetime. Further, the inclusion of "worldwide" in the detail about today's McDonalds' franchises alludes to the fact that the influence has transcended American borders since 1968.

The frame below may help you both analyze and create connections between evidence and commentary when using comparison-contrast. This frame offers a simplified way of recognizing how comparison-contrast can be used to analyze similarities and differences; however, when developing your own writing, you will want to use your own words and ideas.

Connecting Evidence and Commentary with Methods of Development
Evidence such as [(1) description of evidence] [(2) verb: supports, challenges, refutes, substantiates] Schlosser's claim that [(3) restatement of claim] **because** [(4) commentary].

Table 4-5

A completed frame based on the Schlosser essay might appear as follows:

Evidence such as (1) the comparison between the 1,000 McDonald's restaurants in 1968 and the 30,000 restaurants in operation now (2) underscores Schlosser's claim that (3) the fast food industry is inescapable and infiltrating every nook and cranny of our lives **because** (4) such extreme growth in 30 years is not only a result of changes in our culture but, with that momentum, is also a force defining some of the changes in our culture.

Remember: Methods of development are common approaches writers frequently use to develop and organize the reasoning of their arguments. A method of development provides an audience with the means to trace a writer's reasoning in an argument. When developing ideas through comparison-contrast, writers present a category of comparison and then examine the similarities and/or differences between the objects of the comparison. When analyzing similarities and/or differences, like categories of comparison must be used. (REO-1.G–K)

3.1 Checkpoint

Close Reading: Professional Text

Reread the anchor text on homelessness on pages 187–189. Then answer the open response and multiple-choice questions.

1. Examine how the writer uses some sort of comparison or contrast to address issues with the collection of data on homelessness.

2. In the first paragraph, the author suggests that data about homelessness may be unreliable because of
   (A) the frequent changes in methods for counting and measuring homelessness
   (B) failure to consider the needs of families when collecting data
   (C) insufficient numbers of people responsible for collecting data
   (D) the frequent problems among homeless populations
   (E) the unwillingness of governmental agencies to cooperate and share data

Evaluating Writing: Student Text

Reread the student draft on pages 189–190. Then answer the following open response and multiple-choice questions.

1. What revisions to the draft would clarify the comparison between the challenges faced by homeless mothers and the challenges faced by other homeless people?

2. The writer is considering adding the following sentence to the beginning of the fourth paragraph.

   It is not just abused or hungry mothers and children being forced into these situations.

   Should the writer make this addition?

(A) Yes, because it creates a comparison between mothers who "have been forced from their homes" and those who have jobs but have become homeless.
(B) Yes, because it will clarify the contrast between those who "have been forced from their homes" and all other homeless people.
(C) Yes, because it will highlight that abused or hungry mothers often face impossible choices.
(D) No, because it will create an unnecessary connection between homeless who "have been forced from their homes" and those who still have jobs."
(E) No, because the intended audience is likely to reject the idea that those who "have been forced from their homes" are abused or hungry mothers and children.

Composing on Your Own
Review all the writing you have done on the subject of homelessness and check to see if your thesis has a claim that reveals a line of reasoning. When you are satisfied with your thesis, brainstorm or free write about how you might use comparison-contrast to advance your argument and trace your line of reasoning. Look for areas in your essay where comparison-contrast may help clarify key ideas. As you refine your work, be sure to consider the rhetorical situation, including your audience, context, and purpose. Save your work for later use.

3.2 Methods of Development: Description and Definition | REO-1.L

When developing ideas through a description or definition, writers relate the characteristics, features, or sensory details of an object or idea, sometimes using examples or illustrations. As in all cases, certain subjects—or parts of subjects—are better suited to these methods of development than to others.

Appealing to the Senses through Description

Description provides details of appearance and other physical characteristics. Description recreates or describes a person, place, event, or action so that the reader can picture it. Description relies on *sensory details*: words that evoke the experiences of our five basic senses. This method of development can enlist people's emotions, since everyone has memories and feelings associated with sensory experiences. Description, like comparison, can also make something unfamiliar feel more familiar.

Consider how Schlosser uses description in his introduction as it relates to the argument set forth in the introduction. As you read the following example from Schlosser's introduction, notice how description serves a purpose as a method of development.

Description Example from Schlosser's Introduction	Explaining Example and the Method of Development
Pull open the glass door, feel the rush of cool air, walk in, get on line, study the backlit color photographs above the counter, place your order, hand over a few dollars, watch teenagers in uniforms pushing various buttons, and moments later take hold of a plastic tray full of food wrapped in colored paper and cardboard. The whole experience of buying fast food has become so routine, so thoroughly unexceptional and mundane, that it is now taken for granted, like brushing your teeth or stopping for a red light. It has become a social custom as American as a small, rectangular, hand-held, frozen, and reheated apple pie.	The description here is recreating the event or action of going into a fast food restaurant—not just McDonald's, but any fast food chain—which makes this description resonate with more audiences, not just those who frequent McDonald's. The description is packed with sensory details, ranging from a tactile detail—"the rush of cool air"—to the visual of the "backlit color photographs above the counter."

Table 4-6

Once again you can use a simple frame to consider how the descriptive evidence connects to the writer's claim. As before, this frame may offer a model for outlining your thoughts, but when writing your own material, you will want to use your own words. In particular, be sure to use vivid words that appeal to the senses and help your reader hear, see, and feel what you are describing.

Connecting Evidence and Commentary with Methods of Development
Evidence such as [(1) description of evidence] [(2) verb: supports, challenges, refutes, substantiates] Schlosser's claim that [(3) restatement of claim] **because** [(4) commentary].

Table 4-7

A completed frame based on the Schlosser example might appear as follows:

> Evidence such as (1) the sensory-loaded description of a fast-food buying experience (2) reinforces Schlosser's claim that (3) fast food has become a routine staple in American culture **because** (4) all readers—even those who do not eat fast food—can picture the experience of buying fast food as it is described in this paragraph so vividly. In so doing, the descriptive details validate Schlosser's claim that fast food is, in fact, a common, routine part of American culture.

Developing Shared Meanings through Definition

Definition establishes a common meaning for a subject or an aspect of a subject between the writer and the audience. To help define a subject or concept, a writer might use comparison to show what else it is like and contrast to show negative examples.

Consider how Schlosser uses definition in his introduction and how it relates to his argument. As you read the following example from Schlosser's introduction, notice how definition serves a purpose as a method of development.

Definition Example from Schlosser's Introduction	Explaining Example and the Method of Development
In the early 1970s, the farm activist Jim Hightower warned of "the McDonaldization of America." He viewed the emerging fast food industry as a threat to independent businesses, as a step toward a food economy dominated by giant corporations, and as a homogenizing influence on American life. In *Eat Your Heart Out* (1975), he argued that "bigger is not better." Much of what Hightower feared has come to pass. The centralized purchasing decisions of the large restaurant chains and their demand for standardized products have given a handful of corporations an unprecedented degree of power over the nation's food supply. Moreover, the tremendous success of the fast food industry has encouraged other industries to adopt similar business methods. The basic thinking behind fast food has become the operating system of today's retail economy, wiping out small businesses, obliterating regional differences, and spreading identical stores throughout the country like a self-replicating code.	Schlosser warns of Hightower's fear of "the McDonaldization of America" to open this paragraph. As the paragraph continues, it explains what this concept means. Schlosser explains that this fear came from fast food chains being a "a threat to independent businesses." He then gradually increases the scope of what this means—from being controlled by big corporations to having a "homogenized" society. Further, the paragraph ends with more discussion of what this phrase came to mean—similar business methods, identical stores, and the perpetuating of consumerism and conformity. Using the term "McDonaldization of America" in the first place is effective because it directly connects McDonald's—the quintessential fast food chain—with the "self-replicating code" that has, in fact, happened since the warning by Hightower.

Table 4-8

You can use the same frame you used with other methods of development to explain how the evidence from definition connects to the writer's claim.

Connecting Evidence and Commentary with Methods of Development
Evidence such as [(1) description of evidence] [(2) verb: supports, challenges, refutes, substantiates] Schlosser's claim that [(3) restatement of claim] **because** [(4) commentary].

Table 4-9

A completed frame based on the Schlosser example might appear as follows:

> Evidence such as (1) the definition of what Hightower referred to as "The McDonaldization of America" (2) extends Schlosser's claim (3) that the fast food industry has influenced not only our diet but also our culture and economy **because** (4) this term makes the most famous fast food franchise into a noun representing the process of "McDonaldization" that has taken place in many industries. In this way, Schlosser establishes the responsibility of McDonald's for the changes that have forced conformity and uniformity through mass marketing and standard business practices.

> **Remember:** When developing ideas through a definition or description, writers relate the characteristics, features, or sensory details of an object or idea, sometimes using examples or illustrations. (REO-1.L)

3.2 Checkpoint

Close Reading: Professional Text

Reread the anchor text on homelessness on pages 187–189. Then answer the open response and multiple-choice questions.

1. Give an example of a definition and a description from the passage. Then explain how each one supports the author's thesis.

2. What solution does the author describe in paragraph 3 that may improve the reliability of the data collected about homelessness?

- (A) Improved software for collecting, archiving, and interpreting data about homelessness
- (B) Having private companies gather more information about homelessness
- (C) Hiring census data workers to also collect data about homelessness
- (D) Enhancing education and training for those responsible for gathering the data
- (E) Allowing the homeless themselves to be involved in collecting necessary data

3. In the final paragraph, what method of improving data collection is described in most detail?
    (A) "a common vocabulary" (sentence 1)
    (B) "effective programs" (sentencel)
    (C) "additional data" (sentence 2)
    (D) "consistent data" (sentence 3)
    (E) "key agencies" (sentence 4)

Evaluating Writing: Student Draft

Reread the student draft on pages 189–190. Then answer the following open response and multiple-choice questions.

1. Identify a part of the student draft that you found unclear or hard to understand. Give an example of one definition or one description that would help clarify and support the writer's argument and write it as it might appear in the draft.

2. The writer is considering adding the following sentence to the third paragraph to describe other choices that women may be forced to make when they become homeless.

    They may also have been forced to choose between paying rent or utilities and buying food.

    Which of the following is the most logical place to insert this sentence in the paragraph?
    (A) Before sentence 7
    (B) Before sentence 8
    (C) Before sentence 9
    (D) Before sentence 10
    (E) Before sentence 11

Composing on Your Own

Review all the writing you have done on the subject of homelessness. Evaluate all your ideas in the context of your rhetorical situation and begin to develop them into an essay. If needed, conduct online research or a library search to find evidence to support your claim. Use the checklist below as you are writing. Use it again when you are finished to evaluate your work. While your writing does not have to follow every point in the checklist, the list should help you review whether your ideas and arguments are thorough and well-reasoned.

Checklist for Composing
✓ Does your introduction use effective strategies for orienting, focusing, and engaging your audience? (1.1)
✓ Does your conclusion respond to or consider the rhetorical situation and use effective concluding strategies? (1.2)
✓ Does your thesis statement establish a defensible claim and suggest a line of reasoning? (2.1)
✓ Did you use comparison-contrast if that method of development best suits your purpose? (3.1)
✓ Did you use definition or description if those methods of development best suit your purpose and line of inquiry? (3.2)
✓ Did you check your writing for mistakes in spelling and mechanics and make an effort to correct them?

Table 4-10

Part 3 Apply What You Have Learned

Look back at the report by the Government Accountability Office or the excerpt from the introduction to *Fast Food Nation* in Unit 3, including the introductory information. Reread the passage carefully. Write a short response that identifies multiple methods of development and then explains how different methods of development work together to achieve the purpose of the passage. Using table 4-2 as guide, cite specific examples of different types of evidence the author uses to orient, focus, and engage the audience. Explain how the author uses this evidence build the argument. In addition, show how the author uses comparison-contrast, description, and definition to clarify the line of reasoning.

Reflect on the Essential Questions: Write a brief response that answers these essential questions: *As a reader, how do I recognize and explain the methods of development a writer uses to achieve a purpose? As a writer, how can I advance my argument with appropriate methods of development?* In your answer, correctly use the key terms listed on page 215.

Unit 4 Review

Section 1: Reading

Questions 1–9. Read the following passage carefully before you choose your answers.

(The following is an excerpt from a speech given by workers' rights leader Cesar Chavez in 1990 to honor Dr. Martin Luther King Jr.)

1 My friends, today we honor a giant among men: today we honor the reverend Martin Luther King Jr.

2 Dr. King was a powerful figure of destiny, of courage, of sacrifice, and of vision. Few people in the long history of this nation can rival his accomplishment, his reason, or his selfless dedication to the cause of peace and social justice.

3 Today we honor a wise teacher, an inspiring leader, and a true visionary, but to truly honor Dr. King we must do more than say words of praise.

4 We must learn his lessons and put his views into practice, so that we may truly be free at last.

5 Who was Dr. King?

6 Many people will tell you of his wonderful qualities and his many accomplishments, but what makes him special to me, the truth many people don't want you to remember, is that Dr. King was a great activist, fighting for radical social change with radical methods.

7 While other people talked about change, Dr. King used direct action to challenge the system. He welcomed it, and used it wisely.

8 In his famous letter from the Birmingham jail, Dr. King wrote that "The purpose of direct action is to create a situation so crisis-packed that it will inevitably open the door to negotiation."

9 Dr. King was also radical in his beliefs about violence. He learned how to successfully fight hatred and violence with the unstoppable power of nonviolence.

10 He once stopped an armed mob, saying: "We are not advocating violence. We want to love our enemies. I want you to love our enemies. Be good to them. This is what we live by. We must meet hate with love."

11 Dr. King knew that he very probably wouldn't survive the struggle that he led so well. But he said, "If I am stopped, the movement will not stop. If I am stopped, our work will not stop. For what we are doing is right. What we are doing is just, and God is with us."

12 My friends, as we enter a new decade, it should be clear to all of us that there is an unfinished agenda, that we have miles to go before we reach the promised land.

13 The men who rule this country today never learned the lessons of Dr. King, they never learned that non-violence is the only way to peace and justice.

14 Our nation continues to wage war upon its neighbors, and upon itself.

15 The powers-that-be rule over a racist society, filled with hatred and ignorance.

16 Our nation continues to be segregated along racial and economic lines.

17 The powers-that-be make themselves richer by exploiting the poor. Our nation continues to allow children to go hungry, and will not even house its own people. The time is now for people, of all races and backgrounds, to sound the trumpets of change. As Dr. King proclaimed, "There comes a time when people get tired of being trampled over by the iron feet of oppression."

18 My friends, the time for action is upon us. The enemies of justice want you to think of Dr. King as only a civil rights leader, but he had a much broader agent. He was a tireless crusader for the rights of the poor, for an end to the war in Vietnam long before it was popular to take that stand, and for the rights of workers everywhere.

19 Many people find it convenient to forget that Martin was murdered while supporting a desperate strike on that tragic day in Memphis, Tennessee. He died while fighting for the rights of sanitation workers.

20 Dr. King's dedication to the rights of the workers who are so often exploited by the forces of greed has profoundly touched my life and guided my struggle.

21 During my first fast in 1968, Dr. King reminded me that our struggle was his struggle too. He sent me a telegram which said "Our separate struggles are really one. A struggle for freedom, for dignity, and for humanity."

22 I was profoundly moved that someone facing such a tremendous struggle himself would take the time to worry about a struggle taking place on the other side of the continent.

23 Just as Dr. King was a disciple of Gandhi and Christ,[1] we must now be Dr. King's disciples.

24 Dr. King challenged us to work for a greater humanity. I only hope that we are worthy of his challenge.

---

1. Which of the following best describes the strategy Chavez uses to develop his argument?

(A) Chavez draws a contrast between his methods and methods of Dr. King.

(B) Chavez defines the beliefs and methods of Christ and Gandhi.

(C) Chavez narrates the key points in the life of Dr. King.

(D) Chavez defines racism as a cause and nonviolence as an effect.

(E) Chavez compares Dr. King's values and strategies with his own.

2. Which line from the passage best captures the thesis of Chavez's speech?

(A) "My friends, as we enter a new decade, it should be clear to all of us that there is an unfinished agenda, that we have miles to go before we reach the promised land." (paragraph 12)

(B) "...Dr. King was a great activist, fighting for radical social change with radical methods." (paragraph 6)

(C) "Dr. King knew that he very probably wouldn't survive the struggle that he led so well." (paragraph 11, sentence 1)

(D) "Our nation continues to be segregated along racial and economic lines." (paragraph 16)

(E) "Many people find it convenient to forget that Martin was murdered while supporting a desperate strike . . . ." (paragraph 19, sentence 1)

---

1 Gandhi and Christ were both advocates for nonviolent opposition and peaceful protest.

3. Which of the following best expresses the main purpose of Chavez's speech?
   (A) To encourage the audience to recognize historical similarities between himself, Dr. King, and Gandhi
   (B) To inform the audience by memorializing Dr. King, explaining who he was, and describing his experiences
   (C) To influence the audience to join Dr. King's cause by relating key moments from King's struggle for racial equality
   (D) To inspire the audience by showing them that their movement for social justice is similar to Dr. King's movement
   (E) To motivate his audience to study Dr. King's legacy of nonviolent protest

4. The first five sentences of Chavez's speech appeal to his audience's
   (A) awe and reverence for the legacy of Dr. King
   (B) sense of sympathy for Dr. King's death
   (C) doubts about the legacy and memory of Dr. King
   (D) fears that a leader like Dr. King can never be replaced
   (E) hope that Chavez will honor Dr. King

5. Which of the following pieces of evidence most likely has the greatest effect on Chavez's credibility?
   (A) He memorializes Dr. King as an honorable and wise teacher of timeless truths.
   (B) He quotes a letter from Dr. King that emphasizes direct action.
   (C) He provides specific examples of Dr. King's accomplishments.
   (D) He compares Dr. King's methods to those of Gandhi and Christ.
   (E) He reveals that Dr. King sent him a telegram stating that they shared the same struggle.

6. Chavez uses the adjectives "unfinished" and "promised" (paragraph 12) to
   (A) disparage the false promises made by the government
   (B) motivate his listeners to continue striving for their goals
   (C) imply that there is simply too much to do to accomplish their goals
   (D) suggest that Dr. King would be disappointed in how little progress had been made in the fight for justice
   (E) argue that God will guide him and his followers in their struggle

7. Which example from Dr. King's life directly supports the speaker's claims about the power of nonviolence?
   (A) Dr. King's telegram to the speaker
   (B) Dr. King's ability to stop an armed mob
   (C) Dr. King's letter from a Birmingham jail
   (D) Dr. King's insistence that the struggle for equality will continue
   (E) Dr. King's fight to help protect the rights of sanitation workers

8. Paragraph 11 serves what purpose in the reasoning of the speech?
   (A) It demonstrates that Dr. King's struggle failed but that the movement he started "will not stop."
   (B) It explains the relationship between the "armed mob" and the failure of Dr. King's movement.
   (C) It explains that Chavez inherited Dr. King's legacy for "doing . . . right."
   (D) It connects Dr. King's "just" and "right" movement with that of Chavez and his followers.
   (E) It contrasts Dr. King's legacy with the fact that the "nation continues to be segregated along racial and economic lines."

9. By stating "that we have miles to go before we reach the promised land," Chavez
   (A) challenges the audience to rise-up like "an armed mob" but without violence
   (B) affirms that what the audience is "doing is right"
   (C) evokes feelings of a journey to complete their "unfinished agenda"
   (D) shows his audience how to "open the door to negotiation" with unjust leaders
   (E) asks his audience to accept "the men who rule this country today"

Section I: Writing

Questions 10–15. Read the following passage carefully before you choose your answers.
The passage below is a draft.

(1) In July of 2005, the reigning and long-term "king of pop" passed away. (2) So much more than just a singer, Michael Jackson's performances had become part of American and worldwide culture since his debut as a 6-year-old member of the boy band, *The Jackson 5*, in 1964. (3) His performances and music were so powerful that, in 1989, Jackson was called "the king of pop" while being presented an award. (4) The name stuck. (5) While there are many talented male performers in pop music today, few have the history of long-term popularity and influence on so many other artists to allow them to earn the title of "king." (6) Whoever should take his place must demonstrate similar long-term success and influence. (7) A look at popular music over the last two or three decades reveals one name. (8) Justin Timberlake is one male performer who, like Jackson, started performing as a child and has succeeded in remaining popular over two decades while also allowing his music and performances to evolve over time. (9) It is Timberlake who most deserves to inherit Jackson's crown. (10) Timberlake shows few signs of slowing down as he continues to tour very successfully and still releases number one songs more than twenty years following his 1995 debut with his own boy-band, *NSYNC*.

---

10. The writer wants to create a cause-effect relationship between Jackson's fame and Timberlake's success. Of the following sentences, which one would most clearly establish that relationship if added after sentence 8?

(A) Jackson's 2005 death contributed to the rise of Timberlake's popularity.

(B) Timberlake even holds Jackson as one of his most important influences, a fact that is obvious when listening to their music.

(C) Timberlake's increasing fame may have been the reason that Jackson remained popular into the 2000s.

(D) Pop music relies on stars like Jackson and Timberlake to retain fans and maintain its popularity.

(E) The loss of a star such as Jackson left room for other, younger stars to rise up through the ranks of pop music and take their place as leaders for their time.

Question 11 is covered in Unit 1.

11. The writer wants to better emphasize the exigence for this argument. Which of the following, if added after sentence 4, would accomplish this?

(A) Jackson's death was a terrible loss for all pop artists and their fans.

(B) That is now a title to be taken by someone else.

(C) As a result, however, his death left the world of popular music without its king—without its number-one personality.

(D) In fact, it became the most popular way of referring to Jackson—people seemed to just know that he was the "king of pop."

(E) But all kings die.

Question 12 is covered in Unit 2.

12. In an attempt to better involve the reader emotionally, the writer wants to add the following sentence into the draft.

Though the tragic and unexpected loss of such an influential person will be felt for many years, someone must assume Jackson's crown and carry pop music forward.

Where would the sentence best be placed?

(A) Before sentence 2

(B) Before sentence 6

(C) Before sentence 7

(D) Before sentence 9

(E) After sentence 10

Questions 13–15 are covered in Unit 5.

13. To suggest a closer connection between Jackson and Timberlake, the writer wants to add a transitional phrase to the beginning of sentence 10. Which of the following would be the best choice?

(A) Like Jackson,

(B) Though not identical to Jackson,

(C) While Jackson was famous for more than 40 years,

(D) In fact,

(E) Unlike other musicians,

14. In sentence 2 (reproduced below), the writer would like to further emphasizes Jackson's status as a history-making artist and performer.

So much more than just a singer, Michael Jackson's performances had become part of American and worldwide culture since his debut as a 6-year-old member of the boy band, The Jackson 5, in 1964.

Which of the follow adjectives, if added before the word "performances," would best accomplish this goal?

(A) technical

(B) live

(C) concert

(D) amazing

(E) legendary

15. The writer wants to include evidence of Jackson's long-term popularity and success by adding the following sentence.

Jackson made music for more than 45 years, including 30 top-ten hits and 13 number-ones.

Where would the sentence best be placed?

(A) Before sentence 1

(B) Before sentence 3

(C) Before sentence 5

(D) Before sentence 6

(E) Before sentence 8

JOIN THE CONVERSATION: RHETORICAL ANALYSIS (PART 3)

Before moving on to the rhetorical analysis prompt in the free-response portion of the unit review, do one more revision of the rhetorical analysis practice prompt you started in Unit 2 (pages 104–106) and continued in Unit 3 (pages 178–180). The rhetorical analysis prompt for Unit 4 remains mainly the same as it was in Unit 3. As before, the first part of the prompt provides background, the second states your task, and the third provides a checklist for fulfilling the requirements. However, the third bullet changes the expectation of this list one last time. Instead of a brief explanation, you are now expected to provide a *full* explanation. This list is the version you will see on the exam. Everything the prompt asks you to do has been covered in Units 1–4.

The speech on pages 53–55 was delivered on "Malala Day"—July 12, 2013—by Malala Yousafzai, a girls' and children's education rights activist who survived an assassination attempt in 2012 when she was 15. She delivered this speech to the "Youth Take Over the UN" assembly, a campaign that stressed the importance of global education rights. This was the first speech that she delivered since the assassination attempt.

Read the passage carefully. Write an essay that analyzes some of the rhetorical choices Yousafzai makes to convey her message that all children around the world deserve an equal education.

In your response you should do the following:

- Respond to the prompt with a thesis that analyzes the writer's rhetorical choices .
- Select and use evidence to develop and support your line of reasoning.
- Explain how the evidence supports your line of reasoning.
- Demonstrate an understanding of the rhetorical situation.
- Use appropriate grammar and punctuation in communicating your argument.

To address the changed requirement in the **third bullet** (that your explanation is now *full*, not brief, even though the word *fully* is not stated), develop commentary that explains how the evidence you have thoughtfully and strategically selected supports the overarching claim in your thesis. You cannot simply state, as you might have in Unit 3, that Yousafzai uses repetition to move the argument away from herself to focus instead on the audience. Now the task demands analysis—that is, you must explain *how* repetition achieves that purpose by looking at the different examples of it throughout the passage and explaining the effect of each instance.

As you saw in Unit 3, the thesis for this task could very simply state the choices Yousafzai uses to develop her argument and be sufficient. However, you also saw how linking the choices and the argument to a larger abstract idea helps make the argument about a more universal idea (underlined).

> Malala Yousafzai uses appeals to ethos and her terrifying personal story to convey her message that all children around the world deserve an equal education, and to illustrate <u>the value of education to develop independent and self-sufficient people</u>.

You will now work to create a more cohesive essay by relating your examination of Yousafzai's rhetorical choices in the body of the essay to the abstract idea from the thesis.

Evidence and Line of Reasoning As in Unit 3, you are expected to select and use evidence to support your line of reasoning. The strategies Yousafzai uses in her speech become your line of reasoning—that is, your claims and your line of reasoning are nearly identical. As you state your thesis, you might identify the broad category of rhetorical choices you will explore in the essay, or you might state specific choices you will explore. For example, a thesis statement might list three broad categories of the choices as 1) repetition, 2) personal anecdotes, and 3) use of compare-contrast. Or the thesis might list instead the more specific instances of those examples, such as 1) repetition that allows her to shift the focus toward purpose, 2) the story of an attempt on her life, and 3) a comparison of the Taliban and true Islam.

Organizing Your Analysis You could organize your analysis by moving from one type of rhetorical choice to another, or you could instead move through the speech, from beginning to end, identifying where Yousafzai uses certain choices and their effects on her argument. In either case, the thesis for a rhetorical analysis essay identifies the choices you will analyze and the line of reasoning you will follow. It also links to the abstract idea the argument embodies.

Introductions and Conclusions The exam does not require introductions. Many students successfully state only their thesis and then proceed to the essay that supports and explains the claim. If included, an introduction should remain brief, and it should engage, orient, and focus the reader using any of the strategies you have learned. (See pages 192–195.)

Conclusions are also not required. If a conclusion is included, it should use the strategies for effective conclusions you learned in this unit. (See pages 198–200.) While you might briefly mention the examples you provided in the essay, *do not summarize your argument*.

Remember to leave time to check that you fulfilled the requirement of the **final bullet** point.

Use the organizer on the following page to help you "upgrade" your earlier drafts into a full rhetorical analysis.

Apply

Follow the same process to respond to the rhetorical analysis prompt on page 238. For current free-response question samples, visit the College Board website.

Unit 4: Rhetorical Analysis and Argument Full Essay Drafting Organizer

Abstract Idea that runs throughout (What is it really about?)

Introduction	Lead-in addressing an abstract concept	
	Thesis:	
Body Paragraph 1	Supporting Claim 1	Connection to abstract idea in thesis
	Lead-in to evidence	Describe evidence
	Explain how that evidence supports the reasoning that justifies that claim and appeals to the audience.	
	How does the evidence lead to or connect with next paragraph?	Reconnect to abstract idea in thesis
Body Paragraph 2	Supporting Claim 2	Connection to abstract idea in thesis
	Lead-in to evidence	Describe evidence
	Explain how that evidence supports the reasoning that justifies that claim and appeals to the audience..	
	How does the evidence build upon or connect to previous paragraph?	Reconnect to abstract idea in thesis
Body Paragraph 3	Supporting Claim 3	Connection to abstract idea in thesis
	Lead-in to evidence	Describe evidence
	Explain how that evidence supports the reasoning that justifies that claim and appeals to the audience.	
	How does the evidence build upon or connect to previous paragraph?	Reconnect to abstract idea in thesis
Conclusion	Statement about essay topic that leads to abstract idea	
	Call to the reader about the essay topic (call to act or think differently)	
	General statement about the importance of the abstract idea(s)	
	Full Essay Draft	

JOIN THE CONVERSATION: THE ARGUMENT ESSAY (PART 4)

The argument prompt for Unit 4 remains the same as it was in Unit 3.

> For decades, movies and music have included messages or labels to signal that they have material in them that some people may find troubling. Advocates for such things argue this is important to prevent people from being exposed to things they do not want to encounter. However, Erika Christakis, a lecturer at the Yale Child Study Center, says that "free speech and the ability to tolerate offense are the hallmarks of a free and open society."
>
> Write an essay that argues your position on the use of warning labels or warning messages to signal potentially troubling content.
>
> In your response you should do the following:
>
> - Respond to the prompt with a thesis that presents a defensible position.
> - Provide evidence to support your line of reasoning.
> - Explain how the evidence supports your line of reasoning.
> - Use appropriate grammar and punctuation in communicating your argument.

Previous units have focused on gradually developing a simple claim into a thesis statement. While this unit further develops the idea of a thesis statement, it also addresses building an introduction and conclusion that revolve around the thesis to begin improving the cohesion of the essay.

In previous units, you focused on the development of a thesis that stated "the main, overarching claim" and then worked on attaching that thesis to an abstract idea. This unit suggests that you preview the line of reasoning in the thesis as well. You might list specific ideas you will examine, or you might simply state a broad category of ideas you will explore in the essay. For example, a thesis statement might list your three examples/pieces of evidence to support the claim as 1) when I stayed overnight at my friend's and saw my first R-rated film, 2) recent deaths in my city related to vaping, and 3) McDonald's restaurants deciding to put "hot" labels on their coffee. Or, to present them more generally, that thesis might list the broader categories of those examples: 1) my own experiences with film ratings, 2) recent vaping deaths, and 3) restaurants and hot beverage labels. Or, the thesis might not list these at all. The exam requires ONLY a clear and defensible (arguable) claim, though previewing your line of reasoning and including the abstract idea is likely to strengthen your argument.

Methods of Development Unit 2 asked you to think strategically about the purpose of your evidence in the essay. Does it explain, illustrate, contradict, or serve another purpose? Unit 3 and now Unit 4 ask you to think strategically about everything you are writing. Is a paragraph meant to show cause-effect? Do you need to develop a comparison for the audience? Maybe you need to define something before you discuss it. Likely, small narratives, such as the sleepover that left you sleepless, find their way into arguments as anecdotes that offer examples as evidence. Although the exam does not require these extras, your awareness of them will help you strengthen your essay.

Introductions and Conclusions The exam does not require introductions. Many students successfully state only their thesis and then proceed to the essay that supports and explains the claim. If included, an introduction should remain brief, and it should engage, orient, and focus the reader using any of the strategies you have learned. (See pages 192–195.)

Conclusions are also not required. If a conclusion is included, it should use the strategies for effective conclusions you learned in this unit. (See pages 198–200.) While you might briefly mention the evidence you provide in the essay, *do not summarize your argument.*

Remember to leave time to check that you fulfilled the requirement of the **final bullet** point.

Use the organizer on page 235 to help you "upgrade" your earlier drafts into a full argument.

Apply

Follow the same process to respond to the argument prompt on page 238. For current free-response question samples, visit the College Board website.

Section II: Free Response

The first free-response question on the AP® exam is a synthesis task. See Join the Conversation on pages 364–373, 448–455, and 540–544 for guidance in responding to that kind of prompt. You will be provided synthesis prompts in Units 6–9.

Rhetorical Analysis: "Lessons of Dr. Martin Luther King Jr."

The excerpt on pages 224–226 is from a 1990 speech given by Cesar Chavez (1927–1993). Chavez was an American farm worker, labor leader, and civil rights activist. His birthday, March 31st, is a state holiday in several states and is also celebrated by many as a day to promote service to the community in honor of his life and work. He originally gave this speech just before the celebration of Martin Luther King Jr. Day.

Read the passage carefully. Write an essay that analyzes the rhetorical choices Chavez makes (such as methods of development, organization, or line of reasoning) to convey his message of unity and emphasize similarities between his and King's methods and movements.

In your response you should do the following:

- Respond to the prompt with a thesis that analyzes the writer's rhetorical choices.
- Select and use evidence to develop and support your line of reasoning.
- Explain how the evidence supports your line of reasoning.
- Demonstrate an understanding of the rhetorical situation.
- Use appropriate grammar and punctuation in communicating your argument.

Argument: Hell is Other People

In the play *No Exit* from 1944, French philosopher and playwright Jean Paul Sartre (1905–1980) wrote what is arguably his most famous line, "Hell is other people." By that he meant, among other things, that we are defined and limited by the way others perceive us—that by the power of their perceptions others can lock us into being someone we are not.

Write an essay that argues your position on the role that other people's perceptions of us play in shaping our perspectives of ourselves.

In your response you should do the following:

- Respond to the prompt with a thesis that presents a defensible position.
- Provide evidence to support your line of reasoning.
- Explain how the evidence supports your line of reasoning.
- Use appropriate grammar and punctuation in communicating your argument.

UNIT 5

Structuring and Supporting Coherent Arguments

Part 1: Constructing Cohesive Arguments
Part 2: Maintaining Coherence and Using Transitions
Part 3: The Many Meanings of Language

ENDURING UNDERSTANDINGS AND SKILLS: Unit Five

Part 1

Understand

Writers guide understanding of a text's lines of reasoning and claims through that text's organization and integration of evidence. (REO-1)

Demonstrate

Describe the line of reasoning and explain whether it supports an argument's overarching thesis. (Reading 5.A)

Develop a line of reasoning and commentary that explains it throughout an argument. (Writing 6.A)

Part 2

Understand

Writers guide understanding of a text's lines of reasoning and claims through that text's organization and integration of evidence. (REO-1)

Demonstrate

Explain how the organization of a text creates unity and coherence and reflects a line of reasoning. (Reading 5.B)

Use transitional elements to guide the reader through the line of reasoning of an argument. (Writing 6.B)

Part 3

Understand

The rhetorical situation informs the strategic stylistic choices that writers make. (STL-1)

Demonstrate

Explain how word choice, comparisons, and syntax contribute to the specific tone or style of a text. (Reading 7.A)

Strategically use words, comparisons, and syntax to convey a specific tone or style in an argument. (Writing 8.A)

Source: *AP® English Language and Composition Course and Exam Description*

Unit 5 Overview

In a way, every well-constructed argument is like a sturdy bridge. All bridges have the same purpose: they allow people to cross or connect from one area to another. Though they share the same basic function, not all bridges are constructed the same way. Construction of any bridge is influenced by its context. For example, a bridge that is supposed to allow many cars to cross over a body of water should not be constructed of rope and wood. On the other hand, if the purpose of the bridge is to allow people to cross a chasm through a mountainous jungle, it would be appropriate to construct the bridge from rope and wood.

A bridge made of vines in Japan

The same is true for writing an argument. Although all arguments attempt to convey and support the writer's claim, each is constructed based on a particular context—the needs and understandings of the audience—and the amount of support the writer needs to substantiate his or her claim. Like different types of bridges, different arguments require different types of support and materials. Your job as the writer is to construct an argument that will move your audience to agree with your claim. The line of reasoning you establish determines the path your audience will travel.

Source: Pexels
More than 100,000 cars cross the Brooklyn Bridge each day.

In the previous unit, you read about how to contextualize your arguments by constructing introduction and conclusion paragraphs. You also read about a number of other techniques writers use to develop and organize their ideas. These organizational techniques will also be useful as you build your supporting paragraphs.

In this unit, you'll discover how writers support their argument and maintain a strong line of reasoning to bridge the gap between their introduction and conclusion. You'll also learn how to build and support arguments of your own and how to use clear language that drives your argument through to the end. By the time you finish this unit, you'll have the tools to develop and construct an argument that accurately and purposefully conveys your perspective by encouraging your audience to cross the bridge you have built.

Close Reading: Professional Text
Aung San Suu Kyi's Speech Accepting the Sakharov Prize for Freedom of Thought

The following speech is by Aung San Suu Kyi (ung sun su chee), former Nobel Peace Prize recipient and current state counsellor (equivalent to prime minister) of Myanmar (also known as Burma). In 1990 she was awarded the Sakharov Prize for Freedom of Thought, an award that celebrates those who promote human rights and freedom, while advocating for greater democratic opportunities within the military state of her home country. She received the award in absentia, however, since she was under house arrest for her actions against the tyrannical government, and she remained confined for almost 15 years. You will return to this speech throughout this unit. For now, read it to understand Aung San Suu Kyi's central message on the subject of fear and oppression and to follow her ideas as they unfold.

1 It is not power that corrupts but fear. Fear of losing power corrupts those who wield it and fear of the scourge of power corrupts those who are subject to it. Most Burmese are familiar with the four *a-gati*, the four kinds of corruption. *Chanda-gati*, corruption induced by desire, is deviation from the right path[1] in pursuit of bribes or for the sake of those one loves. *Dosa-gati* is taking the wrong path to spite those against whom one bears ill will, and *moga-gati* is aberration due to ignorance. But perhaps the worst of the four is *bhaya-gati*, for not only does *bhaya*, fear, stifle and slowly destroy all sense of right and wrong, it so often lies at the root of the other three kinds of corruption. Just as *chanda-gati*, when not the result of sheer avarice, can be caused by fear of want or fear of losing the goodwill of those one loves, so fear of being surpassed, humiliated or injured in some way can provide the impetus for ill will. And it would be difficult to dispel ignorance unless there is freedom to pursue the truth unfettered by fear. With so close a relationship between fear and corruption it is little wonder that in any society where fear is rife corruption in all forms becomes deeply entrenched.

2 Public dissatisfaction with economic hardships has been seen as the chief cause of the movement for democracy in Burma, sparked off by the student demonstrations in 1988.[2] It is true that years of incoherent policies, inept official measures, burgeoning inflation and falling real income had turned the country into an economic shambles. But it was more than the difficulties of eking out a barely acceptable standard of living that had eroded the patience of a traditionally good-natured, quiescent[3] people—it was also the humiliation of a way of life disfigured by corruption and fear.

---

1 **right path**: In Buddhism, the right path is a spiritual discipline that leads to enlightenment and the end of suffering..

2 Students and people from all walks of life joined nationwide protests against the military government. In August of 1988, soldiers shot and killed protesters. During this time, Aung San Suu Kyi rose to prominence as a voice for democracy and nonviolence.

3 **quiescent**: inactive; passive

3 The students were protesting not just against the death of their comrades but against the denial of their right to life by a totalitarian regime which deprived the present of meaningfulness and held out no hope for the future. And because the students' protests articulated the frustrations of the people at large, the demonstrations quickly grew into a nationwide movement. Some of its keenest supporters were businessmen who had developed the skills and the contacts necessary not only to survive but to prosper within the system. But their affluence offered them no genuine sense of security or fulfillment, and they could not but see that if they and their fellow citizens, regardless of economic status, were to achieve a worthwhile existence, an accountable administration was at least a necessary if not a sufficient condition. The people of Burma had wearied of a precarious state of passive apprehension where they were "as water in the cupped hands" of the powers that be.

4 Emerald cool we may be
As water in cupped hands.
But oh that we might be
As splinters of glass
In cupped hands.[4]

5 Glass splinters, the smallest with its sharp, glinting power to defend itself against hands that try to crush, could be seen as a vivid symbol of the spark of courage that is an essential attribute of those who would free themselves from the grip of oppression. Bogyoke Aung San[5] regarded himself as a revolutionary and searched tirelessly for answers to the problems that beset Burma during her times of trial. He exhorted the people to develop courage: "Don't just depend on the courage and intrepidity of others. Each and every one of you must make sacrifices to become a hero possessed of courage and intrepidity. Then only shall we all be able to enjoy true freedom."

6 The effort necessary to remain uncorrupted in an environment where fear is an integral part of everyday existence is not immediately apparent to those fortunate enough to live in states governed by the rule of law. Just laws do not merely prevent corruption by meting out impartial punishment to offenders. They also help to create a society in which people can fulfill the basic requirements necessary for the preservation of human dignity without recourse to corrupt practices. Where there are no such laws, the burden of upholding the principles of justice and common decency falls on the ordinary people. It is the cumulative effect on their sustained effort and steady endurance which will change a nation where reason and conscience are warped by fear into one where legal rules exist to promote man's desire for harmony and justice while restraining the less desirable destructive traits in his nature.

7 In an age when immense technological advances have created lethal weapons which could be, and are, used by the powerful and the

---

4 A traditional Burmese poem

5 **Bogyoke Aung San**: the father of Aung San Suu Kyi, who led the fight to free Burma from British rule but was killed in July 1947, six months before independence

unprincipled to dominate the weak and the helpless, there is a compelling need for a closer relationship between politics and ethics at both the national and international levels. The Universal Declaration of Human Rights of the United Nations proclaims that "every individual and every organ of society" should strive to promote the basic rights and freedoms to which all human beings regardless of race, nationality or religion are entitled. But as long as there are governments whose authority is founded on coercion rather than on the mandate of the people, and interest groups which place short-term profits above long-term peace and prosperity, concerted international action to protect and promote human rights will remain at best a partially realized struggle. There will continue to be arenas of struggle where victims of oppression have to draw on their own inner resources to defend their inalienable rights as members of the human family.

8 The quintessential revolution is that of the spirit, born of an intellectual conviction of the need for change in those mental attitudes and values which shape the course of a nation's development. A revolution which aims merely at changing official policies and institutions with a view to an improvement in material conditions has little chance of genuine success. Without a revolution of the spirit, the forces which produced the iniquities of the old order would continue to be operative, posing a constant threat to the process of reform and regeneration. It is not enough merely to call for freedom, democracy and human rights. There has to be a united determination to persevere in the struggle, to make sacrifices in the name of enduring truths, to resist the corrupting influences of desire, ill will, ignorance and fear.

9 Saints, it has been said, are the sinners who go on trying. So free men are the oppressed who go on trying and who in the process make themselves fit to bear the responsibilities and to uphold the disciplines which will maintain a free society. Among the basic freedoms to which men aspire that their lives might be full and uncramped, freedom from fear stands out as both a means and an end. A people who would build a nation in which strong, democratic institutions are firmly established as a guarantee against state-induced power must first learn to liberate their own minds from apathy and fear.

10 Always one to practice what he preached, Aung San himself constantly demonstrated courage—not just the physical sort but the kind that enabled him to speak the truth, to stand by his word, to accept criticism, to admit his faults, to correct his mistakes, to respect the opposition, to parley[6] with the enemy and to let people be the judge of his worthiness as a leader. It is for such moral courage that he will always be loved and respected in Burma—not merely as a warrior hero but as the inspiration and conscience of the nation. The words used by Jawaharlal Nehru[7] to describe Mahatma Gandhi[8] could well be applied to Aung San:

---

6 **parley**: have discussions
7 **Jawaharlal Nehru**: activist in the movement for India's independence from Great Britain and India's first prime minister
8 **Mahatma Gandhi:** a leader in the nonviolent movement for India's independence

11 "The essence of his teaching was fearlessness and truth, and action allied to these, always keeping the welfare of the masses in view."

12 Gandhi, that great apostle of non-violence, and Aung San, the founder of a national army, were very different personalities, but as there is an inevitable sameness about the challenges of authoritarian rule anywhere at any time, so there is a similarity in the intrinsic qualities of those who rise up to meet the challenge. Nehru, who considered the instillation of courage in the people of India one of Gandhi's greatest achievements, was a political modernist, but as he assessed the needs for a twentieth-century movement for independence, he found himself looking back to the philosophy of ancient India: "The greatest gift for an individual or a nation was *abhaya*, fearlessness, not merely bodily courage but absence of fear from the mind."

13 Fearlessness may be a gift but perhaps more precious is the courage acquired through endeavour, courage that comes from cultivating the habit of refusing to let fear dictate one's actions, courage that could be described as "grace under pressure"—grace which is renewed repeatedly in the face of harsh, unremitting pressure.

14 Within a system which denies the existence of basic human rights, fear tends to be the order of the day. Fear of imprisonment, fear of torture, fear of death, fear of losing friends, family, property or means of livelihood, fear of poverty, fear of isolation, fear of failure. A most insidious[9] form of fear is that which masquerades as common sense or even wisdom, condemning as foolish, reckless, insignificant or futile the small, daily acts of courage which help to preserve man's self-respect and inherent human dignity. It is not easy for a people conditioned by fear under the iron rule of the principle that might is right to free themselves from the enervating[10] miasma[11] of fear. Yet even under the most crushing state machinery courage rises up again and again, for fear is not the natural state of civilized man.

15 The wellspring of courage and endurance in the face of unbridled power is generally a firm belief in the sanctity of ethical principles combined with a historical sense that despite all setbacks the condition of man is set on an ultimate course for both spiritual and material advancement. It is his capacity for self-improvement and self-redemption which most distinguishes man from the mere brute. At the root of human responsibility is the concept of perfection, the urge to achieve it, the intelligence to find a path towards it, and the will to follow that path if not to the end at least the distance needed to rise above individual limitations and environmental impediments. It is man's vision of a world fit for rational, civilized humanity which leads him to dare and to suffer to build societies free from want and fear. Concepts such as truth, justice and compassion cannot be dismissed as trite when these are often the only bulwarks which stand against ruthless power.

---

9 **insidious**: stealthy
10 **enervating**: energy-draining
11 **miasma**: oppressive atmosphere

Source: Claude Truong-Ngoc

Aung San Suu Kyi, State Counsellor of Myanmar (Burma) and leader of the National League for Democracy

Composing on Your Own

Respond to Aung San Suu Kyi's ideas by writing your own ideas on freedom of thought and democratic government. Carefully consider how you define freedom based on your own knowledge and experiences. Your definition may be a single sentence or a brief explanation consisting of a few sentences. Then list short examples and evidence to support your definition. You will be returning to these ideas throughout the unit, so save your work for future use.

Evaluating Writing: Student Draft
Tyrannical Rule

Following is the student draft anchor text you will use in this unit to better understand the skills you need to evaluate writing. A student wrote it for a class debate based on the following question: *The United States is often called "The Land of the Free and the Home of the Brave." Based on your own knowledge and experience, is the United States a free country?* The following draft still needs work. As you read it, consider what it adds to the discussion of governmental power and corruption. Write down your thoughts so you have notes for reference. Later you'll have an opportunity to suggest ways to improve the written argument.

(1) When most Americans think of tyranny, they think of Soviet Russia, Nazi Germany, or contemporary North Korea. (2) These same Americans are unaware of the oppressive ruling practices which have existed, and have even been celebrated, in their own *Land of the Free* and *Home of the Brave*. (3) This, of course, is because tyranny is universally accepted as being viciously oppressive and inhumane, something that a *civilized nation* like the U.S. could never be. (4) If an American considers the most common tyrannical practices—instigating or retaliating with violence, generating fear, scapegoating minority classes, and engaging in governmental corruption—they will have to admit that history offers plenty of examples to prove that tyrannical practices have been just as alive and

well in the U.S. as they have been in other countries. (5) Consequently, there were the Japanese internment camps during World War II. (6) But many people may question how a government founded upon the "unalienable rights" of "life, liberty, and the pursuit of happiness" can consistently allow such practices to crawl into its ruling protocol. (7) Now, is this tyranny to the same extent as actual dictatorships? (8) No. (9) It seems as though the common denominator in all of the governments mentioned above is this: humankind. (10) So, it might be time to realize that in the depths of human nature, no matter how well-intentioned, everyone is capable of compromising even the greatest of virtues for the sake of gaining and maintaining more power.

What Do You Know?

This unit provides instruction on clearly supporting your thesis, organizing your text, including transitional elements, and using appropriate and precise words to convey a specific tone. Before proceeding, assess what you already know about these concepts by answering questions about the anchor text by Aung San Suu Kyi and the student draft on tyrannical rule. Answering questions on subjects before formally studying them is a good way to learn.

CLOSE READING: PROFESSIONAL TEXT

1. Identify four claims that Aung San Suu Kyi makes in the text. Use specific quotes from the text.
2. Identify evidence or examples in Aung San Suu Kyi's speech that support the four claims you cited. Your evidence or examples should consist of four quotes from the passage.
3. Identify two areas of text where Aung San Suu Kyi explicitly (clearly) provides commentary by connecting her evidence to her thesis. Your answers should consist of two quotes from the passage.
4. Identify one way Aung San Suu Kyi builds a bridge between one claim and another.

EVALUATING WRITING: STUDENT DRAFT

1. Summarize the student writer's thesis in the draft paragraph.
2. Identify examples that the student writer offers in the paragraph to support this thesis.
3. Identify two areas where explicit, not implied, commentary or reasoning is offered in the paragraph.

Part 1

Constructing Cohesive Arguments

Enduring Understanding and Skills

Part 1

Understand

Writers guide understanding of a text's lines of reasoning and claims through that text's organization and integration of evidence. (REO-1)

Demonstrate

Describe the line of reasoning and explain whether it supports an argument's overarching thesis. (Reading 5.A)

Develop a line of reasoning and commentary that explains it throughout an argument. (Writing 6.A)

Source: *AP® English Language and Composition Course and Exam Description*

Essential Question: What role do body paragraphs play in laying out a line of reasoning?

Earlier an argument was compared to a bridge. As a reader, you cross the bridges the writer's reasoning provides so the major claims and conclusions seem coherent, logical, and meaningful. Experienced readers recognize those bridges and can evaluate how effectively they and the material they connect support the argument's overarching thesis. As a writer, your job is to guide your reader through a line of reasoning by providing support and connectors that clearly validate your argument. You build that support throughout your essay's body paragraphs. The connectors, columns, and foundations in Figure 5-1 represent an argument's supporting claims, commentary, and evidence.

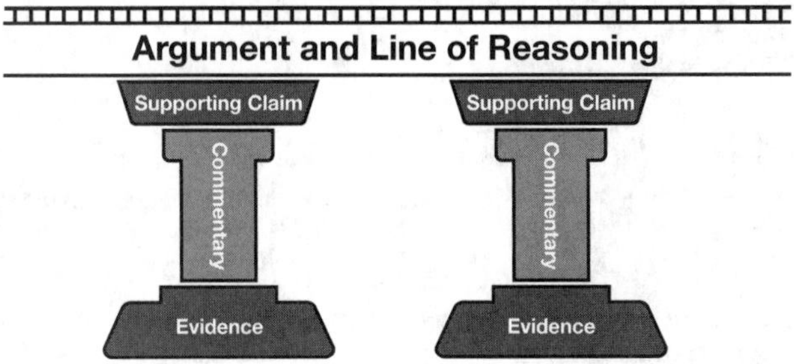

Figure 5-1

Part 1 of the unit will help you understand the purpose and construction of an argument's body paragraphs, which make up the largest part of any essay. You will read about different functions of body paragraphs and types of support body paragraphs that serve useful rhetorical purposes. You will use what you learned about effective, purposeful paragraphs in earlier units to help you build well-developed arguments and essays.

KEY TERMS

body paragraph	commentary
evidence	reasoning

1.1 Functions of Body Paragraphs | REO-1.M

Body paragraphs—those between the introduction and conclusion—have several different functions. They include making claims, supporting them with evidence, and providing commentary that explains how each paragraph contributes to the reasoning of the main argument and supports the overarching thesis. As your writing advances, you will see other purposes for body paragraphs, such as clarifying a point or introducing a complication.

One body paragraph might fulfill only a single function. Another might fulfill two or three at once. In most student essays, body paragraphs include three functions: making claims, providing evidence, and providing commentary. If you use the pattern of making a claim, supporting it with evidence, and providing commentary, you'll have a consistent model to help ensure that you communicate your arguments as effectively as possible.

A typical body paragraph in general academic writing opens with a topic sentence that makes a claim to support the thesis, the overarching claim. Topic sentences may also indicate what evidence will be presented or explored in the paragraph. As a result, the topic sentence connects evidence to the thesis. Read the following section from a book by Timothy Snyder, *On Tyranny: Twenty Lessons from the Twentieth Century.* The excerpt on the next page is Lesson 13, "Practice corporeal politics," which explores the necessary elements of successful political resistance.

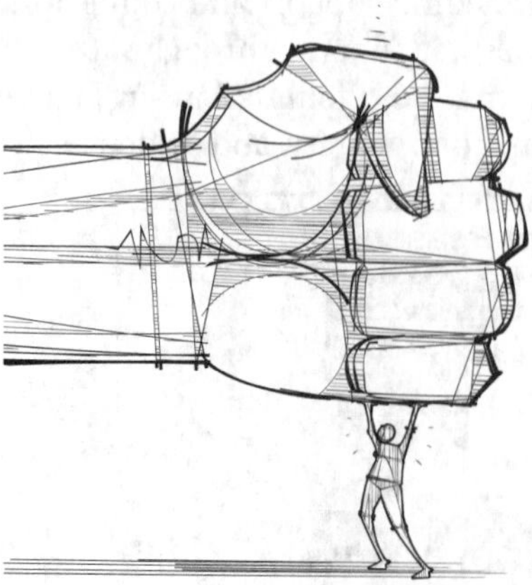

Source: Getty Images

What does this drawing suggest about how to fight oppression? What details led you to that inference?

Thesis

Power wants your body softening in your chair and your emotions dissipating on the screen. Get outside. Put your body in unfamiliar places with unfamiliar people. Make new friends and march with them.

Body Paragraph 1

For resistance to succeed, two boundaries must be crossed. First, ideas about change must engage people of various backgrounds who do not agree about everything. Second, people must find themselves in places that are not their homes, and among groups who were not previously their friends. Protest can be organized through social media, but nothing is real that does not end on the streets. If tyrants feel no consequences for their actions in the three-dimensional world, nothing will change.

Body Paragraph 2

The one example of successful resistance to communism was the Solidarity labor movement in Poland in 1980–81: a coalition of workers and professionals, elements of the Roman Catholic Church, and secular groups. Its leaders had learned hard lessons under communism. In 1968, the regime mobilized workers against students who protested. In 1970, when a strike in Gdańsk on the Baltic coast was bloodily suppressed, it was the workers' turn to feel isolated. In 1976, however, intellectuals and professionals formed a group to assist workers who had been abused by the government. These were people from both the Right and the Left, believers and atheists, who created trust among workers—people whom they would not otherwise have met.

Body Paragraph 3

When Polish workers on the Baltic coast went on strike again in 1980, they were joined by lawyers, scholars, and others who helped them make their case. The result was the creation of a free labor union, as well as government guarantees to observe human rights. During the sixteen months that Solidarity was legal, ten million people joined and countless new friendships were created amid strikes, marches, and demonstrations. The Polish communist regime put down the movement with martial law in 1981. Yet eight years later, in 1989, when they needed negotiating partners, the communists had to turn to Solidarity. The labor union insisted on elections, which it then won. This was the beginning of the end of communism in Poland, eastern Europe, and the Soviet Union.

The Role of Supporting Claims in an Essay

The thesis in this excerpt—a call to action—is expressed colorfully in the first paragraph, repeated below. Each of the three paragraphs that follow supports the thesis by presenting and providing evidence for additional claims. In body paragraphs 1 and 2, the supporting claim is the first sentence. In body paragraph 3, the supporting claim is the final sentence.

> **Thesis:** Power wants your body softening in your chair and your emotions dissipating on the screen. Get outside. Put your body in unfamiliar places with unfamiliar people. Make new friends and march with them.
>
> **Supporting Claim**: (Body paragraph 1) For resistance to succeed, two boundaries must be crossed.
>
> **Supporting Claim**: (Body paragraph 2) The one example of successful resistance to communism was the Solidarity labor movement in Poland in 1980–81: a coalition of workers and professionals, elements of the Roman Catholic Church, and secular groups.
>
> **Supporting Claim**: (Body paragraph 3) This [the power of Solidarity] was the beginning of the end of communism in Poland, eastern Europe, and the Soviet Union.

Snyder's overarching claim is that to stand up to power, people need to march in unfamiliar places with unfamiliar people.

A topic sentence typically introduces a key supporting claim that is further expanded within the paragraph. The topic sentence of body paragraph 1 above supports that thesis by introducing another claim that specifies the requirements for successful resistance. The topic sentence of body paragraph 2 supports the thesis by introducing the claim that the Solidarity movement in Poland was a successful example of resistance. The topic sentence of body paragraph 3 supports the overarching thesis by introducing a claim about the significance of the resistance movement—it was the beginning of the end of the grip a major world ideology and political structure had on Eastern Europe.

The Role of Topic Sentences in a Paragraph

While the supporting claims in each body paragraph bolster the overarching thesis of the essay, the topic sentences also present their own claims that need support. **Evidence,** as you know from previous units, is support for a claim. The more concrete, or solid, the evidence is, the more strongly it will support the argument.

Evidence on its own, though, is not enough to support an argument. So in addition to laying out a claim in the topic sentence and supporting it with evidence, a body paragraph may also provide **commentary**, which explains the relationship between the evidence and the topic sentence's claim and typically supports the argument as stated in the thesis. The commentary explains a writer's **reasoning**, which is his or her thinking about how the evidence supports and relates to the overarching argument.

The analysis below shows how Snyder uses a typical body paragraph pattern to provide evidence following the topic sentence. The evidence is a number of specific details that expand on the topic sentence. He then adds commentary to explain why the evidence supports the claim in the topic sentence.

Topic Sentence: (Body paragraph 1) For resistance to succeed, two boundaries must be crossed.

Evidence: First, ideas about change must engage people of various backgrounds who do not agree about everything. Second, people must find themselves in places that are not their homes, and among groups who were not previously their friends. Protest can be organized through social media, but nothing is real that does not end on the streets.

Commentary: If tyrants feel no consequences for their actions in the three-dimensional world, nothing will change.

Commentary in the body paragraphs also explains how each paragraph contributes to the line of reasoning.

Thesis: Power wants your body softening in your chair and your emotions dissipating on the screen. Get outside. Put your body in unfamiliar places with unfamiliar people. Make new friends and march with them.

Commentary in body paragraph 1: If tyrants feel no consequences for their actions in the three-dimensional world, nothing will change.

Role in line of reasoning: This sentence explains why people have to make new friends and march with them to successfully resist power.

Commentary in body paragraph 2: These were people from both the Right and the Left, believers and atheists, who created trust among workers—people whom they would not otherwise have met.

Role in line of reasoning: This paragraph shows concrete examples of both unsuccessful resistance (1968 student protest with workers mobilized against them and 1970 workers' strike with no support from others) and the power of unity with others (formation of diverse group in 1976 to support abused workers). The commentary ties the latter example back to the thesis by pointing out that the people in the new group were a diverse mix with different views. The importance of their working together was to create trust.

Commentary in paragraph 3: During the sixteen months that Solidarity was legal, ten million people joined, and countless new friendships were created amid strikes, marches, and demonstrations. The Polish communist regime put down the movement with martial law in 1981. Yet eight years later, in 1989, when they needed negotiating partners, the communists had to turn to Solidarity.

Role in line of reasoning: This paragraph shows the lasting power of the trust diverse people working together can create. Even though Solidarity had been crushed under martial law, it was still vibrant enough to be a negotiating partner for those in power.

Writers can also synthesize information, quotes, and ideas from others to help shape their commentary, as in the example below from another part of Snyder's book, Lesson 18, "Be calm when the unthinkable arrives." Those parts are noted in the margin.

Thesis	Modern tyranny is terror management. When the terrorist attack comes, remember that authoritarians exploit such events in order to consolidate power. The sudden disaster that requires the end of checks and balances, the dissolution of opposition parties, the suspension of freedom of expression, the right to a fair trial, and so on, is the oldest trick in the Hitlerian book. Do not fall for it.
Body paragraph 1 Primary source quotes	The Reichstag fire was the moment when Hitler's government, which came to power mainly through democratic means, became the menacingly permanent Nazi regime. It is the archetype of terror management. On February 27, 1933, at about nine p.m., the building housing the German parliament, the Reichstag, began to burn. Who set the fire that night in Berlin? We don't know, and it doesn't really matter. What matters is that this spectacular act of terror initiated the politics of emergency. Gazing with pleasure at the flames that night, Hitler said: "This fire is just the beginning." Whether or not the Nazis set the fire, Hitler saw the political opportunity: "There will be no mercy now. Anyone standing in our way will be cut down." The next day a decree suspended the basic rights of all German citizens, allowing them to be "preventively detained" by the police. On the strength of Hitler's claim that the fire was the work of Germany's enemies, the Nazi Party won a decisive victory in parliamentary elections on March 5. The police and the Nazi paramilitaries began to round up members of left-wing political parties and place them in improvised concentration camps. On March 23 the new parliament passed an "enabling act," which allowed Hitler to rule by decree. Germany then remained in a state of emergency for the next twelve years, until the end of the Second World War. Hitler had used an act of terror, an event of limited inherent significance, to institute a regime of terror that killed millions of people and changed the world. . . .

(continued)

Concluding paragraph

For tyrants, the lesson of the Reichstag fire is that one moment of shock enables an eternity of submission. For us, the lesson is that our natural fear and grief must not enable the destruction of our institutions. Courage does not mean not fearing, or not grieving. It does mean recognizing and resisting terror management right away, from the moment of the attack, precisely when it seems most difficult to do so. [Fourth U.S. president and "Father of the Bill of Rights"] James Madison nicely made the point that tyranny arises "on some favorable emergency." After the Reichstag fire, [political philosopher and German Jew] Hannah Arendt wrote that "I was no longer of the opinion that one can simply be a bystander."

Primary source quotes and ideas of others

Commentary bridges the evidence to the claim. It can be the most important part of supporting an argument. It provides the direct link between the evidence and the writer's line of reasoning. If the commentary fails to clearly support this link, the argument collapses.

Use the following template to help you provide commentary in the paragraphs you write.

> This evidence proves [claim] because [explain how].

Notice how this template works with the commentary from the first body paragraph on page 252. The bracketed parts in the template are underlined in the example below.

> This evidence proves that <u>modern tyranny is terror management,</u> because in the example of Hitler's rise to power, <u>Hitler said that the fire was "just the beginning." He saw the political opportunity: "There will be no mercy now. Anyone standing in our way will be cut down."</u>

The template shows a simplified version of providing commentary. Not all body paragraphs follow this or any other one specific model. Many paragraphs are *deductive,* meaning that they present a claim, offer evidence, and provide commentary. However, some arguments are *inductive,* meaning the writer presents evidence and commentary before introducing the reasonable argument that derives from the evidence. A deductive argument might state: *all species of bats use echolocation to guide themselves at night.* The author would have to support this statement with multiple examples to support the point. An inductive argument might state: *the common brown bat uses echolocation to guide itself at night, so all species of bats likely use echolocation.* The writer starts with a specific example, and then seeks to apply this example to a larger supposition or argument.

Not all body paragraphs need to fulfill all functions—making a supporting claim, providing evidence, and providing commentary to tie the evidence to the claim. When constructing body paragraphs, keep a balance between evidence and commentary, allowing readers to connect the dots in a chain of reasoning and fill any gaps they might encounter. Returning to the bridge metaphor: You take care to construct your argument in the way you believe will make most sense to your readers and achieve your purpose; you guide your readers, but in the end the readers cross the bridge on their own. If you thoughtfully consider how best to support your argument with evidence and commentary, you can create a well-reasoned argument that a reader will follow.

> **Remember:** The body paragraphs of a written argument make claims, support them with evidence, and provide commentary that explains how the paragraph contributes to the reasoning of the argument. (REO-1.M)

1.1 Checkpoint

Close Reading: Professional Text

Reread Aung San Suu Kyi's speech on pages 241–244. Then complete the following open response activity and answer the multiple-choice questions.

1. Select several body paragraphs from the speech. On separate paper, describe how each paragraph is constructed. Your descriptions should reveal the paragraphs' presentation of a claim within a topic sentence, evidence, and/or commentary. Remember that some body paragraphs contain only claims, only evidence, or only commentary. Others contain a blend of those elements. Avoid selecting more than three consecutive paragraphs. Instead, choose paragraphs from across the speech.

2. Which of the following best describes the line of reasoning the author develops in the body paragraphs of her speech?
   - (A) She describes a series of injustices with escalating seriousness and tragic consequence.
   - (B) She presents a series of arguments and refutes them one by one.
   - (C) She illustrates the cause-and-effect relationship between fear and injustice.
   - (D) She alludes to past historical figures who agreed with her central argument in the speech.
   - (E) She uses strong emotional descriptions that help her redefine the meaning of courage.

3. In paragraph 2, the author suggests that political uprisings may be caused most of all by

    (A) political corruption among leaders
    (B) economic concerns among student demonstrators
    (C) strife between warring political factions
    (D) high inflation
    (E) feelings of humiliation among the populace

Evaluating Writing: Student Draft

Reread the student draft about tyrannical rule on pages 245–246. Then on separate paper complete the following open response activities and answer the multiple-choice question.

1. Use your knowledge and understanding of history and consider the claims this paragraph makes. Then rewrite sentence 5 by adding at least two more examples to support the claim the writer is making.

2. Add sentences to the student paragraph to clearly explain how the evidence relates to the writer's claim. You should consider adding a sentence after sentence 5, 8, or 9.

3. The student writer is considering adding the following language to the end of sentence 5, adjusting the punctuation as needed:

    the Trail of Tears incident and unjust treatment of native Americans, the Jim Crow laws of the 20th century, and the Supreme Court's decision in Plessy v. Ferguson

    Should the writer add this language?

    (A) No, because the example provided already accurately illustrates the writer's claim.
    (B) No, because the added examples are not contextually appropriate.
    (C) Yes, because the examples act as a transition between abstract concepts.
    (D) Yes, because the additional examples help strengthen the claim.
    (E) Yes, because the added examples illustrate how American democracy differs from tyrannical governments.

Composing on Your Own

Skim the response you wrote after your first reading of Aung San Suu Kyi's speech and any notes you made regarding the student paragraph about tyrannical rule. You will now begin developing these ideas and continue throughout the unit.

As you have read, the elements of the rhetorical situation greatly influence the choices a writer makes. Before you do more writing, take time to choose or create a rhetorical situation. Choose or adapt any of the contexts, audiences, and purposes below or create your own. Write down the choices you make.

Contexts/Formats
▪ A school-run website focused on improving school governance ▪ A student YouTube channel focused on local policing ▪ A school task force to encourage more student representation in local government
Audiences
▪ Students and teachers ▪ Students, teachers, parents, and local government leaders
Purposes
▪ Promote a greater role for student involvement ▪ Encourage closer communication to avoid misunderstandings ▪ Address concerns that students face within the community

On the topic of tyranny or another topic you find particularly interesting, write a paragraph in which you articulate a thesis statement and then follow it with two body paragraphs that supply supporting claims and evidence. Provide brief commentary to connect the evidence to your claims. Keep your rhetorical situation in mind as you write so you can effectively target your message. Save your work for later use.

Part 1 Apply What You Have Learned

Read or listen to "Tuskegee University Commencement Address" delivered by Michelle Obama on May 9, 2015. You can find it easily online. Bookmark it for future use. Then answer the questions below.

1. What thesis about "double-duty" does Obama make in this speech?
2. What evidence for this thesis does she present in the first half of the speech? What evidence does she present in the final half of the speech?
3. Summarize Obama's line of reasoning and find two examples where she provides commentary to help support that line of reasoning.

Reflect on the Essential Question: Write a brief response that answers this essential question: *What role do body paragraphs play in laying out a line of reasoning?* In your response, use and explain the key terms listed on page 248.

Part 2

Maintaining Coherence and Using Transitions

Enduring Understanding and Skills

Part 2

Understand

Writers guide understanding of a text's lines of reasoning and claims through that text's organization and integration of evidence. (REO-1)

Demonstrate

Explain how the organization of a text creates unity and coherence and reflects a line of reasoning. (Reading 5.B)

Use transitional elements to guide the reader through the line of reasoning of an argument. (Writing 6.B)

Source: AP® English Language and Composition Course and Exam Description

Essential Question: How does a text create unity and coherence and use transitions to guide readers through a line of reasoning?

Source: Pixabay

Imagine you had to cross the brook shown in this photo. Which path forward would you take? Would you choose the stepping-stone bridge, with its disconnected, unevenly positioned parts? Or would you instead opt for the solid support of the interconnected bridge?

Most people would naturally choose the solid bridge because it is the easier option and offers little risk of slipping into the muddy water below. Though the stepping-stone bridge allows crossing from one side to the other, why choose the uneven and treacherous option? In the same way, why settle for an argument that is supported by insufficient evidence when you can create one that is well-constructed and highly effective? As a writer, you want to create a unified, coherent line of reasoning that smoothly guides your reader from point to point.

In Part 1 of this unit, you explored the importance of producing body paragraphs with evidence and reasonable commentary to support your argument. In Parts 2 and 3, you'll read about how to create coherence and make stylistic choices to ensure that your arguments will be unified and logical, with clear connections between your claims and other aspects of your argument.

KEY TERMS

clause	phrase	sentence
coherence	pronoun	synonym
parallel structure	repetition	transitional elements

2.1 Levels of Coherence | REO-1.N

Coherence—the quality of being logically organized and smoothly connected—occurs at different levels in a piece of writing. In a coherent sentence, the idea in one clause logically links to an idea in the next clause. In a coherent paragraph, the idea in one sentence logically links to an idea in the one that follows. In a coherent text, one paragraph's ideas logically link to those in the next paragraph.

A coherent argument is consistently logical and also unified. In a unified argument, all the examples and commentary logically work together to support the main claim and build the central argument. When an argument is unified, its logic is coherent—or clearly understandable—to the reader. Effective writers make strategic choices about how to organize the argument's ideas to ensure that each one links to another and that the relationships between them serve to further the argument. To make sure that an argument maintains the three main qualities of coherence—consistency, logical reasonability, and unity—writers link the ideas on three levels: sentence, paragraph, and the overall argument.

Coherence within Sentences

Sentences are the most common building block of essays. At its most basic level, a **sentence** is simply a group of words that together present a complete idea. To qualify as a complete idea it must contain at least one **clause**, a group of words that contains a subject and a verb. A clause that makes sense on its own is called an independent clause. A sentence with only one independent clause is called a *simple sentence.* If a clause cannot stand on its own, it is a *dependent clause.*

For example, look at the simple sentence below.

(S) (V)
At the river, **I crossed** the solid bridge.

At the river is an introductory **phrase**; it does not contain a subject and verb. *I crossed the solid bridge* is an independent clause that can function as a complete idea on its own.

Logically Linked Clauses within a Sentence Both parts of the following sentence contain a clause.

(S) (V) (S) (V)
When **I reached** the river, **I crossed** the solid bridge.

The first clause in the sentence is *When I reached the river,* which is incomplete on its own. It leaves the reader or listener wondering, "then what?" The clause has a subject and a verb, but because the idea is not complete, it is a *dependent clause.* To complete the idea and create a cohesive sentence, you have to add a second clause: *I crossed the solid bridge,* or something else to answer the "then what?" question.

The following sentence from Snyder's essay shows internal coherence in the same way. The dependent clause is in italics.

> *If tyrants feel no consequences for their actions in the three-dimensional world*, nothing will change.

The first clause is a dependent clause, leaving the reader to ask, "then what?" or some similar question to see where the thought will lead. In this case, the thought leads smoothly to the independent clause in the sentence: "nothing will change." (See Part 2.3 for more on connectors, or *transitional elements,* within sentences.)

Simple Sentences When you write an argument or other type of essay, strive to use a blend of sentence types. The type of sentence you use will depend on how you want to organize your ideas. For example, a simple sentence with just one subject and one verb is an excellent choice when you want to present important information concisely. The most basic sentence can highlight significant information, especially when it is not surrounded by many other simple sentences. If you were to write in only simple sentences, however, your work would sound stilted and mechanical, qualities that typically harm coherence.

Compound Sentences A *compound sentence* is one that contains at least two independent clauses linked by some form of punctuation. If you were to take the sentence apart, you would have two complete thoughts. When you create a compound sentence, your goal is to link your ideas through *coordination,* the connection between two or more ideas having equal importance. Some of the ways that you can coordinate a sentence are shown on the next page.

WAYS TO CREATE SENTENCE COHERENCE THROUGH COORDINATION

Punctuation: Comma and a coordinating conjunction

, *and* (in addition) , *but* (in contrast)	, *or* (in contrast; choice or possibility) , *nor* (in contrast) , *for* (cause/effect; reason)	, *so* (cause/effect) , *yet* (in contrast) , *and then* (time order)

Purpose

Demonstrates balance and equality in the relationship of ideas

Caution: Commas typically come *before* coordinating conjunctions when the conjunction is before the last word (or phrase) in a list or when the conjunction connects two independent clauses.

Example

I reached the river**,** ***and*** I crossed the solid bridge.

Punctuation: Semicolon. [;]

Purpose

Tells the reader that the ideas of each independent clause are closely related. It's like using a comma, but without the conjunction. In fact, it functions exactly as its parts look—semicolons provide the pause of a comma (bottom part) and yet can be replaced by a period (top part) and the sentence will still make sense.

Example

I reached the river**;** I crossed the solid bridge.

Punctuation: Colon [:]

Purpose

Separates full clauses by defining or clarifying an element found in the first clause; often introduces an explanation or list

Examples

I reached the river**:** it was quite swampy.

We need four ingredients to make muffins**:** flour, sugar, milk, and butter.

Punctuation: Semicolon, a conjunctive adverb, and a comma

; however, (contrast) *; consequently,* (cause/effect) *; therefore,* (cause/effect)	*; accordingly,* (cause/effect) *; furthermore,* (in addition to)

Purpose

The conjunctive adverb connects the equal idea; however, it indicates an adverbial relationship such as those shown in parentheses.

Example

I reached the river**;** consequently**,** I crossed the solid bridge.

Table 5-1

Complex Sentences Sometimes the ideas you present in a single sentence may not be of equal importance or emphasis. In that case, a complex sentence will convey the relationship. A *complex sentence* is one in which one clause, the independent clause, can stand on its own, while the other, the dependent clause, cannot. The purpose of a dependent clause is to show that the idea it contains is related to the idea in the independent clause but is not as important. These dependent clauses are called *subordinate clauses* (derived from the Latin words meaning "under" and "rank"). Like a compound sentence, a complex sentence can demonstrate relationships between ideas that suggest contrast, cause and effect, or time order. The dependent clause adds information to the independent clause through the use of a *subordinating conjunction*, a joining word that shows the connection between independent and dependent clauses. The subordinating conjunction always precedes the dependent clause.

Subordinating Conjunctions (and Relationships)	Comma Rule	Examples
*after** (chronology) *as* (chronology or cause/effect) *before** (chronology) *until** (chronology) *while* (chronology) *because* (cause/effect) *if* (cause/effect) *since** (cause/effect) *unless* (cause/effect) *when* (cause/effect) *although* (contrast) *as if* (in addition to) *so that* (logical outcome) *These words can also function as prepositions.	If your sentence begins with a subordinating conjunction, you must add a comma after the first clause. The same does not always apply to sentences in which the subordinating conjunction comes after the independent clause because there is typically no forced pause in speech.	When I reached the river, I crossed the solid bridge. After we ate dinner, we washed the dishes. He should be more careful since he often misplaces things.

Table 5-2

In the first example in the chart, although there are two clauses in the sentence, the more important information is *I crossed the solid bridge.* What is the more important information in the following two sentences in the chart?

Writers typically vary their sentence length depending on the needs of the writing. Short, simple sentences may be used for emphasis. Compound sentences may be used to link ideas. Complex sentences can explicitly show the relationship of various ideas, while giving the writing a smooth, forward flow.

Coherence between Sentences

Just as different parts of a sentence should be logically linked and coherent, different sentences within a paragraph should stand in relation to one another. Notice how tightly linked the sentences are in the following paragraph.

> For resistance to succeed, *two boundaries* must be crossed. *First,* ideas about change must engage people of various backgrounds who do not agree about everything. *Second,* people must find themselves in places that are not their homes, and among groups who were not previously their friends. Protest can be organized through social media, but nothing is real that does not end on the streets. If tyrants feel no consequences for their actions in the three-dimensional world, nothing will change.

Sentence 1 refers to "two boundaries" that must be crossed. From this sentence, the reader expects those boundaries to be identified, which Snyder does in the next sentence. The word *First* starting the second sentence draws a connection back to the previous sentence, since the reader knows this is one of the two boundaries mentioned in that sentence. In the following sentence, the word *Second* fulfills the same purpose, linking back to both the second and first sentences. These connecting words are transitional elements, meaning they help the writing move smoothly from one idea or subject to another..

Coherence between Paragraphs

In the same way that sentences within a paragraph should be logically connected to one another, paragraphs within an essay should link logically to other paragraphs. Notice how **repetition**, repeated words, ideas, and structure tie the following paragraphs together (see Part 2.2). Other transitional elements can also tie paragraphs together (see Part 2.3).

Thesis	Modern tyranny is *terror management*. When the terrorist attack comes, remember that authoritarians exploit such events in order to consolidate power. The sudden disaster that requires the end of checks and balances, the dissolution of opposition parties, the suspension of freedom of expression, the right to a fair trial, and so on, is the oldest trick in the Hitlerian book. Do not fall for it.
1st Body Paragraph	The Reichstag fire was the moment when Hitler's government, which came to power mainly through democratic means, became the menacingly permanent Nazi regime. It is the archetype of *terror management*.
Concluding Paragraph	For tyrants, the lesson of the Reichstag fire is that one moment of shock enables an eternity of submission. For us, the lesson is that our natural fear and grief must not enable the destruction of our institutions. Courage does not mean not fearing, or not grieving. It does mean recognizing and resisting *terror management* right away, from the moment of the attack, precisely when it seems most difficult to do so.

The paragraphs in Snyder's essay are also linked through their line of reasoning. The first paragraph presents a general statement that equates tyranny with terror management wherever it might occur. The second paragraph, to develop that idea logically, provides a strong example: the rise to power of Hitler after the fire at the German parliament building and the consequences of letting down your democratic guard as the result of an act of terror. The final paragraph takes the argument to its conclusion by stating the lessons to be learned from that example and explaining how to recognize and react to terror management when it is happening around you.

Remember: Coherence occurs at different levels in a piece of writing. In a sentence, the idea in one clause logically links to an idea in the next clause. In a paragraph, the idea in one sentence logically links to an idea in the one that follows. In a text, one paragraph's ideas logically link to those in the next paragraph. (REO-1.N)

2.1 Checkpoint

Close Reading: Professional Text

Reread Aung San Suu Kyi's speech on pages 241–244. Then complete the chart below and answer the multiple-choice questions.

1. On separate paper, create a chart similar to the one below. Using Aung San Suu Kyi's speech, fill in the chart to show how she uses clauses, sentences, and paragraphs to create coherence by logically linking ideas. First, in the middle column, list examples of the text parts that appear in the paragraphs cited. Then, in the last column, explain how each text part helps Aung San Suu Kyi connect ideas in her speech.

Text Part	Example from Text	Explanation of Logical Link
Clauses (paragraph 3)		
Sentence (paragraph 1)		
Paragraph (paragraph 11)		

2. In the last sentence of paragraph 7, the phrase "inner resources" most likely links to the essay's earlier appeals for people to address social injustices with

   (A) violence
   (B) protests
   (C) courage
   (D) reckless abandon
   (E) democracy

3. The main idea expressed in the first sentence of paragraph 9 echoes which of the following words in the last sentence of paragraph 8?

   (A) united
   (B) persevere
   (C) truths
   (D) corrupting
   (E) ignorance

Evaluating Writing: Student Draft

Reread the student draft on pages 245–246. Then answer the following open response and multiple-choice questions.

1. Identify several places where repetition or another strategy helps link sentences and clauses together.

2. Identify a place where the linking could be stronger and suggest a way to revise it to accomplish that goal.

3. In the paragraph, the writer wants to ensure that the sentences progress coherently so that the ideas in one sentence link to the ideas in the next. What should the writer do with sentence 6 (reproduced below) to best achieve this goal?

   But many people may question how a government founded upon the "unalienable rights" of "life, liberty, and the pursuit of happiness" can consistently allow such practices to crawl into its ruling protocol.

   (A) Move it before sentence 2.
   (B) Move it after sentence 3.
   (C) Move it before sentence 5.
   (D) Move it after sentence 8.
   (E) Move it after sentence 9.

Composing on Your Own

Review the paragraphs you wrote on the subject of tyranny or another subject of interest to you. Check to make sure you provide at least one piece of evidence and brief commentary to connect evidence to each of your claims. Then look for ways of increasing the coherence of your sentences by using effective coordination, punctuation, and subordinating conjunctions. When reviewing your work, keep the rhetorical situation in mind and make choices and changes accordingly. Save your work for later use.

2.2 Repeated Words and Patterns that Strengthen Coherence | REO-1.O

As you have seen, repetition is one way to make connections. In the example from Snyder's book, the repeated use of the phrases *terror management* and *Reichstag fire* help tie together different paragraphs and serve as guideposts for readers to follow the writer's line of reasoning. But anything that draws a reader's attention back to something already stated creates a connection. Repeating ideas, syntactical patterns, evidence, and even individual words helps maintain logical coherence in an essay. Writers consciously choose how and when to repeat language and language structures. Done well, repetition through various techniques helps your meaning come through clearly, logically, and smoothly.

Using Synonyms

Experienced writers tend to repeat ideas throughout their work as they develop their line of reasoning. Rather than use the same word each time, however, writers often use **synonyms**—words that have similar meanings and can in some cases be used interchangeably. One practical value of this approach is to avoid monotony. For example, in an essay about the natural habits of wild boars, readers might soon grow tired of hearing only the term *wild boars* to identify them. Good writers learn to shift their language to avoid monotony, and in this case they might refer to wild boars using synonyms for them, such as *feral pigs*, *warthogs*, or *peccary*, throughout the essay.

Synonyms also have an important role in engaging readers and in so doing strengthening coherence. Like repetition, synonyms draw readers' attention back to something they have read already, but the tie is now between what the words stand for, not the words themselves. In the following passage from *Horizon*, nature writer Barry Lopez uses several different terms for rain and for the arrangement of clouds in the sky as a storm approaches.

> At dusk the coming rain is still little more than mist beading up on my cheekbones, a chill on the back of my hands. In the agitated air, droplets of water tremble on my fingernails when I hold my hands still.

> Somewhere, once, someone must have composed a list of the gradations of color I now see before me in the sky: the grays of pigeon feathers, of slate and pearls; in one sector the puce [reddish brown] of a fresh bruise, in another the whites of eggshells. In the taxonomic language of meteorology, the sky is heaped with nimbostratus and cumulonimbus. Tiers of clouds are decked shoulder to shoulder in every direction.

The synonyms Lopez uses for *rain* are *mist beading up* and *droplets of water.* The synonyms for the arrangement of the clouds are *heaped with, tiers of clouds*, and *decked shoulder to shoulder*. These words serve almost as magnets back to other words that mean the same or nearly the same thing, creating coherence. However, since no two words mean *exactly* the same thing, synonyms can provide additional meaning or nuance to a subject. Each synonym for the cloud arrangement, for example, adds another piece to the scene unfolding before the reader's eyes.

For another example, consider the words *irritated, annoyed, angry, mad, irate*, and *furious*. They are all synonyms, but they describe different degrees of the same feeling. People frequently use *angry* and *mad* to generically describe their feelings, but these adjectives lack specificity. However, feeling *irate* or *furious* is a more extreme sensation than feeling *irritated* or *annoyed*. Different words often reveal the degree of a feeling or sensation.

Using Pronouns and References

A **pronoun** is a word that can replace a noun in a sentence. The most commonly used pronouns are *I, you, he, she, it, they, that,* and *this*. Readers would have no trouble knowing to whom the pronouns *I* and *you* refer. But other pronouns would not make sense if they are not preceded by the noun they are replacing. That noun is called a reference, or antecedent (which derives from the Latin words meaning "going before"). Like repetition and synonyms, pronouns and their antecedents have a magnetic effect; pronouns pull a reader back to the antecedent, creating coherence and flow. Readers actively engaged in making these connections are also actively engaged in the text as a whole.

The following passage is from *Talking to Strangers: What We Should Know about the People We Don't Know* by Malcolm Gladwell. It narrates the arrival of the first Spanish people in Mexico. All of the pronouns are bracketed. What are their antecedents, or references?

> Cortés landed in Mexico in February of 1519 and slowly made [his] way inland, advancing on the Aztec capital of Tenochtitlán. When Cortés and [his] army arrived, [they] were in awe. Tenochtitlán was an extraordinary sight—far larger and more impressive than any of the cities Cortés and [his] men would have known back in Spain. [It] was a city on an island, linked to the mainland with bridges and crossed by canals. [It] had grand boulevards, elaborate aqueducts, thriving marketplaces, temples built in brilliant white stucco, public gardens and even a zoo. [It] was spotlessly clean—which, to someone raised in the filth of medieval European cities, would have seemed almost miraculous.

After you've found the antecedents for all the pronouns, try reading the passage with the antecedents in place of the pronouns. You would not have to read far to see how clumsy that becomes: Cortés landed in Mexico in February of 1519 and slowly made [Cortés's] way inland, advancing on the Aztec capital of Tenochtitlán. When Cortés and [Cortés's] army arrived, [Cortés and Cortés's army] were in awe.

Once you establish an antecedent, you need provide only enough context for your reader to know to whom or what your pronoun refers. You may also decide *not* to use a pronoun and instead repeat the antecedent, as Gladwell does in several places. In sentence 2, for example, Gladwell repeats *Cortés* instead of using *he*. In the third sentence he repeats the antecedent *Tenochtitlán* instead of using the pronoun *it*. Striking the perfect balance between pronouns and their antecedents gives your writing coherence and smoothness. Learn to maintain coherence and clarity when shifting between pronouns and their antecedents.

Using Repetition and Parallel Structure

While writers want to use a variety of words to express themselves, purposeful repetition—whether of words, phrases, sentences, or sentence structures—is one of the most valuable tools available to writers. Used effectively, it will help you emphasize ideas in your writing. When you discover elements of repetition as you read, you should ask yourself what the writer is specifically trying to emphasize. Emphasizing important points helps focus readers' attention and create coherence.

Notice the emphasis in the following passage from the speech by Malala Yousafzai (Unit 2).

> **We call upon** all governments to ensure free, compulsory education all over the world for every child. **We call upon** all the governments to fight against terrorism and violence. To protect children from brutality and harm. **We call upon** the developed nations to support the expansion of education opportunities for girls in the developing world. **We call upon** all communities to be tolerant, to reject prejudice based on caste, creed, sect, color, religion or agenda to ensure freedom and equality for women so they can flourish. **We cannot all succeed** when half of us are held back. **We call upon** our sisters around the world to be brave, to embrace the strength within themselves and realize their full potential.

There are two types of repetition in the above quote. One is called *anaphora*, which means the repetition of the same phrase at the beginnings of clauses. The second is **parallel structure**, which means using the same or a similar pattern of words to show that two or more ideas have equal importance.

Notice that even when a sentence doesn't begin with the phrase "We call upon," all the sentences are still structured the same way. The repetition of "We call upon" emphasizes Yousafzai's charge to world leaders. By repeating the word *we*, she emphasizes the idea that multitudes of people are calling on world leaders for support. There is strength in numbers, and Yousafzai recognizes this. Toward the end of the speech, Yousafzai purposely breaks the pattern by introducing the phrase "We cannot all succeed," which establishes a link between those who are held back from success and those "calling upon" people in power to bring change. She doesn't have to explain the idea because her repetitive language does the job for her.

As you write, make strategic decisions about varying pronouns, choosing synonyms, or using repetition with a specific purpose in mind. They are all tools to increase coherence and keep your reader engaged and on track.

> **Remember:** Repetition, synonyms, pronoun references, and parallel structure may indicate or develop a relationship between elements of a text. (REO-1.O)

2.2 Check Point

Close Reading: Professional Text

Reread Aung San Suu Kyi's speech on pages 241–244. Then answer the following open response and multiple-choice questions.

1. Identify and document any examples of repetition in the text. Look for repeated words, phrases, and sentence structures.

2. Explain why Aung San Suu Kyi repeats the ideas, words, and/or syntactical structures you have identified.

3. In the final sentence of paragraph 8, the author appeals to the reader's sense of emotional resolve by
   (A) constructing a complex analogy
   (B) employing a deliberate fragment
   (C) alluding to previous acts of valor among famous leaders
   (D) using parallel sentence structure
   (E) speaking with abstract metaphors

4. In the context of the passage, the parallel structure throughout the second sentence ("Fear of . . . failure") of paragraph 14
   (A) highlights the daily lives and needs of individuals
   (B) reminds individuals of their current state and calls them to action
   (C) focuses on the detrimental aspects of life and offers multiple solutions
   (D) shames people for their failure to find the courage necessary to address injustice
   (E) emphasizes the pervasive fears that grip the lives of individuals

5. The parallel structure used in the first sentence of paragraph 10 allows the author to portray Aung San primarily as
   (A) courageous and not apathetic
   (B) restrained by the beliefs of his followers
   (C) politically savvy and tactical
   (D) heroic but occasionally imprudent
   (E) well-educated but somewhat reticent

Evaluating Writing: Student Draft

Reread the student draft on pages 245–246. Then answer the following questions by suggesting edits or additions to particular sentences. If no edit is needed, you may write "fine as is."

1. Repeated words or phrases
   (a) Where can the writer repeat language to improve coherence or emphasize the argument?
   (b) Where can the writer change language to be less repetitive?

2. Synonyms and pronouns
   (a) Where can the writer use synonyms or other substitutions to avoid being overly repetitive?

3. Sentence structure
   (a) Where can the writer construct parts of sentences, or full sentences, in a repetitive manner to emphasize a point?
   (b) Are there places where the writer should eliminate repeated structures to avoid being redundant?

Composing on Your Own

Review the paragraphs you wrote on the subject of tyranny or another subject of interest to you. Try to improve coherence by using the following at least one time: repetition, synonyms, pronouns and references, and parallel structure. As you revise, keep the rhetorical situation in mind, including your audience, context, and purpose. Save your work.

2.3 Transitions | REO-1.P REO-1.Q

Another way to logically link elements in an essay is by using **transitional elements**, words that assist in creating coherence among sentences, paragraphs, or sections in a text by showing relationships among ideas. Transitional elements also allow for smooth ways to introduce evidence or to indicate its relationship to other ideas and evidence, either in a specific paragraph or in the text as a whole.

The purpose of any transition is to link the sentences and paragraphs together. As you produce your sentences, consider how each one will relate to future sentences, so you can use transitions appropriately. When moving from one idea or claim to another, use transitional language that establishes a relationship between a new paragraph and the one that came before it. Failing to establish coherent links will leave your reader struggling to follow.

Transitional Language

Transitions give your ideas coherence and allow you to seamlessly unify your ideas. Study the following chart of transitional language to see ways you can produce logical coherence within your writing.

Purpose	Transitional Language
In addition to	*and, again, and then, besides, equally important, finally, further, furthermore, next, what's more, moreover, in addition*
Comparison-contrast	*whereas, but, yet, on the other hand, however, nevertheless, on the contrary, by comparison, compared to, up against, balanced against, vis-à-vis, but, although, conversely, meanwhile, after all, in contrast, in the same way*
Cause-effect	*because, for, since, for the same reason, evidently, furthermore, moreover, besides, indeed, in fact, in addition, in any case, that is*
Indicate exceptions	*yet, still, however, nevertheless, in spite of, despite, of course, once in a while, sometimes*
Emphasize	*definitely, extremely, obviously, in fact, indeed, in any case, absolutely, positively, naturally, surprisingly, emphatically, unquestionably, without doubt, certainly, undeniably, without reservation*
Indicate sequence and chronology (time order)	*immediately, first, second, third . . ., then, following this, at this time, now, at this point, after, thereafter, afterward, soon, later, subsequently, finally, consequently, previously, formerly, before this, simultaneously, concurrently, thus, therefore, hence, next, and then, soon, while*
Provide examples	*for example, for instance, in this case, in another case, on this occasion, in this situation, take the case of, to demonstrate, to illustrate, as an illustration*

Table 5-3

Logically Linked Ideas

Not only phrases (as in the chart above) but also whole sentences and paragraphs can serve to transition between ideas. *Logically linked ideas*—ideas connected to make the line of reasoning clear—help readers make sense of your argument. These work at the phrase, clause, sentence, and paragraph levels.

The chart on the next page provides examples of logical links at each of those levels from Malala Yousafzai's speech (Unit 2) and explains how each serves to link her ideas.

Logical Links at Different Levels	
Phrase	**Relationship Established (Logical Link)**
We realize the importance of our voice when we are silenced. **In the same way,** when we were in Swat, the north of Pakistan, we realized the importance of pens and books when we saw the guns.	The phrase *in the same way* sets up a comparative link that equates the importance of education with social activism.
Clause	**Relationship Established (Logical Link)**
And if we want to achieve our goal, then let us empower ourselves with the weapon of knowledge **and** let us shield ourselves with unity and togetherness.	The dependent clause creates a cause-effect relationship to the first independent clause about empowerment with knowledge. The second independent clause links the importance of knowledge with unity. Because the final clause is connected with the word *and*, Yousafzai establishes the equal value of knowledge and unity.
Sentence	**Relationship Established (Logical Link)**
I do not even hate the Talib who shot me.	In context, this sentence works to link Yousafzai's general claim about education for all of the Taliban's children to Yousafzai's personal experience and character.
Paragraph	**Relationship Established (Logical Link)**
In India, innocent and poor children are victims of child labor. Many schools have been destroyed in Nigeria. People in Afghanistan have been affected by extremism. Young girls have to do domestic child labor and are forced to get married at an early age. Poverty, ignorance, injustice, racism and the deprivation of basic rights are the main problems, faced by both men and women.	This paragraph offers direct evidence for the global atrocities referenced in the preceding paragraph when Yousafzai states, "Women and children are suffering in many ways in many parts of the world." Because the examples in this paragraph primarily focus on the violations against women and children, this whole paragraph logically links back to the preceding paragraph as well as to the paragraph that follows it in which Yousafzai focuses on "women's rights and girls' education because they are suffering the most."

Table 5-4

Remember: Transitional elements are words or other elements (phrases, clauses, sentences, or paragraphs) that assist in creating coherence among sentences, paragraphs, or sections in a text by showing relationships among ideas. Transitional elements can be used to introduce evidence or to indicate its relationship to other ideas and evidence in that paragraph or in the text as a whole. (REO-1.P, Q)

2.3 Checkpoint

Close Reading: Professional Text

Reread Aung San Suu Kyi's speech on pages 241–244. Then complete the following open response activity and answer the multiple-choice questions.

1. Review the chart you made in response to the activity in Close Reading 2.1 on page 263. Also reread Aung San Suu Kyi's speech. Drawing from your list of repeated features and identifying new examples along the way, write a paragraph explaining why Aung San Suu Kyi repeats the ideas, words, and/or syntactical structures you have identified.

2. The first sentence of paragraph 5 ("Glass splinters . . . oppression") provides an effective transition from paragraph 4 because it

(A) transforms the metaphor introduced in paragraphs 3 and 4
(B) explains the relationship between glass and emeralds
(C) connects the imagery with the author's main argument
(D) links the author's concrete examples to a series of abstract images
(E) illustrates the causes of the current problem under discussion

3. The author uses paragraph 13 to transition from praising fearlessness to

(A) promoting specific forms of action and civil disobedience
(B) providing claims about the topic that represent her own original thinking
(C) encouraging the kind of universal action that fosters democracy
(D) focusing on the courage formed through experience and perseverance
(E) conceptualizing normal behaviors in the lives of the Burmese people

4. At the beginning of paragraph 13, the author effectively transitions from paragraph 12 by

(A) elaborating on her beliefs about the positive results of humankind being free from fear
(B) alluding to specific acts by historical leaders like Gandhi and Nehru
(C) sustaining the image of a well or spring that was introduced earlier
(D) employing parallel structure at the end of paragraph 12 and the beginning of paragraph 13
(E) reinforcing images of violence and political corruption earlier

Evaluating Writing: Student Draft

Reread the student draft on pages 245–246. Then answer the following open response and multiple-choice questions.

1. Identify two places the writer can add transitional phrases, clauses, or sentences to more accurately relate pieces of the argument.

2. Are there places where the writer can eliminate transitional elements because they are not needed? If so, identify them.

3. The writer needs to add a transitional sentence before the two concluding sentences (9 and 10). Which of the following sentences would best achieve this goal?
   - (A) Perhaps the reason for this consistent behavior demands a deeper look into the human psyche.
   - (B) To prove this claim, all governments must be adequately considered.
   - (C) For example, humans have been ruling one another ever since societies were created.
   - (D) Contemporary psychology may be able to offer simple answers for complex questions.
   - (E) Interestingly enough, governmental action is typically tied to individual humans.

4. In sentence 5 (reproduced below), the writer wants to use a transitional phrase to show the relationship between the evidence in the sentence and the other ideas in the paragraph.

   <u>Consequently,</u> there were the Japanese internment camps during World War II.

   Which of the following versions of the underlined text best achieves this goal?
   - (A) (as it is now)
   - (B) For example,
   - (C) In a similar sense,
   - (D) Furthermore,
   - (E) In contrast,

Composing on Your Own

Return to the argument you began writing in Part 1. Revise and expand the draft to build coherence using transitional elements (words, phrases, clauses, sentences) to guide readers through your line of reasoning. You don't have to create a clean draft now. If you are working on paper, mark up the earlier draft, using arrows, text inserts, and notes in the margins to show your thinking. If you are working on a computer, you can use the comment function in your word processor to remind you of things to think about, leave yourself notes in the manuscript itself, or just make the revisions as you go. As you revise, keep the elements of your rhetorical situation in mind.

Part 2 Apply What You Have Learned

Reread or listen again to "Tuskegee University Commencement Address" delivered by Michelle Obama on May 9, 2015. Then write a short essay about how Obama's use of logically linked ideas—such as repetition and parallel structure—creates coherence within the speech.

Source: The White House

The official portrait of First Lady Michelle Obama, 2013

Reflect on the Essential Question: Write a brief response that answers this essential question: How does a text create unity and coherence and use transitions to guide readers through a line of reasoning? Use the key terms on page 258 in your response.

Part 3

The Many Meanings of Language

Enduring Understanding and Skills

Part 3

Understand

The rhetorical situation informs the strategic stylistic choices that writers make. (STL-1)

Demonstrate

Explain how word choice, comparisons, and syntax contribute to the specific tone or style of a text. (Reading 7.A)

Strategically use words, comparisons, and syntax to convey a specific tone or style in an argument. (Writing 8.A)

Source: AP® English Language and Composition Course and Exam Description

Essential Question: How do word choice, comparisons, and the arrangement of words convey a writer's attitudes toward readers and the chosen subject?

"Sticks and stones may break my bones, but words will never hurt me." Many children, maybe even you, might have been taught to say or think this after being verbally taunted. However, this saying attempts to ignore the power words have to convey emotions and meaning.

Think about it: You speak and write in different ways depending on your mood and your audience. When you're angry you may use more aggressive language. If you're agitated as you write an email or text message, you may be more inclined to use all capital letters and choose words with negative meanings. When you're excited or happy, your words and language patterns will be more upbeat. The language you use in speaking and writing conveys your position (how you generally feel about something) and your perspective (how your own life experiences influence your attitude toward it).

Words *are* powerful. They are the essential tools you use to communicate. Words allow you to interpret your reality and express that interpretation to others. The more coherently you can do both, the more effectively you'll communicate.

Throughout Part 3, you'll explore how language generates and changes meaning based on its ties to many different elements of the rhetorical situation. You'll also explore how the rhetorical situation influences writers to choose precise language that accurately presents their argument and their perspective on their topic.

KEY TERMS

adjective (adjectival)	connotative meaning	perspective
adverb (adverbial)	denotative meaning	precise word choice

3.1 The Meaning of Words | STL-1.A

Mark Twain famously said, "The difference between the almost right word and the right word is . . . the difference between the lightning bug and the lightning." Twain knew that writers rely on the meanings and interpretations of words as the foundation of their arguments. How a writer's words connect with the audience has a huge influence on the argument's overall effectiveness.

Connotative and Denotative Meanings

Think about a typical day in your life. Do you use the same language with your grandparents that you use with your friends during the school day? Do you use the same language on social media as you do in face-to-face encounters? If you're like most people, the answer is probably no. Your language and behaviors are tied to your surroundings, circumstances, relationships, and emotions. The same is true of the words you use when writing a paper.

Words have both denotative and connotative meanings. A word's **denotative meaning**, or denotation, is simply its definition as it might appear in a dictionary. But the same word's **connotative meaning**, or connotation, is the emotional content associated with a word when in a specific context. Connotative meanings are typically either positive or negative, and they can have a profound effect on a writer's tone.

Consider the following words and phrases:

1. Wicked
2. Wicked cool
3. Wicked man
4. Wicked cool man
5. Wicked cool, man

These examples show that when words are put into new contexts their meanings change. In example 1, *wicked* can be used in two ways. It can be an adjective with a strong negative connotation meaning "bad." Alternatively, it can be a slang term, also an adjective, that holds the positive connotation of "wonderful" or "amazing." In example 2, the word relates to the slang connotation, but in example 3, the word has a denotative meaning and describes a man who is bad.

Depending on the language surrounding it, a word can project different meanings. Examples 4 and 5 illustrate this effect. Example 4 describes a man who is either really cold or really terrific, while the addition of a comma in example 5 creates an expression that describes something really terrific.

Though simple, the phrases on page 276 show that small changes in context, punctuation, and wording can significantly change the meaning of words. Choose your words with precision, because such choices mean *everything*.

Remember: Words have both connotative and denotative meanings. (STL-1.A)

3.1 Checkpoint

Close Reading: Professional Text

Reread Aung Sun Suu Kyi's speech on pages 241–244. Then complete the following open response activity and answer the multiple-choice questions.

1. Write the denotative meaning of the following words from Aung Sun Suu Kye's speech. Use the dictionary if needed. Then write *neutral, positive*, or *negative* after it to describe its connotative meaning in the speech.

a. corruption (paragraph 1)
b. avarice (paragraph 1)
c. quiescent (paragraph 2)
d. comrades (paragraph 3)
e. freedom (paragraph 5)
f. revolution (paragraph 8)
g. sacrifices (paragraph 8)
h. liberate (paragraph 9)
i. moral courage (paragraph 10)
j. Mahatma Gandhi (paragraph 10)
k. fearlessness (paragraph 11)
l. authoritarian rule (paragraph 12)
m. wisdom (paragraph 14)
n. enervating (paragraph 14)
o. power (paragraph 15)
p. suffer (paragraph 15)

2. In the first sentence of paragraph 12, the word *apostle* is understood to mean

    (A) a follower of a particular religious figure or institution
    (B) an individual who produced ancient texts of great value
    (C) one who exemplifies a valuable, potentially radical message
    (D) a religious leader or chief authority of a religious movement
    (E) a person who embraces and champions a belief system

3. Which of the following words in paragraph 3 conveys a connotation of the fear once felt by the people in Burma?

    (A) protesting (sentence 1)
    (B) demonstrations (sentence 2)
    (C) keenest (sentence 3)
    (D) sufficient (sentence 4)
    (E) precarious (sentence 5)

Evaluating Writing: Student Draft

Reread the student draft on pages 245–246. Then answer the following open response and multiple choice questions.

1. On separate paper, explain the connotations associated with the numbered, underlined part in each sentence. First, state whether the language is positive, negative, or neutral. Then briefly explain the common associations, assumptions, and feelings the language evokes.

> These same (1) Americans are unaware of the oppressive ruling practices which have existed, and have even been (2) celebrated, in their own *Land of the Free and Home of the Brave.* This, of course, is because (3) tyranny is universally accepted as being viciously oppressive and inhumane, something that a ***civilized nation*** like the U.S. could never be. If an American considers the most common tyrannical practices—(4) instigating or retaliating with violence, generating fear, scapegoating minority classes, and engaging in governmental corruption—they will have to admit that history offers plenty of examples to prove that tyrannical practices have been just as alive and well in the U.S. as it has been in other countries. Consequently, there were the (5) Japanese internment camps during World War II. But many people may question how a government founded upon the (6) "unalienable rights" of "life, liberty, and the pursuit of happiness" can consistently allow such practices to (7) crawl into its ruling protocol.

2. The student wishes to revise sentence 9 (reprinted below) to clarify what she means by the word "humankind" following the colon near the end of the sentence. Which of the following substitutions, adjusted for proper structure and punctuation, would best accomplish her goal?

It seems as though the common denominator in all of the governments mentioned above is this: humankind.

(A) (as it is now)

(B) "the human desire for power and control."

(C) "people are always trying to show they know more than others."

(D) "it seems like there are always people who let themselves be oppressed."

(E) "the lust and greed of bad people."

Composing on Your Own

Return to your draft in progress. First, review the denotative meanings of your words to make sure you are using them correctly. Second, highlight words with strong, effective connotations that successfully convey your intentions, and revise words that could convey a stronger or more precise connotative meaning. Finally, make sure your word choice reflects the needs of the rhetorical situation.

3.2 Word Choice and Perspective | STL-1.B STL-1.C

As you have read, words do not have a static meaning. Descriptive words such as adjectives and adverbs, for example, not only qualify or modify the subjects they describe, but they also convey a perspective or point of view on those subjects. **Precise word choice** reduces the possibility of confusion and may help the audience perceive the writer's true **perspective**—the writer's attitude toward a topic based on a number of factors, including life experiences.

Description and Perspective

Although all word choices help to convey a writer's perspective, adjectives and adverbs are the words that most obviously project attitudes and views. **Adjectives** are words that modify, or describe, nouns and pronouns. Sometimes whole parts of sentences can function as adjectives. These sentence parts are known as *adjectivals.*

More versatile than adjectives, **adverbs** can modify verbs and adjectives as well as other adverbs. As with adjectives, parts of sentences can function as adverbs; in that case, they're called *adverbials.* The best way to tell the difference between these types of describing words is by learning what questions each word type answers. See Table 5-5 on the next page.

Adjectives (Adjectivals)	Adverbs (Adverbials)
What kind?	When?
Which one?	Where?
How many?	How?
What color?	How often?
What size?	How much?
	To what degree?
	Why?

Table 5-5

As you can see from the questions in Table 5-5, adjectives usually describe objects or concepts, while adverbs usually describe actions or elaborate on a description.

Writers use descriptive language to clarify their attitude about their topic, which is often called the writer's *tone* (see Unit 6). The choice of adverbs and adjectives helps convey a particular perspective or tone to the audience.

What tone or perspective about power do you pick up from the following sentence that begins Snyder's piece on successful resistance?

> Power wants your body softening in your chair and your emotions dissipating on the screen.

Probably the two key words that convey perspective in this sentence are *softening* and *dissipating,* both adjectives. Power—in this sentence given human qualities since it "wants" something—does not want your body to be fit and strong, able to march in protests. It wants your body softening, couch-potato style, and your emotions to evaporate, siphoned off by your dependence on the screen. That power wants those things of people conveys through well-chosen adjectives a strongly negative view of power.

Precision and Perspective

The more precise the words, the more clearly they communicate the writer's meaning and perspective. Consider again Gladwell's description of Tenochtitlán. Notice how precise the underlined descriptive words are. Also notice how the *comparisons* between what the newcomers found in Mexico and what they knew from Spain sharpen the focus and convey perspective.

> Tenochtitlán was an <u>extraordinary</u> sight—<u>far larger</u> and <u>more impressive</u> than any of the cities Cortés and his men would have known back in Spain. It was a city on an island, linked to the mainland with bridges and crossed by canals. It had <u>grand</u> boulevards, <u>elaborate</u> aqueducts, <u>thriving</u> marketplaces, temples built in <u>brilliant white</u> stucco, public gardens and even a zoo. It was <u>spotlessly</u> clean—which, to someone raised in the filth of medieval European cities, would have seemed almost <u>miraculous</u>.

Readers should understand a written work without having to wonder what the writer is trying to communicate. Unless writing is clear, readers may be left with questions that weaken an argument, or they may misunderstand entirely.

> **Remember:** Descriptive words, such as adjectives and adverbs, not only qualify or modify the things they describe but also convey a perspective toward those things. Precise word choice reduces confusion and may help the audience perceive the writer's perspective. (STL-1.B, STL-1.C)

3.2 Checkpoint

Close Reading: Professional Text

Reread Aung Sun Suu Kyi's speech on pages 241–244. Then answer the following open-response and multiple-choice questions.

1. Write a response explaining the way Aung Sun Suu Kyi conveys her perspective on how fear influences the lives of both tyrannical rulers and oppressed people. Be sure to cite relevant evidence from the text.

2. In context, the word "intrepidity" in paragraph 5 means

(A) caution
(B) fortitude
(C) diligence
(D) virtue
(E) morality

3. In paragraph 6, the author argues that the primary purpose of "just laws" is to promote

(A) strict punishments for lawbreakers
(B) respect and fear for those who enforce the laws
(C) human dignity and social harmony
(D) a clearly defined code of morality for all to follow
(E) an economic environment that allows businesses to succeed

Evaluating Writing: Student Draft

Reread the student draft about tyrannical rule on pages 245–246. Then complete the following activity.

1. On separate paper, write five examples of adjectival words or phrases, adverbial words or phrases, or a mixture of both. Then in a sentence or two explain how these words or phrases influence the coherence of the argument as a whole.

Composing on Your Own

Return to your draft in progress. Review your writing, looking for ways to make your ideas and perspective clearer and more precise by using vivid and accurate descriptive language and comparisons. Make any revisions necessary to improve the effectiveness of your word choice in conveying what you intend.

Now give your composition a critical review to make sure your writing is coherent and unified. First, check to make sure that you have each element shown in the chart below. If you do not, make a copy of the organizer on separate paper and complete it before revising your work. (Your composition may include other elements as well, but be sure it has a claim, evidence, and commentary.) Next, check your descriptive words and phrases to make sure you're using precise, vivid language that conveys the appropriate tone and connects with your audience. Remember, your word choices should reflect the needs of your rhetorical situation.

Claim:		
Evidence	**Evidence**	**Evidence**
Commentary	**Commentary**	**Commentary**

Use the checklist below as you are writing or revising. Use it again when you are finished to evaluate your work.

Checklist for Composing
✓ Do your body paragraphs make claims, support them with evidence, and provide commentary that explains how the paragraph contributes to the reasoning of the argument? (1.1)
✓ Does your essay have coherence at all levels? Within a sentence, does the idea in one clause lead logically to the next? In a paragraph, does the idea in one sentence link logically to the one that follows? In the essay as a whole, do the ideas in one paragraph link logically to the ideas in the next? (2.1)
✓ Did you use repetition, synonyms, pronoun references, and parallel structure to indicate or develop a relationship between elements of your text? (2.2)
✓ Did you show relationships among ideas by using such transitional elements as words, phrases, clauses, sentences, or paragraphs that assist in creating coherence among sentences, paragraphs, or sections in a text? Did you use transitional elements to introduce evidence or to indicate its relationship to other ideas and evidence in a specific paragraph or in the text as a whole? (2.3)
✓ Did you choose words carefully, aware of both their denotative and connotative meanings? (3.1)
✓ Did you use descriptive words such as adjectives and adverbs to qualify or modify what they describe and also to convey your perspective? (3.2)
✓ Did you check your writing for mistakes in spelling and mechanics and make an effort to correct them?

Table 5-6

Part 3 Apply What You Have Learned

Reread or listen again to "Tuskegee University Commencement Address" delivered by Michelle Obama on May 9, 2015. Identify Obama's perspective on her subject. Then write a paragraph detailing how she uses description and precise language to convey that perspective.

Reflect on the Essential Question: Write a brief response that answers this essential question: *How do word choice, comparisons, and the arrangement of words convey a writer's attitudes toward readers and the chosen subject?* In your response, correctly use the key terms listed on page 276.

Unit 5 Review

Section I: Multiple Choice

Section II: Free Response

Section I: Reading

Questions 1–6. Read the following passage carefully before you choose your answers.

(The following is an excerpt from an article titled "Is Dance a Sport?" that appeared in the *Journal of Dance Education* in 2015.)

1 It appears that a new debate has emerged for dancers. For many years dancers debated dance as art versus entertainment. This age-old debate still exists without a consensus, yet there is suddenly a new generation of dancers with a fresh debate. Legions of young performers are fervently proclaiming that their dance is actually a sport. How did this debate emerge? Is dance a sport? Perhaps more important, should dance be considered a sport?

2 The *Oxford Dictionary* defines sport as "an activity involving physical exertion and skill in which an individual or team competes against another or others for entertainment" ("Sport" n.d.-b). The *Merriam-Webster Dictionary* offers two definitions: "a contest or game in which people do certain physical activities according to a specific set of rules and compete against each other," and "a physical activity that is done for enjoyment" ("Sport" n.d.-a). These definitions use vocabulary that is at odds with the very essence of dance. Activity. Exertion. Compete. Contest. Rules. These ideas do not suggest an act of expression, nor do they describe a craft that relies on creativity. Dance can be defined as "an art performed by individuals or groups of beings, existing in time, space, forces, and flow, in which the human body is the instrument, and movement is the medium" (Krauss, Chapman, and Dixon 1999, 24). The phrase "dance is an art" is found in countless other definitions of dance, from

Nora Ambrosio's (2010, 3) *Learning About Dance* textbook to Wikipedia. The phrase "dance is a sport" is nowhere to be found. So why the debate?

3 From the beginning of time, dance has been a method of communication. Cave paintings from prehistory suggest that dance was used to celebrate, mourn, teach skills and tasks from one generation to the next, and communicate with the gods (Anderson 1992, 13–14). Throughout history, dance has been a language that transcends sociocultural barriers; it is a means of expression that is deeply and profoundly human. People of different nationalities might not understand one another's culture or language, but viewing dance can result in a unique sense of communication and understanding. Just like the adage "a picture is worth a thousand words," dance offers a complex exchange of information between dancer and audience.

4 In today's society, dancers train to develop skill, but skill alone does not make a dancer "great." It is artistry that separates a capable dancer from a truly memorable one; this quality transforms the physicality of movement into something more profound. This consideration is at the heart of the debate when dance is called a sport. Bodies moving in space could be absent of formal technique and still be appreciated as art. When dancers use their bodies in physically impressive and athletic ways, they must also possess creative intention, a sense of self, and a desire for originality for them to be considered artists. Athletes might demonstrate similar qualities while playing sports, but their work is only publicly revered where there is obvious skill and measurable success. In art there does not have to be a "winner" or a "loser" for the dancer and the audience to feel something.

References

Ambrosio, N. 2010. *Learning about dance: Dance as an art form and entertainment.* 6th ed. Dubuque, IA: Kendall Hunt.

Anderson, J. 1992. *Ballet & modern dance: A concise history.* 2nd ed. Pennington, NJ: Princeton Book Company.

Kraus, R., S. Chapman, and B. Dixon. 1999. *History of the dance in art and education.* Englewood Cliffs, NJ: Prentice Hall.

Sport. n.d.-a. In *Merriam-Webster dictionary.* http://www.merriam-webster.com/dictionary/sport (accessed March 10, 2014).

———. n.d.-b. In *Oxford dictionary.* http://www.oxforddictionaries.com/us/definition/american_english/sport (accessed March 10, 2014).

1. The second paragraph contributes to the writer's reasoning primarily by

(A) highlighting answers to universal questions

(B) providing definitions that help the author evaluate the claim

(C) suggesting that no answer can be given to age-old questions

(D) exploring sources that contradict one another and the argument at hand

(E) amplifying the mysterious nature of dance as both a sport and art

2. By repeatedly and definitively referring to dance as "art" throughout the piece, the writer suggests which of the following?

(A) The argument about dance being a sport ignores dance's purpose.

(B) There is no actual debate about the status of dance being a sport.

(C) Many questions about dance still need to be answered.

(D) Dance is difficult to understand; therefore, it can't be a sport.

(E) The noncompetitive nature of dance eliminates its need for rules and standards.

Question 3 is covered in Unit 1.

3. Which of the following represents an assumption the writer makes about some members of her audience?

(A) They believe dance is only an art form due to its ability to allow for personal expression.

(B) They think dance is too complex for non-dancers to understand.

(C) They feel that since art is expressive, it doesn't require the skills necessary for competition.

(D) They believe dance requires immense physical skill, so it is fair to consider it a sport.

(E) They believe many individuals enjoy dance as expressive art despite not participating in it.

Question 4 is covered in Unit 2.

4. Which of the following best states the writer's thesis?

(A) Dance can sometimes be sport, but is best labeled as a way of expressing communication.

(B) Great dancers practice their skills in both competitive and noncompetitive arenas.

(C) Dance competitions are sports, but ballet productions are art.

(D) There will always be a debate about whether dance is art or a sport.

(E) Dance is not a sport; it is an expressive artform that can be profoundly moving.

Question 5 is covered in Unit 3.

5. The third paragraph functions as
   (A) a shift from clarified definitions in paragraph 2 to a clear argument in paragraph 4
   (B) a way to make broad claims about assumptions others make in their view of dance
   (C) a historical context allowing the reader to understand why some consider dance a sport
   (D) an exploration of art in general and its profound influence on humans
   (E) a way to detail different forms of human communication throughout history

Question 6 is covered in Unit 4.

6. The article presents a contrast between
   (A) skill and talent
   (B) sport and competition
   (C) competition and art
   (D) dance and art
   (E) sport and appreciation

Section I: Writing

Questions 7–9. Read the following passage carefully before you choose your answers.

(The passage below is a draft.)

(1) Horace Mann experienced life, within his early years, in a culture that began shifting from being rural toward becoming more industrial. (2) This shift was due in large part to the *Industrial Revolution*. (3) The burgeoning movement's influence on the social structure began to agitate the family-oriented nature of U. S. culture. (4) This began blurring the lines of social-governmental roles. (5) New industries separated parents and children in order to fulfill employment vacancies, while in the past the children would have worked for the parents. (6) With parents and children continually interacting less, the education and morals that families were once expected to bestow upon their children became more and more nonexistent. (7) Although the rise of industrial capitalism began to produce large profits, a healthy market, and supply individuals with jobs, it "wreaked havoc on the family. . . [leaving children]

to largely fend for themselves." (8) This issue of having a large amount of uneducated, seemingly immoral, and perhaps unpatriotic individuals began to fuel the institution of a state-funded public education. (9) The government-funded education system would step in as "the custodial role, assuming some of the absent parents' responsibilities," which Altenbaugh also notes. (10) The new governmental role would assist in educating children and producing good citizens that would provide value not only for society and the workplace.

(11) The economy played a large role in the beginning of public education, not only in that it began to strip parents of their ability to enact their responsibilities, but also in that it mandated that employees maintain productivity and routine. (12) Thus, the influence this had on education is clear. (13) Routine, work ethic, and a totalitarian outlook were seen as desirable management models that should be promoted within the walls of public schools. (14) With the fragmentation of education, due in large part to companies, it seemed only right that, "education had to become formal and institutionalized." (15) The industrial revolution should not be solely blamed for the breakdown of the family in the 18th and 19th centuries. (16) It should also be noted that parents of this time period were indeed more and more willing to "surrender educational responsibilities to institutions."[1]

---

7. Which of the following words or phrases, if placed at the beginning of sentence 4, would create the most logical connection between sentence 3 and sentence 4?
   (A) As exemplified,
   (B) For instance,
   (C) Although,
   (D) Consequently,
   (E) Surprisingly,

1 All quotes are taken from Altenbaugh, Richard J. *The American People and Their Education: A Social History*. Merrill/Prentice Hall, 2003.

8. In the underlined portion of sentence 11 (reproduced below), the writer is looking to create coherence among his paragraphs.

The economy played a large role in the beginning of public education, not only in that it began to strip parents of their ability to enact their responsibilities, but also in that it mandated that employees maintain productivity and routine.

Which answer choice would best replace the underlined language?

(A) (as it is now)

(B) The government

(C) The local schools

(D) The changing political atmosphere

(E) Social pressure

Question 9 is covered in Unit 3.

9. The writer wants to attribute the quote in sentence 7 (reproduced below) to a valid source.

Although the rise of industrial capitalism began to produce large profits, a healthy market, and supply individuals with jobs, it "wreaked havoc on the family . . . [leaving children] to largely fend for themselves."

Which of the following additions, adjusting punctuation as needed, best achieves this purpose?

(A) writes one contemporary author.

(B) says Altenbaugh.

(C) argues Richard.

(D) posits one critic.

(E) according to professor Richard J. Altenbaugh.

JOIN THE CONVERSATION: RHETORICAL ANALYSIS (PART 4)

Before moving on to the rhetorical analysis prompt in the free-response portion of the unit review, spend more time on the practice prompt you started in Unit 2 and continued developing in Units 3 and 4. The rhetorical analysis prompt for Unit 5 remains as it was in previous units. This is the last unit in which you will specifically focus on learning about the rhetorical analysis prompt. Study the sample prompt below.

The speech on pages 53–55 was delivered on "Malala Day"—July 12, 2013—by Malala Yousafzai, a girls' and children's education-rights activist who survived an assassination attempt in 2012 when she was 15. She delivered this speech to the "Youth Take Over the UN" assembly, a campaign that stressed the importance of global education rights. This was the first speech she delivered after the assassination attempt.

Read the passage carefully. Write an essay that analyzes the rhetorical choices Yousafzai makes to convey her message that all children around the world deserve an equal education.

In your response you should do the following:

- Respond to the prompt with a thesis that analyzes the writer's rhetorical choices.
- Select and use evidence to develop and support your line of reasoning.
- Explain how the evidence supports your line of reasoning.
- Demonstrate an understanding of the rhetorical situation.
- Use appropriate grammar and punctuation in communicating your argument.

As you upgrade your practice rhetorical analysis for the last time, focus on creating a more cohesive and coherent argument using strategies you learned in this unit.

- Transitioning between paragraphs, parts of paragraphs, and sentences will help to guide your reader through the reasoning of your analysis; effectively, it helps make your argument more coherent (logical and consistent) and cohesive (unified into a single, whole piece).
- Few issues are simplistic, so you might find success exploring how readers with other perspectives might see the rhetorical choices you are highlighting. You can use transitions to introduce some of those ideas.
- Carefully consider the words you use to convey your attitude about different parts of your analysis.

Using an organizer like the one on the following pages may help you gather your thoughts and cover each required aspect of the prompt.

- The first page of the organizer (page 292) provides a template for the introduction, including your thesis, and first body paragraph.
- The second page of the organizer (page 293) provides a template for the second body paragraph.
- The third page of the organizer (page 294) provides a template for the third body paragraph.
- The final page of the organizer (page 295) provides a template for the conclusion.

Use the draft you started in earlier units and check it against the organizer to look for ways to improve the coherence of your essay. Although there are other ways to develop a rhetorical analysis than by following this template, this approach followed carefully will likely result in a well-developed analysis. As you will see, you can also use it for the argument essay.

<table>
<tr><th colspan="4">Unit 5: Drafting Organizer for Rhetorical Analysis and Argument Essay (Final)</th></tr>
<tr><td rowspan="2">Introduction</td><td colspan="2">Lead-in addressing an abstract concept</td><td rowspan="10">Abstract Idea that runs throughout (What is it really about?)</td></tr>
<tr><td colspan="2">Thesis</td></tr>
<tr><td rowspan="8">Body Paragraph 1</td><td colspan="2">Transitional clause or sentence:</td></tr>
<tr><td>Supporting Claim 1</td><td>Connection to abstract idea in thesis</td></tr>
<tr><td>Lead-in to evidence</td><td>Describe evidence</td></tr>
<tr><td colspan="2">Explain how that evidence supports the reasoning that justifies that claim and appeals to the audience.</td></tr>
<tr><td colspan="2">Transition to complex discussion or another example? (Not only . . . , but also . . .)</td></tr>
<tr><td colspan="2">Additional discussion</td></tr>
<tr><td>How does it lead to or connect with the next paragraph?</td><td>Reconnect to abstract idea in thesis</td></tr>
</table>

Body Paragraph 2			Abstract Idea that runs throughout (What is it really about?)
	Transitional clause or sentence:		
	Supporting Claim 2	Connection to abstract idea in thesis	
	Lead-in to evidence	Describe evidence	
	Explain how that evidence supports the reasoning that justifies that claim and appeals to the audience.		
	Transition to complex discussion or another example? (Not only . . . , but also . . .)		
	Additional discussion		
	How does it build upon or connect to previous paragraph?	Reconnect to abstract idea in thesis	

<table>
<tr><td rowspan="7">Body Paragraph 3</td><td colspan="2">Transitional clause or sentence:</td><td rowspan="7">Abstract Idea that runs throughout (What is it really about?)</td></tr>
<tr><td>Supporting Claim 3</td><td>Connection to abstract idea in thesis</td></tr>
<tr><td>Lead-in to evidence</td><td>Describe evidence</td></tr>
<tr><td colspan="2">Explain how that evidence supports the reasoning that justifies that claim and appeals to the audience.</td></tr>
<tr><td colspan="2">Transition to complex discussion or another example?
(Not only . . . , but also . . .)</td></tr>
<tr><td colspan="2">Additional discussion</td></tr>
<tr><td>How does it build upon or connect to previous paragraph?</td><td>Reconnect to abstract idea in thesis</td></tr>
</table>

Conclusion	Statement about essay topic that leads to abstract idea.	Abstract idea that runs throughout
	Call to the reader about the essay topic (call to act or think differently)	
	General statement about the importance of the abstract idea(s)	

Apply

Use the template to respond to the rhetorical analysis prompt on page 298. For current free-response question samples, check the College Board website.

JOIN THE CONVERSATION: THE ARGUMENT ESSAY (PART 5)

This is also the last unit in which you will practice developing the argument prompt. The argument prompt for Unit 5 is the same as it was in Unit 4 and reflects what you will see on the exam.

> For decades, movies and music have included messages or labels to signal that they have material in them that some people may find troubling. Advocates for such things argue this is important to prevent people from being exposed to things they do not want to encounter. However, Erika Christakis, a lecturer at the Yale Child Study Center, says that "free speech and the ability to tolerate offense are the hallmarks of a free and open society."
>
> Write an essay that argues your position on the use of warning labels or warning messages to signal potentially troubling content.
>
> In your response you should do the following:
>
> - Respond to the prompt with a thesis that presents a defensible position.
> - Provide evidence to support your line of reasoning.
> - Explain how the evidence supports your line of reasoning.
> - Use appropriate grammar and punctuation in communicating your argument.

As with the rhetorical analysis prompt, as you revise your practice argument essay, focus on the strategies covered in this unit to achieve coherence.

- Transitioning between paragraphs, parts of paragraphs, and sentences will help to guide your reader through your line of reasoning; effectively, it helps make your argument more coherent (logical and consistent) and cohesive (unified into a whole, one piece).
- Few issues are simplistic, so you might find success exploring the evidence for your claims from other perspectives. Units 7 and 9 will look at the issue of complexity more closely, but you can begin to use what you've learned about transitions to introduce some different perspectives in this draft of your argument essay.

- Carefully consider the words that you use to convey your attitude about different parts of your argument.
- When you finish your draft, check it over to make sure you meet the requirements of each bullet point in the prompt. The final point reminds you to use appropriate grammar and punctuation, so double check for possible grammatical and punctuation errors.

Using an organizer like the one on pages 292–295 may help you gather your thoughts and cover each required aspect of the prompt.

- The first page of the organizer (page 292) provides a template for the introduction, including your thesis, and first paragraph.
- The second page of the organizer (page 293) provides a template for the first body paragraph.
- The third page of the organizer (page 294) provides a template for the second body paragraph.
- The final page of the organizer (page 295) provides a template for the conclusion.

Use the draft you started in earlier units and check it against the organizer to look for ways to improve the coherence of your essay. Although there are other ways to develop an argument essay than by using this template, this approach followed carefully will likely result in a well-developed argument. You can also use it for the rhetorical analysis essay.

Apply

Use the template to respond to the argument prompt on page 298. For current free-response question samples, check the College Board website.

Section II: Free Response

The first free-response question on the AP® exam is a synthesis task. See Join the Conversation on pages 364–373, 448–455, and 540–544 for guidance in responding to that kind of prompt. You will have synthesis prompts to respond to in Section II of the Unit Review in units 6–9.

Rhetorical Analysis: "Is Dance a Sport?"

In her article "Is Dance a Sport?" Lindsay Guarino, an assistant professor of dance at Salve Regina University, argues that dance's qualities transcend what typically constitutes sports.

Read the passage on pages 284–285 carefully. Then write an essay that analyzes the rhetorical choices Guarino makes to convey her message about the importance of dance.

In your response you should do the following:

- Respond to the prompt with a thesis that analyzes the writer's rhetorical choices.
- Select and use evidence to support your line of reasoning.
- Explain how the evidence supports your line of reasoning.
- Demonstrate an understanding of the rhetorical situation.
- Use appropriate grammar and punctuation in communicating your argument.

Argument: How Background Influences Character

Consider the following observations from two prolific American authors:

"We are the sum of all of our parts."
—Thomas Wolfe (1900–1938)

"Our past may shape us, but it doesn't define who we become."
—Alyson Noel (b. 1965)

Write an essay that argues your position on how an individual's background influences his or her character.

In your response you should do the following:

- Respond to the prompt with a thesis that presents a defensible position.
- Provide evidence to support your line of reasoning.
- Explain how the evidence supports your line of reasoning.
- Use appropriate grammar and punctuation in communicating your argument.

UNIT 6

Synthesizing Perspectives and Refining Arguments

Part 1: Synthesizing Perspectives
Part 2: Considering and Accounting for New Evidence
Part 3: Strategic Use of Tone

ENDURING UNDERSTANDINGS AND SKILLS: Unit Six

Part 1

Understand

Writers make claims about subjects, rely on evidence that supports the reasoning that justifies the claim, and often acknowledge or respond to other, possibly opposing, arguments. (CLE-1)

Demonstrate

Identify and explain claims and evidence within an argument. (Reading 3.A)

Develop a paragraph that includes a claim and evidence supporting the claim. (Writing 4.A)

Part 2

Understand

Writers make claims about subjects, rely on evidence that supports the reasoning that justifies the claim, and often acknowledge or respond to other, possibly opposing arguments. (CLE-1)

Demonstrate

Identify and describe the overarching thesis of an argument, and any indication it provides of the argument's structure. (Reading 3.B)

Write a thesis statement that requires proof or defense and that may preview the structure of the argument. (Writing 4.B)

Part 3

Understand

The rhetorical situation informs the strategic stylistic choices that writers make. (STL-1)

Demonstrate

Explain how word choice, comparisons, and syntax contribute to the specific tone or style of a text. (Reading 7.A)

Strategically use words, comparisons, and syntax to convey a specific tone or style in an argument. (Writing 8.A)

Source: *AP® English Language and Composition Course and Exam Description*

Unit 6 Overview

On February 2, 2020, pop stars Shakira and Jennifer Lopez, two Latinx singers and dancers, hit the stage at the Super Bowl halftime show. It was reported that Shakira and Lopez were selected to reflect the Latin culture in Miami, the host city for the Super Bowl game. Following the performance, Twitter exploded with reactions that ranged from absolute glorification to deep disgust to utter confusion. *Forbes* magazine reported, "There were more than 1 million tweets mentioning Lopez and Shakira directly, according to social analytics firm ListenFirst, which is up 431% from last year's 127,576 mentions about Maroon 5. There were 1,114,545 tweets mentioning the halftime show, in general, and 69% of them expressed a positive sentiment." Read the brief excerpt below from *Time* magazine reporting on the halftime show:

> [The show] highlighted both performers' extensive back catalogues of hits, super-charged by guest appearances from fellow Latin artists Bad Bunny and J Balvin. But they also made sure to nod at the importance and political potential of the moment, showcasing support for Puerto Rico[1] and recognizing the immigration crisis[2] with their set pieces. Here were the biggest moments of the Super Bowl LIV halftime show, which was ultimately a high-energy, sparkling celebration of dance and Latin pop . . . .
>
> Shakira kicked things off, dressed in glittering red Peter Dundas[3] with a veritable army of female dancers at her command. She ran through her biggest songs . . . . She whipped out her notorious belly-dancing skills, played a searing guitar . . . and crowd-surfed her way through a mosh pit. There was a horn section and a salsa dance break. And when she closed out with "Hips Don't Lie" and the famous "No fightin" intro to that song, the crowd went wild. . . .
>
> The Halftime Show transitioned directly over to Lopez for a rousing set that she kicked off with her classic song "Jenny from the Block," surrounded by a cadre of dancers, decked out in Versace[4] black leather and dancing exuberantly. But the highlight came after Lopez made a costume change to a sparkling body suit and sang "Waiting for Tonight" while pole dancing[5]. . . .
>
> Lopez's 11-year-old daughter Emme got her time to shine as well—and to prove she follows in her mom's footsteps—coming out to sing with a chorus of girls for a sweet rendition of the Lopez classic "Let's Get Loud;" the camera also panned over to Shakira during the song, who was playing the drums . . . .

---

1 **Puerto Rico**: a U.S. territory in the Caribbean Sea that damaged by Hurricane Maria in 2017 and a series of strong earthquakes in 2019–2020.
2 **immigration crisis**: During the administration of President Trump, authorities greatly limited immigration, refusing entry even to those who claimed they had legitimate cases for sanctuary. Detention centers along the U.S.-Mexico border held thousands of immigrants, including many children separated from their parents, waiting for their cases to be heard.
3 **Peter Dundas:** Norwegian fashion designer
4 **Versace:** Italian fashion designer
5 **pole dancing:** a combination of dancing and acrobatics that uses a vertical pole and is associated with adult entertainment and erotic dance

> For "Let's Get Loud," Lopez appeared draped in a giant flag coat—one side featuring the red, white and blue of Puerto Rico, and the other the red, white and blue of the U.S. It was a poignant—and pointed—show of support to the territory, which was recently hit by a damaging earthquake. . . .
>
> In a marked gesture of solidarity toward the Latin community and those impacted by anti-immigration policies, the set design featured glowing cages housing child performers. To drive the point home, they sang a snippet of "Born in the U.S.A." . . .
>
> Shakira threw it back to her 2010 World Cup song "Waka Waka" for their joint finale, which also featured some exuberant cheerleading-style basket tosses. . . . Lopez and Shakira closed out their set with impressive synchronized shimmies, the ultimate power move.

Reaction on Twitter ranged from praise for the show's cultural infusion and celebration of strong women to condemnation for its sexual innuendos and suggestive performances. Some tweeted their confusion about the children in cages and about Shakira's tongue wag that millions of viewers saw when the camera zoomed in for a close-up.

In the days following the Super Bowl performance, production managers, artists, and Internet trolls responded to the issues posed on social media, addressing complaints and adding questions that continued the conversation about the performance. Many who watched the halftime performance chimed in, expressing in their initial response a general position on the subject. In the ongoing (if not "unending") conversation, participants likely began to sharpen their positions, understanding and being able to explain *why* they liked or didn't like the halftime performance. The more information they received from the many other participants, the more they bounced their own ideas off those they may have disagreed with, the more they shaped their initial positions into claims. Maybe some who thought the political overtones were distracting changed their minds after learning more about conditions in Puerto Rico and detention centers. Maybe some who thought the stars' sexual innuendos were out of line came around to thinking that these powerful women used their ability to get the attention of a nation to make important social comments.

Source: Getty Images

Visual sources often succinctly convey ideas and feelings that would take many words to explain. What does this image of the Puerto Rican flag painted on cracked earth convey?

This public debate about a halftime performance shows how participants bring their own perspective to a subject and this perspective informs their position. In a sense, every social media user is a new source of information. Some sources are mainly objective; others are more biased. Participants in the conversation must determine which information is credible and which is not. If the information is relevant and credible enough, it might even lead you to change your own position. (See Part 1.1 for information on evaluating sources.)

In this unit, you will continue to identify and explain claims and evidence within arguments. You will also consider how biases and limitations within the evidence might render an argument weak or ineffective. Sometimes, as more evidence is introduced into the "unending conversation" about a topic, writers may need to revise their thesis statements to account for the new evidence. Readers may need to rethink their positions as well.

The focus of this unit is to help you identify reliable and credible information and also determine information that is biased or that has limited abilities to further an argument. It will also help you revise your argument and line of reasoning to account for new evidence. Finally, this unit will explore ways the tone of a text affects the reader and how tone can shift as a writer's attitude toward a topic changes.

Close Reading: Professional Text
"The Ways We Lie" by Stephanie Ericsson

Following is an essay by screenwriter and advertising copywriter Stephanie Ericsson called "The Ways We Lie." It originally appeared in a 1992 issue of the *Utne Reader*. Ericsson breaks down the act of lying to make a larger point about the role lying plays in our lives and our culture. Read it to understand the position Ericsson takes as she contributes to the conversation about truth and lies.

1 The bank called today, and I told them my deposit was in the mail, even though I hadn't written a check yet. It'd been a rough day. The baby I'm pregnant with decided to do aerobics on my lungs for two hours, our three-year-old daughter painted the living-room couch with lipstick, the IRS put me on hold for an hour, and I was late to a business meeting because I was tired.

2 I told my client that traffic had been bad. When my partner came home, his haggard face told me his day hadn't gone any better than mine, so when he asked, "How was your day?" I said, "Oh, fine," knowing that one more straw might break his back. A friend called and wanted to take me to lunch. I said I was busy. Four lies in the course of a day, none of which I felt the least bit guilty about.

3 We lie. We all do. We exaggerate, we minimize, we avoid confrontation, we spare people's feelings, we conveniently forget, we keep secrets, we justify lying to the big-guy institutions. Like most people, I indulge in small falsehoods and still think of myself as an honest person. Sure I lie, but it doesn't hurt anything. Or does it?

4 I once tried going a whole week without telling a lie, and it was paralyzing. I discovered that telling the truth all the time is nearly impossible. It means living with some serious consequences: The bank charges me $60 in overdraft fees, my partner keels over when I tell him about my travails, my client fires me for telling her I didn't feel like being on time, and my friend takes it personally when I say I'm not hungry. There must be some merit to lying.

5 But if I justify lying, what makes me any different from slick politicians or the corporate robbers who raided the S&L[1] industry? Saying it's okay to lie one way and not another is hedging. I cannot seem to escape the voice deep inside me that tells me: When someone lies, someone loses.

6 What far-reaching consequences will I, or others, pay as a result of my lie? Will someone's trust be destroyed? Will someone else pay *my* penance because I ducked out? We must consider the *meaning of our actions*. Deception, lies, capital crimes, and misdemeanors all carry meanings. *Webster's* definition of *lie* is specific: *1: a false statement or action especially made with the intent to deceive; 2: anything that gives or is meant to give a false impression.* A definition like this implies that there are many, many ways to tell a lie. Here are just a few.

The White Lie

A man who won't lie to a woman has very little consideration for her feelings. —Bergen Evans

7 The white lie assumes that the truth will cause more damage than a simple, harmless untruth. Telling a friend he looks great when he looks like hell can be based on a decision that the friend needs a compliment more than a frank opinion. But, in effect, it is the liar deciding what is best for the lied to. Ultimately, it is a vote of no confidence. It is an act of subtle arrogance for anyone to decide what is best for someone else.

8 Yet not all circumstances are quite so cut-and-dried. Take, for instance, the sergeant in Vietnam who knew one of his men was killed in action but listed him as missing so that the man's family would receive indefinite compensation instead of the lump-sum pittance the military gives widows and children. His intent was honorable. Yet for twenty years this family kept their hopes alive, unable to move on to a new life.

Façades

Et tu, Brute?[2] —Caesar

9 We all put up façades to one degree or another. When I put on a suit to go to see a client, I feel as though I am putting on another face, obeying the expectation that serious businesspeople wear suits rather than sweatpants. But I'm a writer. Normally, I get up, get the kid off to school, and sit at my computer in my pajamas until four in the afternoon.

1 **S&L**: Savings and Loan

2 **Et tu, Brute?:** "You as well?" asks Caesar, in Shakespeare's play *Julius Caesar*, when he sees that his supposed friend Brutus has joined in his assassination.

When I answer the phone, the caller thinks I'm wearing a suit (though the UPS man knows better).

10 But façades can be destructive because they are used to seduce others into an illusion. For instance, I recently realized that a former friend was a liar. He presented himself with all the right looks and the right words and offered lots of new consciousness theories, fabulous books to read, and fascinating insights. Then I did some business with him, and the time came for him to pay me. He turned out to be all talk and no walk. I heard a plethora of reasonable excuses, including in-depth descriptions of the big break around the corner. In six months of work, I saw less than a hundred bucks. When I confronted him, he raised both eyebrows and tried to convince me that I'd heard him wrong, that he'd made no commitment to me. A simple investigation into his past revealed a crowded graveyard of disenchanted former friends. . . .

Deflecting

When you have no basis for an argument, abuse the plaintiff. —Cicero

11 I've discovered that I can keep anyone from seeing the true me by being selectively blatant. I set a precedent of being up-front about intimate issues, but I never bring up the things I truly want to hide; I just let people assume I'm revealing everything. It's an effective way of hiding.

12 Any good liar knows that the way to perpetuate an untruth is to deflect attention from it. When Clarence Thomas[3] exploded with accusations that the Senate hearings were a "high-tech lynching," he simply switched the focus from a highly charged subject to a radioactive subject. Rather than defending himself, he took the offensive and accused the country of racism. It was a brilliant maneuver. Racism is now politically incorrect in official circles—unlike sexual harassment, which still rewards those who can get away with it.[4]

13 Some of the most skilled deflectors are passive-aggressive people who, when accused of inappropriate behavior, refuse to respond to the accusations. This you-don't-exist stance infuriates the accuser, who, understandably, screams something obscene out of frustration. The trap is sprung and the act of deflection successful, because now the passive aggressive person can indignantly say, "Who can talk to someone as unreasonable as you?" The real issue is forgotten and the sins of the original victim become the focus. Feeling guilty of name-calling, the victim is fully tamed and crawls into a hole, ashamed. I have watched this fighting technique work thousands of times in disputes between men and women, and what I've learned is that the real culprit is not necessarily the one who swears the loudest.

---

3 **Clarence Thomas**: African American Supreme Court Justice accused during his 1991 confirmation hearings of sexual harassment

4 This article appeared in 1992, long before the now widely known #MeToo movement and other high-profile efforts to expose sexual harassment.

Omission

The cruelest lies are often told in silence. —R. L. Stevenson

14 Omission involves telling most of the truth minus one or two key facts whose absence changes the story completely. You break a pair of glasses that are guaranteed under normal use and get a new pair, without mentioning that the first pair broke during a rowdy game of basketball. Who hasn't tried something like that? But what about omission of information that could make a difference in how a person lives his or her life?

15 For instance, one day I found out that rabbinical legends tell of another woman in the Garden of Eden before Eve. I was stunned. The omission of the Sumerian goddess Lilith from Genesis—as well as her demonization by ancient misogynists[5] as an embodiment of female evil—felt like spiritual robbery. I felt like I'd just found out my mother was really my stepmother. To take seriously the tradition that Adam was created out of the same mud as his equal counterpart, Lilith, redefines all of Judeo-Christian history.

16 Some renegade Catholic feminists introduced me to a view of Lilith that had been suppressed during the many centuries when this strong goddess was seen only as a spirit of evil. Lilith was a proud goddess who defied Adam's need to control her, attempted negotiations, and when this failed, said adios and left the Garden of Eden.

17 This omission of Lilith from the Bible was a patriarchal strategy to keep women weak. Omitting the strong-woman archetype of Lilith from Western religions and starting the story with Eve and the Rib has helped keep Christian and Jewish women believing they were the lesser sex for thousands of years.

Stereotypes and Clichés

Where opinion does not exist, the status quo becomes stereotyped and all originality is discouraged. —Bertrand Russell

18 Stereotype and cliché serve a purpose as a form of shorthand. Our need for vast amounts of information in nanoseconds has made the stereotype vital to modern communication. Unfortunately, it often shuts down original thinking, giving those hungry for the truth a candy bar of misinformation instead of a balanced meal. The stereotype explains a situation with just enough truth to seem unquestionable.

19 All the "isms"—racism, sexism, ageism, et al.—are founded on and fueled by the stereotype and the cliché, which are lies of exaggeration, omission, and ignorance. They are always dangerous. They take a single tree and make it a landscape. They destroy curiosity. They close minds and separate people. The single mother on welfare is assumed to be cheating. Any Black male could tell you how much of his identity is obliterated daily by stereotypes. Fat people, ugly people, beautiful people, old people, large-breasted women, short men, the mentally ill, and the homeless all could tell you how much more they are like us than we want to think. I

5 **mysogynists:** people with a strong prejudice against women

once admitted to a group of people that I had a mouth like a truck driver. Much to my surprise, a man stood up and said, "I'm a truck driver, and I never cuss." Needless to say, I was humbled.

Groupthink

Who is more foolish, the child afraid of the dark, or the man afraid of the light? —Maurice Freehill

20 Irving Janis, in *Victims of Group Think*, defines this sort of lie as a psychological phenomenon within decision-making groups in which loyalty to the group has become more important than any other value, with the result that dissent and the appraisal of alternatives are suppressed. If you've ever worked on a committee or in a corporation, you've encountered groupthink. It requires a combination of other forms of lying—ignoring facts, selective memory, omission, and denial, to name a few.

21 The textbook example of groupthink came on December 7, 1941. From as early as the fall of 1941, the warnings came in, one after another, that Japan was preparing for a massive military operation. The navy command in Hawaii assumed Pearl Harbor was invulnerable—the Japanese weren't stupid enough to attack the United States' most important base. On the other hand, racist stereotypes said the Japanese weren't smart enough to invent a torpedo effective in less than 60 feet of water (the fleet was docked in 30 feet); after all, U.S. technology hadn't been able to do it.

22 On Friday, December 5, normal weekend leave was granted to all the commanders at Pearl Harbor, even though the Japanese consulate in Hawaii was busy burning papers. Within the tight, good-ole-boy cohesiveness of the U.S. command in Hawaii, the myth of invulnerability stayed well entrenched. No one in the group considered the alternatives. The rest is history.

Out-and-Out Lies

The only form of lying that is beyond reproach is lying for its own sake. —Oscar Wilde

23 Of all the ways to lie, I like this one the best, probably because I get tired of trying to figure out the real meanings behind things. At least I can trust the bald-faced lie. I once asked my five-year-old nephew, "Who broke the fence?" (I had seen him do it.) He answered, "The murderers." Who could argue? At least when this sort of lie is told it can be easily confronted. As the person who is lied to, I know where I stand. The bald-faced lie doesn't toy with my perceptions—it argues with them. It doesn't try to refashion reality, it tries to refute it. *Read my lips. . . .* No sleight of hand. No guessing. If this were the only form of lying, there would be no such things as floating anxiety or the adult-children-of-alcoholics movement.

Dismissal

Pay no attention to that man behind the curtain! I am the Great Oz! —The Wizard of Oz

24 Dismissal is perhaps the slipperiest of all lies. Dismissing feelings, perceptions, or even the raw facts of a situation ranks as a kind of lie that

can do as much damage to a person as any other kind of lie. The roots of many mental disorders can be traced back to the dismissal of reality. Imagine that a person is told from the time she is a tot that her perceptions are inaccurate. *"Mommy, I'm scared."* "No you're not, darling." *"I don't like that man next door, he makes me feel icky."* "Johnny, that's a terrible thing to say, of course you like him. You go over there right now and be nice to him."

25 I've often mused over the idea that madness is actually a sane reaction to an insane world. Psychologist R. D. Laing supports this hypothesis in *Sanity, Madness and the Family*, an account of his investigation into the families of schizophrenics. The common thread that ran through all of the families he studied was a deliberate, staunch dismissal of the patient's perceptions from a very early age. Each of the patients started out with an accurate grasp of reality, which, through meticulous and methodical dismissal, was demolished until the only reality the patient could trust was catatonia.[6]

26 Dismissal runs the gamut. Mild dismissal can be quite handy for forgiving the foibles of others in our day-to-day lives. Toddlers who have just learned to manipulate their parents' attention sometimes are dismissed out of necessity. Absolute attention from the parents would require so much energy that no one would get to eat dinner. But we must be careful and attentive about how far we take our "necessary" dismissals. Dismissal is a dangerous tool, because it's nothing less than a lie.

Delusion

We lie loudest when we lie to ourselves. —Eric Hoffer

27 I could write the book on this one. Delusion, a cousin of dismissal, is the tendency to see excuses as facts. It's a powerful lying tool because it filters out information that contradicts what we want to believe. Alcoholics who believe that the problems in their lives are legitimate reasons for drinking rather than results of the drinking offer the classic example of deluded thinking. Delusion uses the mind's ability to see things in myriad ways to support what it wants to be the truth. But delusion is also a survival mechanism we all use. If we were to fully contemplate the consequences of our stockpiles of nuclear weapons or global warming, we could hardly function on a day-to-day level. We don't want to incorporate that much reality into our lives because to do so would be paralyzing.

28 Delusion acts as an adhesive to keep the status quo intact. It shamelessly employs dismissal, omission, and amnesia, among other sorts of lies. Its most cunning defense is that it cannot see itself. . . .

The liar's punishment [. . .] is that he cannot believe anyone else. —George Bernard Shaw

29 These are only a few of the ways we lie. Or are lied to. As I said earlier, it's not easy to entirely eliminate lies from our lives. No matter how pious we may try to be, we will still embellish, hedge, and omit to lubricate the daily machinery of living. But there is a world of difference between telling

6 **catatonia:** stupor

functional lies and living a lie. Martin Buber[7] once said, "The lie is the spirit committing treason against itself." Our acceptance of lies becomes a cultural cancer that eventually shrouds and reorders reality until moral garbage becomes as invisible to us as water is to a fish.

30 How much do we tolerate before we become sick and tired of being sick and tired? When will we stand up and declare our right to trust? When do we stop accepting that the real truth is in the fine print? Whose lips do we read this year[8] when we vote for president? When will we stop being so reticent about making judgments? When do we stop turning over our personal power and responsibility to liars?

31 Maybe if I don't tell the bank the check's in the mail, I'll be less tolerant of the lies told me every day. A country song I once heard said it for me: "You've got to stand for something or you'll fall for anything."

Composing on Your Own

Respond in writing to Ericsson's text. What are your views about lying? What types of lies, if any, are you willing to commit? How does lying affect your personal life, your academic life, and your life in society? Write freely to answer these and any other questions that come to mind. Save your work for future use.

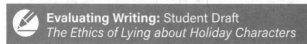

Evaluating Writing: Student Draft
The Ethics of Lying about Holiday Characters

Following is the student anchor text you will use in this unit to practice evaluating writing. A student wrote this as the first draft of a paper for a psychology class project, an anthology of student papers on "The Consequences of Lying" that was to be printed and distributed to the entire school after a cheating scandal was uncovered there. The draft still needs work. As you read it, think about what it contributes to the conversation about lying and compare it with Ericsson's essay. Later you will have an opportunity to suggest ways the essay might be improved.

(1) Many of our most cherished memories are of holiday celebrations. (2) While adults frantically search for the best deals on the year's hottest new toys, children approach this time of year with joy and wonder. (3) Undoubtedly, some of the most memorable life experiences—for both adult and child—stem from imagining Santa coming down the chimney to deposit gifts under the tree, or the baskets of candy left by the Easter Bunny. (4) While both child and adult recall these times of magic and consumerism with warm nostalgia, it is up to the adults to maintain these fanciful images for children.

7 **Martin Buber**: Jewish philosopher (1878–1965)

8 "Read my lips: no new taxes" was a line spoken by George H. W. Bush at the 1988 Republican nominating convention.

(5) Parents everywhere are plagued by the ethics of lying to children in order to foster a childhood full of magic. (6) Should adults, from parents and grandparents to schoolteachers and religious leaders, continue to perpetuate lies about Santa Claus, the Easter Bunny, and the Tooth Fairy in order to instill magic into these holidays and, ultimately, childhood?

(7) David Johnson, a professor of philosophy, has an ethical objection to parents promoting literal belief in Santa Claus, believing that it discourages critical thinking. (8) When kids begin to ask questions, many adults pull out "proof." (9) This promotes credulous thinking, since it teaches kids to believe something in spite of the evidence against it, and sets a dangerous precedent. (10) And, since children trust their parents to tell them the truth, this lie is a betrayal of their trust.

(11) Conversely, Cyndy Scheibe, a professor of psychology, recalls the look on children's faces when they start to question their belief in Santa. (12) That shift comes at a stage of cognitive development when their thinking grows more organized. (13) Scheibe qualifies her belief that children should be allowed to believe in these holiday characters by saying that when children start questioning how Santa can get down every chimney or how reindeer can fly, it is time for adults to answer honestly.

(14) Ultimately, parents and other adults in children's lives need to instill their own traditions and ways of celebrating that can either enhance or replace the traditions and celebrations connected to fictional characters.

What Do You Know?

This unit will provide instruction on synthesizing perspectives and refining arguments, considering and accounting for new evidence, and understanding how writers convey a tone through word choice and writing style.

Maybe you already know some or most of this information. Check what you know by trying to answer the following questions about the anchor texts. Taking stock of prior knowledge before formally studying a topic is a good way to reinforce learning, according to learning scientists. What you don't know now you will likely learn as you complete the activities in this unit.

CLOSE READING: PROFESSIONAL TEXT

1. How does Ericsson indicate that she anticipates others' reactions to her claims?

2. At what point in the introductory paragraphs (paragraphs 1–6) does Ericsson suggest she has reevaluated her initial claim about lying?

3. At what points in her essay does Ericsson show that she has considered new evidence and shifted her line of reasoning as a result?

4. What is Ericsson's tone? Why does Ericsson maintain this tone in the essay?

5. Cite at least one instance where Ericsson shifts her tone in order to suggest a qualification, refinement, or reconsideration of her perspective.

EVALUATING WRITING: STUDENT DRAFT

1. Briefly describe the perspectives of the two sources the writer cites in the student draft.

2. What position(s) do the two sources take? Do they agree or disagree?

3. Based on the writer's word choice, would this draft be an example of formal, informal, or neutral diction?

4. What is the overall tone of the piece?

5. Is there any place where the tone shifts? If so, where is it, and how does it shift?

Source: Getty Images

What does this image suggest about Santa and his reindeer? What does the image contribute to the ongoing conversation about promoting children's belief in fictitious characters?

Part
1

Synthesizing Perspectives

Enduring Understanding and Skills

Part 1

Understand

Writers make claims about subjects, rely on evidence that supports the reasoning that justifies the claim, and often acknowledge or respond to other, possibly opposing, arguments. (CLE-1)

Demonstrate

Identify and explain claims and evidence within an argument. (Reading 3.A)

Develop a paragraph that includes a claim and evidence supporting the claim. (Writing 4.A)

Source: *AP® English Language and Composition Course and Exam Description*

Essential Question: How can you identify and develop a sound argument that synthesizes or incorporates multiple sources?

Reread the Unit Overview about the Super Bowl halftime show on pages 300–301. The magazine article tries to share multiple viewpoints, including some that are biased. (See Part 1.3 for a discussion of bias.). What position, if any, does the *Time* magazine description take? Does the writer of the article show bias? If you watched the show (and you can do so on YouTube by searching for Halftime Show, Superbowl 2020), does the description tally with your own opinion of the show? Review the reactions described in the paragraphs following the excerpt, and try to imagine the perspectives from which they came—parents watching with young children, fans of J. Lo and Shakira who watched just for their performance, football fans with no interest in either of the performers, people who were offended by the show's political messages, and people who applauded those messages.

Part 1 of this unit will explore the need and process for creating source-informed arguments. To effectively **synthesize**—collect and combine information about a topic—invest time in understanding others' positions and perspectives, which will likely influence your own as well. When reviewing source material, identify biased information or information that has limitations as evidence to support your argument. Be open to reading and analyzing sources that may not jibe with your current position or perspective on a topic so that you adjust as needed.

KEY TERMS

bias	perspective	source
evidence	position	synthesis/synthesize
credible/credibility	reasoning	
limitation	reliable/reliability	

1.1 Evaluating and Synthesizing Source Material | CLE-1.P CLE-1.Q

When synthesizing, writers find reliable and credible sources, strategically select the most relevant information, and deftly incorporate this information into their own argument.

Reliable and Credible Sources

A **source** is any origin of information—a written text, a spoken text, an image, a website or other digital resource, to name a few—that provides **evidence** or insight. Often, a source is written or produced by a person with a particular voice or viewpoint. Every day, you synthesize information from many different sources. You seek information to help decide what to buy and where to buy it (think Black Friday ads), you search for videos to show how to fix something at home, you look for tutorials to help troubleshoot technology, and you scour the Internet researching all the colleges you are interested in attending. In all of these instances, you want the most reliable information to help you make an informed decision. In all of these examples, you *synthesize*—collect and combine—information from several sources to come to a conclusion.

In the same way that you sort through sources to find the best deal or decide which college to attend, you also sort through a variety of sources when writing an argument. To be strategic about which sources to choose, first evaluate the source to see if it is credible and reliable.

The term ***credibility*** generally refers to the trustworthiness of the author or source. **Credible** writers tend to have advanced degrees and experience with the subject and often collaborate with others who are well-versed on the subject. Writers who have been published in reputable journals, magazines, and books are likely to be credible. (See Table 6-1 on pages 313–314 for sources ranked by credibility.) Citations of a writer's work by other authors or organizations also enhance a writer's credibility, since they acknowledge the writer's expertise. Credible writers present information logically, fairly, and respectfully, acknowledging opposing perspectives with careful consideration.

If a source is credible, it uses information that is trustworthy and factual. If a source is **reliable,** it consistently includes information from credible sources and often analyzes different sides of an issue. Information is not purposely distorted to fit the writer's perspective or position without acknowledging others' perspectives or positions. In addition, a reliable source will often include a range of information and viewpoints from the subject's "unending conversation," even if the writer does not necessarily agree. If a reliable source includes quantitative data, it is likely to be reproducible, corroborated, or confirmed by others. Evidence is corroborated when it is supported by multiple reliable sources. Reporters must corroborate news stories by interviewing multiple people; only when numerous people tell the same story does a reporter know that story is probably true. Similarly, when you write an essay, you must access difference sources to corroborate your information. If you find the same information corroborated by a subject-area expert, a university study, and a well-regarded book, then the information is likely reliable.

In earlier units, you read that claims must be supported with evidence, evidence must be explained using commentary, and commentary must connect the two logically, reflecting a clear line of **reasoning**. Authors whose strategic choices take into account all of the elements of the rhetorical situation (see page 8) increase their credibility with readers.

The following table lists types of sources from most reliable and credible to least. Examples of credible sources are included for each type.

Type	Writers and Audience	Where to Find
Scholarly, peer-reviewed articles or books (print or online) <u>General/Academic</u> academicjournals.org jstor.org academic.microsoft.com <u>Science</u> sciencemag.org/journals omicsonline.org <u>Humanities/Literature</u> acla.org muse.jhu.edu	*Writers*: researchers *Audience:* students and other researchers	Academic databases Google scholar
Trade or professional articles or books (print or online) <u>Medical</u> jamanetwork.com pubmed.gov <u>Construction</u> *Construction and Building Materials* journals.elsevier.com/construction-and-building-materials	*Writers*: practitioners in a field *Audience:* other practitioners	Professional databases

(continued)

Type	Writers and Audience	Where to Find
Magazine articles, books, and newspaper articles from well-established newspapers <u>Newspapers</u> *The New York Times* *The Wall Street Journal* *The Washington Post* <u>News Sources</u> BBC Reuters Associated Press <u>Magazines</u> *The New Yorker* *The Economist* *The Atlantic* *Foreign Affairs*	*Writers:* authors and journalists who have consulted reliable sources and whose work has been vetted by an editor *Audience*: general public	Websites and print versions of magazines and newspapers
Websites, blogs, and social media <u>Science</u> science.gov <u>U.S. Government</u> usa.gov <u>The Word Fact Book</u> cia.gov/library/publications/resources/the-world-factbook/ <u>Encyclopedia Britannica</u> britannica.com <u>The Smithsonian</u> smithsonianmag.com	*Writers:* Some are written by experts, but others are written by people with a biased agenda. Websites published by research foundations or people who are subject-area experts are more reliable than those created by individuals who are promoting commercial interests or a particular viewpoint. *Audience:* anyone	Personal websites and social media accounts
Wikipedia* *Studies since 2005 in a variety of subject areas have shown that Wikipedia compares favorably to sources widely recognized as reliable. However, some articles on Wikipedia may not be reliable. Wikipedia can be used as a research tool that provides links to reliable sources, but Wikipedia should not be cited as a source.	*Writers:* anonymous sources Editors oversee entries and post warnings if the article appears to lack credible sources. Most entries include footnotes with links to sources. *Audience:* anyone	Website

Table 6-1

Evaluate Sources

Suppose you are developing an argument to present to state lawmakers that the voting age should be lowered to 16. You find the following sources. Which ones are most relevant to the argument? To your audience and purpose? Which ones provide specific information that would make the argument stronger? Which ones are from credible sources? Which ones seem to be less credible? What further information is needed to decide if the source is reliable and credible? As you read the sources, take notes evaluating their credibility.

Source A

A study in the *Annals of the American Academy of Political and Social Science* found that, "On measures of civic knowledge, political skills, political efficacy, and tolerance, 16-year-olds, on average, are obtaining scores similar to those of adults. . . . Adolescents in this age range are developmentally ready to vote."

Source B

Social scientists Tak Wing Chan and Matthew Clayton say that 16- and 17-year-olds wouldn't be competent voters because "research in neuroscience suggests that the brain, specifically the prefrontal cortex, is still undergoing major reconstruction and development during the teenage years," and added that the prefrontal cortex is what "enables us to weigh dilemmas, balance trade-offs and, in short, make reasonable decisions in politics."

Source C

Austria lowered the voting age to 16 in 2007. According to Markus Wagner, social sciences professor at the University of Vienna, et al., studies of subsequent elections show "the quality of these [younger] citizens' choices is similar to that of older voters, so they do cast votes in ways that enable their interests to be represented equally well."

Source D

On *The Federalist* website, Robert Tracinski, political writer, states, "Seeing Parkland students go on television and agitate for gun control has people on the Left excited at the prospect of lowering the voting age to 16. That is, they're excited about the small subset of Parkland students opportunistic talk-show hosts have paraded in front of television cameras—not the ones who dropped out of scripted "town halls" when they refused to let CNN tell them what they could say. . . . But what I've seen from the teenagers getting the most television coverage has confirmed their poorly considered political views should not have binding power over anyone and explained why they should not be given any kind of authority on matters of national importance."

Source E

Only 12.5% of 18-year-olds participated in the 2014 midterm election, compared to 42% of the general population. According to the United States Elections Project's analysis of US Census Bureau data, just 16% of eligible voters ages 18–29 voted in the 2014 election, compared to 30% for ages

30–44, 43% for 45–59, and 55% for age 60 and up. Over the last 30 years, voter turnout for 18- to 29-year-olds has never exceeded 21% in a midterm election.

Source F

David Davenport, research fellow at the Hoover Institution, said, "My concern is if 16-year-olds were allowed to vote on any kind of broad scale, what we'd actually be doing is bringing the least politically informed, the least politically experienced, the least mature in terms of making long-term judgments and trade-offs, directly into and potentially affecting our voter turnout and results."

Source G

A 2018 poll from *The Atlantic* and the Public Religion Research Institute found that 81% of Americans oppose lowering the voting age to 16, with a scant 16% in favor. Only 19% of young people support the idea, and just 9% of seniors. Among Democrats, 25% would like to see the voting age lowered; support among Republicans is a mere 6%.

Source H

The D.C. City Council had considered legislation that would allow 16- and 17-year-olds in the nation's capital to vote in all elections, including the 2020 presidential election, but they tabled the bill indefinitely after losing support from council members.

Some of the sources support your claim and others do not. Some appear more credible because they are studies by academic or professional bodies. Source G describes a poll about lowering the voting age. Polls can be useful, but you need to consider the limitations of a poll as well. A poll is used to explain popular opinion and may not be as relevant as other types of evidence. Source H states a fact about a city council that may be too local to be relevant to the argument about national voting.

Synthesize Sources

Your claim is that the voting age should be lowered to 16. How can you synthesize information from the sources to refine and support your position? You probably want to start with those sources that support your claim. Sources A and C both offer supporting information, and both are credible. One quotes from a reliable source: *Annals of the American Academy of Political and Social Science*, a scholarly publication that explains how it carefully screens its articles. The other source cites a credible person from the University of Vienna reporting on a study completed by social sciences professors.

To begin synthesizing these sources, identify as precisely as possible what each adds to the conversation about young voters. You might notice that Source A focuses on the "civic knowledge, political skills, political efficacy, and tolerance" that shows 16-year-olds are developmentally ready to vote. To know for sure how the researchers measured "political skills" and "political efficacy," you would need to look at the original research. Fortunately, the source is very reliable so you can assume the journal would have screened all its publications for academic integrity.

Source C approaches the question from a somewhat different perspective, focusing on how well, compared to older voters, 16-year-olds use their votes to represent their interests. This focus might align with the idea of "political efficacy" mentioned in Source A. The information in Source C, however, is derived from actual experience rather than experimental testing, since Austria granted 16-year-olds the right to vote in 2007. That gives Source C solid credibility, assuming the election studies used reasonable ways to assess the votes of young people.

So how might you synthesize the perspective and information in these two sources to support your position? Although there are many ways to synthesize sources, you might start by expressing in one sentence how both together support your claim. For example:

> Both testing and actual experience have shown that sixteen-year-olds have the civic knowledge to be informed voters capable of representing their interests.

After you pin down a statement like the one above, you might want to go back into the sources and find quotes you can use to provide specific information supporting your synthesis. Figure 6-1 shows how key ideas and quotes from different sources can be synthesized into a paragraph.

Source A

"On measures of civic knowledge, political skills, political efficacy, and tolerance, 16-year-olds, on average, are obtaining scores similar to those of adults."

Source C

Younger voters "cast votes in ways that enable their interests to be represented equally well" as older voters.

Synthesis

The voting age in the United States should be lowered to age 16. Both testing and actual experience have shown that 16-year-olds have the civic knowledge to be informed voters capable of representing their interests. "On measures of civic knowledge, political skills, political efficacy, and tolerance, 16-year-olds, on average, are obtaining scores similar to those of adults," concluded a study in the *Annals of the American Academy of Political and Social Science*. In 2007, Austria granted sixteen-year-olds the right to vote. University of Vienna studies of elections since 2007 reveal that younger voters take voting seriously and "cast votes in ways that enable their interests to be represented equally well" as older voters.

Figure 6-1

The credible sources in the table on pages 313–314 share some features that distinguish them as credible and reliable. Use these in your own writing to increase your credibility and reliability.

Writing Choices that Increase Credibility	
Writing Choice	**Purpose**
Using domain-specific vocabulary and details associated with the subject or issue	To demonstrate a knowledge of and expertise of the subject/issue
Quoting from an expert associated with the subject or issue	To use another's expertise of the subject/issue and ethos to substitute for or enhance the writer's knowledge of the subject/issue
Attributing (citing) quoted, summarized, and paraphrased sources (see pages 34–35)	To promote transparency, reveal sources of borrowed information, and allow readers to examine those sources
Conditioning your language so you do not express ideas in absolute terms (see pages 149–150 and Unit 7)	To recognize complexity by acknowledging that other perspectives may be worth considering
Maintaining a respectful tone with appropriate diction (See Unit 8)	To avoid language that reveals bias, which would weaken your credibility

Table 6-2

Remember: When synthesizing, writers draw upon arguments from multiple sources, strategically select the most relevant information, and combine apt and specific source material as part of their own argument. A source provides information for an argument, and some sources are more reliable or credible than others. (CLE-1.P, Q)

1.1 Checkpoint

Close Reading: Professional Text

Reread "The Ways We Lie" by Stephanie Ericsson on pages 302–308. Then complete the open response activity and answer the multiple-choice questions that follow.

1. Evaluate the reliability and credibility of the sources Ericsson used for her examples. As you reread Ericsson's essay, on separate paper make note of the different types of information she synthesizes to strengthen her argument about lying. The specific details she provides likely came from books or articles she consulted on subjects such as history and psychology, as well as from her personal experiences. Try to determine possible types of sources, such as scholarly articles, popular magazines, or philosophy texts, for each example she gives. Then write a paragraph in which you assess the reliability of her possible sources and the credibility of the examples she draws from them.

2. Which of the following best describes the purpose of the writer's use of source material in the essay?
   (A) The writer moves beyond her personal experiences to show the negative effects of lying on a wide range of people and events.
   (B) The writer refers to outside sources to justify her belief that lying is part of our culture.
   (C) The writer describes a series of hypothetical cause-and-effect sequences to show the dangers of lying.
   (D) The writer exploits real and hypothetical situations where lying had adverse effects to warn parents about the dangers of lying.
   (E) The writer integrates excerpts from others' personal experiences to underscore the ubiquity of lying in our culture.

3. The writer's descriptions in the first two paragraphs of the essay
   (A) establish the writer's professional credentials to speak on the subject of lying
   (B) create the impression that the writer begs for the reader's sympathy and pity
   (C) provide context for understanding the everyday factors that cause lying
   (D) reject the argument that lying is a pathological feature of human nature
   (E) furnish evidence that most lying is prompted by a desire for compassion

4. By using short quotations or epigrams to introduce various forms of lying, the writer
   (A) acknowledges diverse perspectives to prove that lying is indefinable
   (B) implies that her audience should recognize the type of lies she describes
   (C) establishes a thoughtful context for the descriptions that follow
   (D) introduces diverse perspectives about lying to prove her belief that all people lie
   (E) validates her claim that creative people are more effective liars

Evaluating Writing: Student Draft
Reread the student draft on pages 308–309. Then answer the following open response and multiple-choice questions.

1. How does the writer use the information provided by the two professors?

2. What is the relationship between the sources used by the writer?

3. The writer wants to support the main argument of the essay by adding information from another reliable source. Which of the following would best achieve this purpose?
   (A) a report organized by age that shows the number of children who believe in fictional holiday characters
   (B) a blog post from a mother of five who describes her family's holiday traditions and experiences with Santa
   (C) an article published in a scholarly journal that discusses the negative results of parents promoting fictional characters to their children
   (D) an entry on a live website that tracks the amount of money spent on toys during the holiday season
   (E) a newspaper article about community events that offers children an opportunity to get their pictures taken with Santa

Composing on Your Own
Review the notes you made after reading Ericsson's article. Did you raise any questions you would like to try to answer with help from sources? Try to zero in on a subject you would like to develop that would rely on sources, not just your own experiences. You may choose to write about some aspect of lying, or you may want to write about one of the following subjects or another of your choice:

- civil liberties versus public safety
- fair allocation of scarce resources during an emergency
- social media and bullying
- gender identity and discrimination
- an ethically ambiguous situation

In writing, develop and explain your position on the subject you chose. Choose a rhetorical situation from the following possibilities as a context for your writing, or create one of your own. Feel free to change any part of the situations in the chart on the next to make the task more interesting to you. For example, you may want to write about the stay-at-home orders but direct your remarks to protesters demanding to go back to work. Write down the choices you make so you can keep them in mind as you write.

Exigences
▪ Pandemic stay-at-home orders ▪ Instance of social media bullying ▪ Realizing a cashier at a "big box" store charged you only half the price of an item by mistake
Audiences
▪ Business owners ▪ School officials ▪ Friends
Purposes
▪ Analyze conflicting values and reach a position ▪ Explore people's responsibilities to others and assert a thesis ▪ Evaluate the ethics of a situation and persuade others of your view

Use a variety of sources, not just your own experience, to develop your position. In the library and online, find reliable and credible sources and make sure they are appropriate for your rhetorical situation. Make a list of the information you will need to support with examples from sources. Take notes when you find information or a quotation you might be able to weave effectively into your argument. Make a list of your sources, and be sure to identify each source with the publishing information (author, date of publication, type of publication, publisher, page number if appropriate). Save your work for future use.

1.2 Position Versus Perspective | CLE-1.R

Sources may take the same position on a subject while viewing it from different perspectives.

Identifying Positions and Perspectives

A **position** is personal idea about a subject. It identifies what someone believes to be true about a topic. Different people may hold the same position, but they may arrive at the position from different perspectives. **Perspective** is the complex interplay among a writer's background, interests, and experiences that inform their personal convictions, or their positions on ideas.

Think back to the responses to the 2020 Superbowl halftime show. Two people may share the position that the show was overly sexualized and sent the wrong message to women. However, one person may have arrived at that position because she believes that female performers often feel unfairly pressured to appeal to a male-dominated audience. Another person may have arrived at the same position based on a moral or religious code that emphasizes modesty.

Consider the sources on pages 315-316. Sources B and D both hold the position that 16-year-olds should not be allowed to vote, but they arrive at that position from different perspectives. The social scientists in Source B are interested in how the teenage brain works. They come to their position based on their expertise. However, the writer from Source D is not interested in science; he focuses on his own views of the right to bear arms and fears that young voters will not agree with his ideas.

Understanding the background, interests, and experiences that shape perspectives helps writers by

- allowing them to recognize, acknowledge, and respond to other positions by providing insight into *why* others might believe differently
- underscoring the many different perspectives that can lead to a position, which may make readers more open to arriving at that position as well
- connecting with a wider audience, since the writer appears to have considered others' experiences and interests—even if the writer is acknowledging a position opposite his or her own
- establishing the writer's credibility because he or she appears to have taken into consideration others' experiences and interests

When you synthesize differing views, you may learn something along the way that will inspire you to edit or revise an original claim or thesis. You may start out with a position on a subject based on your own perspective, but when considering information from different sources—or different perspectives—you are likely to develop a more nuanced and informed position. (See 2.1.)

> **Remember:** A position and a perspective are different. Sources may have the same position on a subject, yet each comes from a different perspective based on their background, interests, and expertise. (CLE-1.R)

1.2 Checkpoint

Close Reading: Professional Text

Review Stephanie Ericsson's essay on pages 302–308. Then answer the following open response and multiple-choice questions.

1. Ericsson's *subject* is lying, but what is her *position* on lying?

2. Her perspective is shaped by the personal experiences she relates in her essay as well the examples she discusses. In what paragraph(s) does she acknowledge a change in her perspective?

3. The writer's relation to the reader is best described as that of
   (A) an informed commentator
   (B) a sympathetic ally
   (C) a passionate critic
   (D) an amused colleague
   (E) an aloof judge

4. Which of the following quotations from paragraphs 1–6 best captures the writer's position on the importance or significance of her topic?
   (A) "We lie. We all do." (paragraph 3, sentences 1 and 2)
   (B) "I discovered that telling the truth all the time is nearly impossible." (paragraph 4, sentence 2)
   (C) "There must be some merit to lying." (paragraph 4, sentence 4)
   (D) "I cannot seem to escape the voice deep inside me that tells me: When someone lies, someone loses." (paragraph 5, sentence 3)
   (E) "A definition like this implies that there are many, many ways to tell a lie." (paragraph 6, sentence 7)

5. In paragraph 3, the writer implies that most people lie
   (A) with malicious intent
   (B) in a state of self-denial
   (C) casually and without concern
   (D) to deceive or gain power over others
   (E) with regret and a sense of guilt

6. Which of the following best describes the argumentative structure the writer follows after paragraph 6?
   (A) she moves from personal anecdotes to showing that most people throughout history have lied
   (B) she classifies, defines, and illustrates specific types of lies and shows their consequences
   (C) she begins each section with personal anecdotes followed by cited professional research
   (D) she arranges her descriptions of lying from those that are least consequential to those that are most consequential
   (E) she provides cited opinions of professional research psychologists followed by counterarguments and rebuttals

Evaluating Writing: Student Draft

Reread the student draft on pages 308–309. Then answer the following open response and multiple-choice questions.

1. What is the writer's position on lying to children?
2. Is the position stated after a consideration of different perspectives?
3. How do different perspectives inform the writer's argument, if at all?
4. What are some possible positions held by the writer's audience? How do you know?
5. The writer feels it necessary to summarize the perspectives of both the philosopher and the psychologist. Which of the following sentences, if inserted at the beginning of the conclusion, would best summarize both perspectives?
    (A) While Johnson explores the ethics of maintaining a false narrative in order to create magic during holidays, Scheibe relies on the psychological perspective to inform her position that nurturing these beliefs can be appropriate depending on the cognitive development of the child.
    (B) Both Johnson and Scheibe believe that magic can be found in a variety of ways for children during the holiday season, not only through fictional characters.
    (C) While both Johnson and Scheibe acknowledge the importance of children believing in something magical, Johnson focuses on the strain parents feel while Scheibe focuses on the changes in children that comes when they learn the truth.
    (D) Even though Johnson and Scheibe have the same position, Johnson explains his position from an economic ethical standpoint while Scheibe explains her position from a psychological standpoint.
    (E) Johnson and Scheibe believe that it is up to the parents to decide the extent to which they want to foster the belief in fictional characters.

Composing on Your Own

Review the writing you did as you developed and explained your position on a subject of interest to you. Keeping your rhetorical situation in mind, try to express your key idea in a claim that might serve as your thesis statement. Analyze the positions and perspectives of the writers of your sources and others on your chosen topic. How do they compare with one another's and with your own? Begin to sketch out your argument—in a literal sketch like the one on page 210 of Unit 4 describing the speech by President Bush or a more traditional outline—and how you intend to use your source material. Save your work for later use.

1.3 Recognizing and Acknowledging Biases in Source Material | CLE-1.S CLE-1.T

The strongest arguments recognize and take into account the biases and limitations of the source material.

Limitations in Source Material

Credible sources are trustworthy sources. Credible writers present information logically, fairly, and respectfully, acknowledging opposing perspectives with careful consideration. However, some writers have an agenda and may not provide information from opposing sources. Read the opinion section of any newspaper and you will find editorials that defend a particular viewpoint. Although an editorial writer usually backs up his or her claims with information from specific sources, the writer is primarily interested in promoting a particular viewpoint and is less concerned with integrating opposing views or a wide variety of support. The exaggerated, emotional language in some editorials—sometimes called "loaded language" and used to belittle opposing positions—reveals the writer's slant on the subject.

To be credible, writers also need to acknowledge their *own* possible biases and limitations as well as those of their sources. **Bias** is a tendency to react prejudicially either for or against someone or something in an unfair way, often unconsciously. Everyone has personal biases. For example, some people are biased toward certain types of music or genres of movies. In the opening illustration, people of Puerto Rican descent may have a positive bias toward the halftime performance because they share the heritage of the performers. Viewers who are fans of popular music may also be more inclined to praise the performance, while people with no connection to the language or culture of the performers and no connection to the music they sing may have a biased negative view of the performance. While these are superficial examples, they help show that all people naturally entertain biases and preferences.

Beyond acknowledging biases, strong arguments acknowledge the **limitations** of any evidence or any sources provided. Limitations may include

- focusing on one aspect of a subject to the exclusion of others
- faulty reasoning, such as overgeneralization (basing a conclusion on too few examples), red herring (missing the point of the argument or getting off on a tangent that has nothing to do with the argument), and false cause (assuming that because one thing happened before another, the first caused the second)
- the intentional omission of evidence that doesn't support the claim
- evidence that only partially supports a claim or supports only certain aspects of a claim

Writers may either highlight the limitations of their own sources or openly recognize certain merits of others' arguments. Usually a writer does not accept an opposing argument in its entirety but may admit that part of a different perspective has validity. When writers acknowledge the limitations of their evidence or arguments, they build their credibility by showing they have educated themselves about the weaknesses of their own arguments. Readers are more likely to believe a writer who has analyzed all sides of an issue.

Stephanie Ericsson acknowledges her own bias and the limitations of her logic in her essay. For example, consider the line of reasoning she develops in her description of "The White Lie."

> The white lie assumes that the truth will cause more damage than a simple, harmless untruth. Telling a friend he looks great when he looks like hell can be based on a decision that the friend needs a compliment more than a frank opinion. But, in effect, it is the liar deciding what is best for the lied to. Ultimately, it is a vote of no confidence. It is an act of subtle arrogance for anyone to decide what is best for someone else.
>
> Yet not all circumstances are quite so cut-and-dried. Take, for instance, the sergeant in Vietnam who knew one of his men was killed in action but listed him as missing so that the man's family would receive indefinite compensation instead of the lump-sum pittance the military gives widows and children. His intent was honorable. Yet for twenty years this family kept their hopes alive, unable to move on to a new life.

Ericsson's first example describes something we all do: give someone a compliment even when we don't really mean it. The audience is more likely to believe the ubiquity of lying when the author incorporates common everyday examples. Ericsson then shifts at the beginning of the second paragraph ("Yet not all circumstances are quite so cut-and-dried") to introduce a much more morally ambiguous example that speaks to the deeper effects of lying that aren't as obvious. By making this shift, she acknowledges the limitation of her first example—the fact that it is a fleeting moment with no lasting impact. Her second example addresses this limitation by showing the severity and greater implications of "the white lie."

A biased source doesn't take into account other positions, or, if it describes opposing positions, it may dismiss them in a condescending tone without giving them credence. Unbiased writers acknowledge positions other than their own and are able to see the limitations and flaws in their own arguments. Of course, good writers also offer evidence to support their own views. Taking others' experiences and interests into consideration establishes a writer's credibility by showing open-mindedness and honesty.

Read the following excerpt from the article "Give a lower voting age a try" by the Editorial Board of *The Washington Post.*

Source I

When D.C. Council member Charles Allen (D-Ward 6) introduced legislation in 2015 to lower the voting age to 16, he was pretty much laughed down. He recalled the skeptical questions: "'How can you convince me that a 16-year-old is mature enough, smart enough, engaged enough?" The bill died in committee.

When the proposal was reintroduced this week, a majority of council members signed on as co-sponsors and Mayor Muriel E. Bowser (D) expressed support. One reason for the different reception—and why the nationwide push for lowering the voting age has been reinvigorated—is the thoughtful and influential activism of young people following February's mass school shooting in Parkland, Fla.

Upending decades of political tradition is clearly provocative, and the council should proceed carefully in deciding whether to allow 16- and 17-year-olds to vote in local and federal elections. A case could be made that 16-year-olds lack the life experience to make informed choices. But we think a more compelling argument can be made in favor of lowering the voting age as a measure that could encourage lifelong civic engagement.

In the underlined section above, the writers acknowledge the limitations of their evidence. They are focusing on a recent example of student engagement, but there is established research that teenagers are not as prepared as older people to make important decisions that affect the lives of all citizens. This choice by the writers helps their argument. They are perceived as reasonable, thoughtful people who can step back and view their argument from other perspectives. By doing so, they appear unbiased and credible. Without this information, the argument would be less convincing. Imagine if the underlined section, instead of acknowledging its limitations, had dismissed the opposing viewpoint. In the following example, notice how dismissing the opposing view tends to undermine rather than strengthen the writer's argument: *It is clear that those who oppose this proposed legislation are caught in their own narrowminded views and fail to value the intelligence and civic engagement of young people.*

Source: Getty Images

Remember: When incorporating evidence or sources into an argument, the strongest arguments recognize and acknowledge the biases and limitations of the material and account for those limitations in their reasoning. The degree to which a source does or does not consider other positions reflects the degree to which that source is biased. (CLE-1.S, T)

1.3 Checkpoint

Close Reading: Professional Text

Review Ericsson's essay on pages 302–308. Then complete the following open response activities and answer the multiple-choice questions that follow.

1. Identify two instances in which Ericsson addresses the limitations of her experiences and examples. Explain how this strategy works to strengthen her argument.

2. Then identify two instances where either her biases show within her essay or she does *not* acknowledge the limitations of her evidence.

3. Which of the following sections of the essay provides anecdotal evidence that prevents the writer from seeming to be self-righteous or moralizing in her discussion of lying?
   (A) her reference to wearing pajamas in the "Façades" section
   (B) her descriptions of Clarence Thomas in the "Deflecting" section
   (C) her discussion of Catholic feminists in the "Omission" section
   (D) her story about the truck driver in the "Stereotypes and Clichés" section
   (E) her questioning of her nephew in the "Out-and-Out Lies" section

4. The evidence in the "Omission" section of the essay allows the writer to
   (A) carefully reflect on the ways accidental misuse of language distorts the truth
   (B) expose the many lies that we believe and how they perpetuate stereotypes
   (C) resolve the long-standing debate about society's stereotypes surrounding gender roles
   (D) illustrate the sometimes negative consequences of lies based on purposely ignoring the larger truth
   (E) depict the lasting effects of outdated religious traditions

5. Which section of the essay provides evidence of the author's belief that lying may be essential to human survival and well-being?
   (A) the section entitled "Deflecting"
   (B) the section entitled "Omission"
   (C) the section entitled "Groupthink"
   (D) the section entitled "Dismissal"
   (E) the section entitled "Delusion"

Evaluating Writing: Student Draft
Reread the student draft on pages 308–309. Then answer the following open response and multiple-choice questions.

1. What evidence, if any, is there of biases in the sources cited by the writer?
2. The writer wants to account for possible limitations within the source material used. Which of the following sentences, if placed in the last paragraph, best accounts for possible limitations while still maintaining the writer's position?
   (A) Both perspectives are research-based and offer great insight into the argument and, thus, both need to be considered when deciding whether or not to celebrate fictional characters and in what way.
   (B) Although both perspectives are well-researched and credible, they fail to consider factors such as family dynamics, cultural customs, or religious traditions and, therefore, each family needs to make its own decisions about what is best.
   (C) While Schiebe's psychological perspective focuses on the complex interplay between cognitive and behavioral theories, Johnson's philosophical perspective focuses more on the ethics of maintaining a false narrative.
   (D) Children do not realize the financial burden that is placed upon their parents in order to maintain these false narratives and perpetuate a belief in magic that really isn't magic at all.
   (E) Clearly it is unreasonable to expect philosophers, who deal with hypothetical ethical questions rather than real people, ever to agree with psychologists, who deal with real-life situations.

Composing on Your Own

Reexamine your list of sources.

- Is each credible? If not, replace the source.
- Do any show obvious bias or have any other limitations that might render them unsuitable for your purpose? If so, find one or more sources to replace them.
- Have you accessed a source that represents a different position or perspective on this issue?
- Review your chosen rhetorical situation. With that in mind, write a first draft of your essay. Embed source materials by quoting, paraphrasing, or summarizing to strengthen your argument. (See Unit 1, Part 3, pages 34–35.) Save your work for future use.

Part 1 Apply What You Have Learned

Read "Liars: It Takes One to Know One" by Travis Riddle, published in *Scientific American*, July 24, 2012, and reproduced below. (The parenthetical citations refer to sources listed in the Works Cited section at the end.) Then answer the questions that follow.

Liars: It Takes One to Know One

In the final hand of the 2011 World Series of Poker, Pius Heinz, a 22-year-old German who had honed his poker chops online was matched up against 35-year-old Martin Staszko—a former Hyundai automobile plant foreman. Staszko was in bad shape, having only about a quarter of the chips his younger opponent had, and had been dealt a relatively mediocre hand. Despite this, he decided to risk it all in an attempt to wage a comeback. In effect, he was lying, and Heinz, fortunately blessed with a relatively good hand, called him on his lie. Heinz, having successfully detected his opponents attempt at deceit, won the hand, the tournament, and $8.7 million while Staszko, the failed deceiver, took runner up and had to console himself with just $5.4 million.

Although humans are the only species that plays poker, we are far from the only species that uses deception (Searcy and Nowicki, 114). And though several million dollars may seem like a high stakes game to us, the stakes for animals which use deception are even higher—often life or death. A frog which successfully fakes its croak to make itself seem bigger will be more likely to succeed in life than a similarly sized one which unsuccessfully fakes its croak. However, the ability to detect deception is just as important as the ability to deceive. A female frog with a talent for detecting deception will be more likely to mate with the actual biggest frog in the pond, rather than the one which only sounds the biggest, ensuring a greater likelihood of success for her genes. And so the evolutionary arms race continues, with liars and lie detectors successively attempting to one-up each other in reproductive fitness.

This is how deception is usually considered. The separate processes of deception and deception detection competing against each other, with the genes associated with each waxing and waning in success relative to the other. However, psychological and neuroscience theories of how lying and lie detection actually work seem to make a different prediction. Specifically these theories suggest (Sip et al.) that lying and detecting lies both rely on theory of mind, which is the ability to think about what someone else is thinking, and executive processes, an umbrella term which includes abilities like problem solving, attention, reasoning, and planning. Thus, rather than two separate processes competing against each other, these models suggest that improvements in one area will be directly related to improvements in the other. Good liars, in other words, should also make for good lie detectors.

Until now, however, no one has considered looking at whether this idea is true or not. In fact, previous research (Bond and DePaulo) has failed to show any relationship at all between lie detection ability and any individual differences. That is, there is no evidence indicating which individuals are likely to be good or bad at lie detection. To answer these questions, researchers at the University of London and the University College London had participants play a game (Wright et al.) they designated the Deceptive Interaction Task.

Participants playing the game are told that the object is to simultaneously be the best at lie detection as well as the most credible. The participants were told that the individuals who score highest in these two areas would each receive a prize of £50 (about $62 USD). This ensured that all participants were motivated to lie effectively and to attempt to detect lies in others. Participants played in groups of five or six, and on each trial, one participant was chosen randomly to be the sender. The sender was given a card, on which was printed an opinion (for example "Smoking should be banned in all public places") and an instruction to lie or tell the truth. Participants had privately indicated whether they agreed or disagreed with these opinions prior to the start of the game. After reading their card, the sender then presented either their actual opinion, or lied about their opinion, and gave some supporting arguments to back up what they had said. The other participants, designated as receivers, then indicated whether they thought the sender was lying or telling the truth.

The results revealed the first ever demonstration of what kinds of people are likely to be good lie detectors: those who are good liars. Interestingly, and in line with what past research has established, participants took significantly less time to start speaking when they were telling the truth than when they were lying. In particular, when lying, participants started speaking after an average of 6.5 seconds. When telling the truth, participants began speaking after an average of 4.6 seconds. The researchers also had IQ and emotional intelligence scores for each of the participants, but neither of these measures were related to lying or lie detection abilities.

Though this research is primarily about deception, it also speaks to a body of work showing that the way in which the brain and mind represent other people is remarkably similar to the way in which the self is represented. For example, when seeing someone else experience emotion, people will respond to tasks as if they were feeling that emotion themselves (Decety and Jackson). Similarly, other work (Casile and Gieses) shows that if you twitch your finger, it enhances your ability to perceive someone else twitch their finger in the same way. That deception and deception detection abilities are associated seems to point to a similar conclusion—the representation of self and the representation of other must bear some striking similarities.

Though this study features a more realistic experimental setting than many previous investigations of deception, there are still some shortcomings of the study that deserve to be addressed in future work. First, the requirement of stringent experimental control meant that participants were explicitly instructed when to lie. However, the authors do point out that there are many instances in which individuals are either explicitly instructed to lie (for example, by a boss or parent), or are compelled to lie by the situation. Just think of the last time someone asked you if their new, awful haircut looked nice, and it's easy to see how we are often forced to lie for one reason or another.

Also, as this is a correlational study, the reason for the association between lying and lie detection abilities remains unknown. While the authors suggest that one likely explanation is that both of these abilities draw on theory of mind and executive functioning, other hypotheses could also be reasonably entertained, and future work should be able to falsify those hypotheses which are not actually true.

This is the first example effectively showing who is likely to be a good liar. Specifically, those who are also good at lie detection. This is an important demonstration of a phenomenon with which our culture is justifiably fascinated. Lying, whether from a politician, an athlete, a poker player, or a frog is an important determinant of who wins and loses. Elections, court cases, card games, and the ability to reproduce all rely on lying and lie detection abilities. With such high stakes, it's no wonder that we spend so much time trying to figure out who is bluffing and who isn't. Given these findings, perhaps we can begin to be just a little more accurate.

Works Cited

Bond, C. F., Jr., & DePaulo, B. M. (2008). "Individual differences in judging deception: Accuracy and bias." *Psychological Bulletin, 134*(4), 477–492. https://doi.org/10.1037/0033-2909.134.4.477

Casile, Antonio & Giese, Martin A. "Nonvisual Motor Training Influences Biological Motion Perception." *Current Biology, 16*(1), 10 January 2006, 69–74.

Decety, John & Jackson, Philip L. "The Functional Architecture of Human Empathy." *Behavioral and Cognitive Neuroscience Reviews,* 3(2), 2004.

Searcy, William A. & Nowicki, Stephen. "Bird Song and the Problem of Honest Communication." *America Scientist*, *96*(2), March–April 2008, 114.

Sip, Kamila E, et al. "Detecting Deception: The Scope and Limits." *Trends in Cognitive Sciences*, Elsevier Current Trends, 31 Jan. 2008.

Wright, Gordon R. T., Berry, Christopher J., Bird, Geoffrey. " 'You can't kid a kidder': association between production and detection of deception in an interactive deception task." *Frontiers in Human Neuroscience*, 2012, 6, 87.

---

1. Identify the different positions on lying Riddle includes in his article.
2. Choose three of the sources Riddle used, and write a brief evaluation of their credibility. If possible, look them up online or in the library to learn more about them.
3. According to Riddle, what are two limitations of the research by Wright et al. that he reports in this article?

Reflect on the Essential Question: Write a brief response that answers this essential question: *How can you identify and develop a sound argument that incorporates and synthesizes multiple sources?* In your answer, explain the key terms listed on page 312.

Part 2

Considering and Accounting for New Evidence

Enduring Understanding and Skills

Part 2

Understand

Writers make claims about subjects, rely on evidence that supports the reasoning that justifies the claim, and often acknowledge or respond to other, possibly opposing, arguments. (CLE-1)

Demonstrate

Identify and describe the overarching thesis of an argument, and any indication it provides of the argument's structure. (Reading 3.B)

Write a thesis statement that requires proof or defense and that may preview the structure of the argument. (Writing 4.B)

Source: *AP® English Language and Composition Course and Exam Description*

Essential Question: How does the consideration of new evidence influence an already-established thesis or line of reasoning?

As more praise, questions, and criticisms of the Superbowl Halftime performance continued to flood social media outlets, those responsible for the artistic decisions—including Shakira and Lopez themselves—spoke out about their choices, offering reasons for what they did and shifting the conversation. For example, Shakira's close-up tongue wag combined with a high-pitched trill that left many viewers confused turned out to be a nod to her father's Lebanese heritage and thus carried cultural significance. This sound and movement, called a *zaghrouta*, is a traditional Arabic expression of joy and celebration. When this information was reported, many who were initially confused were now informed and many who ridiculed the gesture as being unflattering or inappropriate recognized their cultural ignorance and subsequently revised their original claim—or qualified it—based on this new information.

In the same way, when writers continue to engage in the ongoing conversation, they will continue to gain more information and insight. As a result, they may find themselves revising their **thesis statement**, the sentence or sentences that communicate the writer's central claim. Other times, they may not change the thesis, but they may change *why* they think the way they do and then qualify their claim, refining their understanding based on this new information. The **line of reasoning**—the reasons and evidence that support the thesis—may change to account for this new information. The willingness to consider and synthesize new information into an argument can strengthen the entire argument.

This part will help you recognize the need for revising your thesis statement or line of reasoning when new evidence is introduced.

KEY TERMS	
line of reasoning	thesis statement

2.1 Consideration and Use of New Evidence | CLE-1.U

Consideration and use of new evidence may require revision of the thesis statement and/or line of reasoning.

Revising a Thesis Statement or a Line of Reasoning

Unit 1 introduced the idea of the "unending conversation," a metaphor for an ongoing discussion with people joining and leaving, privy only to the part of the conversation that took place during the time they were in the room. The nature of a conversation is always changing as more voices, more perspectives, and more evidence are introduced. Claims and reasoning may be challenged with new evidence.

History has many examples of how positions evolve—especially in the wake of new discoveries. In the early 1900s, scientists discovered radium, which was quickly deemed a miracle element. Because it glowed in the dark, green phosphorescent radium was painted on the faces of clocks and wristwatches. Many young women were employed in factories and given the task of painting the radium on watches. In order to get a perfect point on their brushes, factory workers would twist the tips of their paintbrushes in their lips before dipping it in the paint. Their ingestion of radium made their skin glow, giving them the appearance of health. But after a while, these women mysteriously began to get sick. Their teeth started to fall out, and their bones began to disintegrate. But Americans would not believe that their ailments were caused by radium, which was believed to be a miracle cure for everything from blindness to mental hysteria. As more factory workers fell ill, scientists finally determined that the radium was poisoning them. Naturally, this new evidence and the testimony of the women who worked in the factories changed the claims about radium, and laws were created to prohibit its use in household items, cosmetics, and medicines.

An effective writer is able to hold somewhat loosely to his or her thesis statement, allowing it to be influenced by the research process. In Unit 1, the circular process of developing and refining arguments is represented in Figure 1-5 (page 23). Ideas begin as a seed of thought and develop as the writer gathers more information. Even after a thesis statement is formulated, new evidence should continue to shape the thesis and the reasoning used to support the thesis.

Consider the student who is researching the claim that the voting age should be lowered to 16. Reading through his sources, he reviews the *Washington Post* editorial.

Source I

When D.C. Council member Charles Allen (D-Ward 6) introduced legislation in 2015 to lower the voting age to 16, he was pretty much laughed down. He recalled the skeptical questions: "'How can you convince me that a 16-year-old is mature enough, smart enough, engaged enough?" The bill died in committee.

When the proposal was reintroduced this week, a majority of council members signed on as co-sponsors and Mayor Muriel E. Bowser (D) expressed support. One reason for the different reception—and why the nationwide push for lowering the voting age has been reinvigorated—is the thoughtful and influential activism of young people following February's mass school shooting in Parkland, Fla.

Based on this information, a student might incorporate this information into his line of reasoning.

Claim: Voting rights should be extended to 16-year-olds.

Reason: Some state and local governments are supportive of allowing 16-year-olds to vote.

Example: Though originally opposed, a majority of Washington D.C. council members signed on to support a bill to lower the voting age.

However, later he finds the following source:

Source J

The D.C. City Council had considered legislation that would allow 16- and 17-year-olds in the nation's capital to vote in all elections, including the 2020 presidential election, but they tabled the bill indefinitely after losing support from council members.

After closely investigating both sources, the student realizes that Source I was written in April 2018 and the events in Source J occurred in November 2018. Ultimately, the D.C. council did not support the legislation. This example no longer supports the reasoning, and unless the writer can find other examples of local governments that are considering opening voting rights to younger people, the reasons may not be viable. Even if the D.C. City Council voted in favor of the proposal, having only one example limits the strength of the argument. This may be an example of a hasty generalization, in which a conclusion is based on too few examples. Just because one local government considered lowering the voting age doesn't mean that most or many local governments are in favor of it.

If the student wants to stay on the subject of 16-year-old voting rights, a new claim and line of reasoning would be necessary to incorporate new information and qualify the limitations of the evidence.

> **Revised Claim:** Although a subject of continuing debate, voting rights should be extended to 16-year-olds in the United States.
>
> **Revised Line of Reasoning:** Some state and local governments waver in their support of allowing 16-year-olds to vote, but where it has been tried—in Austria, for example, since 2007—16-year-olds demonstrated the same competence for voting for their interests as other groups of young people.
>
> **Example:** Though originally opposed, a majority of Washington D.C. Council members signed on to support a bill to lower the voting age, influenced in part by the articulate and mature student leaders who gained wide publicity after the school shootings in Parkland, Florida, in 2015. When it finally came up for a vote, however, the bill failed to pass.
>
> **Limitations:** There are only a few places in the United States the issue has been brought before a legislature, so a full public debate on the issue is yet to happen. Evidence may emerge during those debates that would shed new light on the decision to let 16-year-olds vote.

Sometimes you may even decide to make a dramatic change in your position and your thesis statement if the information you find is convincing enough to change your mind. Notice the conflicting evidence about the maturity of the teenage brain presented in the sources in Part 1.1. After reviewing the scientific evidence used in Source B, you may begin to doubt your original thesis. As you continue to research how the law treats minors, you realize that the law and the courts support the idea that children aren't capable of handling the same rights as adults, and even the courts have come to understand that sentencing a minor in the same way as an adult is cruel and unusual punishment. In the end, you may decide that the voting laws should not be changed.

Remember: Consideration and use of new evidence may require revision of the thesis statement and/or changes to the line of reasoning. (CLE-1.U)

2.1 Checkpoint

Close Reading: Professional Text

Review the text by Ericsson on pages 302–308. Then complete the open response activities and answer the multiple-choice questions that follow.

1. In Part 1.3, you found instances in which Ericsson addresses the limitations of her experiences and examples as well as instances where she does *not* acknowledge the limitations of her evidence. Explain how adding the following legal element to the section titled "The White Lie" might change the author's line of reasoning:

   However, it is against the law for a military sergeant to lie to families about the status of a soldier, even if the family benefits.

2. Identify a concern or a possible limitation that you find within Ericsson's argument.

3. Much of Ericsson's evidence is relatively general, yet she also uses very specific examples. How would the line of reasoning change if she were to include more specific details in her examples? How would that change add to or detract from her argument?

4. In paragraph 6, the writer considers *Webster's* definition of a lie in order to
   (A) analyze the existing definition of lying in order to show that it is wrong
   (B) undermine a common misunderstanding about how lying hurts people
   (C) criticize those who lie, especially when they knowingly create false impressions and expectations
   (D) examine the motives of those who lie but not the effects those lies have on victims
   (E) suggest that the standard definition of "lie" requires further interpretation and elaboration

5. In the last paragraph, the writer returns to the lie she told her bank in order to
   (A) cast doubt on the ubiquity of lying in everyday situations
   (B) show that society has grown too comfortable with immoral actions
   (C) suggest that being personally honest might expose other people's lies
   (D) describe how her situation would have been improved if she had told the truth
   (E) concede she will continue to lie but reassess her motives for lying

Evaluating Writing: Student Draft
Reread the student draft on pages 308–309. Then complete the following open response activities and answer the multiple-choice questions.

1. How does the writer's thesis at the end of the essay show consideration of different positions introduced into the discussion?

2. What kinds of additional evidence might the writer examine to add strength to the argument?

3. The writer would like to add the following sentence to the passage.

   After all, children will eventually discover the truth about their favorite childhood holiday characters, and the resulting distrust they feel toward their parents can alter the integrity of that relationship.

   Which of the following changes would the writer need to make in order to incorporate this new information into the passage's overall line of reasoning?

   (A) changing the second paragraph to focus on the changes in the parent-child relationship after children realize their parents have lied to them
   (B) updating the thesis statement to indicate that lying can destroy relationships among family and friends
   (C) adding statistics to the first paragraph about the amount of money spent on toys during the holiday season
   (D) anticipating that opposition to this new information would include claims about the many different ways that children are lied to, not just those concerning fictional holiday characters
   (E) removing the contrast between the way parents and children view the holiday season from the introduction and moving this to the second paragraph

Composing on Your Own
Review the draft you wrote in the previous Composing on Your Own exercise. Did the sources you selected cause you to rethink or refine your position on the subject? If so, revise your thesis statement and line of reasoning, if necessary, to account for your new understanding. Save your work for future use.

Part 2 Apply What You Have Learned

Reread "Liars: It Takes One to Know One" on pages 330–332. Suppose the author came across the following new information after writing the article. Read this information and then answer the questions that follow.

Studies over the past two decades using fMRIs (functional magnetic resonance images), which show blood flow to certain parts of the brain during certain activities, have provided evidence that lying involves the frontal cortex. These studies also suggested that lying takes more mental effort than telling the truth. German researcher Ahmed Karim conducted a twist on those studies by using electrodes from outside of the head to deliver safe and painless electrical current aimed at the anterior prefrontal cortex, which plays a key role in moral and ethical decision-making. The current blocked the ability of that part of the brain to operate well. As a result, subjects were able to develop better lies (not as easily detected as others) and to reduce their response time. One possible explanation is that the cognitive effort to lie was made easier without the complicating factors of ethics and morality.

1. Does the information in this passage require revising the thesis or line of reasoning in the article by Travis Riddle? If so, how? If not, why not?

2. If so, where in the article would be the best place to work in this new information?

Reflect on the Essential Question: Write a brief response that answers this essential question: *How does the consideration of new evidence influence an already-established thesis or line of reasoning?* In your answer, explain the key terms listed on page 335.

Part 3

Strategic Use of Tone

Enduring Understanding and Skills

Part 3

Understand

The rhetorical situation informs the strategic stylistic choices that writers make. (STL-1)

Demonstrate

Explain how word choice, comparisons, and syntax contribute to the specific tone or style of a text. (Reading 7.A)

Strategically use words, comparisons, and syntax to convey a specific tone or style in an argument. (Writing 8.A)

Source: *AP® English Language and Composition Course and Exam Description*

Essential Questions: How does a writer's strategic word choice convey his or her tone, and what does a shift in tone suggest about the writer's line of reasoning?

In music, tone has a literal meaning, a sound with a specific pitch and frequency. But music also has an emotional impact or tone. A song can reflect a listener's mood or be played to create a mood. For example, someone might listen to a sad song when going through the break-up of a relationship or grieving the loss of a loved one. Or someone might listen to love songs when preparing for a special date. Note the relationship: perspective—the complex interplay of experiences and emotions that shape one's outlook or inform one's position on something—is akin to tone, a writer's (or musician's or any other artist's) general attitude or feeling about something.

Source: Stan Eales, cartoonstock

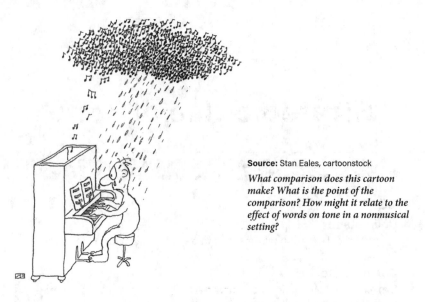

What comparison does this cartoon make? What is the point of the comparison? How might it relate to the effect of words on tone in a nonmusical setting?

In Part 3, you will make inferences about a writer's tone based on the strategic choice of words and writing style. You will also see how these choices influence the way a message is received.

KEY TERMS

connotation	style
denotation	tone
diction	word choice

3.1 Tone | STL-1.D STL-1.E

Tone is a writer's attitude or feeling about a subject conveyed through his or her strategic choice of words, with particular attention to the connotations of the words. Depending on the writer's choice of words, the tone of a piece may be serious or playful, optimistic or pessimistic, sincere or ironic.

Tone and Word Choice

In effective writing, the writer's choices work together to engage a targeted audience, establish the writer's credibility, develop a convincing line of reasoning, and achieve the writer's purpose(s) arising from the rhetorical situation. One choice a writer makes is about what tone to use. Tone is communicated through various techniques and strategies but especially through word choice and writing style.

Word choice, or **diction,** in a text includes the vocabulary, the use of standard or nonstandard language, even the use (or not) of contractions. *Standard English* is used by almost all academics and professionals. It conforms to the conventions of language that are accepted most widely by English speakers. While many dialects of English are used throughout the nation and world, Standard English provides a consistent way to communicate with people across regions and cultures. For this reason, even though writers may occasionally include dialect or informal language for affect, Standard English is the preferred form for rhetorical writing that can be clearly understood by a wide audience. *Nonstandard English* reflects regional variations, slang, and colloquial expressions. Many people use it in nonprofessional or nonacademic settings. Fiction writers often use it to capture the flavor of a character.

Diction is often classified as formal, informal, or neutral. *Formal diction* is free of slang and contractions and often academic or dignified in tone. It is the language of scholarly publications, legal documents, and other serious communications. *Informal diction* is marked by contractions and slang—the language of everyday speech. *Neutral diction* has a conversational or personal tone and is commonly used in popular magazine and newspaper articles. It is characterized by words that are free of emotional undertones. It may contain contractions, but it tends to avoid slang. All types of diction have their place.

For example, Ericsson includes both formal and informal diction when introducing her discussion of "Delusion":

> I could write the book on this one. Delusion, a cousin of dismissal, is the tendency to see excuses as facts. It's a powerful lying tool because it filters out information that contradicts what we want to believe. Alcoholics who believe that the problems in their lives are legitimate reasons for drinking rather than results of the drinking offer the classic example of deluded thinking.

Notice that Ericsson begins her paragraph with an informal colloquialism: "I could write the book on this one." This common saying, which people often use conversationally, helps ease the reader into the subject matter. But after her first sentence, Ericsson begins using formal, standard English; she employs serious language to discuss how the psychology of "delusion" can have serious consequences.

Writers set their tone by using appropriate words to elicit emotions in the reader. Words have denotation and connotation. **Denotation** is the dictionary definition of a word; **connotation** is the emotional implication or association of a word. Take, for example, two words with a similar denotation: *house* and *home*. Denotatively, there is little difference between these terms. But connotatively, *house* implies a physical structure where people live and *home* implies a place of security and belonging. The word *home* has positive connotations. By using highly connotative words, writers are able to evoke specific feelings and emotions within their audiences.

Consider the connotations of the following excerpt from a short essay called "Green Dreams: The All-American Lawn."

> The ideal American lawn represents a perfect symmetry of greenness, each blade nearly identical, not a weed in sight to distract the eye. It is nature minutely sculpted and carefully shaped into uniform harmony that calms the eye with its unblemished regularity. With the help of endless watering and invigorating nutrients, the American lawn even thrives in areas that would otherwise be landscapes of desert rock and sand. One can almost imagine our mythic settler forefathers, who attempted to tame the Wilderness, looking upon this expanse of crewcut green and smiling with satisfaction.

Many of the words and phrases in this passage have positive connotations: *perfect, carefully shaped, harmony, invigorating, thrives,* and *satisfaction.* The descriptive details about nature and the strong verbs work to create a calm and peaceful tone. Though formal, the word choice is creative instead of academic.

Tone and Writing Style

Word choice and style work together to create a writer's tone. Writing **style** is the way in which a writer expresses thoughts and ideas and creates the "voice" readers hear when they read. A number of factors combine to create a writer's style. Word choice is one important element. The style of sentences a writer uses is another: Some writers rely on long, flowing sentences with descriptive adjectives; others rely on more formal language, academic terms, and complex sentence structure that reveals their expertise on a topic. Sometimes in less formal writing, sentence fragments and slang can help a writer create a down-to-earth style.

Both of the following texts are on the same topic: protection of the environment. As you read each, identify words with positive or negative connotations. Also consider the style of the writing and how the word choice supports the style and creates an overall tone. The first repeats the excerpt you read earlier from "Green Dreams: The All-American Lawn," but then moves on to the rest of the essay.

> The ideal American lawn represents a perfect symmetry of greenness, each blade nearly identical, not a weed in sight to distract the eye. It is nature minutely sculpted and carefully shaped into uniform harmony that calms the eye with its unblemished regularity. With the help of endless watering and invigorating nutrients, the American lawn even thrives in areas that would otherwise be landscapes of desert rock and sand. One can almost imagine our mythic settler forefathers, who attempted to tame the Wilderness, looking upon this expanse of crewcut green and smiling with satisfaction.
>
> But what looks so green and peaceful at first glance is, in actuality, more barren than a desert. The perfect lawn consists of one plant—grass—and represents a monoculture devoid of the diversity necessary to support a thriving ecosystem. To achieve this uniform greenness requires

wasting billions of gallons of water and applying endless killing chemicals that destroy all the insect life. Every year, Americans spend billions of dollars buying fuel, fertilizers, and pesticides to ensure that our houses are surrounded by a manicured ecological wasteland.

However, each homeowner has the power to change this narrative. If you want to see more birds and bunnies—and aren't worried about the occasional dandelion—you can stop drenching your lawn in pesticides and herbicides. Who knows? You might spend less time applying chemicals and more time enjoying nature.

The second is familiar to you—it is from Greta Thunberg's Speech at The UN Climate Action Summit, the anchor text in Unit 1.

"How dare you pretend that this can be solved with just 'business as usual' and some technical solutions? With today's emissions levels, that remaining CO_2 budget will be entirely gone within less than $8\frac{1}{2}$ years.

"There will not be any solutions or plans presented in line with these figures here today, because these numbers are too uncomfortable. And you are still not mature enough to tell it like it is.

"You are failing us. But the young people are starting to understand your betrayal. The eyes of all future generations are upon you. And if you choose to fail us, I say: We will never forgive you.

"We will not let you get away with this. Right here, right now is where we draw the line. The world is waking up. And change is coming, whether you like it or not."

These two sources convey their messages through two very different writing styles and tones. Each uses word choice, writing style, and connotation to convince the reader. "Green Dreams: The All-American Lawn" uses inviting language in the first paragraph to engage the reader but, in the second paragraph, tactically switches tone to suggest that the inviting appearances described in the introduction hide a more problematic reality. In contrast, Thunberg confronts the audience with short, clipped sentences and shame-evoking rhetorical questions. Her words are highly negative: *failing us, your betrayal, never forgive you.* The writers employ vastly different tones, but both effectively communicate their message.

Other elements also contribute to an writer's style. These characteristics include

- Punctuation, such as a dashes and semicolons
- Text features such as headings within an article or speech
- Questions, sometimes rhetorical, within the writing
- Comparisons
- Syntax, or arrangement of words, phrases, and paragraphs
- Contractions, colloquialisms, sentence fragments, and slang

Compare the word choice, style, and tone of the following two passages, both written by women on the subject of writing and both delivered as speeches by request at universities. In the first, Virginia Wolff (1882–1941) attempts to figure out what to say on the subject of women and fiction. This is how Chapter 1 of *A Room of One's Own* (1929) begins.

> But, you may say, we asked you to speak about women and fiction—what has that got to do with a room of one's own? I will try to explain. When you asked me to speak about women and fiction I sat down on the banks of a river and began to wonder what the words meant. They might mean simply a few remarks about Fanny Burney; a few more about Jane Austen; a tribute to the Brontës and a sketch of Haworth Parsonage under snow; some witticisms if possible about Miss Mitford; a respectful allusion to George Eliot; a reference to Mrs. Gaskell and one would have done.[1] But at second sight the words seemed not so simple. The title women and fiction might mean, and you may have meant it to mean, women and what they are like; or it might mean women and the fiction that they write; or it might mean women and the fiction that is written about them; or it might mean that somehow all three are inextricably mixed together and you want me to consider them in that light. But when I began to consider the subject in this last way, which seemed the most interesting, I soon saw that it had one fatal drawback. I should never be able to come to a conclusion. I should never be able to fulfill what is, I understand, the first duty of a lecturer—to hand you after an hour's discourse a nugget of pure truth to wrap up between the pages of your notebooks and keep on the mantelpiece for ever. All I could do was to offer you an opinion upon one minor point—a woman must have money and a room of her own if she is to write fiction; and that, as you will see, leaves the great problem of the true nature of woman and the true nature of fiction unsolved. . . .
>
> *[She sits by the side of a river to contemplate this question.]*
>
> The river reflected whatever it chose of sky and bridge and burning tree, and when the undergraduate had oared his boat through the reflections they closed again, completely, as if he had never been. There one might have sat the clock round lost in thought. Thought—to call it by a prouder name than it deserved—had let its line down into the stream. It swayed, minute after minute, hither and thither among the reflections and the weeds, letting the water lift it and sink it, until—you know the little tug—the sudden conglomeration of an idea at the end of one's line: and then the cautious hauling of it in, and the careful laying of it out? Alas, laid on the grass how small, how insignificant this thought of mine looked; the sort of fish that a good fisherman puts back into the water so that it may grow fatter and be one day worth cooking and eating. I will not trouble you with that thought now, though if you look carefully you may find it for yourselves in the course of what I am going to say.

1 All of the women mentioned in these lines played a role in shaping English literature. Haworth Parsonage was the home of the Brontës and is now a museum.

Here's what you might notice about elements of Virginia Wolff's style.

Punctuation, such as dashes and semicolons	Long sentences connected with semicolons are common, which gives the effect of a pile-up of ideas. Dashes are also used for some parenthetical comments that reflect a tone ("to call [thought] by a prouder name than it deserved," "you know the little tug").
Questions	First sentence is a question asked from the audience's perspective; a question is also used to address the audience in the sentence about her thought as something caught on the end of a fishing line.
Comparison	Comparison between the content of her speech and a nugget of truth that can be placed on the mantel. Also lengthy comparison between how a thought takes shape (or not) like something at the end of a fishing line and how it is "hauled in" for examination and thrown back if not good enough.
Syntax	First sentence begins as if in mid-stream with "But, you may say," an unusual opening syntax; repetition of clauses beginning with "or" in the first paragraph.

Table 6-3

Together with her word choice, Wolff's writing style helps create a serious tone, suggesting she took her audience of educated readers seriously and devoted much thought to the subject of women's roles that was emerging as a social issue at the time. But she does not use distant academic language, and her comparison of thought to a fish on a line is a down-to-earth analogy.

The second passage was delivered almost 100 years later by novelist Zadie Smith, who was asked in 2008 to address writing students at Columbia University on "some aspect of [her] craft." She presents her ideas in ten points. The excerpt below is point #8 from her speech "That Crafty Feeling."

8. Step Away from the Vehicle

You can ignore everything else in this lecture except number eight. It is the only absolutely 24-carat-gold-plated piece of advice I have to give you. I've never taken it myself, though I intend to next time around. . . . The advice is as follows:

When you finish your novel, if money is not a desperate priority, if you do not need to sell it at once or be published that very second—*put it in a drawer*. For as long as you can manage. A year or more is ideal—but even three months will do. *Step away from the vehicle*. The secret to editing your work is simple: you need to become its reader instead of its writer. I can't tell you how many times I've sat backstage with a line of novelists at some festival, all of us with red pens in hand, frantically editing our published novels into fit form so that we might go on stage and read from them. It's an unfortunate thing, but it turns out that the perfect state of mind to edit your own novel is two years after it's published, ten minutes before you go on stage at a literary festival. At that moment every redundant phrase, each show-off, pointless metaphor, all the pieces of deadwood, stupidity, vanity and tedium are distressingly obvious to you. Two years earlier, when the proofs came, you looked at the same page and couldn't see a comma out of place. And by the way, that's true of the professional editors, too; after they've read a manuscript multiple times, they stop being able to see it. You need a certain head on your shoulders to edit a novel, and it's not the head of a writer in the thick of it, nor the head of a professional editor who's read it in 12 different versions. It's the head of a smart stranger who picks it off a bookshelf and begins to read. You need to get the head of that smart stranger somehow. You need to forget you ever wrote that book.

Punctuation, such as dashes and semicolons	Sentences are long in this passage as well, but they are mixed with shorter sentences so the feeling of ideas piling up is softened.
Text features	Dividing her speech into ten points and numbering them provides chunks of text (similar to Ericsson's categories).
Comparison	The title of #8 compares standing back from your writing as if you were a criminal being asked to stand away from your car. That comparison makes a light-hearted comparison to the "crimes" an author can commit when she lacks distance from her work.
Contractions, colloquialisms, sentence fragments, and slang	Uses a sentence fragment ("For as long as you can manage."). Uses contractions (can't, I've, it's)

Table 6-4

Smith's word choice and writing style help create a more light-hearted tone, and she makes it clear that she doesn't take herself too seriously (she doesn't follow her own advice; she sees "every redundant phrase, each show-off, pointless metaphor, all the pieces of deadwood, stupidity, vanity and tedium" in her own work). Smith is addressing an audience of college students, so she uses an informal tone that readily connects with the language and life experience of her listeners. The comparison to stepping away from a vehicle, the clever title, and other self-deprecating remarks help create a humorous tone.

Since tone is the writer's attitude or feeling about a subject, it can take as many forms as there are attitudes and feelings. These are just a few.

- Sarcastic—uses mockery by saying the opposite of what is really meant
- Heartfelt—expresses genuine emotion
- Scornful—expresses a very critical attitude
- Playful—uses lighthearted language and images and easy-going, informal style
- Somber—uses dark language and formal style

Remember: A writer's tone is the writer's attitude or feeling about a subject, conveyed through word choice and writing style. Readers infer a writer's tone from the writer's word choice, and especially the positive, negative, or other connotations of those words. (STL-1.D, E)

3.1 Checkpoint

Close Reading: Professional Text

Review the anchor text, "The Ways We Lie," on pages 302–308. Then complete the following open response activities, and answer the multiple-choice questions.

1. On separate paper, complete the following chart to help you identify the relationship between tone, word choice, style, and subject.

Describe the author's tone.	Identify strategic word choices to help set the tone.	Identify at least three characteristics of the author's style.

2. The website of *Utne Reader*, in which Ericsson's essay was published, describes its audience this way: "*Utne* readers are enthusiastic and motivated agents of social change who want to spend their time and resources making the world a better place. They crave a well-rounded perspective on current events that moves beyond the headlines and sound bites." In what specific ways does Ericsson's tone connect to her intended audience? Does it enhance the strength of her argument? Why or why not?

3. The writer's use of rhetorical questions in paragraph 6 (sentences 1–3) establishes a tone of
   (A) hopelessness and despair
   (B) soul-searching and urgency
   (C) revulsion and disgust
   (D) self-righteousness and rage
   (E) apathy and acceptance

4. When discussing those who get away with lying in sections like "Deflecting," "Omission," and "Groupthink," the writer's tone is best described as
   (A) forgiving
   (B) critical
   (C) aloof
   (D) respectful
   (E) detached

5. In context, the tone of the author's remark that "Of all the ways to lie, I like this one the best" (paragraph 23, sentence 1) is most accurately described as
   (A) dismissive and flippant
   (B) indifferent and apathetic
   (C) judgmental and condescending
   (D) ironic and sarcastic
   (E) accepting and tolerant

6. The author's description of "the daily machinery of living" (paragraph 29, sentence 4) implies that she believes
   (A) lying is a mechanical, automatic response in contemporary culture
   (B) lying is a distraction from our daily routines
   (C) lying often appears to help make daily life easier
   (D) lying helps people maintain good relationships
   (E) lying keeps the most important aspects of daily life running

Evaluating Writing: Student Draft

Reread the student draft on pages 308–309. Then answer the following open response and multiple-choice questions.

1. To what extent is the writer's tone consistent? Explain your answer.

2. Does the tone reflect the position, perspective, and audience of the writer's argument?

3. The writer wants to ensure that the first three sentences maintain a tone of nostalgic warmth. Which of the following revisions should the writer make to convey this tone?

   (1) Many of our most cherished memories are of holiday celebrations. (2) While adults frantically search for the best deals on the year's hottest new toys, children approach this time of year with joy and wonder.

(3) Undoubtedly, some of the most memorable life experiences—for both adult and child—stem from imagining Santa coming down the chimney to deposit gifts under the tree, or the baskets of candy left by the Easter Bunny.

(A) (as it is now)

(B) Remove sentence 2.

(C) Remove sentence 3.

(D) Remove the word *cherished* in sentence 1.

(E) Delete the first part of sentence 2, and begin with the word *Children.*

Composing on Your Own

Review the latest draft of your essay. Read it like the "smart stranger who picks it off a bookshelf and begins to read" as Zadie Smith describes a detached reader. Pay special attention to the words you use and their connotations, since they help set the tone. Evaluate these points:

- Is your language formal, informal, or neutral? Make sure your diction is consistent throughout and appropriate for your audience.
- Does the tone suit the message you are trying to convey and the audience you are trying to reach? If not, revise appropriately.
- Check to make sure you have used appropriate grammar and punctuation.

Save your work for future use.

3.2 Shifts in Tone | STL-1F

A shift or change in tone may suggest a writer's qualification, refinement, or reconsideration of his or her perspective on a subject.

Sometimes a writer maintains the same tone throughout a text, as Greta Thunberg does in her UN speech. Never once does she temper her harsh tone and stinging words. At the end of her speech, the audience knows they have been taken to task by a young woman with a mission. In contrast, "Green Dreams: the All-American Lawn" begins with soothing tone that shifts when the author describes the negative effects of pesticides on the land. But in the final lines, the tone shifts again:

> However, each homeowner has the power to change this narrative. If you want to see more birds and bunnies—and aren't worried about the occasional dandelion—you can stop drenching your lawn in pesticides and herbicides. Who knows? You might spend less time applying chemicals and more time enjoying nature.

With this final statement, the tone turns cautiously optimistic and directly implicates the reader by suggesting that everyone can take action to facilitate change.

A shift in tone often indicates a change in the direction of the argument or in the purpose of the speaker. A shift in tone can indicate the following changes in the author's perspective:

- Qualification—introduces details to indicate gradations of meaning or that a claim is not always true or may be valid only in certain circumstances
- Refinement—clarifies a point by offering more precise details or examples
- Reconsideration—introduces alternate evidence or commentary to reveal different viewpoints

Often a shift in tone will be signaled by such transitions as the following:

- Qualification—*but, possibly, most likely, basically, generally, unless, however*
- Refinement—*in addition, to clarify, not, occasionally, in particular, specifically, furthermore*
- Reconsideration—*on the other hand, but, however, yet, from another perspective*

On December 10, 2007, former vice president and climate activist Al Gore gave his Nobel Lecture. Here is a short excerpt that demonstrates shifts in tone:

> And most important of all, we need to put a *price* on carbon—with a CO_2 tax that is then rebated back to the people, progressively, according to the laws of each nation, in ways that shift the burden of taxation from employment to pollution. This is by far the most effective and simplest way to accelerate solutions to this crisis.
>
> The world needs an alliance—especially of those nations that weigh heaviest in the scales where earth is in the balance. I salute Europe and Japan for the steps they've taken in recent years to meet the challenge, and the new government in Australia, which has made solving the climate crisis its first priority.
>
> But the outcome will be decisively influenced by two nations that are now failing to do enough: the United States and China. While India is also growing fast in importance, it should be absolutely clear that it is the two largest CO_2 emitters—most of all, my own country—that will need to make the boldest moves or stand accountable before history for their failure to act.
>
> Both countries should stop using the other's behavior as an excuse for stalemate and instead develop an agenda for mutual survival in a shared global environment.

> These are the last few years of decision, but they can be the first years of a bright and hopeful future if we do what we must. No one should believe a solution will be found without effort, without cost, without change. Let us acknowledge that if we wish to redeem squandered time and speak again with moral authority, then these are the hard truths . . .

In the first two paragraphs, Gore explains two important steps the world needs to take in order to stop the trajectory of climate change. The second paragraph ends positively with praise for nations that are taking climate change seriously: "I salute Europe and Japan for the steps they've taken in recent years to meet the challenge, and the new government in Australia, which has made solving the climate crisis its first priority." Then the tone changes with the opening lines of the next paragraph: "But the outcome will be decisively influenced by two nations that are now failing to do enough: the United States and China." Here, Gore, makes a qualification on his claim that the world needs an alliance of nations that includes the greatest offenders and potentially the greatest heroes in the climate wars. He explains that unless China and the United States get on board with other nations that are enacting changes to curb climate change, little progress will be made.

In the fifth paragraph, Gore's tone changes again, from accusatory to optimistic: "These are the last few years of decision, but they can be the first years of a bright and hopeful future if we do what we must." Gore seems to be offering a reconsideration of his previous gloomy predictions. Why? Because he wants the audience to join him in his fight—he needs to motivate his listeners to action. When convincing an audience, and especially when using emotional appeals, the right tone can move an audience from listeners to doers.

Remember: A writer's shift in tone from one part of a text to another may suggest the writer's qualification, refinement, or reconsideration of their perspective on a subject. (STL-1.F)

3.2 Checkpoint

Close Reading: Professional Text

Review the anchor text, "The Ways We Lie," on pages 302–308. Then complete the following tasks and answer the multiple-choice question.

1. Copy the following template on separate paper, and complete it to help you articulate the tonal shift in Ericsson's essay.

   In "The Ways We Lie," Stephanie Ericsson's tone shifts from one of ________________ when describing ____________________ to a tone of ________________ when describing ____________________, which highlights the writer's realization that ____________________.

2. What words or phrases signal a shift in tone within Ericsson's writing?

3. Which of the following best describes the writer's shift in tone as she turns from discussing her daily lies in paragraphs 1–4 to her reflection on these lies in paragraphs 5–6?
   (A) honest to mocking: she acknowledges her own lies and then ridicules those who lie, including herself
   (B) matter-of-fact to uncertain: she seems assured about the necessity of her own lies but expresses concern about their effects
   (C) casual to indignant: she speaks of her lies in a casual manner but grows angry when describing how other would view her if they discovered her lies
   (D) flippant to serious: she treats her own lies dismissively until she realizes that others are likely judging her
   (E) neutral to sympathetic: she objectively describes her lies she told but adopts sympathy and concern when realizing others will atone for her lies

Evaluating Writing: Student Draft

Reread the student draft on pages 308–309. Then answer the following open response and multiple-choice questions.

1. Where could the writer shift his or her tone in order to suggest a qualification, refinement, or reconsideration of his or her perspective?

2. The writer wants to add a transition that emphasizes the shift that occurs between sentence 4 and sentence 5. Which of the following would best fulfill this purpose?
   (A) And
   (B) Unfortunately,
   (C) Although,
   (D) Until
   (E) Conversely,

Composing on Your Own

Review the latest draft of your essay. Does your tone shift or change at any point in the essay? If yes, why? Is it effective? If no, consider changing your tone in order to qualify, refine, or change your perspective. Revise your essay one last time, using the following checklist. Then save your work.

Checklist for Composing
✓ Did you strategically select from multiple reliable sources the most relevant information to weave into your argument? (1.1)
✓ Did you consider both the position and perspectives of your sources and use your understanding to enhance your argument? (1.2)
✓ Did you recognize and address the biases or limitations of your sources? (1.3)
✓ Does your thesis statement incorporate any changes that new evidence you encountered might require? (2.1)
✓ Does your word choice and writing style convey a tone appropriate for your audience and other aspects of your rhetorical situation? (3.1)
✓ To clarify your message by qualification, refinement, or reconsideration of perspective, did you shift your tone? (3.2)
✓ Did you check your writing for mistakes in spelling and mechanics and make an effort to correct them?

Table 6-5

Part 3 Apply What You Have Learned

Reread "Liars: It Takes One to Know One" by Travis Riddle on pages 330–332. Write two paragraphs comparing Riddle's word choice, writing style, and tone with those of Ericsson. Address at least three of the following that are relevant, and draw a conclusion about how the rhetorical situation for each influenced the writers' tone.

- Word choice (connotations, denotations)
- Punctuation, such as a dashes and semicolons
- Text features such as headings within an article or speech
- Questions, sometimes rhetorical, within the writing
- Comparisons
- Syntax, or arrangement of words, phrases, and ideas
- Contractions, colloquialisms, sentence fragments, and slang

Reflect on the Essential Question: Write a brief response that answers this essential question: *How does a writer's word choice convey his or her tone, and what does a shift in tone suggest about the writer's line of reasoning?* In your answer, explain the key terms listed on page 342.

Unit 6 Review

Section I: Multiple Choice

Section II: Free Response

Questions 1–8. Read the following passage carefully before you choose your answers.

Section I: Reading

(The following is a 1978 essay from The Washington Post *by Pulitzer Prize-winning journalist Ellen Goodman in which she describes the experience of a group of fourth graders who visit the Museum of Fine Arts to see a Monet exhibit).*

1 She was on what the school called a "field trip," as if the fourth graders were anthropologists and the Museum of Fine Arts were a foreign land.

2 It was, in some ways, a meeting of different cultures. The nine-year-old chatter splintered in huge marble hallways built to echo 19th-century discussions of ART. The blue jeans and T-shirts jarred with the gilt frames holding priceless paintings.

3 The class had gone to meet one of the woman's favorite people—Claude Monet—and so, she had gone along. Not to introduce them, you understand, but to accompany them.

4 There she was struck, not by the contrasting cultures, but by the contrasting values of one culture. The children had been taken en masse[1] to meet an individualist. They had come, clutching worksheets in one hand and best friends in the other—the channel markers of the social system—to see the work of a man who rebelled against his own artistic system. Watching them giggling together and sharing answers she thought again: They are becoming socialized, for better and for worse.

---

1 **en masse:** in a group

5 The worksheets and friends were, in one way or another, the constraints of society on the ego. How they performed on paper and with each other would inevitably be marked down on the up-to-date report card under the headings "Learning Skills" and "Social Skills."

6 Yet the paintings on the wall were the work of the disciplined but essentially "unsocialized" ego of the artist who believed in the primary value of self-expression. If, like Monet, they skipped school to go to the sea, or drew cartoons of their teacher, they would be labeled "social problems." If they had the nerve to believe that their own rebellious notions were better than the collected wisdom of the École des Beaux-Arts[2], they, too, would be considered antisocial egotists.

7 The nine-year-olds, scattered around the rooms full of luscious landscapes, were, on the whole, good kids. You didn't have to remind them to keep their hands off. They had been almost civilized out of the real Me-Decade, the first years of life. Totally selfish at one, outrageously self-centered at two, by now the cutting edges of their egos had rubbed off against each other and the adults. They raised their hands and waited their turns and followed directions. They had learned the art of survival—cooperation, and orderliness, laced with hypocrisy and covered with suppression.

8 They were becoming socialized. For better and for worse.

9 She thought of all the conflicting feelings and messages that went into this process. Be yourself but get along with others. Be popular but don't follow the crowd. Write an imaginative story within these margins and in this time. Paint . . . by numbers.

10 They say that societies get the children that they want. The imaginative three-year-old becomes the reasonable 10-year-old. The nursery-school child who asks, "How do they get the people inside the television set?" becomes the middle-school child who reads the ingredients on the cereal box. The two-year-old exhibitionist becomes the 12-year-old conformist who won't wear the wrong kind of blue jeans.

---

2 **École des Beaux-Arts**: (School of Fine Arts) a famous and influential art school in Paris

11 As kids grow up, they are less exhausting and less imaginative, less selfish and less creative. They are easier to live with. Their egos come under control. They become socialized, for better and for worse.

12 We train selfishness out of them. Yet, ironically, some who resist, like the artists, may end up giving the most to others. The product of the most egotistical self-expression may become a generous gift available on the museum wall or the library shelf.

13 The fourth graders finished their hour with Monet. They were impressed with Impressionism and would, for a while, remember the man they'd met. They left, with their worksheets in one hand and their best friends in the other, still chattering. They passed, in reasonable order, through the doorway and down the massive staircase.

14 Very few of them had read or understood the words printed on the wall of the exhibit. They were copied from a letter Monet had written to a friend: "Don't you agree that on one's own with nature, one does better? Me, I'm sure of it . . . What I'm going to do here will at least have the merit of not resembling anyone else, or so I think, because it will be simply the expression of what I myself have felt."

---

1. The writer's choice to compare worksheets and friends to constraints

(A) illustrates the importance of structure in early education

(B) explains the various benefits of art outside of the classroom

(C) emphasizes the value of beauty in all artistic mediums

(D) highlights the tension between socialization and noncomformity

(E) juxtaposes the unjust expectations of school to the emotive aspects of art

2. In paragraph 7, the writer's diction in the line "They had learned the art of survival—cooperation, and orderliness, laced with hypocrisy and covered with suppression" serves to establish a

(A) critical and patronizing tone toward traditional education systems

(B) dismissive tone when discussing parenting in the 1970s

(C) nostalgic tone reflecting on the evolving lives of elementary students

(D) despairing and hopeless tone about society's shifting values

(E) darker tone admitting the trade-offs of compliance for survival

3. Which of the following best describes the overall tone created by the writer's style?
   (A) pointed and resentful
   (B) upbeat and hopeful
   (C) objective and factual
   (D) droll and sarcastic
   (E) resigned yet accepting

4. In paragraph 3, the writer's choice to include the second item, "Not to introduce them, you understand, but to accompany them," mostly has the effect of
   (A) helping the reader understand the reason the woman accompanied the children
   (B) highlighting the personality of the woman
   (C) establishing a direct relationship with the reader
   (D) clarifying that the woman did not want to intrude
   (E) reiterating the woman's high regard for Monet

5. The writer's statement "Yet, ironically, some who resist, like the artists, may end up giving the most to others," serves to
   (A) contradict her previous arguments and undermine her credibility
   (B) create a feeling of ridicule for educators
   (C) dramatically shift her sense of exigence
   (D) strengthen her credibility in speaking of educational concerns
   (E) shift the perspective from which she approaches the subject

Question 6 is covered in Unit 1.

6. Which of the following best describes the writer's exigence?
   (A) recognition of the power of memory in the aging process
   (B) a new understanding of the limiting viewpoints of art imposed by museums and art teachers
   (C) seeing the disparity between the romantic views of childhood and realistic views of adulthood
   (D) the desire to celebrate the virtues of fitting in by following social conventions
   (E) the realization that cultural values are riddled with ironies and incongruencies

Question 7 is covered in Unit 3.

7. In the context of the passage, paragraphs 4 and 13 serve respectively to

(A) underscore contrasting values in one culture and then acknowledge the socializing process likely to prevail

(B) describe a nostalgic experience the writer recalls from her childhood and then shift to a more general example

(C) provide generalizations about the education system and then move to descriptions of authentic educational experiences

(D) offer a narrative regarding the author's respect for Monet's art and then shift to a statement about nonconformity

(E) juxtapose a personal perspective and then describe a cultural perspective regarding the need for socialization

Question 8 is covered in Unit 5.

8. The chief effect of the repeated phrase "for better or worse" throughout the essay is to

(A) describe the benefits of conformity while lamenting a loss of imaginative creativity

(B) highlight the shift from childhood naiveté to adulthood socialization and accomplishment

(C) convey the writer's dismay at educational trends and their influence on aesthetic values

(D) contrast conventional vies of conformity with the views of artists

(E) acknowledge other perspectives about the positive effects of socialization and conformity

Section I: Writing

Questions 9–14. Read the following passage carefully before you choose your answers. *(The passage below is a draft.)*

(1) The Super Bowl is the most-watched television broadcast in the United States. (2) The game unites people of all different cultures, backgrounds, religions, and races. (3) That, and late-night celebrations, explain why 11.1 million workers used a day off (4.7 million called in sick) the following day. (4) Businesses scramble to fill the roles of those who have called into work. (5) Kids come to school tired and cranky, if they show up. (6) Host cities lose revenue because game-goers have to make quick exits. (7) It is no surprise that the number of people who think the day following this epic game should be a national holiday is up to 52.4 percent.

(8) Currently, schools are closed for Columbus Day and President's Day, but how many celebrate the historic events and people these holidays honor? (9) It is likely this number doesn't compare to the 102 million people who watched the 2020 Super Bowl. (10) The Super Bowl is an experience, and not just for die-hard sports fans anymore.

(11) This argument is not just about the one out of ten people who don't show up to work the following day. (12) Yes, business will likely continue and the person who calls in may lose his or her pay or a sick day. (13) But there are bigger things to consider. (14) This change would reaffirm American values and help the local and national economies. (15) Tourists who travel to the Super Bowl are projected to spend $350 dollars each day they're in town. (16) If the day after the Super Bowl was declared a national holiday, the die-hard fans who travel to the Super Bowl host cities would be able to linger and spend more money.

(17) The resurgence of old-fashioned American values—celebrating with friends and family, bonding over a favorite team, Super Bowl halftime performance, or creativity and entertainment value of the commercials—would be affirmed by declaring the day after the Super Bowl a national holiday.

9. The writer wants to support the main argument of the essay by adding information from another reliable source. Which of the following sources would best achieve this purpose?

(A) a report showing that school-age students want the day after the Super Bowl to be a national holiday

(B) a blog post from an avid sports follower who wants to see live coverage of the Super Bowl on every channel

(C) an article published in a scholarly journal that discusses the psychological effects of secular celebrations

(D) an entry on a live website that records the amount of money spent during the Super Bowl

(E) an economic study showing that declaring the day after the Super Bowl as a national holiday would greatly increase consumer spending

10. The writer wants to show how many people with different perspectives support his or her position. To do so, the writer wants to add the following sentence. Where would this sentence best be placed to achieve the writer's purpose and maintain the line of reasoning?

It has become a bonding experience for friends and strangers who represent the same city, pop culture enthusiasts, and those from different generations who share stories about "the best from my day" compared to their favorite Super Bowl, past or present.

(A) before sentence 5

(B) after sentence 7

(C) after sentence 10

(D) before sentence 14

(E) before sentence 17

11. The writer is considering removing the information provided in sentences 15 and 16. Should the writer delete these sentences?

(A) Yes, because they fail to support a perspective that is discussed in subsequent paragraphs.

(B) Yes, because they present evidence that is unrelated to the writer's position.

(C) Yes, because they fail to clarify the writer's position regarding similarities between the Super Bowl and other holidays.

(D) No, because they provide necessary context about the position so the writer can refute other perspectives.

(E) No, because they provide evidence for the claim that a Super Bowl holiday would help boost the economy.

12. The writer wants the underlined portion of sentence 13 (reproduced below) to be consistent with the overall tone and style of the passage.

But there are bigger things to consider.

Which revision best accomplishes this goal?

(A) (as it is now)

(B) consider the far-reaching effects of declaring a Super Bowl holiday.

(C) the economy is the most important implication that we need to consider.

(D) there is no way that businesses are going to listen; a petition needs to circulate that encourages policy makers to hear this plea.

(E) we are headed for a decline in sports viewing, a decline in revenue, and a decline in American values if we don't enact this change.

13. The writer is considering moving sentence 7 to the beginning of the paragraph and placing it after sentence 1.

Should the writer make this change?

(A) Yes, moving it will provide evidence upfront and add credibility to the writer's assertion.

(B) Yes, the evidence should be introduced earlier so that the reader can understand the reasoning behind the argument being made.

(C) Yes, the sentence should be moved to create a cause-and-effect relationship that better supports the argument being made.

(D) No, the first five sentences contextualize the argument, making the evidence in sentence 7 relevant to the writer's position.

(E) No, sentence 7 relies on sentence 6 to form the writer's position about the subject.

14. The writer has found additional information about the negative educational impact of the Super Bowl. According to the current line of reasoning, where is the best place to include this information in the passage?

(A) (as it is now)

(B) after sentence 5

(C) after sentence 8

(D) after sentence 13

(E) after sentence 17

JOIN THE CONVERSATION: SYNTHESIS ESSAY (PART 1)

Section II of both the AP® exam and this unit review consists of free-response tasks. The purpose of this "Join the Conversation" feature is to help prepare you to respond to these prompts, whether in college or on the exam.

You have already developed argument essays and rhetorical analysis in Units 1–5. For the remaining units, you will focus on developing your skill in writing synthesis essays, the first free-response task on the exam. Although it has some additional complexity, the synthesis task is like other argument prompts you have worked on in many ways. The difference is that with the synthesis task, you now need to use sources that are provided for you as you make the argument. Study the prompt below.

Immigration and the settlement of people are facts of history. Culture and language barriers often lead to similar groups settling in "enclaves"—that is, smaller areas surrounded by larger areas where the population in the smaller area is culturally or ethnically distinct from that of the larger area. Terms like "Chinatown," "Little Italy," "Little Havana," and "Little Senegal" have become common, but there are even entire cities that have come to represent enclaves. Dearborn, Michigan, for example, has one of the largest concentrations of Middle Eastern people in North America. Recent conversations about immigration, diversity, and national/cultural identity have brought attention to the role of these enclaves in larger society.

Carefully read the following three sources, including the introductory information for each source. Write a thesis and two paragraphs that synthesize material from at least two of the sources and develop your position on the role of cultural or ethnic enclaves.

Source A (Dearborn)
Source B (Greenholtz)
Source C (Denmark)

In your response you should do the following:

- Respond to the prompt with a thesis that presents a defensible position.
- Select and use evidence from at least two of the provided sources to support your line of reasoning. Indicate clearly the sources used through direct quotation, paraphrase, or summary. Sources may be cited as Source A, Source B, etc., or by using the description in parentheses.
- Explain how the evidence supports your line of reasoning.
- Use appropriate grammar and punctuation in communicating your argument.

As in the argument prompt, the **first part** provides some background to establish the situation. The **second part** states your task. The **third part**, unique to the synthesis prompt, lists your sources (up to seven on the actual exam).

The **fourth part** is nearly identical to the checklist from the argument prompt, with one exception—the **second bullet**. As in the argument prompt, this bullet requires you to select evidence, but now the evidence must come from at least two of the sources provided instead of from only your own ideas and experiences. The prompt suggests how you might use that evidence in your essay and reminds you to cite the sources of your information.

Despite these differences, you are still expected to draw your ideas from the different contexts of argument—the different "worlds of an argument"—as you did with the argument prompt. (See Unit 1, pages 1 and 49.) In so doing you ,can make a unique argument connecting to an abstract idea using the sources as support for your own conclusions and not merely summarizing the argument of the sources.

The body paragraphs of your essay should provide examples and include information from multiple sources. For example, in the argument about enclaves, you might draw on a personal example of getting together with family members during a holiday or a reunion and how such a gathering makes you feel secure in who you are and where you come from. Although a family reunion or holiday is not an idea addressed in any of the sources, you could relate this personal experience to information from the sources in order to provide commentary. Source B communicates that enclaves might be very helpful if people choose to live in them (are not forced), and Source A explains that early Middle Eastern immigrants flocked together in Dearborn most likely because they wanted to feel secure and connected. You might therefore connect the idea that choosing to return to a homogeneous group—such as your family—doesn't mean you don't like people who are different from you, but it does help you to feel supported and encouraged as a person.

The Sources

The three sources from which you must choose at least two for the synthesis task in this unit appear on the following pages.

The source information provides the title, publication, and date of the passage. This information may become part of your argument. What information is provided here that may be helpful?

Source A

"How Dearborn, Michigan became the heart of Arab America" *The National*, 5 July 2017.

This lead-in statement provides context and sometimes a bit of commentary about the source. What do you learn about this source that you otherwise would not have known?

The following is from an English language media outlet focusing on news about and for the Middle East.

Two very different buildings stand on either side of Michigan Avenue in the Detroit suburb of Dearborn, the historic home of Henry Ford and his eponymous[1] motor company.

Built in warm brick and limestone with very English-looking windows and a steeply hipped roof, the Dearborn City Hall was designed in 1921 in a Colonial revival style and built using tax revenues largely generated by the car-maker, whose headquarters and colossal assembly plants still dominate the landscape. Only 12 years old and funded from charitable donations, the grey building at 13624 Michigan Avenue could not be more different.

Not only is it decorated with ornate turquoise tiles and geometric patterns on its facade, but it is also topped with a very Islamic-looking dome.

To the uninitiated, the building looks like a mosque, but actually it is home to the strictly non-denominational Arab-American National Museum (AANM), the only national institution in the United States dedicated to the Arab-American experience. . . .

Dearborn now boasts the largest and most diverse Arab community in the US, and of the city's 98,000 residents, more than 30 per cent identify as Arab-American or claim some form of Arab descent.

"There are more than 35,000 museums in this country, but not a single one was telling the Arab-American story in a way that the community deemed appropriate, they weren't really hitting the mark," [museum director Devon] Akmon tells me. . . . .

"So we set out to illustrate the diversity of the Arab-American community but also to humanize their experiences, so that even if a visitor isn't an Arab-American, they can connect with the displays to understand the Arab immigrant experience as an American story."

1 **eponymous:** named for a person

"One of the things that we all gravitate to as Arab-Americans is our culture, so no matter if you're Lebanese or Palestinian, Muslim or Christian, we revert back to that shared commonality of our cultural experiences and try to uplift the community and bring people together, despite their differences." . . .

Inside the museum, the temporary exhibitions accompany four permanent displays dedicated to the contribution the Arab world has made to global culture, the experience of Arab immigrants arriving in America, the lives of Arabs in America and people of Arab heritage who have made a significant contribution to the US.

With *Epicenter X* [an exhibit of Saudi Contemporary Art], the AANM has joined a growing list of American institutions that have chosen to exhibit major displays of contemporary art from the Middle East, including the Los Angeles County Museum of Art, which mounted *Islamic Art Now: Contemporary Art of the Middle East* in 2015 and the Yale University Art Gallery, which recently celebrated the 175th anniversary of Arabic studies at Yale with the exhibition Modern Art from the Middle East.

When it comes to mounting shows at the AANM however, Akmon insists that the museum's motivations are quite different. "

Our focus is primarily on Arab-Americans, so when we think about exhibitions that point back to the homeland, so to speak, it's usually with a different kind of message in mind," he explains. "

Most Americans are not aware that there is a vibrant art scene emerging in Saudi Arabia and that there are some very interesting voices and philosophies emerging in that work, some of which is critical of its own society and some of which is critical of American society," Akmon adds.

"We are interested in providing space for the examination of that work to happen and for creating a safe space where those dialogues can happen."

Source B

Greenholtz, Joe. "Fear and the 'problem' of the city's ethnic enclaves." *Richmond News*, 13 June 2012.

The following is an article published by a newspaper in a Canadian city on the west coast.

CBC Radio hosted a public forum earlier this week entitled "Choosing Segregation: Ethnic Enclaves in Metro Vancouver." Regular readers know that I believe the transformation of immigrants into dyed-in-the-wool Canadians to be a multi-generational process and research shows second and following generations are less likely to choose to live in an ethnic enclave.

There is contrary research from the U.S. that says increased diversity leads to "turtling" of ethnic communities (i.e., withdrawing into their shells). But I would humbly submit that U.S. society and its approach to diversity is nothing like Canada's and that U.S. results can tell us very little about what is likely to happen in Canada.

Ethnic enclaves have existed throughout human history, let alone Canadian history. The most important difference between then and now is that ethnic enclaves, which used to be called ghettos, were imposed upon "undesirables" who were forced into segregation by the ruling establishment. When ghettos were formed voluntarily, it was to provide mutual protection for their residents from violence and abuse by the mainstream.

As the title of the CBC forum suggests, today's ethnic enclaves are a matter of choice, not necessity, and whatever you think of segregation itself, that's a big step in the right direction and speaks volumes about the progress we've made—here in our little slice of paradise, at the very least.

Participants thought the fact that the composition of these ethnic enclaves—voluntary segregation by the South Asian and Chinese communities, in particular—was the reason that it had become a topic of public conversation. Sixty per cent of Richmond's population is made up of "visible minorities" so ethnic enclaves in Richmond are somehow a cause for concern. Sixty per cent of White Rock's population is made up of people of European origin, but that is somehow not seen as an ethnic enclave nor a cause for concern. Makes one wonder, at the very least. I believe that it's part of all of us getting used to the changing dynamic of Canadian society, but that's not to say racism has been vanquished in Canada, by any means.

The most moving part of the forum came when an immigrant from Jamaica stood up to describe his experience of life in Canada. He said that he'd never "realized" he was Black until he moved here, but that fact is now made clear to him every day, in ways both subtle and overt. He talked about walking along the street, minding his own business when the woman walking in front of him glanced back and then suddenly clutched her purse more tightly and quickened her pace.

The man, sensing her fear and thinking she knew something about the neighborhood that he didn't, also quickened his pace. And as she walked faster and faster, it finally dawned on him that he was the source of her fear—a middle-aged, middle class, educated man in a suit, who happened to be Black.

There is no doubt ethnic clumping has its irritants. I think one of the reasons we feel so annoyed when people carry on loud cellphone conversations near us is that we are excluded from the conversation. The same is true of conversations in languages we can't understand. But these are irritants, not significant social issues. People are hard wired to discriminate, speaking of evolution. But we are also hard wired to reflect, to learn, and to improve ourselves. We need to keep our eye on the real issue—fear of the unfamiliar and the unthinking discrimination it engenders.

Source C

"Denmark Wants to Break Up Ethnic Enclaves. What Is Wrong with Them?"
Homeland Security News Wire, 2 December 2019.

The following was originally published by an online daily news source focusing on government, business, finance, science and technology, and homeland security issues.

In 2018, following a series of violent incidents in Mjolnerparken, a sprawling housing project on the outskirts of Copenhagen which is home mostly to Muslim immigrants, the Danish government drafted, and the Danish parliament approved, a new "ghetto" law, aimed at dealing more effectively with the ills—especially high levels of poverty, unemployment, and crime—afflicting ethnic enclaves in Denmark. *The Economist* writes that crimes in those areas were to be punished more harshly and public day care for toddlers made mandatory to inculcate Danish values. Public-housing corporations were ordered to sell off some apartments to wealthier newcomers.

"Denmark's ghetto law reflects growing European discomfort with districts dominated by ethnic-minority groups," *The Economist* notes. "From Oslo to Milan, grumpy natives complain of districts that no longer feel like the country they grew up in."

There are two main objections that Danes and other Europeans raise when they explain their objections to the current system of ethnic enclaves. First, the very existence of poor immigrant districts undermines public support for their generous welfare systems. "That claim is hard to prove or disprove. But a second objection is easier to examine—that ghettos harm their residents, in part by keeping them poor," *The Economist* writes, adding:

> Such a bold policy [as reflected in the Danish ghetto law] suggests that the evidence for ghettos being bad is overwhelming. In fact, it is mixed. In the 1920s, at the end of a wave of immigration to America, sociologists at the University of Chicago argued that ethnic enclaves facilitated assimilation. Immigrants first settled in big cities, drawing on the knowledge and contacts of their former compatriots. Over generations, they adapted culturally and climbed the economic ladder, mixing with the native population.

Economists say that there is evidence to support both the argument that ghettos are harmful for their residents, and the argument that they are beneficial. In a 1997 paper, two Harvard economists noted that theoretical arguments could point either way. On the one hand, ethnic enclaves limit their residents' exposure to economic opportunities and cultural knowledge outside their own ethnicities. On the other, they give new immigrants access to information and connections acquired by earlier arrivals, and may provide them with role models.

The Economist says that the free market offers at least a partial solution to the problem of ethnic enclaves in big European cities:

> Gentrification[1] is the main engine of free-market desegregation in cities these days. Even native Danes like some diverse districts. Mjolnerparken borders Norrebro, an ethnically mixed district where shops selling hijabs sit next to vegan cafés. Not all such areas are central or attractive enough to appeal to gentrifiers. But even in concrete *banlieues*[2], there are less punitive ways for governments to encourage integration than by labelling them ghettos and pushing some of their residents out.

Keeping Track of Ideas and Sources

Use a web graphic organizer like the one on the next page to organize ideas from your reading of the sources. Notice that in addition to areas for each source, there is a fourth area titled "Complexity." In this space, write notes about any clashes you may see in the perspectives of the sources, any overlaps, or any areas of limitation or bias in the perspectives. Also note the abstract idea you believe these ideas connect to.

The organizer on the next page has been completed to show one way it can be filled in. You can add to it in Units 7 and 8 as more sources are introduced.

1 **gentrification**: the process of renovating or "improving" a property or an area of a city to conform to more middle-class or upper-class tastes. Sometimes it involves controversial movement of residents.

2 ***banlieues***: outlying areas; suburbs

Source A

Perspective:

Focuses on vibrancy of and diversity within Arab community in Dearborn, MI and efforts to make the experiences and perspectives of Arab-Americans known to others through artwork.

Quote:

". . . we all gravitate to as Arab-Americans is our culture, so no matter if you're Lebanese or Palestinian, Muslim or Christian, we revert back to that shared commonality of our cultural experiences and try to uplift the community and bring people together, despite their differences."

Source C

Perspective:

There are both good and bad aspects of ethnic enclaves; the Danish government interpreted it as bad and passed strict laws to break them up.

Quote:

"From Oslo to Milan, grumpy natives complain of districts that no longer feel like the country they grew up in."

Cultural Enclaves

Source B

Perspective:

Voluntary segregation into ethnic enclaves provides a safe place, especially for those experiencing racism.

Quote:

"We need to keep our eye on the real issue-fear of the unfamiliar and the unthinking discrimination it engenders."

Complexity

Complications with different perspectives:

- Source A: Focuses on how the Arab-American community reaches out to show a diversity of views
- Source B: brings up the possibility of the opposite of reaching out: "turtling"
- Source C: Danish government seems to ignore argument that ethnic enclaves help prepare immigrants for assimilation, but it's also true that they keep residents from economic opportunities and cultural knowledge.
- Abstract idea underlying all: what is the best way to interact with people who are different from us

From Organizer to Essay

Use the information from the graphic organizer to write a thesis that encapsulates your views based on your sources. Then use a table like the following to organize your main ideas into an introduction, which includes your thesis, and two supporting paragraphs that include references to the sources. The table that follows has been completed to provide a model.

<table>
<tr><th colspan="4">Unit 6: Synthesis (Part 1) Two Paragraph Drafting Organizer (with Introduction and Optional Conclusion)</th></tr>
<tr><td rowspan="2">Introduction</td><td colspan="2"><u>Lead-in addressing an abstract concept</u>:
Immigration patterns have resulted in diversifying populations in most parts of the developed world. With that diversification the challenges of how to understand, appreciate, and interact with people who are different from us have become the subject of frequent debate. In particular, people wonder if the ethnic enclaves that have grown in many areas are beneficial or harmful to the people who live in them and the people who live around them.</td><td rowspan="2">Abstract idea that runs throughout</td></tr>
<tr><td colspan="2"><u>Thesis:</u>
While there may be harms associated with "segregated" ethnic enclaves, if the residents live there voluntarily, the benefits likely outweigh the harms, since they provide the comfort of cultural community and the opportunity to preserve cultural traditions and even share them with the larger society.</td></tr>
<tr><td rowspan="5">Body Paragraph 1</td><td colspan="2"><u>Transitional clause or sentence:</u>
Imagine arriving in a foreign country whose language you do not speak. If you have been invited by a family member or friend, and you would naturally seek them out and live where they live.</td><td rowspan="5">Abstract idea that runs throughout</td></tr>
<tr><td><u>Supporting Claim 1</u>
People can feel out of place. (Story of Jamaican experiencing racism for first time)</td><td><u>Connection to abstract idea in thesis</u>
People in new country may harbor prejudice against those different from themselves.</td></tr>
<tr><td><u>Lead-in to source references</u>
Newcomers might have heightened sense of how they appear different in new country.</td><td><u>Source information</u>
Jamaican at public forum reported on in Source B; assimilation in Source C</td></tr>
<tr><td colspan="2"><u>Explain how source information relates to the evidence/claim and to the reasoning that justifies that claim and appeals to the audience.</u>
Imagine yourself arriving at an airport in a foreign country, possibly one whose primary language you do not speak. Chances are, if you are like most people who had a choice in immigrating to a new country, you have been invited by a family member or friend, and you would naturally seek out those people and live where they live. Until you reach them, you may have a heightened sense of ways in which you might appear different to people around you. At a public forum in Canada, for example, an immigrant from Jamaica told the story of how he never even realized he was Black until he arrived in Canada, "but the fact is now made clear to him every day, in ways both subtle and overt," such as when White women clutch their bags tighter and walk faster when he is near in a neighborhood other than his own (Source B). It's no wonder that a person in such a situation would prefer to live in the comfort of cultural community where he feels he does not have to worry about being seen as a threat.</td></tr>
<tr><td colspan="2"><u>Transition to complex discussion or another example? (Not only..., but also...)</u>
Voluntary "segregation," then, provides a way to stay safe given that people in majority communities do not often have effective skills for interacting with those who are different, even if living in those enclaves does deprive people economic and other opportunities that assimilation in the larger community may offer. Assimilation can and does often occur, but it typically takes place over several generations. In fact, according to Source C, "ethnic enclaves facilitated assimilation."</td></tr>
</table>

Body Paragraph 2

Transitional clause or sentence:

Representing a different approach, in Dearborn, Michigan, Arab-Americans, who make up more than 30% of the city's population (Source A), have both found comfort in living in ethnic enclaves and also reached out to the larger community to try to make themselves better known and understood.

Supporting Claim 2	Connection to abstract idea in thesis
People can both find comfort and reach out to larger society.	This approaches bridges gaps between people of different backgrounds.

Lead-in to source reference(s)	Source information
A key institution in this initiative is the Arab-American National Museum, "the only national institution in the United States dedicated to the Arab-American experience."	Through the museum, the Arab-Americans have "set out to illustrate the diversity of the Arab-American community but also to humanize their experiences, so that even if a visitor isn't an Arab-American, they can connect with the displays to understand the Arab immigrant experience as an American story."

Explain how source information relates to the evidence/claim and to the reasoning that justifies that claim and appeals to the audience.

Representing a different approach, in Dearborn, Michigan, Arab-Americans, who make up more than 30% of the city's population (Source A), have both found comfort in living in ethnic enclaves and also reached out to the larger community to try to make themselves better known and understood. A key institution in this initiative is the Arab-American National Museum, "the only national institution in the United States dedicated to the Arab-American experience." This experience demonstrates that there may be ways for immigrant communities to cherish and preserve their cultures and at the same time actively work toward improving understanding between people who are different from one another.

Transition to complex discussion or another example? (Not only..., but also...)

There is even diversity among Arab-Americans, since they have varied backgrounds. According to Akmon, "One of the things that we all gravitate to as Arab-Americans is our culture, so no matter if you're Lebanese or Palestinian, Muslim or Christian, we revert back to that shared commonality of our cultural experiences and try to uplift the community and bring people together, despite their differences."

Abstract idea that runs throughout

Optional Conclusion

Reconnect to abstract idea in thesis:

Whether people voluntarily live in ethnic enclaves for the sake of comfort or, like many Arab-Americans in Dearborn, reach across differences for better understanding, those outside the enclaves owe it to themselves, the immigrants, and this nation to get to know, appreciate, and respect people different from themselves. As Greenholz (Source B) concludes, "We need to keep our eye on the real issue—fear of the unfamiliar and the unthinking discrimination it engenders."

Apply

Follow the same process as above to respond to the synthesis prompt on the next page. For current free-response question samples, check the College Board website.

Section II: Free Response

Synthesis: Snowflakes

Free speech on campuses has been a center of controversy over the years. Recent conversations about speech on college campuses have staked differing claims about whether speech that could trigger strong reactions in sensitive people should be moderated or even banned.

Carefully read the following sources, including the introductory information for each source. Write a thesis and two paragraphs that synthesize material from the two sources, and develop your position on the role of free speech on campus.

Source A (Svrluga)
Source B (Hatch)

In your response you should do the following:

- Respond to the prompt with a thesis that presents a defensible position.
- Select and use evidence from both of the provided sources to support your line of reasoning. Indicate clearly the sources used through direct quotation, paraphrase, or summary. Sources may be cited as Source A or Source B or by using the description in parentheses.
- Explain how the evidence supports your line of reasoning.
- Address the different perspectives presented by the two sources.
- Use appropriate grammar and punctuation in communicating your argument.

Source A

Svrluga, Susan. "College President: 'This is not a day care. This is a university!' " *The Washington Post*, 30 November 2015.

Reporter Susan Svrluga provides context in her introduction to the letter that follows.

This fall, protests at Yale, Princeton, Duke and the University of Missouri—where the chancellor and system president resigned in the midst of turmoil—drew national attention to the concerns many students have about how minorities are treated on campus. The protests have also prompted debate about freedom of speech and whether students should be protected from words and ideas that make them uncomfortable. Everett

Piper, president of Oklahoma Wesleyan University, weighed in with a letter to the campus community:

This past week, I actually had a student come forward after a university chapel service and complain because he felt "victimized" by a sermon on the topic of 1 Corinthians 13. It appears that this young scholar felt offended because a homily on love made him feel bad for not showing love! In his mind, the speaker was wrong for making him, and his peers, feel uncomfortable.

I'm not making this up. Our culture has actually taught our kids to be this self-absorbed and narcissistic! Any time their feelings are hurt, they are the victims! Anyone who dares challenge them and, thus, makes them "feel bad" about themselves, is a "hater," a "bigot," an "oppressor," and a "victimizer."

I have a message for this young man and all others who care to listen. That feeling of discomfort you have after listening to a sermon is called a conscience! An altar call is supposed to make you feel bad! It is supposed to make you feel guilty! The goal of many a good sermon is to get you to confess your sins—not coddle you in your selfishness. The primary objective of the Church and the Christian faith is your confession, not your self-actualization!

So here's my advice:

If you want the chaplain to tell you you're a victim rather than tell you that you need virtue, this may not be the university you're looking for. If you want to complain about a sermon that makes you feel less than loving for not showing love, this might be the wrong place.

If you're more interested in playing the "hater" card than you are in confessing your own hate; if you want to arrogantly lecture, rather than humbly learn; if you don't want to feel guilt in your soul when you are guilty of sin; if you want to be enabled rather than confronted, there are many universities across the land (in Missouri and elsewhere) that will give you exactly what you want, but Oklahoma Wesleyan isn't one of them.

At OKWU, we teach you to be selfless rather than self-centered. We are more interested in you practicing personal forgiveness than political revenge. We want you to model interpersonal reconciliation rather than foment personal conflict. We believe the content of your character is more important than the color of your skin. We don't believe that you have been victimized every time you feel guilty and we don't issue "trigger warnings" before altar calls.

Oklahoma Wesleyan is not a "safe place", but rather, a place to learn: to learn that life isn't about you, but about others; that the bad feeling you have while listening to a sermon is called guilt; that the way to address it is to repent of everything that's wrong with you rather than blame others for everything that's wrong with them. This is a place where you will quickly learn that you need to grow up!

This is not a day care. This is a university!

Source B

Hatch, James. "My Semester With the Snowflakes." *medium.com*, 21 December 2019.

The following edited article was published by James Hatch in December of 2019.

In May of 2019, I was accepted to the Eli Whitney student program at Yale University. At 52, I am the oldest freshman in the class of 2023. Before I was accepted, I didn't really know what to expect. I had seen the infamous YouTube video of students screaming at a faculty member. I had seen the news stories regarding the admissions scandal and that Yale was included in that unfortunate business. I had also heard the students at Yale referred to as "snowflakes" in various social media dumpsters and occasionally I'd seen references to Ivy League students as snowflakes in a few news sources.

I should give a bit of background information. I was an unimpressive and difficult student in public schools. I joined the military at 17 and spent close to 26 years in the U.S. Navy. I was assigned for 22 of those years to Naval Special Warfare Commands. I went through SEAL training twice, quit the first time and barely made it the second time. I did multiple deployments and was wounded in combat in 2009 on a mission to rescue an American hostage. . . .

After a few classes, I started to get to know some of my classmates. Each of them is a compelling human who, in spite of their youth, are quite serious about getting things done. . . .

Let me address this "snowflake" thing. According to the Urban Dictionary, a "snowflake" is a "term for someone that thinks they are unique and special, but really are not. It gained popularity after the movie *Fight Club* from the quote 'You are not special. You're not a beautiful and unique snowflake. You're the same decaying organic matter as everything else.' " I hear the term occasionally from buddies of mine who I love. They say things like, "How are things up there with the liberal snowflakes?"

Let me assure you, I have not met one kid who fits that description. None of the kids I've met seem to think that they are "special" any more than any other 18–22-year-old. These kids work their asses off. I have asked a couple of them to help me with my writing. One young woman volunteered to help me by proof-reading my "prose" and, for the record, I believe she will be the President someday. I recently listened while one of my closer pals, a kid from Portland, Oregon, talked to me about the beauty of this insane mathematics problem set he is working on. There is a young man in our group who grew up in Alaska working on fishing boats from a young age and who plays the cello. There is an exceptional young woman from Chicago who wrote a piece for the *Yale Daily News* expressing the importance of public demonstrations in light of a recent police shooting. She and I are polar opposites. I am the "patriarchy" at first glance, and she is a young Black woman who is keen on public protests. Not the type of soul I generally find myself in conversation with. We come from different worlds and yet we both read classic works with open hearts and minds.

We recently met with a prominent writer from a think tank who is researching the state of the humanities in the university setting. There were four of us students: two young men, the young woman from Chicago, and me, the old guy. As the younger students started to express their thoughts, the young woman (truly a unicorn of a human) used the word "safe space" and it hit me forcefully. I come from a place where when I hear that term, I roll my eyes into the back of my vacant skull and laugh from the bottom of my potbelly. This time, I was literally in shock. It hit me that what I thought a "safe space" meant, was not accurate. This young woman, the one who used the phrase, isn't scared of anything. She is a life-force of goodness and strength. She doesn't need anyone to provide a comfortable environment for her. What she meant by "safe space" was that she was happy to be in an environment where difficult subjects can be discussed openly, without the risk of **disrespect or harsh judgment**. This works both ways. What I mean is, this young woman was comfortable, in this university setting, wrestling with things like the Aristotelian idea of some humans being born as "natural slaves." She was quite comfortable in that space. The question was, how comfortable was the 52-year-old White guy in that discussion? Did it make me uncomfortable? Yes. I'm grateful for the discomfort. Thinking about things I don't understand or have, for most of my life, written off, is a good thing.

Being uncomfortable is KEY in this world of ours. Not altogether different from the world of special operations, where the work needs to be done, regardless of weather or personal feelings. The climate in this educational institution is one where most students understand that there HAS to be a place where people can assault ideas openly and discuss them vigorously and respectfully in order to improve the state of humanity. I'll call that a "safe space" and I'm glad those places exist. . . .

In my opinion, the real snowflakes are the people who are afraid of that situation. The poor souls who never take the opportunity to discuss ideas in a group of people who will very likely respectfully disagree with them. I challenge any of you hyper-opinionated zealots out there to actually sit down with a group of people who disagree with you and be open to having your mind changed. I'm not talking about submitting your deeply held beliefs to your twitter/facebook/instagram feeds for agreement from those who "follow" you. That unreal "safe space" where the accountability for one's words is essentially null. I have sure had my mind changed here at Yale. To me there is no dishonor in being wrong and learning. There is dishonor in willful ignorance and **there is dishonor in disrespect**. . . .

Rhetorical Analysis: "Nine-Year-Olds, Meet Monet"

Reread the passage, "Nine-Year-Olds, Meet Monet," on pages 356–358. Write a response analyzing the rhetorical choices Goodman makes to convey the account of students on a field trip to an art museum from different perspectives.

In your response you should do the following:

- Respond to the prompt with a thesis that analyzes the writer's rhetorical choices.
- Select and use evidence to support your line of reasoning.
- Explain how the evidence supports your line of reasoning.
- Demonstrate an understanding of the rhetorical situation.
- Demonstrate your understanding of tone and tonal shift.
- Use appropriate grammar and punctuation in communicating your argument.

Argument: Declaration in Charlie Chaplin's *The Great Dictator*

In the 1940 cinematic political satire, *The Great Dictator*, Charlie Chaplin spoke the following declaration when his character, the antagonist, a ruthless dictator named Adenoid Hynkel, acknowledges his change of heart in an impassioned plea for brotherhood and kindness.

Read the following statement carefully. Then write a response in which you argue a position on Hynkel's declaration. Use appropriate, specific evidence to illustrate and develop your position.

> *We think too much and feel too little. More than machinery, we need humanity. More than cleverness, we need kindness and gentleness. Without these qualities, life will be violent and all will be lost.*

In your response you should do the following:

- Respond to the prompt with a thesis that presents a defensible position.
- Provide evidence to support your line of reasoning.
- Explain how the evidence supports your line of reasoning.
- Use appropriate grammar and punctuation in communicating your argument.

UNIT 7

Style as Substance

Part 1: Introduction and Conclusions
Part 2: Qualifying Claims
Part 3: Sentences
Part 4: Clarity

ENDURING UNDERSTANDINGS AND SKILLS: Unit Seven

Part 1

Understand

Individuals write within a particular situation and make strategic writing choices based on that situation. (RHS-1)

Demonstrate

Identify and describe components of the rhetorical situation: the exigence, audience, writer, purpose, context, and message. (Reading 1.A)

Write introductions and conclusions appropriate to the purpose and context of the rhetorical situation. (Writing 2.A)

Part 2

Understand

Writers make claims about subjects, rely on evidence that supports the reasoning that justifies the claim, and often acknowledge or respond to other, possibly opposing, arguments. (CLE-1)

Demonstrate

Explain ways claims are qualified through modifiers, counterarguments, and alternative perspectives. (Reading 3.C)

Qualify a claim using modifiers, counterarguments, or alternative perspectives. (Writing 4.C)

Part 3

Understand

The rhetorical situation informs the strategic stylistic choices that writers make. (STL-1)

Demonstrate

Explain how writers create, combine, and place independent and dependent clauses to show relationships between and among ideas. (Reading 7.B)

(Note: Students should be able to read and analyze these complexities but are not expected to write with them on timed essays.)

Write sentences that clearly convey ideas and arguments. (Writing 8.B)

(continued)

Part 4

Understand

The rhetorical situation informs the strategic stylistic choices that writers make. (STL-1)

Demonstrate

Explain how grammar and mechanics contribute to the clarity and effectiveness of an argument. (Reading 7.C)

Use established conventions of grammar and mechanics to communicate clearly and effectively. (Writing 8.C)

Source: *AP® English Language and Composition Course and Exam Description*

Unit 7 Overview

On-camera actors learn to control their facial expressions so they can express not only the seven basic universally recognized facial expressions—happiness, sadness, contempt, fear, disgust, anger, and surprise—but also the nearly limitless range of smaller and subtle expressions that shade the basic emotions into more complex feelings. Actors develop the skills to express the universal as well as the detailed and nuanced feelings to serve their main purpose: deception. Although the word *deception* often has negative connotations, the audience willingly gives the actors permission to practice this deception; the audience members know they are witnessing a pretense for their entertainment. When viewing a movie or play, people put aside their disbelief for the sake of enjoying an interesting story and becoming invested in the characters. The goal of an actor is to be skilled enough to convince the audience that the feelings being portrayed are the genuine emotions of a real character. Furthermore, if the actors are truly convincing, they may make viewers reflect on their own lives and characters; people often see movies not only to be entertained, but to learn something about life.

Source: Wikimedia Commons

Can you identify each of the seven universally recognized facial expressions?

Writers use similar skills for achieving their goals. When writers have mastered the essential skills of narrowing topics and making claims that can be defended with reasoning and evidence, they may move on to more complex expressions as their writing skills advance. Author Pawan Mishra says that as writers improve, the writing becomes more difficult. Writers often start wanting more information and paying closer attention to ideas they may not have thought much about before. They might begin to seek out other perspectives, knowing that their ideas fit somewhere within that larger conversation. They frequently become more thoughtful about the words they choose or the way they organize a sentence, spending time moving ideas and words around within a sentence to make it clearer or to emphasize certain points, just as actors work to perfect the clear expression of complex emotions. While the actor's goal is to master deception to fool a willing audience, often a writer's goal is to master transparent, clear, and engaging reasoning to convince a sometimes unwilling or wary audience.

Actors and writers can make similar mistakes. Actors' overuse of certain facial expressions, especially with eyebrows, can ruin the deceit through overacting: suddenly the audience becomes more aware of the actor than the character. Writers can also "overwrite"—they can use obscure words when common words will do and use more words than necessary. Suddenly the reader is more aware of the author than the message.

Source: Bradford Veley, cartoonstock.com

As a writer, don't try to sound smart or flashy—**be** smart and be yourself.

When you write clearly, you show readers that you are aware of the time and effort close reading requires. Using precise words and concise sentences can help you achieve a clear style that effectively and thoughtfully engages your reader in the conversation. This unit explores a variety of ways to move beyond the basics of writing and to put your style to work in supporting and clarifying complex ideas.

Close Reading: Professional Text
"How the Loss of the Landline Is Changing Family Life" by Julia Cho

Source A

Cho, Julia. "How the Loss of the Landline Is Changing Family Life." *The Atlantic*, 12 December 2019.

A writer from New Jersey, Julia Cho describes her work as focused on "themes of love and loss, time and memory, faith and doubt, intuition and synchronicity, and hope as a way of knowing." Her work has appeared in a number of major newspapers and magazines across the United States. This article was originally published in the December 12, 2019 issue of *The Atlantic*, a magazine that the *Chicago Tribune* newspaper called "a gracefully aging . . . 150-year-old granddaddy of periodicals." In the article, Cho discusses the effects that the growth of mobile phone use across family generations has on family relationships.

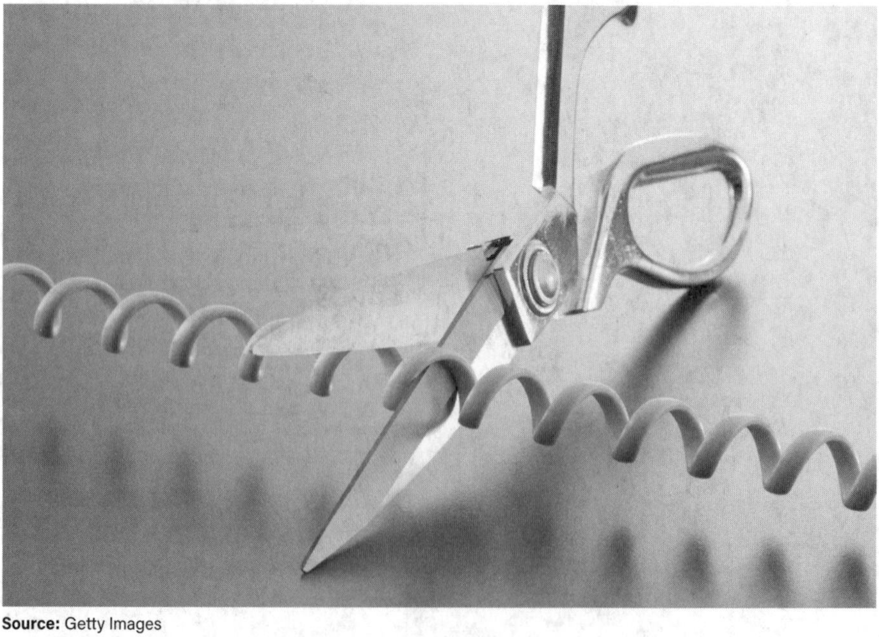

Source: Getty Images

The shared phone was a space of spontaneous connection for the entire household.

1 My tween will never know the sound of me calling her name from another room after the phone rings. She'll never sit on our kitchen floor, refrigerator humming in the background, twisting a cord around her finger while talking to her best friend. *I'll get it*, *He's not here right now*, and *It's for you* are all phrases that are on their way out of the modern domestic vernacular. According to the federal government, the majority of American homes now use cellphones exclusively. "We don't even have a landline anymore," people began to say proudly as the new millennium progressed. But this came with a quieter, secondary loss—the loss of the shared social space of the family landline.

2 "The shared family phone served as an anchor for home," says Luke Fernandez, a visiting computer-science professor at Weber State University and a co-author of *Bored, Lonely, Angry, Stupid: Feelings About Technology, From the Telegraph to Twitter*. "Home is where you could be reached, and where you needed to go to pick up your messages." With smartphones, Fernandez says, "we have gained mobility and privacy. But the value of the home has been diminished, as has its capacity to guide and monitor family behavior and perhaps bind families more closely together."

3 The home telephone was a communal invention from the outset. "When the telephone rang, friends and family gathered 'round, as mesmerized by its magic flow of electrons as they would later be by the radio," according to *Once Upon a Telephone*, a lighthearted 1994 social history of the technology. After the advent of the telephone, in the late 19th century, and through the mid-20th century, callers relied on switchboard operators who knew their customers' voices, party lines were shared by neighbors (who would often eavesdrop on one another's conversations), and phone books functioned as a sort of map of a community.

4 The early telephone's bulky size and fixed location in the home made a phone call an occasion—often referred to in early advertisements as a "visit" by the person initiating the call. (One woman quoted in *Once Upon a Telephone* recalls the phone as having the "stature of a Shinto shrine" in her childhood home.) There was phone furniture—wooden vanities that housed phones in hallways of homes, and benches built for the speaker to sit on so they could give their full attention to the call. Even as people were defying time and space by speaking with someone miles away, they were firmly grounded in the space of the home, where the phone was attached to the wall.

5 Over the course of the 20th century, phones grew smaller, easier to use, and therefore less mystical and remarkable in their household presence. And with the spread of cordless phones in the 1980s, calls became more private. But even then, when making a call to another household's landline, you never knew who would pick up. For those of us who grew up with a shared family phone, calling friends usually meant first speaking with their parents, and answering calls meant speaking with any number of our parents' acquaintances on a regular basis. With practice, I was capable of addressing everyone from a telemarketer to my

mother's boss to my older brother's friend—not to mention any relative who happened to call. Beyond developing conversational skills, the family phone asked its users to be patient and participate in one another's lives.

6 Cellphones, which came on the market in the '80s and gained popularity in the '90s, rendered all of this obsolete as they displaced landlines. When kids today call "home," they may actually be calling one parent and bypassing the other; friends and bosses and telemarketers (if they get through) usually reach exactly the person they are hoping to speak with. Who will be on the other end of the line is no longer a mystery.

7 What's more, the calls, texts, and emails that pass through cellphones (and computers and tablets) can now be kept private from family members. "It keeps everybody separate in their own little techno-cocoons," says Larry Rosen, a retired psychology professor at California State University at Dominguez Hills and a co-author of *The Distracted Mind: Ancient Brains in a High-Tech World*. Whereas early landlines united family members gathered in a single room, cellphones now silo them.

8 Cheryl Muller, a 59-year-old artist living in Brooklyn, raised her two sons, now 30 and 27, during the transition from landline to cellphone. "I do remember the shift from calling out 'It's for you,' and being aware of their friends calling, and then asking them what the call was about, to pretty much . . . silence," she says. Caroline Coleman, 54, a writer in New York City whose children grew up during the same transition, recalls how at age 10 her son got a call from a man with a deep voice. "I was horrified. I asked who it was—and it was his first classmate whose voice had changed," she said. "When you get cells, you lose that connection."

9 These days, this dynamic is also often reversed. A shared family phone meant that kids overheard some of their parents' conversations, providing a window into their relationships, but today, children frequently see a parent silently staring at a screen, fingers tapping, occasionally furrowing a brow or chuckling. "Sometimes there are people that I've never even heard of that you're texting," my 11-year old once told me. Sherry Turkle, a professor at MIT and the author of *Reclaiming Conversation: The Power of Talk in a Digital Age*, has described this as "the new silences of family life."

10 Central to the smartphone's pull is the fact that it is not just a phone. The original telephone was designed exclusively for the back-and-forth rhythm of speaking and listening, while today's phones perform that function and so many others. "When it was just a phone, you could only have one conversation at a time," says Mary Ellen Love, a teacher in New Jersey who raised two sons—22 and 24—during the landline era, and is now raising an 11-year-old daughter named Grace. "Now Grace can look at [her phone] and be involved in five conversations in a second."

11 "Nobody had separation-anxiety issues when they walked out of the house without their [landline] phone," says Catherine Steiner-Adair, a clinical psychologist and a co-author of *The Big Disconnect: Protecting Childhood and Family Relationships in the Digital Age*. "Nobody used to say that their princess phone was their life. It's not your phone—it's the

news, it's YouTube, it's your bank account, it's shopping . . . You can engage in every aspect of your life, and some of that is wonderful."

12 Meanwhile, the physical medium of communication has shifted from telephone poles, visually linking individual homes, to the elusive air. The environment of each call has shifted from a living room or a kitchen to anywhere, and as a result, callers spend time placing each other: In the early days of the phone, they often asked, "Are you there?," but now they have graduated to "Where are you?" When people look up after whiling away time in their virtual homes—their homepages, their home screens—they must adjust back to their physical surroundings. "You don't lose yourself in the same way when you're talking on the phone on the wall," says Steiner-Adair. "You don't lose your sense of where you are in time and space."

13 Plenty of people don't lament the passing of the family phone. Michael Muller, the 27-year-old son of Cheryl, the artist in Brooklyn, says he enjoys the constant proximity of a cellphone and prefers texting over calling, which he says people only use when they want to "extract an answer." "Text is so much easier to take as much time as you want to think about it," he told me. If he has kids, he's not sure he'll get a landline for his family to share.

14 Even in its infancy, the telephone wasn't always celebrated. Its rise prompted a London editor in the late 19th century to ask, "What will become of the privacy of life? What will become of the sanctity of the domestic hearth?" Some viewed the phone as supernatural (they struggled to understand how sound could travel through wire) or impractical (aboveground phone lines in the early days were often highly obtrusive). When people first shouted into phones, they felt awkward, as though they were performing.

15 Even as the family phone recedes into history a century and a half later, we can preserve the togetherness it promoted in other ways. Rosen, the psychology professor, says that "creating special family time is really critical," and Turkle writes of the importance of device-free "sacred" spaces in the home. The family phone was hardly a necessary ingredient for family bonding.

16 And perhaps the spirit of the family phone can live on. Margaret Klein, an educational researcher living in New Jersey and a mother of three girls, ages 6, 9, and 11, has tried to ease into giving her daughters their own phones. Her girls share a stripped-down cellphone with *no* internet access, and call it "the family phone." When her oldest went to a ballet program in Manhattan this summer, she brought it. Klein's 9-year-old has used it a few times to text her camp friends. But "it always goes back and lives in its place at the end of the day," she tells me—right next to their landline in the living room.

17 Indeed, even as smartphones have taken over, some people stand by their landlines. "I mainly want to keep it because it works when there is no power," says Peter Eavis, a New York City–based journalist in his 50s and a

father of two. "And as a veteran of 9/11, an actual NYC blackout, Hurricane Irene, and Superstorm Sandy, it gives me comfort."

18 But Eavis's landline is on its way to being an anomaly, and a generation of children who never had one are coming of age. Eventually, for those who enjoyed—or at least grew accustomed to—the sound of a communal phone ringing in their homes, a moment of silence will be in order.

Composing on Your Own

Respond to the ideas in Cho's article by writing your own thoughts on technology and family. Consider the effects of technology on your family and in what ways they are positive and what ways they are negative. You will develop these ideas throughout this unit. To help you focus, you may adapt any of the following contexts, audiences, and purposes for your writing or create a rhetorical situation of your own. Write down your choices and begin drafting your initial ideas. Save your work for future use.

Contexts/ Formats	▪ Blog for a website titled "Unplug" ▪ Speech on technology and family closeness ▪ Letter to the editor
Audiences	▪ Young adults ▪ Members of your faith community ▪ Adult readers
Purposes	▪ Warn about the dangers of dependence on technology ▪ Argue for increasing family activities ▪ Persuade people to use cell phones in more socially meaningful ways

Evaluating Writing: Student Draft
The Amish and Technology Use

Following is the anchor text you will use in this unit to practice evaluating and editing writing. A student wrote it as part of a school-wide initiative that is examining the impact of technology on the lives of families. This draft still needs work. As you read it, think about what it contributes to the conversation about technology and compare it to the ideas you wrote down. Later you will have an opportunity to suggest ways the writing might be improved.

[1] The Amish[1] people first came to the United States in the early part of the 18th century. [2] Today, most people think of the Amish as people in horse drawn buggies who wear plain clothes and refuse use of any modern technology. [3] They reject most technology that they feel will separate family or community members from one another. [4] The Amish reflect a desperate need that many other Americans have today—the need to

1 **Amish**: a division of Christianity arising in the 16th century and advocating church membership of adult believers only, nonresistance, and the separation of church and state

explore how technology affects our relationships with people. [5] Amish communities ask themselves one question. [6] How will this new thing affect our relationships with one another?

[7] A study conducted between 2015 and 2019 by the Pew Research Center shows the percentage of Americans with a positive view of technology companies plummeted from 71% to 50%. [8] Meanwhile, a 2015 article from the Open Technology Institute and republished by the World Economic Forum expressed the concern of "researchers, policymakers, popular pundits, and journalists" that newer digital technologies have disrupted our personal and family relationships while exposing people to things to which they would rather not be exposed. [9] However, outright rejection of emerging technologies cannot be the answer. [10] Luddites[2] trying to work in today's economy will certainly suffer as more jobs require online interaction, smartphone communication, and other digitally-based activities.

[11] Jeff Smith, author of *Becoming Amish: A Family's Search for Faith, Community and Purpose,* offers a few anecdotes to illustrate what he calls the Amish "humane practice of technology." [12] One such story tells of a farmer who wanted to buy a machine to roll hay into bales—one that he would be able to use alone—in order to make his farming more efficient. [13] The families living in his community came together to discuss the request. [14] "The conversation centers on how a device will strengthen or weaken relationships within the community and within families," Smith explains. [15] Despite the obvious benefits the machine would offer, his request was denied. [16] The "social cohesion" created by working together to bale hay was not worth the risk of allowing the machine. [17] Another example, offered by Smith, involves an Amish family who wanted to run propane gas to every room in their house. [18] (The Amish do not use public electrical services and only allow propane lights in the kitchen and living room.) [19] What if night fell and the members of the family could all more easily separate into their own rooms instead of gathering in the living room? [20] Community members discussed if this would negatively affect the family's relationships. [21] It certainly would negatively affect the family, the community decided, and voted against allowing it.

[22] Both of these circumstances have related examples in the rest of the United States that isn't Amish. [23] Think about the effect of installing televisions in every child's room in a house and of allowing every family member to have a smartphone during a meal. [24] Each of these situations, and others like them, creates circumstances where family members spend less time together because of the adoption of some kind of technology.

[25] This is not to say that we should consider the Amish way of life for all Americans. [26] That would leave behind our growing global and technological community. [27] It is to say that the Amish provide an example of how we should consider the effects of technology as we learn to use it.

2 **Luddite**: A person opposed to new technology or ways of working

What Do You Know?

CLOSE READING: PROFESSIONAL TEXT

In the rest of this unit, you will read about ways writers engage readers in introductions and conclusions, develop nuanced positions, and style their writing to stress the relationship of their ideas. You may know some of these techniques already. Try to answer the following questions about the anchor text by Julia Cho and the student draft on technology. Don't worry if you have trouble with some of the terms and ideas—you will have a clearer understanding of them by the end of the unit. Answering questions on subjects before formally studying them is a proven way to learn.

1. How does Cho orient the reader to the topic and claims of this article?

2. Does Cho claim that the loss of the landline has had largely positive or negative effects? In your answer, briefly summarize Cho's main argument.

3. Why would Cho use a semicolon to combine the two independent sentences into a single sentence (from paragraph 6, reproduced below)? What might be the larger idea she is trying to communicate?

> When kids today call "home," they may actually be calling one parent and bypassing the other; friends and bosses and telemarketers (if they get through) usually reach exactly the person they are hoping to speak with.

4. Cho uses dashes throughout her article; how does this punctuation mark help her organize information in a way that contributes to her argument?

EVALUATING WRITING: STUDENT DRAFT

1. What words and phrases in the student draft might you add or change to better qualify the argument? Consider words that could help emphasize, clarify, or temper the writer's statements.
2. According to the conclusion of the student draft, what course of action or change in attitude does the writer hope to motivate in the reader?
3. Would rearranging or deleting any sentences in paragraph 1 of the student draft (sentences 1–6) help clarify the logic of the paragraph?

Source: Getty Images

Part 1

Framing an Argument

Enduring Understanding and Skills

Part 1

Understand

Individuals write within a particular situation and make strategic writing choices based on that situation. (RHS-1)

Demonstrate

Identify and describe components of the rhetorical situation: the exigence, audience, writer, purpose, context, and message. (Reading 1.A)

Write introductions and conclusions appropriate to the purpose and context of the rhetorical situation. (Writing 2.A)

(See also Unit 4)

Source: *AP® English Language and Composition Course and Exam Description*

Essential Question: What are good strategies for engaging your audience at the beginning of your writing and for providing a unified end?

Actors are trained to "claim the stage" at the beginning of a performance, to immediately engage the audience in the drama from their first step onto the stage. All the tools of the theater support that effort—the actors' placement and movement on the stage, props, sets, and maybe even a spotlight. If all participants play their parts well, the audience remains under the spell of the actors and production crew until the last line of the play is uttered and the storyline first introduced in Act I wraps up. The audience comes back to reality, ideally somewhat changed from the experience—more inspired, more angry, more comforted—depending on the nature of the play.

In the same way, effective writers "claim the stage" of their rhetorical situation, engaging their audience using all the tools at their disposal. Clear in their purpose and tuned into their audience, they grab the attention of their readers, carry them along a well-reasoned argument, and return full circle to create a sense of completeness. Ideally at the end of the essay, readers, like audience members in the theater, are somewhat changed from the experience. Maybe they are now motivated to think in a different way or take action they may not otherwise have taken.

Part 1 will explore ways to begin and end your argument so that you claim the stage and keep control until you have forcefully conveyed your message.

KEY TERMS	
engage	orient
focus	unified end

1.1 Beginning with the End in Mind | RHS-1.I

The introduction—a writer's first step onto the stage—serves to introduce both the writer and the subject to the audience. It may express the thesis of the argument, and it often tries to orient, engage, and focus the reader with striking and provocative details, such as quotations, anecdotes, and statistics.

Orienting, Engaging, and Focusing the Reader

When a play first starts, chances are that the audience will not know immediately what is taking place—who the characters are, what the problem is, and why the setting is designed as it is. The playwright's job is to **orient** the audience—to situate them within the circumstances of the play. (The derivation of *orient* is from a Latin word meaning "east," suggesting a meaning related to proper alignment with the points of a compass.) The introduction of an essay often has a similar function: it gives readers enough information to understand the scope of the topic and the author's position on it.

When actors or writers claim the stage, they **engage**, or involve, the audience by finding a way to grab their attention. And when they **focus** their audience, they seek to eliminate distractions and clarify their subjects and claims as precisely as possible. They shine a light along the path they want their readers to follow. To do that, however, they need to have a clear roadmap in their minds leading to the destination. For this reason, writers need to begin with the ending in mind.

Writers also need to be attuned to the needs, beliefs, and values of their audience to engage them effectively in an introduction. By knowing these aspects of their audience, writers can choose the best ways to reach readers. In Unit 4 (see pages 194–195) you saw some of the strategies writers can use to introduce their subjects. Which to use and how to use them depends on what will work best for the targeted audience.

Consider Julia Cho's article on the family and the landline. Her audience was the half million adult readers of *The Atlantic*. Most would be old enough to at least remember the landline. Many would be parents likely concerned about raising children in the age of cell phones. The table on the next page shows common methods authors use in their introductions and explains a few ways Cho uses some of them to orient, engage, or focus her particular readers.

Methods for Introductions	Used?	Possible Purpose(s): Orient, Engage, Focus
interesting examples		
quotations	√	The quote from Luke Fernandez explains the importance of the family phone to families that had them. This quote helps to orient the reader who may not be familiar with or who may never have thought about the value of a family phone. It also helps to focus the reader on the relationship between the landline and families.
intriguing statements		
anecdotes		
questions		
statistics	√	The statistic from the federal government about the nearly exclusive use of cell phones orients the reader to today's reality while possibly engaging someone who would be surprised by that statistic. It also helps focus on the need for this discussion because the changed reality affects most Americans.
data		
contextualized information	√	While recognizing the advantages of cell phones at the end of the second paragraph, the writer contextualizes information on the use of smartphones within the social sphere to orient the reader with the feelings of loss and change and also to focus on the narrowed problem/topic.
scenario	√	The scenario of the writer's "tween" engages readers who are old enough to remember themselves in that scenario and also younger readers who try to picture themselves in the scene. It also helps orient the reader to the source of the concern while focusing the reader on the change that has occurred and feeling of loss brought on by that change.

Table 7-1

Cho uses multiple methods in the introduction. And all of the methods also do multiple things: the scenario both orients and focuses, while the statistic also engages. Further, the author heightens readers' interest by including a scenario from her own home, linking that scenario to a statistic, and then contextualizing that statistic with commentary from an area expert. Cho includes evidence from multiple sources, each piece building and expanding on the others, which takes the reader, step-by-step, deeper into her line of reasoning.

Remember: The introduction of an argument introduces the subject and/or writer of the argument to the audience. An introduction may present the argument's thesis. An introduction may orient, engage, and/or focus the audience by presenting quotations, intriguing statements, anecdotes, questions, statistics, data, contextualized information, or a scenario. (RHS-1.I)

1.1 Checkpoint

Close Reading: Professional Texts

Complete the open response activity and answer the questions that follow.

1. Read the article below. Because it is shorter than Julia Cho's article, it uses fewer introductory methods. On separate paper, recreate a table like Table 7-1 to identify and explain the introductory methods used in this article.

Source B

Malatesta, Matt. "Phone-Gate: North Shore's Evans to miss state title game." *VypeMedia.com*, 21 December 2019.

The following article was published on a website dedicated to "promotion and coverage of high school and youth sports." Note that it has a breezier style than Cho's article and uses single-sentence paragraphs—a feature of some news reporting.

1 North Shore's Zach Evans is considered by the national recruiting pundits as a 5-Star[1] running back.

2 He is the most coveted recruit in the country.

3 On the eve of the Class 6A Division-I State Title Game against Duncanville, Evans was sent back home to Houston.

4 The news started hitting social media this morning and rumors were a plenty.

5 The North Shore Mustangs were asked to give up their phones last night to focus on their much-anticipated rematch with Duncanville.

6 Everyone complied. Zach Evans did not.

7 He was asked repeatedly. He would not.

8 Knowing coach Jon Kay, athletic director Vivian Dancy and superintendent Dr. Angi Williams, every "I" was "dotted" and every "T" was crossed. Galena Park ISD is first class and always does the "right" thing.

9 According to sources close to the situation, the decision went up the chain-of-command and the decision was made. Zach Evans, the nation's top recruit, was sent home.

1 High school student athletes are ranked by many colleges based upon their skills and potential for success at the college level. 5 stars is the highest ranking a student athlete can receive.

10 Keep in mind, this is not an isolated incident. Evans was suspended earlier in the season for three games. It was handled in-house.

11 What Jon Kay, Vivian Dancy and Dr. Angi Williams did last night should be applauded by every high school coach in the state.

12 Why?

13 If the No. 1 player in the country can be suspended for the Class 6A Division-I State Title Game, then anyone can. It sets the entire tone for the overall program. No wonder the 'Stangs are so successful.

14 It starts at the top. These coaches do EVERYTHING in their power to help their student-athletes. The hours away from their families are countless. They are more than fair. They don't do it for the money. They are fearless in teaching life lessons to kids that some parents are afraid to do.

15 One player does not make a team. There is no "I" in team. No one is bigger than the team. Team, team, team!

16 Evans didn't comply.

17 Coaches in every sport regardless of gender preach this every day. EVERY DAY!

18 Don't get it twisted. This is a gut-wrenching decision for a coach. It will keep you up at night. It probably did for Jon Kay, his assistants and the rest of his team.

19 North Shore is the beacon of light for Houston's rough-and-tumble #Eastside. Now it might be the guiding light for the entire state as they make the right decision on the biggest stage.

20 And it has nothing to do with X's and O's.

Review the text by Julia Cho on pages 383–386 before answering the following questions.

2. Cho introduces her essay by mentioning her daughter ("My tween. . . her best friend") primarily to

(A) introduce the need to bring back landline phones

(B) highlight the author's desire to give her child new experiences

(C) establish a sense of loss that is repeated throughout the piece

(D) reinforce common occurrences between generations of phone users

(E) engage multiple perspectives stressing the importance of communication

3. In sentences two and three of paragraph 1, the author engages readers primarily by

(A) increasing the formality of her vocabulary

(B) shifting from third to first person pronouns

(C) establishing a contrast

(D) using italics

(E) adopting a nostalgic tone

4. The quotation in the last sentence of paragraph 2 echoes the author's earlier concern regarding
   (A) her daughter's inability to experience the use of a landline
   (B) the changing nature of modern American domestic vernacular
   (C) people who brag that they no longer have any need for landlines
   (D) the consequences of losing shared social spaces in family life
   (E) government intrusions in American family life

Evaluating Writing: Student Draft

Reread the student draft on pages 386–387. Then answer the following open response activity and multiple-choice question.

1. On separate paper, recreate a table like Table 7-1 to identify and explain the introductory methods used in the student draft. Then rewrite or add one sentence to help the writer create a more engaging introduction. Be sure to explain what method your sentence employs, where you would add the sentence within the introduction, and why it is likely to engage the reader.

2. The writer is considering adding the following information after the first sentence in the first paragraph.

   By 1840, the first recognizably Amish community in the United States, the Northkill Amish settlement, was established in Berks County, Pennsylvania. Having migrated to the United States to escape religious persecution in Europe, they found the religious tolerance of Pennsylvania nurturing for their beliefs.

   Should the writer include this information? Why or why not?
   (A) Yes, because it provides historical information necessary to understanding the passage.
   (B) Yes, because it explains why Amish people came to America from Europe.
   (C) Yes, because it explains why so many Amish settled in Pennsylvania and surrounding states.
   (D) No, because the content is not relevant to the passage's focus on technology's impact.
   (E) No, because it focuses on specific historical dates, which the rest of the passage avoids.

Composing on Your Own

Review the writing you did in response to Cho's article and the rhetorical situation you chose. Think about the methods you might use in your introduction. You may use an organizer like Table 7-1 to try out different approaches to see what works best. As you continue to work on your draft, put yourself in your reader's shoes. What would orient, engage, and focus you as a reader? Use only those approaches that help you create an engaging introduction that focuses and orients your reader. Hold off on writing your introduction formally, however. Save your work for future use.

1.2 Ending at the Beginning: A Unified End | RHS-1.J

An effective argument comes to a **unified end**, a conclusion that arrives at a meaningful understanding resulting from

- an interesting and well-constructed thesis
- body paragraphs that lay out a line of reasoning and support it with evidence and commentary
- strong links between ideas and sections

Like an introduction, an effective conclusion seeks to engage and focus the reader, and it uses a variety of methods to do so. Usually, conclusions avoid providing new claims and information that don't directly relate to or support ideas and information in the essay. If the conclusion links back to the introduction and no new ideas are introduced, a writer can bring the argument to a unified end. Often, a conclusion brings together the key ideas of an essay in a clear, concise paragraph that leaves the reader with an intriguing thought or a compelling image. However, while a conclusion typically ends the essay by unifying the writer's ideas, it does not always end the argument because it may provide additional ideas or questions for the audience to consider. In this way, a good conclusion engages the audience in the ongoing conversation and could form the thesis for an additional essay.

Drawing Meaning from the Argument

While the introduction establishes a claim that reflects the rhetorical situation and seeks ways to *orient, engage,* and *focus* the audience, the conclusion emphasizes the *topic* and *purpose* of the argument for the audience. The introduction heightens the audience's interest in the argument, while the conclusion encourages the audience to consider the larger meaning of the argument and, if appropriate, to take action. The writer may suggest that the audience take immediate physical action (such as registering people to vote), or the writer may encourage the audience to think a different way (such as questioning voter I.D. laws that prevent thousands from voting).

Look back at Julia Cho's article to identify some of the methods she uses in her last three paragraphs to bring her argument to a unified end. The first column in Table 7-2 below lists a number of methods a conclusion can use to bring the argument to a unified end and shows which methods Cho uses and how she uses them. While this list includes common effective options for conclusions, writers can use a variety of approaches in their conclusions to unify their ideas.

Methods for Conclusions	Used?	How Cho Uses This Option
Explain the significance of the argument within a broader context	√	She shows that there are other ways to promote family togetherness.
Make connections to something beyond the essay	√	She acknowledges the importance of the broader concept of comfort that having a landline can still bring for some people.
Call the audience to act		
Suggest a change in behavior or attitude		
Propose a solution	√	She offers the example of the "family phone" used by Margaret Cline.
Leave the audience with a compelling image	√	She provides a sharp contrast in the last paragraph between the phone ringing and the moment of silence.
Explain implications		
Summarize the argument		
Connect to the introduction	√	The last sentence connects back to the first sentence of the article, reinforcing the social sharing concept.

Table 7-2

Remember: The conclusion of an argument brings the argument to a unified end. A conclusion may present the argument's thesis. It may engage and/or focus the audience by explaining the significance of the argument within a broader context, making connections, calling the audience to act, suggesting a change in behavior or attitude, proposing a solution, leaving the audience with a compelling image, explaining implications, summarizing the argument, or connecting to the introduction. (RHS-1.J)

1.2 Checkpoint

Close Reading: Professional Texts

Complete the following open response activity and answer the multiple-choice questions.

1. Reread the article "Phone-Gate" on pages 393–394. Look closely at the last two short paragraphs. On separate paper, recreate a table like Table 7-2 to explain what options the writer uses, explain why they are used, and describe how they help bring this brief article to a unified end. Not all options are used in the passage. If you can think of other ways the conclusion functions in addition to the options listed in the chart, you may write them also and explain your reasoning.

Review Julia Cho's text on pages 383–386 before answering the following questions.

2. The last paragraph of the passage places the author's argument in a broader context by
   (A) asking older readers to reminisce about the past
   (B) amplifying the importance of slowing down cultural changes
   (C) welcoming the inevitable passing of a valued social norm
   (D) challenging the future benefits of social communication
   (E) underscoring the author's lament for an outdated technology

3. The author provides closure in her last paragraph by
   (A) exposing the fallacy of Peter Eavis's argument in paragraph 17
   (B) using dashes in the second sentence to set off a phrase that helps clarify the author's meaning
   (C) implying a sense of loss, because younger people, such as her daughter, will never experience a landline
   (D) using the abstract academic terms of "anomaly" and "communal"
   (E) employing descriptive language to help readers visualize landline usage

Evaluating Writing: Student Draft

Reread the student draft on pages 386–387. Then answer the following open response activity and multiple-choice question.

1. On separate paper, recreate a table like Table 7-2 to analyze the conclusion of the student draft. Explain what options the writer uses and why they are used, and describe how they help bring this brief article to a unified end. Note that not all options are used in the passage. Then rewrite or add one sentence to help the writer unify the conclusion. Identify how your sentence affects the conclusion and where your sentence fits in the concluding paragraph.

2. The writer is considering adding the following sentence to the end of the last paragraph:

   All communities and families should ask themselves the same question as the Amish do: How will this new thing affect our relationships with one another?

   Should the writer make this addition? Why or why not?

   (A) Yes, because it summarizes the Amish attitude toward technology, making it easily understood.

   (B) Yes, because it extends the idea in the previous sentence and reiterates the importance of relationships.

   (C) Yes, because it requires the reader to think about the Amish in a unique way.

   (D) No, because it requires more knowledge about the Amish than what the passage reveals.

   (E) No, because it shifts focus to "all communities" when it should focus only on the Amish.

Composing on Your Own

Review the rhetorical situation you chose, the writing you did, and the experiments you did with introductory methods. Sketch out a draft of the body paragraphs (see Unit 5, Part 1). Then consider which methods will ensure that your conclusion accomplishes your purpose and helps achieve the desired response from your audience. Use an organizer like Table 7-2 to test different approaches to see what works best. Again, put yourself in your reader's shoes—what would help you draw the most meaning from the argument if you were the reader?

As backwards as it may seem, some writers save writing their formal introduction until the very end. They collect their evidence, outline their thesis, draft their paper, draft their conclusion, and only then draft their introduction and give their argument a title. A title and introduction that come first can fence you in and prevent your ideas from going places. Sometimes, the places outside the fence are more interesting and reflect how writing about an idea can lead you to other ideas. Once you have drafted the body, the conclusion, and then an introduction, revise the rest of your paper so that your conclusion comes back around to the introduction.

Part 1 Apply What You Have Learned

Reread the student draft titled "The Amish and Technology Use" on pages 386–387. Explain the strategies the author uses in the introduction and conclusion. Then identify some additional methods you might use in a revision of the introduction and conclusion to make the writing more effective. If necessary, do some research. You may use the common options outlined in the previous table, or you may consider your own options. On separate paper, rewrite the introduction and conclusion with your revisions.

Reflect on the Essential Question: Write a brief response that answers this essential question. *What are good strategies for engaging your audience at the beginning of your writing and for providing a unified end?* Correctly use the key terms on page 391 in your answer.

Part 2

Qualifying Claims

Enduring Understanding and Skills

Part 2

Understand

Writers make claims about subjects, rely on evidence that supports the reasoning that justifies the claim, and often acknowledge or respond to other, possibly opposing, arguments. (CLE-1)

Demonstrate

Explain ways claims are qualified through modifiers, counterarguments, and alternative perspectives. (Reading 3.C)

Qualify a claim using modifiers, counterarguments, or alternative perspectives. (Writing 4.C)

(See also Unit 9)

Source: *AP® English Language and Composition Course and Exam Description*

Essential Question: How does a writer address complexity and nuance in an argument?

In 2009, a former basketball star for the University of California, Los Angeles (UCLA) saw a face that looked very familiar being used to advertise the newest edition of a video game version of college basketball. It was his own. The player, Ed O'Bannon, had played for UCLA in the mid 1990s and was on the team when it won the College Basketball National Championship in 1995. O'Bannon had then gone on to nine seasons of professional basketball, so he was used to being paid for his talents and his endorsement of products. When he saw his face being used in this video game, he was very upset. Here was this company making money from his face—and the faces of many other players—without paying them a cent, though they paid the NCAA, the organization that governs big-time college sports, for the rights to use the images. The NCAA argued that O'Bannon had been a college athlete while at UCLA and he could not be paid for his play or appearances during that period because he was an amateur. But in the years since, he had been paid for both, so he did not think he was being treated fairly when he saw his photo being used to advertise a video game. Eventually, he and several other players took the NCAA to court and won. The case forever changed the way student athletes are seen by colleges and companies and resulted in hundreds of thousands of former athletes receiving thousands of dollars each. Who was right in this case? Did both sides have fair points?

Arguments are rarely simple. Though simplifying an argument down to right/wrong or pro/con is all too easy, doing so fails to acknowledge the nuanced differences over which people often actually disagree. Not all arguments even take a pro or con position but instead may explore an idea, policy, or quality. Arguments are **complex**, often with as many differences as there are people in the conversation. One way a writer can address the nuances, subtleties, and complexities of an argument is to **qualify**—or temper the meaning of—that argument using words, phrases, and information as modifiers. These modifiers emphasize, intensify, or even lessen certain aspects of the claims and reasoning of an argument.

Take, for example, the running debate about whether or not college athletes should be paid. Some people say yes, they should be because they help universities bring in so much money that they deserve to have some of it. Others say no, they should not be because they are getting free educations from their scholarships. As simple as it seems to split this argument into a binary, or simple two-sided, "yes they should" or "no they should not" division, doing so ignores much information and **complexity** that significantly affects the argument. While college football and basketball often make money, few other college sports do, so should athletes in those other sports be paid as well? Even the sports that make money do so at only a few hundred of the thousands of colleges and universities in the United States. Schools that make money from those sports bring in millions and millions of dollars, so maybe just *those* schools should pay athletes in just *those* sports a portion of the profit. What about schools and companies that continue to use the faces of particularly popular athletes to market themselves or to sell merchandise, as was the case with Ed O'Bannon? Should those former athletes be paid? As this example shows, issues and subjects are rarely simplistic and need careful consideration. As a writer, you need to understand and address the complexities in your arguments.

When you are arguing, you are claiming the "rightness" of your perspective over that of others. However, arguments are not often about right or wrong or even about one side or the other. More often, they are about what essayist and sociolinguist Deborah Tannen calls "the complex middle" where "truth does not reside on one side or the other but is rather a crystal of many sides."

For these reasons, writers need to make certain choices in their writing that reflect how complex these issues can become. Effective and useful arguments usually avoid expressing positions in **absolute terms**—absolutely one way or absolutely the other. Instead, they carefully choose words to point out the small differences in opinion and perspective. These choices reflect a self-awareness and the importance of recognizing the limits of one's understanding, including the way unconscious bias shapes our perception of an issue.

KEY TERMS	
absolute terms	counterarguments
clauses	modifiers
complex	phrases
complexity	qualify

2.1 Complexity and Absolute Terms | CLE-1.V CLE-1.W

As you read above, arguments and issues are rarely simple. Someone who simplifies an argument risks oversimplifying it, losing worthwhile perspectives. Trying to simplify an argument might also lead to unsound generalizations. Looking at only the two most obvious positions on a topic may be an acceptable place to start an inquiry, but the "complex middle" is where the heart of a good argument beats.

Acknowledging Different Perspectives

Universally associated with acting, the well-known comedy/tragedy mask demonstrates two opposing emotions—happiness and sadness. Ancient Greek actors actually wore masks showing exaggerated emotions since people sitting far away in the open-air theaters would not have been able to see more subtle facial expressions.

Shakespeare's plays are categorized broadly as tragedies or comedies. Knowing the category of a play is an appropriate perspective for an actor approaching a role. But the best dramas, whether tragedies or comedies, are those that evoke a wide range of emotions in between those two extremes.

In the same way, when you try to understand someone else's argument, you might start with identifying the simple "sides" of the argument—the pro and the con—but you can't stop there because most arguments cannot simply be divided into two opposing positions. In addition, even people who largely agree about an argument or position still may have important differences in their perspectives. For example, consider three people who are against a new bridge linking two towns. One person argues that the long-term financial costs of the bridge are too high. Another person argues that the increased flow of traffic will create more congestion and smog. Yet another person argues against the bridge because it could disrupt a fragile river ecosystem.

Nuance, counterarguments, and complex ideas all become a part of your thinking as you try to understand not just the argument in front of you but also the larger ongoing conversation into which this argument fits. When you find yourself once again in the metaphorical parlor, you know you are on the right track for both understanding an argument as a reader and developing an argument as a writer.

If an argument you are reading or writing uses such absolute terms as *always, never, completely,* or *absolutely*, then its perspective may be limited by a mask of one side or the other. Authors may use absolute terms to express a factual truth, but such terms often ignore or disregard the larger conversation happening around them. They may appear to make the argument more immediately forceful and effective, but, in the long run, the argument will suffer.

Consider the Cho article you read as the anchor text for this unit (pages 383–386). You might say simply that the article contrasts families with home phones with those who have only cell phones. However, that assessment would ignore the nuance of a family having a home phone for emergencies while also having cell phones or having a family cell phone that is called the family phone. Both of these circumstances appear in the article and cannot be easily classified into one side or the other.

The graphic below shows how binary perspectives with careful thought break into more complex perspectives. Cho shows her readers that the topic has more perspectives than a simple longing for family phones and dislike of cell phones.

The top level of the graphic shows the starting simplicity of the "either-or." The second level provides explanation of those two positions. The third level, however, introduces more complex perspectives. The bottom branches of the family phone side of the argument show more subtle views: that landlines have practical value and that they are not really necessary for family closeness. On the cell phone branch of the diagram, the same pattern plays out. The second level elaborates on a benefit of cell phones, while the bottom level shows nuances in cell phone use: Grace is all-in with multiple conversations, while in another family, the cell phone with no internet has become the family phone.

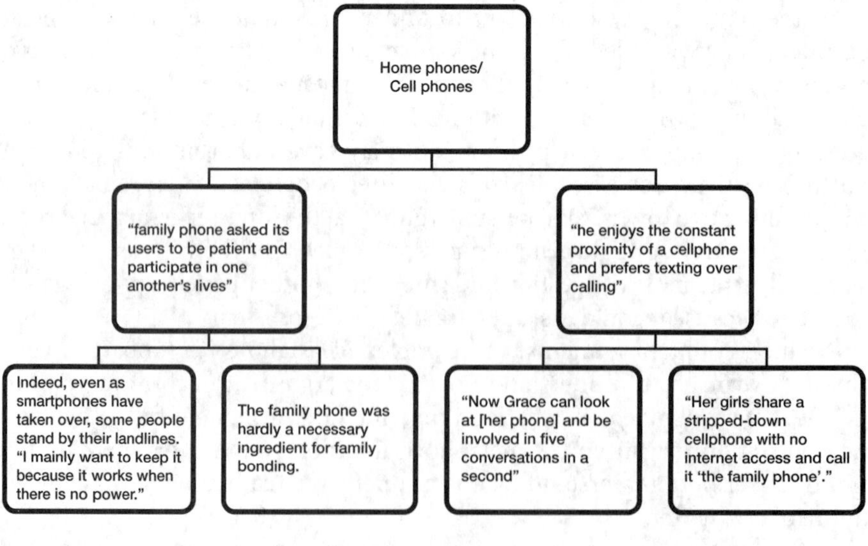

Figure 7-1

Also, Cho's article focuses on one aspect of cell phones and family life. Other perspectives might focus on safety issues—the security of knowing a child can contact a parent or caregiver in an emergency or, from a more negative perspective, the increased vulnerability of a child to cyber dangers. Writers are careful to limit and clarify their scope without suggesting that other perspectives are either nonexistent or unworthy of investigating.

Remember: A lack of understanding of the complexities of a subject or issue can lead to oversimplification or generalizations. Because arguments are usually part of ongoing discourse, effective arguments often avoid expressing claims, reasoning, and evidence in absolute terms. (CLE-1.V,W)

2.1 Checkpoint

Close Reading: Professional Texts

Complete the following open response activity and then answer the multiple-choice questions.

1. Reread "Phone-Gate" on pages 393–394. Then, starting with the binary perspectives shown in the box as the top level, on separate paper create a graphic like Figure 7-1 to recognize different possible perspectives and ideas in the passage.

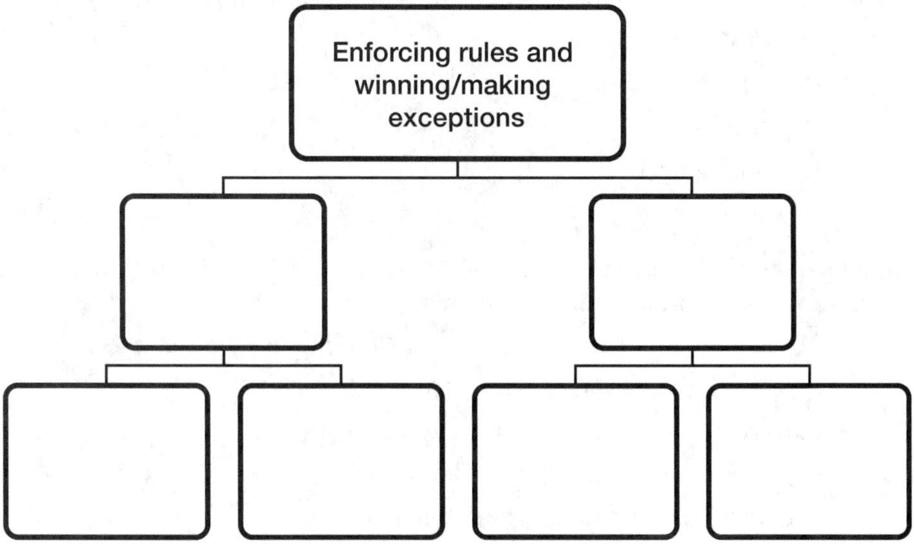

2. Reread the beginning of the anchor text by Julia Cho and answer the following multiple-choice questions.

In paragraph 2, the author develops her argument by

(A) providing generalizations substantiated by a detailed example
(B) using citations from Fernandez that contrast the past with the present
(C) referencing personal experiences that refute Fernandez's arguments
(D) following her own assertions with qualified recommendations from Fernandez
(E) offering counterarguments from Fernandez followed by her own position

3. The examples the author marshals into paragraph 5 function primarily as evidence of

(A) shared social space
(B) changing household habits
(C) limited privacy
(D) the inconveniences of landlines
(E) her desire to abolish cell phones

4. The author's citation from Sherry Turkle in paragraph 9 further develops her argument that cell phones encourage behavior that is

(A) inconvenient
(B) quiet
(C) antisocial
(D) impractical
(E) anti-family

5. In paragraph 10, the author uses the citation from Mary Ellen Love to advance the argument that cell phones

(A) are better at connecting users with multiple people at once
(B) may be more versatile than landlines
(C) are not necessarily harmful to family life
(D) have become essential to adolescent life
(E) may be altering important social skills

Evaluating Writing: Student Draft

Reread the student draft on the Amish and technology. Then answer the following open response and multiple-choice questions.

1. What information might the author of the student draft include to add complexity to the argument?

2. The writer is considering inserting the following sentence after sentence 2.

   Many people are under the impression that the Amish religion—they are "Anabaptists"—requires that they reject technology, but this ignores the real reason for their rejection of technology.

   Should the writer insert this sentence? Why or why not?

   (A) Yes, it clarifies the beliefs of the Amish that confuse people unfamiliar with their faith.

   (B) Yes, it clarifies the Amish concerns about technology and addresses a misperception.

   (C) Yes, it introduces an important new term to clarify the Amish religion.

   (D) No, it attempts to make statements about the Amish in absolute terms.

   (E) No, it demeans the reader and harms the overall effectiveness of the argument.

Composing on Your Own

Review your own draft, analyzing it for complexity and nuance just as you did with "Phone-Gate." Does your argument divide too neatly into right and wrong or two opposing viewpoints? If so, revise to integrate other viewpoints, even those that are only a shade of difference away from yours. Remaking the organizer in Figure 7-1 may help you think of nuances and complexities you may have left out. While revising, keep the rhetorical situation in mind. Save your work for future use.

2.2 Using Modifiers to Qualify Claims | CLE-1.X

Writers who wish to avoid stating the terms of an argument in pro and con strategically use words, phrases, and clauses as modifiers to qualify or limit the scope of an argument, to add shades of nuance. These efforts tend to make an argument more accurate and, usually, more interesting.

Finding the Complex Middle

What do the following claims have in common?

- Shakespeare is the best playwright of all time.
- Capital punishment is warranted for people who commit murder.

- Providing healthcare to all is the job of the government.
- The new 5G broadband technology is harmful to people's health.

You can probably see that all of these claims present a simplistic view of their subjects. Trying to defend them would require disregarding the many ongoing conversations on these topics and the many different perspectives of people who have given these matters much thought. Fortunately, though, strategic use of words, phrases, and clauses as modifiers will chisel the broad granite topics into unique and sculpted claims.

Words as Modifiers

Grammatically, **modifiers** add information to clarify or pin down broader concepts. Some workhorses in this category are the words *one, some, many, most, may, might, possibly, probably*, and *arguably*. Notice the job they do if they are added to the above claims.

- Shakespeare is *arguably one of* the best playwrights of all time.
- Capital punishment *may be* warranted for *some* people who commit murder.
- Providing healthcare to all *may be* the job of the government.
- The new 5G broadband technology is *possibly* harmful to people's health.

All of these words limit the scope of the claims, shading them a bit by acknowledging other perspectives. "Shakespeare is arguably one of the best playwrights of all time" opens the door to the views of people who would argue against that conclusion. The statement on capital punishment acknowledges the possibility of special circumstances and cases. While the government *could* provide healthcare, so could other institutions. And the dangers of 5G technology are still unknown for certain, only possible.

Modifiers can also make information more precise and accurate by answering questions, such as

- how many?
- how frequently?
- to what extent?
- under which circumstances?
- for what purpose or reason?

Some common examples are the words *sometimes, frequently, often, habitually, usually, rarely*, and *precisely*.

Phrases as Modifiers

Phrases—one or more words functioning together as a unit within a clause—provide many ways to qualify a claim to limit its scope. Some of the common phrase types are shown in the table on the next page.

Type of Phrase	Definition	Examples
Prepositional phrase	Begins with a preposition and ends with a noun or pronoun	*in the morning, on the table, in the 20th century, under the surface, from the right, with the understanding, to most people*
Appositive phrase	A phrase with a noun that explains or identifies another noun nearby	Shakespeare, *an Elizabethan playwright, . . .* 5G, *a broadband technology, . . .*
Participial phrase	A phrase beginning with a participle (the -ing or -ed form of a verb)	*Depending on the circumstances, capital punishment . . .*

Table 7-3

- Shakespeare is *arguably one* of the best playwrights of all time *in the development of complex characters and poetic language.* [prepositional phrase]
- Capital punishment *may be* warranted for *some* people who commit murder *in certain circumstances.* [prepositional phrase]
- Providing healthcare to all, *an expensive endeavor*, *may be* the job of the government. [appositive phrase]
- *According to a number of studies*, the new 5G broadband technology is *possibly* harmful to people's health. [participial phrase]

Clauses as Modifiers

Clauses—groups of words within a sentence that include a subject and a verb—provide some of the most valuable ways to qualify a claim to limit its scope. The two broad categories of clauses are *independent*, those that can stand alone because they express a complete thought, and *dependent*, those which, as their name suggests, cannot stand on their own but must be attached to an independent clause. (Part 3.2 explores in more detail how independent and dependent clauses relate to one another.) Every complete sentence includes at least one independent clause, the main subject and the verb that explains what the subject is or is doing.

Two of the most commonly used types of clauses in argument and the ways they can qualify or limit a claim are shown in the table below.

Types of Clauses	Definition	Examples
Adverbial clause	A dependent clause that functions as an adverb (modifying verbs, adjectives, or other adverbs)	*Although many studies have shown that capital punishment is not a deterrent to crime,* capital punishment may be warranted for some people who commit murder in certain circumstances.
Adjectival clause	A dependent clause that functions as an adjective (modifying nouns or pronouns)	Shakespeare, *who was an Elizabethan playwright, . . .* 5G, *which is a broadband technology making possible a new era in connectivity, . . .*

Table 7-4

- Shakespeare, *whose work has influenced generations of dramatists*, is arguably one of the best playwrights of all time in the development of complex characters and poetic language. [adjectival clause]
- Capital punishment may be warranted for some people who commit murder in certain circumstances *because some murders are more egregious than others.* [adverbial clause]
- *Although many in the healthcare industry disagree*, providing healthcare to all, an endeavor requiring vast amounts of funding, may be the job of the government. [adverbial clause]
- *Because the number of studies is too limited to be conclusive*, the new 5G broadband technology is *possibly* harmful to people's health. [adverbial clause]

Clauses are especially useful for addressing **counterarguments**—arguments developed to oppose another argument—and alternative perspectives.

- **Counterargument addressed in adverbial clause:** *Although many in the healthcare industry point to inefficiencies in the federal bureaucracy as a reason why government-funded healthcare would be a mistake*, some economists have argued that government-provided healthcare would actually save the government money over a ten-year period.
- **Alternative perspectives addressed in adverbial clause:** *While many approach the question of the death penalty from a moral perspective,* courts rely on legal precedence and process to hand down such decisions, so those are the channels through which change might emerge.

All of these approaches help shape an overly simplified claim into one that leads readers into the complex and more interesting middle. All of them also bring to mind author Pawan Mishra's quote that "as you become a better writer, the writing becomes more difficult." You become more thoughtful about how what you say will be received by other people, especially those who have already taken part in the ongoing conversation.

Remember: Writers may strategically use words, phrases, and clauses as modifiers to qualify or limit the scope of an argument. (CLE-1.X)

2.2 Checkpoint

Close Reading: Professional Texts

Reread the "Phone-Gate" article on pages 393–394. Then answer the following open response questions.

1. Identify a limiting word, phrase, or clause in each of the following paragraphs: 1, 7, 9.

2. Choose one of the limiting modifiers you identified in question 1 and explain its effect on the statement it limits.

Reread the anchor text by Julia Cho and answer the following multiple-choice questions.

3. Which of the following statements includes a modifier to limit an absolute statement?
   (A) "My tween will never know the sound of me calling her name from another room after the phone rings." (paragraph 1, sentence 1)
   (B) "According to the federal government, the majority of American homes now use cellphones exclusively." (paragraph 1, sentence 4)
   (C) "Whereas early landlines united family members gathered in a single room, cellphones now silo them." (paragraph 7, sentence 3)
   (D) "A shared family phone meant that kids overheard some of their parents' conversations, providing a window into their relationships . . . ." (paragraph 9, sentence 2)
   (E) "And perhaps the spirit of the family phone can live on." (paragraph 16, sentence 1)

4. The qualifying modifier in the first sentence of paragraph 17 serves as a
   (A) statement that further supports the evidence in the previous paragraph
   (B) transition from counterarguments to the author's argument
   (C) limiting statement for a previous claim from a cited source
   (D) recognition of alternative perspectives that differ from the author's
   (E) description of those who are opposed to cell phone use

5. The word "bypassing" in the second sentence of paragraph 6 implies that cell phones can be used for purposes of
   (A) convenience
   (B) efficiency
   (C) avoidance
   (D) favoritism
   (E) manipulation

Evaluating Writing: Student Draft
Reread the student draft on the Amish and technology. Then answer the following open response and multiple-choice questions.

1. What modifiers might improve the student draft? Add or delete clauses, phrases, or words to help the writer qualify or limit the scope of the argument.

2. The writer wants to qualify this statement so it is less absolute.

   The Amish reflect a desperate need that many other Americans have today—the need to explore how technology affects our relationships with people.

   Which of the following would best accomplish that goal if it were added to the beginning of the sentence?
   (A) Despite their differences,
   (B) While others disagree,
   (C) Contrary to popular opinion,
   (D) In some respects,
   (E) Quiet and law-abiding,

Composing on Your Own
Review your draft in progress. Ask yourself if you have found "the complex middle" in the expression of your thesis statement. Is it appropriately qualified, given your rhetorical situation? If not, work on revising it by using words, phrases, and clauses to tighten it. Then carefully read every other sentence in your draft. Identify places where modifying words, phrases, and clauses could clarify and enrich your ideas, and revise your draft to include them. While revising, keep the rhetorical situation in mind. Save your work for future use.

Part 2 Apply What You Have Learned

Read the following transcript of a broadcast on National Public Radio and complete the task that follows it.

Source C

Kamenetz, Anya. From "It's A Smartphone Life: More Than Half of U.S. Children Now Have One." National Public Radio, 31 October 2019.

Just over half of children in the United States—53 percent—now own a smartphone by the age of 11. And 84 percent of teenagers now have their own phones, immersing themselves in a rich and complex world of experiences that adults sometimes need a lot of decoding to understand.

These stats come from a new, nationally representative survey of media use among children ages 8–18, by Common Sense Media, which has been tracking this since 2003. . . .

Here are some other highlights of the report, paired with context from our other reporting:

- As it has for decades, video viewing beats all other screen media activity—averaging 2 hours, 52 minutes per day for teens and 2 and a half hours for tweens.
- Online video viewing has doubled—and most children say it is their most enjoyable online activity. There is a corresponding decrease in watching old-fashioned TV, whether broadcast, or time-shifted onto a digital recorder.
- About 1 in 5 children has a phone by age 8. There *could* be a silver lining to children getting their first phones closer to elementary school than high school. Scholars like Jordan Shapiro and Stacey Steinberg have argued that parents need to model healthy social media use with younger children, and let them participate. And parenting expert Ana Homayoun says that parents can help establish healthier habits with the first phone by taking a heavier hand while children are younger—by checking the phone periodically, actively coaching kids on social media etiquette and handing the phone over only at certain designated times.
- Young people from families making $35,000 or less a year spend much more time with screen media—nearly two hours per day more when compared with families making more than $100,000. Vicky Rideout notes that gap has been pretty persistent over time. "Entertainment media is an affordable alternative to after-school programs or private piano lessons," she says. And there can be opportunities for "informal learning"—with the right guidance.

- There are big gender differences, particularly over video games. Almost three-fourths of boys say they enjoy playing video games "a lot," whereas fewer than 1 in 4 girls say the same. Video games are the online activity most associated with problematic overuse or addiction.
- The favorite media-based activity among girls is listening to music—like Ashley Mingo's K-pop faves.
- And girls also report liking social media much more than boys do. Seven in 10 teen girls use social media every day. Compared with other online activities, social media use is more associated with anxiety, depression, cyberbullying and self-image issues.
- African-American and Hispanic teens have distinctive patterns of use. Each group reports spending more than two hours a day on social media, whereas for white teens it's about an hour and a half. (Mingo, who is African-American, would qualify as a high user of social media between Pinterest, Snapchat and Tumblr). They also report enjoying social media more than white teens. Other research has suggested that people of color are more likely to value social media as a means of getting involved in politics, that youth of color follow more celebrities and public figures than white teens do, and that social media is sometimes a path to political participation and civic engagement.
- Screens are a bigger-than-ever part of schoolwork. Nearly 6 in 10 teens do homework on a computer every day. This can be a problem given the temptation to multitask. It's also an equity issue. Although lower-income teens spend more time consuming entertainment media, they are less likely to have access to laptops, and they spend more time doing homework on mobile phones instead.
- Teens report spending only 3 percent of their screen time on creative pursuits like writing, or making art, or music—outside of homework or school projects. But some researchers, like Emily Weinstein at Harvard, and Mimi Ito at the University of California, Irvine, note that social media platforms like TikTok, Snapchat or Instagram can be platforms for creative expression in ways that aren't necessarily captured by a survey like this. It also may be that teens use their consumption to inform and inspire their creative expression, like Mingo, an aspiring animator, does.

Review the draft you have been working on throughout this unit on technology and the family. You now have three sources with three different perspectives to consider—Source A ("How the Loss of Landlines is Changing Family Life," pages 382–386), Source B ("Phone-Gate," pages 393–394) and Source C ("It's A Smartphone Life," pages 413–414). Read them carefully to determine if what you learned in Sources B and C may lead you to qualify your original claim to allow for complexity and nuance. How might you work some of the ideas and information from Sources B and C into your draft? Make any useful revisions, and save your work for future use.

Source: Getty Images

Visuals as well as texts convey perspectives and positions. What message or perspective on children and cell phones might this artwork convey? To answer that question, carefully analyze the image and describe the details you see. Then draw a conclusion about what the details convey.

Reflect on the Essential Question: Write a brief response that answers this essential question: *How does a writer address complexity and nuance in an argument?* Correctly use the key terms on page 403 in your answer.

Part 3

Sentences

Enduring Understanding and Skills

Part 3

Understand

The rhetorical situation informs the strategic stylistic choices that writers make. (STL-1)

Demonstrate

Explain how writers create, combine, and place independent and dependent clauses to show relationships between and among ideas. (Reading 7.B)

(Note: Students should be able to read and analyze these complexities but are not expected to write with them on timed essays.)

Write sentences that clearly convey ideas and arguments. (Writing 8.B)

Source: *AP® English Language and Composition Course and Exam Description*

Essential Question: How can sentences express relationships among ideas?

In elementary school, you probably learned that a **sentence** has a noun and a verb, a thing (or person) [noun] and something that thing does [verb].

Lanisha paints.

You probably also learned about direct objects.

Lanisha paints *landscapes.*

Any number of sentence elements can be added to expand on the basic idea presented by the first two-word sentence.

Lanisha paints *beautiful* landscapes.

The modifier "beautiful," an adjective in this case, describes the quality of her paintings.

Lanisha paints beautiful landscapes *alone.*

The new modifier, "alone," may make you start to wonder why the writer mentions that. You may even ask why she is alone or if she is lonely.

Lanisha *painfully* paints beautiful landscapes alone.

Now another modifier, an adverb, raises more questions. Is the physical act of painting painful for Lanisha? Is it emotionally painful for her? Is it both?

The idea of a painter doing beautiful work expands and become more complex as that beauty mixes with the idea of being alone and then with some sort of pain. Beauty, isolation, and pain all enrich the meaning of one another in a sentence.

As a writer, you may draft your sentences by first just writing your ideas on paper (or typing them) until you have your rough ideas laid out, but then you revisit your sentences and arrange them—moving ideas and placing words as Lanisha might places brushstrokes for certain effects in her art.

You will move words, phrases, clauses, and even entire sentences around in your writing to better communicate your ideas. You join some thoughts as relatively equal in importance, and you join other thoughts to emphasize one over the other. Close readers recognize the effect of these relationships within and between sentences and not only understand the meaning they express as clearly as possible but also come to appreciate the craft of writing such expressive sentences.

KEY TERMS

arrangement	phrase
clause	sentence
coordination	subordination

3.1 Arranging Sentences | STL-1.G STL-1.H STL-1.L

Writers express ideas in sentences, which are made up of clauses, at least one of which must be independent. The arrangement of sentences in a text can emphasize certain thoughts. Certain patterns of joining thoughts, known as subordination and coordination, express the intended relationship between ideas in a sentence.

The Power of Structure

A **clause** has a noun and a verb. An independent clause can stand alone as a sentence, which makes it a complete thought. A dependent clause must be attached to an independent clause. Take the underlined sentence above, for example.

> An independent clause can stand alone as a sentence, which makes it a complete thought.

The double-underlined clause is independent. If you put a period at the end, it still makes sense. It can function *independent* of anything else.

> An independent clause can stand alone as a sentence. Which makes it a complete thought.

However, the period after the first clause means the single-underlined clause cannot stand alone—it *depended* on the first clause to make sense. If you read them together you will still understand, but if you take it out of context, you can see that it cannot stand as a complete thought by itself.

> Which makes it a complete thought.

It is *dependent* on its connection to the independent clause to make sense.

Independent/dependent clauses in sentences are the basic structures that help writers convey ideas to their audiences. How ideas are constructed and arranged in an argument reflect the writer's purposes and how the writer wants the audience to understand the argument. The order of the ideas in a single sentence, as well as the order and arrangement of the sentences throughout a text, together demonstrate the line of reasoning (see Units 3 and 5).

Arrangement of Sentences

Both within and between sentences, **arrangement** plays a key role in conveying and emphasizing ideas. Look at this sentence from "Phone-Gate."

> On the eve of the Class 6A Divison-I State Title Game against Duncanville, Evans was sent back home to Houston.

The sentence leads off with the evening of the state championship, which establishes the idea that something big and important is happening and creates some suspense. That suspense bursts, however, when you learn in the independent clause that Evans was sent home to Houston. Not just home, but "back" home—from where he had just come.

The independent clause comes at the end: "*Evans was sent back home to Houston.*" That part of the sentence carries the most meaning. Conveying when it happened does add to the effect, but the argument of the entire text is that anyone—even a star player like Evans—will be held to the same rules as the rest of the team.

You could easily rearrange the sentence by inverting the sentence structure.

> Evans was sent back home to Houston on the eve of the Class 6A Divison-I State Title Game against Duncanville.

That still makes sense and gets across the main idea, but the suspense is gone. You know *what* happened already, so *when* it happened is a little less important.

Now consider the arrangement between sentences.

> (2) [Evans] is the most coveted recruit in the country.
>
> (3) On the eve of the Class 6A Division-I State Title Game against Duncanville, Evans was sent back home to Houston.
>
> (4) The news started hitting social media this morning and rumors were a plenty.

In this arrangement, you learn first that Evans is an important player, next what the event is and when it happened, and finally that the news spread quickly. Sentence 4 has almost no bearing on the article at all, and the writer could have deleted it. Look at what happens, though, if the sentences are rearranged.

> (2) [Evans] is the most coveted recruit in the country.
>
> (4) The news started hitting social media this morning and rumors were a plenty.
>
> (3) On the eve of the Class 6A Division-I State Title Game against Duncanville, Evans was sent back home to Houston.

That almost useless information in sentence 4 now contributes to the suspense created by the first part of sentence 3. There is now A LOT of space between the mention of Evans's importance and when the reader learns what happened to him. In that space, there is talk about rumors and social media and then the mention of how important the event is. Now when the reader learn that Evans was sent back to Houston, the news hits a little bit harder.

This example clearly shows how the order of information and ideas in sentences affects the way you take in and respond to information. Studying how writers arrange sentences and how that arrangement affects your response will add depth to your understanding of the argument as a whole and may even provide access points for you to argue with their reasoning. When you write, thoughtfully arrange the ideas in your sentences and the order of your sentences to accurately reflect your reasoning and to make the greatest impact.

✔ **Remember:** Writers express ideas in sentences. Sentences are made up of clauses, at least one of which must be independent. The arrangement of sentences in a text can emphasize particular ideas. The arrangement of clauses, phrases, and words in a sentence can emphasize ideas. (STL-1.G, H, L)

3.1 Checkpoint

Close Reading: Professional Text

Review the anchor text, "How the Loss of the Landline Is Changing Family Life," on pages 383–386. Then complete the open response activity and answer the multiple-choice questions.

1. List three examples of how the arrangement of sentences within the excerpt below helps the writer build the argument.

> Over the course of the 20th century, phones grew smaller, easier to use, and therefore less mystical and remarkable in their household presence. And with the spread of cordless phones in the 1980s, calls became more private. But even then, when making a call to another household's landline, you never knew who would pick up. For those of us who grew up with a shared family phone, calling friends usually meant first speaking with their parents, and answering calls meant speaking with any number of our parents' acquaintances on a regular basis. With practice, I was capable of addressing everyone from a telemarketer to my mother's boss to my older brother's friend—not to mention any relative who happened to call. Beyond developing conversational skills, the family phone asked its users to be patient and participate in one another's lives.

2. The details in the third sentence of paragraph 3 ("After the advent . . . one of a community") are mostly arranged by
   - (A) chronology
   - (B) cause-effect
   - (C) order of importance
   - (D) comparison and contrast
   - (E) spatial order

3. In the second sentence of paragraph 12, the relationship between the first and second clauses ("The environment of each.... 'where are you' ") is best described as one of
   - (A) comparison and contrast
   - (B) general to specific
   - (C) specific to general
   - (D) cause-effect
   - (E) question and answer

4. The structure of the final sentence in paragraph 4 permits the author to capture a sense of
   - (A) irony
   - (B) hypocrisy
   - (C) history
   - (D) defiance
   - (E) hopefulness

Evaluating Writing: Student Draft

Reread the student draft on pages 386–387. Then complete the following open response activity and answer the multiple-choice question.

1. Analyze the arrangement of sentences 7 through 10 and evaluate the effectiveness of that arrangement.

2. The writer is considering swapping the order of sentences 19 and 20 (reproduced below).

   (19) What if night fell and the members of the family could all more easily separate into their own rooms instead of gathering in the living room? (20) Community members discussed if this would negatively affect the family's relationships.

   Should the writer swap the order of these two sentences?
   - (A) Yes, because it will clarify for the reader the difference between the family and community.
   - (B) Yes, because the question exemplifies the concerns that the community discussed.
   - (C) Yes, because questions should never follow parenthetical statements.
   - (D) No, because the question represents the family members' desires for the change.
   - (E) No, because the question is more important than the community discussion.

Composing on Your Own

Reread your draft in progress, and ask yourself if any of your sentences would be more effective if their parts were in a different order. If so, make revisions. Also ask yourself if any sentences would be more effective if they were moved to a different location within your text. If so, make revisions. Save your work for future use.

3.2 Subordination and Coordination | STL-1.I STL-1.J STL-1.K

Sometimes a writer wants to connect ideas that have equal importance, while at other times a writer wants to join one idea with a less important but related idea. Often the less important idea helps in the understanding of the more important one.

Emphasis and Weight

The title of this unit is "Style as Substance." In essence, that means that style can be more than just the *way* you say something; it can also be *what* you say. Relating parts of sentences through coordination and subordination—an aspect of style—conveys clear meaning to readers.

As you read in Unit 5, **coordination** is the joining of words or sentence elements to convey that they have relatively equal importance or emphasis. The connectors writers use to join these elements are called *coordinating conjunctions*. The table below shows common coordinating conjunctions and the relationships they convey.

Coordinating Conjunction	Use it to . . .	Example Sentences
and	add information	We began hiking in the morning **and** didn't stop until dusk.
but	show a difference or another viewpoint	She wanted to go jogging, **but** it was raining outside.
so	show a result or cause-effect	We need to arrive at her house before breakfast, **so** we must set an early alarm.
or	show another possibility or choice	We may go to the movies, **or** we may stay home.
yet	reveal a "surprising" opposite comment or a noteworthy contrast	He complains about his cavities, **yet** he continues to eat sweets.

Table 7-5

Subordination is the joining of sentence elements to convey that one has greater importance or emphasis than the others. The words and phrases that show these relationships are called *subordinating conjunctions*. The clause that follows one of these terms is the subordinate clause.

Subordinating Conjunctions	Use it when . . .	Example Sentences
after, before, during, when, while	show time sequence	We can go out skiing **after** the snowstorm stops.
as	reveal extent or make a comparison	It isn't **as** rainy **as** it was yesterday.
because, since	explain why	She convinced the crowd to accept her proposal, **because** she is an articulate speaker.
although, unless	reveal a contrast or a condition	**Although** the United States has become a very wealthy country, most of the wealth has gone to small number of people. We will make sweetcorn for dinner, **unless** the store is sold out.

Table 7-6

Look closely at the coordination in these sentences from "It's A Smartphone Life" and the analysis that follows.

> Other research has suggested that people of color are more likely to value social media as a means of getting involved in politics, **[and]** that youth of color follow more celebrities and public figures than white teens do, **and** that social media is sometimes a path to political participation and civic engagement.

This long sentence combines multiple complete thoughts (independent clauses) that are all given equal weight. The coordinating conjunction *and* signals the addition of more information to go along with what has already been provided. By adding those ideas on at the same level, the writer gives them equal weight. Note that the first *and* is implied. In a series connecting equal items, *and* precedes the final item.

> . . . people of color are more likely to value social media as a means of getting involved in politics
>
> **[and]**
>
> youth of color follow more celebrities and public figures than white teens do
>
> **and**
>
> social media is sometimes a path to political participation and civic engagement

Rhetorical Analysis: These informative clauses are all significant ideas contributing to an understanding on social media's importance to people of color, so they are all treated equally.

Now consider the following sentence, which shows an imbalance in the clauses through subordination.

> Each group reports spending more than two hours a day on social media, **whereas** for white teens it's about an hour and a half.

This sentence presents two ideas, but the subordinating conjunction "whereas" demonstrates a contrast between the two ideas.

Each group (African American and Hispanic teens) reports spending more than two hours a day on social media

whereas

for white teens it's about an hour and a half.

Rhetorical Analysis: By putting the information about African American and Hispanic teens in an independent clause and subordinating the information about white teens in a dependent clause, the writer keeps the emphasis on African American and Hispanic teens. The information about white teens is not expressed on its own terms but rather in its relation to the information about the other teens.

The writer could have written two separate sentences.

Separate sentences rather than combined through coordination: . . . people of color are more likely to value social media as a means of getting involved in politics. Youth of color follow more celebrities and public figures than white teens do. Social media is sometimes a path to political participation and civic engagement.

Separate sentences rather than combined through subordination: Each group (African American and Hispanic teens) reports spending more than two hours a day on social media. For white teens it's about an hour and a half.

While the surface-level information still would have been communicated in separate sentences, the reader would have had to infer the relationships among the ideas—and those relationships are critical to the reasoning of the writing. By signaling those relationships, the conjunctions also help smooth out choppy writing.

As you read the arguments of other writers, pay close attention to how they develop relationships among ideas and how those relationships affect your understanding of the argument. The arrangement of clauses can change the meaning or create particular effects, particularly with the subordinated sentences. As you write, look for places where you can convey relationships to help your reader see nuances and complexity in your argument and reasoning.

Remember: Subordination and coordination are used to express the intended relationship between ideas in a sentence. Writers frequently use coordination to illustrate a balance or equality between ideas. Writers frequently use subordination to illustrate an imbalance or inequality between ideas. (STL-1.I–K)

3.2 Checkpoint

Close Reading: Professional Text

Review the anchor text, "How the Loss of the Landline Is Changing Family Life," on pages 383–386. Then complete the following open response activity and answer the multiple-choice questions.

1. Using the analyses on the previous pages as a guide, write an analysis of the coordinate and subordinate relationships in the three sentences below.

   Coordinate:

   A shared family phone meant that kids overheard some of their parents' conversations, providing a window into their relationships, but today, children frequently see a parent silently staring at a screen, fingers tapping, occasionally furrowing a brow or chuckling.

   Subordinate:

   Even as people were defying time and space by speaking with someone miles away, they were firmly grounded in the space of the home, where the phone was attached to the wall.

   Both:

   After the advent of the telephone, in the late 19th century, and through the mid-20th century, callers relied on switchboard operators who knew their customers' voices, party lines were shared by neighbors (who would often eavesdrop on one another's conversations), and phone books functioned as a sort of map of a community.

2. In the second sentence of paragraph 10, the author strategically arranges the clauses in a way that
   (A) emphasizes the importance of a smartphone's multifunctional abilities
   (B) challenges the need for any communication device to complete more than one task
   (C) keeps the focus on the old technology while showing how the new technology is different
   (D) contrasts the ease of speaking on a phone with the complexity of texting
   (E) contradicts earlier points lauding the creation of the smartphone

3. Which of the following best describes the effect of the author's structural choices in the first three sentences of paragraph 5 ("Over the course . . . would pick up")?
   (A) Use of the conjunction "And" at the beginning of sentence 2 suggests lesser significance.
   (B) Use of the conjunction "But" at the beginning of sentence 3 establishes a contrast.
   (C) The opening phrase of each sentence shows their ideas are of equal importance.
   (D) The use of subordination in each sentence reflects nuance and complexity.
   (E) The adverb "therefore" in sentence 1 minimizes the best features of cell phones.

4. The second sentence of paragraph 2
   (A) clarifies the older generation's communication methods
   (B) emphasizes the value of family in contemporary communication
   (C) associates the value of the home with the function of the landline
   (D) refutes an unpopular opinion about cell phones and their value in social life
   (E) contrasts the impact of smartphones and landlines on cultural norms

5. The repeated use of the quotation " 'You don't lose' " in the final two sentences of paragraph 12
   (A) highlights the important role cell phones play in keeping people connected
   (B) suggests the superiority of landlines over cell phones
   (C) casts doubt on the ability of cell phones to fully replace the need for landlines
   (D) underscores the self-absorption that occurs with cell phones
   (E) praises cell phone for providing valuable information regarding all facets of our daily lives

6. The author's use of parallelism in the final sentence of paragraph 3 illustrates her belief that
   (A) landlines encouraged more communal behavior than cell phones
   (B) privacy was often compromised in the days of landlines
   (C) modern cell phones are more efficient than landlines
   (D) switchboard operators seldom respected caller privacy
   (E) telephone technology advanced slowly in 19th and 20th centuries

Evaluating Writing: Student Draft

Reread the student draft on pages 386–387. Then complete the open response activity and answer the and multiple-choice question.

1. Help the author clarify the relationship among ideas by combining two sentences to create a sentence with a main clause and subordinate clause.

2. The writer is consider revising the underlined portion of sentence 23 (reproduced below) to demonstrate that either scenario illustrates the problem with technology.

   Think about the effect of installing televisions in every child's room in a house <u>*and*</u> *of allowing every family member to have smartphones during a meal.*

   Which of the following versions of the underlined portion of sentence 23 best accomplishes this goal?

   (A) (as it is now)
   (B) but
   (C) yet
   (D) or
   (E) also

Composing on Your Own

Reread your draft, paying close attention to how, if it all, you have combined sentences. Just as you can make words and phrases more vivid by adding modifiers to them, you can make short independent clauses more nuanced and interesting when you revise them to include a subordinate clause. Also, a subordinate clause is an excellent way to introduce an opposing viewpoint to a claim or even qualify a full thesis statement. Review your qualified thesis statement, and if you think adding a subordinate clause would clarify or sharpen its nuance, revise it accordingly. Save your work for future use.

Part 3 Apply What You Have Learned

Source C ("It's a Smartphone Life," pages 413–414) uses bullets, a handy way to list separate pieces of information. However, a bulleted list is not usually effective in showing relationships and nuances among ideas. Choose three or four items from the bulleted list in Source C, and combine them into a paragraph that uses coordination and subordination to show relationships among ideas.

Reflect on the Essential Question: Write a brief response that answers this essential question: *How can sentences express relationships among ideas?* Correctly use the key terms on page 417 in your answer.

Part 4

Clarity Through Conventions

Enduring Understanding and Skills

Part 4

Understand

The rhetorical situation informs the strategic stylistic choices that writers make. (STL-1)

Demonstrate

Explain how grammar and mechanics contribute to the clarity and effectiveness of an argument. (Reading 7.C)

Use established conventions of grammar and mechanics to communicate clearly and effectively. (Writing 8.C)

Source: *AP® English Language and Composition Course and Exam Description*

Essential Question: How do grammar and mechanics contribute to clarity in writing?

Why do actors stand onstage where they do? Why and where do they move? How close should they be to other actors onstage? These are some of the questions a director answers when planning out the staging of a play. Every placement, every movement, every space between characters needs to contribute to the meaning of a scene and reveal aspects of characters and their relationships with one another. Over centuries of dramatic presentations, a number of theatrical conventions have developed that directors use to guide these decisions: place actors on an angle, arrange actors to direct the audience's eyes to focal points, limit distracting movement but use movement to punctuate a change in scene, position characters in relation to one another to reveal the nature of their relationship—friends may stand closer than rivals, for example. And while a director follows these conventions to enhance the audience's understanding of the play, a director also tries to compose a pleasing stage picture so the whole arrangement conveys a message as well as the parts.

Source: Getty Images

Directors use theatrical conventions to reveal relationships among characters and convey both details and an overall effect. ***What details direct the audience to the focal point of this arrangement?***

Writers, like directors, follow conventions so *their* message and meaning come through in as many ways as possible. These conventions of grammar and mechanics assure that your carefully coordinated, subordinated, qualified, supported, and elaborated language and ideas do not get lost in a tangle of confusion. Using the conventions of grammar and mechanics will likely also earn you the respect of certain audiences, especially in academic and professional settings, who expect a command of grammar and mechanics from writers.

Fortunately, writers, like actors, have a chance to rehearse. Each round of revision improves the substance of your argument just as each rehearsal helps the actors and director clarify and refine their emphasis and message. Finally, with the substance of your argument solid, you can move to the "dress rehearsal" stage and edit your writing to be sure that even the small details of mechanics, punctuation, and spelling support your meaning.

KEY TERMS

boldface	italics
design features	mechanics
grammar	punctuation

4.1 Grammar, Mechanics, and Punctuation for Meaning | STL-1.M STL-1.N STL-1.O

Grammar and mechanics that follow established conventions of language enable clear communication. Writers use punctuation strategically to demonstrate the relationships among ideas in a sentence. Punctuation advances a writer's purpose by clarifying, organizing, emphasizing, indicating purpose, supplementing information, or contributing to tone.

Grammar and Mechanics

Grammar is the whole system of a language—the "rules" used to structure ideas into units to convey meaning by showing relationships among the grammatical elements. You have been absorbing the rules of grammar ever since you learned how to talk, though they may have been rules distinct to your community rather than the rules of Standard English. The grammar rules you have learned tell you (without your having to think about it) how to structure a sentence if you are asking a question or how to refer back to your sister Mariana after you have previously named her by simply using the word "she."

In the course of learning by doing—the way children learn to speak and write—chances are good that you may never have had the need to know or use some of the finer points of grammatical conventions. As you establish your footing in academic writing, you will absorb these conventions as well. They are valued because they help make written communication clear and effective to a wide range of readers.

For example, suppose you come across this sentence in your reading about technology and families:

> Trying to bring their families together, cell phone use may be limited by parents.

There are no misspellings, and the punctuation and capitalization are all fine. But you very well might stumble on that sentence because its structure is at odds with its meaning. No doubt you got the general idea of the sentence: Parents may limit cell phone use to bring their families together. But the structure of the sentence communicates that *cell phones* are trying to bring their families together, not parents, since the phrase "trying to bring their families together" modifies cell phones as it is placed in the sentence. Even if that confusing structure caused only a momentary stumble in your reading, it set you a bit off course. Writers who follow grammatical conventions prevent such stumbles and clearly communicate their message to their audience.

Mechanics are the rules of capitalization, punctuation, and spelling that govern written language. In speech you don't have to worry about capitalizing, spelling, or adding commas; your spoken words, vocal inflections, and pauses communicate clearly enough. In writing, however, you have to replace those cues for understanding and the rules of mechanics take their place. Punctuation is an especially effective way to provide cues for readers.

Punctuation

At the most basic level, **punctuation** lets readers know where a sentence begins and ends.

Anything between two "end marks" (periods, exclamation marks, and question marks) is a complete sentence. Anything that is not essential to understanding the independent clause or clauses of a complete sentence is set off by other punctuation (commas, parentheses, and dashes). Punctuation, then, is another way to show relationships among ideas.

Reread "It's a Smartphone Life" on pages 413–414. Then consider these sentences from it and how they make use of punctuation to indicate relationships between ideas.

> Just over half of children in the United States—53 percent—now own a smartphone by the age of 11.

The dashes emphasize the exact number provided to qualify what the writer means by "just over half." This information is not strictly necessary, but it is likely provided to illustrate just how close the statistic is to the 50% halfway mark.

> And there can be opportunities for "informal learning"—with the right guidance.

Here, another dash creates a dramatic emphasis on the need for proper and effective—or "right"—guidance necessary for informal learning opportunities. In the context of the excerpt, the dash and what follows it stand as a warning that informal learning would be difficult without proper procedures and supervision.

> African-American and Hispanic teens have distinctive patterns of use. Each group reports spending more than two hours a day on social media, whereas for white teens it's about an hour and a half. (Mingo, who is African-American, would qualify as a high user of social media between Pinterest, Snapchat and Tumblr).

The information in the parentheses is not really necessary to the argument as a whole, though it does provide a specific example of a teen who fits into this category. The effect of the information within the parentheses is to make the broad, generalized comments about "African-American and Hispanic teens" more individual and specific to a real person.

In each of these cases, the information is not necessary to the argument, but it does provide more context for understanding the issues surrounding the argument.

Learn to use the following punctuation to further your idea development and rhetorical expression.

Punctuation Mark	Not just . . .	Also, think of it as . . .
Comma	a mark to pause or take a breath during a sentence	a way to organize ideas in a sentence by separating words, phrases, and dependent clauses from the independent clauses.
Colon	a mark placed before a list	a way of indicating an explanation or clarification of what came before it (which may include a list). What follows the colon is also the modifying information.

(continued)

Punctuation Mark	Not just . . .	Also, think of it as . . .
Semicolon	a mark to combine two sentences/independent clauses	a way to combine the complete thoughts in separate sentences for consideration together; the relationship between the two clauses is inferred since there is no conjunction to assert the relationship.
Dash	a way of separating extra information from the main part of a sentence.	a way to include nonessential information that may be interesting or influence the understanding of information in the rest of the sentence.
Hyphen	a simple way of combining words.	a way to combine words to indicate a combined idea or concept.
Quotation Mark	a way to indicate when something is being quoted.	a way to indicate sarcastic or figurative usage of a word.
Period	the end of a sentence.	the end of a complete thought.
Exclamation Mark	the end of a sentence that is meant to loudly declare something.	a way of emphasizing or elevating a sentence and expressing strong emotion.
Question Mark	the end of a sentence that is asking a question.	a way to get readers to consider an idea on their own.

Table 7-7

Remember: Grammar and mechanics that follow established conventions of language enable clear communication. Writers use punctuation strategically to demonstrate the relationships among ideas in a sentence. Punctuation (commas, colons, semicolons, dashes, hyphens, parentheses, quotation marks, or end marks) advances a writer's purpose by clarifying, organizing, emphasizing, indicating purpose, supplementing information, or contributing to tone. (STL-1.M–O)

4.1 Checkpoint

Close Reading: Professional Text

Review the anchor text, "How the Loss of the Landline Is Changing Family Life," on pages 383–386. Then complete the open response activity and answer the multiple-choice questions.

1. Find examples of a few different kinds of punctuation marks in the text and explain how they develop relationships in sentences. Also explain how the relationships of those sentences contribute to the argument.

2. In the third sentence of paragraph 12 ("When people look up . . . physical surroundings"), the writer's use of dashes to offset a nonessential phrase serves to
   (A) illustrate the versatility of cell phones
   (B) warn the audience about complacency with cell phone use
   (C) indicate the changes required when landlines disappear
   (D) describe the purposes of home pages and home screens
   (E) underscore the social disconnect caused by cell phones

3. In the third sentence of paragraph 14, the writer's use of two phrases in parenthesis
   (A) inserts a definition into her discussion of landlines
   (B) defines vocabulary essential to the argument presented
   (C) explains why some had negative views of early phones
   (D) qualifies the primary assertion within this paragraph
   (E) admits that there are similarities between cell phones and landlines

4. The use of the dash in the next to last sentence of paragraph 8 creates a sense of
   (A) measured judgment
   (B) thoughtless pessimism
   (C) overprotectiveness
   (D) increasing anxiety
   (E) momentary suspense

5. The writer's use of a dash in the final sentence of paragraph 1 allows her to establish a tone of
   (A) impending tragedy
   (B) nostalgia and regret
   (C) playful whimsicality
   (D) positivity and optimism
   (E) empathetic criticism

Evaluating Writing: Student Draft

Reread the student draft on pages 386–387. Then complete the open response activity and answer the multiple-choice question.

1. Identify two sentences in which the writer uses punctuation to clarify "extra" information from the essential information. Explain why the author sets aside this information. Then rewrite two sentences by adding your own additional information, being sure to use the appropriate punctuation to set off your "extra" information.

2. The writer is considering editing the punctuation between sentence 5 and 6 (reproduced below) to a colon (:) to clarify the relationship between the two sentences.

(5) Amish communities ask themselves one question. (6) How will this new thing affect our relationships with one another?

Should the writer make this edit?

(A) Yes, because the second sentence expands on the first.

(B) Yes, because they are both independent clauses.

(C) Yes, because there is not a conjunction present.

(D) No, because they are both complete sentences.

(E) No, because the second sentence asks a question already implied by the first.

Composing on Your Own

On the last few revisions of your writing, you have qualified claims, moved sentences around, and combined sentences using subordinate clauses. Check over each of these changes and any others you have made to make sure the mechanics, especially the punctuation, serve the purpose of clarifying your ideas within your rhetorical situation. When you are satisfied with your decisions, use the spelling and grammar check on your computer or tablet to see if it questions any of your choices. If it does, think through why that might be and edit your work accordingly. Save your work for future use.

4.2 Design Features | STL-1.P

Writers also use some **design features**, such as italic type or boldface, to create emphasis.

Adding Emphasis

You may have learned that certain titles are correctly presented in *italic type,* as are some foreign terms and other words. However, **italics** can also be used to express meaning by indicating emphasis. Consider the difference between these two sentences.

> *You* are the reason I have succeeded.
> You are the *reason* I have succeeded.

In the first sentence above, notice that the writer wants to emphasize the importance of the person who is being addressed, while in the second sentence, the writer wants to emphasize the reason. You can see how the writer of "It's A Smartphone Life" (pages 413–414) used italics to express meaning in the following sentences.

> About 1 in 5 children has a phone by age 8. There *could* be a silver lining to children getting their first phones closer to elementary school than high school.

Notice the italics on the word "could." Likely, uncertainty and unpredictability are what the writer means to emphasize here. That explanation would fit with the next sentences, which call for parents to model healthy social media use. The effect is to say that if parents do that modeling, then there will be a silver lining.

Boldface text is also used to draw attention to particular words, to make them stand out so a reader can quickly see them when scanning the page. You may have noticed words in boldface in this book—those are the key terms for each unit. Boldface type is also often used for headings, as in "The Ways We Lie" in Unit 6 on pages 302–308.

Writers use both italics and boldface to press certain ideas or concepts related to their argument that lie *just* outside of written explanation. Italics and boldfaced should be used rarely, saved for the ideas that really need them.

Remember: Some design features, such as italics or boldface, create emphasis. (STL-1.P)

4.2 Checkpoint

Close Reading: Professional Text

Review "How the Loss of the Landline Is Changing Family Life" on pages 383–386. Then complete the following open response activity and answer the multiple-choice questions.

1. On separate paper, identify the places where italics are used in the article to emphasize text and explain how those italics might be related to the argument of the passage. (Do not include the italicized titles of books.)

2. The author most likely italicizes the word *no* in the third sentence of paragraph 16 to

(A) establish a tone of sarcasm aimed at overprotective parents

(B) emphasize the need for all families to avoid the internet

(C) highlight the contradictory nature of the initial message

(D) accentuate the idea that the children's phone is atypical

(E) instruct parents on the proper use of cell phones

Evaluating Writing: Student Draft

Review the student draft on pages 386–387. Then complete the open response activity and answer the multiple-choice question.

1. Make a list of words from the student draft that could be italicized for emphasis.

2. The writer is considering editing the passage by italicizing the underlined words in sentences 25 and 27 (reproduced below).

   This <u>is not</u> to say that we should consider the Amish way of life for all Americans. That would leave behind our growing global and technological community. It <u>is</u> to say that the Amish provide an example of how we should consider the effects of technology as we learn to use it.

   Should the writer make this edit to the passage?

   (A) Yes, because it better emphasizes the contrast between the two sentences.

   (B) Yes, because these terms are essential to understanding the argument.

   (C) Yes, because each is preceded in the sentence by pronouns.

   (D) No, because these words are not significant terms of the argument.

   (E) No, because it adds new ideas that will likely confuse the reader at the end of the passage.

Composing on Your Own

Review your draft to see if there are any places where italic or boldface types would enhance the meaning of your writing. If so, add them. When in doubt, leave them out.

Revise your essay one last time, using the checklist on the following page. Then save your work.

Checklist for Composing, Revising, and Editing
✓ Did you consider possible introductory methods by putting yourself in your reader's shoes? (1.1)
✓ Did you draft body paragraphs and experiment with possible concluding methods? Did you write your introduction and conclusion so that they tie together? (1.2)
✓ Did you revise your draft to integrate other viewpoints and avoid presenting only a binary view of your topic? (2.1)
✓ Have you found the "complex middle" in the expression of your thesis statement by qualifying it as necessary with words, phrases, and clauses? Did you clarify and enrich your ideas with modifying words, phrases, and clauses? (2.2)
✓ Did you review and, if needed, revise your arrangement of parts within a sentence to make their presentation as effective as possible? Did you review and, if needed, revise the placement of your sentences within your text? (3.1)
✓ Did you combine sentences and use subordinate clauses to clarify or sharpen nuances? (3.2)
✓ Did you review and, if needed, edit the punctuation of your text, given the adjustments you made to it through the course of revision? (4.1)
✓ Did you judiciously use italics or boldface or choose to leave them out if you felt they would not add anything significant to your message? (4.2)
✓ Did you edit your writing for mistakes in spelling and other mechanics and make an effort to correct them?

Table 7-8

Part 4 Apply What You Have Learned

Review the writing you did when you combined bullet points from Source C into a paragraph with subordination and coordination. Evaluate how effectively you used punctuation to clarify and emphasize the ideas and the relationships among them, and make changes as needed to enhance your reworking of the bullet points. Choose among these revision options.

- Revise so that you use a colon after an independent clause and the word, phrase, or clause that follows clarifies or emphasizes the first clause.
- Revise so that you use quotation marks around a word, phrase, or clause to create a particular tone.
- Revise so that you use a rhetorical question.

Reflect on the Essential Question: Write a brief response that answers this essential question: *How do grammar and mechanics contribute to clarity in writing?* In your answer, correctly use the terms on page 429.

Unit 7 Review

Section I: Multiple Choice

Section II: Free Response

Section I: Reading

Questions 1–12. Read the following passage carefully before you choose your answers.

(The following excerpt is from a book by Anne Lamott, an American writer, political activist, public speaker, and a writing teacher. Arguably her most famous work, *Bird by Bird: Some Instruction on Writing and Life* (1994), has been in print nonstop for more than 25 years. The passage below is from the chapter "False Starts.")

1 I found out something important about false starts when I began accompanying some members of my church to a convalescent home[1] once a month, where we were conducting a worship service. After that first dismal visit, I thought I knew who the residents were and what they were capable of, what they were all about. If I had started to write, I would have written about them with confidence, and I would have been all wrong.

2 I have been going there for four years now. I don't ever really look forward to it, but I keep going back for reasons I do not quite understand. Perhaps I am subconsciously hoping it will help me get into the Junior League[2] someday. Still, the moment I walk in and smell those old people again, and find them parked in the hallways like so many cars abandoned by the side of the road, I start begging God not to let me end up like this. But God is not a short-order cook, and these people were once my age. I bet they used to beg God not to let them end up as they have.

3 At first many of them look strangely alike. Then you start to notice that some have lambskin chaps or blankets, some have manicures, some have the teeth they were

---

1 **convalescent home:** nursing home; place for people to rehabilitate during or following an illness or surgery
2 **Junior League:** educational and charitable women's organizations

born with, some have sores, some don't, some were clearly beautiful in earlier days, some weren't, some seem to know where they are, some remember lines from the Lord's Prayer, some sleep, some try to sing along on the simple hymns and clap in rhythm. But even the ones who clap all clap differently. Some clap along frailly, almost in silence. One woman claps with great gusto, as if she's at a polka. One old man claps once, as if to kill a fly. My favorite, a woman named Anne like me, is someone I'd first pegged as a muzzy,[3] emaciated woman who smelled of urine and baby powder without a whole lot going on inside.

4 She isn't what I thought, though. I still don't know who she is, but I do know now who she isn't. She can never remember my name, and when I tell her every month, she pantomimes smiting her own forehead. Then we both smile. I suspect she is pulling my leg. When we sing "Amen," she always sits with her hands in her lap, palms cupped together as if there might be a tiny bird inside. With each clap, she moves her hands a tiny bit apart, as if she really does want to clap along, but at the same time she doesn't want to let the bird get out.

5 If I'd written about her and the other old people after the first few visits, the smells and confusion would have dominated my description. I would have recorded our odd conversations—one woman is convinced we went to school together; another once asked if Sam[4] was a dog—and I would have tried to capture my sense of waste. Instead, I continued to go there, and I struggled to find meaning in their bleak existence. What finally helped was an image from a medieval monk, Brother Lawrence, who saw all of us as trees in winter, with little to give, stripped of leaves and color and growth, whom God loves unconditionally anyway. My priest friend Margaret, who works with the aged and who shared this image with me, wanted me to see that even though these old people are no longer useful in any traditional meaning of the word, they are there to be loved unconditionally, like trees in the winter.

6 When you write about your characters, we want to know all about their leaves and colors and growth. But we also want to know who they are when stripped of the surface show. So if you want to get to know your characters, you have to hang out with them long

---

3 **muzzy:** confused
4 **Sam:** the writer's son

enough to see beyond all the things they aren't. You may try to get them to do something because it would be convenient plotwise, or you might want to pigeonhole them so you can maintain the illusion of control. But with luck their tendrils will sneak out the sides of the box you've put them in, and you will finally have to admit that who they are isn't who you thought they were.

---

1. Which of the following words in the first paragraph (lines 1–8) qualifies the nature of the writer's first visit to the home?

(A) "important" (line 1)

(B) "convalescent" (line 3)

(C) "dismal" (line 4)

(D) "confidence" (line 7)

(E) "wrong" (line 8)

2. The introduction and conclusion in this excerpt are connected by the idea that

(A) the elderly are complicated

(B) surface impressions of others are too limited

(C) it is impossible to truly know anyone

(D) a writer must develop a character with confidence

(E) unconditional love is redemptive

3. Read the following sentence from paragraph 5.

If I'd written about her and the other old people after the first few visits, the smells and confusion would have dominated my description.

What is the purpose of the underlined clause in the sentence?

(A) to qualify the writer's thesis

(B) to add contradictory information

(C) to highlight Anne's character traits

(D) to add descriptive details about the home

(E) to establish a confident tone

4. Which of the following best describes the effect of the author's structural choices in the first sentence of paragraph 6?
   (A) She begins with a dependent clause to provide context for her descriptive images of "leaves," "colors," and "growth."
   (B) She shifts from second to first person pronouns to objectify her tone.
   (C) She modifies the noun "characters" by using the modifying phrase "all about."
   (D) She arranges "leaves," "colors," and "growth" in the order of their importance.
   (E) She uses nonessential clauses to demonstrate the complexity of her idea.

Questions 5–7 are covered in Unit 2.

5. The writer establishes her credibility in paragraph 1 by
   (A) demonstrating that she cares more for other people than herself
   (B) illustrating her commitment to her religion and sharing it with others
   (C) offering a personal experience and admitting flaws that illustrate her candor
   (D) demonstrating her ability to read and understand people based on first impressions
   (E) offering reasons for the choices she made to improve her writing

6. Which of the following most likely describes the intended audience of this text?
   (A) convalescent-home volunteers
   (B) website editors
   (C) award-winning novelists
   (D) inexperienced writers
   (E) experienced writing instructors

7. The writer uses experiences at the convalescent home to illustrate that
   (A) our first impressions of people tell us a great deal about their character
   (B) understanding people requires seeing beyond the traits we think they lack
   (C) all people have a purpose regardless of their physical or mental disabilities
   (D) volunteering to help the elderly is an effective expression of respect
   (E) even at the end of their lives, the elderly have a great deal to teach others

Questions 8–9 are covered in Units 3 and 4.

8. The author develops her arguments in the essay primarily through
  (A) comparison and contrast
  (B) definition and narration
  (C) cause and effect
  (D) division and classification
  (E) narration and description

9. The writer most likely explains that the residents of the home "are there to be loved unconditionally" (paragraph 5, last sentence) to
  (A) connect with the reader's own sense of aging
  (B) explain how her priest friend matters in the passage
  (C) assert that age is nothing but a number
  (D) imply that unconditional love can solve any problem
  (E) appeal to the reader's sense of empathy

Question 10 is covered in Unit 3.

10. The writer's line of reasoning throughout the passage might best be described as moving from
  (A) initial impressions to realizations about people that can be applied to writing
  (B) justifying her visit to a convalescent home to a description of the people she met there
  (C) descriptions of people to advice on how writers can cope with death and dying
  (D) observations about convalescent homes to arguments about a writer's need for faith
  (E) descriptions of a worship service to the author's own spiritual realizations

Question 11 is covered in Unit 4.

11. The writer's use of tree imagery in paragraph 6 assists in her attempt to
  (A) contrast the examples in the previous paragraphs
  (B) imply that writers must consider the age of their characters
  (C) articulate her thesis for the entire passage
  (D) suggest the image shared by her priest friend was unhelpful
  (E) develop claims about the cyclical nature of aging and death

Question 12 is covered in Unit 5.

12. The image provided by her "priest friend Margaret" (paragraph 5) allows the author to develop a logical connection between

(A) the view of the writing process and its similarity to the aging process

(B) the need for religious conviction and artistic integrity

(C) her experiences as a creative writer and feelings of uselessness

(D) her experience at the convalescent home and advice about writing

(E) organic processes and her own views of religion's value

Section I: Writing

Questions 13–21. Read the following passage carefully before you choose your answers.

(1) The New York City subway was an astonishing achievement of engineering and technology when it opened its first official underground line in 1904. (2) That first line, the "Manhattan Main Line," ran 9.1 miles from City Hall to 145th Street in Harlem. (3) The subway—including its aboveground segments—has grown to 840 miles of track and more than a billion riders a year. (4) Needless to say, the city would stop working if the subway system stopped working. (5) Maintaining the subway to ensure its future is the target of a recent plan by the Metropolitan Transit Authority, or MTA, to update the subway. (6) Called "Fast Forward," this plan to drastically update the subway would cost taxpayers about 37 billion dollars.

(7) The problem is no one can seem to agree on which taxpayers should pay for the "Fast Forward" plan. (8) New York City Mayor Bill de Blasio has said that the subway is the responsibility of the state of New York. (9) In a recent speech, he explained that the subway is really the responsibility of state government and "ultimately the governor." (10) On the other hand, Governor Andrew Cuomo responded that "if that's the case, then the real problem is you're not going to be able to do anything significant to fix the subways."

(11) It is neither a part of just the city nor just the state. (12) While the subway is often seen as a symbol of New York City, the money generated by the billions of fares paid, jobs worked, and tourists moved throughout the city benefits New Yorkers throughout both the city and the state.

13. The writer wants to revise sentence 5 (reproduced below) to better emphasize the reason for writing the passage.

Maintaining the subway to ensure its future is the target of a recent plan by the Metropolitan Transit Authority, or MTA, to <u>*update the subway*</u>*.*

Which possible revision of the underlined portion best accomplishes this goal?

(A) (as it is now)

(B) update it as a symbol of the city and better please the great people who live there

(C) update and recreate the subway as representative of the modern city and its progressive—and increasingly diverse—population

(D) update, but not change, the subway since it is an American icon we must preserve

(E) update and modernize the 115-year-old system that has seen regular, though not comprehensive, updates over the decades

14. The writer would like to add a sentence to the end of the second paragraph (sentences 7–10) to help the casual reader better relate to the situation facing the subway riders and taxpayers. Which of the following sentences would best accomplish this goal?

(A) Taxpayers now must choose whom to believe most—the governor or the mayor.

(B) Both the mayor and the governor need the trust of taxpayers.

(C) Failure to follow through with the "Fast Forward" plan will ultimately benefit taxpayers who will not have to pay the billions for the plan, not have to endure delays of construction, and not have to listen to the arguments between the governor and the mayor.

(D) It is becoming increasingly clear that the governor has no intention of helping either riders or New York City taxpayers.

(E) Caught in the middle are the millions of daily subway riders and taxpayers relying on the trains to carry them to work, to school, to family, and to vacation.

15. To emphasize the mayor's comments and avoid unnecessarily repeating information, the writer would like to combine sentences 8 and 9 (reproduced below).

New York City Mayor Bill De Blasio has said that the subway is the responsibility of the state of New York. In a recent speech, he explained that the subway is really the responsibility of state government and "ultimately the governor."

Which of the following revisions best accomplishes this?

(A) "Ultimately the governor" will be responsible, claims the mayor.

(B) New York City Mayor Bill de Blasio has said that the subway is the responsibility of New York State and "ultimately the governor."

(C) Responsibility for the safety of subway riders belongs to the state and "ultimately the governor."

(D) It is the state, not the city, that will be responsible.

(E) The governor and the state will carry the burden of paying for the "Fast Forward" plan, regardless of what they may think.

16. The writer is considering moving the third paragraph (sentences 11–12) to become the first paragraph. Should the writer make this revision?

(A) Yes, moving the third paragraph would better establish the reasoning of the first two paragraphs (sentences 1–10).

(B) Yes, the third paragraph introduces information that is necessary to understanding the first two paragraphs (sentences 1–10).

(C) Yes, the third paragraph better engages the audience than the first two paragraphs (sentences 1–10).

(D) No, the reasoning of the third paragraph relies on information provided in the first two paragraphs (sentences 1–10).

(E) No, the third paragraph sets up a contrast between the ideas presented in the first two paragraphs (sentences 1–10).

17. The writer would like to add a sentence after sentence 3 to demonstrate the cause-effect relationship between the increasing load of passengers and the need to repair the subway. Which of the following sentences would best accomplish this?

(A) Failure to update or repair the subway now will mean greater failures in the future.

(B) Stranding passengers is the greatest nightmare of New York City officials because stranding people in the subway or without transit means people don't work or travel and also don't trust the government.

(C) With so many riders, the subway has endured much more wear-and-tear than originally predicted.

(D) Simply put, failure to update the subway means more car and bus traffic, resulting in more congested—and more dangerous—roads, bridges, and tunnels.

(E) With so many people relying on the subway, not repairing it is not an option.

18. The writer wants to add the following question to the passage to establish the relationship between the comments from the mayor and governor and the purpose of the passage.

Should it be just the residents of the city or should people from throughout the state pay for the plan?

Where would the sentence best be placed?

(A) Before sentence 8

(B) Before sentence 9

(C) After sentence 10

(D) Before sentence 11

(E) After sentence 12

Question 19 is covered in Unit 4.

19. The writer wants to add the following sentence to the passage to act as the thesis.

An agreement must be reached regarding the "Fast Forward" plan that involves sharing the cost and responsibility for the subway between the city and the state.

Where would the sentence best be placed?

(A) Before sentence 1

(B) After sentence 5

(C) Before sentence 7

(D) Before sentence 11

(E) After sentence 12

Questions 20 and 21 are covered in Unit 5.

20. The writer wants to revise sentence 11 (reproduced below) to include parallel structure that gives equal weight to both the city and the state.

It is neither a part of just the city nor just the state.

Which of the following revisions best accomplishes this?

(A) (as it is now)

(B) It is not just a part of the city; it is also a part of the state.

(C) Whether you see it as part of the city or part of the state doesn't matter—it belongs to both.

(D) Not just a part of the city and not just a part of the state; the subway belongs to both.

(E) It belongs to all New Yorkers, regardless of its place in the city or its place in the state.

21. The writer would like to add a transition to the beginning of sentence 3 (reproduced below), adjusting the capitalization as needed, to create a more coherent connection between the past and present of the subway.

The subway—including its aboveground segments—has grown to 840 miles of track and more than a billion riders a year.

Which of the following choices best accomplishes this goal?

(A) Although more than 100 years has past,

(B) Afterward,

(C) Even if the city didn't grow like it has,

(D) Without a doubt,

(E) Since then,

JOIN THE CONVERSATION: SYNTHESIS ESSAY (PART 2)

The purpose of this "Join the Conversation" feature between Section I and Section II of the Unit Review is to help prepare you to respond to free-response prompts, whether in college or on the exam.

As you know, the first free-response task on the exam is the synthesis task. You had your first chance at practicing it in Unit 6 on pages 374–377. The practice synthesis prompt for Unit 7 is nearly identical to that of Unit 6, with just a few small changes. Study the prompt below.

Immigration and the settlement of people are facts of history. Culture and language barriers often mean that similar groups settle in "enclaves," that is, smaller areas surrounded by larger areas where the population in the smaller area is culturally or ethnically distinct from that of the larger area. Terms like "Chinatown," "Little Italy," "Little Havana," and "Little Senegal" have become common, but there are even entire cities that have come to represent enclaves. Dearborn, Michigan, for example, has one of the largest concentrations of Middle Eastern people in North America. Recent conversations about immigration, diversity, and national/cultural identity have brought attention to the role of these enclaves in larger society.

Carefully read the following four sources, including the introductory information for each source. Write an essay that synthesizes material from at least three of the sources and develops your position on the role of cultural or ethnic enclaves.

Source A (Dearborn)
Source B (Greenholtz)
Source C (Denmark)
Source D (Pew)

In your response you should do the following:

- Respond to the prompt with a thesis that presents a defensible position.
- Select and use evidence from at least three of the provided sources to support your line of reasoning. Indicate clearly the sources used through direct quotation, paraphrase, or summary. Sources may be cited as Source A, Source B, etc., or by using the description in parentheses.
- Explain how the evidence supports your line of reasoning.
- Use appropriate grammar and punctuation in communicating your argument.

As before, the **first part** of the prompt provides some background to establish the situation. The **second part** states your task. Now, instead of writing two paragraphs as you did in Unit 6, you will write a full essay, similar to the argument essay from Unit 5 but with sources synthesized. The **third part** of the prompt lists your sources (up to 7 on the actual exam).

A new source has been added to the list for this unit. It is on the next page. This source provides more information for consideration. It is a graph, called a "quantitative" visual since it relates to numbers and quantities. You will see at least one quantitative visual on the synthesis portion of the actual exam.

The **fourth part** provides a helpful checklist with requirements for fulfilling the task.

The Sources

As you read the different sources, you should carefully consider how they affect the argument you are planning to make. Be careful that you do not simply summarize the sources. The purpose of the sources in your synthesis is to support *your* argument.

As you consider visual quantitative sources, first identify what is being represented by the visual. Often, the introductory information of the source will state this information, but you should still look closely to be sure you understand. Second, consider how this new information relates to the other sources. (See page 451 for more on analyzing quantitative sources.)

Additional sources will add complexity to the issue. Some sources may seem contradictory. Their purpose is not to confuse you, but rather to reflect the different possible perspectives on the issue.

The way you integrate different sources and their perspectives will affect the development of your argument. Consider what you studied in Parts 2 and 3 of this unit as you look closely at the arrangement of sentences, the use of subordinate and coordinate clauses, and the general arrangement of clauses, phrases, and words in sentences.

Source D

"The Rise of Asian Americans." *Pew Research Center*, 19 June 2012.

Below is a graph relating to data from the 2010 census of the United States.

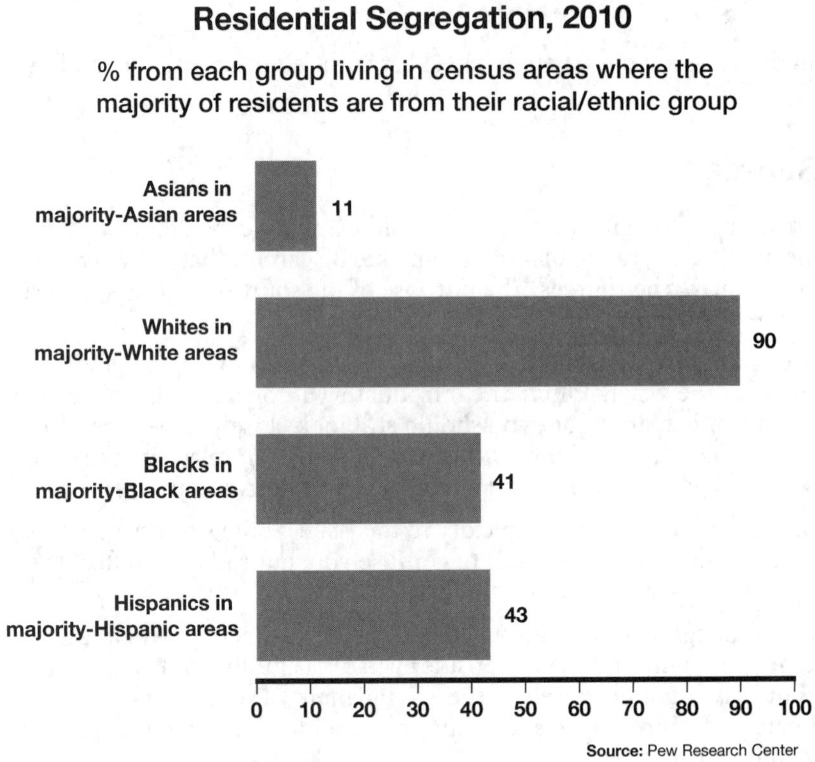

Analyzing Quantitative Sources

Since you are sure to have at least one quantitative, or numbers-based, source on the exam, learn the process for analyzing such visual sources, extracting information from them, and drawing conclusions based on them. The following steps will help you understand what each source conveys.

Steps for Analyzing Quantitative Sources
1. **Identify the title** of the graphic. Either on page or in your mind, express the title in your own words. Note the date, if any.
2. **Understand the key.** Often the key is at the bottom of the graphic. In Source D, it is right under the title: "% from each group living in census tracts where the majority of residents are from their racial/ethnic group." Again, on paper or in your head, restate the key so you know exactly what information the graphic is providing. In this case, for example, you might restate it this way: "This graph shows the percent of people from various racial or ethnic groups who live in neighborhoods where the majority of the population is the same as theirs."
3. **Understand the labeling** of the graph. In this case, the labels along the left-hand side identify different racial and ethnic groups that live in neighborhoods in which the majority of the population is of the same racial or ethnic group. The numbers on the right-hand side are the percentages, and the bars between the two are a visual representation of the differences for easy comparison. The *x*-axis (horizontal) shows the range of percentages by 10s.
4. **Understand how the information conveyed relates to the title.** In this case, for example, ask, "What is the relationship between each ethnic/racial percentage to segregated residential areas?"
5. **Explain the relationships.** The relationship between the racial/ethnic groups and segregated living shows the percentage of people who live in segregated communities. So while only 11% Asians live in segregated areas, 90% of Whites do. Another way to say the same thing is to note that 89% of Asians (100% minus 11%) live in integrated areas, while only 10% of Whites do. Make similar calculations for each group represented.
6. **Draw a conclusion** based on the information you have interpreted. Many conclusions are possible. A few in this case include: Far more Whites live in White-majority areas than other groups; Blacks and Hispanics live in integrated areas in about the same percents; in the groups represented, Asians are least segregated.

Keeping Track of Ideas and Sources

A new web graphic organizer is provided on the next page to account for the new additional source. Several more sources will be added over the next several units, so hold onto your graphic organizers and drafts for future use.

As more sources are added, you may want to revise the "Complexity" space in your organizer, noting any additional clashes in the perspectives of the sources, any overlaps, or any areas of limitation or bias you may see in the perspectives. Also note the abstract idea you believe these ideas connect to, including those in the new source.

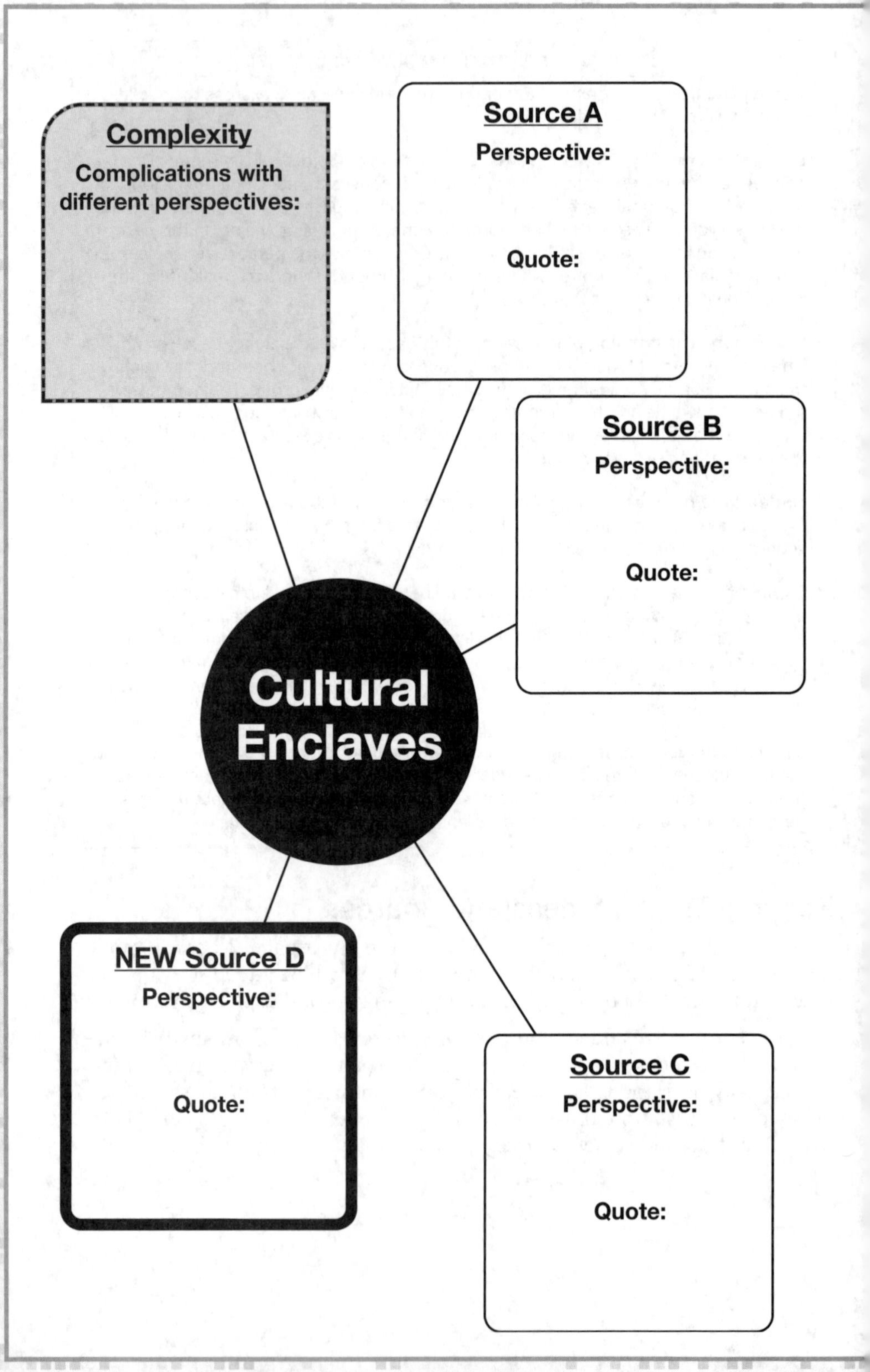
Complexity
Complications with different perspectives:
Source A
Perspective:
Quote:
Source B
Perspective:
Quote:
Cultural Enclaves
NEW Source D
Perspective:
Quote:
Source C
Perspective:
Quote:

From Organizer to Essay

Use the information on the graphic organizer to write a thesis that encapsulates *your* views based on your sources. Use a table like the one below to organize your main ideas into an introduction that includes your thesis and three supporting paragraphs that include references to the sources.

<table>
<tr><th colspan="4">Unit 7: Synthesis Full Essay Drafting Organizer</th></tr>
<tr><td rowspan="2">Introduction</td><td colspan="2">Lead-in addressing an abstract concept:</td><td rowspan="2">Abstract idea that runs throughout</td></tr>
<tr><td colspan="2">Thesis with subordinate clause lead-in:</td></tr>
<tr><td rowspan="8">Body Paragraph 1</td><td colspan="2">Transitional clause or sentence:</td><td rowspan="8">Abstract idea that runs throughout</td></tr>
<tr><td>Supporting Claim 1</td><td>Connection to abstract idea in thesis</td></tr>
<tr><td>Lead-in to source information</td><td>Source information</td></tr>
<tr><td colspan="2">Explain how source information relates to the claim and to the reasoning that justifies that claim and appeals to the audience.</td></tr>
<tr><td colspan="2">Transition to complex discussion or another example? (Not only...but also...)</td></tr>
<tr><td>Lead-in to source information</td><td>Source information</td></tr>
<tr><td colspan="2">Explain how source information relates to the claim and to the reasoning that justifies that claim and appeals to the audience.</td></tr>
<tr><td colspan="2">Reconnect to abstract idea in thesis</td></tr>
</table>

<table>
<tr><td rowspan="9">Body Paragraph 2</td><td colspan="2">Transitional clause or sentence:</td><td rowspan="9">Abstract idea that runs throughout</td></tr>
<tr><td>Supporting Claim 2</td><td>Connection to abstract idea in thesis</td></tr>
<tr><td>Lead-in to source information</td><td>Source information</td></tr>
<tr><td colspan="2">Explain how source information relates to claim 2 and to the reasoning that justifies that claim and appeals to the audience.</td></tr>
<tr><td colspan="2">Transition to complex discussion or another example? (Not only..., but also...)</td></tr>
<tr><td>Lead-in to source information</td><td>Source information</td></tr>
<tr><td colspan="2">Explain how source information relates to the example and to the reasoning that justifies that claim and appeals to the audience.</td></tr>
<tr><td colspan="2">Reconnect to abstract idea in thesis</td></tr>
<tr><td colspan="2"></td></tr>
<tr><td rowspan="8">Body Paragraph 3</td><td colspan="2">Transitional clause or sentence:</td><td rowspan="8">Abstract idea that runs throughout</td></tr>
<tr><td>Supporting Claim 3</td><td>Connection to abstract idea in thesis</td></tr>
<tr><td>Lead in to source information</td><td>Source information</td></tr>
<tr><td colspan="2">Explain how source information relates to the claim and to the reasoning that justifies that claim and appeals to the audience.</td></tr>
<tr><td colspan="2">Transition to complex discussion or another example? (Not only..., but also...)</td></tr>
<tr><td>Lead-in to source Information</td><td>Source information</td></tr>
<tr><td colspan="2">Explain how source info relates to claim 3 and to the reasoning that justifies that claim and appeals to the audience.</td></tr>
<tr><td colspan="2">Reconnect to abstract idea in thesis</td></tr>
</table>

<table>
<tr><td rowspan="3">Conclusion</td><td>Statement about essay topic that leads to abstract idea:</td><td rowspan="3">Abstract idea that runs throughout</td></tr>
<tr><td>Call to the reader about the essay topic (call to act or think differently):</td></tr>
<tr><td>General statement about the importance of the abstract idea(s):</td></tr>
</table>

Apply

Follow the same process as above to respond to the synthesis prompt on the next page. For current free-response question samples, visit the College Board website.

Section II: Free Response

Synthesis: Students and Farm Jobs

For decades, American farmers would hire high school students or other part-time workers to do the planting and harvesting of various crops. However, in the last 15–20 years, many farmers report that hiring American students or simply American workers to fill seasonal—or temporary—farm jobs has become increasingly difficult or even impossible. Some claim that these are jobs that Americans simply will not do any longer because the jobs are too difficult for people who have grown used to easier work. Others claim that the jobs do not pay enough for this laborious work, so people are not motivated to take them.

Carefully read the following sources, including the introductory information for each source.

Write an essay that synthesizes material from the three sources and develops your position on the relationship between American workers and farm jobs.

Source A (Johnson)
Source B (Mataconis)
Source C (Kirby)

In your response you should do the following:

- Respond to the prompt with a thesis that presents a defensible position.
- Select and use evidence from the three provided sources to support your line of reasoning. Indicate clearly the sources used through direct quotation, paraphrase, or summary. Sources may be cited as Source A, Source B, etc., or by using the description in parentheses.
- Explain how the evidence supports your line of reasoning.
- Use appropriate grammar and punctuation in communicating your argument.

Source A

Johnson, Kirk. "Hiring Locally for Farm Work Is No Cure-All." *The New York Times*, 11 October 2011.

The following is an excerpt from an American newspaper.

Mr. [John] Harold, a 71-year-old Vietnam War veteran who drifted [to western Colorado] in the late '60s, has participated for about a decade in a federal program called H-2A that allows seasonal foreign workers into the country to make up the gap where willing and able American workers are few in number. He typically has brought in about 90 people from Mexico each year from July through October.

This year, though, with tough times lingering and a big jump in the minimum wage under the program, to nearly $10.50 an hour, Mr. Harold brought in only two-thirds of his usual contingent. The other positions, he figured, would be snapped up by jobless local residents wanting some extra summer cash.

"It didn't take me six hours to realize I'd made a heck of a mistake," Mr. Harold said, standing in his onion field on a recent afternoon as a crew of workers from Mexico cut the tops off yellow onions and bagged them.

Six hours was enough, between the 6 a.m. start time and noon lunch break, for the first wave of local workers to quit. Some simply never came back and gave no reason. Twenty-five of them said specifically, according to farm records, that the work was too hard. On the Harold farm, pickers walk the rows alongside a huge harvest vehicle called a mule train, plucking ears of corn and handing them up to workers on the mule who box them and lift the crates, each weighing 45 to 50 pounds.

"It is not an easy job," said Kerry Mattics, 49, another H-2A farmer here in Olathe, who brought in only a third of his usual Mexican crew of 12 workers for his 50-acre fruit and vegetable farm, then struggled to make it through the season. "It's outside, so if it's wet, you're wet, and if it's hot you're hot," he said.

Still, Mr. Mattics said, he can't help feeling that people have gotten soft.

"They wanted that $10.50 an hour without doing very much," he said. "I know people with college degrees, working for the school system and only making 11 bucks."

A mismatch between employers' requirements and the skills and needs of the jobless—repeated across industries—has been a constant theme of this recessionary era[1] But here on the farm, mismatch can mean high anxiety.

The H-2A program, in particular, in trying to avoid displacing American citizens from jobs, strongly encourages farmers to hire locally if they can, with a requirement that they advertise in at least three states. That forces participants to take huge risks in guessing where a moving target might land—how many locals, how many foreigners—often with an entire season's revenue at stake. Survival, not civic virtue, drives the equation, they say.

"Farmers have to bear almost all the labor market risk because they must prove no one really was available, qualified or willing to work," said Dawn D. Thilmany, a professor of agricultural economics at Colorado State University. "But the only way to offer proof is to literally have a field left unharvested."

---

1 **recessionary era:** a period of low economic activity, loss of investment value, and widespread unemployment

Source B

Mataconis, Doug. "Farmers Finding Few Americans Willing To Do Jobs Immigrants Do" *Outside the Beltway*, 5 October 2011.

The following was originally published on a website dedicated to "politics and foreign affairs analysis."

The unemployment rate is above 9% and some people have been out of work for more than a year, but one segment of the economy is finding that there are indeed jobs Americans won't do:

[The article then reposts the entirety of source A.]

This isn't entirely surprising, of course. We saw the same thing in operation in Georgia earlier this year when a new law aimed at illegal immigrants[1] caused migrant farm workers to flee the state, leaving farmers with crops rotting in the field. When those farmers tried to make alternative arrangements and hire locally, they found very few people willing to do the work, and even fewer who could do the job as quickly and efficiently as the illegal immigrants who used to do it. A similar law enacted in Alabama was seen to have a similar impact on the construction industry.

Immigrants, regardless of their legal status, are uniquely suited for this type of work for many reasons. Farming requires quick action with harvest time comes; crops need to be picked when they're ready to be picked. Farmers simply can't afford to wait for someone to apply for a picker's job when they're not even sure they'll keep up with it. Migrant workers exist because there's a market for them. They don't stay in one place very long (hence the migrant part) because once they're done picking in one place, they move on to another. That's why it's the kind of job that attracts undocumented immigrants, because most of them don't have fixed addresses to begin with so the idea of spending the summer traveling the country doesn't bother them as much as it would the average American worker.

Immigration opponents constantly repeat the refrain that immigrants take jobs away from Americans. In reality, most immigrants are doing jobs that Americans don't want to do, or that they'd only for an exorbitantly high rate of pay that would make the price of ordinary goods prohibitively high, thus harming American competitiveness. Today, they're the people doing things like picking crops in the field or framing houses. A hundred years ago they were mining coal and digging railroad tunnels. They're willing to do the work because they're willing to sacrifice to make a better life for themselves and their families. If they were really stealing jobs from Americans, then we'd see some evidence of it. Instead, we get farmers like Mr. Mattics who took a gamble on the idea that out-of-work Americans would be grateful for a chance to work, and lost.

---

1 **illegal immigrants:** people who enter a country without the required documentation

Source C

Kirby, Brendan. "New Study Explodes Myth of 'Jobs Americans Won't Do.' " *Lifezette.com*, 28 August 2018.

The following is an excerpt from an online media source.

Native-born Americans make up a majority of workers in nearly every occupation—including jobs Americans supposedly won't do, according to a study released Monday.

The report by the Center for Immigration Studies (CIS), which examined census data, pierces the oft-repeated "jobs American's won't do" myth. Steven Camarota, who co-wrote the study, said immigrants certainly dominate certain occupations in some parts of the country.

But he said the experience of other parts of the country dispels the fear that jobs would be left undone if not for immigration.

"That argument assumes a form of segregation in the workforce that does not exist," said Camarota, director of research at the Washington, D.C.-based think tank.

The report updates research CIS performed a couple of years ago, only with a more sophisticated model that not only breaks down employees by national origin but also estimates the share of jobs held by illegal immigrants. It is based on the Census Bureau's American Community Survey (ACS) from the years 2012 through 2016.

The authors examined all 474 civilian occupations as defined by the Department of Commerce and found only six in which non-natives hold a majority—graders and sorters of agricultural products; plasterers and stucco masons; sewing machine operators; tailors, dressmakers and sewers; miscellaneous personal appearance workers; and miscellaneous agricultural workers.

But Camarota said workers in those professions make up only about 1 percent of the U.S. workforce. "They're almost irrelevant," he said.

Even among the six occupations with foreign-born majorities, some of the immigrant laborers have become naturalized citizens. And about 755,000 workers were born in the United States, according to the study.

"They still make up almost half even in those occupations," Camarota said.

If there truly were jobs that Americans refuse to do, Camarota said, it would be impossible for businesses to fill vacancies in parts of the country where the foreign-born population is small. But that is not the case, he said.

"Where there are not immigrants, Americans do the jobs," he said.

Rhetorical Analysis: "False Starts"

Anne Lamott is an American writer, political activist, public speaker, and writing teacher. Arguably her most famous work, *Bird by Bird: Some Instruction on Writing and Life* has been in print nonstop for 25 years. The passage on pages 438–440 is from the chapter "False Starts."

Read the passage carefully. Write an essay that analyzes the rhetorical choices Lamott makes to convey her message about false starts in writing.

In your response you should do the following:

- Respond to the prompt with a thesis that analyzes the writer's rhetorical choices.
- Select and use evidence to support your line of reasoning.
- Explain how the evidence supports your line of reasoning.
- Demonstrate an understanding of the rhetorical situation.
- Demonstrate your understanding of tone and tonal shift.
- Use appropriate grammar and punctuation in communicating your argument.

Argument: It Takes a Village

The Igbo people from the African country of Nigeria are credited with originating the now well-known saying that "it takes a village to raise a child."

Write an essay that argues your position on the role (if any) that extended family and/or communities play in raising children.

In your response you should do the following:

- Respond to the prompt with a claim that presents a defensible position.
- Provide evidence to support your line of reasoning.
- Explain how the evidence supports your line of reasoning.
- Use appropriate grammar and punctuation in communicating your argument.

UNIT 8

Using Style Strategically

Part 1: Considering Audience through Strategic Choices
Part 2: Writer's Style and Perspective
Part 3: Using Modifiers Strategically

ENDURING UNDERSTANDINGS AND SKILLS: Unit Eight

Part 1

Understand

Individuals write within a particular situation and make strategic writing choices based on that situation. (RHS-1)

Demonstrate

Explain how an argument demonstrates understanding of an audience's beliefs, values, or needs. (Reading 1.B)

Demonstrate an understanding of an audience's beliefs, values, or needs. (Writing 2.B)

Part 2

Understand

The rhetorical situation informs the strategic stylistic choices that writers make. (STL-1)

Demonstrate

Explain how word choice, comparisons, and syntax contribute to the specific tone or style of a text. (Reading 7.A)

Strategically use words, comparisons, and syntax to convey a specific tone or style in an argument. (Writing 8.A)

Part 3

Understand

The rhetorical situation informs the strategic stylistic choices that writers make. (STL-1)

Demonstrate

Explain how writers create, combine, and place independent and dependent clauses to show relationships between and among ideas. (Reading 7.B)

Write sentences that clearly convey ideas and arguments. (Writing 8.B)

Source: *AP® English Language and Composition Course and Exam Description*

Unit 8 Overview

Take a look at the image below. What do you see?

Source: Getty Images

Most people see the same image in this picture: two people, maybe a mother and daughter. There isn't much room for disagreement at this obvious level. People simply agree the image shows two women and the conversation stops there.

Now examine this zoomed-in, close-up section of the image. With the image modified this way, you can see that the picture is not just two people, but hundreds of people. This view is from the upper right-hand corner of the original image. When you look more closely at the image—and pay attention to the specific parts that make up the whole—you see the details that went into creating the whole. You get a sense of the people by looking at their faces, their clothing, their positions, their activities, and their relationships to one another. None of that insight is possible when you view the image from the initial perspective.

Argument—from the perspective of both reader and writer—works in much the same way. An obvious or simplistic presentation of a claim grinds the conversation to a halt. There is no further discussion of evidence, cause-effect hypotheticals, or significance over the long term. But think of each specific photograph in the image above as a strategic word choice, sentence arrangement, or audience acknowledgment. Together, these elements form a worthwhile argument and contribute to a far richer conversation.

A critical reader recognizes and appreciates the elements of style that make an argument effective and convincing, that account for complex perspectives, and that allude to deeper issues underlying the surface argument. An effective writer, once initial ideas are generated, focuses on fine-tuning and honing the argument so it delivers those elements to readers. In this unit, you will refine your understanding of an argument in its context and how rhetorical strategies—specifically the blend of word choices, sentence and paragraph organization, comparisons, and conventions—fit within that context.

Close Reading: Professional Text
"On Morality" by Joan Didion

Following is an essay by American writer Joan Didion. Didion's style, defined as "new journalism," communicates facts and real-life experiences through narrative storytelling. Over the years, she has often used this technique to comment on elements of pop culture, such as the dangers of California subcultures in the 1960s. The following essay, "On Morality," was written in 1965 in the midst of the war in Vietnam, the civil rights movement, the Cold War and nuclear tension, and political division throughout the United States. The anchor icon next to the heading tells you that this essay is a reading you will return to throughout this unit. For now, read it to understand the main or central ideas Didion expresses as she discusses her interpretation and implied definition of morality. Take your time reading it. When you encounter a word, term, or name you don't know, use the footnotes to help you figure out the meaning.

1 As it happens I am in Death Valley,[1] in a room at the Enterprise Motel and Trailer Park, and it is July, and it is hot. In fact it is 119°. I cannot seem to make the air conditioner work, but there is a small refrigerator, and I can wrap ice cubes in a towel and hold them against the small of my back. With the help of the ice cubes I have been trying to think, because *The American Scholar*[2] asked me to, in some abstract way about "morality," a word I distrust more every day, but my mind veers inflexibly toward the particular.

---

1 **Death Valley:** a desert in eastern California, one of the hottest places on Earth.
2 ***The American Scholar***: a general-interest journal published by the Phi Beta Kappa society.

2 Here are some particulars. At midnight last night, on the road in from Las Vegas to Death Valley Junction, a car hit a shoulder and turned over. The driver, very young and apparently drunk, was killed instantly. His girl[friend] was found alive but bleeding internally, deep in shock. I talked this afternoon to the nurse who had driven the girl to the nearest doctor, 185 miles across the floor of the Valley and three ranges of lethal mountain road. The nurse explained that her husband, a talc[3] miner, had stayed on the highway with the boy's body until the coroner could get over the mountains from Bishop, at dawn today. "You can't just leave a body on the highway," she said. "It's immoral."

3 It was one instance in which I did not distrust the word, because she meant something quite specific. She meant that if a body is left alone for even a few minutes on the desert, the coyotes close in and eat the flesh. Whether or not a corpse is torn apart by coyotes may seem only a sentimental consideration, but of course it is more: one of the promises we make to one another is that we will try to retrieve our casualties, try not to abandon our dead to the coyotes. If we have been taught to keep our promises—if, in the simplest terms, our upbringing is good enough—we stay with the body, or have bad dreams.

4 I am talking, of course, about the kind of social code that is sometimes called, usually pejoratively, "wagontrain morality." In fact that is precisely what it is. For better or worse, we are what we learned as children: my own childhood was illuminated by graphic litanies of the grief awaiting those who failed in their loyalties to each other. The Donner Reed Party,[4] starving in the Sierra snows, all the ephemera[5] of civilization gone save that one vestigial taboo, the provision that no one should eat his own blood kin. The Jayhawkers,[6] who quarreled and separated not far from where I am tonight. Some of them died in the Funerals[7] and some of them died down near Badwater[8] and most of the rest of them died in the Panamints. A woman who got through gave the Valley its name. Some might say that the Jayhawkers were killed by the desert summer, and the Donner Party by the mountain winter, by circumstances beyond control; we were taught instead that they had somewhere abdicated their responsibilities, somehow breached their primary loyalties, or they would not have found themselves helpless in the mountain winter or the desert summer, would not have given way to acrimony, would not have deserted one another, would not have *failed.* In brief, we heard such stories as cautionary tales, and they still suggest the only kind of "morality" that seems to me to have any but the most potentially mendacious[9] meaning.

---

3 **talc:** a mineral used in talcum powder and other products
4 **Donner-ReedPparty**: A group of 87 people who tried to cross the mountains into California during the stormy winter of 1846. The 47 who survived ate the flesh of those who died.
5 **ephemera:** passing niceties
6 **Jayhawkers**: Another group of easterners heading to California to mine for gold.
7 The Funerals and the Panamints are mountain ranges close to Death Valley.
8 Badwater Basin has the lowest elevation in North America.
9 **mendacious:** untruthful

5 You are quite possibly impatient with me by now; I am talking, you want to say, about a "morality" so primitive that it scarcely deserves the name, a code that has as its point only survival, not the attainment of the ideal good. Exactly. Particularly out here tonight, in this country so ominous and terrible that to live in it is to live with antimatter,[10] it is difficult to believe that "the good" is a knowable quantity. Let me tell you what it is like out here tonight. Stories travel at night on the desert. Someone gets in his pickup and drives a couple of hundred miles for a beer, and he carries news of what is happening, back wherever he came from. Then he drives another hundred miles for another beer, and passes along stories from the last place as well as from the one before; it is a network kept alive by people whose instincts tell them that if they do not keep moving at night on the desert they will lose all reason. Here is a story that is going around the desert tonight: over across the Nevada line, sheriff's deputies are diving in some underground pools, trying to retrieve a couple of bodies known to be in the hole. The widow of one of the drowned [young men] is over there; she is eighteen, and pregnant, and is said not to leave the hole. The divers go down and come up, and she just stands there and stares into the water. They have been diving for ten days but have found no bottom to the caves, no bodies and no trace of them, only the black 90° water going down and down and down, and a single translucent fish, not classified. The story tonight is that one of the divers has been hauled up incoherent, out of his head, shouting—until they got him out of there so that the widow could not hear—about water that got hotter instead of cooler as he went down, about light flickering through the water, about magma,[11] about underground nuclear testing.

6 That is the tone stories take out here, and there are quite a few of them tonight. And it is more than the stories alone. Across the road at the Faith Community Church a couple of dozen old people, come here to live in trailers and die in the sun, are holding a prayer sing. I cannot hear them and do not want to. What I can hear are occasional coyotes and a constant chorus of "Baby the Rain Must Fall"[12] from the jukebox in the Snake Room next door, and if I were also to hear those dying voices, those Midwestern voices drawn to this lunar country for some unimaginable atavistic[13] rites, *rock of ages cleft for me,*[14] I think I would lose my own reason. Every now and then I imagine I hear a rattlesnake, but my husband says that it is a faucet, a paper rustling, the wind. Then he stands by a window, and plays a flashlight over the dry wash outside.

---

10 **antimatter:** matter composed of antiparticles of ordinary matter. The meeting of matter and antimatter in sufficient quantities would produce an explosion that could annihilate the world. During the Cold War, the U.S. Air Force paid for studies evaluating this potential.

11 **magma:** melted rock; magma

12 The No. 2 hit on the popular music charts in 1965, with the refrain "Wherever my heart leads me, baby I must go."

13 **atavistic:** primitive

14 The first line of a Christian hymn: "Rock of ages cleft [split open] for me, let me hide myself in thee."

7 What does it mean? It means nothing manageable. There is some sinister hysteria in the air out here tonight, some hint of the monstrous perversion to which any human idea can come. "I followed my own conscience." "I did what I thought was right." How many madmen have said it and meant it? How many murderers? Klaus Fuchs[15] said it, and the men who committed the Mountain Meadows Massacre[16] said it, and Alfred Rosenberg[17] said it. And, as we are rotely and rather presumptuously reminded by those who would say it now, Jesus said it. Maybe we have all said it, and maybe we have been wrong. Except on that most primitive level—our loyalties to those we love—what could be more arrogant than to claim the primacy of personal conscience? ("Tell me," a rabbi asked Daniel Bell[18] when he said, as a child, that he did not believe in God. "Do you think God cares?") At least some of the time, the world appears to me as a painting by Hieronymus Bosch;[19] were I to follow my conscience then, it would lead me out onto the desert with Marion Faye, out to where he stood in *The Deer Park* looking east to Los Alamos and praying, as if for rain, that it would happen:[20] "*. . . let it come and clear the rot and the stench and the stink, let it come for all of everywhere, just so it comes and the world stands clear in the white dead dawn.*"

8 Of course you will say that I do not have the right, even if I had the power, to inflict that unreasonable conscience upon you; nor do I want you to inflict your conscience, however reasonable, however enlightened, upon me. ("We must be aware of the dangers which lie in our most generous wishes," Lionel Trilling[21] once wrote. "Some paradox of our nature leads us, when once we have made our fellow men the objects of our enlightened interest, to go on to make them the objects of our pity, then of our wisdom, ultimately of our coercion.") That the ethic of conscience is intrinsically insidious seems scarcely a revelatory point, but it is one raised with increasing infrequency; even those who do raise it tend to *segue*[22] with troubling readiness into the quite contradictory position that the ethic of conscience is dangerous when it is "wrong," and admirable when it is "right."

---

15 Klaus Fuchs fled Germany to the United States, where he worked on the development of the atomic bomb during World War II. He moved to Great Britain to assume an important position at the British atomic energy center. He was convicted and imprisoned for providing atomic energy secrets to the Soviet Union.

16 The Mountain Meadows Massacre occurred in September 1857 in Utah. A group of 130 to 140 emigrants heading for California were attacked by Native Americans who were incited and joined by Mormons angry at the treatment they had received during their earlier trek across the continent. All but 17 children were massacred.

17 Alfred Rosenberg was a Nazi leader often called "The Grand Inquisitor of the Third Reich." He was hanged for war crimes in 1946.

18 Daniel Bell was a sociologist and was considered a leading intellectual following World War II.

19 Hieronymus Bosch (ca. 1450–ca. 1516), a Dutch painter of fantastic and hellish images.

20 Marion Faye is a character in the Hollywood novel *The Deer Park* by Norman Mailer. Los Alamos, New Mexico, was the site of atomic bomb testing. The "it" Faye refers to is the dropping of the atomic bomb.

21 Lionel Trilling (1905–1975), an eminent critic of literature and modern culture.

22 **segue:** move without interruption

9 You see I want to be quite obstinate about insisting that we have no way of knowing—beyond that fundamental loyalty to the social code—what is "right" and what is "wrong," what is "good" and what "evil." I dwell so upon this because the most disturbing aspect of "morality" seems to me to be the frequency with which the word now appears; in the press, on television, in the most perfunctory kinds of conversation. Questions of straightforward power (or survival) politics, questions of quite indifferent public policy, questions of almost anything: they are all assigned these factitious[23] moral burdens. There is something facile going on, some self-indulgence at work. Of course we would all like to "believe" in something, like to assuage our private guilts in public causes, like to lose our tiresome selves; like, perhaps, to transform the white flag of defeat at home into the brave white banner of battle away from home. And of course it is all right to do that; that is how, immemorially, things have gotten done. But I think it is all right only so long as we do not delude ourselves about what we are doing and why. It is all right only so long as we remember that all the *ad hoc* committees, all the picket lines, all the brave signatures in *The New York Times,* all the tools of agitprop[24] straight across the spectrum, do not confer upon anyone any *ipso facto*[25] virtue. It is all right only so long as we recognize that the end may or may not be expedient, may or may not be a good idea, but in any case has nothing to do with "morality." Because when we start deceiving ourselves into thinking not that we want something or need something, not that it is a pragmatic necessity for us to have it, but that it is a *moral imperative* that we have it, then is when we join the fashionable madmen, and then is when the thin whine of hysteria is heard in the land, and then is when we are in bad trouble. And I suspect we are already there.

Composing on Your Own

After you read, respond to Didion's ideas in writing. What questions did it raise about morality? What parts, if any, were confusing, and which parts were clear? What do you think her main point is about morality? Does she say what morality is, or does she suggest instead what it isn't? How do her views jibe with your views of morality? Write freely to answer these questions and any others that occur to you. You will be developing these ideas throughout the unit, so save your work for future use.

23 **factitious:** artificial
24 **agitprop:** political propaganda
25 ***ipso facto*:** just by the fact of it

Evaluating Writing: Student Draft
Morality

Following is a student draft on morality as seen through a historical example. It was written as a script for a multimedia presentation for a community event called Culture Clash, sponsored by the local library. This unedited draft is similar to the type of text in one of the multiple-choice sections of the AP® English Language and Composition test. This draft still needs work. As you read it, think about how it contributes to the conversation about morality. Later you will have the opportunity to suggest ways the writing might be improved.

(1) Throughout history, when a country reaches its peak, it believed it had to share its success with the rest of the world. (2) At no time was this truer than during the Age of Exploration, when Spain and other European nations stumbled upon the brave new world that was inhabited by Indians. (3) European morality was based on the philosophy of the Catholic church whereas Native Americans found their sense of morality to be rooted in nature and their ancestral tradition. (4) Spain and other European countries, under the pretense that they were saving the Native Americans by giving them eternal salvation, worked them to death searching for gold. (5) Entire Native American communities were destroyed, communities that had been based on sharing and compassion. (6) The Spanish believed themselves to be godly, yet they found themselves destroying civilizations that were built on a natural moral code born out of nature and the strength of community.

(7) Was Hernán Cortés a moral leader? (8) He destroyed an entire people and enslaved those who were remaining so that he could discover as much wealth as possible. (9) Even though we know the means by which he achieved "greatness," Cortés is immortalized in history because he expanded his nation's empire while gaining Catholic followers and discovering gold. (10) It is this characterization that is published in history books but not where we get the real low down. (11) Montezuma, the Aztec emperor, was one of the greatest kings in Aztec history, and he was deceived by Cortés, the Spanish Conquistador. (12) As such, Montezuma has gone down in history as one of the greatest fools compared Cortés. (13) Cortés goes down in history as a quintessence of greatness for burning his own ships to prevent his men from returning to Cuba and ultimately destroying an entire empire with his mere 150 men. (14) Montezuma has been immortalized as the fool that lost an empire of millions to 150 men. (15) While we think that morality comes from a standard, innate moral code, morality is a fluid abstract notion that changes based on who tells the story—because the stories we tell often become evidence to prove our morality.

What Do You Know?

The rest of Unit 8 will continue to explore how the situation in which an argument is presented influences the stylistic choices the writer makes. But before learning new skills and information, assess what you already know about the concepts in Unit 8 by reviewing and answering questions about the anchor text by Joan Didion and the student draft on morality. Don't worry if you find these questions challenging. Answering questions on a subject before formally learning about it is one way to deepen your understanding of new concepts. You may wish to work with a classmate as you try to answer the questions.

CLOSE READING: PROFESSIONAL TEXT

1. Give an example of a comparison the author makes in order to connect with her audience. How does this comparison advance her purpose?
2. How does Didion's use of anecdotes within her essay add to the strength of her argument about morality?
3. How do Didion's diction and syntax influence how she is perceived? How does Didion show her consideration of different perspectives and contexts?

EVALUATING WRITING: STUDENT DRAFT

1. What is the author's purpose for writing? Does the writer acknowledge different viewpoints that might exist within the audience—such as the audience's beliefs, values, and needs?
2. How does the writer make use of comparisons to enhance the argument?
3. How might the writer's syntax and word choice influence how her main claim is perceived?

Part 1

Considering Audience through Strategic Choices

Enduring Understanding and Skills

Part 1

Understand

Individuals write within a particular situation and make strategic writing choices based on that situation. (RHS-1)

Demonstrate

Explain how an argument demonstrates understanding of an audience's beliefs, values, or needs. (Reading 1.B)

Demonstrate an understanding of an audience's beliefs, values, or needs. (Writing 2.B)

Source: *AP® English Language and Composition Course and Exam Description*

Essential Question: How do the audience's beliefs, values, and needs inform stylistic choices regarding comparisons, syntax, and diction?

If a tree falls in the forest and no one is there to hear it, does it still make a sound? If a text has no reader, does it still have a message? Both of these questions center on the idea that someone must be on the receiving end for an event, or text, to come into existence and have meaning. However, author Joan Didion seems sure that the writer controls the meaning of the message. In an essay called "Why I Write," she said, "there's no getting around the fact that setting words on paper is the tactic of a secret bully, an invasion, an imposition of the writer's sensibility on the reader's most private space."

Yet the fact remains that communication requires a sender, a receiver, and a message, and all influence one another, despite any bullying an author claims to do. The audience has great influence on the message a writer presents and the way it is presented. As you write to communicate a message within a rhetorical situation, what you know about who will be reading it guides the stylistic choices you make. Your stylistic choices, in turn, shape your readers' responses. The impact of your writing is the result of accumulated stylistic choices—how you use comparisons, what words you choose (diction), and how you arrange those words (syntax). Each small choice, like each of the individual photos that make up the image on page 462, plays a role in communicating your message.

KEY TERMS

analogy	dynamic
anecdote	metaphor
bias	simile
comparison	syntax
diction	unique

1.1 Effective Comparisons in Context | RHS-1.K

Putting a point across effectively in an argument or essay often requires the writer to coax readers to think about the topic in a new way. One way writers can accomplish that goal is by illustrating relationships among situations or ideas using comparisons. The effectiveness of comparisons depends on a mutual understanding of them by the audience and the writer and their ability to advance the writer's purpose.

Making Comparisons

Writers use different kinds of **comparison**—the identification of similarities—to link their feelings or perceptions to something the reader will understand or relate to. Comparisons are a tool of everyday living—they play a key role in how humans make sense of the world. Authors can explain complex subjects by comparing their ideas to things or experiences their audience finds familiar; the audience then uses the familiar references as a bridge to understand something less familiar. For example, in 2020, a meme began circulating via social media during the period of social distancing restrictions due to the coronavirus pandemic. The meme, which read: "'The viral curve is flattening; we can start lifting restrictions now' is like saying, 'The parachute has slowed our rate of descent; we can take it off now.'" The comparison made the point that reopening the nation to business as usual before the pandemic was brought under control was dangerous. Readers understood that the comparison was apt because in both situations—shedding a parachute too soon or reopening a nation before it is safe to do so—the probable outcome is similar: needless harm and/or death.

Similes and Metaphors

Similes and metaphors are two of the most common types of comparisons writers use.

- A **simile** is a direct comparison of two different things using the word *like* or *as*.
  Anchor Text Example: *At least some of the time, the world appears to me* ***as*** *a painting by Hieronymus Bosch.*

If the reader does not share an understanding of Hieronymus Bosch's paintings, the comparison is useless. But for readers who do know the painter, vivid images come to mind of a weird, phantasmagoric, sometimes joyful, sometimes threatening universe. Think of how efficient the comparison between the world and such a painting is; then consider how many words it would take to create a verbal image that would conjure the same effect.

The Garden of Earthly Delights by Hieronymus Bosch

- A **metaphor** is an implied comparison of dissimilar things, stated without using the words *like* or *as*.
  Anchor Text Example: *Particularly out here tonight, in this country so ominous and terrible that to live in it is to live with antimatter, it is difficult to believe that 'the good' is a knowable quantity.*

The metaphor in this passage compares living in a desolate environment like Death Valley to experiencing "antimatter"—which is something that can potentially destroy matter. The comparison suggests that when our presumptions of morality are stripped away, our carefully constructed ideas about what is good and bad quickly dissipate into nothing. Harsh realities undermine our moral pieties and, as Didion points out, what is considered "the good" is no longer a "knowable quality." In comparing the "terrible and ominous" realities of Death Valley to the annihilating properties of antimatter, Didion quickly conveys her ideas about the subjectivity of morality without having to explain each conceptual step—she depends on her audience being able to make the link between two concepts.

Comparisons are not always explicitly stated; very often they must be inferred. For example, in his opening statement to the Senate Judiciary Committee in 2005 after President George W. Bush nominated him to be chief justice of the Supreme Court, then-Judge John Roberts used a metaphor implying a comparison between judges and umpires when he said, "... it's my job to call balls and strikes and not to pitch or bat." Sometimes the comparisons are between two things even more different than judges and umpires. For example, you might not make an immediate connection between such vastly different things as agricultural silos and shame. Yet the following cartoon makes that comparison clearly and simply: shame can accumulate and cause so much internal pressure that it needs to be vented like the over-pressurized contents of farm silos.

"Sometimes, son, the guilt inside builds up so much you have to vent the shame silo."

Analogies

An **analogy** is a direct comparison between one idea or thing and another idea or thing based on their being alike in some way. Even though the two things or ideas are distinctly different, they share a key similarity or similarities. Metaphors and similes are both tools writers can use to draw an analogy.

Consider the famous line from the classic film, *Forrest Gump*: "My mama always said life was like a box of chocolates. You never know what you're gonna get." *Life* and *a box of chocolates* are two very different things, obviously, yet they are comparable because they both involve making decisions without knowing the outcome. When you choose a chocolate from the box, you are unsure of the filling. The uncertainty about the filling of a chocolate parallels the feeling of uncertainty about life experiences. In both situations, people make choices without really knowing how they will turn out. The analogy uses something that nearly everyone can relate to—choosing a chocolate—to explain another, much larger idea—having to make choices in life.

In another passage from "Why I Write," Didion compares writing to composing a photo using camera angles. Notice that she opens with a simile but then adds more details to create a fully developed analogy.

> To shift the structure of a sentence alters the meaning of that sentence, as definitely and inflexibly as the position of a camera alters the meaning of the object photographed. Many people know about camera angles now, but not so many know about sentences. The arrangement of the words matters, and the arrangement you want can be found in the picture in your mind. The picture dictates the arrangement.

Didion creates an analogy that compares positioning a camera to capture an image to the ways an author uses words to capture an image in her mind. To say that two things are analogous is to say that they are comparable in *some relevant* way. Many analogies are used to explain or clarify a difficult, obscure, or abstract concept by relating it to something that is easier to understand or more concrete for the audience.

For example, recall Didion's vivid analogy between writing and bullying: "there's no getting around the fact that setting words on paper is the tactic of a secret bully, an invasion, an imposition of the writer's sensibility on the reader's most private space." She explains one intellectual and abstract concept—the relationship between a writer and reader—by using a vivid physical concept—bullying and invasion—and in so doing puts a unique and violent gloss on the relationship. By comparing the act of writing to bullying, Didion suggests that writing can be manipulative; the writer's words enter the mind of the reader and have the potential to change the way he or she thinks.

Less poetically, analogies can also be used in a line of reasoning. In Unit 3, you read about a deductive pattern of reasoning that begins with a premise and leads to a logical conclusion. In an argument by analogy, the deductive logic, also called a *syllogism*, is meant to prove that because two things are similar, what is true of one is also true of the other.

Here is how it might look:

1. *A* is similar to *B* in certain (known) respects.

2. A has the feature X.

3. Therefore, B is likely to have the feature X.

For example:

> Jupiter's moon Europa is similar to Earth because they both have an atmosphere that contains oxygen.
>
> Earth supports life.
>
> Therefore, Europa might have life on it.

Note the qualification of the conclusion with the word *might*. Just because two things are similar in some ways does not mean they are similar in all ways.

Comparisons work when two things are related in some logical way. If a writer fails to show the reader how two things or ideas are connected, the comparison fails. If the comparison is overly obvious, the writing may seem simplistic or too obvious. Be aware that some analogies, similes, and metaphors are overused and considered clichés. Writers may also fall into the trap of using *false analogies*, which assume that because two things are similar in some ways, they must be similar in all ways. You may be familiar with such dubious comparisons in advertising; the young man wearing a certain brand of jeans is compared to a famous rock star, or the flavor of certain type of ice cream is compared to experiencing heaven. These overwrought comparisons cause readers or viewers to doubt the underlying validity of the message. In another example, many contemporary writers like making analogies between people's minds (or brains) and computers. Not only has this analogy become somewhat clichéd, but it is also simplistic and fails to take into account the complexity of the human mind, which in addition to computing data, is also creative, analytical, tuned in to emotions, able to abstract, self-aware, and able to work on many levels beyond what can be processed by a machine. For instance, a computer could never recognize the expression of a loved one whose feelings you have just hurt through a careless choice of words.

Anecdotes

An **anecdote** is a short, interesting story about a real incident or person. For example, Didion begins to lay out her ideas on morality in paragraph 2 of her essay, using a brief anecdote about the aftermath of the drunk driving accident. Although not technically a comparison like the simile, metaphor, and analogy, an anecdote gives readers a real-life event to compare to a general concept.

Writers often use anecdotes to shift or challenge the audience's perception of a subject or situation, as Didion does with her analogy between writing and invasion. Often, the purpose of analogies is to appeal to readers' emotions or leave the reader with questions—questions that a good writer will investigate, explore, and sometimes resolve by the end of the piece. In writing, an anecdote may

- present a hypothetical situation that describes a concrete example of key ideas
- compare different perspectives about a subject
- make the argument more personal or more emotional
- connect with the audience by providing insight into the writer's personal experience

Didion is known for her use of storytelling within her arguments. When exploring wrongs in society or commenting on political corruption, she includes anecdotes as evidence or to help develop her argument. Consider again the story Didion shares in the second paragraph of "On Morality." She provides a short anecdote (the drunk driving story) that emphasizes why she values particulars, not just abstract ideas like *morality*. Here, she actually acknowledges the power of the anecdote: anecdotes allow writers to speak in *particulars*. Her argument is not about the nurse's husband who stayed with the boy's body after the car accident. Instead, her argument is about morality, and this anecdote is a specific example of morality in the real world.

Purposes and Effects of Comparisons

While all of the techniques above serve the same general purpose—to compare explicitly or implicitly—they do so in different ways. The differences determine which strategy will be most appropriate for the writer's argument, message, and audience. Similes and metaphors are especially useful when they are concrete and describe a situation, experience, feeling, or entity that cannot otherwise be communicated with accuracy.

The chart below shows why a writer might use a comparison to make an argument resonate with the audience.

Purposes of comparison are . . .
▪ to create a body of associations in order to amplify a point ▪ to create a richer, layered reading ▪ to convey complex meaning in a few words ▪ to make a connection between the subject and a larger context ▪ to make an abstraction more concrete and accessible to an audience ▪ to increase emotional response
Possible effects of comparisons are that the . . .
▪ audience feels specific emotions ▪ audience relates ideas from previous texts to the ideas in the current text ▪ the writer connects with a larger or more specific audience ▪ writer connects to audience by expressing old ideas in new ways and vice versa ▪ writer's attitude or perspective on a subject is conveyed

Table 8-1

Using the chart above, consider how the purpose of a comparison influences the effect or meaning of a sentence from Martin Luther King Jr.'s "I Have a Dream" speech, which was delivered on August 28, 1963, from the steps of the Lincoln Memorial to a crowd of 250,000. The speech was also broadcast on all three major networks of the time.

> No, no, we are not satisfied, and we will not be satisfied until justice rolls down like waters and righteousness like a mighty stream.

You might generate the following commentary about the significance of the comparison to the message.

> King compares "justice" to rolling waters and "righteousness" to a "mighty stream." In this comparison, King suggests that justice and righteousness are powerful, natural, and inevitable; just as one cannot keep back a river, laws that promote racial inequality cannot hold back the human spirit. In addition, King, who was an experienced minister, purposely echoes soaring Biblical language to increase the emotional response in the audience. Many in King's

audience would make the connection between King's language and the biblical story of Noah's Ark, in which God flooded the world to punish humanity's misdeeds but saved Noah and his family because of their righteousness.

Whether reading another writer's argument or evaluating your own, ask the following questions to evaluate comparisons.

Questions to Evaluate Effectiveness of Comparison
1. What are the audience's beliefs, needs, and values that the writer is trying to reach through this comparison?
2. Why might the writer want to appeal to this particular audience?
3. What are the relationships among the speaker, audience, and subject?
4. What abstraction is made more concrete, and is the abstraction characterized positively or negatively?
5. What emotion is evoked with this comparison?

Table 8-2

Shared Understandings

A writer's comparisons must be both shared with and understood by the audience to fulfill the writer's purposes. As you saw earlier, without knowing about the paintings of Hieronymus Bosch, the reader would not be able to take away meaning from Didion's statement that the world appeared to her sometimes as one of his paintings.

Following is another example that makes a comparison to a perhaps more popular and widely known example than the Bosch paintings. It comes from Texas Governor Ann Richards's keynote address at the 1988 Democratic National Convention, in which she noted she was only the second female in more than 150 years to address the convention.

> Twelve years ago, Barbara Jordan, another Texas woman, Barbara made the keynote address to this convention, and two women in a hundred and sixty years is about par for the course. But if you give us a chance, we can perform. After all, Ginger Rogers did everything that Fred Astaire did. She just did it backwards in high heels.

In this brief excerpt, Richards points out the general lack of opportunity for women that is a factor in American politics. First, she relates her own invitation to serve as the DNC's keynote speaker to that of the last woman invited to deliver the keynote, Barbara Jordan—the only other woman in U.S. history to serve the function. She goes on to make a larger point about the general competence of women by comparing the male and female genders with the famed dance team of Fred Astaire and Ginger Rogers. Both Rogers and Astaire were gifted, highly trained dancers. But as Richards notes, Rogers had to do the same complicated steps Astaire did, with the added difficulty of moving backwards while wearing high-heeled, no doubt uncomfortable shoes. Richards knows that she might make some people defensive if she immediately lectures her audience about gender inequalities. So, instead of pointing out that highly competent women often have to overcome gender discrimination to be successful, she eases into her subject matter by wrapping her main claim inside a joke that humorously alludes to the many difficulties women face. Often, humor relaxes an audience and puts them in a positive frame of mind, which makes them more receptive to a writer's ideas—the audience can laugh together at a shared joke. With the help of her colorful comparison, Richards is able to move into a speech about the inequities and hard work that affect the lives of women and families in America.

> **Remember:** Writers may make comparisons (similes, metaphors, analogies, or anecdotes) in an attempt to relate to an audience. Effective comparisons must be shared and understood by the audience to advance the writer's purpose. (RHS-1.K)

1.1 Checkpoint

Close Reading: Professional Text
Review Didion's essay "On Morality." Then complete the open response activity and answer the multiple-choice questions that follow.

1. On separate paper, make a copy of the chart below. For each column complete the stem with specific details related to Didion's essay. Choose two of the following comparisons to help focus your analysis or choose your own example from the essay: the desert, childhood promises, Jayhawkers, bodies fallen in the hole, Faith Community Church.

The purpose of the comparison is to . . .	The possible effects of the comparison are . . .

2. Answer all the questions from Table 8-2 on page 477 about your chosen examples.

3. In context, the "social code" Didion mentions in the first sentence of paragraph 4 refers to
   (A) the promise of cautionary tales
   (B) wagon-train morality
   (C) immorality and amorality
   (D) particulars not abstractions
   (E) conventional beliefs

4. In the final paragraph of "On Morality," Didion employs the metaphor of "the white flag of defeat" to
   (A) connect with readers by acknowledging her own unjust acts
   (B) reassure readers that their mistakes are forgivable and common
   (C) emphasize that claims of morality often mask selfish motives
   (D) succumb to the notion that the times change and therefore morality is harder to define
   (E) exploit the common delusion that we are innately moral

5. Toward the end of the passage, the author uses the phrase "monstrous perversion" to refer to
   (A) innate immorality
   (B) decisions made in the name of conscience
   (C) tamped down self-righteousness
   (D) primacy of personal conscience
   (E) conscience that succumbs to reason

Evaluating Writing: Student Draft

Reread the student draft about Cortés and Montezuma on page 468. Then complete the following open response activities and answer the multiple-choice questions.

1. How does the comparison between these leaders support the writer's larger point?

2. Write a short response in which you develop a comparison between two historical leaders showing that historical respect is or is not measured by one's morality. For example, you may choose to compare James Buchanan and Abraham Lincoln. Both men go down in history books with the stature of presidents, but Buchanan is remembered for his proslavery agenda, whereas Lincoln, who succeeded Buchanan, oversaw a Civil War that eventually ended slavery.

3. The writer is considering adding the following sentence after sentence 3.

While it is true that the Aztecs, one of the tribes exploited by Spain and other European countries, sacrificed people from other tribes they conquered or destroyed, their sacrifices did not compare to the Europeans' mass-slaughter and the force with which they acquired the land of the Native Americans and claimed the New World.

Should the writer make this revision?

(A) No, this detail is better placed in paragraph 2.

(B) No, this detail is redundant and therefore not necessary.

(C) Yes, the new information helps the writer show that the Aztecs committed many immoral acts.

(D) Yes, this detail clarifies the differing degrees to which the Aztecs and Cortés acted immorally.

(E) Yes, this detail offers a counterargument that will be refuted in paragraph 2.

Composing on Your Own

Joan Didion uses the "particulars" of specific anecdotes and examples to develop her definition of the abstract concept of morality. Review what you wrote after your first reading of Didion's essay. Choose a single abstract or universal concept—including morality if that draws your interest more than others—as the focus of an essay that you will develop with the techniques from this unit, starting with analogy, anecdote, metaphor, and simile. Realize that you, like Didion, live in turbulent times. The issues have changed, but there are still mass protests, economic hardship, systemic racism and sexism, divided government, and gaping wealth differences. To focus your thoughts and narrow your topic, choose a context, purpose, and audience to shape your rhetorical situation or create one of your own. Write down the choices you make and the concept you choose to define.

Exigences/Contexts
▪ An invitation from *American Scholar* to write a thoughtful piece relevant to today's times ▪ Witnessing an example of injustice ▪ A student-created TED-type talk on matters of urgent concern to young people
Purposes
▪ Explore your best understanding of an abstract concept ▪ Hold someone accountable for unjust behavior and prevent it in the future ▪ Engage listeners on an intriguing topic with the hope of reorienting attitudes
Audiences
▪ Well-read students, teachers, and other adults ▪ Readers of a local newspaper or members of a local government council ▪ Students, parents, teachers, school administrators, and community members

Once you have established the boundaries of your rhetorical situation, make a chart on separate paper like the one below to gather evidence to support your definition and your argument. Try to develop a variety of imaginative examples, evidence, and anecdotes to support your definition. Didion, for example, uses these anecdotes: "diving to retrieve bodies in an underground pool" or "staying with a dying boy to keep him from being eaten by coyotes." Save your completed chart for future use.

Abstract concept to define	
Analogies	
Anecdotes	
Similes	
Metaphors	

1.2 Diction and Syntax in Crafting Argument | RHS-1.L RHS-1.M

Writers know that the words they choose and the order in which they arrange those words influence how an audience perceives them—even to the point of leading the audience to agree or disagree with an argument. Bias seeps through in word choice especially, and a writer's bias may alienate certain audiences. For these reasons, writers choose words and their arrangement strategically.

Diction

Every word counts in an argument. A writer's word choice—**diction**—can serve to clarify or muddy the meaning (or to add no meaningful substance at all). For example, in May 1920, one small word in a speech delivered by presidential nominee Warren G. Harding kicked off a political and grammatical controversy. In the speech, Harding declared, "America's present need is not heroics but healing; not nostrums [fake remedies] but normalcy; not revolution but restoration...." Harding's use of the word *normalcy* sparked political pushback from people who wondered if "normalcy" meant a return to the low wages, high taxes, and unemployment of the earlier part of the century. It led to public ridicule and diminished credibility on another level as well—from newspaper writers and editors, who assumed Harding simply hadn't known any better than to substitute a made-up word to take the place of *normality*. The *Boston Globe* went so far as to insert *normality* in place of *normalcy* in their reprint of Harding's speech. (It turned out that *normalcy* was in fact a real word that had existed for a long time; it simply wasn't used as often as *normality*. Since those days, *normalcy* has moved into relatively common usage, while *normality* is used less often.) This example shows the power of a single word to complicate rather than clarify a message and to negatively affect credibility.

Words also gain power when they arouse the five senses. Sensory words help readers see, hear, feel, taste, and touch a subject, and the more they can imagine experiencing what the writer describes, the more engaged they are likely to be in the writer's argument.

Diction, however, describes more than just individual word choices. Word choices have a cumulative effect and work together to help establish a writer's voice. If you remember having been told to use your "inside voice" when you were a child, you know that certain voices are appropriate for certain contexts and not for others. Diction, one aspect of voice, is sometimes categorized according to those contexts: for example, *academic diction* is the word choice you make in formal, academic writing; *poetic diction* is the choice of more flowery words to evoke feelings; *informal diction* is the word choice you use in relaxed contexts; it includes slang and colloquialisms. Consider the same idea expressed using some different categories of diction:

> **Academic diction:** The temperature in Death Valley had reached 102 degrees by 3 p.m.
>
> **Poetic diction:** The heat strengthened throughout the morning and by afternoon pressed down its merciless hand on the landscape.
>
> **Informal diction:** It was hot this morning but it was way hotter this afternoon.

Each diction has its place; the rhetorical situation guides a writer's word choices and diction.

Diction and Bias The words a writer chooses to use in an argument can reflect personal values or **bias**—the writer's personal prejudices or preferences about a topic. Writers may reveal their biases by leaving out or taking for granted certain facts or information or using words loaded with connotation, vague language, generalizations, or stereotypes. If an audience notices bias in the writer's word choice, they may be less likely to find the writer credible and accept the argument.

For example, take a look at the following excerpt from the film *Wall Street.* In one pivotal scene millionaire corporate raider Gordon Gekko addresses a crowd of angry shareholders at Teldar Paper, a company he is attempting to acquire through a hostile takeover. Here is the end of that speech:

> The point is, ladies and gentlemen, that greed—for lack of a better word—is good. Greed is right. Greed works. Greed clarifies, cuts through, and captures the essence of the evolutionary spirit. Greed, in all of its forms—greed for life, for money, for love, for knowledge—has marked the upward surge of mankind. And greed . . . will not only save Teldar Paper, but that other manufacturing corporation called the USA. Thank you very much.

Notice the powerful, positive adjectives the speaker applies to the word *greed*: it's "right," it "works," it "captures the essence of the evolutionary spirit." It will not only save the shareholders' company—it will save the entire nation. Notice as well that Gordon Gekko uses the gender-biased term *mankind* instead of the gender-neutral term *humankind*. Also think about all the things Gordon Gekko does not mention in this speech. For example, how might his takeover of Teldar Paper affect the company's employees? If you are someone who sees "greed" in its more familiar light—as the motivation for inequality, exploitation, environmental degradation, and compromise of principles—the words Gekko uses with positive connotations would likely alarm you and set your mind against accepting his argument. (See Unit 6, Part 2.)

Syntax

While diction refers to the selection of individual words, **syntax** refers to the grouping and arranging of words into clauses, sentences, and paragraphs. The way a writer chooses to group words, like the specific words the writer chooses, influences how likely the audience will be to accept or reject the argument.

Consider this excerpt from Joan Didion's essay "Why I Write," which provides some context for her idea of writing as an act of bullying.

> [Writing is] an aggressive, even hostile act. You can disguise its aggressiveness all you want with veils of subordinate clauses and qualifiers and tentative subjunctives, with ellipses and evasions—with the whole manner of intimating rather than claiming, of alluding rather than stating—but there's no getting around the fact that setting words on paper is the tactic of a secret bully, an invasion, an imposition of the writer's sensibility on the reader's most private space.

The excerpt above consists of just two sentences: one short and one very long. The short first sentence grabs the reader's attention with a declarative statement that signals the reader to ask why or in what way writing is an aggressive, even hostile act. The second sentence vividly supplies the answer. It also subtly supplies humor in that its form follows its function; at the same time Didion is describing the "veils of subordinate clauses and qualifiers and tentative subjunctives," she is creating those structures in the essay itself. At the same time she is saying that writers evade and allude rather than making direct statements, she provides an example of a writer—herself—doing just that.

Syntax and Sentence Length One aspect of syntax is sentence length. Compare the syntax in the following three statements about the fate of polar bears in an era of climate change. When reading the following examples, notice how sentence length influences the effectiveness of the author's argument, and pay particular attention to how sentence length mirrors the descriptive qualities within each sentence.

Example 1: Polar bears are losing their habitat. The sea ice is dwindling. Soon there will be no polar bears. They'll be extinct by 2050. It will be a loss for the planet.

Example 2: Due to enormous changes in habitat involving a precipitous loss of sea ice, polar bears will soon find themselves without a place to live, hunt, or raise their cubs. As a result of this sad phenomenon, many researchers believe that polar bears will be extinct by 2050, another huge and dangerous loss to our climate-challenged planet.

Example 3: It paddled closer, close enough now we could see it clearly, its paws working feverishly beneath the surface of the water, its long neck straining to keep its head above the surface, its eyes fixed eagerly on the steel grail ahead of it, its small ears flat against the side of its head. A passing ice floe provided welcome respite and the bear took advantage, clambering out of the ocean, its fur thick with water. It shook itself briefly, walked from one end of the floe to the other to stay level with the ship as the ice drifted past, then plunged back into the water.—Kieran Mulvaney, *The Great White Bear: A Natural and Unnatural History of the Polar Bear*

Example 1 uses short sentences, all about the same length, and they all follow the same structure—subject–verb—almost like a list or an outline of factual data. A single short sentence amidst longer sentences can disrupt the rhythm and flow of the writing and powerfully call attention to the idea in the short sentence. In addition, a string of short sentences can be effective for hammering home some strong points. However, to many readers, the short sentences in Example 1 may have the stilted, redundant cadence of a text written for a grade-school student. The language lacks descriptive words and phrases to engage the reader; beyond the bare facts, there is almost no language that evokes an emotional response or helps the reader picture the subject matter. The first example gives facts in simple sentences, but it does little else.

Example 2 consists of two longer sentences (28 words in the first sentence and 27 in the second), and they too follow a similar structure—both begin with this pattern: prepositional phrase–subject–verb. These sentences relate most of the same information as Example 1, but the writer smoothly combines the information into two sentences and includes a wider variety of descriptive words—such as "precipitous," "sad," "huge," "dangerous"—that connect emotionally with the reader. The combination of longer sentences with more description creates a structure with more flow and nuance than Example 1.

Example 3 has three sentences of mixed lengths—53 words, 22 words, and 31 words. The first sentence—the longest by far—reflects the polar bear's struggle as it tries to catch up with the boat; the repeated and parallel phrases "its paws . . . its long neck . . . its eyes . . . its small ears . . ." build tension through their repetition. When the bear reaches the safety of the ice floe, the author uses a short sentence to pause the forward narrative flow, which mirrors the bear's momentary respite. The level of detail provided also shows the author's intent observation and deep experience with his subject. Unlike the first two examples, Example 3 does not include statistical data and instead opts for a narrative that interests the reader in the bear's struggle—the reader becomes emotionally invested in the bear's survival. The crisp descriptions and varied sentence length clearly convey the actions of the bear, which helps make the reader more receptive to the author's argument.

Notice how the syntax in the examples matches the descriptive style of the writing. While in the first example the author uses short sentences to mostly recount dry facts, the third example uses varied sentence length to match the movements of the bear. Good writing depends on using sentences of varying lengths: some short, some longer, and some in between. Most important, syntax should reflect and enhance the ideas the writer is communicating.

The way a writer orchestrates sentences—whether long, complex sentences, a series of rhetorical questions, or some other form—influences the way the message is sent to and received by the audience. These structures and patterns are most effective when they serve one or more of the following purposes:

- clarifying meaning
- establishing or disrupting sentence rhythm
- evoking specific emotions relevant to the specific audience, occasion, and message
- emphasizing a point or manipulating the audience's attention
- establishing cause-and-effect or compare-contrast relationships

Punctuation and Syntax Punctuation is an integral part of the rhythm and cadence of the writer's message. Writers who use punctuation effectively can exercise great control over meaning and tone in their writing. For example, a writer's punctuation might serve to emphasize the syntax of a description, calling out a modifier or a phrase.

> **Original sentence**: The tired, hungry, and frantic polar bear paddled for his life to get to the ice floe.
>
> **Revised syntax:** The polar bear, tired, hungry, and frantic, paddled for his life to get to the ice floe.
>
> **Punctuation to offset modifiers**: The polar bear—tired, hungry, and frantic—paddled for his life to get to the ice floe.

Punctuation such as semicolons can establish parallel relationships between subjects, such as cause-effect relationships.

> The ice melted; the habitat shrank. The habitat shrank; polar bears starved.

Syntax and Patterns and Repetition Syntax applies not only to the arrangement of words within a sentence but also to the arrangement of sentences within a longer passage. Repetition and patterns are especially communicative. Consider again a passage by Joan Didion from "Why I Write," this time with a little more context.

(1) Grammar is a piano I play by ear, since I seem to have been out of school the year the rules were mentioned. (2) All I know about grammar is its infinite power. (3) To shift the structure of a sentence alters the meaning of that sentence, as definitely and inflexibly as the position of a camera alters the meaning of the object photographed. (4) Many people know about camera angles now, but not so many know about sentences. (5) The arrangement of the words matters, and the arrangement you want can be found in the picture in your mind. (6) The picture dictates the arrangement. (7) The picture dictates whether this will be a sentence with or without clauses, a sentence that ends hard or a dyingfall sentence, long or short, active or passive. (8) The picture tells you how to arrange the words and the arrangement of the words tells you, or tells me, what's going on in the picture.

Note especially the patterns and repetitions in sentences 5–8:

(5) The arrangement of the words matters, and the arrangement you want can be found in the picture in your mind. (20 words)

(6) The picture dictates the arrangement. (5 words)

(7) The picture dictates whether this will be a sentence with or without clauses, a sentence that ends hard or a dyingfall sentence, long or short, active or passive. (28 words)

(8) The picture tells you how to arrange the words and the arrangement of the words tells you, or tells me, what's going on in the picture. (26 words)

All the repeated words are underlined. The underlined words—*arrangement, pictures, words, sentences*—offer an at-a-glance outline of the four key ideas that are interwoven within this paragraph. Didion repeatedly stresses that the *arrangement* of *words* is important, because it is the way a writer transfers the thoughts—or *pictures*—in her head into *sentences* that connect with the reader. By repeating key words, Didion keeps the reader focused on her main idea. In addition, you might note that each sentence starts the same way, three of them with a key idea: the picture. Sentence 5 starts with another key idea: arrangement. Sentence 7, explaining whether a sentence will be long or short, is the longest sentence. Its length, however, would not really even be noticed except that it is preceded by such a short sentence. Each sentence depends on those around it for its effectiveness. Notice that the repetition of words is not redundant; Didion still uses a variety of descriptive words and sentence structure, and she only repeats key words to emphasize her ideas.

Remember: Writers' choices regarding syntax and diction influence how the writer is perceived by an audience and may influence the degree to which an audience accepts an argument. Word choice may reflect writers' biases and may affect their credibility with a particular audience. (RHS-1.L, M)

1.2 Checkpoint

Close Reading: Professional Text

Review Joan Didion's essay "On Morality." Then complete the following open response activities and answer the multiple-choice questions.

1. Analyze the syntax and diction in this passage from the end of the essay by completing the second column of the chart below on separate paper.

> Of course we would all like to "believe" in something, like to assuage our private guilts in public causes, like to lose our tiresome selves; like, perhaps, to transform the white flag of defeat at home into the brave white banner of battle away from home. And of course it is all right to do that; that is how, immemorially, things have gotten done. But I think it is all right only so long as we do not delude ourselves about what we are doing and why. It is all right only so long as we remember that all the *ad hoc* committees, all the picket lines, all the brave signatures in *The New York Times,* all the tools of agitprop straight across the spectrum, do not confer upon anyone any *ipso facto* virtue. It is all right only so long as we recognize that the end may or may not be expedient, may or may not be a good idea, but in any case has nothing to do with "morality." Because when we start deceiving ourselves into thinking not that we want something or need something, not that it is a pragmatic necessity for us to have it, but that it is a *moral imperative* that we have it, then is when we join the fashionable madmen, and then is when the thin whine of hysteria is heard in the land, and then is when we are in bad trouble. And I suspect we are already there.

Diction

(a) What descriptive words or phrases have strong connotations, and what connotations do they have?

(b) What words appeal vividly to the senses?

(c) What do think she means by "brave" signatures?

(d) How might you describe the category of diction Didion uses? (See page 482.) Give examples.

Syntax

(a) Identify places where Didion uses repetition to emphasize her ideas. Explain what ideas she is trying to emphasize.

(b) Give three examples of how Didion uses different sentence lengths in the paragraph to emphasize her ideas.

(c) Explain why "believe" and "morality" are in quotation marks.

2. Write a paragraph of rhetorical analysis describing Didion's diction and syntax and explain the effect of the items you noted in your response to question 1 on your understanding of the essay.

3. In paragraph 6 the author uses the phrase "unimaginable atavistic rites" primarily to
   - (A) provide an example of people searching for meaning and comfort in an environment of primal darkness
   - (B) emphasize that she disagrees with religious prayers and songs because morality transcends religion
   - (C) restate her assumption that human morality can be defined differently by each person
   - (D) compare her own definition of morality to the socially acceptable understanding of morality
   - (E) suggest that notions or morality evolve with the social code as societal trends change

4. In the context of the passage, the writer's use of "cautionary tales" serves to
   - (A) warn others about the dangers of using morality as a defense of immoral actions
   - (B) connect with the audience by sharing her own childhood stories about morality
   - (C) suggest that our founding sense of morality comes from the concepts we are taught as children
   - (D) refute her audience's teachings on morality in order to alter their viewpoint on the subject
   - (E) expose that bogus values in cautionary tales have no merit or influence on individuals or society

5. In stating that she "distrusts" the word "morality" more every day, the author establishes herself as
   - (A) an amoral if not immoral person
   - (B) an individual who trusts almost no one
   - (C) a whimsical and satirical person
   - (D) a person with a critical and analytic viewpoint
   - (E) a person with fixed and unchanging ideals

Evaluating Writing: Student Draft

Reread the student draft on morality. Then complete the open response activities and answer the multiple-choice questions.

1. Study the following sentences from the student passage:

> (1) Throughout history, when a country reaches its peak, it believed it had to share its success with the rest of the world. (2) At no time was this truer than during the Age of Exploration, when Spain and other European nations stumbled upon the brave new world that was inhabited by Indians. (3) European morality was based on the philosophy of the Catholic church whereas Native Americans found their sense of morality to be rooted in nature and their ancestral tradition.

On separate paper, revise one or all of the sentences using the prompts below and evaluate the changes.

- Change key words that affect the tone of the excerpt. Then explain how changing these words changes the tone and the way the message might be received.
- Change the structure of the sentences. You might consider adding questions, dashes for emphasis, or longer or shorter sentences. When you have finished, write a brief paragraph explaining how changing the structure changed the tone and the way you think the message might be received.

2. The student writer is considering revising sentence 1 (below) to give it more formality and precision that specifically conveys the claim.

Throughout history, when a country reaches its peak, it believed it had to share its success with the rest of the world.

Which of the following phrases would best accomplish this goal?

(A) (as it is now)

(B) Throughout history, there have been many examples of clashing cultures and the rise of nations.

(C) Throughout history, when a country becomes successful, it often feels entitled to impose its culture and values on other societies.

(D) Textbooks tell us only one side of a complicated history, so it is very important to read with a critical eye.

(E) It is commonly presumed that a country's duty is to tell other countries what to do based on their own definitions of success.

3. The writer wants to avoid revealing any potential biases in sentences 7 and 8 (below) while still maintaining an appropriate line of reasoning connecting the evidence and the claim.

(7) Was Cortés a moral leader? (8) He destroyed an entire people and enslaved those who were remaining so that he could discover as much wealth as possible.

Which of the following versions of sentence 7 accomplishes this goal?

(A) (as it is now)

(B) Remove sentence 7.

(C) Though he found riches for his country, Cortés was an immoral leader who deserves no place in history.

(D) There are instances where one has to sacrifice the sense of morality to ensure the greater good.

(E) Though he is remembered as a successful leader, historians question Cortés's moral conscience.

Composing on Your Own

Referring to the chart on page 481 you completed for Composing on Your Own, write a first draft of your definition of an abstract concept. Use whatever ideas from your chart work well, but you likely will not use everything. Also, as you write, new ideas will come to mind; work those in when they help make your point.

After you have finished your first draft, read it over, evaluating your diction and syntax. Ask yourself these questions:

- Where could you use a stronger or clearer word?
- Do the connotations of your words reflect your ideas?
- Do any of your words convey an overly biased perspective?
- Did you use a mix of short, medium, and long sentences?
- Do the structures of your sentences enhance and help communicate your ideas?
- Where might repetition or other patterns enhance your meaning?
- Have you used punctuation to effectively convey your ideas?
- What other revisions can you make to improve your draft?

Make revisions as warranted based on your evaluation of your diction and syntax and save your work for future use.

1.3 Unique and Dynamic Audiences | RHS-1.N

Although writers make every effort to understand the values, needs, beliefs, and backgrounds of their audiences, audiences are never made up of only one kind of people from identical backgrounds with identical beliefs. For example, some in Warren G. Harding's audience might not have agreed with the press when they ridiculed Harding for his poor public speaking, disregarding it completely when they voted for him—or for his opponent—for president. Some might even have agreed with the press but decided to vote for Harding nonetheless because other criteria related to their values and beliefs were more important in making that decision than his public speaking. Further, some in the audience may have been initially embarrassed for Harding when the press pointed out what they believed to be an error in Harding's speech but later learned that it was after all a legitimate word.

Audiences are **unique**—that is, different audiences can be identified by generally shared beliefs, values, and backgrounds, as you have been doing when you have considered your audience as part of your rhetorical situation. In different rhetorical situations, you will have different audiences. However, while audiences may generally share beliefs, each member in an audience does not share the exact same beliefs as other members. Common interests and values may unite people into a group, but people still retain distinct differences. Consider the speech of Governor Richards at the Democratic National Convention. Richards knew that Democrats would likely be generally receptive to a speech that focused on the inequities women face. But she also knew that this receptiveness would not be universal; some members of her audience would be more receptive than others. As a result, Richards decided to introduce her subject matter with humor, to help create a bridge for those more reluctant members in her audience. Imagine how differently the audience would respond to Richards' speech if she used the scolding language—"How dare you!"—of Thunberg's speech in Unit 1.

Even audiences that share most values, beliefs, and backgrounds can change over time. That is, they are **dynamic**, evolving in their views and beliefs as they learn new information, have new experiences, and consider different perspectives. Writing that endures over time reaches audiences very different from the original audience, and its endurance is partly owing to the acknowledgment that audiences are dynamic. Writers try to use evidence, organization, and language that carefully considers the multiplicity of perspectives of the audience as well as the evolving contexts in which the argument may be presented.

Changing Contexts

Consider the context at the time the Declaration of Independence was written. Take a look at the edits in the excerpt reprinted below. The writers labored over every word and phrase to ensure that the message not only reflected their intention but also considered the perspectives of the other colonies. For example, during the revision process, the committee chose not to mention slavery or any derivative of that term directly. Their reason? They feared that if the document took a specific antislavery stance they might lose colonial unity.

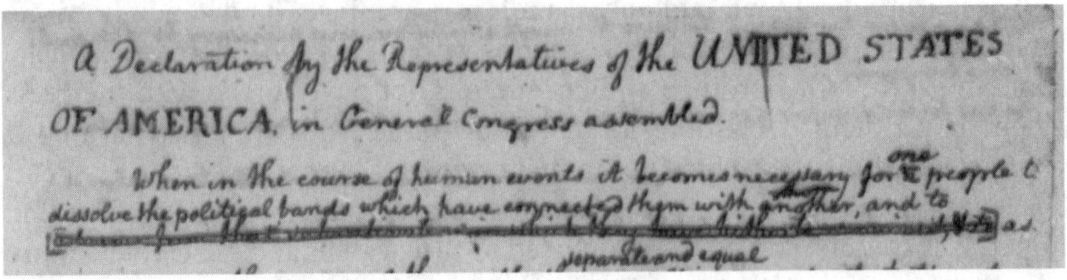
A Declaration by the Representatives of the UNITED STATES OF AMERICA, in General Congress assembled.
When in the course of human events it becomes necessary for one people to dissolve the political bands which have connected them with another, and to
separate and equal

The most important of Benjamin Franklin's edits to the draft involved only a few words, but it changed the entire thrust of the argument. He crossed out the last three words of Jefferson's observation that "We hold these truths to be *sacred and undeniable*." In their place he inserted the words that now complete the famous phrase: "We hold these truths to be *self-evident*..." According to Franklin, the word *sacred* implied that the message that "all men are created equal" was religious in nature. With the removal of the word *sacred*, the argument was no longer religious but human, even scientific by virtue of its truths being objectively observable. Removing the religious sentiment helped promote the idea of unity through something other than religion. Indeed, the Declaration of Independence inspired the colonists to unite under a common political ideology, which in turn would strengthen their resolve toward independence and eventually help them gain foreign alliance and break free of British rule.

The revisions to the original draft of the Declaration of Independence reflect the writers' careful consideration of the perspectives, contexts, and needs of multiple audiences—the colonists who supported independence, the colonists who opposed independence, potential foreign allies, their friends and family in Great Britain, and the British king and parliament. During the revolutionaries' process of mobilizing support, each of these audiences no doubt had shifting and evolving views. Those initially opposed might have become supportive; those eager for separation might have had second thoughts. The drafters of the Declaration of Independence had to keep all these considerations in mind as they chose the evidence, organization, and language of one of the most important documents in Western history.

Audience Perspectives, Contexts, and Needs

Joan Didion wrote her essay "On Morality" at the request of *The American Scholar*, a general-interest journal published by the Phi Beta Kappa Society. That she was given that subject implies a need for clarity, insight, and explanation of the term from a respected thinker. The members of Phi Beta Kappa, a highly selective honor society, are top academic achievers in liberal arts and sciences. Didion chose evidence for the well-educated and well-read audience of *The American Scholar* who are skilled in critical reading. The immediate physical context—time and place—of her essay also influenced its content, specifically inspiring her choices for the essay's use of the desert as a metaphor for society at large. Didion sits in a hot motel room (immediate context) during a time of cultural uncertainty (broader concept). However, that she does not mention current events directly suggests that she understands she is writing about larger principles that would speak to later audiences whose "current" events would be different in details but similar in moral uncertainties. The morally ambiguous stories she includes parallel morally ambiguous times—then as well as now and in the future—and highlight the way people use the term *morality* as a cover-up for doing what they think is right.

Given those audience perspectives, contexts, and needs, what evidence, organization, and language would best deliver Didion's message?

Evidence Didion is not a philosopher—she is a "new journalist"—a writer known for her personal and literary observations of society. She understood that *The American Scholar* knew that about her and was looking for a piece in her style of writing. So she did not turn to the great philosophers for their definitions of morality and assess in what ways they were accurate and in what ways they fell short and then write a scholarly dissection of the concept for readers of *The American Scholar*. Instead, she imaginatively steeped herself in the unusual and desolate environment she found herself in and looked for explanations in that context. She also brought to the surface a number of other life and death incidents from history that demonstrated moral ambiguity.

Suppose, instead, a prominent Jewish scholar had been asked to write about morality for an audience of the highly regarded magazine *Southern Jewish Life*. Such a scholar would approach the task of finding evidence in a different way. No doubt the writer would understand that the readers have a particular interest in Judaism and the South, though the depth of their knowledge of both might vary. The scholar would likely consider evidence from the Torah (the Hebrew Bible) or Talmud (the collection of interpretation of the Torah by famous rabbis through history), possibly with examples to tie the religious-based explanations to modern Jewish life in the South.

Organization Again, the needs and expectations of the audience, the nature of the evidence itself, and the writer's purpose help shape decisions writers make about how to organize their evidence. Didion takes all three into account in the organization of her essay. Her audience is specialized—intellectual and critical—and she uses an organization that requires the readers to put some effort into following her thought process.

In paragraph 1, after setting the scene in the hot desert and aided to some extent by the ice cubes, Didion gets around to her purpose: "to think . . . in some abstract way about 'morality,' " yet she acknowledges she is drawn to particulars rather than the abstract. Her stated purpose is indefinite enough to allow the organization of the essay to develop in a number of different ways. A key to her purpose, however, is that she going to "think" about morality. She does not say she is going to define it or trace the history of philosophical explanations of it—she is going to think about it. And although she has taken great care to organize her essay, as it flows she makes it seem sometimes as if she is thinking out loud about it.

In paragraphs 2–3, Didion lays out local examples of a type of morality she trusts, one built on the conviction that we should keep our promises, in this case to retrieve our casualties. In paragraph 4, Didion expands from the current time to look back on historical examples that were the substance of cautionary tales about what happens when we "breach our primary loyalties." She trusts the basic lessons behind these cautionary tales—never betray those you love—while also suggesting that these historical examples are oversimplified so children can easily understand them.

In paragraphs 5 and 6, Didion's thinking takes a turn to explore why it may be so difficult to act with morality. With some ambiguity, she writes, "Particularly out here tonight, in this country so ominous and terrible that to live in it is to live with antimatter, it is difficult to believe that 'the good' is a knowable quantity." Although she seems to refer to the environment as the one she finds herself in "here tonight," she also continues the description with "in *this country* so ominous and terrible that to live in it is to live with antimatter. . . ." (Antimatter, recall, when touched with matter, has enormous explosive force.) "The good"—a necessary anchor for morality—seems unknowable, and the stories of traveling through this wilderness suggest that reason has only a slight hold on the mind, that madness is always possible when you don't know for sure what anything means. Water that should get colder as it gets deeper gets hotter instead, possibly the result from underground nuclear testing. Is that noise a lethal rattlesnake or just a benign rustling paper? Nothing is certain.

In paragraphs 7 and 8, Didion addresses problems with the ethic of conscience and provides many examples of people whose conscience told them they were doing the "right" thing who nonetheless committed atrocities. She contemplates the "sinister hysteria" and the "monstrous perversion" of doing what you think is right—that is the path of "madmen." And trying to inflict your conscience on someone else is "intrinsically insidious." She writes, "Except on that most primitive level—our loyalties to those we love—what could be more arrogant than to claim the primacy of personal conscience?"

Paragraph 9 is the heart of the argument: if people use morality as a justification for what may be simply expedient, a good idea or a bad idea, a grab for power or a push for public policy, then reason has lost its grip and the "whine of hysteria" last associated with the desert spreads everywhere.

A very rough summary of the organization might appear as follows:

- Introduction and statement of purpose—paragraph 1
- What trusted morality is—paragraphs 2–4
- Why morality is so hard to pin down when "the good" in unknowable—paragraphs 5–6
- Why the ethic of conscience is not morality—paragraphs 7–8
- What morality is not, and the current dangers of using it as justification—paragraph 9

This kind of organization that follows the writer's thoughts as they develop and flow one into the next is sometimes called *developmental order.*

Language Most high school students would find the language of Didion's essay difficult, at least on the first reading. The audience she had in mind when she wrote it was made up of high-achieving college students or graduates. At the same time, some of her language is straight and simple. The language in paragraphs 2 and 3, for example, in which she discusses the morality she trusts, is plain and ordinary. In paragraph 4, however, the language changes as she tries to untangle people's conflicting views of morality: ". . . my own childhood was illuminated by graphic litanies of the grief awaiting those who failed in their loyalties to each other. The Donner-Reed Party, starving in the Sierra snows, all the ephemera of civilization gone save that one vestigial taboo, the provision that no one should eat his own blood kin." Her alternating diction reflects her attitudes toward the concepts of morality. When she writes about particulars, her language is simple and clear; when she writes about explanations of morality, her language becomes academic.

Remember: Because audiences are unique and dynamic, writers must consider the perspectives, contexts, and needs of the intended audience when making choices of evidence, organization, and language in an argument. (RHS-1.N)

1.3 Checkpoint

Close Reading: Professional Text

Review Didion's "On Morality" and then complete the open response activities and answer the multiple-choice questions.

1. Choose five of the anecdotes or examples of evidence on the next page. For each one, write a sentence explaining why you think Didion chose it to advance her argument—in other words, what it conveys about morality. (If necessary, do research to learn more about it.) Write a second sentence evaluating its suitability for Didion's audience and purpose.

- the car accident
- Donner-Reed party
- Jayhawkers
- underwater rescue attempts
- Mountain Meadows Massacre
- Alfred Rosenberg

2. Explain how the organization of Didion's essay could be described as a conversation with the reader. Point to at least four specific places to clarify your explanation. Write a few sentences explaining the effect of that pattern on Didion's argument.

3. The rhetorical purpose of paragraph 1
   (A) suggests the author writes from her own perspective and a personal, journalistic lens
   (B) encourages readers to compare their own assumptions about morality to the author's
   (C) establishes excuses for possible lapses that may occur later in the author's arguments
   (D) allows readers to connect with the author when she classifies herself as morally delinquent
   (E) clearly articulates the author's thesis and establishes an organizational pattern for the essay

4. The author's use of an extended quotation at the end of paragraph 7 supports her perspective that
   (A) a world void of the sense of a "higher good' is doomed to suffer a tragic end
   (B) moral conscience may be used to justify atrocities
   (C) whether people are moral or not, they will in the end destroy themselves
   (D) some forms of morality do not allow for violence in the name of a higher good
   (E) moral codes require too much education

Evaluating Writing: Student Draft

Reread the student draft on page 468. Then complete the following open response activities and answer the multiple-choice question.

1. Evaluate the quality of evidence the writer used in light of the purpose and audience.

2. Describe the author's diction and note any places where word choice surprised you.

3. The student writer wants to alter the passage for an audience that is unfamiliar with the historical details of the examples chosen. Which of the following changes best accomplishes this goal?
   (A) In sentence 2, changing "Age of Exploration" to "Age of Discovery"
   (B) After sentence 2, adding "(as Columbus called those he encountered)"
   (C) In sentence 11, changing "emperor" to "king"
   (D) In sentence 11, adding "who was searching for gold to enrich Spain," after Conquistador
   (E) In sentence 13, adding "(the Aztecs)" after the word "empire"

Source: The Museum of the Netherlands

This print by a Dutch artist shows the meeting of Cortés and Montezuma outside Tenochtitlan.

Look closely at this print and try to identify the people and their actions. How would you describe the dynamic between Cortés and Montezuma in this depiction? What details would you use as evidence to support your interpretation?

Composing on Your Own

Didion referenced an array of disciplines as she chose evidence: an artist's hellish paintings, a novel by Normal Mailer, Klaus Fuchs (science/technology), Mountain Meadows Massacre (history), and Alfred Rosenberg (politics). Didion's span of evidence across a range of disciplines allows her message to resonate with audiences of different backgrounds and interests. You have already considered possible analogies, anecdotes, metaphors, and similes that could advance your argument with your audience. You have also thought about the denotative and connotative meaning of your words and have put diction and syntax to work to deliver your message.

Now stand back and expand your evidence to accommodate a unique and dynamic audience by looking for examples from different areas and perspectives. Use the graphic below to help you think of evidence from different perspectives to help you clarify your abstract concept and explain its relevance to today. Try to think of at least three additional pieces of evidence from these broader categories, and synthesize them into your draft. Save your work for future use.

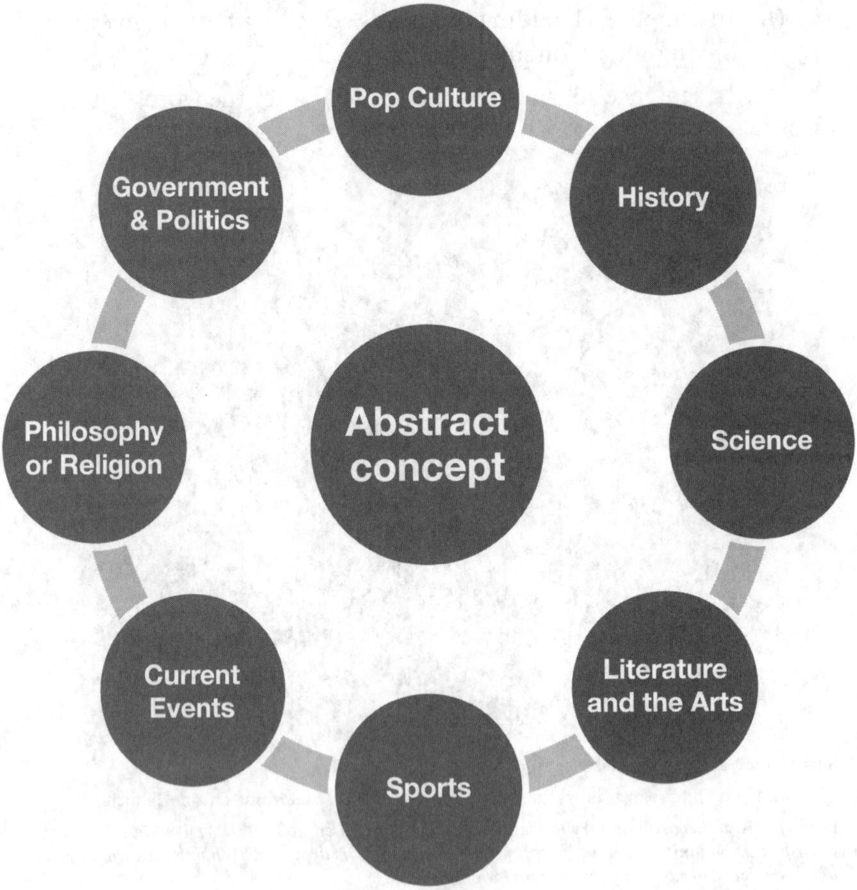

Figure 8-1

Part 1 Apply What You Have Learned

Following are the beginning paragraphs of a 2008 article in *The New York Times Magazine* titled "The Moral Instinct" by psychologist Stephen Pinker. Read them and then complete the task that follows.

> Which of the following people would you say is the most admirable: Mother Teresa, Bill Gates or Norman Borlaug? And which do you think is the least admirable? For most people, it's an easy question. Mother Teresa, famous for ministering to the poor in Calcutta, has been beatified[1] by the Vatican, awarded the Nobel Peace Prize and ranked in an American poll as the most admired person of the 20th century. Bill Gates, infamous for giving us the Microsoft dancing paper clip and the blue screen of death,[2] has been decapitated in effigy[3] in "I Hate Gates" Web sites and hit with a pie in the face. As for Norman Borlaug . . . who the heck is Norman Borlaug?

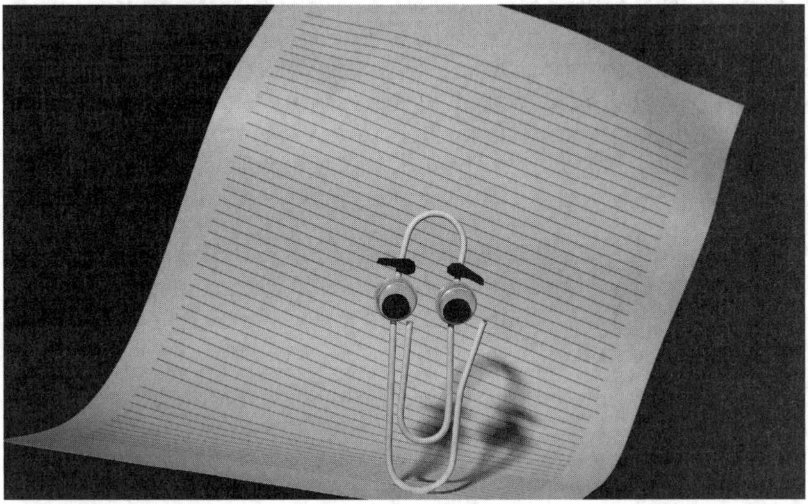

> Yet a deeper look might lead you to rethink your answers. Borlaug, father of the "Green Revolution" that used agricultural science to reduce world hunger, has been credited with saving a billion lives, more than anyone else in history. Gates, in deciding what to do with his fortune, crunched the numbers and determined that he could alleviate the most misery by fighting everyday scourges in the developing world like malaria, diarrhea and parasites. Mother Teresa, for her part, extolled the virtue of suffering and ran her well-financed missions accordingly: their sick patrons were offered plenty of prayer but harsh conditions, few analgesics[4] and dangerously primitive medical care.

1 **beatified:** made a saint
2 **blue screen of death:** blue screen that indicates the computer has reached a point where it can no longer function
3 **effigy:** sculpture or model of a person
4 **analgesics:** pain relievers, such as aspirin

It's not hard to see why the moral reputations of this trio should be so out of line with the good they have done. Mother Teresa was the very embodiment of saintliness: white-clad, sad-eyed, ascetic and often photographed with the wretched of the earth. Gates is a nerd's nerd and the world's richest man, as likely to enter heaven as the proverbial camel squeezing through the needle's eye. And Borlaug, now 93, is an agronomist who has spent his life in labs and nonprofits, seldom walking onto the media stage, and hence into our consciousness, at all.

I doubt these examples will persuade anyone to favor Bill Gates over Mother Teresa for sainthood. But they show that our heads can be turned by an aura of sanctity, distracting us from a more objective reckoning of the actions that make people suffer or flourish. It seems we may all be vulnerable to moral illusions the ethical equivalent of the bending lines that trick the eye on cereal boxes and in psychology textbooks. Illusions are a favorite tool of perception scientists for exposing the workings of the five senses, and of philosophers for shaking people out of the naïve belief that our minds give us a transparent window onto the world (since if our eyes can be fooled by an illusion, why should we trust them at other times?). Today, a new field is using illusions to unmask a sixth sense, the moral sense. Moral intuitions are being drawn out of people in the lab, on Web sites and in brain scanners, and are being explained with tools from game theory, neuroscience and evolutionary biology.

Write a rhetorical analysis of the introduction to Pinker's essay to describe how the author uses rhetorical strategies to address context, purpose, and audience. Your analysis should focus on two of the following rhetorical strategies discussed in Part 1:

- comparisons (similes, metaphors, analogies, anecdotes)
- diction
- bias (connotation)
- syntax
- punctuation
- awareness of unique and dynamic audience
- evidence
- organization
- language

Reflect on the Essential Question: Write a brief response that answers this essential question: *How do the audience's needs, beliefs, and values inform stylistic choices regarding comparisons, syntax, and diction?* In your answer, correctly use the key terms listed on page 471.

Part 2

Writer's Style and Perspective

Enduring Understanding and Skills

Part 2

Understand

The rhetorical situation informs the strategic stylistic choices that writers make. (STL-1)

Demonstrate

Explain how word choice, comparisons, and syntax contribute to the specific tone or style of a text. (Reading 7.A)

Strategically use words, comparisons, and syntax to convey a specific tone or style in an argument. (Writing 8.A)

Source: *AP® English Language and Composition Course and Exam Description*

Essential Question: How do word choice, syntax, and conventions define a writer's style and help to clarify the message and create perspective?

The way you interpret an argument depends to a large extent upon its **style**, the manner in which the writer portrays the subject and expresses a unique perspective or vision. Style varies widely depending upon the discipline and the genre, but it is an important aspect of every creative endeavor—from music to dance to the visual arts and writing.

For example, although all of the paintings on the next page have the same subject, a woman's face, each has a distinct style—the artists use widely different shadings, brushstrokes, and approaches to depicting the human face. Their perspectives, or viewpoints, on the subject are also different. The painting in the upper left from 1911 shows a woman's face from the perspective of a slight side view; the intense shadings of the face contrast sharply with the outline of the woman's large black eyes, which seem to stare at the viewer. The top right picture, painted around 1941, shows the perspective of someone looking at a woman straight on, while the muted tones create a style that is calming and restful. The bottom left picture, following an impressionistic style developed in the late 19th century, uses muted tones to show a woman in profile. This picture doesn't attempt to carefully reproduce each feature of the woman but gives a general impression of form and tone; it seems more of a sketch, with the clearly seen brush strokes calling attention to the act of painting while the exact expression on the woman's face is hard to determine. The bottom right illustration, created in 1892, uses a perspective from behind a woman who is looking in a mirror, so the viewer can see both the back of her head and a frontal reflection of her face. Further, the artist has designed the painting so that from a farther perspective the viewer sees the outline of a skull; the artist uses this image to comment on the transitory nature of beauty—life quickly succumbs to death. Notice that all these artists make careful decisions about style. Like the precise words and perspectives that writers use, each artist makes particular stylistic choices to elicit certain reactions in the audience.

Source: Wikimedia Commons

Top left: Alexej von Jawlensky, c. 1911, Woman's Face
Top right: Rabindranath Tagore, before 1941, Woman's Face
Bottom left: János Tornyai, before 1935, Woman's Face
Bottom right: Charles Allen Gilbert, 1892, All is Vanity

Though it does not depend on visual images, writing works in a similar way. The words, conventions, and the organization of sentences and paragraphs embody an overall perspective and work together to define a writer's style.

KEY TERMS	
conventions	irony
ironic perspective	style

2.1 Writer's Style | STL-1.Q

Style is the mix of word choice, syntax, and conventions writers use to express their message. Readers analyze these elements to learn from and define a writer's style, a practice that can be inspirational for young writers. However, writers try to find their *own* sense of style that reflects their perspectives, personality, and craft.

Every writer's style is created as a result of choices. In her essay "On Morality," Joan Didion *chose* to use the word *mendacious* instead of *dishonest* for a reason; out of all of the other synonyms that she could have inserted in that sentence, she chose *mendacious*. Only she knows for sure why she chose that word. Maybe she liked the rhythm of the word in the sentence; maybe she liked having two words beginning with "m" together at the end of the sentence; maybe she understood a nuanced connotation of the word compared to other synonyms; maybe she chose a word of Latin origin—more typical of her diction in the parts of her essay where she is not discussing down-to-earth particulars. All a reader can do is speculate and assess the effect of that word on the reader.

Style is not prescriptive. Though there is plenty to admire in Joan Didion's writing, a student learning the craft cannot imitate Didion's (or any other writer's) style and trick readers into thinking the message is authentic. Why? Because style comes from experience, from understanding the different ways that language can be manipulated, and from communicating—both successfully and unsuccessfully—within a variety of situations. Many people learning to write look for a checklist that will tell them they have achieved a style—or they seek to imitate other writers who have their own identifiable style. But style is subjective. That is the essential problem when analyzing another writer's style to try to create your own. Different readers may have very different ideas about why certain rhetorical choices were made and the effect of those choices on a reader's response to the writer's message.

Elements of Style

Review the list of style-defining elements in the chart on the next page. How these elements are used can make the difference between a clean or embellished style, a conversational or formal style. Styles may be as varied as adjectives to describe them: declamatory, discursive, eloquent, lyrical, formal, sarcastic, informal, angry, succinct, turgid, and many others.

Word Choice	Syntax	Conventions
The strategic use of words based on their denotative meanings (those with specific definitional meanings) and connotative meanings (those with strong associations or emotional underpinnings) to enhance or reinforce meaning in the given context	The way that words, phrases, clauses, and grammar are arranged for effect. Syntax reflects the writer's choices about using long versus short sentences, rhetorical questions, interruptions within sentences for effect, parallel sentence patterns, varied sentence patterns, and other arrangements.	Language that follows the customs of a community (such as business, legal, academic). Conventions should be appropriate to the medium, the writer's purpose, and the rhetorical situation. Conventions likely follow rules of punctuation, capitalization, and grammar, though they can be broken for effect.

Table 8-1

Consider how you might identify and analyze the word choice, syntax, and conventions of Didion's essay to articulate her style. Reread the third paragraph, reproduced below, and note the *words* that are strategically in line with Didion's purpose; a *sentence structure* that reflects syntactic purpose; the *conventions* that reflect both her rhetorical situation and basic writing rules; and, finally, the way these elements work together to reflect *her style*.

> It was one instance in which I did not distrust the word, because she meant something quite specific. She meant that if a body is left alone for even a few minutes on the desert, the coyotes close in and eat the flesh. Whether or not a corpse is torn apart by coyotes may seem only a sentimental consideration, but of course it is more: one of the promises we make to one another is that we will try to retrieve our casualties, try not to abandon our dead to the coyotes. If we have been taught to keep our promises—if, in the simplest terms, our upbringing is good enough—we stay with the body, or have bad dreams.

Word Choice This is a paragraph in which Didion's diction is down to earth. A number of the words in this category have origins in Old English or other northern European languages: *word, body, close in, eat, flesh, torn, dead, taught, keep, upbringing, good, enough, stay, bad dreams.* She seems to prefer that diction when discussing the kind of morality she trusts. At the same time, the language is powerful. She does not write, "the coyotes close in and eat the *remains*," which somewhat sanitizes the idea of a dead body. Instead she uses a much stronger life-or-death word, *flesh*, with its connotation of soft, vulnerable tissue or its association with "flesh and blood."

Syntax By far the longest and most complex sentence in this passage is the following.

> Whether or not a corpse is torn apart by coyotes may seem only a sentimental consideration, but of course it is more: one of the promises we

make to one another is that we will try to retrieve our casualties, try not to abandon our dead to the coyotes.

The sentence begins with an independent clause in which the subject is itself a clause (*Whether or not a corpse is torn apart by coyotes may seem only a sentimental consideration*) that has a feel of uncertainty to it because of the words "may seem," which suggest that it *really* is something else. Didion then adds an independent clause—*but of course it is more*—to signal that there is more at stake than first impressions. The thought does not end there, though, since the sentence continues after the colon, providing through another independent clause an example of the kind of promise people make to one another that, when kept, can be considered a truly moral act. The repetition of the word *try*—first in *try to* and then in *try not to*—places an emphasis on the effort to fulfill that promise rather than the absolute achievement of it. The complexity of the syntax reflects the complexity of the thought.

Conventions In the sentence analyzed above, Didion also made the choice to use a colon where she could have used a period or semicolon instead. Why? One use of the colon is to separate two independent clauses when the second reflects, illustrates, or expands on the first, which would explain her choice here. After the colon, readers may well ask, "What more is it?" Her answer then follows the colon.

Didion also uses the dash effectively. A dash separates words into parenthetical statements; here, what she includes between the two dashes is grammatically nonessential, meaning that the sentence is a complete thought without the phrase inserted in the middle. Why would she make this choice? Although the phrase is grammatically nonessential, it still contains a key idea that helps clarify the writer's point. As a result, Didion uses the dashes to amplify this "nonessential" information. She uses the convention of the dashes to restate and correlate a good upbringing with being taught to keep promises. Without a good upbringing, people will likely not make the moral decision in this situation.

Reread paragraph 3, reproduced below. Then on the next page see how you might pull all of the above observations together in a rhetorical analysis of paragraph 3.

> [3] It was one instance in which I did not distrust the word, because she meant something quite specific. She meant that if a body is left alone for even a few minutes on the desert, the coyotes close in and eat the flesh. Whether or not a corpse is torn apart by coyotes may seem only a sentimental consideration, but of course it is more: one of the promises we make to one another is that we will try to retrieve our casualties, try not to abandon our dead to the coyotes. If we have been taught to keep our promises—if, in the simplest terms, our upbringing is good enough—we stay with the body, or have bad dreams.

> In paragraph 3, Joan Didion provides an example of what she would consider honest morality—keeping our promises to others. Since this is a relatively simple and fundamental concept, she conveys the message appropriately through down-to-earth but powerful language with vivid connotations, such as her statement: "we will try to retrieve our casualties, try not to abandon our dead to the coyotes." Didion suggests that none of us wants to be abandoned, either in life or death, and we depend on our loved ones to keep a basic social contract ensuring that we respect and look out for each other. In sentence 3, Didion's syntax appropriately focuses the reader's attention on the points that matter the most, with an independent clause introducing the idea that not leaving a body behind may seem like only a "sentimental" consideration, followed by a second independent clause that clarifies what it actually is. Didion enhances her syntax in this sentence with conventions that clarify the message, including a colon that signals "here's what I really mean," which is followed by her insights about specific "promises we make to one another." In the final sentence, she uses a pair of dashes that emphasize the correlation between "keeping promises" and a "[good upbringing]," emphasizing the relative simplicity of her vision of morality.

As a writer, the more you focus on *why* you make specific choices within your own writing, the more likely you are to have control over how the audience will receive your message. As you work on developing a style of your own, remember writing's most organic purpose: to communicate a message to an audience. Everything about your style should support that purpose. For example, using large "impressive" words that don't fit the context of your argument will work against that purpose. Using *clichés*, overused phrases or expressions, works against the originality and clarity of your message.

So what is the best advice for developing your writing style? Read and study writers who came before you. Carefully consider the message you are trying to convey. Question every choice you make—choose your specific words, sentence structures, and conventions thoughtfully and strategically. And write often.

Remember: Writers' style is made up of the mix of word choice, syntax, and conventions employed by the writer. (STL-1.Q)

2.1 Checkpoint

Close Reading: Professional Text

Review Didion's essay. Then complete the open response task and answer the multiple-choice questions on the next page.

1. Review the rhetorical analysis of the word choice, syntax, and conventions in paragraph 3 of "On Morality." Then complete a similar analysis of paragraph 8, reproduced below. Begin by answering the questions below.

> Of course you will say that I do not have the right, even if I had the power, to inflict that unreasonable conscience upon you; nor do I want you to inflict your conscience, however reasonable, however enlightened, upon me. ("We must be aware of the dangers which lie in our most generous wishes," Lionel Trilling once wrote. "Some paradox of our nature leads us, when once we have made our fellow men the objects of our enlightened interest, to go on to make them the objects of our pity, then of our wisdom, ultimately of our coercion.") That the ethic of conscience is intrinsically insidious seems scarcely a revelatory point, but it is one raised with increasing infrequency; even those who do raise it tend to segue with troubling readiness into the quite contradictory position that the ethic of conscience is dangerous when it is "wrong," and admirable when it is "right."

   (a) How would you describe Didion's choice of words? How do her choices affect her message? Provide and analyze specific examples.
   (b) How would you describe Didion's syntax? How does her syntax affect her message? Provide and analyze specific examples.
   (c) Give examples of how Didion effectively uses conventions. How does her use of conventions affect her message? Provide and analyze specific examples.

2. Write a rhetorical analysis of the word choice, syntax, and conventions in paragraph 8 of "On Morality" using your answers from the previous question. Review the commentary on page 506 for a model.

3. In paragraph 9, the author uses the words "factitious," "facile," and "assuage" to develop her belief that the act of asserting one's moral supremacy is
   (A) necessary for social order
   (B) a form of cultural identity
   (C) conveniently self-serving
   (D) ironically immoral
   (E) complex and requires education

4. The author's decision to use the word "Exactly" as a single-word sentence suggests that she
   (A) must compensate for her lack of certainty
   (B) realizes that all her arguments so far have been vague or confusing
   (C) regrets trying to discuss a difficult concept like morality
   (D) must speak forcefully to hold the reader's attention
   (E) desires to reinforce a key idea about morality

Evaluating Writing: Student Draft

Reread the student draft on page 468. Then complete the following open response activity and answer the multiple-choice question.

1. Describe the author's style by identifying specific words, phrases, or organizational patterns. Be sure to explain how her word choice, syntax, and adherence to conventions creates her style.

2. The writer wants to revise the underlined portion of sentence 10 (below) to be stylistically consistent with the passage overall.

   It is this characterization that is published in history books <u>but not where we get the real low down</u>.

   Which revision of the underlined text best achieves this goal?
   (A) (as it is now)
   (B) remove the underlined portion and adjust the punctuation adding a period.
   (C) but it does not address the moral infractions that came with the success.
   (D) which is a good reason not to trust most books about history.
   (E) and why we must keep Cortes's name alive for future generations.

Composing on Your Own

Review the latest draft of your essay on an abstract concept. Analyze each paragraph as you have analyzed the paragraphs from "On Morality" in the activities above. Ask yourself:

- How might I describe my word choice? Does my word choice support my message? How might I improve it?
- How might I describe my syntax? Does my syntax support my message? How might I improve it?
- How might I describe my us of conventions? Does my use of conventions support my message? How might I improve it?

Based on the answers to your analytic questions, make revisions to improve your word choice, syntax, and use of conventions so they integrate smoothly with your message. Save your work for future use.

Extension: While style is personal and organic, one of the ways writers develop style is through exposure to other writers and experimentation with stylistic paths. Choose a sentence from Didion's essay that you think represents an aspect of her style. Using that sentence as a model, write a sentence or two of your own that reflect Didion's word choice, syntax, and conventions but relate to your own abstract idea and evidence. Does that style feel like a fit for your topic? Do you see any other places in your essay you might want to incorporate elements of Didion's (or another writer's) style? If so, make those changes.

2.2 Complex and Ironic Perspectives | STL-1.R

Style helps support and convey more than just the literal message of the writer. Through stylistic choices, writers may also signal their perspective or the stance they take toward their subject. One of those perspectives is **irony**, the expression of meaning through language that usually means the opposite of the writer's true meaning. Irony often results from the differences between an argument and the readers' expectations or values.

Complex Perspective

Like fiction writers, nonfiction authors speak through the voice of a persona—a created personality. Just as comedians or musicians design an onstage persona, nonfiction writers develop a persona through whom to voice their thoughts, ideas, and attitudes. Just as there is a real-life Ariana Grande and a stage version ("The girl you see in photographs is only a part of the one I am," she sings), so is there a real-life writer and a published persona. The persona a writer adopts cues the readers to the writer's perspective—at how much distance does the writer stand from the subject, audience, and themselves?

In some cases, there may be very little difference between the writer and the writer's persona. Eric Schlosser, for example, speaks with a straightforward perspective on his subject and his readers in *Fast Food Nation* (see Unit 3), as if to say, "Here's what I learned about fast food; I can make it pretty interesting for you if you want to learn about it too; and I'm trying to get my message to you as directly as possible."

In contrast, Didion adopts a persona with more distance. In a review in *The New York Times* of a 2017 documentary about Joan Didion ("The Center Will Not Hold"), Glenn Kenny describes the persona Didion has developed through her career and the tools she used to create it. He writes, "Joan Didion's meticulously calibrated prose has the effect of placing her at a particular remove from the reader. The persona she creates on the page is always frank but never ingratiating." In "On Morality," Didion has a more complex perspective than Schlosser did in *Fast Food Nation*. It's as if she's saying, "I have interesting and powerful thoughts about morality; I'm going to pretend I'm thinking them through in a conversation with you, preempting your questions and concerns ('You are quite possibly impatient with me by now; I am talking, you want to say, about a 'morality' so primitive that it scarcely deserves the name"), assuming I know how you are reacting, and by so doing, I am placing some distance between us, because now it's not just my ideas that I am communicating but also my 'meticulously calibrated prose.' "

Ironic Perspective

One way to define **irony** is "the difference between an author's argument and the reader's expectations and values." In 1729, Jonathan Swift (author of *Gulliver's Travels*) published an anonymous essay that many consider the best example of sustained irony in the English language. Its full original title is "A Modest Proposal For preventing the Children of Poor People in Ireland From being a Burden to Their Parents or Country, and For making them Beneficial to the Public," but it is more commonly known as "A Modest Proposal." A reader picking up this pamphlet may be hoping to find a workable solution to a difficult problem. *Note: the spelling has been modernized.*

> It is a melancholy object to those, who walk through this great town, or travel in the country, when they see the streets, the roads and cabin-doors crowded with beggars of the female sex, followed by three, four, or six children, all in rags, and importuning every passenger for an alms. These mothers instead of being able to work for their honest livelihood, are forced to employ all their time in strolling to beg sustenance for their helpless infants who, as they grow up, either turn thieves for want of work, or leave their dear native country . . .
>
> I think it is agreed by all parties, that this prodigious number of children in the arms, or on the backs, or at the heels of their mothers, and frequently of their fathers, is in the present deplorable state of the kingdom, a very great additional grievance; and therefore whoever could find out a fair, cheap and easy method of making these children sound and useful members of the common-wealth, would deserve so well of the public, as to have his statue set up for a preserver of the nation.
>
> But my intention is very far from being confined to provide only for the children of professed beggars: it is of a much greater extent, and shall take in the whole number of infants at a certain age, who are born of parents in effect as little able to support them, as those who demand our charity in the streets.
>
> As to my own part, having turned my thoughts for many years, upon this important subject, and maturely weighed the several schemes of our projectors, I have always found them grossly mistaken in their computation. It is true, a child just dropped from its dam [mother], may be supported by her milk, for a solar year, with little other nourishment: at most not above the value of two shillings, which the mother may certainly get, or the value in scraps, by her lawful occupation of begging; and it is exactly at one year old

that I propose to provide for them in such a manner, as, instead of being a charge upon their parents, or the parish, or wanting food and raiment for the rest of their lives, they shall, on the contrary, contribute to the feeding, and partly to the clothing of many thousands. . . .

There is likewise another great advantage in my scheme, that it will prevent those voluntary abortions, and that horrid practice of women murdering their bastard children, alas! too frequent among us, sacrificing the poor innocent babes, I doubt, more to avoid the expense than the shame, which would move tears and pity in the most savage and inhuman breast.

[Here Swift continues, straight-faced, to make an accounting for the number of children in the kingdom and to point out that they cannot be gainfully employed.]

I shall now therefore humbly propose my own thoughts, which I hope will not be liable to the least objection.

I have been assured by a very knowing American of my acquaintance in London, that a young healthy child well nursed, is, at a year old, a most delicious nourishing and wholesome food, whether stewed, roasted, baked, or boiled; and I make no doubt that it will equally serve in a fricassee, or a ragout.

I do therefore humbly offer it to public consideration, that of the hundred and twenty thousand children, already computed, twenty thousand may be reserved for breed, whereof only one fourth part to be males; which is more than we allow to sheep, black cattle, or swine, and my reason is, that these children are seldom the fruits of marriage, a circumstance not much regarded by our savages, therefore, one male will be sufficient to serve four females. That the remaining hundred thousand may, at a year old, be offered in sale to the persons of quality and fortune, through the kingdom, always advising the mother to let them suck plentifully in the last month, so as to render them plump, and fat for a good table. A child will make two dishes at an entertainment for friends, and when the family dines alone, the fore or hind quarter will make a reasonable dish, and seasoned with a little pepper or salt, will be very good boiled on the fourth day, especially in winter.

When you have read far enough to know Swift's idea, you realize that the first instance of irony is in the title itself: Nothing in this proposal is "modest." The persona's sympathy for the poor at the beginning of the essay does, no doubt, align with Swift's own views, and an ironic perspective is not immediately obvious. By the time he proposes his idea, which he hopes "will not be liable to the least objection," the distance between the writer's persona and the real-life writer becomes a gaping chasm. Swift's ridiculous, extreme proposal helps him deliver his true message: that the poor, especially the Irish, suffer greatly; that they are humans entitled to human comforts; and that the rich and privileged cannot commoditize poor people or treat them as economic resources. Notice how Swift heightens the irony by presenting his horrifying proposals as being entirely rational and logical; his perspective seems to be that of a rational man who is coolly assessing cost-benefits based on basic mathematical calculations. This strategy heightens Swift's point: he shows that the English government doesn't respect the Irish as human individuals but instead treats them as if they were livestock. In addition, Swift uses exaggeration when he suggests different recipes for preparing children and also advises on breeding strategies to maximize the output of children. Although Swift's words may be humorous today, his suggestion shocked his original audience; Swift knew his audience expected a standard speech about the conditions in Ireland, and instead they received biting satire. Writers typically use satire by employing irony, humor, and exaggeration to criticize foolishness and corruption.

Didion also uses irony in a few places in "On Morality." "Of course we would all like to 'believe' in something," she writes, enclosing the word *believe* in quotation marks to subtly question the integrity of such beliefs. The quotation marks signal a split between what she says and what she means. She also refers to *New York Times* signatures, calling them brave but conveying the obvious opposite—that there is little bravery in signing a letter to the *New York Times*.

Remember: Writers may signal a complex or ironic perspective through stylistic choices. Irony may emerge from the differences between an argument and the readers' expectations or values. (STL-1.R)

2.2 Checkpoint

Close Reading: Professional Text

Review "On Morality" and complete the open response activity and answer the multiple-choice questions.

1. Explain why Didion may use such conventions as quotation marks and italic type for the following words and phrases.
    - "wagon-train morality" (paragraph 4)
    - *failed* (paragraph 4)
    - "morality" (paragraphs 4, 5, 9)
    - "the good" (paragraph 5)
    - "wrong" versus "right" (paragraphs 8, 9)
    - "believe" (paragraph 9)
    - *moral imperative* (paragraph 9)

2. In the context of her argument about morality, the story Didion tells in paragraphs 2 and 3 offers a perspective that is
   - (A) ironic
   - (B) straightforward
   - (C) complex
   - (D) satirical
   - (E) distant

3. In paragraph 5, the author's primary rhetorical strategy is to
   - (A) use the perspective of one individual's life to generalize about other groups throughout the desert
   - (B) progressively expand the focus of her narrative from the description of Death Valley to American society
   - (C) acknowledge the likely reactions of her readers before illustrating her claim with an example
   - (D) chronicle stories from all over the world that question the authenticity of moral ideals
   - (E) appear uncertain about matters of morality only to shift to a firm stand on morality in modern society

4. In paragraph 8, which of the following statements best describes the author's perspective on ethic of conscience?
   - (A) Individuals can change their own sense of morality, which will affect the morals of society as a whole.
   - (B) Despite the different ways people view good and bad, the cultural understanding of morality comes from childhood stories.
   - (C) Whereas many people choose to keep their ethic of conscience hidden, this concealment is part of our innate moral code.
   - (D) Because of the nature of morality, neither writer nor reader has the right to assume their own moral code is superior.
   - (E) Although discussing the ethics of conscience can be dangerous, it is necessary when we believe deeply in something.

Evaluating Writing: Student Draft

Reread the student draft on page 468. Then complete the open response activity and answer the multiple-choice question.

1. The writer seems to allude to additional complex ideas at the end of the last paragraph. Add two sentences (or more) to the final paragraph: one that includes an ironic tone, and one that includes a new or different perspective.

2. When evaluating whether or not the writer has addressed the complexity of the issue, which of the following is most important for the writer to consider?
   (A) the reader's familiarity with this period and additional historical facts the writer needs to provide
   (B) which other Native American leaders the writer should include to show a pattern throughout history
   (C) whether the audience is likely to acknowledge their own moral shortcomings after the moral dilemma posed in sentence 15
   (D) whether the writer has offered equal amounts of research about the biographies of Montezuma and Cortés
   (E) why some history books choose to show only one side of the story, resulting in biased presentations of ideas and facts

Composing on Your Own

1. Evaluate your perspective in your composition. Does your style help make your perspective clear? Is your perspective appropriately complex for your topic? Revise your work if your style is inconsistent or your perspective lacks complexity.
2. Experiment with irony on the concept that is at the center of your essay. Try rewriting a key sentence from an ironic perspective. For example, if you were writing on morality, you might start your ironic essay as follows:

"Nothing could be easier to define than morality," or "It's a good thing everyone can agree on what morality means," or "I would write an essay on morality but it's such an unimportant concept."

You might also consider adopting a persona, as Swift did in "A Modest Proposal," through whom to express the opposite of what you actually believe. For example, you might adopt the character of a politician trying to justify a policy that most feel is immoral.

Decide whether irony would be appropriate to introduce in your composition. If so, make further revisions to integrate irony into your work. Save your work for future use.

Part 2 Apply What You Have Learned

Reread the opening paragraphs from Steven Pinker's article, "The Moral Instinct," on pages 499–500. Write a paragraph describing his perspective and explain what textual details make his perspective clear. Identify any irony in those paragraphs and its impact on the message.

Reflect on the Essential Question: Write a brief response that answers these essential questions: *How do word choice, syntax, and conventions define a writer's style and help to clarify the message and create perspective?* In your answer, explain the key terms listed on page 503.

Part 3

Modifiers and Parenthetical Elements

Enduring Understanding and Skills

Part 3

Understand

The rhetorical situation informs the strategic stylistic choices that writers make. (STL-1)

Demonstrate

Explain how writers create, combine, and place independent and dependent clauses to show relationships between and among ideas. (Reading 7.B)

Write sentences that clearly convey ideas and arguments. (Writing 8.B)

Source: *AP® English Language and Composition Course and Exam Description*

Essential Questions: How do writers create, combine, and place clauses to show relationships and clearly convey ideas and arguments?

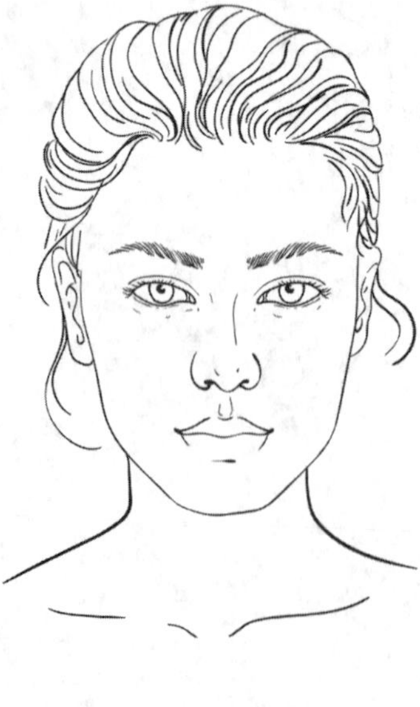

You've probably seen time-lapse drawings on YouTube. An artist stands before a work-in-progress, pencil in hand. After making an initial general shape—an oval for a face, for example—the artist adds more detail, modifying the original shape with new shapes inside it for eyes and an outline for a nose and mouth. With more pencil tracings, shadows, and highlights, the artist—at what appears to be breathtaking speed—starts to modify a general face to a very specific face. Of course, the illusion of speed is only that—an illusion. Without the time-lapse, you would see the careful, thoughtful, deliberate placement of each element that brings the face to life.

Writers work in a similar way. They start with a claim or argument in their minds and gradually add details to make their ideas conform to the unique vision in their heads. Instead of lines, highlights, and shadings, of course, writers use rhetorical skills to bring their shape to life and then grammatical and mechanical details to give readers the clearest expression possible. The grammatical and mechanical details covered in this unit will help you improve your revision process and increase your stylistic maturity and sophistication.

Source: Getty Images

This sketch from Leonardo da Vinci's notebooks shows how artists start with basic lines and shapes, study the different parts of their subjects, combine them, and then artfully modify and refine them to create a unique image.

KEY TERMS

commas
dashes
modifiers
parentheses
parenthetical elements

3.1 Modifiers | STL-1.S

Writers also make significant modifications to their work in progress. When revising an argument from a rough draft, for example, a writer may add words, phrases, and clauses to qualify, clarify, or specify particular information.

A **modifier** is a word, phrase, or clause that functions as an adjective or adverb to give more information about another word or phrase in a sentence. Modifiers can qualify, or limit, the meaning of other words; clarify another word or subject; or specify information about the thing with which the modifier is associated. As such, they can be a very useful tool for creating more precise constructions. However, use caution: while modifiers can certainly add more depth and precision to the writing, if used too frequently or inserted in the wrong place in a sentence, modifiers can disrupt the rhythm and meaning can be lost.

Purposes of Modifiers

In Units 4 and 7 you read about the rhetorical purposes of modifiers—how they limit or qualify an argument. This part will focus on how modifiers function on a more granular level within sentences where they *clarify, qualify,* or *specify* an idea to make their message more precise for readers.

Modifiers that Clarify Words, phrases, and clauses serve to clarify the writer's ideas by adding information, nuance, and specificity to writing. They can also add color to a sentence and breathe life into writing. Without modifiers, writing lacks the appropriate shadings and distinction between ideas. Notice the underlined modifiers in the following passage by Peter Singer ("The Drowning Child and Expanding Circle," *New Internationalist,* April 5, 1977). First read the passage just for the meaning. Then reread it with attention to the underlined modifiers, which add descriptive detail and/or specificity to the text. You might even want to try to read it without the modifiers to appreciate how important they are. Most of the modifiers in this passage clarify the writer's thoughts.

> [1] To challenge my students to think about the ethics of what we owe to people in need, I ask them to imagine that their route to the university takes them past a shallow pond. [2] One morning, I say to them, you notice a child has fallen in and appears to be drowning. [3] To wade in and pull the child out would be easy but it will mean that you get your clothes wet and muddy, and by the time you go home and change you will have missed your first class.
>
> [4] I then ask the students: do you have any obligation to rescue the child? [5] Unanimously, the students say they do. The importance of saving a child so far outweighs the cost of getting one's clothes muddy and missing a class, that they refuse to consider it any kind of excuse for not saving the child. [6] Does it make a difference, I ask, that there are other people walking past the pond who would equally be able to rescue the child but are not doing so? [7] No, the students reply, the fact that others are not doing what they ought to do is no reason why I should not do what I ought to do.
>
> [8] Once we are all clear about our obligations to rescue the drowning child in front of us, I ask: would it make any difference if the child were far away, in another country perhaps, but similarly in danger of death, and equally within your means to save, at no great cost—and absolutely no danger—to yourself? [9] Virtually all agree that distance and nationality make no moral difference to the situation. [10] I then point out that we are all in that situation of the person passing the shallow pond: we can all save lives of people, both children and adults, who would otherwise die, and we can do so at a very small cost to us: the cost of a new CD, a shirt or a night out at a restaurant or concert, can mean the difference between life and death to more than one person somewhere in the world—and overseas aid agencies like Oxfam overcome the problem of acting at a distance.

Modifiers are of three main types: those that modify nouns (or words, phrases, or clauses that function as nouns), those that modify verbs (or words or phrases that function as verbs), and those that modify adjectives (or words, phrases, or clauses that function as adjectives). They also fall into several different grammatical elements: single words, phrases, and clauses. Examples of each type from the excerpt by Peter Singer and the sentences they appear in are in the chart on the next page.

Grammatical Element	Word	Phrase	Clause
Modify nouns or words functioning as nouns	shallow (pond) [1] small (cost) [10]	(one person) somewhere in the world [10] (lives) of people [10]	(other people) who would equally be able to rescue the child [6] (children and adults) who would otherwise die [10]
Modify verbs or words functioning as verbs	then (point out) [10] Unanimously (the students say) [5]	(do so) at a very small cost to us [10]	(agree) that distance and nationality make no moral difference [9] (point out) that we are all in that situation [10]
Modify adjectives or words functioning as adjectives	similarly (in danger of death) [8] very (small cost) [10]	(clear) about our obligations . . . [8]	

Table 8-2

Modifiers that Qualify In Unit 7 you read about modifiers that qualify claims. These modifiers can also qualify single ideas or words. Some are especially useful to help avoid making statements in absolute terms. (See Unit 3, Part 2.)

Modifiers that Qualify	
a few	many
a little	most
a lot of	much
all	none
any	several
both	some
enough	
Examples from the Singer excerpt: ▪ do you have any obligation [4] ▪ would it make any difference [8] ▪ we can all save lives of people [10]	

Table 8-3

Modifiers that Specify Modifiers that specify are those that answer the question, "which one?" These are either demonstrative or possessive pronouns. They are called modifiers that specify because they indicate that what they are modifying is not a general thing (the students, a route) but rather a very specific thing (my students, your route).

Modifiers that Specify	
Demonstrative	**Possessive**
that	your
this	their
those	our
these	my
	ours
	whose
	his
	hers
	its
Examples from the Singer excerpt: ▪ <u>my</u> students [1] ▪ <u>their</u> route [1] ▪ <u>your</u> clothes [3]	

Table 8-4

Placement of Modifiers

Modifiers are effective only if they are correctly placed. To reduce ambiguity and confusion, writers typically place modifiers closest to the word, phrase, or clause they are meant to modify.

Sometimes the placement of a modifier actually changes rather than simply confuses meaning. Read the following two sentences and note how placement of the modifier *almost* affects meaning. In the first sentence *almost* is an adverb that modifies the verb *got*. In the second sentence, *almost* is also an adverb, but this time it modifies the adjective *every.*

She **almost** got to the front row at every concert she went to.
She got to the front row at **almost** every concert she went to.

Notice how placement of the word *only* changes its meaning in the following sentences.

The student body can **only** nominate four students for the community scholarship.

Meaning: The student body cannot actually select the recipient of the scholarship; it can only nominate possible candidates.

The student body can nominate **only** four students for the community scholarship.

Meaning: The student body cannot nominate any more than four students.

Only the student body can nominate four students for the community scholarship.

Meaning: No one else other than the student body can nominate students for the scholarship.

The modifier *only* is sometimes called a determiner—a word that functions as an adjective to modify nouns. This type of modifier usually should be placed in front of a noun to modify the major subject in the sentence.

Phrases and clauses also need to be placed accurately. A modifier in the wrong place in a sentence is called a misplaced modifier, which can make the sentence clunky or difficult to understand. Take a look at the two sentences below.

A man ran toward the bus **carrying a leather briefcase.** (misplaced modifier)

A man **carrying a leather briefcase** ran toward the bus. (correct)

The placement of the modifier in the first sentence suggests that the bus was carrying the briefcase, not the man.

Modifiers must also modify a clear subject. A *dangling modifier* modifies a word or phrase that is not actually stated in a sentence. Below, the first sentence lacks a subject that is modified, while the second sentence is constructed accurately with a subject present. The modifier is underlined.

Having learned her lesson the hard way, the first step in Alyssa's fitness program was to warm up. (dangling modifier)

Having learned her lesson the hard way, Alyssa vowed to make warming up the first step in her fitness program. (correct)

Clearly the phrase "having learned her lesson the hard way" is meant to modify Alyssa, but the first sentence is constructed so that "the first step" is in the grammatical position to be modified by that phrase instead. In fact, Alyssa appears only as a possessive noun modifying "fitness program." In the second sentence, Alyssa is the subject of the sentence, so the modifier correctly applies to her.

To help you check the placement of your modifiers, understand what different phrases and clauses actually modify.

- A **prepositional phrase** is a group of words consisting of a preposition (a part of speech that denotes a relationship to something else), its object, and any word(s) that modify the object. Most of the time, a prepositional phrase modifies a verb or a noun. When a prepositional phrase modifies a noun, it is said to be behaving **adjectivally** because adjectives **modify nouns**. When a prepositional phrase modifies a verb, it is said to be behaving **adverbially** because adverbs modify verbs. In the following sentences, the prepositional phrases are underlined once and the words they modify are underlined twice.

Prepositional phrase modifying a noun
Angelica reached for the book on the table.

Prepositional phrase modifying a verb
The puppy ran behind the sofa to chew on his new toy.

- An **adjectival clause** modifies a noun, so the clause should be placed near the noun. In the following example, the adjectival clause is underlined once and the word it modifies is underlined twice.

  Adjectival clause modifying a noun
  The professor whose expertise was psychology was a compelling witness at the trial.

- An **adverbial** phrase should be placed near the verb because that is what it modifies.

  Adverbial phrase modifying a verb
  The toddler woke every morning at the same time.

Just as the artist skillfully adds contour and clarity to a picture or a photographer changes the angle of a camera, a writer revises and modifies and revises again until the meaning is just right. As Didion wrote, "To shift the structure of a sentence alters the meaning of that sentence, as definitely and inflexibly as the position of a camera alters the meaning of the object photographed."

Remember: Modifiers—including words, phrases, or clauses—qualify, clarify, or specify information about the thing with which they are associated. To reduce ambiguity, modifiers should be placed closest to the word, phrase, or clause that they are meant to modify. (STL-1.S)

3.1 Checkpoint

Close Reading: Professional Text

Review "On Morality" on pages 463–467. Then answer the following open response and multiple-choice questions.

For each of the five sentences on the next page, identify and explain

- the main subject of each sentence
- a key modifying phrase or clause in each sentence
- how the modifiers qualify, clarify, or specify information
- how each sentence would be different without the modifier(s)

1. "The driver, very young and apparently drunk, was killed instantly."

2. "I am talking, of course, about the kind of social code that is sometimes called, usually pejoratively, 'wagon-train morality.' "

3. "Particularly out here tonight, in this country so ominous and terrible that to live in it is to live with antimatter, it is difficult to believe that 'the good' is a knowable quality."

4. "They have been diving for ten days but have found no bottom to the caves, no bodies and no trace of them, only the black 90-degree water going down and down and down, and a single translucent fish, not specified."

5. "Across the road at the Faith Community Church a couple of dozen old people, come here to live in trailers and die in the sun, are holding a prayer sing."

6. At the end of paragraph 5 of "On Morality," Didion uses "not classified" to modify the translucent fish in order to
   - (A) acknowledge that she was an outsider looking in on the events of the town, and therefore her evaluation is limited
   - (B) characterize the efforts of those trying to maintain their sense of good, especially during trying times
   - (C) stress the importance of details in discussing abstract issues, making them more concrete for readers
   - (D) reinforce the idea of the strangeness of the environment where many things are not knowable
   - (E) celebrate the resolute nature of those who try to do "good" even when they are challenged to do otherwise

7. The phrase "our loyalties to those we love" (paragraph 7) serves mainly to
   - (A) qualify her claim that morality changes but we maintain loyalty to the original moral code
   - (B) refute the claim that we too often give in to self-righteousness under the pretext of morality
   - (C) emphasize the foundational moral teachings the author remembers from her youth
   - (D) validate our fears of uncertainty when we question our own innate sense of morality
   - (E) interrupt a string of accusations with a sense of humility and emotion

Evaluating Writing: Student Draft
Reread the student draft on page 468. Then complete the following open response activity and answer the multiple-choice question.

1. Choose one sentence that includes a modifier that emphasizes key details about the main subject of the sentence or paragraph. Rewrite the sentence without the modifiers, noting how the evidence and argument presented *without* the modification changes the effect of the argument.

2. The writer wants to reduce confusion and ambiguity in sentence 11 (reproduced below) while maintaining the line of reasoning.

   Montezuma, the Aztec emperor, was one of the greatest kings in Aztec history, and he was deceived by Cortés, the Spanish conquistador.

   Which of the following is the best revision?

   (A) (as it is now)
   (B) Montezuma, the Aztec emperor who was considered one of the greatest kings in Aztec history, lost his title when the Spanish conquistador Cortés deceived him.
   (C) Montezuma, the Aztec emperor, eventually became considered one of the greatest kings in Aztec history after his fight against Cortés, the Spanish conquistador.
   (D) Montezuma, the Aztec emperor who stood his moral ground, lost his fight against Cortés, the Spanish conquistador.
   (E) The Aztec emperor, Montezuma, eventually became considered one of the greatest kings in Aztec history after his death.

Composing on Your Own
Review your draft. Identify the modifiers you used and think about why you chose them. Are they doing the job you want them to or would other modifiers do a better job of clarifying, quantifying, or specifying? Are the modifiers placed correctly in the sentences? Make changes as you see fit based on your evaluation. Save your work for future use.

3.2 Parenthetical Elements | STL-1.T

Parenthetical elements include any information that interrupts a sentence to provide information that, though not completely necessary, adds useful insights or examples or other material that may advance the understanding of an audience and the purpose of a writer. They are often enclosed in parentheses, but they can also be expressed in other ways.

Sentence, Interrupted

A **parenthetical element** is any word, phrase, or clause that adds detail to a sentence or any sentence that adds detail to a paragraph but is not essential for understanding the core meaning. Often, parenthetical elements in sentences or paragraphs appear in parentheses; however, commas and dashes may be used to separate parenthetical elements within a sentence. While all of these conventions function the same way in a sentence, they have different rhetorical purposes and effects on the reader. Compare the following treatments of a sentence from "On Morality." Then consider how each of the versions below flows and reads a little differently.

WITH PARENTHESES: The driver (very young and apparently drunk) was killed instantly.

The parenthetical element in this sentence is *very young and apparently drunk*. If the nonessential phrase is removed, the sentence is still a complete thought that can stand alone. Without the parenthetical element it reads, *The driver was killed instantly*. **Parentheses** tell the reader that information has less importance or emphasis than the other information in the sentence, that the inserted phrase is just a "by-the-way." Parentheses offer a softer separation than commas and dashes.

WITH COMMAS: The driver, very young and apparently drunk, was killed instantly.

In this instance, **commas** are used to set aside the parenthetical information. The phrase inside the **commas** adds important details about the driver of the car and the anecdote the author is presenting as evidence. The commas, however, do not call much attention to the phrase; the phrase flows as part of the larger sentence.

WITH DASHES: The driver—very young and apparently drunk—was killed instantly.

Most readers would probably agree that if the writer's purpose is to call attention to the extra information, the use of **dashes** is most effective. The visual separation is very noticeable. Dashes create a stronger separation than commas and signal the importance of the information within the sentence more than parentheses. Understanding the nuances among different parenthetical elements and knowing how they can shift the emphasis in a sentence or paragraph can help you bring the audience into your message.

Remember: Parenthetical elements—though not essential to understanding what they are describing—interrupt sentences to provide additional information that may address an audience's needs and/or advance a writer's purpose. (STL-1.T)

3.2 Checkpoint

Close Reading: Professional Text

Review "On Morality." Then answer the following open response and multiple-choice questions.

1. In what places does Didion use parentheses? What message is within each set of parentheses? Why do you think she used parentheses there? How do those messages contribute to Didion's argument? Write a paragraph answering these questions.

2. In what places does Didion use dashes? What is the message within each set of dashes? How do the use of dashes and the points they emphasize advance her argument? Write a paragraph answering these questions.

3. In the third paragraph, the clause set off by dashes ("if, in the simplest terms, our upbringing is good enough") relates to the rest of the sentence by

(A) simplifying her claim so that more readers are able to relate to her message
(B) acknowledging the assumption upon which the rest of the sentence depends
(C) offering a potential explanation for what the rest of the sentence describes
(D) restating the influence of the lessons we learn in childhood on our morality
(E) detailing a scenario in which morality is upheld

4. The clause "you want to say" inserted in the first sentence of paragraph five

(A) introduces a specific yet very common experience that supports the central thesis
(B) introduces the definition of morality in the context of the argument
(C) prepares the reader for a controversial idea about self-righteousness and morality
(D) provides additional context for the writer's argument that the notion of morality changes
(E) asks that readers maintain patience as she begins to lay out her argument

5. Why is the following sentence in paragraph 7 in parentheses?

("Tell me," a rabbi asked Daniel Bell when he said, as a child, that he did not believe in God. "Do you think God cares?")

(A) The author wants to show that this information is of little importance and not vital to her larger discussion.

(B) The author wants to include this information to support her point, but it is an aside that is not essential to understanding her argument.

(C) The author wants to show that this information is an insightful joke, but it does not match the tone of her larger argument.

(D) The author wants to include additional viewpoints that are important to understanding her argument, but she does not want to distract readers from her main argument.

(E) The author wants to show that religious concerns have validity but are only parenthetical to her main argument.

6. The phrasing inside the dashes in the first sentence of paragraph 9 allows the author to establish a distinction between

(A) right and wrong beliefs

(B) morality and social codes

(C) subjective and objective beliefs

(D) conventional and unconventional views of morality

(E) religious and secular moral codes

Evaluating Writing: Student Draft

Reread the student draft on page 468. Then complete the open response activity and answer the following multiple-choice question.

1. Choose one sentence that includes a parenthetical element. Change the parenthetical element and discuss how the change affects the message. Then consider additional details the writer could have included to modify key subjects or ideas, complex perspectives, or diverse audiences, and add these details using the most appropriate parenthetical element. Finally, articulate *why* this change is an improvement in the context of the argument as a whole.

2. The writer is considering deleting the phrase "—because the stories we tell often become evidence to prove our morality," in sentence 15 (reproduced below).

While we think that morality comes from a standard, innate moral code, morality is a fluid abstract notion that changes based on who tells the story—because the stories we tell often become evidence to prove our morality.

Should the writer delete the phrase that follows the dash?

(A) Yes, because it distracts from the focus of the paragraph by introducing a new claim.

(B) Yes, because it restates the idea in the main sentence and is redundant.

(C) Yes, because it detracts from the central argument by offering a personal perspective.

(D) No, because it gives the audience a clue to understand a key counterargument.

(E) No, because it attempts to persuade the audience of claims about reexamining history.

Composing on Your Own

Review your revised draft. Add any parenthetical elements that you think would genuinely enhance your message. While you are learning many strategies in this course, they are only useful when they make an argument clearer or more persuasive than it was without them—the ideas at the heart of the argument are always the most valuable part. Use the checklist on the next page to remind you of the strategies you learned and how you might apply them to your writing. Seek feedback from a teacher or peer and then use that feedback as appropriate to make further revisions. Finally, edit your paper to make it as error free as possible.

Checklist for Composing, Revising, and Editing
✓ Did you choose or create a rhetorical situation for your writing and seek to understand its elements?
✓ Did you develop your discussion of an abstract idea through comparisons (similes, metaphors, analogies, or anecdotes) that your readers would understand? (1.1)
✓ Would your audience appreciate your syntax and diction and the way they advance your argument, and have you avoided bias? (1.2)
✓ Did you consider the perspectives, contexts, and needs of your intended audience when making choices of evidence, organization, and language in your argument? (1.3)
✓ Did you develop a style with conscious choices about the words, syntax, and conventions you used? (2.1)
✓ Did you consider and possibly use a complex or ironic perspective? (2.2)
✓ Did you use modifiers to clarify, qualify, and specify, and did you place them appropriately in the sentence? (3.1)
✓ Did you use parenthetical elements to suit your argument and the points you want to highlight? (3.2)
✓ Did you edit your writing for mistakes in spelling and other mechanics and make an effort to correct them?
✓ Did you edit your writing to ensure that your conventions are appropriate for your audience and type of writing?

Table 8-5

Part 3 Apply What You Have Learned

Review Pinker's opening paragraphs and identify places where he uses parenthetical elements and other conventions to good effect. Write a paragraph explaining the effect of his rhetorical choices on his argument and you as a reader.

Reflect on the Essential Question: Write a brief response that answers this essential question: *How do writers create, combine, and place clauses to show relationships and clearly convey ideas and arguments?* In your answer, explain the key terms listed on page 517.

Unit 8 Review

Section I: Multiple Choice

Section II: Free Response

Section I: Reading

Questions 1–9. Read the following passage carefully before you choose your answers.

(This passage is excerpted from a speech Charlton Heston, president of the National Rifle Association, delivered in May 1999, in Denver, Colorado, just a few weeks after the Columbine Massacre: a school shooting that happened in Littleton, Colorado, and claimed the lives of 13 persons.)

1 Thank you. Thank you very much. Good morning. I am very happy to welcome you to this abbreviated annual gathering of the National Rifle Association. Thank you all for coming and thank you for supporting your organization.

2 I also want to applaud your courage in coming here today. Of course, you have a right to be here. As you know, we've canceled the festivities, the fellowship we normally enjoy at our annual gatherings. This decision has perplexed a few and inconvenienced thousands. As your president, I apologize for that.

3 But it's fitting and proper that we should do this. Because NRA members are, above all, Americans. That means that whatever our differences, we are respectful of one another and we stand united, especially in adversity.

4 I have a message from the mayor, Mr. Wellington Webb, the mayor of Denver. He sent me this and said don't come here, we don't want you here. I said to the mayor, well, my reply to the mayor is, I volunteered for the war they wanted me to attend when I was 18 years old. Since then, I've run small errands for my country, from Nigeria to Vietnam. I know many of you here in this room could say the same thing. But the mayor said don't come.

5 I'm sorry for that. I'm sorry for the newspaper ads saying the same thing, don't come here. This is our country. As Americans, we're free to travel wherever we want in our broad land.

6 They say we'll create a media distraction, but we were preceded here by hundreds of intrusive news crews. They say we'll create political distraction, but it's not been the NRA pressing for political advantage, calling press conferences to propose vast packages of new legislation.

7 Still they say don't come here. I guess what saddens me the most is how that suggests complicity. It implies that you and I and 80 million honest gun owners are somehow to blame, that we don't care. We don't care as much as they do, or that we don't deserve to be as shocked and horrified as every other soul in America mourning for the people of Littleton.

8 Don't come here. That's offensive. It's also absurd because we live here. There are thousands of NRA members in Denver, and tens upon tens of thousands in the state of Colorado.

9 NRA members labor in Denver's factories, they populate Denver's faculties, run Denver corporations, play on Colorado sports teams, work in media across the Front Range, parent and teach and coach Denver's children, attend Denver's churches and proudly represent Denver in uniform on the world's oceans and in the skies over Kosovo at this very moment.

10 NRA members are in city hall, Fort Carson, NORAD, the Air Force Academy and the Olympic Training Center. And yes, NRA members are surely among the police and fire and SWAT team heroes who risked their lives to rescue the students at Columbine.

11 Don't come here? We're already here. This community is our home. Every community in America is our home. We are a 128-year-old fixture of mainstream America. The Second Amendment ethic of lawful, responsible firearm ownership spans the broadest cross section of American life imaginable.

12 So, we have the same right as all other citizens to be here. To help shoulder the grief and share our sorrow and to offer our respectful, reassured voice to the national discourse that has erupted around this tragedy.

13 One more thing. Our words and our behavior will be scrutinized more than ever this morning. Those who are

hostile towards us will lie in wait to seize on a sound bite out of context, ever searching for an embarrassing moment to ridicule us. So, let us be mindful. The eyes of the nation are upon us today.

14 . . . We have work to do, hearts to heal, evil to defeat, and a country to unite. We may have differences, yes, and we will again suffer tragedy almost beyond description. But when the sun sets on Denver tonight, and forever more, let it always set on we the people, secure in our land of the free and the home of the brave.

---

1. The speaker's style is best described as

(A) defensive and critical

(B) aggressive and antagonistic

(C) compassionate and empathetic

(D) optimistic and hopeful

(E) sarcastic and jeering

2. The speaker's perspective in the passage is that of

(A) a civically engaged leader who calls for reform of gun laws

(B) a concerned citizen who calls for more access to guns

(C) a loyal organization leader who defends his organization despite criticism

(D) a disgruntled organization leader, disappointed in his members for their complacency

(E) a citizen who is outraged over disparities in the community he loves

3. The first line of paragraph 3, "But it's fitting and proper that we should do this" serves primarily to

(A) issue a disclaimer about the message he is about to deliver in the aftermath of a tragedy

(B) qualify and explain the need to interrupt normally scheduled activities

(C) sharpen the contrast between his organization and the Denver audience

(D) warn his audience about the way their message is likely to be received in Littleton

(E) unite his audience under a common goal and rally them to be—and do—their best

4. The rhetorical purpose of the last paragraph is to
   (A) suggest that he is speaking from the perspective of all members of the NRA
   (B) encourage the audience to support others in light of the recent tragedy
   (C) excuse the hostility of NRA members in response to others' judgments
   (D) prompt the audience to support and advertise for the NRA
   (E) clearly articulate his call to action, warning his members of the stakes

5. In context, the "128-year-old fixture of mainstream America" to which the speaker refers is
   (A) Littleton, Colorado
   (B) the NRA
   (C) the second amendment
   (D) the Columbine school district
   (E) democratic unity

6. The passage ends on a note of
   (A) exhausted defeat
   (B) ominous warning
   (C) mocking cynicism
   (D) regret and grief
   (E) great determination

7. In paragraphs 4, 5, and 6, the speaker criticizes the mayor and the newspaper on the grounds that they have
   (A) assumed NRA members contributed to the tragedy and feel less grief than others
   (B) misconstrued the reason that Heston and his organization wanted to be in Littleton
   (C) failed to alert the press that the NRA desired to support efforts responding to the tragedy
   (D) overlooked the benefit of gun sales for the local economy and community of Littleton
   (E) encouraged citizens and media to reject the NRA because of its pro-gun stance

Question 8 is covered in Unit 2.

8. The speaker contrasts his own experience volunteering for the draft with general jobs of other NRA members to

(A) illustrate the double standards of those who claim the NRA is not welcome in Littleton

(B) explain the effects of gun sales on the local economy and the community at large

(C) emphasize the influence of the NRA on many other areas in the United States

(D) suggest that NRA members are upstanding members of the community

(E) highlight the obstacles that the NRA has had to overcome over the years

Question 9 is covered in Unit 6.

9. In context, sentences 2–4 of paragraph 4 ("I said to the mayor…don't come") could be used to support which of the following claims about the speaker's tone?

(A) His tone when discussing the people of Littleton, Colorado, is patronizing.

(B) His tone when discussing the mayor of Denver, Colorado, is conciliatory.

(C) He adopts a bold, forthright tone when acknowledging his reply to the mayor.

(D) He adopts an admiring tone when discussing those who welcomed him to the city.

(E) He adopts an impersonal tone when discussing the tragedy of what has just occurred.

Section I: Writing

Questions 10–16. Read the passage carefully before you choose your answers. (The passage below is a draft.)

(1) Apparently, our nation was built on the idea that every person should hold as many guns as possible, and through this logic, we will all be safer because we will have to act in a world where we know everyone has a gun. (2) The titans of our history were at the forefront of the idea that Americans are obligated to have weapons to not only protect themselves, but also that the right to bear arms helps us to protect others. (3) It was through the approval of the Second Amendment that these titans of history guaranteed our right to bear arms, and consequently, protect an American, democratic liberty.

(4) In 1789, it took an average of 20 seconds to reload a musket. (5) Further, the United States lacked a standing army of any sort and relied on militias to be ready and waiting for a foreign or domestic threat. (6) There presented a strong purpose for the ratification of this amendment yet the firearms were not, and are not, exempt from regulation. Automatic and semi-automatic weapons were not in the dreams of our founding fathers.

(7) After each mass shooting, the parents, families, and classmates of those affected appeal their state legislatures, begging them to regulate these types of weapons that are able to destroy so many lives in such a short time.

(8) Upon reaching the state legislature, gun-control activists quickly find that special interest groups such as the National Rifle Association (NRA) have endorsed and assisted in getting the legislatures at the state level elected, which creates a conflict of interest. (9) The NRA has set a ceiling on gun regulation—capping the acquisition and use of firearms at nuclear weapons. (10) That's it. (11) If you want a tank, a machine gun, a grenade—go for it. (12) That is your right; and, be sure to thank the ratification of the second amendment on your way out the door.

10. The writer wants to avoid revealing any potential biases in the first sentence (below) but still maintain the central claim.

Apparently, our nation was built on the idea that every person should hold as many guns as possible, and through this logic, we will all be safer because we will have to act in a world where we know everyone has a gun.

Which of the following versions of the sentences accomplishes this goal?

(A) (as it is now)

(B) Our nation was built on the idea that every person has the right and responsibility to own a gun, which logically suggests that society is safer when everyone is armed.

(C) Apparently, our nation was built on the idea that every person should hold as many guns as possible which means that we can all be safer because we will have to act in a world where we know everyone has a gun.

(D) We are the safest nation because we were founded on the idea that everyone should own as many guns as possible.

(E) Apparently, we will all be safer because we will be in a world where we know everyone has a gun.

11. The writer wants to alter the passage for an audience that is unfamiliar with the historical details embedded within this argument. Which of the following changes best accomplishes this goal?

(A) Add to sentence 2: *The titans of our history—James Madison, Thomas Jefferson, and George Washington—*

(B) Edit sentence 3 to include: *It was through the Second Amendment—the right to bear arms—*

(C) Edit sentence 4 by changing the word *musket* to the more era-neutral term *firearm.*

(D) Edit sentence 6 by substituting the word *ratification* for the word *approval.*

(E) Edit sentence 12 by replacing *the ratification of the second amendment* with *the nation's founders.*

12. The writer wants to add the following sentence to the argument to provide additional explanation. Where would this sentence best be placed?

Our founding fathers did not envision a world where mass shootings would become the norm as a result of a semi-automatic weapon being able to shoot at the rate of 500–1,000 rounds per minute.

(A) before sentence 1

(B) after sentence 3

(C) before sentence 7

(D) after sentence 10

(E) after sentence 12

13. The writer is considering adding the following sentence at the beginning of the second paragraph, before sentence 4.

However, at the time that this amendment was ratified, the America as we know it today looked completely different.

Should the writer make this revision?

(A) No, this detail assumes that the reader has historical knowledge about the second amendment.

(B) No, this detail would be better placed before sentence 7 to help to clarify the transition between the past and present.

(C) Yes, this detail introduces the expert evidence of historians.

(D) Yes, this detail transitions from the introductory ideas about the second amendment to discussing the history of firearms.

(E) Yes, this detail anticipates responses prior to the writer's claim being presented.

Question 14 is covered in Unit 4.

14. The writer wants to expand the acknowledgement of the power of the democratic idea while still ensuring the claim is clear. Which of the following would best achieve this purpose if placed in the last paragraph?

(A) The second amendment has created a safer society overall even though our firearms are different today.

(B) Many attempts to regulate firearms for the American public have been made with no success.

(C) Gun control was not needed in 1789, but as gun technology advances, we must add protections to ensure the safety of American citizens.

(D) It is our responsibility to maintain the vision of our forefathers and uphold the democratic oath upon which this country is built.

(E) It would be incredibly costly and time-consuming to ensure safeguards for gun control, which ultimately wouldn't impact the mass shootings that occur.

Question 15 is covered in Unit 5.

15. The writer wants to add a phrase at the beginning of sentence 6 (adjusting the capitalization as needed) to set up a cause-effect relationship between sentences 5 and 6. Which of the following choices best accomplishes this goal?

(A) Further,

(B) Similarly,

(C) By contrast,

(D) In fact,

(E) Consequently,

Question 16 is covered in Unit 7.

16. The writer wants to ensure that the argument has addressed the complexity of the issue. When evaluating whether or not complexity has been addressed, which of the following questions would be most important for the writer to address?

(A) Is the reader familiar with this time period in history or does the writer need to provide more historical facts?

(B) Should the writer discuss other founding fathers who were involved in the creation of the Bill of Rights and ratification of certain amendments?

(C) What other attempts have been made to control firearms and what other options exist to regulate weapons?

(D) Have firearms been regulated in other countries and can such examples be used as a basis for comparison in the argument?

(E) Has the writer described or addressed reasons why many citizens oppose firearm regulation in modern America?

JOIN THE CONVERSATION: SYNTHESIS ESSAY (PART 3)

This final instructional guide on responding to the synthesis prompt in the Unit Review and on the AP® exam uses the exact same prompt as that of Unit 7. (See pages 364–373 and 448–455 for Parts 1 and 2 of the instructional guide on synthesis.) However, you will now encounter two new sources.

Immigration and settlement of people are facts of history. Culture and language barriers often mean that similar groups settle in "enclaves," that is, smaller areas surrounded by larger areas where the population in the smaller area is culturally or ethnically distinct from that of the larger area. Terms like "Chinatown," "Little Italy," "Little Havana," and "Little Senegal" have become common, but there are even entire cities that have come to represent enclaves. Dearborn, Michigan, for example, has one of the largest concentrations of Middle Eastern people in North America. Recent conversations about immigration, diversity, and national/cultural identity have brought attention to the role of these enclaves in larger society.

Carefully read the following sources, including the introductory information for each source.

Write an essay that synthesizes material from at least three of the sources and develops your position on the role of cultural or ethnic enclaves.

Source A (Dearborn)—Unit 6, page 366
Source B (Greenholtz)—Unit 6, page 367
Source C (Denmark)—Unit 6, page 369
Source D (Pew)—Unit 7, page 450
Source E (Miami)—NEW, page 542
Source F (Slattery)—NEW, page 543

In your response you should do the following:

- Respond to the prompt with a thesis that presents a defensible position.
- Select and use evidence from at least three of the provided sources to support your line of reasoning. Indicate clearly the sources used through direct quotation, paraphrase, or summary. Sources may be cited as Source A, Source B, etc., or by using the description in parentheses.
- Explain how the evidence supports your line of reasoning.
- Use appropriate grammar and punctuation in communicating your argument.

The new sources provide more information for consideration. One of these new sources (Source E) is a "qualitative" visual. It does not relate to numbers, as the graph in Source D does; instead, it provides some images that are open to interpretation. Throughout this book, captions have raised questions about interpretations of photos and other graphics to focus your thinking on images as "texts." Use what you have learned to analyze the qualitative visual sources in the synthesis task. You will always see two visual sources on the synthesis task and at least one of those will be quantitative.

Most of what you need to be able to do in the overall essays has been covered, so the essay organizer will not appear here. Now you need to focus on revising your writing style and making certain that your paragraphs and sentences are cohesive and coherent.

- Carefully consider different perspectives as they are presented in the synthesis task.
- Remember, this task requires you to not only make your argument but also to show you understand other perspectives and can argue with/against them.
- Work on revision of individual sentences based on the things you learned about clauses, phrases, and words in parts 1 and 3 of this unit.

Keeping Track of Ideas and Sources

If you started a web graphic organizer in Unit 6, use it again to continue with the additional sources in this unit. In the organizer on page 544, notice that in addition to areas for each source, including the visual source, there is a fourth area titled "Complexity." In this space, write notes about any clashes you may see in the perspectives of the sources, any overlaps, or any areas of limitation or bias in the perspectives. Also note the abstract idea you believe these ideas connect to. Then use the drafting organizer on pages 453–455 as a guide to complete your essay.

Source E
"Exploring Little Havana."
19 June 2020.

The following is a collection of pictures related to La Pequeña Havana (Little Havana) in Miami, Florida.

Source F

Slattery, Gram. "In Defense of the Ethnic Enclave." *Harvard Political Review*, 29 May 2019.

Following is an excerpt from a journal on politics, policy, and culture published by college students at Harvard University.

As a Bostonian, I lament a shrinking Chinatown that has been boxed in over time by two interstate highways and a remarkably bland, expanding medical center. Furthermore, I'm angered to see the attempts of the city's redistricting commission to divide Chinatown between three councilmen, a measure that would effectively destroy the community as a political entity. On the other hand, I applaud a North End, now wedged between beautiful post-Big Dig[1] green space and the Atlantic, a neighborhood that has grown hip and professional, but remained distinctively Italian even as Italian-Americans have grown wealthier as a whole.

As a last-ditch effort, when ethnic enclaves slowly degrade, failing to follow the path of the North End, it is possible to artificially celebrate the ethnic heritage of an enclave even after the enclave has been demographically diminished. For instance, the Feast of San Gennaro in New York's Little Italy, originally instituted as a celebration of Neapolitan immigrants in 1924, continues today. The festival seems to admit that if one can no longer celebrate the heritage of one's country of origin in a collective way, he or she might as well celebrate the heritage of the enclave that was itself derived from that now distant country of origin.

On the whole, it is only by embracing new urban ethnic groups, avoiding the nativist slings of our past, and buttressing the integrity, cultural, architectural, and otherwise, of our existing immigrant communities, that we can avoid, or at least delay the disappearance of the Little Italies, Chinatowns, and host of other enclaves. I do not mean to imply that we should strive for ethnic compartmentalization, but a connection to one's heritage has always existed in a nation of immigrants, and I would much prefer a spicy jambalaya model of living to a homogenous rice pudding culture of mush. Perhaps, it is time to take the required steps to protect the integrity of ingredients in this cultural jambalaya, not to stress our differences, but rather to protect the vibrancy of pluralism in a homogenizing American society.

1 The Big Dig was a 16-year construction project to run major highways through Boston, Massachusetts, into tunnels

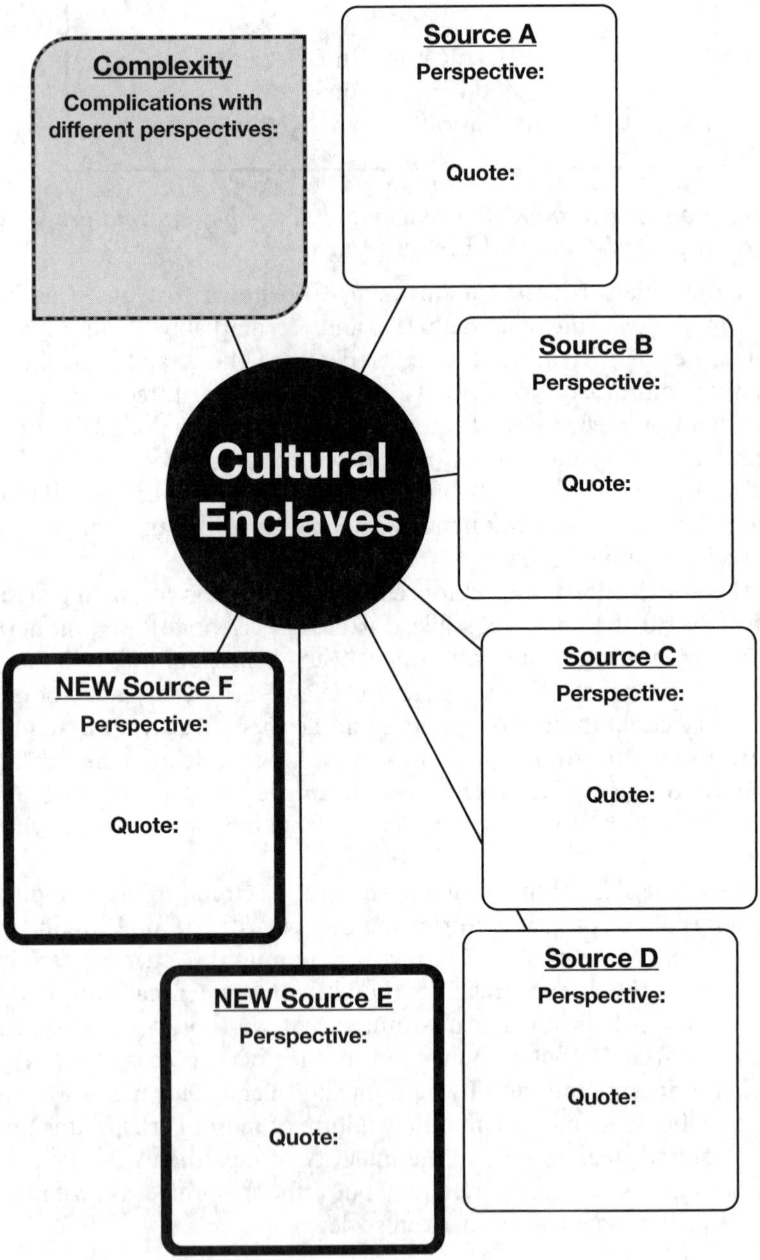

Apply

Follow the same process as above to respond to the synthesis prompt on page 545. For current free-response prompt samples, visit the College Board website.

Section II: Free Response

Synthesis: Circumstance and Morality

The question of what constitutes moral and immoral behavior has perplexed humankind for centuries. When questioned in surveys, people generally hold similar opinions of what they consider moral and immoral acts, which suggests we have a shared sense of what is right and wrong. Yet people consistently act against these moral codes. Furthermore, when faced with their transgressions, people often try to justify them. So what factors cause people to act in ways that are immoral? To find an answer, scientists, psychologists, philosophers, and other thinkers have created and studied countless experiments. In 1971, Phillip Zimbardo, a psychology professor at Stanford University, oversaw an experiment called the Stanford Prison Experiment. During the experiment, Stanford students were assigned roles as guard or prisoner and were then observed. The experiment ended when the guards began to brutalize the prisoners. Many questions arose from this experiment—did the circumstances drive these students to commit immoral acts? Were they powerless against situational forces? If so, how are we to explain German doctors during World War II who lied to Nazi soldiers about the health of some Jews to spare their lives?

Carefully read the following six sources, including the introductory information for each source. Write an essay that synthesizes material from at least three of the sources and develops your position on the extent to which the circumstances of a person's life influence that person's moral decisions.

Source A: Virginia O'Hanlon Letter to the Editor and Response (The Sun)
Source B: Speech and Immorality (Simply Philosophy Study)
Source C: "Are These 10 Lies Justified?" (Dworkin)
Source D: "Ten Reasons Why You Shouldn't Lie" (Greenberg)
Source E: "How Do We Make Moral Decisions?" (Dartmouth Study)
Source F: "Correlation of Sibling Traits" (Graph)

In your response you should do the following:

- Respond to the prompt with a thesis that presents a defensible position.
- Select and use evidence from at least three of the provided sources to support your line of reasoning. Indicate clearly the sources used through direct quotation, paraphrase, or summary. Sources may be cited as Source A, Source B, etc., or by using the description in parentheses.
- Explain how the evidence supports your line of reasoning.
- Use appropriate grammar and punctuation in communicating your argument.

Source A

O'Hanlon, Virginia. "Letter to the Editor," and response in unsigned editorial, *New York Sun*, 21 September 1897.

Eight-year-old Virginia O'Hanlon wrote a letter to the editor of New York's Sun, and the quick response was printed as an unsigned editorial Sept. 21, 1897.

DEAR EDITOR: I am 8 years old.

Some of my little friends say there is no Santa Claus.

Papa says, 'If you see it in THE SUN it's so.'

Please tell me the truth; is there a Santa Claus?

VIRGINIA O'HANLON.
115 WEST NINETY-FIFTH STREET.

VIRGINIA, your little friends are wrong. They have been affected by the skepticism of a skeptical age. They do not believe except they see. They think that nothing can be which is not comprehensible by their little minds. All minds, Virginia, whether they be men's or children's, are little. In this great universe of ours man is a mere insect, an ant, in his intellect, as compared with the boundless world about him, as measured by the intelligence capable of grasping the whole of truth and knowledge.

Yes, VIRGINIA, there is a Santa Claus. He exists as certainly as love and generosity and devotion exist, and you know that they abound and give to your life its highest beauty and joy. Alas! how dreary would be the world if there were no Santa Claus. It would be as dreary as if there were no VIRGINIAS. There would be no childlike faith then, no poetry, no romance to make tolerable this existence. We should have no enjoyment, except in sense and sight. The eternal light with which childhood fills the world would be extinguished.

Not believe in Santa Claus! You might as well not believe in fairies! You might get your papa to hire men to watch in all the chimneys on Christmas Eve to catch Santa Claus, but even if they did not see Santa Claus coming down, what would that prove? Nobody sees Santa Claus, but that is no sign that there is no Santa Claus. The most real things in the world are those that neither children nor men can see. Did you ever see fairies dancing on the lawn? Of course not, but that's no proof that they are not there. Nobody can conceive or imagine all the wonders there are unseen and unseeable in the world.

You may tear apart the baby's rattle and see what makes the noise inside, but there is a veil covering the unseen world which not the strongest man, nor even the united strength of all the strongest men that ever lived, could tear apart. Only faith, fancy, poetry, love, romance, can push aside that curtain and view and picture the supernal beauty and glory beyond. Is it all real? Ah, VIRGINIA, in all this world there is nothing else real and abiding.

No Santa Claus! Thank God! he lives, and he lives forever. A thousand years from now, Virginia, nay, ten times ten thousand years from now, he will continue to make glad the heart of childhood.

Source B

"Speech and Immorality." simplyphilosophy.org, accessed 13 June 2020.

Speech is naturally used to communicate to other people. But not all communications to other people are valuable. Some kinds of speech are wrong by their very nature. There are five ways that speech may go wrong: by lying, deception, gossip, harm and rash promises.

One of the ways in which speech may go wrong is by lying. Lying is deliberately telling something that we believe to be false. Since speech is naturally aimed at communication, this is contrary to the purpose of communication. Whether or not lying is sometimes acceptable is another issue. Most of the time it is not acceptable. Even people who argue that it is sometimes acceptable usually limit acceptability to those times that someone's life is in danger.

Another way that speech may go wrong is by deception. Deception is arranging for someone to believe something that is false. It does not necessarily require speech, but most of the time some form of communication is required. Almost everyone admits that deception is sometimes acceptable. Like lying, these times are usually limited to those situations in which someone's life or health are in danger.

A third way for speech to go wrong is by gossip. Gossip is sharing information with those people who have no right to that information. This can include sharing classified information with another country, sharing personal information with strangers, and giving out another's password. In these sorts of cases, deception is not necessary, but giving away information that we have no right to share is the problem.

A fourth way for speech to go wrong is by using it to harm someone. It is possible to speak without any sort of deception, lying or gossip and to intentionally <u>cause</u> harm to another person. This includes such things as pointing out their faults, reminding them of past transgressions, nagging and 'fighting words'. Name calling is also within this category.

The final way for speech to go wrong is by making rash promises. We can promise things without any sort of deception or lying yet find ourselves unable to fulfill them in the future. So making these sorts of promises in the past is rash. This also includes making promises on behalf of others, making contracts, and forcing contracts on third parties.

As far as I can tell, these five ways are all independent ways that our speech might go wrong. If none of them applies, then our speech has nothing wrong with it. I have not proven this, and we need to examine why each of these is usually wrong, and what right principle they are perverting. Doing this will enable us to understand the morality of speech in general.

Source C

Dworkin, Gerald. "Are These 10 Lies Justifed?" *The New York Times*, 14 Dcember 2015.

The following opinion piece by Gerald Dworkin was published on The Stone, *a* New York Times *forum for contemporary philosophers and other thinkers on issues both timely and timeless. Dworkin is distinguished professor of philosophy, emeritus at the University of California, Davis.*

Most of us believe that lying is wrong. We teach our children that it is wrong, and hope or expect that value judgment is shared by our friends and family. In public, we decry politicians and public officials when they lie, which we have frequent occasion to do these days. But the truth about lying is more complicated.

We tell lies to one another every day. But when we commit other acts that are generally believed to be immoral, like cruelty and theft, we do not seek to justify them. We either deny that the acts we committed are appropriately described by these terms, or we feel guilt or remorse. But many of us are prepared to defend our lies: indeed, to advocate their general use. Of course the Nazi at the door inquiring about Jews within ought to be lied to.

But perhaps this example only shows that there is not an absolute prohibition on lying. Such cases are rare, the harm to the innocent clear, the wickedness of the aggressor obvious. I want to argue that the number and types of permissible lies are much wider than one might have thought.

I am not arguing for the view that lying is morally neutral. I accept the fact that there ought to be a strong presumption in favor of honesty. But it is a presumption that not only can be, but ought to be, overridden in many more cases than we assume.

Let me begin by defining what a lie is. If I defined lying so as to include failure to reveal the truth I would be making my case too easy. We all agree that there are many cases where the latter is permissible.

John lies to Mary if he says X, believes X to be false, and intends that Mary believe X.

It should come as no surprise that philosophers have denied, or sought to clarify, each part of this definition. But I think this definition captures most of what people have in mind when they say lying is always, or almost always, wrong. It also captures the morally important feature that explains people's aversion to lying — saying what you believe to be false in order to make other people believe something false. It is usually a bad thing for people to come to believe false things. Even when it is not a betrayal of trust.

Nevertheless, it is my claim that we could not lead our lives if we never told lies — or that if we could it would be a much worse life. But I would like to invite your own views on this to begin a dialogue.

Here is a list of lies that I believe to be either permissible, or, in some cases, obligatory. Readers will certainly disagree with me about some, perhaps many, of these cases. But such disagreement should not be the end of the discussion. I invite your reflection on why you disagree. It may be that I am making some implicit assumption about the case that you are challenging. It might be that you think that there are bad consequences of the lie in question, but I do not, either because I do not think the consequences are likely, or because I do not think they are bad.

In other cases, you might be prepared to accept the verdict as justified lying, but argue it has a special feature that is not present generally. That raises the question of whether there are other such contexts, and how widespread they are.

Some cases may simply involve fundamental differences in judgment. "I can't say why, but it's just wrong." These are much rarer than one might think and I doubt that any of my cases are like that. But we will see.

1. A man lies to his wife about where they are going in order to get her to a place where a surprise birthday party has been organized.
2. A young child is rescued from a plane crash in a very weakened state. His parents have been killed in the crash but he is unaware of this. He asks about his parents and the attending physician says they are O.K. He intends to tell the truth once the child is stronger.
3. Your father suffers from severe dementia and is in a nursing home. When it is time for you to leave, he becomes extremely agitated and often has to be restrained. On the occasions when you have said you would be back tomorrow he was quite peaceful about your leaving. You tell him now every time you leave that you will be back tomorrow knowing that in a very short time after you leave, he will have forgotten what you said.
4. A woman's husband drowned in a car accident when the car plunged off a bridge into a body of water. It was clear from the physical evidence that he desperately tried to get out of the car and died a dreadful death. At the hospital where his body was brought his wife

asked the physician in attendance what kind of death her husband suffered. He replied, "He died immediately from the impact of the crash. He did not suffer."

5. In an effort to enforce rules against racial discrimination "testers" were sent out to rent a house. First, an African-American couple claiming to be married with two children and an income that was sufficient to pay the rent would try to rent a house. If they were told that the house was not available, a white tester couple with the same family and economic profile would be sent. If they were offered the rental there would be persuasive evidence of racial discrimination.
6. In November of 1962, during the Cuban Missile crisis, President Kennedy gave a conference. When asked whether he had discussed any matters other than Cuban missiles with the Soviets he absolutely denied it. In fact, he had promised that the United States would remove missiles from Turkey.
7. A woman interviewing for a job in a small philosophy department is asked if she intends to have children. Believing that if she says (politely) it's none of their business she will not get the job, she lies and says she does not intend to have a family.
8. In order to test whether arthroscopic surgery improved the conditions of patients' knees a study was done in which half the patients were told the procedure was being done but it was not. Little cuts were made in the knees, the doctors talked as if it were being done, sounds were produced as if the operation were being done. The patients were under light anesthesia. It turned out that the same percentage of patients reported pain relief and increased mobility in the real and sham operations. The patients were informed in advance that they either would receive a real or a sham operation.
9. I am negotiating for a car with a salesperson. He asks me what the maximum I am prepared to pay is. I say $15,000. It is actually $20,000.
10. We heap exaggerated praise on our children all the time about their earliest attempts to sing or dance or paint or write poems. For some children this encouragement leads to future practice, which in turn promotes the development—in some—of genuine achievement.

Source D

Greenberg, Barbara. "Ten Reasons Why You Shouldn't Lie." psychologytoday.com, 29 June 2018.

Barbara Greenberg, Ph.D., is a clinical psychologist who specializes in the treatment of adolescents and their well-intentioned but exhausted parents.

Dear Dr. G.,

I am a 17-year-old girl. I am really mad at my parents. Apparently, my mother, who makes most of the money for our family to live on, lost her job a year ago. My parents never told me or my brother. My mother even got up and pretended to go to work every day for the past year.

I was suspicious that something was very wrong in my house when I started to overhear my parents argue about money. My brother and I talked about this and decided to talk about what was going on with my parents.

During that emotional conversation, my mother admitted that she lost her job a year ago and that she didn't want to tell me and my brother because she didn't want us to worry. I think that this was such a stupid thing for my parents to do.

They should have been honest with us. We knew that there was something wrong. We just didn't know what it was. I am so mad at my parents for being so secretive. I wouldn't have asked my parents to buy me things if I knew that they were having financial problems.

An Angry Daughter

Dear Daughter,

I understand why you are angry. It is very difficult to live in a household full of lies because you can feel the tension and you have nothing to attribute it to. As a result, you may come up with all kinds of reasons that this tension exists that may even be worse than the truth.

I am almost always of the opinion that we do better handling the truth than secrets. Secrets create tension and confusion. While the truth may be quite painful, it is almost always easier to deal with than lies and secrets.

Human beings really dislike ambiguity and a lack of clarity. We want to know what is happening in our environments and what we might be able to do to help with the identified problem. I hope that you told your parents what you are telling me. If you haven't, then please find time to tell them that in the future you would like to be told the truth about any stressors going on in the family. You are certainly old enough to be told the truth. Children of most ages usually have a sense when something is not going well. I hope that you and your brother can rebuild trust with your parents and that your anger at your parents dissipates.

Perhaps you can use what happened in your family as a learning opportunity. There are many reasons why lying to children (or to other family members) is not a good idea. Let me explain.

1. Children almost always sense that there are stressors going on and the lack of knowledge about what is going on leads invariably to unnecessary tension and creative speculation. They may believe that the problem is actually worse than it is.
2. When parents withhold the truth in an effort to protect their kids, they are actually decreasing the trust level in the home. After all, when the truth inevitably surfaces, the children will feel lied to and trust will be broken.
3. When parents lie to their kids, they are modeling that lying, is in fact, acceptable. This is never a good message to send.
4. When kids or anyone else for that matter is lied to, they feel irrelevant and unimportant. And, no one wants to feel this way, correct?
5. When parents are honest with their kids, this fosters better communication. And, we know that good communication leads to better relationships, better emotional and physical health, and less susceptibility to peer pressure.
6. When parents lie to their kids, I have to wonder if they are doing this to protect themselves or their kids. In other words, think about what would be most helpful for your family as a system rather than easier for you as a parent. Sometimes, the more difficult thing to do is the right thing to do.
7. If family issues are not shared, then when they are revealed they may be experienced as shocking and alarming. This is why I suggest sharing issues with kids as they occur so that they don't turn into bigger issues than they might actually be.
8. Kids in families want to have a role and be helpful. For example, if a family member is ill then the children can help out in a developmentally appropriate manner. If the stressor is dealt with as a secret, then kids cannot be given a helpful role. Everyone feels better and more important if they are needed.
9. By keeping secrets, parents inadvertently make their kids feel disconnected. It is very important for families to function as a team.
10. Dealing with stressors may actually facilitate the development of resiliency. So, in an effort to raise kids with grit, parents may do well to model how to deal with clearly identified stressors.

So, here's to the telling the truth. I hope that you have learned from your parents' missteps even if they were intended to protect you and your brother.

—Dr. G.

Source E

"How do we make moral decisions?" Dartmouth Study. *sciencedaily.com*, 18 April 2019.

When it comes to making moral decisions, we often think of the golden rule: do unto others as you would have them do unto you. Yet, why we make such decisions has been widely debated. Are we motivated by feelings of guilt, where we don't want to feel bad for letting the other person down? Or by fairness, where we want to avoid unequal outcomes?

Some people may rely on principles of both guilt and fairness and may switch their moral rule depending on the circumstances, according to a Radboud University–Dartmouth College study on moral decision-making and cooperation. The findings challenge prior research in economics, psychology and neuroscience, which is often based on the premise that people are motivated by one moral principle, which remains constant over time. The study was published recently in *Nature Communications*.

"Our study demonstrates that with moral behavior, people may not in fact always stick to the golden rule. While most people tend to exhibit some concern for others, others may demonstrate what we have called 'moral opportunism,' where they still want to look moral but want to maximize their own benefit," said lead author Jeroen van Baar, a postdoctoral research associate in the department of cognitive, linguistic and psychological sciences at Brown University, who started this research when he was a scholar at Dartmouth visiting from the Donders Institute for Brain, Cognition and Behavior at Radboud University.

"In everyday life, we may not notice that our morals are context-dependent since our contexts tend to stay the same daily. However, under new circumstances, we may find that the moral rules we thought we'd always follow are actually quite malleable," explained co-author Luke J. Chang, an assistant professor of psychological and brain sciences and director of the Computational Social Affective Neuroscience Laboratory (Cosan Lab) at Dartmouth. "This has tremendous ramifications if one considers how our moral behavior could change under new contexts, such as during war," he added.

To examine moral decision-making within the context of reciprocity, the researchers designed a modified trust game called the Hidden Multiplier Trust Game, which allowed them to classify decisions in reciprocating trust as a function of an individual's moral strategy. With this method, the team could determine which type of moral strategy a study participant was using: inequity aversion (where people reciprocate because they want to seek fairness in outcomes), guilt aversion (where people reciprocate because they want to avoid feeling guilty), greed, or moral opportunism (a new strategy that the team identified, where people switch between inequity aversion and guilt aversion depending on what will serve their interests best). The researchers also developed a computational, moral strategy model that could be used to explain how people behave in the game and examined the brain activity patterns associated with the moral strategies.

The findings reveal for the first time that unique patterns of brain activity underlie the inequity aversion and guilt aversion strategies, even when the strategies yield the same behavior. For the participants that were morally opportunistic, the researchers observed that their brain patterns switched between the two moral strategies across different contexts. "Our results demonstrate that people may use different moral principles to make their decisions, and that some people are much more flexible and will apply different principles depending on the situation," explained Chang. "This may explain why people that we like and respect occasionally do things that we find morally objectionable."

Source F

"Correlation of Sibling Traits" Wikimedia Commons, accessed 6 April 2020.

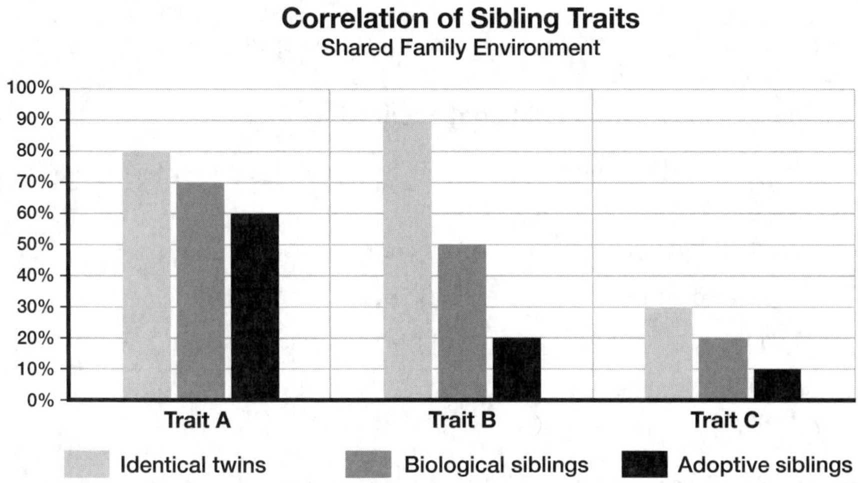

This chart illustrates three patterns of the influence of genes and environment on traits in individuals. Trait A shows a high sibling correlation, whether the siblings are identical twins, biological siblings, or adoptive siblings, but little heritability (ability to be transmitted biologically from parent to offspring). Trait B shows a high heritability, since the correlation of the trait rises sharply with the degree of genetic similarity. Trait C shows low heritability, but also low correlations generally. That is, the degree to which individuals display Trait C has little to do with either genes or environmental factors. Notice also that even identical twins raised in the same family environment rarely show 100% trait correlation.

Rhetorical Analysis: Charlton Heston Speech Excerpt

In May 1999, Charlton Heston, president of the *National Rifle Association*, delivered a speech in Denver just a few weeks after the Columbine Massacre: a school shooting that happened in Littleton, Colorado, and claimed the lives of 13 individuals.

Read the speech on pages 530–532 carefully. Write an essay that analyzes the rhetorical choices Heston makes in order to address his audience and convey his message about the way his organization was presented in Littleton.

In your response you should do the following:

- Respond to the prompt with a thesis that analyzes the writer's rhetorical choices.
- Select and use evidence to support your line of reasoning.
- Explain how the evidence supports your line of reasoning.
- Demonstrate an understanding of the rhetorical situation.
- Use appropriate grammar and punctuation in communicating your argument.

Argument: Fundamental Laws of Nature

NiceArtLife.com is an online magazine that focuses on subjects of the art and graphic world, culture, life, spirituality, science, curiosities, design, photography, and digital arts. People from all over are invited to comment on the stories and art presented, to form a running dialogue among global citizens. Recently, a contributor said:

> In this modern time, [hu]mankind searches almost obsessively for pleasure, materialistic goals and abundance. To obtain this we and our ancestors have exploited nature without any moral restraint to such an extent that nature has been rendered almost incapable of sustaining a healthy life. We have neglected the amazing relationship between [hu]man[s] and nature.

Write an essay that argues your position on the extent to which human interaction with the environment has violated the fundamental state of natural laws. Support your position with evidence from your reading, observation, and experience.

In your response you should do the following:

- Respond to the prompt with a thesis that presents a defensible position.
- Provide evidence to support your line of reasoning.
- Explain how the evidence supports your line of reasoning.
- Use appropriate grammar and punctuation in communicating your argument.

UNIT 9

Contributing to the Conversation

Part 1: Engaging Counterarguments

ENDURING UNDERSTANDING AND SKILLS: Unit Nine

Part 1

Understand

Writers make claims about subjects, rely on evidence that supports the reasoning that justifies the claim, and often acknowledge or respond to other, possibly opposing, arguments. (CLE-1)

Demonstrate

Explain ways claims are qualified through modifiers, counterarguments, and alternative perspectives. (Reading 3.C)

Qualify a claim using modifiers, counterarguments, or alternative perspectives. (Skill 4.C)

Source: *AP® English Language and Composition Course and Exam Description*

Unit 9 Overview

Some people avoid discussing religion and politics at social gatherings. Why? One answer may be that people often define themselves according to their religion and politics, so they may hear opposition to their ideas as a personal attack. Another factor may be the divided and biased news media, those to both the left and right of the newspapers, magazines, and television broadcasts that try for an even-handed presentation. For these reasons and others, no matter how logically sound an argument may be, conversations about religion and politics often devolve into emotionally heated fights. The participants may end up hurling insults rather than working to find a common goal—even if that goal is congenially agreeing to disagree. Emotionally charged responses that ignore the perspectives of others only spread dissension and disregard the importance of social discourse.

Unit 9 addresses this problem and provides tools for contributing to the conversation in respectful and open-minded ways. You have been building your analytical and argumentative skills throughout this course. Now it's time

"I like it. Let's just punch up the bias a bit."

How does the artist use irony in this cartoon?

Source: Cartoonstock

to add the most important skill of all. In this unit, you'll learn to recognize how the ideas of others relate to your own positions and perspectives and how to treat the ideas of others with respect, even when you disagree. Seldom do people change their minds in the middle of a contentious debate. But when others feel that they are respected, listened to, and considered, they are much easier to convince. Creating empathetic responses will not only build your credibility as a speaker, but such responses will also encourage those in the conversation to take matters less personally, listen to the perspectives of others, and possibly change minds, including your own.

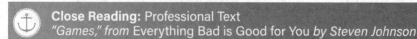

Close Reading: Professional Text
"Games," from Everything Bad is Good for You *by Steven Johnson*

Steven Johnson writes for a variety of sources about the relationships among technology, science, media, and culture. The following chapter from his book *Everything Bad is Good for You* encourages people to reconsider and reevaluate the value of video games and the social biases toward them.

1 You can't get much more conventional than the conventional wisdom that kids today would be better off spending more time reading books, and less time zoning out in front of their video games.

2 The latest edition of *Dr. Spock*[1]—"revised and fully expanded for a new century" as the cover reports—has this to say of video games: "The best that can be said of them is that they may help promote eye-hand coordination in children.

1 Dr. Benjamin Spock (1903–1998) wrote one of the most widely read books ever written, *Baby and Child Care,* and was regarded as an expert in childrearing.

3 The worst that can be said is that they sanction, and even promote aggression and violent responses to conflict.

4 But what can be said with much greater certainty is this: most computer games are a colossal waste of time."

5 But where reading is concerned, the advice is quite different: "I suggest you begin to foster in your children a love of reading and the printed word from the start. . . . What is important is that your child be an avid reader."

6 In the middle of 2004, the National Endowment for the Arts released a study that showed that reading for pleasure had declined steadily among all major American demographic groups.

7 The writer Andrew Solomon analyzed the consequences of this shift: "People who read for pleasure are many times more likely than those who don't to visit museums and attend musical performances, almost three times as likely to perform volunteer and charity work, and almost twice as likely to attend sporting events.

8 Readers, in other words, are active, while nonreaders—more than half the population—have settled into apathy.

9 There is a basic social divide between those for whom life is an accrual of fresh experience and knowledge, and those for whom maturity is a process of mental atrophy. The shift toward the latter category is frightening."

10 The intellectual nourishment of reading books is so deeply ingrained in our assumptions that it's hard to contemplate a different viewpoint.

11 But as McLuhan[2] famously observed, the problem with judging new cultural systems on their own terms is that the presence of the recent past inevitably colors your vision of the emerging form, highlighting the flaws and imperfections.

12 Games have historically suffered from this syndrome, largely because they have been contrasted with the older conventions of reading.

13 To get around these prejudices, try this thought experiment. Imagine an alternate world identical to ours save one techno-historical change: video games were invented and popularized *before* books. In this parallel universe, kids have been playing games for centuries—and then these page-bound texts come along and suddenly they're all the rage. What would the teachers, and the parents, and the cultural authorities have to say about this frenzy of reading? I suspect it would sound something like this:

14 Reading books chronically understimulates the senses. Unlike the longstanding tradition of gameplaying—which engages the child in a vivid, three-dimensional world filled with moving images and musical soundscapes, navigated and controlled with complex muscular movements—books are simply a barren string of words on the page. Only a small portion of the brain devoted to processing written language is

2 Marshall McLuhan (1911–1980) was a philosopher who specialized in media theory.

activated during reading, while games engage the full range of the sensory and motor cortices.

15 Books are also tragically isolating. While games have for many years engaged the young in complex social relationships with their peers, building and exploring worlds together, books force the child to sequester him or herself in a quiet space, shut off from interaction with other children. These new "libraries" that have arisen in recent years to facilitate reading activities are a frightening sight: dozens of young children, normally so vivacious and socially interactive, sitting alone in cubicles, reading silently, oblivious to their peers.

16 Children enjoy reading books, of course, and no doubt some of the flights of fancy conveyed by reading have their escapist merits. But for a sizable percentage of the population, books are downright discriminatory. The reading craze of recent years cruelly taunts the 10 million Americans who suffer from dyslexia—a condition that didn't even exist as a condition until printed text came along to stigmatize its sufferers.

17 But perhaps the most dangerous property of these books is the fact that they follow a fixed linear path. You can't control their narratives in any fashion—you simply sit back and have the story dictated to you. For those of us raised on interactive narratives, this property may seem astonishing. Why would anyone want to embark on an adventure utterly choreographed by another person? But today's generation embarks on such adventures millions of times a day. This risks instilling a general passivity in our children, making them feel as though they're powerless to change their circumstances. Reading is not an active, participatory process; it's a submissive one. The book readers of the younger generation are learning to "follow the plot" instead of learning to lead.

18 It should probably go without saying, but it probably goes better with saying, that I don't agree with this argument. But neither is it exactly right to say that its contentions are untrue. The argument relies on a kind of amplified selectivity: it foregrounds certain isolated properties of books, and then projects worst-case scenarios based on these properties and their potential effects on the "younger generation." But it doesn't bring up any of the clear benefits of reading: the complexity of argument and storytelling offered by the book form; the stretching of the imagination triggered by reading words on a page; the shared experience you get when everyone is reading the same story.

19 A comparable sleight of hand is at work anytime you hear someone bemoaning today's video game obsessions, and their stupefying effects on tomorrow's generations. Games are not novels, and the ways in which they harbor novelistic aspirations are invariably the least interesting thing about them. You can judge games by the criteria desiged to evaluate novels: Are the characters believable? Is the dialogue complex? But inevitably, the games will come up wanting. Games are good at novelistic storytelling the way Michael Jordan was good at playing baseball. Both could probably make a living at it, but their world class talents lie elsewhere.

20 Before we get to those talents, let me say a few words about the virtues of reading books. For the record, I think that those virtues are immense ones—and not just because I make a living writing books. We should all encourage our kids to read more, to develop a comfort with and an appetite for reading. But even the most avid reader in this culture is invariably going to spend his or her time with other media—with games, television, movies, or the Internet. And these other forms of culture have intellectual or cognitive virtues in their own right—different from, but comparable to, the rewards of reading.

21 What are the rewards of reading, exactly? Broadly speaking, they fall into two categories: the information conveyed by the book, and the mental work you have to do to process and store that information. Think of this as the difference between acquiring information and exercising the mind. When we encourage kids to read for pleasure, we are generally doing so because of the mental exercise involved. And Andrew Solomon's words: "[Reading] requires effort, concentration, attention. In exchange, it offers a stimulus to and the fruit of thought and feeling." Spock says: "Unlike most amusements, reading is an activity requiring active participation. We must do the reading ourselves—actively scan the letters, make sense of the words, and follow the threat of the story." Most attributes to the mental benefits of reading also invoke the power of imagination; reading books forces you to concoct entire worlds in your head, rather than simply ingest a series of prepackaged images. And then there is the slightly circular—though undoubtedly true—argument for the long-term career benefits: being an avid reader is good for you because the educational system and the job market put a high premium on reading skills.

22 To summarize, the cognitive benefits of reading involves these faculties: effort, concentration, attention, the ability to make sense of words, to follow narrative threads, to sculpt imagined worlds out of mere sentences on the page. Those benefits are themselves amplified by the fact that society places a substantial emphasis on precisely this set of skills.

23 The very fact that I am presenting this argument to you in the form of a book and not a television drama or video game should make it clear that I believe the printed word remains the most powerful vehicle for conveying complicated information—though the *electronic* word is starting to give printed books a run for their money. The argument of followers is centered squarely on the side of mental exercise—and not content. I aim to persuade you of two things:

1. By almost all the standards we used to measure readings' cognitive benefits—attention, memory, following threads, and so on—the nonliterary popular culture has been steadily growing more challenging over the past thirty years.
2. Increasingly, the nonliterary popular culture is holding *different* mental skills that are just as important as the ones exercised by reading books.

24 Despite the warnings of Dr. Spock, the most powerful examples of both these trends are found in the world of video games. Over the past few years, you may have noticed the appearance of a certain type of story about gaming culture in mainstream newspapers and periodicals. The message of that story ultimately reduces down to: Playing video games may not actually be a *complete* waste of time. Invariably the stories point to some new study focused on a minor side effect of gameplaying—often manual dexterity or visual memory—and explain that heavy gamers show improved skills compared to non-gamers. (The other common let's-take-gamers-seriously story is financial, usually pointing to the fact that the gaming industry now pulls in more money than Hollywood.)

25 Now, I have no doubt that playing today's games does in fact improve your visual intelligence and your manual dexterity, but the virtues of gaming run far deeper than hand-eye coordination. When I read these ostensibly positive accounts of video games, they strike me as the equivalent of writing a story about the merits of the great novels and focusing on how reading them can improve your spelling. It's true enough, I suppose, but it doesn't do justice to the rich, textured experience of novel reading. There's a comparable blindness at work in the way games have been covered today. For all the discussion of gaming culture that you see, the actual experience of playing games has been strangely misrepresented. We hear a lot about the content of games: the carnage and drive-by killings and adolescent fantasies. But we rarely hear accurate descriptions about what it actually *feels like* to spend time in these virtual worlds. I worry about the experiential gap between people who have immersed themselves in games, and people who have only heard secondhand reports, because the gap makes it difficult to discuss the meaning of games in a coherent way. It reminds me of the way social critic Jane Jacobs felt about the thriving urban neighborhoods she documented in the sixties: "People who know well such animated city streets will know how it is. People who do not will always have it a little wrong in their heads—like the old prints of rhinoceroses made from travelers' descriptions of the rhinoceroses."

26 So what does the rhinoceros actually look like? The first and last thing that should be said about the experience of playing today's video games, the thing you almost never hear in the mainstream coverage, is that games are fiendishly, sometimes maddeningly, *hard*.

Composing on Your Own

Write freely in response to Stephen Johnson's text. What experiences specifically related to gaming and reading does it bring to mind? What have you read on the topic? What larger, more universal ideas come to mind? You will be developing your ideas throughout the unit, so save your work.

Evaluating Writing: Student Text
Paradoxically Traditional Life

Following is the anchor text you will use in this unit to further develop your skills in evaluating writing. This is a draft of a student response about traditionalism. It was written as part of a series of short pieces for the Progressive Student Book Club that attempt to understand progressivism vs. traditionalism. This unedited draft is similar to the type of text found in the multiple-choice section of the AP® Language and Composition test.

(1) People like to believe that society has advanced over the years. (2) If a person were to observe even the most modest selection of historical literature, they would notice that although items have become a bit *flashier,* society has remained paradoxically constant. (3) Consistently, social progress has produced generational disputes about the value of what is traditional and what is contemporary. (4) It just so happens that the characteristics of what can be considered *traditional* hardly change, and the same goes for the characteristics of what can be considered *contemporary*. (5) What is *traditional* is seemingly obsolete, old-fashioned, and slow. (6) What is *contemporary* is bigger, better, efficient, and faster than its antecedent. (7) To illustrate the aforementioned truth, take how one 19th century philosopher criticizes his culture's obsession with news, drama, efficiency, and speed. (8) The commentary that he makes regarding an individual observing a newspaper, physically watching a neighbor's barn burn down—without lending a helping hand—and even enjoying traveling at "breakneck speeds of 15 miles an hour,"[1] reveals his distaste for what his modern generation stood for. (9) All of the items and actions he scorns exemplify the characteristics of what is contemporary. (10) This is ironic because those very items—newspapers, barns, and slow-moving steam engines—are now criticized as being traditional and obsolete. (11) Or, perhaps, it is better to look historically at the fall of Rome. (12) This sounds all too familiar, not much different from the current day. (13) Life may be different on the surface, but when all of this is considered, individuals should see there is some element of *contemporary* value in embracing things that can be defined as *traditional*.

What Do You Know?

This unit will provide instruction on engaging with others, admitting or challenging limitations in your own and others' arguments, and transitioning to counterarguments. Before digging in, assess what you already know by trying to answer questions about the anchor texts. Learning scientists recommend this approach as a way to solidify learning. You may wish to work with a classmate as you try to answer the questions.

1 Thoreau, Henry David. *Walden*. AMS Press, 1968.

CLOSE READING: PROFESSIONAL TEXT

Using the anchor text about video gaming on pages 558–562, do your best to answer the following questions about how Steven Johnson engages with other perspectives throughout his argument.

1. List the different perspectives that Johnson engages with throughout his piece.
2. Explain why Johnson brings up each of the perspectives he presents.
3. What is the point of Johnson's hypothetical case, which imagines a world where video games existed before books and reading is considered a new activity?

EVALUATING WRITING: STUDENT DRAFT

Read the anchor text about traditionalism on page 563. Do your best to answer the following questions about how the writer structures this paragraph.

1. Summarize the writer's main claim.
2. Summarize counterarguments the writer uses to qualify the main claim.
3. Identify any areas where the writer offers evidence or alternative perspectives.
4. Identify any arguments that could work as counterarguments for this writer's work.

Part 1

Engaging Counterarguments

Enduring Understanding and Skills

Part 1

Understand

Writers make claims about subjects, rely on evidence that supports the reasoning that justifies the claim, and often acknowledge or respond to other, possibly opposing, arguments. (CLE-1)

Demonstrate

Explain ways claims are qualified through modifiers, counterarguments, and alternative perspectives. (Reading 3.C)

Qualify a claim using modifiers, counterarguments, or alternative perspectives. (Writing 4.C)

Source: *AP® English Language and Composition Course and Exam Description*

Essential Question: How do writers qualify claims using modifiers, counterarguments, and alternative perspectives when engaging others' ideas?

After the American Revolution, political superstar Alexander Hamilton emerged as a leading supporter of the Federalist ideology—a belief in a strong central government and the power of that government to issue credit and pay debts through a national bank. One of his chief opponents was southerner Thomas Jefferson, a defender of states' rights and individual liberties who feared a too-powerful central government and opposed the national bank. Their disagreement came crackling to life centuries later in the wildly popular stage play *Hamilton*, in a scene imagined by its creator Lin Manuel-Miranda as a rap battle (search for Cabinet Battle #1 on YouTube to hear or view it). When Hamilton fails to persuade Jefferson, he muses, "Such a blunder sometimes it makes me wonder why I even bring the thunder."

"Bringing the thunder" is rarely the way to persuade, and although Hamilton ended up getting the national bank, he succeeded because he compromised: He agreed to his opponents' demands that the permanent capital of the United States be established where it is now—nestled between two southern states, Maryland and Virginia.

Compromise is often perceived as a weakness, but it paves the way for people to work together in the midst of disagreement. Paradoxically, compromise is union stemming from disunion, and it is arguably the most practical way to move forward to obtain results. Compromise typically works the same way in argumentative writing, though the compromise is at an intellectual rather than a practical or political level.

This unit will help you engage with the perspectives of others in ways that can support your argument yet still address problems that may arise during such conversations. You'll read about how to anticipate opposing positions, or **counterarguments**, and decide the most appropriate way to address them. You'll also read about how to strengthen the validity of your argument by incorporating the ideas of others who share your position.

Thoughtful writers address the arguments and perspectives of others, and when they do, they leave the thunder behind and remain respectful and considerate.

KEY TERMS

alternative evidence	modifier
complement	qualify
counterargument	rebut
concede	refute
contradict	support
invalid argument	

1.1 Engaging with Others | CLE-1.Y CLE-1.Z

Throughout this course you have been "listening in on" enduring conversations on a range of topics, often adding your own views to the conversation. A key part of joining in any argument is to acknowledge and engage the perspectives of others in the conversation. Writers can use those perspectives to support or complement their own arguments or show how their arguments contradict those of others.

Modifying and Qualifying Claims

As you read in Units 7 and 8, modifiers serve a number of purposes. One is to limit the scope of an argument and avoid absolute terms. Instead of claiming "Video games are underrated," you might more reasonably claim, "Some video games may be underrated given the skills they help develop."

Also, a simple way to engage with the perspectives of others in an argument is to **qualify** a claim with **modifiers** that acknowledge other views exist. For example, the claim "the value of video games is underrated" can be qualified by placing it in the context of the ongoing conversation: "While parents may rightly worry about the potentially isolating effects of video gaming, overall the value of video games is underrated." The dependent clause added to the beginning of the sentence modifies the claim, acknowledging that other views not only exist but may also have merit. (See pages 401–410.)

However, merely acknowledging other viewpoints is usually not putting them to good rhetorical use. Engaging with other viewpoints deepens and strengthens an argument, as the following sections explain.

Using Perspectives that Support, Complement, or Contradict

Perhaps as a child your parents reprimanded you with the following adage: *The world doesn't revolve around you.* Even though most people have heard this adage and claim to believe it, their personal behavior often proves otherwise. Instead of considering other perspectives, people formulate their arguments based on beliefs they assume their audience will accept as obviously true. Inexperienced writers may think all members of their audience have shared the same experiences and background they have, but that perception is rarely true.

Writers at all experience levels need to recognize their own biases (see page 325) and strive not to project their views on the audience. To avoid this misstep, writers engage with the perspectives of others who hold contrary positions. By including the perspectives of others, writers demonstrate their effort to eliminate personal biases. These different perspectives may have their source in

- academic or professional learning
- personal experience
- cultural attitudes (for example, the collectivist mindset common to many Asian cultures as opposed to the individualistic mindset of many Americans)
- assumptions (concepts commonly taken for granted, such as "wealth is desirable" or "democracy is the best political system")
- common social observations (such as "people tend to socialize with others like themselves")
- hypothetical considerations (if this were to happen, then what would follow?)

Which perspectives to include depends in part on the audience for the argument. Throughout this course you have been reminded of the influence the audience has on the shape of a writer's or speaker's argument. Knowing the values, needs, and beliefs of your audience will guide you in deciding which alternative perspectives to include in your argument. Thoughtful writers or speakers anticipate possible objections or disagreements their audience may have and try to address them head-on.

Consider, for example, the famous speech by Frederick Douglass, American orator, social reformer, abolitionist, and statesman, "What to the Slave is the Fourth of July?" He delivered the speech at the invitation of the Rochester Ladies' Anti-Slavery Society in Rochester, New York, on July 5, 1852. Following are excerpts. As you read, notice the perspectives Douglass engages at the beginning of the speech, recognizing the audience he is addressing and the purpose and occasion for the speech.

> The signers of the Declaration of Independence were brave men. They were great men too—great enough to give fame to a great age. It does not often happen to a nation to raise, at one time, such a number of truly great men. The point from which I am compelled to view them is not, certainly, the most favorable; and yet I cannot contemplate their great deeds with less than admiration. They were statesmen, patriots and heroes, and for the good they did, and the principles they contended for, I will unite with you to honor their memory.
>
> They loved their country better than their own private interests; and, though this is not the highest form of human excellence, all will concede that it is a rare virtue, and that when it is exhibited, it ought to command respect. He who will, intelligently, lay down his life for his country, is a man whom it is not in human nature to despise. Your fathers staked their lives, their fortunes, and their sacred honor, on the cause of their country. In their admiration of liberty, they lost sight of all other interests. . . .
>
> Fully appreciating the hardship to be encountered, firmly believing in the right of their cause, honorably inviting the scrutiny of an onlooking world, reverently appealing to heaven to attest their sincerity, soundly comprehending the solemn responsibility they were about to assume, wisely measuring the terrible odds against them, your fathers, the fathers of this republic, did, most deliberately, under the inspiration of a glorious patriotism, and with a sublime faith in the great principles of justice and freedom, lay deep the corner-stone of the national superstructure, which has risen and still rises in grandeur around you.
>
> Of this fundamental work, this day is the anniversary. Our eyes are met with demonstrations of joyous enthusiasm . . . a nation's jubilee. . . .
>
> My business, if I have any here to-day, is with the present. . . .
>
> Fellow-citizens, pardon me, allow me to ask, why am I called upon to speak here to-day? What have I, or those I represent, to do with your national independence? Are the great principles of political freedom and of natural justice, embodied in that Declaration of Independence, extended to us? and am I, therefore, called upon to bring our humble offering to the national altar, and to confess the benefits and express devout gratitude for the blessings resulting from your independence to us?
>
> . . . Would you have me argue that man is entitled to liberty? that he is the rightful owner of his own body? You have already declared it. Must I argue the wrongfulness of slavery? Is that a question for Republicans? Is it to be settled by the rules of logic and argumentation, as a matter beset with great difficulty, involving a doubtful application of the principle of justice, hard to be understood? How should I look today, in the presence of Americans, dividing, and subdividing a discourse, to show that men have a natural right to freedom? speaking of it relatively, and positively, negatively, and affirmatively. To do so, would be to make myself ridiculous,

and to offer an insult to your understanding. There is not a man beneath the canopy of heaven, that does not know that slavery is wrong *for him*.

What, am I to argue that it is wrong to make men brutes, to rob them of their liberty, to work them without wages, to keep them ignorant of their relations to their fellow men, to beat them with sticks, to flay their flesh with the lash, to load their limbs with irons, to hunt them with dogs, to sell them at auction, to sunder their families, to knock out their teeth, to burn their flesh, to starve them into obedience and submission to their masters? Must I argue that a system thus marked with blood, and stained with pollution, is wrong? No! I will not. I have better employments for my time and strength than such arguments would imply.

What, then, remains to be argued? Is it that slavery is not divine; that God did not establish it; that our doctors of divinity are mistaken? There is blasphemy in the thought. That which is inhuman, cannot be divine! Who can reason on such a proposition? They that can, may; I cannot. The time for such argument is passed.

At a time like this, scorching irony, not convincing argument, is needed. O! had I the ability, and could I reach the nation's ear, I would, to-day, pour out a fiery stream of biting ridicule, blasting reproach, withering sarcasm, and stern rebuke. For it is not light that is needed, but fire; it is not the gentle shower, but thunder. We need the storm, the whirlwind, and the earthquake. The feeling of the nation must be quickened; the conscience of the nation must be roused; the propriety of the nation must be startled; the hypocrisy of the nation must be exposed; and its crimes against God and man must be proclaimed and denounced.

What, to the American slave, is your 4th of July? I answer: a day that reveals to him, more than all other days in the year, the gross injustice and cruelty to which he is the constant victim. To him, your celebration is a sham; your boasted liberty, an unholy license; your national greatness, swelling vanity; your sounds of rejoicing are empty and heartless; your denunciations of tyrants, brass fronted impudence; your shouts of liberty and equality, hollow mockery; your prayers and hymns, your sermons and thanksgivings, with all your religious parade, and solemnity, are, to him, mere bombast, fraud, deception, impiety, and hypocrisy—a thin veil to cover up crimes which would disgrace a nation of savages. There is not a nation on the earth guilty of practices, more shocking and bloody, than are the people of these United States, at this very hour.

Go where you may, search where you will, roam through all the monarchies and despotisms of the old world, travel through South America, search out every abuse, and when you have found the last, lay your facts by the side of the everyday practices of this nation, and you will say with me, that, for revolting barbarity and shameless hypocrisy, America reigns without a rival.

Douglass engages the perspective of White people celebrating the independence of the United States. He unhesitatingly praises the remarkable men whose intelligence, learning, and principles led to the creation of the nation. By so doing, he establishes an understanding with the audience that he recognizes the same values as they do. That engagement early on opens the door for the audience to take seriously the harsh words Douglass uses later in the speech when he explains that the Independence Day celebrations have nothing to do with Blacks, that those values are not applied equally.

Writers can use the perspectives of others in three main ways: to support, complement, or contradict their argument.

Using Supporting Perspectives Most writers include perspectives from sources that **support** their argument. Other people's supporting perspectives help demonstrate that multiple individuals share the writer's position. Because readers often perceive strength in numbers, adding supportive evidence from others is often convincing, especially if the sources are considered trustworthy and credible. Recall, for example, Thunberg's speech from Unit 1 (pages 3–5), in which she supports her argument about the urgent need for climate-change legislation by integrating statistics from the Intergovernmental Panel on Climate Change. If leading scientists from around the world agree that there is a human-induced climate problem, then most people will likely agree that climate change is the result of human actions and requires immediate efforts to control it.

Using Complementary Perspectives Writers can also include perspectives that will **complement** their argument—enhance it, emphasize certain parts, and clarify essential points. (Note that this is not the same word as *compliment*, which means an expression of praise.) Including a complementary perspective can help you and your audience recognize your argument's layers of complexity. Think back to the Malala Yousafzai speech from Unit 2, on pages 53–55. In it she complements her argument when she includes the perspective of the young boy who claims that Islamic radicals don't know what is written inside a book. Although her speech isn't about providing education to Islamic radicals, this reference to her schoolmate serves to broaden her argument by including ideological ignorance as something that education can work to quell.

Using Contradictory Perspectives Finally, writers not only can but also should include thoughtful perspectives that **contradict**—speak against—their argument. When writers choose to include an opposing perspective, they are recognizing the range of viewpoints that have emerged in the unending conversation. Writers can include contradictions in an argument without weakening their own argument; in fact, including and successfully addressing contradicting perspectives will strengthen an argument, even if doing so requires writers to concede, or admit, that something they generally oppose has merit. However, writers may also need to argue against opposing perspectives, as you will see in the next section.

Always remember that you are entering a larger conversation when you write an argument. If you are generally open to taking other positions seriously in the process of researching and developing your ideas, you'll arrive at a complex and interesting thesis and advance your own thinking to produce a better, stronger argument.

Remember: Effectively entering into an ongoing conversation about a subject means engaging the positions that have already been considered and argued about. Evidence and sources will either support, complement, or contradict a writer's thesis. (CLE-1.Y, Z)

1.1 Checkpoint

Close Reading: Professional Text

Reread the anchor text, "Games," by Steven Johnson, on pages 558–562. Then complete the following open response activity and answer the multiple-choice questions.

1. On separate paper, create a chart like the one below, adding four more rows. List five examples of a position Johnson develops, making a new row for each example. Explain the position each example offers on the topic, the source of the perspective, and the function it serves: to support, complement, or contradict. In the final column, also write a sentence about the function of the perspective. One row has been completed for you as an example.

Example from Text	Position on Topic	Perspective	Function
"The best that can be said of them is that they may help promote eye-hand coordination in children. The worst that can be said is that they sanction, and even promote aggression and violent responses to conflict."	Dr. Spock considers video games detrimental to intellectual progress.	☒ Academic/ Professional ☐ Personal Experience/ Testimony ☐ Assumption/ ☐ Common Social Observation ☐ Cultural Attitudes ☐ Hypothetical	This perspective ☐ supports ☐ complements ☒ contradicts the writer's view that . . . . **Sentence:** *This perspective contradicts the writer's view that video games have value and intellectual rigor.*

Table 9-1

2. According to paragraph 7, Andrew Solomon praises reading for its ability to

   (A) encourage people to consider different viewpoints

   (B) communicate important social issues and concerns

   (C) transport individuals to other imaginative realms

   (D) function as a gateway to health and prosperity

   (E) increase people's social connections

3. In the context of the passage as a whole, the author most likely references Dr. Spock in paragraph 2 to
   (A) support his position that reading is the most valuable form of media consumption
   (B) highlight the value of videogaming in contemporary society
   (C) amplify his claim that both reading and video build key skills
   (D) introduce a perspective that the author intends to contradict
   (E) exemplify the need for greater social discourse

Evaluating Writing: Student Draft

Reread the student draft about traditionalism on page 563. On separate paper, write answers to the following questions.

1. What is the writer's position regarding traditionalism?
2. How many perspectives (support, complement, contradict) does the writer engage within the piece?
3. What would you revise to clarify the perspectives the writer includes?
4. Where could you provide more evidence to support the writer's position?
5. How would your suggested clarifications and additions enhance the piece?
6. The writer is considering adjusting the first sentence (reproduced below) by adding the underlined language.

   People like to believe that, as one scholar argues, "over the . . . years, the world has changed tremendously."

   Should the writer add this language to the sentence?
   (A) No, because adding the quotation doesn't add to the validity of the argument.
   (B) No, because the new language makes the sentence harder to understand.
   (C) Yes, because the new language summarizes the writer's main argument.
   (D) Yes, because the language introduces a claim that will be defended throughout the piece.
   (E) Yes, because the new language provides credibility to substantiate a generalized belief.

7. The writer is considering replacing the underlined language in sentence 1 (reproduced below) to show that he or she is engaging an academic perspective.

People like to believe that society has advanced over the years.

Which of the following substitutions would best achieve this purpose?

(A) (as it is now)
(B) individuals
(C) most adults
(D) scientists and philosophers
(E) scholars and nonscholars alike

Composing on Your Own

Think about the many ideas the anchor texts throughout this book have explored: climate change, sustainability, education, consumerism, homelessness, tyranny, technology, lying, morality, and games, among others. Using any of these topics as a springboard and any of the writing you have previously done, generate a position about the topic and make a chart like the one below. When choosing evidence, feel free to use elements and ideas from the anchor text that relate to your topic. Also draw on your reading and life experience. Save your work for future use.

Subject:	
Your Position:	Evidence for your Position:
Complementary Position:	Evidence for Complementary Position:
Counterargument that may be raised against your position:	Evidence for Counterargument:

1.2 Admitting or Challenging Limitations | CLE-1.AA CLE-1.AB CLE-1.AC CLE-1.AD

Writers can argue with the perspectives of others in three main ways: concession, rebuttal, and refutation. When engaging with counterperspectives, writers often challenge other people's arguments, evidence, or both. Engaging with opposing perspectives enhances a writer's credibility.

Building Credibility by Addressing Opposing or Alternate Views

Throughout this course you have examined the importance of building credibility: using ethos to establish yourself as a trustworthy person, supporting your claims with reliable evidence, avoiding logical flaws, and keeping bias in check. However, how a writer interacts with counterarguments in the conversation is one of the most critical aspects of building credibility. Readers judge a writer on how well informed the writer is on the important voices within the conversation and how rigorously and thoughtfully the writer addresses those. Does the writer just "bring the thunder" and then storm out of the room when no one agrees, or does the writer work to understand other viewpoints, accepting those that have merit and showing clearly why others do not? Does the writer simply "cherry-pick" evidence—that is, ignore inconvenient evidence—or does the writer make a sincere effort to address all relevant evidence?

Concessions

When writers **concede** a point to an opposing perspective, they admit the limit of their own arguments and the worth of a perspective they disagree with. A concession does not accept the entirety of another argument, but it does admit that part of another perspective is in some ways valid. Consider, for example, the following concession Mark Twain made in an essay he wrote about the American flag when he was a member of the Anti-Imperialist League, which was protesting the Philippine-American War.

> When it [the American flag] was sent out to the Philippines to float over a wanton war and a robbing expedition I supposed it was polluted, and in an ignorant moment I said so. But I stand corrected. I conceded and acknowledge that it was only the government that sent it on such an errand that was polluted. Let us compromise on that. I am glad to have it that way. For our flag could not well stand pollution, never having been used to it, but it is different with the administration.

Concessions like Twain's can highlight the limitations of the writer's initial argument. For another example, suppose that a writer has built an argument calling for efforts by the gaming industry to eliminate racism from games and the online gaming environment by representing diversity in the characters and in the staff that creates them.

> Admittedly, diversity for diversity's sake is not always a helpful choice. For example, in the multi-player game *Rust*, players are assigned a permanent identity—skin color and gender—and have no choice in the matter. The developers wanted the characters to be consistently recognizable, but they also suggested that playing a character of a race different from yours might build empathy. "I would love nothing more than if playing a black guy in a game made a white guy appreciate what it was like to be a persecuted minority," lead developer Garry Newman said in an NPR interview in 2019.[2] In

2 Code Sw!tch, "Should Your Avatar's Skin Match Yours?" August 31, 2019

> this case, the diversity of the players, removed from meaningful context, had no useful purpose, as Lisa Nakamura, director of the Digital Studies Institute at the University of Michigan, explains. A white kid experiencing racism while playing a game "does not actually improve the suffering of other people who he's aligning himself with, because he still is benefiting from his whiteness in other parts of his life."

The writer, arguing for the worthwhile goal of diversity in video games, concedes the point that diversity for its own sake is not always helpful, suggesting more meaningful ways to achieve it are needed.

In addition to highlighting the limitations of the original argument, a concession can also recognize the merits of another argument in differing circumstances.

For example, if a writer is building an argument against using standardized tests as a consideration for college admission, that writer might make a concession showing some value of standardized tests in differing circumstances, such as admission to graduate school, especially in specialized fields such as law and medicine.

> While standardized tests as criteria for undergraduate college admission have been shown to be worse predictors of success than other factors, such as GPA, at the graduate level they may be more useful. For example, the law school admission test (LSAT) predicts with some accuracy who will pass the bar exam at the end of the graduate studies.

In this case, the writer concedes that in a different context—graduate as opposed to undergraduate admissions—standardized test scores might be a valid criterion.

When writers concede, they build their credibility by showing they have educated themselves about the weaknesses of their arguments and the strengths of others'. In addition, concessions allow writers to admit their own human limitations. Readers are often drawn toward writers who are realistic and not overly pretentious. Audiences may view a concession as an expression of humility, a desirable trait, especially in leaders. The added credibility and reasonability writers gain when conceding a position ultimately help them justify and strengthen their own arguments. Even though their argument may have taken a slight "hit," conceding sets up writers to throw a metaphorical power punch of their own after they have absorbed a blow.

Rebuttals

When engaging counterarguments, writers evaluate both the reasoning and the evidence of the opposing view. If the reasoning is faulty, no amount of evidence will support a counterargument. And even well-reasoned arguments will not stand if they depend on inadequate or faulty evidence. Assessing and questioning both the reasoning and evidence of opposing perspectives will guide a writer in preparing responses to anticipated objections.

Writers can also build arguments by choosing to **rebut** (challenge) or **refute** (disprove completely) their opposition's arguments and/or evidence. A rebuttal may challenge the perspective of the other writer and/or that writer's evidence. Sometimes a writer making a rebuttal may introduce **alternative evidence** to engage their opponent's perspective. Alternative evidence from a reliable source can reveal the weaknesses or inconsistencies in the evidence that supports a differing viewpoint. A writer may also try to show that an opponent's viewpoint is an **invalid argument**. An invalid argument is one founded on faulty reasoning that doesn't follow a logical structure or cannot be fully defended.

Arguments focused on rebuttals are commonplace in politics—just watch any debate. Side A claims that a solution will solve a known problem, while Side B advocates a different solution to the problem. Both sides have support, often from knowledgeable people, and in the ensuing debate each seeks to challenge the other side's argument. For example, many Americans opposed President George W. Bush's plans to invade Iraq in 2003. However, others labeled those Americans unpatriotic for opposing the president. An editorial writer for *The Washington Post* offered this alternative perspective: If they were unpatriotic, "then Abraham Lincoln was an unpatriotic appeaser for opposing the Mexican War as a young congressman in the 1840s." That rebuttal questioned the definition of a term and showed through logical analogy that by the definition implied about Bush's opponents, Abraham Lincoln—known for his undying commitment to preserving the United States—would also have to be called unpatriotic.

Refutations

While the rebuttal might be compared to a knockdown in a boxing match, the refutation, a more extreme version of a rebuttal, is the knockout. When writers refute their opposition, they demonstrate that the argument from their opponent's perspective is either largely or entirely invalid. An argument can be refuted by challenging its evidence, its logic, or a combination of the two.

Rebuttal	challenges an opponent's argument	reveals that an opponent's argument is weak or inconsistent	Both strategies may: • use **alternative evidence** to reveal evidential flaws in an opponent's argument. • reveal an **invalid argument** by pointing out logical flaws in an opponent's argument.
Refutation	disproves an opponent's argument	reveals that an opponent's argument is invalid	

Table 9-2

Consider the case of a writer arguing for strengthening warning labels on vaping products so they resemble those on cigarettes. The writer might reasonably expect readers to challenge the need for stricter labels because they believe that 1) vaping is a safe alternative to cigarette smoking; 2) vaping is an effective means of smoking cessation; and 3) all the flavor additives are generally assumed to be safe. A refutation based on evidence might be constructed as follows:

> Well over half the people surveyed expressed beliefs about vaping that, after further research, have turned out to be unfounded. While vaping may carry fewer risks than smoking cigarettes, its risks are real, according to the latest research. In 2020, the Centers for Disease Control and Prevention reported 60 deaths from lung injuries related to vaping. Further, emerging evidence shows a link between vaping and chronic lung disease and asthma. Evidence reported from Johns Hopkins Medicine notes that vaping as a smoking cessation method is not proven to work, is not approved by the FDA, and often leads to a person both vaping and smoking, which increases cardiovascular risks. And the flavor additives "generally assumed to be safe" are designated as such only in different contexts and products; no evidence proves their safety as chemicals that are inhaled. The government and media need an information campaign so the public understands that what was once believed to be true about vaping has been shown to be false, that its risks are significant, and that the public health hazard of vaping justifies strengthening the warning labels on vaping products.

Writing refutations often includes four steps:

- **Identify the claim you are disputing**. (People express beliefs about vaping that recent research has proven untrue.)
- **State your counterclaim**. (While less risky than cigarette smoking, vaping carries significant risks.)
- **Provide evidence to support your counterclaim**. (CDC data on deaths, link to chronic lung disease and asthma, ineffective smoking cessation method, potentially dangerous chemicals).
- **Explain how your counterclaim fits into the larger conversation**. (Public needs to be made aware of the results of new research and should be protected from the risks by stronger warning labels.)

If you were writing a rhetorical analysis of this argument, you could explain the rhetorical strategy of the counterargument this way:

> In this text, the writer refutes the ideas that vaping is safe and an effective smoking cessation tool in order to anticipate objections from readers who are not up to date on the evidence and who may still hold widespread but disproved beliefs about the relative safety of vaping.

Effective refutations are, by definition, irrefutable. Because this part of an argument is most likely to challenge a reader's or audience's viewpoint, writers try to maintain a respectful tone to avoid denigrating the people who have held the outdated viewpoint. Furthermore, writers who generate well-argued refutations are often viewed as highly reputable, increasing the writer's credibility all the more.

By carefully and respectfully navigating concessions, rebuttals, and refutations, writers who engage opposing viewpoints welcome their observers to join with their reasoning and embrace not only the well-crafted argument but also the process of genuinely improving their understanding.

> **Remember:** Writers enhance their credibility when they refute, rebut, or concede opposing arguments and contradictory evidence. When writers concede, they accept all or a portion of a competing position or claim as correct, agree that the competing position or claim is correct under a different set of circumstances, or acknowledge the limitations of their own argument. When writers rebut, they offer a contrasting perspective on an argument and its evidence or provide alternative evidence to propose that all or a portion of a competing position or claim is invalid. When writers refute, they demonstrate, using evidence, that all or a portion of a competing position or claim is invalid. (CLE-1.AA–1.AD)

1.2 Checkpoint

Close Reading: Professional Text

Reread the anchor piece "Games" by Steven Johnson on pages 558–562. Then complete the following open response activity and answer the multiple-choice questions.

1. On separate paper, create a chart like the one below with two additional rows to show how Johnson develops three counterarguments. In the left-hand column, quote three examples of Johnson's counterarguments. Then mark whether he is using concession, rebuttal, or refutation. Finally, in the right-hand column, explain the purpose of Johnson's counterargument.

Text	Counterargument	Purpose
	☐ Concession ☐ Rebuttal ☐ Refutation	In this text, Johnson [*choose one*: concedes, rebuts, or refutes] [*briefly summarize the perspective and position of the counterargument*] in order to [*explain why Johnson engages with the argument*].

Table 9-3

2. The evidence ("Reading . . . lead.") developed in paragraphs 14–17 primarily serves to
   (A) distract readers from understanding the underlying value of reading
   (B) amplify the need to view video games as superior to reading
   (C) introduce key viewpoints about reading and video games to be discussed later
   (D) reveal that cultural biases influence people's judgments about video games and reading
   (E) reiterate the author's extensive experience with both video games and reading

3. In paragraphs 21–22 ("What are . . . set of skills."), the author acknowledges that reading
   (A) effectively develops important intellectual and social skills
   (B) is commonly accepted as being the best form of media consumption
   (C) quickly transforms the character of those who consistently do it
   (D) is only beneficial when it is done independently
   (E) typically allows people to have more fulfilling and successful careers

4. In paragraph 24, the primary purpose of referencing a "story about gaming culture in mainstream newspapers and periodicals" (sentence 2) and a "new study focused on a minor side effect of gameplaying"(sentence 5) is to
   (A) highlight recent research that refutes the author's main claim
   (B) provide evidence that helps the author's rebuttal of a differing position
   (C) amplify the need for greater communication when the author discusses contentious issues
   (D) engage evidence that support the author's key points
   (E) offer a contrasting perspective that develops the author's counterargument

Evaluating Writing: Student Draft

Reread the student draft about traditionalism on page 563. Then complete the open response activity and answer the multiple-choice questions.

1. Write a one-paragraph response that includes concrete examples disagreeing with the writer's position. When producing this paragraph, make sure your response includes
   - direct quotes from the draft's text
   - a point of concession
   - a clear argument that attempts to refute or rebut the validity of the student writer's argument and/or evidence

2. The writer is considering revising sentence 7 by substituting and adding the underlined language below.

   To illustrate the aforementioned truth, take how <u>throughout his piece,</u> <u>Walden,</u> 19th century philosopher <u>Henry David Thoreau</u> criticizes his culture's obsession with news, drama, efficiency, and speed.

   Should the writer do this?

   (A) Yes, because the added language provides more proof for a claim.

   (B) Yes, because Thoreau was a well-known social critic.

   (C) Yes, because most individuals agree with Thoreau's view about reality.

   (D) No, because adding the author's name and publication adds nothing to the meaning of the sentence.

   (E) No, because there are no direct quotations from the author or the book in the sentence.

3. The writer is considering revising the underlined section of sentence 13 (reproduced below) in order to include a clear concession.

   <u>Life may be different on the surface, but</u> when all of this is considered, individuals should see there is some element of contemporary value in embracing things that can be defined as traditional.

   Which of the following revisions (adjusting for capitalization and punctuation) would best achieve this purpose?

   (A) (as it is now)

   (B) Consequently, life seems different on the surface, but

   (C) Scientists may suggest that lifestyles are substantially different; however,

   (D) Many aspects of modern life are arguably different from those of earlier eras, but

   (E) People think that life changes; however,

4. After sentence 11 (reproduced below), the writer wants to add additional evidence to refute the claim that society has advanced over the years.

Or, perhaps, it is better to look historically at the fall of Rome.

Which of the following sentences would best accomplish this goal?

(A) Take, for example, how the empire crumbled due to corrupt leadership.

(B) For instance, the empire allowed for the conflicting factions to influence their established system.

(C) Ironically, hostile tribes surrounding the once democratic empire overthrew it.

(D) Interestingly enough, Rome faced rapid technological and political advancement.

(E) Like many modern societies, its demise was tied to overexpansion and military overspending.

Composing on Your Own

Review the counterargument you generated for the table in Part 1.1. Write a paragraph presenting that counterargument as clearly and forcefully as possible, using the evidence from the table that supports it. In the next Composing on Your Own activity, you will address that counterargument. Save your work for future use.

1.3 Transitions to Counterarguments | CLE-1.AE CLE-1.AF

Writers typically introduce counterarguments by using transitional language. However, not all arguments conspicuously address, or even include, counterarguments.

Transitions in Counterarguments

When writers address counterarguments, they have to include transitions that link ideas and signal the writers' direction in order to logically hold the argument together. Imagine that a writer begins an argument stating that Toyotas are the most dependable cars. Then the writer starts the second paragraph stating "Chevrolets are the most dependable cars." This direct contradiction of the writer's initial argument about Toyotas creates an invalid argument—both statements can't be true. If the writer wants to address evidence that suggests Chevrolets are more dependable, he or she needs to add transitional language that signals engagement with an opposing perspective: *While Toyotas have long had a reputation of being dependable cars, repair records show that Chevrolets are now the most dependable.*

Writers can transition to their counterarguments using words, phrases or clauses, sentences, and/or paragraphs. These linguistic transitions serve to navigate between the contrasting ideas and establish reasonable relationships to be explored. They also establish whether the writer is going to concede, rebut, or refute the opposing view.

The chart below includes common transitional language that signals how the author will engage the counterargument.

Transitional Language: Words	
Concede: admittedly granted while	**Rebut/Refute:** although but however nevertheless rather since still though yet
***Transitional Language*: Phrases or Clauses**	
Concede: Despite the fact that . . . One cannot deny that . . . While it is true that . . .	**Rebut/Refute:** At the same time . . . Even though . . . It is often argued that . . . Of course . . . On the contrary . . . On the other hand . . . One may argue that . . . Others may say that . . . Some people think that . . .

Table 9-4

Although full sentences or paragraph sections can also function as transitions to counterarguments, there is no standard or typical template for these linguistic structures that signal a transition to counterarguments. However, sentences often include stems from the phrase/clause section of the table, and transitional paragraphs typically begin by presenting the merits of another's perspective and then addressing each merit in turn, conceding, rebutting, or refuting each point.

Although addressing counterarguments generally strengthens arguments, some successful arguments do not address them. For example, a writer may not engage with a counterargument when an audience most likely agrees with the writer's argument. In this case, the writer's perspective already holds credibility with the audience. However, when an audience is antagonistic toward the writer's position and perspective, the writer must engage counterarguments and opposing points of view.

Earlier anchor texts can help illustrate this point. Notice how, throughout her speech, Malala Yousafzai does not engage with a counterargument. She has no reason to provide a counterargument against those who don't value education because most of those who listen to her *do* value it. The number of individuals who support governmental suppression of education is so small that she would be wasting her time engaging with this position.

Writers often imply counterarguments when anticipating objections or counterarguments from a general audience even when they have not been directly challenged. The introduction to *Fast Food Nation* in Unit 3 provides an example. Notice how, near the end of the piece, Schlosser points out that he ate many fast food meals while researching the book. He also concedes that they tasted good! By revealing that he often ate fast food, he anticipates that someone might challenge him by questioning if he has ever eaten any. At no point did Schlosser write, "Some people may question if I have ever eaten fast food"—he did not have to do so explicitly. Instead, he addressed the counterargument without actually stating it. A writer usually addresses general assumptions, rather than specific opposing positions, when responding to an implied counterargument.

Different circumstances call for different types of engagement with the perspectives of others. In any circumstance, though, a thoughtful writer eager to contribute to an unending conversation takes the time to understand the whole context of an argument to make informed and engaging arguments.

Remember: Transitions may be used to introduce counterarguments. Not all arguments explicitly address a counterargument. (CLE-1.AE–AF)

1.3 Checkpoint

Close Reading: Professional Text

Review "Games" on pages 558–562. Then complete the following open response activity and answer the multiple-choice questions.

1. On separate paper, create a chart like the one on the next page, adding three more rows. Then, using the excerpt from "Games," fill in four examples that demonstrate how the writer transitions to and from addressing counterarguments. In the left-hand column, list a specific example of a transition (a concession, rebuttal, or refutation) from the text. In the middle column, identify whether the author uses a word, phrase, sentence, or paragraph as a transition. In the right-hand column, clearly explain the function of the transition by using one of the templates provided. A model answer is provided for you.

Textual Evidence	Transition	Function: Choose One
	☐ Word ☐ Phrase/Clause ☐ Sentence ☐ Paragraph	***Transition to Addressing a Counterargument:*** In this text Johnson transitions from [*summarize argument*] to [*summarize counterargument*] *Or* ***Transition from Exposing a Counterargument:*** In this text Johnson transitions from [*summarize counterargument*] to [*summarize argument*]

Model Answer:

Textual Evidence	Transition	Function: Choose One
From paragraph 10 of "Games": "The intellectual nourishment of reading books is so deeply ingrained in our assumptions that it's hard to contemplate a different viewpoint." (Johnson)	☐ Word ☐ Phrase/Clause ☒ Sentence ☐ Paragraph	**Transition from Counterargument:** In this text Johnson transitions from exposing common arguments for the value of reading to challenging these accepted truths as potentially invalid prejudices.

2. In the context of the passage, the second sentence ("For the record . . . books.") of paragraph 20 serves primarily to

(A) address multiple different perspectives that have been articulated throughout the piece

(B) dismiss the preceding counterargument

(C) transition from a broad generalization to a more precise example

(D) contextualize the importance of the nuanced discussion to follow

(E) anticipate and then dismiss a potential rebuttal

Evaluating Writing: Student Draft

Reread the student draft about traditionalism on page 563. Then complete the following open response activities and answer the multiple-choice question.

1. Write examples from the text that show the writer explicitly addressing counterarguments and including the perspectives of others. Write either the whole quote or cite the specific sentence number(s).
2. Revise the sentences or sections you selected in question 1. Add language (words or phrases) that transitions from the opposing view or different perspective to the writer's perspective. You may have to add, rewrite, and/or recast sentences. Some sentences may not need to be revised.
3. The writer wants to add a word or phrase at the beginning of sentence 2 (reproduced below), adjusting the capitalization as needed, to begin the rebuttal of a common conception.

   If a person were to observe even the most modest selection of historical literature, they would notice that although items have become a bit flashier, society has remained paradoxically constant.

   Which of the following would best achieve this goal?

   (A) For instance,

   (B) In essence,

   (C) Because this is entirely the case,

   (D) However,

   (E) Interestingly,

Composing on Your Own

You have previously stated your position on a subject, and you have defended the reasoning of the counterargument. Now write a two-paragraph argument that justifies your position and either refutes or rebuts the counterargument. When engaging with the counterargument, make sure to use transitional language (e.g., *although*, *though*, *while*, *though it may seem*, *some may argue*).

Part 1 Apply What You Have Learned

Visit "Should Tablets Replace Textbooks in K-12 Schools?" at https://tablets-textbooks.procon.org/. After a brief introduction, you will see a number of arguments for and against replacing physical textbooks with tablets. Read through both sets of arguments. Then instead of looking at the issue as a choice between "yes, tablets should replace textbooks" or "no, they shouldn't," develop a position in the "complex middle" (see page 402) where most interesting arguments are located. Write a brief argument essay on the subject in which you recognize counterarguments. In your response, you should do the following:

- Respond to the prompt "Should Tablets Replace Textbooks in K-12 Schools?" with a claim that presents a defensible position without oversimplifying the issue to a simple "yes" or "no."
- Select and use evidence from at least three of the provided sources to support your line of reasoning. Within each of the Pro and Con arguments on the website, you will notice links to footnotes for sources. Cite the sources for the evidence you use in your essay according to your teacher's guidelines.
- Explain how the evidence supports your line of reasoning.
- Address at least one counterargument through concession, rebuttal, or refutation.
- Use appropriate grammar and punctuation in communicating your argument.

Reflect on the Essential Question: Write a brief response that answers this essential question: *How do writers qualify claims using modifiers, counterarguments, and alternative perspectives?* In your response, explain the key terms listed on page 566.

Source: Getty Images

What position on tablets vs. textbooks does this photograph suggest? What details of the photograph led you to that conclusion?

Unit 9 Review

Section I: Reading

Questions 1–6. Read the following passage carefully before you choose your answers.

(The following is a letter to the editor that appeared in the *New York Times* in response to a prior opinion piece.)

To the Editor:

[1] While "America Needs Its Nerds" (Op-Ed, Jan. 11) by Leonid Fridman, a Harvard student, may be correct in its message that Americans should treat intellectualism with greater respect, his identification of the "nerd" as guardian of this intellectual tradition is misguided.

[2] Mr. Fridman maintains that anti-intellectualism runs rampant across this country, even at the "prestigious academic institution" he attends. However, he confuses a distaste for narrow-mindedness with anti-intellectualism. Just as Harvard, as a whole, reflects diversity in the racial, ethnic and religious backgrounds of its students, each student should reflect a diversity of interest as well.

[3] A "nerd" or "geek" is distinguished by a lack of diverse interests, rather than by a presence of intellectualism. Thus, a nerd or geek is not, as Mr. Fridman states, a student "for whom pursuing knowledge is the top priority" but a student for whom pursuing knowledge is the sole objective. A nerd becomes socially maladjusted because he doesn't participate in social activities or even intellectual activities involving other people. As a result, a nerd is less the intellectual champion of Mr. Fridman's descriptions than a person whose intelligence is not focused and enhanced by contact with fellow students. Constant study renders such social learning impossible.

[4] For a large majority at Harvard, academic pursuit is the highest goal; a limited number, however, refuse to partake in activities other than study. Only these select few are the targets of the geek label. Continuous study, like any other obsession, is not a habit to be lauded. Every student,

no matter how "intellectually curious," ought to take a little time to pursue social knowledge through activities other than study.

[5] Mr. Fridman's analysis demonstrates further flaws in his reference to Japan. He comments that "in East Asia, a kid who studies hard is lauded and held up as an example to other students," while in the United States he or she is ostracized. This is an unfair comparison because Mr. Fridman's first reference is to how the East Asian child is viewed by teachers, while his second reference is to how the American child is viewed by fellow students. Mr. Fridman is equating two distinct perspectives on the student to substantiate a broad generalization on which he has no factual data.

[6] Nerdism may also be criticized because it often leads to the pursuit of knowledge not for its own sake, but for the sake of grades. Nerds are well versed in the type of intellectual trivia that may help in obtaining A's, but has little or no relevance to the real world. A true definition of intellectualism ought to include social knowledge.

[7] While we in no way condone the terms "nerds" and "geeks" as insults, we also cannot condone the isolationist intellectualism Mr. Fridman advocates.

DAVID LESSING
DAVID HERNE
Cambridge, Mass., Jan. 12, 1990
The writers are members of Harvard's class of '93.

---

1. The first sentence of the letter primarily serves to

(A) refute the perspective of another
(B) concede a point and then shift to a rebuttal
(C) complement the credibility of the counterargument
(D) support the points made by the writers
(E) offer multiple contradictory claims

2. In the letter, the writers' primary criticism of Fridman's argument is that it

(A) holds a narrow view of intellectualism and ignores social aptitude
(B) takes the definition of "nerd" out of context
(C) limits his criticism to Harvard instead of society as a whole
(D) relies on overgeneralizing an argument within a specific rhetorical situation
(E) ignores the need for respectful discourse

Question 3 is covered in Unit 3.

3. The purpose of the fifth paragraph is to

(A) support the reasonability Fridman's main argument
(B) list evidence that contradicts the writers' prior claims
(C) expose additional flaws in Fridman's original reasoning
(D) dismiss challenges to the writers' main argument
(E) offer multiple examples that contradict Fridman's previous claim

Question 4 is covered in Unit 4.

4. Which of the following statements best describes the function of the letter's final paragraph?

(A) It ties the writers' perspectives to the claim introduced in first paragraph.
(B) It amplifies the writers' desire to see change.
(C) It encourages the readers to take a specific course of action.
(D) It reassesses the initial argument and clarifies the writers' thinking throughout the letter.
(E) It summarizes the need for social change developed in the letter.

Questions 5 and 6 are covered in Unit 5.

5. In the third paragraph, the writers define the words "nerd" and "geek" primarily to

(A) provide evidence that show how these words are generally used
(B) discuss common assumptions and stereotypes about studious behavior
(C) offer a different, more precise meaning for these words
(D) explain why some students dislike intellectuals
(E) introduce an expert opinion to clarify the meaning of these words

6. Which of the following best explains the writers' decision to repeatedly use the title "Mr. Fridman" in their letter?

(A) It emphasizes whose claims the writers are arguing against.
(B) It reminds readers who wrote the original argument that this response refutes.
(C) It indicates the working relationship between the students who composed both arguments.
(D) It suggests that the writer's opponent uses outdated ideas and claims.
(E) It displays the writers' respect for a person with whom they disagree.

Section I: Writing

Questions 7–10. Read the following passage carefully before you choose your answers. (The passage below is a draft by Elizabeth Hatton, Whitinsville Christian High School.)

Disney Princesses

(1) Disney's portrayal of female figures can have negative effects on the minds of young girls, promoting self-critical attitudes concerning body image. (2) When it comes to the earlier princess movies, there are two common characteristics these heroines share: they are extremely thin, and they are also white. (3) In fairy tales, the princess often serves as the standard of true beauty. (4) When observing the qualities that are given to these characters, a person can determine what qualities in women are considered socially beautiful. (5) Most Disney movies highlight the two mentioned above. (6) Up until some of the newer princesses were portrayed as thin, slender, and fragile. (7) In *Snow White* specifically, the conflict is largely instigated by one woman envying the beauty of another, competing to be the "fairest in the land." (8) And in most others, the princess is praised for her physical beauty. (9) People could even claim that physical beauty is the princess's major asset. (10) In fact, girls with worsening body image tend to see these cartoon princesses as role models.

(11) There are also some recent Disney films promoting beneficial messages that may improve how people empathize with others. (12) The idea of sacrificial love is also a fairly consistent theme throughout Disney movies, especially in the newer ones such as *Lilo and Stitch*, *Tangled*, and *Frozen*. (13) Such films step away from the "true love" and *happily-ever-after* concepts that seemed to dominate many of Disney's previous releases. (14) Instead, these motion pictures promote the belief that "the sacrificing of life for another person is the highest form of love." (15) Such films emulate a more realistic interpretation of life. (16) They do not smother tragedy with an artificial coat of light-heartedness and harmony. (17) They give the audience a holistic perception of what to expect as they age, while not discouraging the dreams of one day finding one's true love. (18) They simply teach that there is more to life than that, and that love is not always found where one might expect.

7. The writer wants to add a transition at the beginning of sentence 11 (reproduced below) to highlight a concession.

There are also some recent Disney films promoting beneficial messages that may improve how people empathize with others.

Which of the following, adjusting for capitalization and punctuation as needed, would be the best choice to achieve this purpose?

(A) Yet, while the messages they send are often detrimental,

(B) Most Disney films negatively affect their viewers; consequently,

(C) Although Disney films may seem to be mostly positive,

(D) The truth is that Disney films are often negative;

(E) Some people may think that Disney films are simplistic, but

Questions 8 and 9 are covered in Unit 5.

8. The writer wants to create a logical connection with sentence 11 by placing a transitional word or phrase at the beginning of sentence 12 (reproduced below), adjusting the punctuation and capitalization as needed.

The idea of sacrificial love is also a fairly consistent theme throughout Disney movies, especially in the newer ones such as Lilo and Stitch, Tangled, *and* Frozen.

Which choice best accomplishes this goal?

(A) Initially,

(B) Consequently,

(C) Although,

(D) For example,

(E) Surprisingly,

9. The writer wants to clarify the relationship between sentences 16 and 17 by adding the word *Instead* to the beginning of sentence 17. Should the writer make this addition?

(A) No, because the ideas in both sentences do not suggest contrast.

(B) No, because the relationship between the ideas in the two sentences is already clear.

(C) No, because contrasting the sentences would undermine the writer's argument.

(D) Yes, because it allows the syntactical progression to be less mechanical.

(E) Yes, because it offers a contrast that transitions between the ideas in the two sentences.

Question 10 is covered in Unit 6.

10. The writer wants to substitute the language in sentence 10 (reproduced below) with information from a credible source.

In fact, girls with worsening body image tend to see these cartoon princesses as role models.

Which of the following substitutions, adjusting punctuation as needed, would best accomplish this goal?

(A) In fact, one study shows that girls with poor body image engage more with the Disney princesses over time, perhaps seeking models of beauty.

(B) In fact, many young girls have expressed that they view Disney princesses as role models of beauty.

(C) In fact, Disney princesses, or their voiceover actors, often grace the covers of popular teen magazines.

(D) In fact, some parents have even revealed that their daughters hold Disney princesses in high regard, striving to be like them.

(E) In fact, the actress who played Princess Audrey in the Disney film *Descendants*, argues that "girls are often poisoned by the belief that they are supposed to appear like imaginary princesses."

Section II: Free Response

Synthesis: Video Games

(Note: For guided practice in writing a synthesis essay, see pages 364–373, 448–455, and 540–544.)

Video games have become increasingly popular and graphically more realistic. Recently, video gaming has become competitive. Now schools and colleges are sponsoring "e-sports" teams, and gamers can even become professionals. Amid this success, though, cultural critics have claimed that gaming is negatively affecting the intellectual and moral character of the culture, which can be seen in anything from the rise in public acts of aggression to the rise in teen sleep deprivation.

Carefully read the following six sources, including the introductory information for each source.

Write an essay that synthesizes material from at least three of the sources and develops your position on the effects of video games.

Source A (Johnson)
Source B (Ratings Guide)
Source C (Interview)
Source D (Graph)
Source E (Blog)
Source F (Survey)

In your response you should do the following:

- Respond to the prompt with a claim that presents a defensible position.
- Select and use evidence from at least three of the provided sources to support your line of reasoning. Indicate clearly the sources used through direct quotation, paraphrase, or summary. Sources may be cited as Source A, Source B, etc., or by using the description in parentheses.
- Explain how the evidence supports your line of reasoning.
- Use appropriate grammar and punctuation in communicating your argument.

Source A

Johnson, Steven. *Everything Bad Is Good for You: How Popular Culture Is Actually Making Us Smarter.* Riverhead Books, 2006.

This reading selection will be found on pages 558–562 of Unit 9.

Source B

"Ratings Guide." *ESRB Ratings*, Entertainment Software Association, www.esrb.org/ratings-guide/.

The following is the rating system for video games.

Everyone

Content is generally suitable for all ages. May contain minimal cartoon, fantasy or mild violence and/or infrequent use of mild language.

Everyone 10+

Content is generally suitable for ages 10 and up. May contain more cartoon, fantasy or mild violence, mild language and/or minimal suggestive themes.

Teen

Content is generally suitable for ages 13 and up. May contain violence, suggestive themes, crude humor, minimal blood, simulated gambling and/or infrequent use of strong language.

Mature 17+

Content is generally suitable for ages 17 and up. May contain intense violence, blood and gore, sexual content and/or strong language.

Adults Only 18+

Content is suitable only for adults ages 18 and up. May include prolonged scenes of intense violence, graphic sexual content and/or gambling with real currency.

Rating Pending

Not yet assigned a final ESRB rating. Appears only in advertising marketing and promotional materials related to a physical (e.g. boxed) video game that is expected to carry an ESRB rating and should be replaced by a game's rating once it has been assigned.

Source C

"Teenager Wins Millions Playing Fortnight," Kyle Giersdorf, interview by David Greene, *Morning Edition*, National Public Radio, August 1, 2019.

The following is an excerpt from a 2019 NPR radio interview.

DAVID GREENE, HOST:
How quickly life can change. Just last week, Kyle Giersdorf was a video game-loving teenager. Today, he is a video game-loving millionaire, all thanks to his talents when it comes to this.

(SOUNDBITE OF ARCHIVED RECORDING)

UNIDENTIFIED ANNOUNCER: For the first game, Victory Royale. Oh, my gosh. Confident play from Bugha.

GREENE: Kyle, who goes by the gamertag Bugha, won the first-ever Fortnite World Cup, a tournament for the video game that boasts 250 million registered players— not bad for a 16-year-old from Potts Grove, Pa.

KYLE GIERSDORF: Nothing pretty much felt real, honestly. But at the same time, I don't know. I just had no emotion coming out of me right then. I was just really happy for all the grind that I put into the game for it to finally pay off.

GREENE: Pay off—pay off? Yeah, what a payoff. It was $3 million. But don't think for a minute that Giersdorf is going to squander this prize money.

GIERSDORF: What I'm going to do with it is invest it and save it, put it towards my future. But most importantly, I think I want to get a new desk. I could use a little bit more space.

GREENE: Kyle says his parents are proud of him and his hard work playing six hours of Fortnite each day.

GIERSDORF: It's like a job. We put in the same amount of hours as many other people would for anything else. So yeah, I just see it as a normal job. I'm doing hard work and just have it pay off.

GREENE: All work and some play.

Source D

Gentile, Douglas. "Pathological Video-Game Use Among Youth Ages 8 to 18: A National Study." *Psychological Science*, vol. 20, no. 5, 2009, pp. 594–602. *JSTOR*, www.jstor.org/stable/40575069. Accessed 5 Apr. 2020.

The following graph is taken from a psychological study about gaming habits.

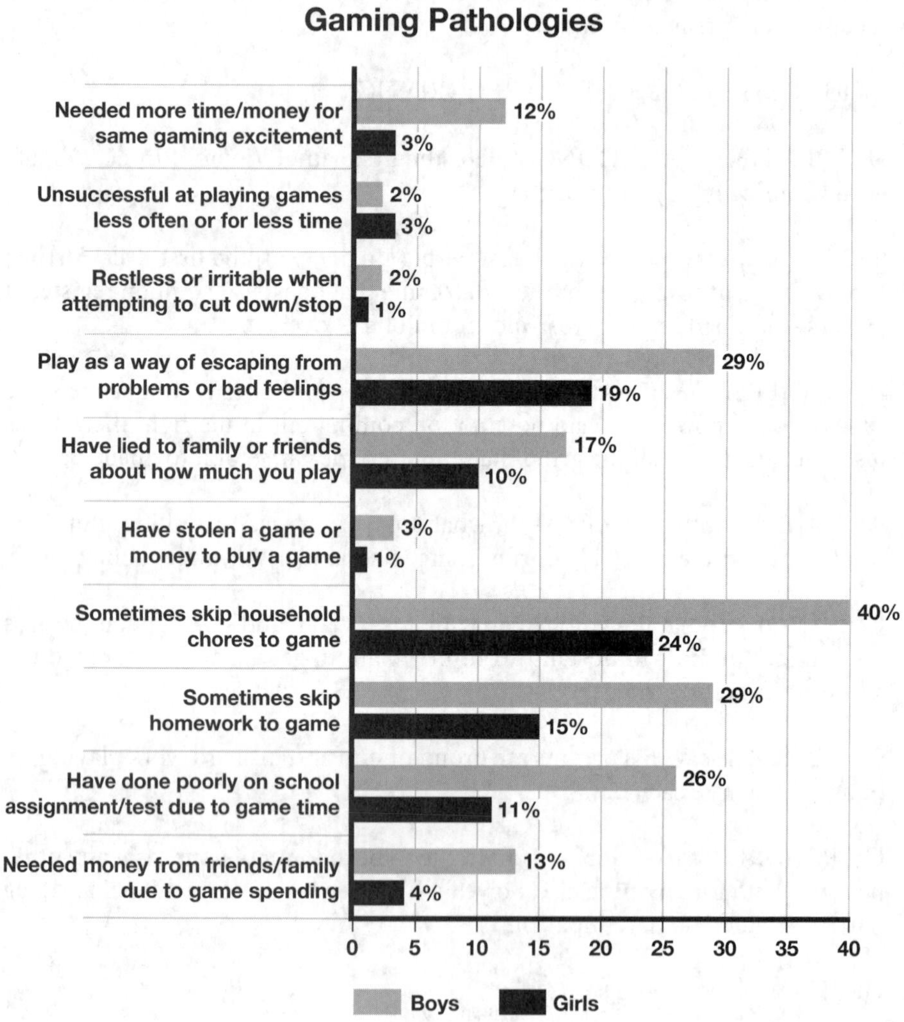

Source E

Juraschka, Ryan. "How Digital Game-Based Learning Improves Student Success." Prodigy Math Blog, 4 Dec. 2019, www.prodigygame.com/blog/digital-game-based-learning/.

The following is taken from an educational gaming website.

Digital game-based learning [DGBL] has been around longer than you might think. . . .

In the world of DGBL, *The Oregon Trail* was one of the first games created for educational purposes.

Back in 1974, *The Oregon Trail* gave children a fun way of learning about what life was like for pioneers. This revolutionary concept helped teachers immerse their students in educational content like never before. As technology has evolved, DGBL has become more useful in and out of the classroom. . . . Since the first instance of DGBL, the teaching method has evolved in both **quality** and **content**.

Now, DGBL learning platforms can easily personalize learning for every student through real-time analytics that pinpoint student strengths and weaknesses.

DGBL platforms track progress in the background—meaning students usually have no idea they're being tested at all! Teachers can use this data to see how far along each student is in their development and make sure the game is helping them progress at the right level.

DGBL software helps educators engage students with content in a way that wasn't possible in the past. But research has shown DGBL works best *in tandem* with in-class lessons—in other words, using the **blended learning** strategy. . . . Several studies have looked at this question [whether game-based and digital-game-based learning improve educational achievement] and the overall conclusion appears to be—**YES!**

Research shows some relation between improved educational achievement and the use of GBL (game-based learned)/DGBL strategies.

Let's look at the effectiveness of DGBL in a little more detail.

The success of DGBL starts with engagement. These platforms help students stay interested in what they're learning in and out of class.

A study from the *International Journal of Serious Games* found that the improved engagement DGBL learning provides also leads to students having **more motivation** to complete school work.

In fact, a 2012 study by the *Mathematics Education Research Journal* showed **93%** of class time was spent on task when using game-based learning, compared to only 72% without it. This shows when students are engaged with content, they're more likely to stay motivated in class.

Teachers who are consistently using DGBL strategies in their classrooms—and adjusting their lessons based on the feedback they receive from the software—are seeing more improvements to learning and grades than those who don't.

DGBL appears to be particularly effective in helping kids improve their overall math knowledge and understanding.

In their 2014 survey, the *Games and Learning Publishing Council* stated, "Nearly three quarters (71%) of digital game-using teachers report that games have been effective in improving their students' mathematical learning."

When students fall behind—especially in cumulative subjects like math—they can lose confidence in their abilities and develop things like a feeling of anxiety. DGBL helps combat these pain points by pinpointing strengths and weaknesses, and letting students practice at their own pace.

Source F

Takeuchi, Lori M., and Sarah Vaala. Level Up Learning: A National Survey on Teaching with Digital Games, The Joan Ganz Cooney Center at Sesame Workshop, 2014.

http://joanganzcooneycenter.org/wpcontent/uploads/2014/10/jgcc_leveluplearning_final.pdf

The following is an excerpt from an executive summary of a survey completed by a private educational research company.

In Fall 2013, the Joan Ganz Cooney Center, on behalf of the Games and Learning Publishing Council, surveyed 694 K-8 teachers from across the United States on whether and how they are using digital games with their students. Here are some key findings and recommendations from this research:

FINDINGS

+ **Digital games have landed in K-8 classrooms.** Nearly three-quarters (74%) of K-8 teachers report using digital games for instruction. Four out of five of these teachers say their students play at least monthly, and 55% say they do so at least weekly. Digital game-using teachers also say they're using games to deliver content mandated by local (43%) and state/national curriculum standards (41%), and to assess students on supplemental (33%) and core knowledge (29%).
+ **Who's using games with their students?** Gender does not predict digital game use in instruction, but younger teachers, those who teach at schools serving low-income students, and teachers who play digital games for their own pleasure are more likely to use games with their

students. Younger teachers and those who play digital games frequently let their students play more often, too. . . .

+ **Teachers who use games more often report greater improvement in their students' core and supplemental skills.** Coincidentally, the teachers that use games more regularly also use games to hit a wider range of objectives (teach core and supplemental content, assess students) and expose students to a wider variety of game genres and devices.
+ **Educational games rule in K-8 classrooms.** Four out of five game-using teachers say their students primarily play games created for an educational audience, compared to just 5% whose students most often play commercial games. Eight percent of game-using teachers say their students mostly play a hybrid of the first two options—entertainment games that have been adapted for educational use. . . .
+ **Mixed marks on STEM [Science, Technology, Engineering, and Mathematics] learning.** Nearly three quarters (71%) of digital game-using teachers report that games have been effective in improving their students' mathematics learning. However, only 42% report the same about their students' science learning, despite research suggesting that games are well suited for teaching complex scientific concepts.
+ **Seeing the benefits of co-play.** Only 37% of game-using teachers report digital games as being effective in improving students' social skills, which is low compared to other skills queried. But teachers whose students primarily play together (in pairs, small groups, as a whole class) were more likely to report improvements in student social skills than teachers whose students play alone.

Rhetorical Analysis: "All Work and No Play Makes Jack a Nerd"

(Note: For guided practice in responding to a rhetorical analysis prompt, see pages 104–106, 178–180, 232–235, and 290–295.)

In a letter to the editor that appeared in *The New York Times,* Harvard students David Lessing and David Herne responded to Leonid Fridman's "America Needs its Nerds." In his piece, Fridman had argued that, because America denigrates rather than extols its intellectuals, the country will not be able to continue as a world power.

Reread the letter on pages 587–588 carefully. Write an essay that analyzes the rhetorical choices Lessing and Herne make to convey their message about being intellectually and socially well-rounded.

In your response you should do the following:

- Respond to the prompt with a thesis that analyzes the writers' rhetorical choices.
- Select and use evidence to support your line of reasoning.
- Explain how the evidence supports your line of reasoning.
- Demonstrate an understanding of the rhetorical situation.
- Use appropriate grammar and punctuation in communicating your argument.

Argument: Social Media and Communication

(Note: For guided practice in responding to an argument prompt, see pages 48–49, 107–109, 181–183, 236–237, and 296–297.)

Social media has been celebrated as a way to easily connect with family, friends, and acquaintances around the world. Distances that could once only be bridged by the mail or phone are now overcome with a few clicks of a button. There are those, however, who condemn social media's value, claiming social media perpetuate hate speech, promote the distribution of inaccurate information, influence individuals to develop negative self-images, and even destroy the foundations of grammar.

Write an essay that argues your position on how social media influence the lives of individuals and the way they communicate.

In your response you should do the following:

- Respond to the prompt with a thesis that presents a defensible position.
- Provide evidence to support your line of reasoning.
- Explain how the evidence supports your line of reasoning.
- Use appropriate grammar and punctuation in communicating your argument.

Practice Examination

Section I

TIME—1 HOUR • 45 QUESTIONS

Directions: *This part consists of selections from nonfiction works and questions on their rhetorical situation, claims and evidence, reasoning and organization, and style. After reading each passage, choose the best answer to each question.*

Questions 1–11. Read the following passage carefully before you choose your answers.

(The following is an excerpt from a humorous essay titled "I Now Have Scientific Proof of How Awesome I Really Am" *published in* TIME Magazine *in 2016.)*

At the end of every Uber ride, not only do you rate your driver from one to five stars, but your driver also rates you. This rating was more or less secret until this spring, when Uber began allowing people to check their personal number through its app. Although my drivers see a full five stars when I ask for a ride, my exact rating is a 4.97, putting me in the very top percentile of Uber customers. This in no way means I'm better than other people, unless you believe in objective, scientific polling.

Over the decades I have wasted minutes worrying if I'm too prying, too loud, too talkative, too cocky. Big Data has provided the previously unknowable answer to what other people think of me, and that answer is 4.97.

The knowledge an Uber rating can offer is incredibly useful. It's also too important to be limited for use in deciding who to pick up for a ride. We could be using it for judgments about dating, electing Presidents and giving raises to columnists. I called Ed Baker, Uber's vice president of growth, who seemed like a great guy even though he's a 4.84. He agreed that Uber had a crucial insight that could really help society. "It would be cool if we put everyone's rider ratings on their desk," he said, considering ways to improve his company. I got off the phone before he tried to give me a job. Since I've become aware of my super rating, I have learned to be careful not to lead people on.

I now knew how much people like me, but I wanted to know exactly why. What if it's just because I'm handsome? Or it's because of pheromones[1]? Or something else that means I can try even less? I called Arun

1 **pheromones**: chemicals an animal produces which changes the behavior of another animal of the same species

Sundararajan, an NYU business-school professor and the author of new book *The Sharing Economy*. "A near perfect rating means you were consistently pleasant, civil, conversational, polite to the wide range of individuals who gave you your Uber rides," he said, "even when you were busy, distracted, late or stressed." I do not know why Sundararajan thinks a person gets busy, distracted or stressed when their job is to write a one-page column. But I think it's that inability to empathize that makes him a 4.33.

My lovely wife Cassandra overheard me mentioning my 4.97 while I was telling her how lucky she is to be married to such a good person. She, however, saw it differently. "You're more of a people pleaser than you are a good person," she said. "When we go out to a restaurant, you make such an effort to talk to the waitstaff, you become a burden to them. Stop asking them about their kid! They have a job to do, and you're slowing them down." Admittedly, Zhirayr missed our highway exit when I asked him about emigrating from St. Petersburg to Armenia during perestroika, but he still gave me five stars.

Cassandra told me she gets exhausted after riding with me in an Uber, since she feels bombarded by the chaotic experiences I draw out of our drivers. Two weeks ago, after a flight was delayed overnight, she was about to ask me not to talk to our driver, but wasn't sure I could do it. "Luckily," she said, "I shut the conversation down because that guy was so annoying. He said, 'You need to have another kid because your son would be so lonely.' Ugh!" Now I know how I lost that 0.03.

I realize that sometimes, if I need to make a phone call or suggest an alternate route, I may have to risk getting a 4. But most of the time, I'm going to suggest that Cassandra and I get separate cars and meet up at home.

1. Which of the following best describes why the author includes the phrase "unless you believe in objective, scientific polling" (paragraph 1, sentence 4)?
   (A) It reveals the author's doubts about the reliability of scientific data.
   (B) It reinforces the author's argument that our opinions are frequently based on science.
   (C) It helps to establish the author's ironic, humorous tone.
   (D) It supports the author's feelings about the increasing importance of technology.
   (E) It introduces a comparison between the author's view of himself and the way others view him.

2. How does the conversation with Arun Sundararajan (paragraph 4, sentence 7) contribute to the passage?
   (A) It supports the writer's claim that a higher rating means he is a nice person.
   (B) It contradicts the writer's claims about Uber ratings being incredibly useful.
   (C) It supports the idea that Uber drivers are good judges of character.
   (D) It illustrates the contradiction in the writer's character that his wife later points out.
   (E) It provides a serious, academic tone that counteracts the writer's arrogance.

3. Which of the following most likely describes the exigence for this text?
   (A) The writer's decision to start using Ubers in order to reinforce his self-worth
   (B) Uber's decision to begin allowing people to check their personal ratings
   (C) The writer's desire to explain why he and his wife no longer share Uber rides
   (D) A disagreement between the writer and his Uber driver, Zhirayr, who missed a turn
   (E) A phone call between the writer and the vice president of growth at the Uber company

4. Which of the following statements best summarizes a main claim that the author explores in the passage?
   (A) "Although my drivers see a full five stars when I ask for a ride, my exact rating is a 4.97, putting me in the very top percentile of Uber customers." (paragraph 1, sentence 3)
   (B) "Over the decades I have wasted minutes worrying if I'm too prying, too loud, too talkative, too cocky." (paragraph 2, sentence 1)
   (C) "The knowledge an Uber rating can offer is incredibly useful." (paragraph 3, sentence 1)
   (D) "I now knew how much people like me, but I wanted to know exactly why." (paragraph 4, sentence 1)
   (E) "I do not know why Sundararajan thinks a person gets busy, distracted or stressed when their job is to write a one-page column." (paragraph 4, sentence 7)

5. Which of the following describe the primary methods of development used in paragraphs 3 and 4?
   (A) narration and description
   (B) cause-effect
   (C) definition and narration
   (D) comparison-contrast
   (E) description and definition

6. At the beginning of the fourth paragraph, why does the writer state "I now knew how much people liked me, but I wanted to know exactly why"?
   (A) to signal a transition from focusing on the writer's personal opinions to including insights from a subject-area expert
   (B) to contrast the author's previous attitude toward ratings with his new understanding of how ratings affect behavior
   (C) to signal a transition from a general discussion of the writer's high ratings to a specific examination of what traits influence ratings
   (D) to contrast the way the author interprets his ratings to how scientific experts interpret his ratings
   (E) to signal a transition from a humorous tone that mocks technology to a serious discussion of how technology affects society

7. Based on the information provided in the passage, what is most likely the author's perspective on Uber's rating system?
   (A) He fears that companies like Uber will share their negative ratings with other companies.
   (B) He suggests that Uber's technology can help reveal aspects of our inner selves.
   (C) He is concerned that Uber drivers will begin rejecting riders based on the app ratings.
   (D) He recognizes the absurdity of using numerical ratings to judge whether someone is good.
   (E) He finds humor in people relying on technology to tell them if they are good.

8. To create a humorous and ironic tone throughout the essay, the writer
   (A) pretentiously alludes to prominent scholars and research
   (B) objectively cites derived statistics to validate his deductions
   (C) consistently employs an ornate and exaggerated academic style
   (D) deliberately constructs illogical claims
   (E) sarcastically refutes a series of counterarguments

9. In the last three paragraphs, the writer primarily describes his interactions with his wife to
   (A) prove that Uber ratings can be used to assess the reliability of drivers, but not passengers
   (B) contrast his own friendly personality with his wife's more aloof nature
   (C) suggest that Uber ratings are too simplistic to accurately gauge someone's character
   (D) affirm his belief that he is a good person, but for reasons only his wife recognizes
   (E) justify the high ratings he has received from Uber drivers

10. Which of the following is the most reasonable thesis implied by this passage?
   (A) We should not place too much importance on electronic ratings.
   (B) Electronic ratings are a superior method for evaluating relationships.
   (C) Uber drivers are better judges of character than most other people.
   (D) Personal relations always provide more reliable assessments of character.
   (E) If we use electronic ratings to judge people, we must use ratings from multiple sources.

11. The perspective of the speaker in the passage can be best described as
   (A) mocking the rating system it seems to be praising
   (B) attacking the rating system for its lack of clarity
   (C) attacking a rating system for being logical and objective
   (D) rational in its approach to the digital rating systems
   (E) addressing the audience and their needs in understanding the topic

Questions 12–24. Read the following passage carefully before you choose your answers.

(The following is an excerpt from a lecture titled "A Latina Judge's Voice" *given by Judge Sonia Sotomayor in 2001, eight years before she became the first Hispanic woman appointed to the US Supreme Court.)*

For me, a very special part of my being Latina[1] is the *mucho platos de arroz, gandoles y pernir* [*pernil*]—rice, beans and pork – that I have eaten at countless family holidays and special events. My Latina identity also

1 **Latina:** a woman or girl of Latin American descent; female version of male *Latino*

includes, because of my particularly adventurous taste buds, *morcilla,*—pig intestines, *patitas de cerdo con garbanzo*—pigs' feet with beans, and *la lengua y orejas de cuchifrito*—pigs' tongue and ears. I bet the Mexican-Americans in this room are thinking that Puerto Ricans have unusual food tastes. Some of us, like me, do. Part of my Latina identity is the sound of merengue at all our family parties and the heart wrenching Spanish love songs that we enjoy. It is the memory of Saturday afternoon at the movies with my aunt and cousins watching *Cantinflas*, who is not Puerto Rican, but who was an icon Spanish comedian on par with Abbot and Costello of my generation. My Latina soul was nourished as I visited and played at my grandmother's house with my cousins and extended family. They were my friends as I grew up. Being a Latina child was watching the adults playing dominos on Saturday night and us kids playing loteria, bingo, with my grandmother calling out the numbers which we marked on our cards with chickpeas.

Now, does any one of these things make me a Latina? Obviously not because each of our Caribbean and Latin American communities has their own unique food and different traditions at the holidays. I only learned about tacos in college from my Mexican-American roommate. Being a Latina in America also does not mean speaking Spanish. I happen to speak it fairly well. But my brother, only three years younger, like too many of us educated here, barely speaks it. Most of us born and bred here, speak it very poorly.

If I had pursued my career in my undergraduate history major, I would likely provide you with a very academic description of what being a Latino or Latina means. For example, I could define Latinos as those peoples and cultures populated or colonized by Spain who maintained or adopted Spanish or Spanish Creole[2] as their language of communication. You can tell that I have been very well educated. That antiseptic description however, does not really explain the appeal of *morcilla*—pig's intestine—to an American-born child. It does not provide an adequate explanation of why individuals like us, many of whom are born in this completely different American culture, still identify so strongly with those communities in which our parents were born and raised.

America has a deeply confused image of itself that is in perpetual tension. We are a nation that takes pride in our ethnic diversity, recognizing its importance in shaping our society and in adding richness to its existence. Yet, we simultaneously insist that we can and must function and live in a race and color-blind way that ignores these very differences that in other contexts we laud. That tension between "the melting pot and the

2 **Spanish Creole**: a language that develops from the simplifying and mixing of different languages into a new one within a fairly brief period of time

salad bowl"—a recently popular metaphor used to describe New York's diversity—is being hotly debated today in national discussions about affirmative action. Many of us struggle with this tension and attempt to maintain and promote our cultural and ethnic identities in a society that is often ambivalent about how to deal with its differences. In this time of great debate we must remember that it is not political struggles that create a Latino or Latina identity. I became a Latina by the way I love and the way I live my life. My family showed me by their example how wonderful and vibrant life is and how wonderful and magical it is to have a Latina soul. They taught me to love being a Puertorriqueña[3] and to love America and value its lesson that great things could be achieved if one works hard for it. But achieving success here is no easy accomplishment for Latinos or Latinas, and although that struggle did not and does not create a Latina identity, it does inspire how I live my life.

12. In the first paragraph, the speaker uses both the Spanish and English names for the food she grew up with in order to
    (A) illustrate the importance of embracing multiple cultures
    (B) appeal to the reasoning of a primarily Spanish-speaking audience
    (C) engage the majority of the audience who do not speak English
    (D) illustrate the importance of a bilingual education in American society
    (E) provide a strong cultural context regarding the hardships of her youth

13. By mentioning how "Mexican-Americans in this room are thinking that Puerto Ricans have unusual food tastes," the speaker reinforces her belief that
    (A) seldom do the experiences of Latino/Latina people differ much based on their origins
    (B) despite cultural similarities, there are dietary differences that often divide people with similar ethnic backgrounds
    (C) Puerto Ricans and Mexicans—though both Latino/Latina—have different cultural backgrounds that neither group is willing to recognize
    (D) there are significant differences between Spanish-speaking and non-Spanish-speaking Latinos/Latinas
    (E) while they are often lumped together, all Latinos/Latinas are not members of a single cultural group

---

3 **Puertorriqueña:** A female person from Puerto Rico or descended from Puerto Ricans. Puerto Ricans are American citizens.

14. The speaker's use of personal memories in the second half of paragraph 1 serves to
    (A) illustrate the childhood events and activities that defined her as a Latina
    (B) contrast the experiences of the non-Spanish-speaking members of the audience
    (C) foreshadow the problems she experienced growing up as both a Puerto Rican and a female.
    (D) define the role American culture played in her combined Latin and American upbringing
    (E) reject the importance of family experiences to the development of one's cultural identity

15. The speaker transitions from paragraph 1 to paragraph 2 by
    (A) bringing the audience back to the present following the flashbacks at the end of paragraph 1
    (B) using personal anecdotes to focus the audience's attention on the political discussions in paragraph 2
    (C) creating a cause-and-effect relationship between paragraph 1 and paragraph 2
    (D) summarizing the effect of the details included in the memory at the end of paragraph 1
    (E) questioning how the details from paragraph 1 have bearing on the claims in paragraph 2

16. The speaker compares herself to her brother in paragraph 2 in order to
    (A) contrast the influence that the English language has had on her life versus its influence on her brother's life
    (B) show that Latinos/Latinas include non-Spanish speakers as well as Spanish-speaking people
    (C) demonstrate the importance of bilingual education in shaping one's sense of cultural identity
    (D) challenge the audience to examine how family relationships shape the identities of young Americans and/or Latinos/Latinas
    (E) advocate for the idea that family relationships should play a role in defining ethnic identity

17. The speaker's use of the word *us* (paragraph 2, sentences 6 and 7, and paragraph 3, sentence 5)
    (A) establishes a contrast between the writer and her audience
    (B) contrasts the writer with her non-American ancestors
    (C) provides a feeling of togetherness for the writer's audience
    (D) divides Latino/Latina into gender groupings
    (E) creates a sense of unity among Latino/Latina people

18. In paragraph 3, by juxtaposing an "antiseptic" description of Latinos with a reference to "*morcilla*—pig's intestine," the speaker
    (A) ridicules most academic efforts to discuss Puerto Rican and Mexican cultures
    (B) mocks white America's attempts to understand Puerto Rican and Mexican cultures
    (C) creates self-effacing humor poking fun at her own inability to defend her culture
    (D) humorously underscores the importance of cultural traditions in Latino identity
    (E) uses crude humor to suggest the inadequacy of all attempts to define *Latino*

19. The speaker's line of reasoning in the paragraph 3 allows her to
    (A) simplify her definition of *Latino/Latina* in order to avoid overly academic language
    (B) qualify the role of Latino/Latina culture in the broader American culture
    (C) show that Latino/Latina Americans possess qualities admired by other Americans
    (D) argue that Latin identity is very complex because of the diverse cultures represented within that ethnicity
    (E) display the contrast between Spanish-speaking and non-Spanish-speaking Latinos/Latinas

20. Which of the following strategies does the speaker employ in paragraph 4 to reinforce her argument about the complexity of Latino/Latina identity?
    (A) repeating the word *tension* (sentences 1, 4, & 5)
    (B) integrating references to "America" (sentence 1 & 9) and the "nation" (sentences 2 & 4)
    (C) alluding to the debate over affirmative action (sentence 4)
    (D) reminding her audience that Puerto Ricans are American citizens
    (E) ironically suggesting that America is not a "melting pot" but a "salad bowl" (sentence 4)

21. The parenthetical statement in paragraph 4, sentence 4 ("a recently . . . diversity") contributes to the speaker's overarching argument by
    (A) indicating that the conflict between ethnic diversity and race or color blindness is currently ongoing
    (B) proving that the speaker still has ties to her home despite her career success
    (C) illustrating that conflicts over ethnic diversity persist but only in big American cities like New York
    (D) providing details about ethnic conflicts within the communities where these arguments matter most
    (E) narrowing the argument to Latina identity instead of expanding it to the entirety of American culture.

22. In paragraph 4, which sentence best indicates the speaker's awareness that America's relationship with race and ethnicity is complex?
    (A) "We are a nation that takes pride in our ethnic diversity, recognizing its importance in shaping our society and in adding richness to its existence." (sentence 2)
    (B) "Yet, we simultaneously insist that we can and must function and live in a race and color-blind way that ignores these very differences that in other contexts we laud." (sentence 3)
    (C) "I became a Latina by the way I love and the way I live my life." (sentence 7)
    (D) "My family showed me by their example how wonderful and vibrant life is and how wonderful and magical it is to have a Latina soul." (sentence 8)
    (E) "They taught me to love being a Puertorriqueña and to love America and value its lesson that great things could be achieved if one works hard for it." (sentence 9)

23. Which of the following sentences from paragraph 4 could best stand as the thesis for the entire passage?

(A) "America has a deeply confused image of itself that is in perpetual tension." (sentence 1)

(B) "Yet, we simultaneously insist that we can and must function and live in a race and color-blind way that ignores these very differences that in other contexts we laud." (sentence 3)

(C) "That tension between "the melting pot and the salad bowl"—a recently popular metaphor used to describe New York's diversity—is being hotly debated today in national discussions about affirmative action." (sentence 4)

(D) "I became a Latina by the way I love and the way I live my life." (sentence 7)

(E) "But achieving success here is no easy accomplishment for Latinos or Latinas, and although that struggle did not and does not create a Latina identity, it does inspire how I live my life." (sentence 10)

24. Which of the following is a logical conclusion that can be derived from the final two paragraphs of the passage?

(A) Labeling individuals based on their experiences is an effective way to define American culture.

(B) National identity is much more important than the complexities of ethnic or racial identity.

(C) National and cultural identities are complex because of the many cultural factors that contribute to them.

(D) Tension within ourselves and between segments of the population is more significant that self-perception.

(E) Education is essential for making meaningful contributions to discussions about culture and identity.

Questions 25–31. Read the following passage carefully before you choose your answers.

(The passage below is a draft.)

(1) In 2011, Swedish video game developer Mojang released a game like no other popular game at the time. (2) This game, Minecraft, surprised the world – and a lot of adults – when its popularity exploded. (3) Even nearly ten years after its release, it continued to win awards, including the 2020 Kids' Choice Award for "Favorite Video Game."

(4) Minecraft is what gamers call a "sandbox" game. (5) There are countless ways for a player to interact with the world around them, including finding

raw materials to "forge" into other things, creating their own games or scenarios, or even engaging in quests or games that other players have created. (6) Part of the game's appeal is its seemingly endless possibilities. (7) Those possibilities also have come to include education.

(8) Teachers can create worlds where students must work together, create things to represent what they are learning, and even use learning from several different classes to build a unique and purposeful world. (9) These are all the things that teachers want students to do in the real world, but there just isn't time or opportunity for that. (10) Doing it in Minecraft makes it possible. (11) Importantly, students can feel free to take risks and try new things in the world of Minecraft – things that would cost a lot of time or money in the real world.

(12) Mojang released "Minecraft: Education Edition" in 2019. (13) With these new teacher support tools added to the myriad of possibilities already available in the game, teachers should take a cue from the large number of their students who are not afraid to take risks in the pixelated, virtual worlds of Minecraft and try it in their classrooms.

25. The writer is considering deleting the introductory phrase "In 2011," from the beginning of sentence 1 (reproduced below).

    In 2011, Swedish video game developer Mojang released a game like no other popular game at the time.

    Which of the following factors is most important for the writer to consider when deciding whether to keep or delete the phrase?

    (A) Identifying whether the reader needs to know when Minecraft began to revolutionize gaming

    (B) Preventing readers from getting lost in the dates and years used throughout the passage

    (C) Explaining why the game continues to be popular with kids, but not with adults

    (D) Acknowledging the limited experiences some readers will have had with video games

    (E) The need to define *video game* to help readers see Minecraft as a classroom tool

26. The writer is considering the addition of the following sentence immediately after sentence 1.

With its pixelated graphics, Minecraft bore little resemblance to other games that opted for more realistic graphics.

Should the writer make this addition?

(A) Yes, because the audience must understand the difference between pixelated and nonpixelated graphics

(B) Yes, because it provides a contrast between Minecraft and previously popular but inferior games

(C) Yes, because it clarifies why people were surprised by the popularity of Minecraft

(D) No, because it creates an unnecessary contrast between Minecraft and inferior games

(E) No, because the audience already knows how Minecraft differs from other popular video games

27. The writer is considering deleting the underlined portion of sentence 3 (reproduced below).

Even nearly ten years after its release, it continued to win awards, including the 2020 Kids' Choice Award for "Favorite Video Game."

Should the writer delete the underlined text?

(A) Yes, because it interferes with the more important point about Minecraft's popularity among educators

(B) Yes, because, in reality, kids do not play Minecraft as much as they play other more realistic games

(C) Yes, because parents are trying to take control over how their children use Minecraft in schools

(D) No, because it provides a specific example of Minecraft's long-term popularity with children

(E) No, because it is important to realize that adults and kids enjoy playing Minecraft for different reasons

28. The writer wants to further explain the comment made in sentence 4 (reproduced below) by adding information from additional reading and research to the end of the sentence, adjusting the punctuation as needed.

Minecraft is what gamers call a "sandbox" game.

Which choice best accomplishes this goal?

(A) and "there's no shortage of sandbox creation games to play" (Cohen, 2019).

(B) it was "inspired by *Infiniminer*, *Dwarf Fortress*, and *Dungeon Keeper*, created by Markus Persson, the founder of Mojang AB" (sandbox-games.net).

(C) a game in which "the player has the ability to create, modify, or destroy their environment" (Davies, 2012).

(D) though "Minetest is perhaps the most complete alternative to Minecraft" (Baker and Kenlon, 2020).

(E) and "early sandbox games came out of space trading and combat games like *Elite* (1984) and city-building simulations and tycoon games like *SimCity* (1989)" (Wikipedia).

29. The writer wants to add the following quotation as evidence to paragraph 3.

"The beauty of the game is in the way it unleashes the creativity of both students and teachers," explains Dan Bloom, a ninth-grade science teacher and writer for Edutopia *(2013).*

Which of the following is the most logical place to insert this sentence in that paragraph?

(A) Before sentence 8

(B) Before sentence 9

(C) Before sentence 10

(D) Before sentence 11

(E) After sentence 11

30. The writer recognizes the need for a transition between the third and fourth paragraphs. Which of the following would be the most logical phrase or clause to add to the beginning of the fourth paragraph, adjusting the punctuation as needed?

(A) Despite Minecraft being nearly a decade old,

(B) Recognizing the educational value of Minecraft,

(C) Feeling a need to keep Minecraft relevant,

(D) Even though it is merely a game,

(E) To please its critics but surprise the video game market,

31. The writer is considering the addition of the following sentence immediately following sentence 12.

This new edition gave teachers many different ways to develop teaching tools and work closely with their students in the game.

Should the writer make this addition?

(A) Yes, because a reader needs evidence that Minecraft is widely used in today's classrooms

(B) Yes, because it describes new features that the "Education Edition" provides for teachers

(C) Yes, because the description gives examples of how Minecraft can be used to teach different subject areas

(D) No, because the writer has already provided enough information about the educational possibilities of Minecraft

(E) No, because too many teachers and parents have argued against use of Minecraft in the classroom.

Questions 32–39. Read the following passage carefully before you choose your answers.

(The passage below is a draft.)

(1) In a speech given just months before he was elected president, Barack Obama addressed the struggles of many Americans:

> "Most working- and middle-class white Americans don't feel that they have been particularly privileged by their race. Their experience is the immigrant experience—as far as they're concerned, no one's handed them anything, they've built it from scratch."

(2) Many people of any race could identify with these observations made by the first Black president. (3) However, for those people, economics, not race, was the central issue of inequality. (4) This is the point President Obama sought to make: that many people feel more affected by economic class than race. (5) But there are Americans in certain parts of the country who felt this way many years before it was said by Obama.

(6) Significant parts of thirteen states fall into what is known as "Appalachia." (7) Historically, the people who settled here were fiercely independent and self-sufficient, but the 1870s saw the discovery of large amounts of coal, while the introduction of railroads saw increased interest by wealthy outsiders. (8) There was a lot of money coming into the region to help remove the coal. (9) The problem was that the money left when the coal did. (10) Companies invested little money into the region. (11) They took the coal, paid what little they had to, and left.

(12) These wealthy outsiders told stories of Appalachians who desperately needed help to be more like the rest of the U.S. (13) The problem was that the rest of the United States was taking and taking from Appalachians and then blaming them as helpless and stupid. (14) "Reformers, philanthropists and missionaries came often to the mountains to offer relief, but lacked the capacity or willingness to alter the way power and wealth worked in our world," explained Elizabeth Catte, author of *What You Are Getting Wrong About Appalachia*. (15) Despite their exploitation, in recent years those same fiercely independent people have started to take back their heritage and reject the prejudice of others. (16) Likewise, outsiders have increasingly accepted the role of Appalachia as a place of natural beauty and cultural heritage.

32. The writer is considering deleting the underlined portion of sentence 2 (reproduced below).

    Many people of any race could identify with these observations made by the first Black president.

    Should the writer delete this portion of the sentence?

    (A) Yes, because mentioning the president's race distracts from the later arguments made about poverty.
    (B) Yes, because the president's race is irrelevant to the economic status of Americans in Appalachia.
    (C) Yes, because there is no logical connection between the president's race and the poverty of people in Appalachia.
    (D) No, because it is relevant that the first Black president is acknowledging the struggles of people of other races.
    (E) No, because discussions about economic class must always be considered in the context of discussions about race.

33. The writer wants to begin narrowing the focus of the passage from all Americans to a smaller portion of the U.S. population with sentence 5 (reproduced below).

    But there are Americans in certain parts of the country who felt this way many years before it was said by Obama.

    Which of the following versions of the underlined portion of sentence 5 best accomplishes this goal?

    (A) (as it is now)
    (B) in this great country
    (C) of different races
    (D) descended from immigrants
    (E) who did not vote for him

34. The writer wants to add the following sentence to the introduction (paragraph 1) in order to better focus the reader on the topic of the overall passage.

"Consider the exploitation of people living in the Appalachian mountain region of the eastern U.S."

Which of the following is the most logical place to insert this sentence in that paragraph?

(A) Before sentence 1

(B) After sentence 1

(C) After sentence 3

(D) After sentence 4

(E) After sentence 5

35. The writer is considering revising sentence 7 (reproduced below) to indicate that the discovery of coal and the coming of the railroads happened simultaneously and were equally harmful in their combination.

Historically, the people who settled here were fiercely independent and self-sufficient, but the 1870s saw the discovery of large amounts of coal, while the introduction of railroads saw increased interest by wealthy outsiders.

Which of the following versions of the underlined portion of sentence 7 best accomplishes this goal?

(A) (as it is now)

(B) coal, but the introduction of

(C) coal; although the introduction of

(D) coal; despite how the introduction of

(E) coal at the same time that

36. The writer wants to add a word or phrase to the beginning of sentence 8 (reproduced below) to clarify the cause-and-effect relationship with the previous sentence.

There was a lot of money coming into the region to help remove the coal.

Which of the following best accomplishes this goal, adjusting for punctuation as needed?

(A) (as it is now)

(B) In fact,

(C) In the meanwhile,

(D) As a result,

(E) Nevertheless,

37. The writer wants to combine sentences 8 and 9 (reproduced below) to most effectively express the relationship between the ideas in each sentence.

(8) There was a lot of money coming into the region to help remove the coal. (9) The problem was that the money left when the coal did.

Which of the following versions of the combined sentences is most effective?

(A) (as it is now)

(B) Despite the money leaving when the coal did, there was a lot of it coming into the region.

(C) There was a lot of money coming into the region to help remove the coal, but unfortunately that money left when the coal did.

(D) There was a lot of money coming into the region to help remove the coal, so the problem was that the money left when the coal did.

(E) Though the money left when the coal did, there had been a lot of money coming into the region to help remove the coal.

38. The writer wants to ensure that sentence 12 (reproduced below) creates a coherent connection between the last two paragraphs.

These wealthy outsiders told stories of Appalachians who desperately needed help to be more like the rest of the U.S.

Which of the following revisions would best accomplish this goal, adjusting punctuation as needed?

(A) (as it is now)

(B) These wealthy outsiders told stories of Appalachian people—a people made up of many different races—who desperately needed help to be more like the rest of the U.S.

(C) Despite their good intentions, these wealthy outsiders told stories of Appalachians who desperately needed help to be more like the rest of the U.S.

(D) These wealthy, thoughtless, and prejudiced outsiders told stories of Appalachians who desperately wanted to be more like the rest of the U.S.

(E) To deflect attention from their dubious business practices, these wealthy outsiders claimed the Appalachian people needed help to become more like the rest of the United States.

39. The writer wants to add commentary before sentence 14 (reproduced below) that provides a transition to the quotation.

"Reformers, philanthropists and missionaries came often to the mountains to offer relief, but lacked the capacity or willingness to alter the way power and wealth worked in our world" explained Elizabeth Catte, author of What You're Getting Wrong About Appalachia.

Which of the following sentences would be the most logical choice for accomplishing that goal?

(A) Appalachian people needed help: help from poverty, help from hunger, help from violence, and help from isolation.

(B) Suddenly outsiders were telling these proud and once-isolated people that they needed to be saved from themselves and rescued from poverty.

(C) A proud and independent people, Appalachians were not able to see themselves and needed help, which made providing that help all the more difficult.

(D) These people did not need help; instead, what they needed was access to the modern comforts that most U.S. citizens enjoyed.

(E) Many good people from around the nation realized something had to be done to rescue these helpless people from themselves.

Questions 40–45. Read the following passage carefully before you choose your answers.

(The passage below is a draft.)

(1) When asked to name past American presidents, people often list George Washington, Abraham Lincoln, and John F. Kennedy. (2) Some may name Barack Obama. (3) Some may name Franklin D. Roosevelt. (4) Some may name Ronald Reagan. (5) President James A. Garfield was assassinated only two months into his term in 1881 and Chester A. Arthur became president. (6) Immediately, all but one of the cabinet secretaries quit. (7) No one thought they could work with him. (8) He was not respected as a politician or leader and was expected to be completely ineffective as a president.

(9) He immediately started with reforms that strengthened the country and improved the lives of many Americans. (10) These included what many both then and now call the "rebirth" of the United States Navy. (11) He is also recognized for leading an administration that provided the consistency and resiliency necessary to help the country recover from the assassination of Garfield. (12) His presidency was not without controversy, though, as he was then and now criticized for signing the 1882 Chinese Exclusion Act.

(13) Suffering from ill health near the end of his first term, he did not campaign strongly for reelection and was demolished by Grover Cleveland in 1885. (14) While he is not often remembered by many as a strong president, he worked to do what was right for the country and remained respectable and scandal free.

40. Which of the following sentences, if placed between sentences 4 and 5, would provide a better transition?
    (A) Hardly anyone, however, names President Chester A. Arthur.
    (B) Everyone should know even the most obscure presidents.
    (C) Rarely, however, do people think of James A. Garfield.
    (D) Most Americans just don't know their history well enough.
    (E) Even if you can name a president, knowing what that president did is more difficult.

41. The writer wants to improve the flow of the first paragraph by rewriting sentence 5 (reproduced below).

    President James A. Garfield was assassinated only two months into his term in 1881 and Chester A. Arthur became president.

    Which of the following best achieves this purpose while emphasizing the cause-effect relationship between Garfield's assassination and Arthur's presidency?
    (A) In 1881, when President James A. Garfield was assassinated only two months into his term, Chester Arthur became president.
    (B) President James A. Garfield's assassination was troubling and many Americans were worried about the future, so they welcomed Chester Arthur as a new president.
    (C) Chester Arthur became president in 1881 after President James A. Garfield was assassinated only two months into his term.
    (D) The consequences of assassinations are always unpredictable and the consequence of the assassination of President James A. Garfield was that Chester Arthur became president.
    (E) Though many thought him unprepared for such a role, Chester Arthur became president after President James A. Garfield was assassinated in 1881.

42. Which of the following, if added to the beginning of the second paragraph, would both create a transition between paragraphs 1 and 2 and qualify the statement about Arthur's reforms?

(A) Despite the death of Garfield,

(B) To the surprise of many,

(C) While Arthur had been a successful politician,

(D) Although many people were disappointed,

(E) Considering Americans were uncertain of their future,

43. In an attempt to avoid any indication of bias, the writer wants to revise the underlined word in sentence 13 (reproduced below).

Suffering from ill health near the end of his first term, he did not campaign strongly for reelection and was <u>*demolished*</u> *by Grover Cleveland in 1885.*

Which of the following versions of the underlined portion of sentence 13 accomplishes this goal?

(A) (as it is now)

(B) destroyed

(C) punished

(D) conquered

(E) defeated

44. The writer is considering revisions to sentence 8 (reproduced below) to emphasize the idea that Arthur was neither respected nor expected to do well as president.

He was not respected as a politician or leader and was expected to be completely ineffective as a president.

Which possible revision of that sentence best accomplishes this goal?

(A) (as it is now)

(B) He was not respected as a politician or a leader, even though he was expected to be completely ineffective as a president.

(C) Despite not being respected as a politician or a leader, he was not expected to be effective as a president.

(D) While he was an ineffective president, historians agree that he was never really respected as a leader.

(E) No one respected him as a politician or a leader and he would be overshadowed by several who followed him.

45. In sentence 14 (reproduced below), the writer wants to qualify the underlined portion in order to summarize information from several credible sources.

While he is not often remembered by many as a strong president, he worked to do what was right for the country and remained respectable and scandal free.

Which of the following, if placed immediately before the underlined portion, would best accomplish this goal?

(A) it is very clear that

(B) no one can argue that

(C) some people claim that

(D) historians widely agree that

(E) even his enemies would say that

Section II

TOTAL TIME—2 HOURS AND 15 MINUTES • 3 QUESTIONS

Question 1

Suggested reading and writing time—55 minutes

It is suggested that you spend 15 minutes reading the question, analyzing and evaluating the sources, and 40 minutes writing your response.

Note: You may begin writing your response before the reading period is over.

(This question counts as one-third of the total essay section score.)

In recent years, increasing costs have forced many schools and school districts in the United States to consider or even switch to a four-day school week.

Carefully read the following sources, including the introductory information for each source.

Write an essay that synthesizes material from at least three of the sources and develops your position on the four-day school week.

Source A (Weis)
Source B (Heyward)
Source C (Edelman)
Source D (Harris)
Source E (Morgan)
Source F (Donis-Keller)
Source G (DeSilver)

In your response you should do the following:

- Respond to the prompt with a thesis that presents a defensible position.
- Select and use evidence from at least three of the provided sources to support your line of reasoning. Indicate clearly the sources used through direct quotation, paraphrase, or summary. Sources may be cited as Source A, Source B, etc., or by using the description in parentheses.
- Explain how the evidence supports your line of reasoning.
- Use appropriate grammar and punctuation in communicating your argument.

Source A

Weis, Kati. "More than 80,000 Colorado students attend school four days a week. What happens on the fifth day?" *Chalkbeat*, 29 May 2019.

The following is from an organization focused on covering stories on education in the United States.

While many children across Colorado are heading to school on Monday mornings, siblings Angelica and Paul Gallegos of Brighton are on their way to Barr Lake State Park's Nature Center to volunteer.

"Every time we go, we all learn something different, something new, and I just think it's awesome that I'm able to give my kids an opportunity to go out and learn something, try something outside," said their mother, Crystal Gallegos.

Angelica, 13, and Paul, 9, have been volunteering once a week at the state park since last August, when the Brighton-based District 27J transitioned to a four-day school week.

As more Colorado school districts cut back to just four days a week in the face of financial pressures, many parents are looking for ways to fill that fifth day—they hope with meaningful learning outside the classroom. Organizations like Boys and Girls Clubs have stepped in to fill the gap, and so have new nonprofits and business partnerships that provide everything from workplace learning to gardening and robotics classes.

This school year, state data shows 104 of Colorado's 178 school districts—serving more than 80,000 students—operated on four-day weeks, up from just 39 in 2000. In fact, Colorado has the highest proportion of school districts operating on four-day weeks in the country, according to the National Conference of State Legislatures.

Source B

Heyward, Georgia. "What Do We Actually Know about the Four-Day School Week?" *Center on Reinventing Public Education*, June 2018.

Below is an infographic published by an organization interested in public education.

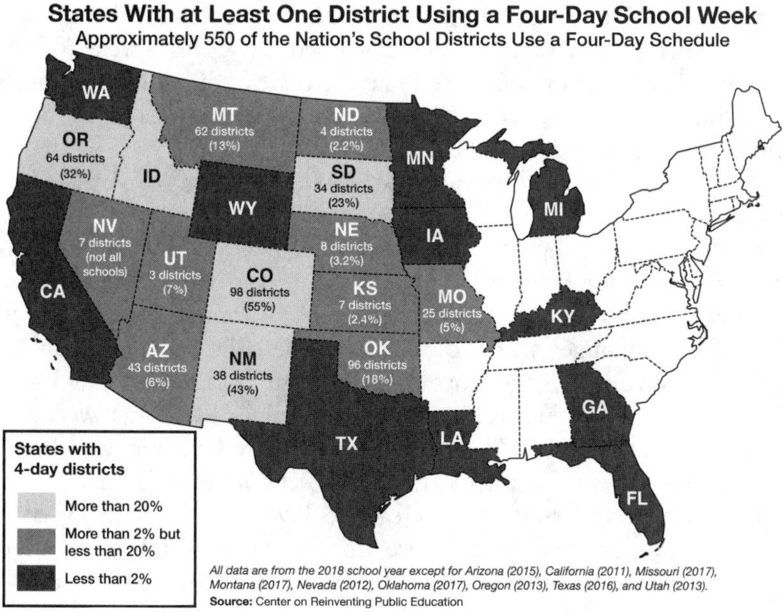

Source C

Edelman, Adam. "A four-day school week? Teachers and kids give it an 'A.' Parents are less enthusiastic." *NBC News*, 28 May 2019.

The following excerpt was originally published in the "Political News" section of the NBC News website.

Teachers and Parents Give it a Grade

For single parents like Jessica Lore, who works full-time for a local sales company and has no family in the area, the four-day schedule was not a welcome change.

"I don't like it one bit, and I feel like the district didn't take seriously my worries about child care," she told NBC News as she picked up her three children from the Boys & Girls Club on a recent Monday.

If it weren't for that free service—Lore's kids receive a scholarship because she can't afford to pay—"I'd have been out of a job," she said.

Even for parents who can afford to have someone at home or who can enlist nearby family to help, the change wasn't universally well received.

Brody Mathews, who has two children at Thimmig Elementary, wasn't thrilled about the longer school days. And while child care wasn't an issue—he and his wife run a business out of their home — a work-related move to Golden, Colorado, will put his kids back in school for five days a week.

"I'll be relieved that they'll be back on a five-day schedule. It's what pretty much every human on earth works or goes to school for," he said.

On the other hand, students and teachers loved the shortened week.

Kids said they enjoyed having more time for play, rest and even homework, while high schoolers tended to pick up extra shifts at their part-time jobs, or volunteer to boost their college prospects.

Alec Alvarez, a third grader at Thimmig Elementary, said he felt the new day was "kind of long" but that it was "worth it" so he could spend his Mondays at his grandmother's house "playing outside."

Zach Felker, a junior at Prairie View High, said he works up to 11 hours on Mondays at a nearby Buffalo Wild Wings to earn money to pay for college.

Teachers, meanwhile, cited having long weekends they can use to prep for the week while still having time for much-needed relaxation.

Ally Hyatt, a seventh-grade science teacher at Vikan Middle, had spent the first four years of her career in Denver Public Schools, and applied for a job last summer specifically in 27J Schools when she learned about their new schedule.

"It was attractive to me because I was essentially working that long of a day in DPS anyway. Here, I could just do it four days week," she a said in an interview in the teachers' lounge at Vikan. "It's been amazing for my personal life, and I love that I have more time to actually plan lessons on Monday and get everything ready for the week."

Source D

Harris, Briony. "Some schools in the US are switching to a four-day week. Here's why." *World Economic Forum*, 17 May 2018.

The following is the full text of an article originally published by an international organization focused on worldwide economic cooperation.

An increasing number of public schools in the US, especially in rural areas, are moving to a four-day school week.

The idea is to save the local authorities money, for example in reduced heating bills or transport costs, as well as saving on the wages of clerical staff and janitors.

Another motivating factor is the need to recruit and retrain teachers, many of whom find the idea of having an extra day to plan and prepare lessons very appealing since this often eats into precious weekend time.

But there are also obvious disadvantages, including the impact on families with two working parents who need to arrange – and pay – for an extra day's childcare every week.

And it is also important to consider the impact on a child's education – whether a four-day school week helps or hinders learning.

Addressing Low Teacher Pay

Oklahoma is a prime example of the trend towards a four-day school week.

More than 200 of the state's schools—in 91 of its 512 school districts—operate on a four-day schedule already.

And thousands of teachers took the decision to walk out of the classroom for nine days in April, demanding more funding and pay rises.

The teachers have been battling real-term wage reductions for 10 out of the past 11 years. . . .

The Oklahoma walkout is part of a wider wave of teacher activism which has also seen strikes in West Virginia, Kentucky and Arizona.

In the US, the lack of morale and pay is having a negative impact on the number of students who decide to train as teachers, with the numbers enrolling in teacher preparation programmes in steady decline.

Anecdotal evidence suggests that a four-day week is helping to address retention and recruitment issues. One Oklahoma school noted that more experienced teachers applied for jobs after a four-day week had been adopted. And another school reported many more applicants for every job opening following the shorter working week.

And an academic study of the four-day week model in the state of Missouri showed that 91% of respondents thought that the school week had improved staff morale in the school district.

France is also notable amongst European countries for experimenting with the school week.

In 2008, the Sarkozy[1] administration decided that children should go to school for six hours a day, four days a week. This was then changed again under President Hollande who instituted a five-day week with Wednesday afternoons off.

Now, President Macron has given local authorities the freedom to choose between a four and a 4.5 day week. Reports suggest that a third of primary schools (mostly in rural areas) will change back to a four-day week, another clear signal that the shorter school week is working for some authorities.

But while a four-day working week may be appealing to teachers and local authorities, what about the impact on children and their families?

Concentration Concerns

Children doing a shorter week do not normally spend fewer hours in lessons. Rather, they are in school for slightly longer on the other four days.

However, some teachers say that longer days are not always the best learning method for younger children, who have shorter concentration spans.

There has also been some discussion around the impact of a three-day weekend, and whether that means younger children struggle to retain what they have learnt during the previous week.

But these concerns were not supported by the Missouri study: 87% of employees surveyed said a four-day week had had a positive impact on what was taught in class, while 76% said the four-day school week had improved the academic quality of their school district.

A different study, conducted by Mark Anderson of Montana State University and Mary Beth Walker of Georgia State University, found that moving to a four-day week had a positive impact on students' maths scores.

However, teachers are also extremely aware that parental support – of both the school and the child – are a critical factor in education.

And the Missouri study also highlighted that some parents had not been supportive of the changes.

The best approach is to make sure all stakeholders, including parents and children, are on board with the changes before they are implemented, that study noted.

1 **Nicolas Sarkozy:** President of France from 2007-2012.

Source E

Morgan, Ron. "40 Hours??" *Cartoonstock*, 5 August 2017. Accessed 8 August 2020.

Below is a cartoon.

"40 hours?? ... All in one *week*?"

Source F

Donis-Keller, Christine, and David L. Silvernail. "Research Brief: A Review of the Evidence on the Four-Day School Week." *Center for Education Policy, Applied Research and Evaluation*, February 2009.

The following is an excerpt from an academic research review.

Challenges to Implementation

The switch to a four-day week is rarely a swift transition and requires districts to research the practice, examine existing models, and weigh advantages and disadvantages. While the research literature and news reports tell the story of many districts that are satisfied with their decision to implement the four-day week, they also caution that districts must consider a range of issues in order to make an informed decision. Some of these concerns are:

- **Childcare:** Often an initial concern with the four-day week, many districts have found that parents prefer having to find good childcare only one day a week, in contrast to some care every day. Some schools have alleviated this concern by using high school students as baby-sitters for those in need, and providing training courses to increase the quality of care provided (Blankenship, 1984; Fager, 1997).
- **Student Fatigue:** There is often concern as to how students, particularly young students, will respond to a lengthened school day. Blankenship (1984) reports that many schools address this concern by creating school schedules that put the bulk of academic work into the earlier parts of the day.
- **At-risk students:** Concerns arise that a three-day break creates additional difficulties for at-risk and special-needs students, though there is limited research to support the claim (Blankenship, 1984; Culbertson, 1982; Fager, 1997).
- **Contact hours:** Despite increasing the length of the school day to accommodate a condensed school schedule, the four-day week appears to run counter to the increased emphasis on more, not less, time in school (Blankenship, 1984; Fager, 1997; Prendergast, Spradlin & Palozzi, 2007).
- **Shift in Costs:** Savings by the school systems are offset by new costs incurred by parents for childcare and food. In addition, savings may be found by reducing hours for some of the school districts' lowest paid, hourly workers (Chmelynski, 2002; Durr, 2003).
- **Legal/Legislative:** State laws typically delimit required instructional time in days per year. Teacher and other labor contracts, as well as retirement and pension plans in many states and districts, are framed in terms of days instead of hours (Darden, 2008; Gains, 2008). While some states allow districts to use the four-day week by applying for a waiver of these requirements, others have sought to change their laws to reflect instructional hours instead of days. For example, in Nebraska, state law does not stipulate a timeframe, but requires a minimum number of hours (1032 hours of instruction in elementary grades and a minimum of 1080 hours of instruction in high school grades). The state department of education reports that "it is up to the school districts to construct their school days and weekly schedule to meet the aforementioned hours of instruction. A few school districts in Nebraska have met the aforementioned hours of instruction using a 4 day school week" (Correspondence with Maine Department of Education).

Conclusion

The four-day week is the preferred calendar of many small rural districts scattered across the country. These districts mostly boast widespread public support, no or positive impact on academic performance, and some financial savings. Savings, however, must be weighed against an increased length of the school day, childcare needs on the off day, and professional development needs to help teachers adapt to an alternative schedule. Thus, it is important for any school district considering changing to a four-day school week to weigh the costs and benefits of such a decision.

References

Blankenship, T. (1984). Update: These school systems swear by the four-day school week because students work harder and face fewer distractions. The American School Board Journal, 171 (8), 32-33.

Chmelynski, C. (2003). Four-day school weeks? Only if they fit. School Board News. Vol. 22 (8).

Culbertson, J. (1982). Four-Day School Week for Small Rural Schools. ERIC Clearinghouse on Rural Education and Small Schools, EDRS 232799.

Durr, G. (2003). Four Day School Week. National Conference of State Legislatures.

Fager, J. (1997). Scheduling Alternatives: Options for Student Success. By Request . . ., Northwest Regional Educational Laboratory. Retrieved October 2008 from: http://www.nwrel.org/request/feb97/schedalts.html.

Prendergast, K. A., Spradlin T. E. & Palozzi, V. J. (2007). Is it Time to Change Indiana's School-Year Calendar? Education Policy Briefs, Vol. 5 (1).

Source G

DeSilver, Drew. "School days: How the U.S. compares with other countries. *Pew Research Center*, 2 September 2014.

The following excerpt was originally part of an article published by a nonprofit organization that provides information on social issues. To read the complete article, visit https://www.pewresearch.org/fact-tank/2014/09/02/school-days-how-the-u-s-compares-with-other-countries/

Among 33 mostly developed nations, annual "total intended instructional time" averaged 790 hours for primary students (ranging from 470 hours in Russia to 1,007 hours in Chile) according to data compiled by the Organization for Economic Cooperation and Development (OECD). For the international equivalent of U.S. middle-schoolers, average annual required hours increased to 925 (ranging from 741 hours in Sweden to 1,167 hours in Mexico). The OECD did not have data for high schoolers. . . .

We used data from the Education Commission of the States, supplemented by examination of relevant rules and statutes and inquiries to individual states, to estimate average instructional-time minimums in the U.S. The numbers we came up with are 943 hours for 1st-graders, 1,016 hours for 7th-graders and 1,025 hours for 11th-graders. (For comparison, a 180-day calendar of 6-hour days would provide 1,080 instructional hours.) . . .

Both sets of numbers, though, mask considerable variation and contain many caveats. Countries may define "instructional time" differently and set their own rules on when, and for how many years, students can attend primary and secondary school. And the OECD data don't include time spent with tutors, in "cram schools" or in other supplemental classes, which are very common in some countries.

Question 2
Suggested time—40 minutes.

(This question counts as one-third of the total essay section score.)

Shirley Chisholm (1924–2005)—the first Black congresswoman in the United States, serving from 1969–1983 and running for president in 1972—gave a speech in 1969 on the campus of Howard University, a historically Black university in Washington, D.C. The campus had recently been through months of violent unrest springing from a variety of factors.

Read the passage from Chisholm's speech carefully. Write an essay that analyzes the rhetorical choices Chisholm makes to convey her message.

In your response you should do the following:

- Respond to the prompt with a thesis that analyzes the writer's rhetorical choices.
- Select and use evidence to support your line of reasoning,
- Explain how the evidence supports your line of reasoning.
- Demonstrate an understanding of the rhetorical situation.
- Use appropriate grammar and punctuation in communicating your argument.

While nothing is easy for the black man in America, neither is anything impossible. Like old man river,[1] we are moving along and we will continue to move resolutely until our goal of unequivocal equality is attained. We must not be docile, we must not be resigned, nor must we be inwardly bitter. We must see ourselves in an entirely new perspective and we cannot sit in our homes waiting for someone to reach out and do things for us.

Every tomorrow has two handles; we can take hold of the handle of anxiety, or the handle of faith. And the first battle is won, my brothers and sisters, when we fight for belief in ourselves, and find that it has come to us while we are still battling. We must not allow petty things to color our lives and stimulate them into vast proportions of evil. To dwell on every slight and clutch it close to our breast and nourish it will corrode our thinking. We're on the move now, and as Frederick Douglass said, "Power concedes nothing without a struggle." It never has, and it never will.

The United States can no longer afford the luxury of costly morally, religiously, and ethically wrong racial discrimination. For America needs all of her citizens with their abilities developed to make a fuller contribution to the future. Many problems scream loudly in this country. The thousands of black citizens disenfranchised, living under degrading conditions. The millions of poor in this nation, white and black, who lack the bare rudiments for fruitful living. The rapidly growing numbers of children caught in a web of disillusionment which destroys their will to learn. The increasing numbers of aged who do not even look forward to rest or retirement.

And despite the historic legislation in our cities and our states, nearly eleven million black citizens today still live in basic ghetto communities[2] of our cities. From decades of non-participation, or only modest participation, the black man has within the last two years shifted his goal to full political participation for full American citizenship. And while on the picket line at the lunch counter and on the bus and the store boycott the black man came face to face with the full breadth and weight of the power of influence exercised by local and state governments intertwining and often stifling the protests.

Indeed, a principle byproduct of the American Civil Rights Movement has been the awakening of the black citizen to his awesome political potential. And just as the picket line and the lunch counter demonstrations and the boycotts were dramatic and effective weapons of protest for the civil rights movement, the polling place is the new phase in the new thrust of the black man's bid for equality of opportunity. "Power concedes nothing." How else can any man rise to power and hold sway over millions or tens of thousands except by smothering dissenting voices?

---

1 **old man river**: This is a reference to the song "Ol' Man River," which contrasts the struggles of African Americans with the ceaseless flow of the Mississippi River

2 **ghetto communities:** sections of a city in which members of a minority group are pressured or forced to live, especially because of social, legal, or economic pressure. Ghettos are often known for being more impoverished than other areas of the city.

Freedom is an endless horizon, and there are many roads that lead to it. We must walk arm in arm with other men, and we must struggle toward goals which are commonly desired and sound. We must give and lend to the youth for stronger voice and encourage their individuality. We must look to the schools and constantly work for their improvement because that is where the future leadership of the country will be coming from to a large extent, particularly in the black communities.

The leaders of today in the black communities must be able to place the goal of freedom ahead of personal ambition. The truly dedicated leader follows what his conscience tells him is best for his people. For whatever else the black man is, he is American. Or whatever he is to become—integrated, unintegrated, or disintegrated—he will become it in America. Only a minority of black people have ever succumbed to the temptation to seek greener pastures of another country or another ideology. You know, so often nowadays we hear people say that we should go back to Africa, we should establish ourselves in Africa, or we should do a lot of other things.

Well if people want to go back to Africa or people want to go to Africa just like people want to go to Europe, that's their own personal business. And you do it voluntarily. I don't intend to go to Africa, I intend to stay here and fight because the blood, sweat, and tears of our forefathers are rooted in the soil of this country. And the reason that Wall Street is the great financial center that it is today is because of the blood sweat and tears of your forefathers who worked in the tobacco and the cotton fields.

Question 3
Suggested time—40 minutes.

(This question counts as one-third of the total essay section score.)

A popular saying states "the clothes make the man" and a 2013 article in *Forbes* magazine (a publication focused on the business world) stated "Like it or not, you are being judged by how you look, how you dress, and how you carry yourself—and, if you're lucky, how you do your job."

Write an essay that argues your position on the role of appearance in society.

In your response you should do the following:

- Respond to the prompt with a thesis that presents a defensible position.
- Provide evidence to support your line of reasoning.
- Explain how the evidence supports your line of reasoning.
- Use appropriate grammar and punctuation in communicating your argument.

Acknowledgments

"Advice to Writers" by Robert Benchley from *Love Conquers All*, copyright © 1922 by Henry Holt and Company.

Afterword to *Fast Food Nation: The Dark Side of the All-American Meal* by Eric Schlosser. Copyright © 2012 by Eric Schlosser.

"All Work and No Play Makes Jack a Nerd" by David Lessing, David Herne. Originally published in *The New York Times* 1/28/90.

"American Sixteen- and Seventeen-Year-Olds Are Ready to Vote" by Daniel Hart and Robert Atkins. Published in *Annals of the American Academy of Political and Social Science*, January 2011.

"Are These 10 Lies Justified?" by Gerald Dworkin. Published in *The New York Times: The Stone* 12/14/15. Reprinted by permission of *The New York Times* via PARS International.

"The Biggest Moments of the Super Bowl 2020 Halftime Show" by Raisa Bruner. Published in *Time* magazine 2/2/20. Reprinted by permission of *Time* magazine via PARS International.

From *Bird by Bird: Some Instructions on Writing and Life* by Anne Lamott, copyright © 1994 by Anne Lamott. Used by permission of Pantheon Books, an imprint of the Knopf Doubleday Publishing Group, a division of Penguin Random House LLC. All rights reserved.

"College president: 'This is not a day care. This is a university!' " introduction by Susan Svrluga. Originally published by *The Washington Post* 11/30/15. Letter by Everett Piper, originally published by *Bartlesville Examiner Enterprise*, 2015. Reprinted with permission.

"Denmark Wants to Break Up Ethnic Enclaves. What is Wrong with Them?" from *Homeland Security News Wire*, 2 December 2019.

"Ditch the GPS. It's Ruining Your Brain" by M. R. O'Connor, originally published in *The Washington Post* on 06/05/2019. Reprinted by permission of the author.

"The Drowning Child and the Expanding Circle" by Peter Singer, as published in the *New Internationalist* (289 issue), 4/5/1997. Reprinted by permission of the New Internationalist.

"Farmers Finding Few Americans Willing to Do Jobs Immigrants Do" by Doug Mataconis, *Outside the Beltway* (outsidethebeltway.com), October 5, 2011.

"Fear and the 'Problem' of City's Ethnic Enclaves" by Joe Greenholtz, originally published in *Richmond News* 6/13/12. Reprinted by permission of LMP Publication Limited.

"Fifty Years Ago We Landed on the Moon. Why Should We Care Now?" by Jill Lepore, from *The New York Times*. © 2019 The New York Times Company. All rights reserved. Used under license.

Final speech from *The Great Dictator* by Charlie Chaplin. Released by United Artists, 1940.

"A Four-Day School? Teachers and Kids Give It an 'A.' Parents Are Less Enthusiastic." by Adam Edelman. NBC News, May 28, 2019.

"Freedom from Fear" by Aung San Suu Kyi. Acceptance speech for the Sakharov Prize for Freedom of Thought, Strasbourg, France, October 22, 2013.

"Games" from *Everything Bad is Good for You* by Steven Johnson, copyright © 2005 by Steven Johnson. Used by permission of Riverhead, an imprint of Penguin Publishing Group, a division of Penguin Random House LLC. All rights reserved.

"Give a lower voting age a try" by the Editorial Board, *The Washington Post*, April 13, 2018.

The Great White Bear: A Natural & Unnatural History of the Polar Bear by Kieran Mulvaney. Published by Houghton Mifflin Harcourt, 2011.

"Hiring Locally for Farm Work Is No Cure-All" by Kirk Johnson. Originally published in *The New York Times* 10/11/11. @ 2011 The New York Times Company. All rights reserved. Used under license.

"Homelessness: A Common Vocabulary Could Help Agencies Collaborate and Collect More Consistent Data." Report to Congressional Requesters from the United States Government Accountability Office (GAO), June 30, 2010.

Horizon by Barry Lopez. Published by Penguin Random House, 2019.

"How Dearborn, Michigan Became the Heart of Arab America" by Nick Leech. Published on *The National* (thenational.ae), July 5, 2017.

"How Digital Game-Based Learning Improves Student Success" by Ryan Juraschka. Published on *Prodigy* (prodigygame.com/blog), September 29, 2019.

"How the Loss of the Landline Is Changing Family Life" by Julia Cho. Originally published in *The Atlantic* 12/12/2019. © 2019 The Atlantic Monthly Group, LLC. All rights reserved. Used under license.

"I Have a Dream" by Martin Luther King Jr. Speech delivered at the March on Washington for Jobs and Freedom, Washington, D.C., August 28, 1963.

"I Now Have Scientific Proof of How Awesome I Really Am" by Joel Stein. Originally published in *Time* magazine 9/12/16. © 2016 TIME USA LLC. All rights reserved. Used under license.

"I'm Not Black, I'm Kanye" by Ta-Nehisi Coates. Published in *The Atlantic*, May 7, 2018.

"In Defense of the Ethnic Enclave" by Gram Slattery. Published in *Harvard Political Review* on 5/29/12. Reprinted by permission of Harvard Political Review.

"Is Dance a Sport?" by Lindsay Guarino. Published in the *Journal of Dance Education* 5/28/15. Reprinted by permission of the *Journal of Dance Education* via the Copyright Clearance Center.

"Islam Is Peace" by President George W. Bush. Remarks by the president at Islamic Center of Washington, D.C., September 17, 2001.

"It's A Smartphone Life: More Than Half Of U.S. Children Now Have One" by Anya Kamenetz. ©2019 National Public Radio, Inc. Originally published on npr.org on October 31, 2019, and is used with the permission of NPR.

Keynote speech by Ann Richards at the 1988 Democratic National Convention, Atlanta, Georgia, July 18, 1988.

"A Latina Judge's Voice" by Sonia Sotomayor. Mario G. Olmos Memorial Lecture at the University of California (Berkeley) School of Law, October 2001.

"Lessons of Dr. Martin Luther King, Jr." by Cesar Chavez. TM/© 2020 The Cesar Chavez Foundation. Reprinted by permission.

"Level Up Learning: A National Survey on Teaching with Digital" by Takeuchi, Lori M., and Sarah Vaala. Originally published on the Joan Ganz Cooney Center website 2014. Used by permission.

"Liars: It Takes One to Know One" by Travis Riddle. Published in *Scientific American* 7/24/12. Reprinted by permission of *Scientific American*, a Division of Springer Nature America, Inc. via the Copyright Clearance Center.

"Living Like Weasels" from *Teaching a Stone to Talk* by Annie Dillard. Copyright © 1982 by Annie Dillard. Used by permission of HarperCollins Publishers.

"Malala Yousafzai's Speech to the UN Youth Assembly" by Malala Yousafzai. Reprinted with permission of the Malala Fund.

"A Modest Proposal: For preventing the children of poor people in Ireland, from being a burthen on their parents or country, and for making them beneficial to the publick" by Jonathan Swift. Published in Dublin and London, 1729.

"The Moral Instinct" by Stephen Pinker. Published in *The New York Times Magazine*, January 13, 2008.

"A More Perfect Union" by Barack Obama. Speech at the National Constitution Center, Philadelphia, PA, March 18, 2008.

"More Than 80,000 Colorado Students Attend School Four Days a Week. What Happens on the Fifth Day?" by Kati Wies. Published on Chalkbeat Colorado (chalkbeat.org), May 29, 2019.

"Much Apu About Nothing" by David S. Cohen. Season 7, Episode 20 of *The Simpsons*, May 5, 1996.

"My Semester with the Snowflakes" by James Hatch. Reprinted by permission of author.

"New Study Explodes Myth of 'Jobs Americans Won't Do' " by Brendan Kirby. Published on LifeZette (lifezette.com), August 28, 2018.

"Nine-Year-Olds, Meet Monet" by Ellen Goodman, from *The Washington Post*. © 1978 The Washington Post. All rights reserved. Used under license.

Nobel lecture by Al Gore, Oslo, Norway, November 10, 2007.

NRA convention speech by Charlton Heston, Denver Colorado, May 1, 1999.

"Obesity prevention: the role of policies, laws and regulations" by Boyd A. Swinburn. Published in *Australia and New Zealand Health Policy*, June 5, 2008.

"On Morality" from *Slouching Towards Bethlehem* by Joan Didion. Copyright © 1966, 1968, renewed 1996 by Joan Didion. Reprinted by permission of Farrar, Straus and Giroux.

On Tyranny: Twenty Lessons from the Twentieth Century by Timothy Snyder, copyright @ 2017 by Timothy Snyder. Used by permission of Tim Duggan Books, an imprint of Random House, a division of Penguin Random House LLC. All rights reserved.

"The Perils of Pesticides Address to Pacific Lutheran University 1989" by Cesar Chavez. TM/© 2020 The Cesar Chavez Foundation. Reprinted by permission.

The Philosophy of Literary Form by Kenneth Burke, copyright © 1941 by Louisiana State University Press.

"Phone-Gate North Shore's Evans to miss state title game" by Matt Malatesta. Reprinted by permission of VYPE Media.

"Politics and the English Language" by George Orwell. Published in *Horizon* (London), April 1946.

Remarks for the United Nations Fourth World Conference on Women by First Lady Hillary Rodham Clinton, Beijing, China, September 5, 1995.

"Replay in Sports Isn't the Problem—Judgment Is" by Christopher L. Gasper. Originally published in *The Boston Globe* 5/13/2019. © 2019 Boston Globe Media Partners. All rights reserved. Used under license.

"Research Brief: A Review of the Evidence on the Four-Day School Week" by Christine Donis-Keller and David L. Silvernail. Published by Center for Education Policy, Applied Research and Evaluation, University of Southern Maine, February 2009.

A Room of One's Own by Virginia Woolf. Published by The Hogarth Press (London), 1929.

"School Days: How the U.S. Compares with Other Countries" by Drew DeSilver. Published by Pew Research Center (pewresearch.org), September 2, 2014.

"Some Schools in the U.S. are Switching to a Four-Day Week. Here's Why." by Briony Harris. Published by the World Economic Forum (weforum.org), May 17, 2018.

"Speech and Immorality" by Hor Victorsson. Originally published on www.simplyphilosophy.org. Reprinted with permission of the author.

Speech at Howard University by Shirley Chisholm. Washington, D.C., April 21, 1969.

Speech by Josephine Baker at the March on Washington for Jobs and Freedom, Washington, D.C., August 28, 1963.

"The Struggle for Human Rights" by Eleanor Roosevelt. Speech given at the Sorbonne, Paris, September 28, 1948.

"Super Bowl Halftime Show 2020: Twitter Reacts To Jennifer Lopez" by Madeline Berg. Published in *Forbes*, February 2, 2020.

Talking to Strangers: What We Should Know about the People We Don't Know by Malcolm Gladwell. Published by Little, Brown and Company, 2019.

"Teenager Wins Millions for Playing Fortnight" by Kyle Gierdorf. ©2019 National Public Radio, Inc. Originally broadcasted on NPR's *Morning Edition* August 2019, and is used with the permission of NPR.

"Ten Reasons Why You Shouldn't Lie" by Dr. Barbara Greenberg. Published in *Psychology Today*, July 29, 2018.

Testimony of Jessica Lynch before the House Committee on Oversight and Reform, April 24, 2007.

"That Crafty Feeling" by Zadie Smith. Lecture to students at Columbia University (New York), March 24, 2008. Included in *Changing My Mind: Occasional Essays*, The Penguin Press, 2009.

"Titanic Movie Review and Film Summary" by Roger Ebert, originally appeared on Rogerebert.com. Used by permission of The Ebert Company, Ltd.

"The Ways We Lie" by Stephanie Ericsson. Published in *Utne Reader*, November/December 1992.

"We Can't Afford to Lose the Postal Service" by Casey Cep. Published in *The New Yorker*, May 2, 2020.

"What to the Slave is the Fourth of July?" by Frederick Douglass. Speech at the Rochester Ladies' Anti-Slavery Society, Rochester, New York, July 5, 1852.

"Why Chinatown Still Matters" by Maurice Berger. Published in *The New York Times* 5/16/16. Reprinted by permission.

"Why I Write" by Joan Didion. Published in *The New York Times*, December 5, 1976.

"Why the French Fries Taste So Good" from *Fast Food Nation: The Dark Side of the All-American Meal* by Eric Schlosser. Copyright © 2001 by Eric Schlosser. Reprinted by permission of Houghton Mifflin Harcourt Publishing Company. All rights reserved.

"The World is Waking Up" (UN General Assembly, NYC 9/23/19) from *No One Is Too Small to Make a Difference* by Greta Thunberg, copyright © 2018, 2019 by Greta Thunberg. Used by permission of Penguin Books, an imprint of Penguin Publishing Group, a division of Penguin Random House LLC. All rights reserved.

"Yes, Virginia," response to a letter from Virginia O'Hanlon, published in *The New York Sun*, September 21, 1897.

Every reasonable effort has been made to properly acknowledge ownership of all material used. Any omissions or mistakes are not intentional and, if brought to the publisher's attention, will be corrected in future editions.

Index

A

B

C

D

E

F

G

H

I

J

K

L

S

T

U

V

W

X

Y

Z